Social Science

Now in its seventeenth edition, *Social Science: An Introduction to the Study of Society* approaches its study from a common sense perspective, rather than a formalistic perspective more common in social science. Readers will see how seemingly diverse disciplines intermingle and connect to one another—anthropology and economics, for example. The goal of the book is to teach students critical thinking and problem-solving skills that will allow them to approach social issues in an objective and informed way.

New to this edition are significant updates on:

- The election of Donald Trump and the emergence of related populist movements
- Trade policy and health care
- Issues involving migration and immigration
- Emerging developments in artificial intelligence
- Comparisons between cultural and biological evolution
- Examples, data, recommended readings, and internet questions

David C. Colander received his PhD from Columbia University and was the Christian A. Johnson Distinguished Professor of Economics at Middlebury College in Middlebury, Vermont from 1982 until 2013, when he was appointed Distinguished College Professor at Middlebury. In 2001–2002 he was the Kelly Professor of Distinguished Teaching at Princeton University. He has authored, co-authored, or edited over 40 books and 200 articles on a wide range of topics. His books have been translated into a number of different languages, including Chinese, Bulgarian, Polish, Italian, and Spanish. He has been president of both the Eastern Economic Association and History of Economic Thought Society and has been on the editorial boards of numerous journals, including the *Journal of Economic Perspectives* and *the Journal of Economic Education*.

Elgin F. Hunt is deceased. He was one of the early authors of this book when it began in the 1930s, and took over as sole author in the 1950s. He continued revising the book until the late 1970s, when David Colander took over.

Social Science

An Introduction to the Study of Society

SEVENTEENTH EDITION

David C. Colander

Elgin F. Hunt

Routledge
Taylor & Francis Group

NEW YORK AND LONDON

Seventeenth edition published 2019
by Routledge
52 Vanderbilt Avenue, New York, NY 10017

and by Routledge
2 Park Square, Milton Park, Abingdon, Oxon, OX14 4RN

Routledge is an imprint of the Taylor & Francis Group, an informa business

First edition published 1955 by MacMillan
Sixteenth edition published 2016 by Routledge

Library of Congress Cataloging-in-Publication Data
A catalog record has been requested for this book

ISBN: 978-1-138-59253-7 (hbk)
ISBN: 978-1-138-32826-6 (pbk)
ISBN: 978-0-429-01955-5 (ebk)

Typeset in Minion Pro
by Servis Filmsetting Ltd, Stockport, Cheshire

Visit the companion website here: www.routledge.com/cw/colander

Dedication

To my granddaughter, Adelaide: May you inherit a peaceful world

Contents

Part II Culture and the Individual

Chapter 4 Society, Culture, and Cultural Change 67

Chapter 5 Geography, Demography, Ecology, and Society 88

Chapter 8   Deviance, Crime, and Society   142

Part III   Institutions and Society

Chapter 13   Stratification, Minorities, and Discrimination   243

Part IV   Politics and Society

Chapter 16   Democratic Government in the United States   315

Part V   Economics and Society

Chapter 17   The Organization of Economic Activities   340

Chapter 18 The Economy, Government, and Economic Challenges Facing the United States 357

Chapter 21   The Political Economies of Developing Countries   418

Preface

Social science is taught in diverse ways. Some courses take a global perspective, some an anthropological perspective, some a psychological perspective, some a sociological perspective, and some a historical perspective—to name just a few. In my view, although each individual social science perspective has something to offer, what distinguishes the social science course is that it looks at problems from as many different perspectives as possible, relying on the scholar's educated common sense to choose the perspective that is most useful for a particular problem. The educated common sense perspective is the social science perspective.

The goal of a social science course is to convey this educated common sense perspective to students. That's not an easy task; as Voltaire once said, common sense is not so common.[1] What he meant by this is that what seems like common sense from one perspective, can seem quite stupid from another. The common sense that we are striving for is an educated common sense—a common sense that has faced vigorous competition from other perspectives. Through the competition of ideas, "common" sense becomes a more and more nuanced common sense. Eventually, with enough competition, common sense becomes educated common sense. Educated common sense involves understanding the nuance in any common sense view, and a recognition of the limits of common sense.

Educated common sense is an important concept for students to learn. At the end of an earlier edition, I included a sheet for students to grade the book and to send me suggestions for improvement. A number of students did this, and their suggestions have played an important role in shaping the book. Most, I'm happy to say, were highly positive, but a few attacked the book and the course. One particularly memorable student flunked me on just about every chapter and wrote the following:

> Until you and this so-called science become legitimized I'd rather spend time gorging myself and then vomiting. Guesses, hypotheses, maybes, might bes don't belong in college; they belong in elementary school.

That student obviously read the book, because he is correct: The book doesn't tell the student what is right or wrong, and it does report guesses, hypotheses, and maybes. But that student is wrong about what does and what doesn't belong in college. Guesses, hypotheses, and maybes are precisely what belong in college, because by the time students are in college they can be expected to have the maturity to understand that knowledge is nothing but good guesses, reasonable hypotheses, and logical maybes. Social science doesn't tell you what's

---

[1] Actually Voltaire was not the only person to have made this point. Many others, before and after, have made the same observation. The reason it has been said so often is that it is just common sense that common sense is not so common.

right. It presents the observations and the theories as fairly as it can and provides you with guidance and training to sift through them and make your own decisions.

The educated common sense perspective blends nuance with facts and truths into a kaleidoscope vision of the world that allows one to see it from multiple perspectives, and to be comfortable with oneself and one's ideas even as one recognizes one's faults and limitations. The goal of the course is to make students open to others' insights but also comfortable with their own insights and sensibilities that they have developed through living and reflection. The skill is often called critical thought, but I prefer to call it educated common sense because critical thought too often is associated with scholars' perspectives, and does not take adequate account of the deep knowledge and sensibility that all people discover by just living. It was that knowledge and sensibility that the original common sense term was meant to capture. Educated common sense modifies, but does not replace, common common sense. It respects knowledge of the mind, but does not make a fetish of it.

In my view colleges teach too little educated common sense. All too often our educational system rushes students into specializations before students have an overall picture—before they know where they want to go. Once they have an overall picture, specialization is necessary, but to make them specialize before having an overall picture is unfair to students. Students who specialize too early don't develop a common sense perspective; they aren't sensitive to the interrelationships and resonances among disciplines. At worst, they become slaves of their discipline's approach. At best, they have the wisdom to recognize that there are many approaches to a problem, but their lack of training forces them to recreate the wheel. Knowledge of the other disciplines would have saved them the trouble and been far more efficient.

That is why I am a strong advocate of the social science course and have been urging colleges to merge their various social science departments into one composite department that focuses more on the interrelationships among the various social sciences than is currently done. The general social science course is one of the most important courses students take in college and, in my view, it is a prerequisite to taking courses in specific social science disciplines. It puts those other disciplines in perspective.

New to This Edition

When the publishers came to me to say that it was time for another edition, I resisted, both because of the work involved and a sense that the last edition would be reasonably acceptable for another year or so. Two events changed my mind, and they are central to the revision of the book.

The first was the election of Donald Trump (and other related populist movements such as Brexit). That election influenced the way we understand both politics and culture. His election brings to the fore issues in economics (trade policy and health care), politics (partisanship, identity of parties, and the divisions within parties) culture (issues of migration and immigration such as DACA), and foreign policy (America First, sovereignty, and globalization) and required revision of all economics and political science focused chapters.

To emphasize its importance, I changed the introduction to capture the differing views on Trump's election, and the recognition that there are different perspectives that need to be acknowledged. Then I integrated a discussion of the issues Trump has raised into many chapters. For example, in Chapter 4, I updated the immigration debate, and explored the different perspectives on immigration. In Chapter 5, I addressed Trump's position on the climate change debate and his pulling the U.S. out of the Paris Climate Accord. In Chapter 16 I discussed how Trump's election reflects forces that may lead to a breaking up of standard political parties, and the emergence of a populist middle that is aligned to neither party. In

Chapter 19 I discuss Trump's America First Policy and how it fits with multilateralism. In Chapter 20 I considered Trump's trade protectionist policy, and the winners and losers from trade. And in Chapter 22 I discussed Trump's war of words with North Korea and potential for conflict. So, if you're wondering why there is another revision—you can blame it on Trump.

The second event is far less known, but, is, I believe, similarly significant. That event is the loss of the top player in the world of the game, Go, to Google's artificial intelligence program, Alpha Go. Go requires far more intuition than chess, so the computer's victory suggests that we are now able to develop algorithms that do better than humans in all types of intuitive activities and jobs in which we previously believed that humans had a unique comparative advantage. This event captures the fact that artificial intelligence is developing much faster than expected, and in the coming decade, expert systems incorporating deep learning algorithms are likely to be a force on the economy and culture as strong as mechanization was in the Industrial Revolution, or globalization was in the 1980s and 1990s.

In short, this development has enormous consequences for culture, economics, psychology and politics, and even for the way we understand humans' role in evolution. It called for substantial revisions in the technology chapter, but also in the discussion of upcoming problems in the economics chapters, and the question of finding meaning to life in the culture and religion chapters.

Those two events were, of course, not the only events that have changed the world in the last three years, and I have also made numerous changes to reflect new scholarship in specific areas. Examples, data, recommended readings and internet questions were all updated. Updates reflecting new scholarly work were also added. For example, in Chapter 2 and Chapter 5 I introduced the new work being done in cooperative and group evolutionary theory, and its implications for the relationship between cultural and biological evolution. I also discuss the new work in epigenetics and its implication of our understanding of the evolutionary process. There were also numerous changes in the political and economic chapters that occurred separately from Trump, such as the ongoing changing political structure in both China and Saudi Arabia. Both are major events with significant implications for the world.

Despite all these changes the book remains what it was in the previous edition—a relatively neutral (at least as neutral as I am able to be), hopefully educated, common sense overview and introduction to the social sciences and social science thinking about the major issues of our day.

*A*cknowledgments

As always, the book benefits from the suggestions of reviewers, colleagues, and students who have e-mailed me. I'd like to thank them all. For this edition, I'd specifically like to thank some great reviewers—Paul Demetriou, Havering College; Edgar Bravo, Miami Dade College Kendall Campus; Victor J. Ingurgio, University of Oklahoma, Norman; Tabitha Otieno, Jackson State University; Alex Gancedo and Harold Silva, Miami Dade College; Caroline Lewis, University of Wales Trinity Saint David; Ruth McGrath, Teesside University; and John Kilburn, Texas A&M International University, among others who wished to remain anonymous.

Over the last few editions the reviewers have included: Tabitha N. Otieno, Jackson State University; Victor J. Ingurgio, University of Oklahoma, Norman; Heather Griffiths, Fayetteville State University; Charles Matzke, Michigan State University; and Ted Williams III, Kennedy-King College, City Colleges of Chicago; William Plants, University of Rio Grande; David S. Schjott, Northwest Florida State College; Emmanuel Agbolosoo, Navajo Community College; Ali Al-Taie, Shaw University; Verl Beebe, Daytona Beach Community College; John Beineke, Kennesaw State College; Thomas J. Bellows, The University of Texas at San Antonio; Dallas A.

Blanchard, University of West Florida; Ducarmel Bocage, Howard University; William K. Callam, Daytona Beach Community College; Pam Crabtree, New York University; Bruce Donlan, Brevard Community College; Anthony Douglas, Lornan, Mississippi; William M. Downs, Georgia State University; Phil A. Drimmel, Daytona Beach Community College; J. Ross Eshleman, Wayne State University; Dana Fenton, City University of New York, Borough of Manhattan Community College; Cyril Francis, Miami Dade College North Campus; Richard Frye, Neuro-Diagnostic Lab, Winchester Memorial Hospital, Winchester, Virginia; Vikki Gaskin-Butler, University of South Florida St. Petersburg; Judy Gentry, Columbus State Community College; Paul George, Miami Dade College; Don Griffin, University of Oklahoma; Heather Griffiths, Fayetteville State University; Charles F. Gruber, Marshall University; Ghulam M. Haniff, St. Cloud State University (Minnesota); Roberto Hernandez, Miami Dade New World Center; Charles E. Hurst, The College of Wooster; Sharon B. Johnson, Miami Dade College; Kenneth C. W. Kammeyer, University of Maryland; Rona J. Karasik, St. Cloud State University; Lynnel Kiely, Truman College; H. D. Kirkland, Lake City Community College; Patricia E. Kixmiller, Miami Dade College; D. R. Klee, Kansas City, Missouri; Casimir Kotowski, Harry S. Truman City College; Errol Magidson, Richard J. Daley Community College; James T. Markley, Lord Fairfax Community College; Stephen McDougal, University of Wisconsin-La Crosse; David J. Meyer, Cedarville University; Karen Mitchell, University of Missouri; Catherine Montsinger, Johnson C. Smith University; Lynn Mulkey, Hofstra University; Roy Mumme, University of South Florida; Eleanor J. Myatt, Palm Beach Junior College; Quentin Newhouse Jr., Howard University; Earl Newman, Henry Ford Community College; Annette Palmer, Howard University; Robin Perrin, Pepperdine University; Joseph Pilkington-Duddle, Highland Beach, Florida; William Primus, Miami Dade College North Campus; Roger Rolison, Palm Beach Community College; William H. Rosberg, Kirkwood Community College; Dan Selakovich, Oklahoma State University; Henry A. Shockley, Boston University; Julie Smith, Mount Aloysius College; Ruth Smith, Miami Dade College; Scharlene Snowden, City University of New York, Medgar Evers College; Ronald Stubbs, Miami Dade College; Larry R. Stucki, Reading Area Community College; Barry Thompson, University of Rio Grande; Judy Thompson, University of Rio Grande; Elizabeth Trentanelli, Miami Dade College; Margaret Tseng, Marymount University; Edward Uliassi, Northeastern University; Angela Wartel, Lewis Clark State College; David Wells, Glendale Community College; Ted Williams, City College of Chicago; W. M. Wright, Lake City Community College; Norman R. Yetman, The University of Kansas; and George Zgourides Primus, Miami Dade College North Campus.

To my knowledge, this is the longest continuing college textbook in the United States. It began in the 1930s when some Chicago professors put together their notes and turned them into a book. It evolved through the 1940s and 1950s into a standard text, and then in the 1960s, Elgin Hunt took it over as the sole author. I took it over in the late 1970s, totally updating and revising it to reflect new developments. I have kept his name on the title to reflect the origins of the book and the fact that it is a collective effort of previous scholars, with a changing group of people working on it.

I always hire students to help me with proofreading, searching for data, reviewing what I have written so that it reflects students' concerns, and they have always done great jobs. This edition is no different, and I would also like to specifically thank Isabella Cass, a student at Middlebury College, who helped with many parts of the revision while she was studying in both China and Russia, keeping me informed of the developments in both those countries. She also updated the test bank and the answers to the end of chapter questions. I would also like to thank all the people at Taylor & Francis involved with this, including Senior Production Editor, Emma Harder and Copyeditor Anna Thomas. Dean Birkenkamp and Tyler Bay did a great job supervising and handling all the editorial issues. I thank them for their hard work. Finally, I want to thank my wife for helping me find the time to work on the book.

D. C. C.

Social Science and Its Methods

After reading this chapter, you should be able to:

- Define social science and explain why it is important
- List the various social sciences
- State the nine steps that make up the scientific method
- Discuss some reasonable approaches to problems in social science
- Differentiate the historical method from the case method and the comparative method
- Distinguish educated common sense from common sense
- Explain why a good scientist is always open to new ways of looking at issues

Theories should be as simple as possible, but not more so.

—Albert Einstein

On November 8, 2016, people gathered around the television at (insert just about any Eastern Seaboard College or University) expecting to cheer Hillary Clinton becoming the first woman president of the United States. The mood was happy; polls predicted a Clinton victory. As the night progressed, the mood changed. Donald Trump, her Republican opponent, who many establishment Republicans had opposed, was doing better than expected; Trump actually had a chance; Trump was leading; Trump had won! Shock and awe is about the only way to describe it. For many in that group, Trump's victory was cataclysmic—they saw it as marking an end of American democracy as they knew it.

That same evening people gathered around the television in (insert just about any southern, rural, mainly white working-class Midwestern non-university town) and had a reverse reaction. Finally, they had been heard. Someone was coming into office who would tell it like it is, drain the swamp, and stick the liberal Eastern establishment elite's political correctness up their collective wazoo, where they felt it belongs. They were concerned about justice for all, but they wanted a justice for all that included justice for them. They were tired of being considered despicable; they were tired of wishy-washy politicians whose views were so filtered that they were at best pablum of the mind. They were tired of politicians who felt they had the right to force their values and world-view on everyone[1].

Other groups dispersed around the country had different reactions. For example, there were those who would be directly affected by the policies Trump had advocated in the

---

[1] The phrasing is, I suspect, jarring for many readers—that's not the way textbooks sound. I use the Trumpesque phrasing in the same way that Trump uses it (as explained in his *Art of the Deal*—to jar, and to set discussion agenda on his terms). I now return to normal textbookeze.

campaign. These included black people, minorities, and immigrants, among others. Their concerns were not intellectual; their concerns were real and pragmatic. What would Trump's election mean for policy? Would immigration be ended? Would Dreamers (children who were brought to the United States illegally, but who had lived just about their entire life there) be deported? Would anti-discrimination policies be ended? . . . Welcome to social science.

Recent previous editions of this book began with a discussion of the 9/11 terrorist attacks on the World Trade Center, and its effect on society and culture. 9/11 served as a focal point for discussions of the interconnections among political, social, cultural, and economic aspects of life. It was an event that pulled the United States together. Trump's victory is a quite different event, but it also serves as a focal point of the interconnections—only this time the focus is on forces pulling U.S. society apart, not pushing it together. The United States has become polarized politically, culturally, and economically. **Social science**—the study of social, cultural, psychological, economic, and political forces that guide individuals in their actions— is the analysis of those forces that push society apart and pull it together.

Formal social science is relatively new. Nevertheless, a vast amount of information has been accumulated concerning the social life of human beings. This information has been used in building a system of knowledge about the nature, growth, and functioning of human societies. Social science is the name given to that system of knowledge.

All knowledge is (1) knowledge of human beings, including their culture and products, and (2) knowledge of the natural environment. Human culture has been changing, and knowledge about it has been gradually accumulating ever since the far distant time when humans first assumed their distinctively human character. But until rather recent times, this knowledge was not scientific in the modern sense. Scientific knowledge is knowledge that has been systematically gathered, classified, related, and interpreted. Science is concerned with learning the concepts and applying those concepts to particulars, rather than just learning a vast amount of information.

Primitive peoples acquired much of their knowledge unconsciously, just as we today still begin the use of our native language and acquire many of the basic elements in our culture unconsciously. For the most part, they accepted the world as they found it, and if any explanations seemed called for, they invented supernatural ones. Some primitive peoples believed that every stream, tree, and rock contained a spirit that controlled its behavior.

In modern times, our emphasis is on the search for **scientific knowledge.** We have divided human knowledge into a number of areas and fields, and every science represents the systematic collection and study of data in one of these areas, which can be grouped roughly into two major fields—social science and natural science. Each of these fields is subdivided into a number of specialized sciences or disciplines to facilitate more intensive study and deeper understanding. Social science is the field of human knowledge that deals with all aspects of the group life of human beings. **Natural science** is concerned with the natural environment in which human beings exist. It includes such sciences as physics and chemistry, which deal with the laws of matter, motion, space, mass, and energy; it also includes the **biological sciences,** which deal with living things. There is more to knowledge than scientific knowledge. There is also **phronesis**, or wisdom, which is a combination of knowledge acquired through philosophical reflection and inquiry, and practical knowledge that one acquires through learning by doing. Whereas scientific knowledge relies on logic, rationality and empirical proofs, phronesis relies on all those plus an instinctual feel for something, and understanding acquired through careful reflection and discussion with others. Some aspects of phronesis are instinctual; for example a bird who instinctually knows they need to migrate south for the winter, or a mother who knows instinctually how to comfort her baby, have knowledge but it is not scientific knowledge. How that knowledge is learned and how one "knows" it, is difficult to determine, but it is knowledge.

These alternative types of knowledge are important for social science since social policy is built on a blend of scientific, philosophical, and practical knowledge. Science tells us what physically is possible; philosophy and practical knowledge tells us what the goals of policy

Street Smarts and Book Smarts

Many of you are taking this course because you have to as part of your degree requirements. A number of you will be somewhat skeptical about the value of the course, and more broadly, the value of the degree. We are sympathetic to your concerns. There is not a lot in this course that will be directly applicable to finding a job, or increasing your pay. Much of it is simply educated common sense. So why is it required?

The answer is that it provides you with the beginning of "book smarts." What are "book smarts"? They are the equivalent to "street smarts"—the instinctual knowledge you get about how to operate successfully in your environment. If you put someone in a new environment, he or she will often flounder—say the wrong thing, miss a joke, interpret an action incorrectly. Over time, one gains street smarts by osmosis—by being in the street; you just know this is how you should act. This is how you can push for something.

There is a similar type of business smarts. Kids who grow up in families in business—where parents have good jobs, and come home and talk about what happened at work—absorb business smarts by osmosis. They become part of their interactions. Depending on the nature of the job, business smarts include street smarts, but they also include knowing when to dump the attitude and fit in—to do what the boss thinks needs to be done, even when the boss is, shall we say, stupid. Business smarts also include what might be called book smarts—a knowledge of how to discuss issues and how to make people realize you are smart. This course involves teaching you book smarts. It conveys to you the thinking of individuals who have been most successful in college and who advise governments and businesses.

Learning the individual facts is less important than learning the reasoning approach that these people use—in a way, it is like learning a foreign language. Making it through the course conveys to employers that you understand the process; and when you get an associate or college degree, this signals employers that you have achieved sufficient book smarts to operate in their world, which you have to do if you want a job.

You probably do not want too much book smarts. Business requires a combination of book and street smarts. People with PhDs in some fields, such as English or Humanities, are as problematic for many business management jobs as are those with no degree at all. Those with PhDs analyze things too much for most businesses. In business, what is wanted is people who understand book smarts, but who can integrate those book smarts with street smarts.

How important is such a signal? That depends. If your name is Kareem, Tamika, Rashid, Ebony, Aisha, or Tyrone, you probably need it more than if your name is Kristen, Greg, Neil, Emily, Brett, Anne, or Jill. How do we know that? Because social scientists have shown it through experiments in which they sent out resumes that were identical except for the names. Resumes with "black-sounding" names had only a 6.7 percent chance of receiving a response, while resumes with "white-sounding" names had a 10.1 percent chance. These researchers found the same amount of built-in "name" discrimination in less-skilled jobs, such as cashier and mailroom attendant, as in more heavily skills-based jobs. How do you get around this? By taking a course such as social science and getting a degree, which signals to the employer that you have "book smarts." We will talk more about these issues in later chapters, but here we just want to point out that it is issues such as these that make up the subject matter of social science.

should be; and a blend of all three tells us how to best achieve those goals. We won't spend a lot of time discussing these alternative types of knowledge other than to acknowledge their importance, and to remind you that science on its own does not lead to policy solutions. Science helps guide, but does not determine, what we should do.

I will, however, introduce you to one tool that moral philosophers use to arrive at philosophical truths—it's called the veil of ignorance or the **impartial spectator tool**. It involves removing yourself from your particular situation, and judging an issue from the perspective of someone who doesn't know which individual he or she will be, and thus will be more likely to be impartial. The goal is to escape one's particular narrow perception of the problem and to arrive at a more neutral view that is more likely to gain broad consensus. Since it is hard to look at issues from other's perspectives, the impartial spectator tool requires extensive discussions and interactions with others who come from different backgrounds and likely disagree with you.

Those discussions are to be carried out not with the goal of winning an argument, but instead with the goal of searching jointly for the truth—a method sometimes called **argumentation for the sake of heaven**—argumentation whose goal is not to win for the sake of winning, but to further one's understanding. Such argumentation leads to what might be called philosophical and moral truths.

In adding these philosophical truths into one's insights, a third field of studies—the humanities—becomes important. Humanities deals with literature, music, art, and philosophy.

The **humanities** are closely related to social science in that both deal with humans and their culture. Social science, however, is most concerned with those basic elements of culture that determine the general patterns of human behavior. The humanities deal with special aspects of human culture and are primarily concerned with our attempts to express spiritual and aesthetic values and to discover the meaning of life. Whereas the social sciences study issues in a systematic, scientific way, the focus of the humanities is more on the emotions and feelings themselves than on the system employed to sharpen that focus. Policy requires a blending of the humanities with science.

The importance of social science goes far beyond the specific social sciences. It is social science thinking that underlies much of the law as well as our understanding of international relations and government. All these fields are the natural by-products of social science inquiry. Thus, a knowledge of social science is necessary for anyone trying to understand current world events.

Social Science

No field of study is more important to human beings than the social sciences. It helps us not only understand society, but also helps us avoid conflict and lead more fulfilling lives. Albert Einstein nicely summed it up: "Politics is more difficult than physics and the world is more likely to die from bad politics than from bad physics."

Because all expressions of human culture are related and interdependent, to gain a real understanding of human society we must have some knowledge of all its major aspects. If we concentrate on some aspects and neglect others, we will have a distorted picture. But social science today is such a vast complex that no one student can hope to master all of it. Thus, social science itself has been broken up into anthropology, sociology, history, geography, economics, political science, and psychology. (The boxes in this chapter provide a brief introduction to each of these disciplines.)

This list of social science disciplines is both too broad and too narrow. It is too broad because parts of the fields of history, geography, and psychology should not be included as social sciences. For instance, parts of history belong in the humanities, and parts of psychology belong in the natural sciences. The list is too narrow because new social sciences are emerging, such as cognitive science and sociobiology, which incorporate new findings and new ways of looking at reality. (See the box on The Evolving Social Sciences.)

Because all knowledge is interrelated, there are inevitable problems in defining and cataloging the social sciences. Often, it is difficult to know where one social science ends and another begins. Not only are the individual social sciences interrelated, but the social sciences as a whole body are also related to the natural sciences and the humanities. The strains of the old song, "The hip bone's connected to the thigh bone, . . ." are appropriate to the social sciences. To understand history, it is helpful, even necessary, to understand geography; to understand economics, it is necessary to understand psychology. Similar arguments can be made for all of the social sciences.

One of the difficulties in presenting definitions and descriptions of the various social sciences is that social scientists themselves do not agree on what it is they do, or should be doing. In preparing this chapter, we met with groups of social scientists specializing in specific fields and asked them to explain what distinguishes their field from others. There was little agreement among specialists in a particular social science, let alone among all social scientists.

*T*he Evolving Social Sciences

The themes of this book are evolution and change. Thus, it would be surprising if the divisions among the social sciences that currently exist still remain ten years from now. Indeed, with the development of new technology and technological advances in the physical sciences, the distinction among the various sciences is blurring and new sciences are developing. As these fields develop, the boundaries of the various social sciences change.

Interaction among the various social sciences is creating new fields, such as economic psychology, psychological economics, and sociopolitical anthropology. In economics and political science, too, a group of economists is calling for the reintegration of these two fields into political economy, and some schools do have departments of political economy.

Change is also occurring in the natural sciences, and there is interaction between the natural and social sciences. New developments in genetic theory, which will be discussed in Chapter 2, have caused many to believe it is time for a new social science, called cognitive science,

which combines psychology, linguistics, philosophy, social anthropology, and molecular biology. Although it is still in the process of formation, a tentative definition of **cognitive science** is the study of how the mind identifies problems and how it solves those problems. For instance, there are more ways to write the letter *s* than there are people who know how to write that letter (all people who write, plus the printing press and computer software and innumerable typefaces designed for them). Let us identify the problem as how to recognize the letter *s* when we see it. We know the result of the exercise: Everyone who knows how to read can instantly recognize most renditions of the letter *s* (the handwriting of a few college students and some physicians excepted). But we do not currently know *how* we do it. Or, how do you distinguish the face of your roommate from the face of your mother, from the face of the letter carrier, from the face of Brad Pitt? There has been speculation about how the mind works for almost as long as there have been minds, theories, and even experiments, but few specific riddles have been conclusively solved. Cognitive science is making inroads in answering such questions.

A cynic once said, "Economics is what economists do." If we replaced "economics" and "economists" with any of the other social sciences and its practitioners, we would have as good a definition as possible. Unfortunately, it would not be very helpful to those who do not know what social scientists do.

One important difference among the individual social scientists did come out of these discussions: Even when two social scientists are considering the same issue, because their training is different, they focus on different aspects of that problem. Geographers fixate on spaces and spatial relativities, economists on market incentives, and political scientists on group decision making. Thus, although we might not be able to define, unambiguously, the domains of the various social sciences, we can give you a sense of the various approaches as we consider issues from various perspectives throughout the book.

The study of social science is more than the study of the individual social sciences. Although it is true that to be a good social scientist you must know each of those components, you must also know how they interrelate. By specializing too early, social scientists can lose sight of the interrelationships that are so essential to understanding modern problems. That is why it is necessary to have a course covering all the social sciences.

To understand how and when social science broke up, you must study the past. Imagine for a moment that you're a student in 1062, in the Italian city of Bologna, site of one of the first major universities in the Western world. The university has no buildings; it consists merely of a few professors and students. There is no tuition fee. At the end of a professor's lecture, if you like it, you pay. And if you don't like it, the professor finds himself without students and without money. If we go back still earlier, say to Greece in the fifth century B.C., we can see the philosopher Socrates walking around the streets of Athens, arguing with his companions. He asks them questions, and then other questions, leading these people to reason the way he wants them to reason (this became known as the *Socratic method*).

Times have changed since then; universities sprang up throughout the world and created colleges within the universities. Oxford, one of the first universities, now has thirty-eight colleges associated with it, and the development and formalization of educational institutions has changed the roles of both students and faculty. As knowledge accumulated, it became more and more difficult for one person to learn, let alone retain, it all. In the sixteenth century, one could still aspire to know all there was to know, and the definition of the Renaissance man (people were even more sexist then than they are now) was one who was expected to know about everything.

Unfortunately, at least for someone who wants to know everything, the amount of information continues to grow exponentially, while the size of the brain has grown only slightly. The way to deal with the problem is not to try to know everything about everything. Today we must specialize. That is why social science separated from the natural sciences and why social science, in turn, has been broken down into various subfields, such as anthropology and sociology.

There are advantages and disadvantages to specialization, and many social problems today are dealt with by teams of various social scientists. Each brings his or her specialty to the table. For example, one of the authors is an economist but works on projects with geographers, sociologists, anthropologists, political scientists, and psychologists. He wrote his most recent book with a physicist. More and more interdisciplinary majors are being created; one of the authors of this book teaches in both the economics department and the international politics and economics department at his school. Interdisciplinary graduate schools of public policy have grown enormously. In these programs, students study all the social sciences while specializing in one. Figure 1.1 provides a graphic overview of the evolution of knowledge and the present social sciences starting with Greece; we could have started earlier, since the Greeks took much of their knowledge from the Middle East and Asia, but we had to cut it off somewhere. (The appendix at the end of this chapter expands on the ideas in this diagram.)

*A*nthropology

Anthropology is the study of the relationship between biological traits and socially acquired characteristics. Sometimes called the study of humans, it consists of two broad fields:

1. Physical anthropology
2. Cultural anthropology

Some of the concerns of physical anthropology are:

- Influence of the evolution of the natural environment on the physical characteristics of humans
- Human evolution: how modern *homo sapiens* evolved from earlier species

Some of the concerns of cultural anthropology are:

- Archaeology, or the remains of extinct civilizations that left no written records
- Organization of preliterate societies
- Characteristics of subgroups or subcultures within contemporary society

Among the topics that interest anthropologists are excavation of formerly inhabited sites, fossils, the gene pool, technology and artifacts, linguistics, values, and kinship.

Social Science as a System of Rules

Today the amount of knowledge is increasing faster than ever. How, then, can a unified social science theory ever be formulated? The answer is found in abstraction and the ability to discover rules or relationships (rather than simply facts) and rules relating rules to other rules.

To understand the importance of knowing rules, think back to grade school when you learned addition. You didn't memorize the sum of 127 and 1,448. Instead you learned an algorithm (a fancy name for a rule) about adding (7 + 8 = 15; write down the 5 and carry the 1 . . .). Then you had to memorize only a few relationships. By changing the number system from a base ten system to a binary system (0 and 1 are the only numbers), you cut substantially the amount of memorization (all you need to know is 0 + 0 = 0; 0 + 1 = 1; and 1 + 1 = 10) and you could apply the same rule again and again, adding all possible numbers (an insight that played an important role in the development of the computer). Knowing the rules saved you from enormous amounts of memorization, but nonetheless gave you access to a large amount of information.

Another way to look at the problem is to think of the library. If you have a small library, you can know nearly everything in it, but once your library gets larger, you will quickly find that having more books makes it harder to know what's in there. However, if you put in place a filing system, such as the Dewey

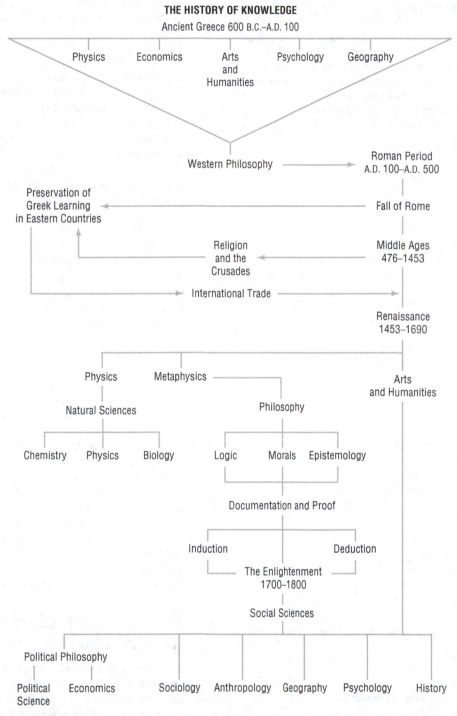

Figure 1.1

Knowledge at a glance. The development of knowledge is messy, but assuming that a picture is worth a thousand words, we offer this sketch of the development of knowledge. Maybe it's worth five hundred words.

Sociology

Sociology is the systematic study of relationships among people. Sociologists assume that behavior is influenced by people's social, political, occupational, and intellectual groupings and by the particular settings in which they find themselves at one time or another. Sociologists differ in their approach. Their three major choices are:

1. Functionalism
2. Conflict
3. Interactionism

Sociology's vast subject matter can be identified as a study of people:

- Where they collect
- How they socialize and organize
- Whom they include in and exclude from their groups
- What they do to their environment
- When they confront formulas for control, such as politics, law, finance, religion, education, and social pressures
- Why they change

Geography

Geography is the study of the natural environment and how the spatial interactions of individuals influence social and cultural development. Some of the concerns of geography are:

- Ecology
- Climate
- Resources
- Accessibility
- Demography

Geography has practical applications manifest in:

- Maps
- Trade patterns
- Industrial and agricultural decisions
- Settlement of population
- Aggression and acquisition

decimal system or the Library of Congress system, you can access the books through a filing system. The rules of the filing system give you the key to great amounts of information, just as the rules of addition, subtraction, or algebra do. General rules, once learned, can be applied to large numbers of particulars. The higher you go (rules about rules about rules), the more you can know with less memorization.[2]

All this is relevant to social science because social science is held together by rules or relationships. If there is to be a unified social science theory, it will be because some student started thinking about rules and how the rules of the various social sciences can fit together. If you understand the general concepts, you can apply them in a variety of circumstances. Thus the future "unified social scientists" will not necessarily know all the facts of a particular social science. Each of the specialties will retain its identity and will likely become even more specialized. But as that specialization occurs, it creates the need for a new specialization that concentrates on tying together the various component parts of social science. The new unified social scientists will know the general rules of the individual social sciences and the rules of how one social science interacts with another, but they will not know all the specific facts of any one of them.

The preceding argument is a heavy one to throw at you in the first pages of a textbook because it asks you not only to know the lessons of the individual social sciences, but also to go beyond and strive for an understanding of their synthesis. Going beyond is ultimately what learning is all about and what makes it so challenging. We would like to be able to say that we can guide you to a unified social science theory, but the truth is that all we can do is give you a boost and encouragement. After surveying the social sciences, you can decide in which one, if any, you want to specialize; whether you should work toward tying them all together; or whether you should bag the whole approach and go into a pre-med program.

The Scientific Method and Its Application

The **scientific method** is a set of rules about how to establish rules. The use of the scientific method is perhaps the most important tool you can have in studying social science because it enables you not only to learn the lessons of the individual social sciences,

---

[2] It was an architect, Ludwig Mies van der Rohe, who compressed such exposition into a famous statement, "Less is more."

*H*istory

History is the study of past events. It is a social science in the sense that it is a systematic attempt to learn about and verify past events and to relate them to one another and to the present. Every event has a historical context within which we commonly say the event must be studied. The subject matter of history is everything that has already happened. The study of history involves:

- Identifying
- Classifying
- Arranging
- Patterning

The fruits of the study of history are:

- Imposition of order
- Appreciation of variety
- Possibilities of prediction
- Realization of limitation

but also to go beyond and strive for an understanding of their synthesis.

Conditions Favorable to Scientific Inquiry. Scientific inquiry is possible only in a society in which certain attitudes are developed or tolerated. Successful scientific investigation requires from the investigator not only intelligence but certain mental attitudes as well. One of these is curiosity, which makes people ask two questions: Why? and How? Another is skepticism, which makes people reexamine past explanations and reevaluate past evidence. To reexamine and reevaluate, investigators need objectivity, which enables them to seek impartially for the truth, to make every effort not to allow personal preconceptions, prejudices, or desires to color the observed facts or influence the interpretation of those facts. When these three attitudes—curiosity, skepticism, and objectivity—come together, scientific inquiry can flourish.

In preliterate tribal societies, the obstacles to the development of scientific methods of inquiry are very great. Such societies are much more bound by custom and tradition than are modern societies. The traditional way of doing things is regarded as the only right way. Moreover, any serious deviation from established procedures is likely to be regarded as a danger to the group.

We cannot classify Europe in the Middle Ages as either preliterate or tribal. Nevertheless, respect for tradition, for ancient authorities, and for religious dictates was so strong then that the growth of a scientific spirit was stunted. The free development of modern science had to wait until such events as the Crusades, the Renaissance, the great voyages of discovery, and the Reformation had loosened the hold of tradition.

Nature of the Scientific Method. Modern science is based on the assumption that this is an orderly universe, ruled by the law of cause and effect. Any given set of circumstances always produces the same result. If seemingly identical situations have different results, they were not really alike; some significant difference existed and was overlooked. Further investigation should disclose what this difference was.

Science offers no final explanations of the universe and its phenomena. Time, space, matter, energy—existence itself—are mysteries the ultimate nature of which is probably forever beyond the grasp of the human search. But an accepted scientific theory may be regarded as an explanation, up to a certain point, of a scientific law.

Scientific investigation is seldom simple. Each field of knowledge has its special problems, and investigators must always adjust their methods to the peculiarities of the situation they are dealing with. A method of investigation that is of great importance in some fields is the setting up and carrying out of controlled experiments.

The Experimental Method and Its Limitations. The **experimental method** is a method of separating out causal factors. It consists of running an experiment many times with only one variant. If the results of the experiments are different, that one variant is most likely the cause.[3] In chemistry, physics, and biology, such controlled experiments play an important role in

---

[3] But it is always possible that some other factor was not "held constant." If you remember chemistry experiments in high school, you know how hard it is to keep all other things constant.

*T*he Saga of Hans, the Thinking Horse

The scientific method can be seen in the saga of Hans, the Thinking Horse. Around 1900, according to reports published in a Berlin, Germany, newspaper, there was a horse that was good at math, and when his owner asked him math questions, the horse could answer by tapping out the correct number with one of his front hooves. People who witnessed the horse's ability were puzzled, and they called in a number of social scientists to investigate the phenomenon. To their amazement, they found that not only could Clever Hans, as he was known, add and subtract when his owner asked him, but he also could calculate square roots. The social scientists were convinced that, against all odds, they had indeed been shown a thinking horse.

Another social scientist, though, a skeptical young psychologist by the name of Oskar Pfungst, had a different idea. He retested Hans, asking a set of questions to which Pfungst himself did not know the answers. He discovered that although Hans succeeded on nearly every question if the questioner knew the answer, the horse failed nearly every question when the questioner did not know the

answer. A social scientist's skepticism had shown that Hans could not really reason, even though it seemed as if he could. This true story demonstrates the important trait of skepticism. The scientific community declared that Hans was just a horse.

But a quality those scientists did not show was imagination. Even though Hans could not think and reason, he had an amazing ability: He could almost read minds. When it came to people who knew the answers to the questions they were asking, he could monitor changes in his questioners' posture, their breathing, their facial expressions, and their inflections and speech patterns. He could interpret the signals they were sending and then provide the responses they wanted. This is an ability that some humans have—although generally to a lesser degree than Hans—and it is an ability that can supplement thinking. Yet it was only at the end of the twentieth century that comparative psychologists showed the imagination to start analyzing this kind of ability in detail.

The lack of imagination exhibited by some scientists in the past limited the scope of the scientific programs they followed. A good scientist must have both skepticism and imagination.

discovering facts and testing hypotheses. In these sciences, an investigator can create a situation in which all the significant factors that bear on a problem can be controlled.

There are, however, limits to the use of the experimental method when a scientist cannot control the situations that are significant for the solution of problems. In the social sciences, less use can be made of the method of controlled experiment, except in dealing with certain relationships that involve rather small groups, because the investigator cannot control the situations. For example, one way to prove or disprove the proposition that high tariffs bring prosperity would be to apply very heavy tariffs to all goods entering the United States for a considerable period of time, while holding constant all other factors affecting business activity. If a sustained increase in prosperity followed, we would then have substantial evidence to support the thesis that high duties are a cause of prosperity. No investigator, let us say an economist, can control the country's tariff policy; and even if she could, while the high tariff was in effect many other social changes would be taking place, such as strikes, the establishment of new industries, and perhaps even wars. Some of these other changes would doubtless have much more influence on the state of national prosperity than would the high tariff and would make it impossible to separate out the effects of the high tariff from the effects of all these other events.

Most problems of interest to social scientists involve very large groups of people, often society as a whole. Controlled experiments cannot be used to solve such problems. When, however, social scientists can gain insight into a problem through laboratory and field experiments, they can, at least partially, control the environment. For example, often firms on Google use field experiments, randomly varying the way an advertisement is presented to people. One ad might state "one-half off"; the other might state "50 percent off." Although these have the same meaning, the way people respond to them is not necessarily the same. The firms then analyze the results and structure future ads to reflect the presentation that was most effective. Every time you are on the Internet, you provide opportunities for firms to conduct field experiments to figure out how to make more money off you. Social scientists also study natural experiments, which occur when two similar areas or entities choose different policies, and the effects of the different policies can be systematically studied. With natural experiments, researchers do not get perfect control, but they get some.

Additionally, social scientists use laboratory experiments, in which they have people come into the lab, where they study their behavior, and then relate that behavior to other information they can find about them. One of the most famous of these is known as the Stanford Marshmallow Experiment, in which psychologists studied 4-year-olds' ability to delay gratification. They gave each child a marshmallow, but promised him or her two if the child would wait twenty minutes before eating it. They then studied the progress of these students for the next twenty years, and found that those students who could delay gratification were psychologically better adjusted, more dependable persons, and received higher grades than those who could not.

In the future, with further advances in computer technology, social scientists will study policy issues using virtual social systems in which a computer model of numerous interacting individuals creates a virtual system that can analog what occurs in the real world. Because of the complexity of social systems, such virtual systems remain a hope for the future, not a reality.

Social experiments are sometimes called experiments, but unless they have a "control" that followed a different path and hence can be studied as a natural experiment, they are not what we mean by experiment. A social experiment is simply the introduction and "trying out" of new social policies. For example, Oregon's change in the financing of health insurance or Florida's experiments with vouchers for financing education might be called social experiments. The distinction involves the ability to have a control and to be able to replicate the experiment. The less the control, and the less the ability to repeat the experiment, the less sure we are of the results.

Methodology and the Social Sciences

Because it is so difficult to experiment in social science, some people have insisted that it is not science. Except for the prestige carried by the word, whether we call the study of society a science is not important. It is merely a question of definition. If we mean by *science* the natural sciences only, then social science is not true science. If we mean by science only the so-called exact sciences, then again social science is not included. If, however, we use the term *science* broadly, to include all systematic attempts to expand knowledge by applying the scientific method, then social science definitely must be included in the scientific family. What is really important is that social scientists have discovered many significant relationships that are sufficiently dependable to add greatly to our understanding of social behavior and to serve as useful guides in dealing with some social problems.

There has been much debate about the correct methodology to be used in social science. Thomas Kuhn, a famous philosopher of science, defined a **paradigm** as a scientific theory and the core of beliefs that surround it. He argued that scientific progression occurs by paradigm shifts in which, for a long time, scientists will resist change and hold on to an old theory even as evidence mounts up against it, and even when another theory better fits the data. Eventually, however, the evidence in favor of the new theory is so

*E*conomics

Economics is the study of the ways in which men and women make a living, the most pressing problem most human beings face. It considers the social organization through which people satisfy their wants for scarce goods and services. Its subject matter is often summarized as:

- Production
- Distribution
- Consumption

Some of the topics it includes are:

- Supply and demand
- Monetary and fiscal policy
- Costs
- Inflation
- Unemployment

Economics seeks to explain, guide, and predict social arrangements by which we satisfy economic wants.

Political Science

Political science is the study of social arrangements to maintain peace and order within a given society. It deals with government, and its interests are:

- Politics
- Laws
- Administration
- Theory of the nature and functions of the state
- International relations

It has both a philosophical and a practical base. It examines the theory of systems of government, but it also studies actual practices of governments, which:

- Levy taxes
- Prohibit
- Regulate
- Protect
- Provide services

Psychology

Psychology deals with the mind and personality of the individual. It is a social science because humans are social creatures. It focuses on the individual and physical processes, such as:

- Biological structure
- Development and maturation

Of the various branches of psychology, the most relevant to social science is social psychology. Social psychology is the study of the individual's behavior as it influences and is influenced by the behavior of others. Some specific topics that interest psychologists and social psychologists are:

- Socialization
- Environment and heredity
- Adjustment and maladjustment

Psychologists deal with natural phenomena such as emotion, memory, perception, and intelligence.

great that suddenly scientists shift their thinking. The process can be likened to the way a drop of water forms on a faucet. It grows larger and larger until it falls. A good example in the sciences is Einstein's relativity theory in physics, which was initially scoffed at but was later adopted because it was consistent with a wider range of physical phenomena than was the earlier gravitational theory of Sir Isaac Newton.

Social scientists have discussed at great length whether Kuhn's theory of paradigm shift is appropriate for the social sciences. If it is, it gives legitimacy to competing theories. If it is not, then the generally accepted theory can be considered the best. The issue has never been resolved, but our understanding of the relevance of theories has advanced.

Imre Lakatos, another famous philosopher of science, has extended Kuhn's arguments by saying that in social science there are generally many competing theories, each being extended through competing **research programs,** or groups of scientists working on a particular problem. For example, in psychology there are the behaviorists and the Freudians. In sociology there are functionalists, conflict theorists, and interactionists. We could cite different theories within each social science. Advocates of each of the research programs compete for researchers. The group of researchers most successful in competing for followers is the one most likely to grow.

Other philosophers of science go further. Some, like Paul Feyerabend, argue that all methodology is limiting and that the correct methodology is no methodology. Still others argue that sociological issues, such as what is likely to advance a scientist's career, rather than the truth of a theory, determine what the scientist believes.

In this book, we emphasize the competition among various theories. By doing so, we hope to show how, in social science, controversy plays an important role in the development of our knowledge.

Probably the best way to understand the scientific method is to consider a couple of examples that do *not* follow the scientific method. For instance, consider astrology or numerology. These pseudostudies hold that by analyzing the alignment of the stars or the position of certain numbers, individuals can discover or predict events that will affect them. However, the accuracy of the discoveries or the reliability of the predictions has never been satisfactorily demonstrated to most social scientists. Even though we might turn to our horoscopes and say, "Aha! That seems to fit my character or my experience," if we critically consider these predictions, often we see that the statements are so broad that they can be applied more or less appropriately to a wide range of happenings or possibilities. This is not to say that the social sciences always avoid that. Economics, for instance, often comes up with predictions from large, highly sophisticated mathematical models (called *econometric models*), and some of these predictions are no better for steering a course than back-of-the-envelope estimates.

A good social scientist generally takes an agnostic (not believing but also not disbelieving) position about claims until they can be tested and retested. Consider, for example, parapsychology, which argues that people can transmit certain information independently of all conventional forms of communication. There is an entire professional association devoted to studying parapsychology issues, such as the ability to transfer thoughts and feeling by means other than the standard senses, and the ability to communicate with the dead. Most social scientists remain unconvinced. They hold that, to date, the theories have not been sufficiently demonstrated. In stating that these theories have not been tested, a good social scientist is not dogmatic. It is possible that we social scientists have become so tied to our way of looking at the world that we are unable to consider the possibilities of other ways. Who is to say that the tests we accept as conclusive are the "right" tests, or that our training has not biased the tests?

Ultimately, however, we must make a working judgment about what is and what is not an acceptable test, and social scientists' methodology is an expression of that working judgment. It should, however, be presented as a working judgment, not as a set of definitive criteria of what is true and what is false. That is why, generally, good social scientists remain agnostic over a wide range of issues that they just do not have time to investigate. Thus, in many ways, what you will get out of a study of social science and an understanding of its methods is a healthy understanding of the limitations of your powers to know.

*T*he Methods of Social Science

The basic procedures of the scientific method are as important in social science as in physical science. Social scientists must observe carefully, classify and analyze their facts, make generalizations, and attempt to develop and test hypotheses to explain their generalizations. Their problem, however, is often more difficult than that of physical scientists for two reasons. First, facts gathered by the social scientist—for example, those concerning the cultures of different peoples—have similarities, but each fact may also be unique in significant respects. Facts of this kind are difficult to classify and interpret. Further, as we have already noted, the generalizations or laws that the social scientist can make are likely to be less definite and certain than those of the physical scientist.

The second reason is that social scientists are generally interested in more than just knowing scientific truths; they are interested in policy. As we stated above, policy requires going beyond science and incorporating moral judgments, which are much more difficult to come to agreement on, into the analysis. This often makes social science policy much more difficult than physical or natural science policy. For example, in the physical sciences we might study the laws of physics—if two objects crash the force exerted by either of the two objects will be equal even if one is much heavier than the other—this is Newton's Third Law of motion. It seems counterintuitive, but once one understands the framework physics uses for understanding relationships among objects, it is almost obvious. No one is going to argue with it.

"I'm a social scientist, Michael. That means I can't explain electricity or anything like that, but if you ever want to know about people, I'm your man."

Now consider economists' law of supply and demand—that if supply exceeds demand, there will be pressures for the price to rise. This law is also obvious once one understands economists' framework. But it is not so easily accepted. Often people don't want the price to rise, and have established institutions to prevent it from doing so, or to implement policy that prevents the rise. That can be done, but it will have consequences, and economists' job as scientists is not to say that policy to hold down price is good or bad. Instead, their role as scientists is to explain—here are the consequences if you do that. Their role as policy advisors is different, and more complex. To decide whether a policy to hold down price is good policy requires an introduction of goals of policy which is determined in moral philosophy—the normative branch of social studies. The policy issue is not resolved by science.

When the physical sciences become closely tied to policy, physical scientists also find that they are mired in conflict and debate just like the social sciences. Consider climate change and global warming. Physical scientists are agreed that global warming is occurring and that the most likely cause is humans' use of fossil fuel. That is a question in the realm of science. What to do about it—the policy implications—requires going out of science and integrating moral philosophy into the analysis. Should we care about global warming? Who should change their actions to stop it? What is the time frame within which we should respond? These and hundreds of similar questions have no easy answer, but they have to be answered if scientists are to provide policy guidance. Science does not deal with such questions. The philosophical way of answering those questions is argumentation for the sake of heaven—having all sides come together to honestly debate the issue in a spirit of mutual acceptance.

The blending of the two roles of a social scientist often leads to difficulties. For example, climate change scientists often have strong views about policy, which is a problem because the science and the policy can become intertwined. When a scientist takes a strong view on a policy question, it leads to a loss of objectivity (or at least in others' perceptions of the scientist's objectivity) of the scientific conclusions. Are the policy views influencing his or her interpretation of the scientific evidence in such a way as to favor his or her policy conclusion. Just as one has a difficult time remaining neutral when judging one's own children relative to others, so too does a scientist have a difficult time judging empirical evidence that relates to a policy he or she believes is necessary.

Because of the blending of science and policy in climate science, the debate has become toxic in both the science and the policy, with both sides not arguing for the sake of heaven, but arguing for the sake of winning and making points, in the same way that many policy debates in social science have become toxic. The same type of problem often exists in social sciences when policy and science become blended. To avoid that toxicity it is important to separate science and policy, and for scientists, in their role as scientists, to have no policy view, or when they have a policy view, to be sure that they have other scientists with opposing policy views on their scientific research team to keep them honest. Often a good social scientist makes all sides mad at him or her.

An Example of the Social Science Method

Let's take an example of the use of the social science method—Joseph Hotz's study of the implications of teen pregnancy. First, he studied all the writing on teen pregnancy. Then he set up the following hypothesis: Teen motherhood causes the mothers to be economically and socially worse off than they otherwise would have been. To test this hypothesis, he used data that had been collected over many years tracking the lives of teenage women. From that he extracted two groups—a set of teenagers who had become pregnant and borne the child and a set of teenagers who had become pregnant but had miscarried. He then compared their economic and social positions when they were in their mid-thirties. If teen motherhood caused the mother to be worse off, then the teens who had borne their babies should have been in a worse position than those who miscarried. They weren't. He found no significant difference between the two groups: Both were low-income, significantly dependent on welfare benefits, and had completed the same number of years of school. The initial hypothesis was false. Teen pregnancy did not make mothers worse off; it was simply a symptom of a larger set of problems. This larger set of problems was so severe that whether mothers had borne a child in their teens made little difference to their economic and social positions.

Hotz's findings were published as the government was conducting a costly campaign against teen motherhood, and his conclusions were unpopular with both liberals and conservatives. Liberals did not like them because his study suggested that much of the family planning advice and sex education developed by liberals was of little help in improving these women's lives. Conservatives did not like them because his study implied that more substantive changes than simply eliminating teen motherhood were needed to improve these women's lives and break the cycle of poverty. But good social science methodology is not about pleasing anybody—it is about understanding social issues and social problems.

Although Hotz's experiment was not fully controlled, it was as close as one could come to a controlled experiment in the social sciences. It selected similar groups to compare in such a way that no obvious reason existed as to why these two groups should differ.

Other Social Science Methods

In addition to the experimental method, social scientists use a variety of different methods. These include the historical method, the case method, and the comparative and cross-cultural methods.

The historical method. Because most social developments—such as the government of the United States—have unique characteristics, in order to understand them as fully as possible the social scientist must rely heavily on a study of their historical background. We can never understand completely how any historical situation came to exist, because there are limits to our historical knowledge and causes become increasingly complex and uncertain as we trace them further into the past. We can, however, make both historical events and present social situations much more intelligible by using the **historical method**—tracing the principal past developments that seem to have been directly significant in bringing about a social situation. To trace these past developments, a historian will use many of the same methods as other social scientists, such as collecting birth and marriage certificates and classifying those data.

It has been noted that history never really repeats itself. Nevertheless, present and past situations often have such striking similarities that a knowledge of the past can give us insights into present situations and sometimes into future trends.

The case method. Writers on the methodology of social research have devoted a great deal of attention to the **case method**—its characteristics, its variations, the uses it can serve, its advantages, and its limitations. Here we only describe its basic nature. The case method involves making a detailed examination and analysis of a particular issue or problem situation. This can involve a case study of a single person, such as that by a psychologist of his or her client; a single area or town, such as a sociologist's study of why a town changes; or even a study of whole countries, such as an economist's study involving comparisons of various countries.

A case study can be intended to discover how to bring about desirable changes in a particular problem situation: for example, to find the most effective ways of upgrading or rehabilitating a slum area. More often, the chief purpose of a case study is to throw light on many similar situations that exist in a society. The hope is that an understanding of one or a few cases will illuminate the others and thus aid in solving the social problems they present. The case or cases selected should be typical of the group they purport to represent.

The preceding requirement can be a limiting factor in the usefulness of the case method. Suppose we wanted to make a study of the class structure of U.S. society as a whole. Obviously, it would be easier to select as cases for study several relatively small and isolated cities in various sections of the country. But it is questionable whether these would give us a true picture of the country as a whole, because today a great proportion of our people lives in large metropolitan areas where the class structure is likely to be much more complex than in smaller and more isolated communities. However, to study and describe in detail the class structure of such an area may be prohibitively difficult and expensive, and therefore impractical.

The comparative and cross-cultural methods.   The **comparative method** was formerly often employed in the hope of discovering evolutionary sequences in the development of human institutions—that is, patterns of social development or progress that would be universal. For example, it was sometimes assumed that definite stages existed in the development of governmental institutions, and it was thought that these stages could be discovered by comparing a society at one level of development with some other society at a different level. Today, this attempt to find patterns of social evolution that can be applied to all societies has been largely abandoned.

Comparison of different societies, however, still plays an important role in anthropological studies through what is called the **cross-cultural method.** This method consists of making detailed studies of the cultural patterns of a number of societies for the purpose of comparing the different ways in which their people meet similar needs. These studies sometimes show surprising similarities in the cultural traits of widely separated peoples who appear to have had no direct or indirect contacts with one another.

Comparison of the characteristics of different societies involves problems. At times, it is difficult to decide whether two or more societies are independent or should be treated as one. Or consider definitions: If we are comparing the family institution in different societies, we must define *family* broadly enough to cover cultural variations, yet specifically enough to make comparisons meaningful. Sociologists do not always agree on just what a family is. Again, if we are comparing unemployment in urban-industrial societies, we must agree on what we mean by *unemployment*. For example, in the early 1980s, the unemployment rate in Mexico, computed by U.S. standards, was approximately 30 percent. Mexican economists, however, argued that this figure was meaningless because Mexican work habits and culture were different from those in the United States. Much of what was measured as unemployment, they said, was actually individuals working at home and not earning money in the marketplace. Thus, although they had nonmarket jobs, they had been counted as unemployed.

Educated Common Sense in the Social Sciences

Probably the most important lesson to remember when conducting any research is that you should use what might be called an **educated common sense.** To see the difference between common sense and *educated* common sense, consider the problem: Does the earth circle the sun or does the sun circle the earth? Uneducated common sense tells us that the sun circles the earth, and that common sense conclusion became built into society and society's view of itself throughout the Middle Ages. To believe otherwise was heresy. In 1540, Copernicus tried to fit that common sense view with observations that classical Greeks had made of the heavens. As he went about this task, he discovered that he could get a good fit of the data with the theory only if he assumed the earth moved around the sun. His was an educated common sense—rational thought based on observation and the best information available. It was that kind of educated common sense that ultimately led to the scientific method. As specialization makes us focus on narrower and narrower issues, it is important to keep in the back of our minds that scientific analysis has made us look at only part of the problem and that we must also use our educated common sense to interpret the results reasonably.

The Use of Statistics

Whenever possible, social scientists rely on quantitative data—data that can be reduced to numbers—but often quantitative data are not available, so social scientists must rely on qualitative data such as interviews or heuristic summaries of information in the literature. When using qualitative data, it is much more difficult to draw specific inferences from the data, because the "facts" one finds depend on how one interprets the qualitative data. One way to partially overcome such "interpretive problems" is the "Delphi method" in which another specialist in the field reviews your interpretation and then you modify your interpretation in response if you see fit, explaining your reasons for accepting or rejecting the suggested modifications. Another way is to translate the qualitative data into quantitative data, creating "proxies" (stand-ins) for any missing quantitative data, although that often simply hides the interpretative issues rather than eliminating them.

If quantitative data are available, social scientists rely on **statistical analysis**—information in numerical form that has been assembled and classified—to provide the social scientist with the information needed to understand social relationships and processes. Statistics do not enable us to measure directly such basic social values as good citizenship, happiness, or welfare, but they are useful in measuring other factors that underlie social life, such as the size of the population of a country, or the number of families whose incomes fall below some level that we set as the minimum for decent and healthful living. Statistical relationships also give us insights into social problems. If we find that the proportion of males in juvenile detention centers who come from broken homes is substantially greater than the proportion of males in the population at large who come from such homes, this suggests that broken homes may be an important factor contributing to juvenile delinquency. But statistics must always be interpreted with care, for it can be easy to read into them conclusions they do not justify. Also, it is sometimes possible to manipulate them so that they appear to show what we want them to show.

Although statistics measure the results of social activity and highlight trends, they have other useful functions: testing theories and discovering relationships. For example, **correlation** is the relationship between two sets of data. A high positive correlation between sets of data means that if an element in one set rises, its corresponding element in the other set is also likely to rise. Other statistics determine how sure we are of a relationship. We do not discuss these statistics because an introductory social science course is not the place to learn them, but it *is* the place to learn that such techniques of testing relationships exist, and they may be worth your while to study at some point in the future.

If we are going to use statistics, we must have data. Data are the raw numbers describing an event, occurrence, or situation. Social scientists' data come from measuring and counting all occurrences of a particular happening. For example, we might find, "In 2019, there were x number of murders and y number of suicides." One way to get data is to conduct a **survey,** a method whereby data are collected from individuals or institutions by means of questionnaires or interviews. For instance, we might conduct a survey in which selected people are questioned or polled on such matters as their incomes, their beliefs on certain issues, or the political candidate for whom they intend to vote. Statistics can tell us how large a portion of a group must be surveyed before we can be reasonably sure that the results will reflect the views of the entire group. Such techniques are used extensively in surveys such as the Gallup or Harris public opinion polls.

The use of statistics has been greatly facilitated, and therefore greatly expanded, by the computer. The computer has made it possible to record, arrange, and rearrange voluminous information quickly and analytically. Today, enormous amounts of data and other resources are available to anyone with a computer or other access to the Internet.

With the expansion of social data and the large increase in computing power, it is increasingly possible for social scientists to look for relationships in the data alone, rather than to be guided in that search by theories. Using highly sophisticated statistical techniques, social scientists analyze data, looking for patterns. After they find a pattern, they fit that pattern to a theory. For example, social scientists Stephen Levitt and John Donohue searched the data and found a relationship between the passage of the abortion rights law in the United States and a decrease in crime in later periods. Based on this evidence, they argued that because abortion reduced the number of unwanted children, those children who were born had more guidance, and that it was the law making abortion legal, not any change in law enforcement or increase in the number of inmates jailed, that was mostly responsible for the decrease in crime rates that the United States experienced in the 1990s.

Whenever making such claims, social scientists should be very careful not to confuse correlation—the simultaneous movement of two variables—with **causation**—in which change in one variable brings about change in the other variable. The difference can be seen in the following example. When it is expected to rain, more people carry umbrellas, so umbrella usage and rain are correlated. But the fact that people carry umbrellas does not cause it to rain, or so most of us believe.

The Interdisciplinary Approach

Modern industrial societies and their problems are becoming increasingly complex, and because no one person today can master all the social sciences, growing emphasis is placed on the interdisciplinary approach to many social problems. The **interdisciplinary approach** means that a group of social scientists with different specialties will work together on a particular problem, not all aspects of which any one of the group fully understands. For some problems, such as those surrounding pollution, it may be necessary to call in, say, a physical scientist, a geologist, and an engineer. But in facing all of these problems, the need for educated people who have a broad sense of problems and interrelationships—who understand the need for a unified social science—is becoming more and more evident.

Though few social relationships can be reduced to exact and invariable laws, human beings in large groups everywhere show great likenesses of behavior when conditions are really similar. Thus, there is reason to believe that we can, through systematic study and research, greatly increase our understanding of the nature and development of human societies, and to hope that the attitudes fostered by the interdisciplinary approach itself and the knowledge to which it leads us can ultimately result in greater tolerance and cooperation among diverse groups and among nations.

The Impartial Spectator and the Veil of Ignorance

As I discussed above, to move from an understanding of the social system—the goal of social science as a science—to guidance on social policy, social scientists need to add values to the analysis—not his or her values, but the values of the group or person he is advising. For example, in advising a society, one uses "society's goals" and explores how to achieve those goals in a way that is consistent with society's values. Science does not determine those values or goals, moral philosophy does. The impartial spectator tool, and the related veil of ignorance, are tools that we will be continually reaching back to in our policy discussions. For example, to many it seems obvious that most tax revenue should come from the rich. But how about from the perspective of a rich person who spent all her time working, while others played? What will she think of her paying more? Most will want to give her likely view—that it would be improper for her to pay more in tax—some weight in the decision of who should pay taxes, and what is fair.

Drawing Policy Implications from Social Science

Much of the relevance of social science is for its policy implications. While we will focus on the scientific aspect of social science—where the goal of study is to understand for understanding's stake, not to solve a problem, throughout the book we will discuss how a social scientist relates that scientific knowledge learned to policy. Here, we will consider some of the key heuristics (general rules) that guide that application.

1. *Put Yourself in All Person's Shoes.* Probably the most important rule about drawing policy implications from social science insights is the "put yourself in all person's shoes" rule. The natural way to approach policy is to approach it from your perspective. The social science approach says that is the wrong way to think about policy—you have to think about it from an outside perspective, not from your perspective alone. Think of yourself as observing the entire social system, and having the ability to put yourself in all other people's shoes. After you have done that, you can pull all the different perspectives together, and come up with a solution that is based on all perspectives, not just yours.

2. *Recognize your inherent bias and adjust for it.* It's impossible to fully take an outside perspective, which leads to the second rule—recognize that you will likely be biased toward your own perspective, and attempt to honestly communicate with people who have different perspectives. Bend over backwards to be open to multiple views.

3. *Distinguish differences in interpretation of facts from differences in normative judgments.* Perspective is based on both interpretation of facts, and on normative judgments you make. Differences in readings of the facts can, in principle, be eliminated by scientific study, and that is what much of what social science does. It discusses facts—information that is true to the best of our current understanding. Differences in normative views can be discussed, but they are not resolvable by science—thus one can expect differences about policy even if all people interpret the facts in the same way. But those differences are likely to be far smaller than they would be if people didn't follow a social scientific approach to policy.

4. *Be Humble.* Even if you follow the above three rules as best you can, there is no way that you are going to be able to fully communicate in a way that you gain other people's perspective, which leads to the final rule—be humble in your policy suggestions—be very hesitant to say, "This is the right policy, and another policy is the wrong policy." Say instead, "Based on the knowledge I have now, this is, in my estimation, the best policy I can come up with now." Be open to criticism and discussion.

Discussing such issues openly and honestly in an environment that encourages argumentation for the sake of heaven is about the only way to come to an agreement on what is meant by social goals, which is why that discussion is a necessary part of social policy.

Values, Terminology, and Rhetoric

This chapter began with a quotation from Albert Einstein, who said, "theories should be as simple as possible, but not more so." The same thing could be said about ideas and the expression of those ideas. Unfortunately, specialists have an incentive to develop a terminology that is anything but simple and that often obscures rather than clarifies. One of the many social science teachers who has written us about this book (and in doing so, these teachers have played an important role in its development) described a history conference she attended where "we were treated to such goodies" as

The sociopolitical internecine amortizations of agronomous proletarization, if solely counterproductive of Jurassic multi-dimensional interstitial extrapolated Augustinian and Aristotelian epistemological diagrammetric middle-sector dichotomies, as measured in the context of paradigmatic vestigiae (though challenged none too effectively, if I am not remiss in saying so, by Freylinghausen's hypothesis delivered at the University of Bordeaux in April 1896) are existentially and polaristically categorized by Nordlinger's Metternichian thermodynamics as tangentially interrelated with studies promulgated by Darffenstangenovich on a scale of one to twenty factored to the 24th power.

Although she may have used a bit of literary license in transcribing the conference proceedings, her point is well taken. She was attending a conference on her specialty; yet she did not understand what was being said. It happens all the time, not only to students, but to teachers as well. Although there may be valuable ideas in what many specialists have to say, we can't profit from them if we can't understand them, or if we must spend hours translating them.

In his wonderful book *The Sociological Imagination*, C. W. Mills made precisely this point. He argued that in many social sciences, "high theory" is top-heavy with jargon. As an example, he interpreted sociologist Talcott Parsons's terminology: He reduced it by 80 to 90 percent and at the same time made it more intelligible. Mills was not making the point that Parsons's insights were not good ones; to the contrary, Mills believed that Parsons was a brilliant sociologist. But Parsons's language obscured his brilliant ideas.

Another characteristic of language is that it embodies value judgments and preserves ways of looking at problems. There is no way to be completely objective; to paraphrase Einstein, the goal is to be as objective as possible but not more so. A good social scientist recognizes the limits of objectivity and is always open to dealing with reality by alternative modes of expression and new ways of looking at issues.

Conclusion

If this chapter has succeeded in its intended purpose, it should have given you a sense of what it means to be a social scientist. As you saw, the social sciences are evolving: They interact and they move among the humanities, the natural sciences, and the individual social sciences, depending on who is working with them. They are fluid, not static, and that fluidity will present problems to anyone who attempts too fixed a definition of any of them.

The ability to handle the fluid definitions, to recognize the shadows as well as the objects without flinching, is an important characteristic that good social scientists exhibit—one which, if learned, will serve you well as you study this book and play the game of life.

 Study and **Review**

Key Points

- Social science is the name given to our knowledge about the nature, growth, and functioning of human society.
- The scientific method is a set of rules about how to establish rules.
- A good social scientist generally takes a wait-and-see position about claims until they are tested and retested.
- A reasonable approach to a problem in social science is to observe, define the problem, review the literature, observe some more, develop a theoretical framework and formulate a hypothesis, choose the research design, collect the necessary data, analyze the results, and draw conclusions.
- Three typical methods in social science are the historical method, the case method, and the comparative method.
- It is important to use educated common sense in the social sciences.
- A good social scientist is always open to new ways of looking at issues.

Some Important Terms

argumentation for the sake of heaven (3)
anthropology (6)
biological science (2)
case method (15)
causation (18)
cognitive science (5)
comparative method (16)
correlation (17)
cross-cultural method (16)
economics (11)

educated common sense (16)
experimental method (9)
geography (8)
historical method (15)
history (9)
humanities (4)
impartial spectator tool (3)
interdisciplinary approach (18)
natural science (2)
paradigm (11)

phronesis (2)
political science (12)
psychology (12)
research program (12)
scientific knowledge (2)
scientific method (8)
Social science (2)
sociology (8)
statistical analysis (17)
survey (17)

Questions for Review and Discussion

General Questions

1. What is scientific knowledge? How does it differ from knowledge acquired "unconsciously"?
2. What is the relationship between phronesis and scientific knowledge?
3. What is the impartial spectator tool, and why is it important for social scientists?
4. What distinguishes argumentation for the sake of heaven from other types of argumentation?
5. Name the principal social sciences and define the field with which each deals.
6. Why would it have been difficult to carry on scientific investigation in primitive societies or even in the Middle Ages?
7. Why is social science policy more difficult than natural science policy?
8. Are there any advantages to having competing research programs?
9. Why is it difficult to formulate precise laws in the field of social science?
10. In what sense is social science scientific?
11. Why is it often impossible to study social problems by means of the experimental method?
12. Explain the ways in which the problems of social science differ from those of the exact natural sciences.
13. What are the advantages of the interdisciplinary approach to the study of many social problems?
14. Social science has been broken down into specialties. Why is it a problem to put them back together through a unified theory?
15. What new social science fields do you think will be important ten years from now? Why do you think so?

Internet Questions

1. In his Ted Talk (https://www.youtube.com/watch?v=FLbEKpL-5Z0), Brian Epstein argues that there are two types of questions that scientists ask: what is it questions, and how does it work questions. Which type does he believe that social scientists are not asking?
2. The website https://www.sciencebuddies.org/science-fair-projects/engineering-design-process/engineering-design-compare-scientific-method distinguishes the scientific method from the engineering method. How do the methods differ?
3. Go to the society portal of Wikipedia (https://en.wikipedia.org/wiki/Portal:Social_sciences) and choose the branches of geography category. How many different types of geography are listed?
4. Take the survey about alcohol use at www.alcoholscreening.org. After taking the survey, look at the feedback you are given based on your answers. What can the results for this survey be used for?
5. In Steven Levitt's defense of his abortion study, (http://freakonomics.com/2005/05/15/abortion-and-crime-who-should-you-believe/) what was one of the alternative suggestions for the increase in crime? What was the alternative argument that critics use to explain why the crime rate has decreased? Did Levitt agree with the alternative argument?

*F*or Further Study

Books to Explore

Easterbrook, Greg, *It's Better than it Looks: Reasons for Optimism in an Age of Fear*, New York: Hachette Books, 2018.

Greene, Brian, *The Fabric of the Cosmos*, New York: Knopf, 2004.

Hecht, Jennifer Michael, *Doubt: A History: The Great Doubters and Their Legacy of Innovation*, San Francisco, CA: Harper, 2004.

Mills, C. Wright, *The Sociological Imagination*, New York: Oxford University Press, 1959.

Pinker, Steven, *Enlightenment Now: The Case for Reason, Science, Humanism and Progress*, New York: Penguin RandomHouse, 2018.

Repcheck, Jack, *Copernicus' Secret: How the Scientific Revolution Began*, New York: Simon & Schuster, 2007.

Salganik, Matthew J., *Bit by Bit: Social Research in the Digital Age*, Princeton, NJ: Princeton University Press, 2017.

Tilly, Charles, *Why*, Princeton, NJ: Princeton University Press, 2006.

Wilson, Edward O., *Consilience: The Unity of Knowledge*, New York: Knopf, 1998.

Internet Sites to Explore

"http://www.americananthro.org/AdvanceYourCareer/Content.aspx?ItemNumber=2150" American Anthropology Association.

"http://psychology.oxfordre.com/" Oxford Research Encyclopedia of Psychology.

"http://www.politicalresources.net/" Political Resources on the Internet.

"http://www.socioweb.com/" Sociological Resources on the Internet.

"https://www.frbatlanta.org/education/publications/extra-credit/2012/spring/i-want-to-study-economics-but-what-do-economists-do.aspx" What Do Economists Do?

Historical Roots of Social Science

Natural scientists tell us that the world has been around for some 6 billion years and that living things have been around for at least 3 billion. We will go back, however, only about 2,600 years, when Western philosophy began on the fringes of ancient Greece (some theorists hold that the Greeks responded to ideas from Eastern civilizations, but there are limits to even our broad sweep). The Greeks came to realize that their ancient account of how the world was created and administered—by an enormous collection of gods, or pantheon—was not the only possible explanation. They are credited with being the first to establish rational theory, independent of theological creed; to grasp rational concepts and use them as a way of looking at reality and seeing logical connections; and to be empirical and antimystical. Two great Greek thinkers of the fifth and fourth centuries B.C., Plato and Aristotle, are responsible for establishing a basis for knowledge as we know it and deal with it today.

The philosophical debates of the Greek period were in many ways the same ones that go on today, explaining how, when all things change, things must also be simultaneously unchanging; otherwise, something would have to be created out of nothing—a logical impossibility. These ideas would later develop into modern physics, including the laws of thermodynamics and the proposition that matter can neither be created nor destroyed—merely transformed. The Greeks also considered many of the issues that later became the social sciences; for example, they considered the role of the state (political science), the way minds interact with society (psychology), and individuals' interaction within the market (economics). Thus, the history of the social sciences begins with the Greeks. The history, however, is not continuous.

Much of the Greek contribution to knowledge would have been lost (Who knows what other contributions actually have been lost?) were it not for its preservation by Eastern civilizations. On their forays into the East during the Crusades (the religious wars from 1095 to 1272 in which Christians in Europe attempted to capture Christianity's traditional territory

in the Middle East), Europeans became reacquainted with the learning of the ancient Greeks, and they brought back the body of ancient Greek learning to Europe, where it was generally available by the twelfth century. These ideas spread slowly throughout Europe over the next three hundred years, and by the middle of the fifteenth century, rediscovery of Greek civilization in Europe was widespread. Because the period from about 1453 (the fall of Constantinople) to the end of the seventeenth century was characterized by the rebirth and proliferation of ancient knowledge, it became known as the **Renaissance** (a French word meaning "rebirth").

The Renaissance must have been a wonderful time for scholars. The totality of knowledge was still comprehensible by the human mind. An ideal in the Renaissance was that an educated person could know everything and exercise all skills and social graces. A true Renaissance man was willing to take on all comers on any issue.

As the store of knowledge grew, it became harder and harder to know everything, and so people began to specialize. A natural division opened, one between the humanities (the study of literature, music, and art) and physics. The physics part of this division was not refined enough, and soon physics was broken up into empirical studies (which developed into the various natural sciences) and metaphysics (nonempirical studies that developed into philosophy).

The Renaissance was preceded by the **Middle Ages** (a period from roughly A.D. 476, and the end of the Roman Empire, to A.D. 1453, the defeat of Christian religious armies in Constantinople by the Islamic Turks). In the Middle Ages, religion was so central to life that the study of religion was taken for granted, and it tied together all the other fields of study. For example, painters painted religious pictures, musicians wrote religious music, and the study of literature was the study of the Bible and its commentators. Questions that today seem the obvious ones, such as "Why are people divided into classes?" and "Why are the poor poor?", were simply not asked. Things were the way they were because that was God's will. Once one knew God's will, the issue was how to carry it out. For example, medieval scholars believed in a "just" price and that collecting interest on savings was immoral. They taught those principles and condemned those who did not follow their teachings.

As the Renaissance dawned and continued, that religious tie provoked tension as scholars in the various fields of study came to conclusions different from the church's doctrines, beginning a long conflict between religious learning and beliefs and so-called rationalist learning and beliefs.

The tension between religious explanations and rationalist explanations was (and still is) inevitable. The rationalist approach places human reason above faith. In a rationalist approach, one looks for logical connections and is continually asking the question "Can you prove it?" This meant that somehow the rationalists had to figure out what it meant to prove something. A religious approach places faith above reason. A religious explanation had no need to prove anything: Explanations were accepted on faith.

Throughout the Renaissance, rationalism more and more replaced religion as the organizing principle of knowledge, and as it did, the various fields of knowledge became divided along rationalist lines. The humanities still reflected religious issues; the rationalist revolution came much later to the humanities. To the degree that they were considered, most of the issues we now classify under social science were studied as part of history. History was part of literature and the humanities. It was simply a documentation of what had happened—it never asked *why* something happened. To ask why meant failure to accept God's will. Thus, it was primarily from philosophy, not history, that most of the social sciences emerged.

The natural sciences and philosophy divided along modes of inquiry and answers to the question "Can you prove it?" The study of philosophy itself evolved into a variety of fields, such as logic, morals, and epistemology (the study of knowledge).

The Enlightenment

The **Enlightenment** is the period in which rationalism definitively replaced religion as the organizing principle of knowledge. The Enlightenment began between A.D. 1650 and A.D. 1700 and continued for about one hundred years. It is in this period that the development of the social sciences took hold and flourished.

By the time of the Enlightenment, it had become evident that to know everything—to be a Renaissance scholar—was impossible. Not only was it impossible to know everything, but it also was impossible to know everything about just one subject—say, all of physics or

all of philosophy. Individuals began to specialize their study. For instance, chemistry and astronomy were separated from physics.

As philosophers delved into their subject, they further divided philosophy into parts. One part was metaphilosophy, the study of issues that most scholars agreed were not empirically testable. One such issue was: Because God is all-powerful, can he create a rock so heavy he cannot move it? The other division of philosophy dealt with issues that could, in principle at least, be empirically tested. For instance: What type of political organization of society is preferable? It is from the second division that the social sciences evolved. (They were called sciences because they were in principle meant to be empirically testable.)

The Enlightenment spawned social science because the Enlightenment rejected the assumption that the classical world of the Greeks and the Romans was perfect. In the Enlightenment (roughly the whole of the eighteenth century), there was a general belief that civilization had improved and so too should the thinking about civilization. Moreover, in the seventeenth century, just preceding the Enlightenment, there was continual turmoil—a long drawn-out war between France and England and a religious conflict between Catholics and Protestants about how to interpret God's will. That fight broke down the religious explanations and made people very much aware of social problems. Which of the two explanations, Catholic or Protestant, was right? Why were they fighting? What could be done about it? The social sciences developed as individuals attempted to explain those social problems and suggest what could be done to solve them.

Although the existence of social problems that require solutions may seem obvious to you, it was not always so obvious. This view is the product of the Enlightenment, which established the "three humiliations" of human beings. These are:

1. The earth is not the center of the universe.
2. Humans are creatures of nature like other animals.
3. Our reasoning ability is subject to passions and subconscious desires.

Before we experienced these humiliations, thinkers could rely on an order they believed was established by God. Social problems were set up by God and were to be accepted or endured. Only after the beginning of the Enlightenment did people begin to believe that society and culture are themselves products of history and the evolution of culture—that they had changed and would continue to change.

Frontispiece from Diderot's Encyclopédie, *written during the Enlightenment.*

As is often the case, the change in viewpoint had a paradoxical counterpoint, and human beings' "humiliation" was accompanied by a belief in human beings' power. If society could change, then the change could be, at least to some extent, guided and directed by human beings.

Since its conception, social science has entwined these two aspects. Sometimes it is simply trying to understand, and it accepts our limited powers and our place in the cosmos, and at other times it is trying to change society.

From Philosophy to Social Science

The evolution of philosophy into the social sciences can be seen in France, where philosophers joined to produce an encyclopedia, edited by Denis Diderot and Jean d'Alembert, which appeared over a span of several years in the mid-1700s. The full title of this encyclopedia proclaimed it to be a rational dictionary of science, art, and industry. Unlike earlier compilations, it contained systematic articles on humans, society, and method, and a number of the first definitions of the social sciences can be traced to this mammoth work.

There are many ways to look at social problems, and as scholars began considering human beings in reference to their social environment, the diversity soon became apparent. The history of each of the social sciences becomes hopelessly tangled with that of each of the others at this point. In the Enlightenment, scholars were debating one another and ideas were quickly evolving. To capture even a flavor of the interaction and debate leads to a formidable morass, hardly conducive to a social science course. So we will stop our consideration here.

Some Important Terms ─────────

Enlightenment (24)
Middle Ages (23)
Renaissance (23)

Human Origins

chapter 2

After reading this chapter, you should be able to:

- Summarize Darwin's theory of evolution
- Explain the role of mutation in the theory of evolution
- Relate DNA to genes and genetic engineering
- Distinguish between the theory of punctuated equilibrium and the theory of continuous equilibrium
- Summarize briefly the evolution of human beings over the last 30 million years

If a single cell, under appropriate conditions, becomes a man in the space of a few years, there can surely be no difficulty in understanding how, under appropriate conditions, a cell may, in the course of untold millions of years, give origin to the human race.

—Herbert Spencer

Our ancestors in the not-so-distant past believed that the globe we live on was the major focus of the universe and that all the heavenly bodies revolved around it. Today, we know that it is only an infinitesimal part of the cosmic universe of space and matter. To human beings, however, this tiny part is more important than all the rest, for the greatest concerns of human beings are themselves, the planet on which they live, their origin, their destiny, and their relationships with each other. Even if they hope for a future life in some far-off heaven, they still long to make their earthly life meaningful and satisfying.

Human beings are first of all social creatures. They normally spend their entire lives in association with other human beings and as members of various organized social groups. The quality of association and membership varies according to the nature of the social group. For members of a family, association normally is constant and close, but as residents of a town or city, human beings' association with the majority of the other residents is only occasional and often impersonal. Modern technology is both increasing and decreasing that association. As social networks (such as Facebook) become central to people's lives, they spend less physical time with their families and geographic neighbors, but they often establish associations with people all over the world.

Physical geography is still important and most people still define themselves as members of a larger society, all bound together to some degree by a common language, common interests, geographic areas, ways of living, common loyalties, and reliance on a common national government for their defense and for much of their general welfare. To a great extent, the ability of people to live happy and satisfying lives depends on the nature of the society they live in.

*T*he Origin of the Human Species

Where and when the human species originated is not known with absolute certainty, but the conventional view is that it was in Africa some 5 to 7 million years ago. Modern scientists believe that millions of years ago, the process of evolution produced our first human ancestors when a humanlike creature branched off from the apes. They believe that then a long series of changes created a group of hominids who displayed over time more and more of the basic physical characteristics that distinguish modern human beings from all other forms of life. Fossils of humanlike species have been found that date back about 5 million years, and research in this field is progressing so rapidly that it is possible that by the time you read this even older evidence will have been found. After splitting off from apes, humanlike species are believed to have continued to gradually change to other types of humanlike species in the evolutionary process.

Darwin and the Theory of Evolution

Evolution in its broadest sense refers to any process of progressive change. Thus, one may speak of the evolution of the novel, of art, or of religion. But when used without qualification, evolution ordinarily means organic evolution, or the theory that all the complex life forms of today have descended from earlier ones that existed long ago, and that they are continually evolving to adapt to their changing surroundings. The theory of evolution was popularized by the English biologist Charles Darwin, who devoted his life to systematically finding evidence to support the concept of evolution and to explaining natural selection, which he believed was the mechanism by which evolution was accomplished.

Darwin, in the capacity of a naturalist, made a five-year voyage with a British surveying expedition on the ship *Beagle* (1831–1836). During this time, he had unusual opportunities to study a great variety of plant and animal life. He was puzzled by the similarities and differences he found and by the progressive steps that often seemed evident in going from the simpler to the more complex forms of life. Ultimately, he developed his theory of natural selection to explain these relationships. The first major work in which he presented his conclusions was *On the Origin of Species* (1859). Later, in another famous book, *The Descent of Man,* he dealt specifically with the evolution of the human race.

Though Darwin was largely responsible for the widespread acceptance by scientists of the concept of evolution, he was neither the first to suggest the idea nor the first to be impressed by the remarkable physical similarity of human beings to certain animals. As far back as the fourth century B.C., Aristotle believed in the gradual development of complex organisms from simpler ones, and a generation before Darwin, the French zoologist J. B. Lamarck had published a theory of evolution. Although flawed, it had many insights. Also, a hundred years before Darwin, the great Swedish naturalist Carolus Linnaeus (1707–1778) organized the various species by similarity of their physical attributes. In doing so, he invented the term *primates*—a group of animals including human beings, apes, and monkeys—whose outstanding characteristics are their larger, complex brains, high intelligence, and hands and feet adapted for grasping. In his studies, Linnaeus could not overlook the resemblances among these three kinds of creatures.

Charles Darwin.

Natural Selection. Darwin's concept of evolution was based in part on **natural selection**, the proposition that individual members of the various species that have characteristics more favorable for meeting the conditions of life are more likely to survive and pass on their characteristics to future generations. Darwin believed that every species is characterized by the appearance of such individuals; thus, the direction that evolution takes is largely determined by "the survival of the fittest."

Genetics studies how the hereditary characteristics of species and individuals are transmitted biologically to their offspring. The precise process of how evolution occurs is still unsettled, but it generally is believed that genetics plays an important role.

The foundation work in genetics was done by Gregor Mendel in the late nineteenth century.[1] He discovered that plants and animals have what he called inheritance factors, now known as **genes,** which he defined as discrete units within cells that retain their original character for generation after generation. Because of this retention, these genes determine the characteristics of future generations. Thus, the study of evolution is closely connected to the study of genetics.

Mutation. Genetics explains the way we are, but it does not explain why and how we change. That occurs through a process called **mutation:** random genetic changes that lead to new characteristics. In mutation, an offspring may have quite different characteristics from those of its parents. Although we do not completely understand why these mutations occur, we do know that if the resulting offspring survive, their new characteristics can be passed on to future generations.

Mutations are random. They seem to be accidents, partial failures of the process by which a species is able to reproduce its kind. We also know that the incidence of mutations is increased by exposure to certain chemicals or types of radiation. Most mutations are neutral, but some are fatal and some are beneficial to the offspring. Beneficial mutations make evolution possible. Over long periods of time, evolution can bring about great changes in the character of a plant or animal species, and in the process the structure and biological functioning of the species often become much more complex.

Examples of changes in a species that seem to be the result of gene mutations and the operation of natural selection (survival of the fittest) are not difficult to find. The peppered moth in Great Britain is a case that has been studied in detail. This moth spends much of its time clinging to trees and is a favorite food of some birds. Until the middle of the nineteenth century, all peppered moths found by naturalists who collected specimens seem to have been light in color. Because the bark of the trees was usually light and often lichen-covered, this served as protection by making it difficult for the birds to see them. But after the Industrial Revolution had been under way for some time, so much soot fell in some areas of central Britain that the tree trunks and branches became darker. This made dark moths harder to see than light ones, and therefore the dark moths lived longer on average and produced more progeny. Because moths go through a great many generations in a relatively short period of time, in some of the more highly industrialized areas of Britain, natural selection almost completely replaced the light peppered moths with the dark ones.

Genes contain two **alleles**, one from each parent, that affect particular characteristics. In sexually reproducing organisms, the alleles transmit characteristics from the parents to the offspring. A **dominant allele** controls the characteristic that is transmitted to offspring. A **recessive allele** will not transmit its characteristics unless both alleles in the pair are recessive. If two recessive alleles are paired, they will determine the characteristic affected. The peppered moth presents a relatively simple example of the operation of natural selection. The color of

---

[1] As is the case with many major scientific breakthroughs, the significance of Mendel's work was not immediately understood. Although he published his results in 1866, their importance was not recognized until 1900.

*T*heories, Proofs, and the Darwinian Story

The peppered moth example has been cited in this text and in most other textbooks about evolution for at least the last twenty years. Why do textbook authors choose this example? We do so in large part because it fits the Darwinian story of evolution so well. Recently, social scientist Michael Majerus pointed out that the moth photos, on which much of the story was based, were staged and that there were serious design flaws with the original peppered moth experiments.

Despite the problems he found in the experiment, Dr. Majerus, and most moth experts, believe that the basic story about the peppered moths holds up and that the story they tell is "qualitatively right." But the recent discussion of the problems with the original experiment provides good insight into the scientific method. The scientific method directs scientists to question everything because there is always a chance that a "proof" will slip through the cracks, leading to false beliefs, especially when a theory comes to be strongly believed by most scientists. The problem is that when reports of observations fit the way we already think, we tend to be less questioning than we otherwise would be. After reviewing the broader evidence, almost all scientists continue to believe that some version of the Darwinian story of evolution holds, but they are continually testing it in order to refine and improve it so that it better fits the empirical data.

However, many people in our society—especially those with a strong Christian affiliation who interpret the Bible literally—are hesitant to accept accounts of evolution. The debate between those who accept it and those who do not is unlikely to be resolved. Science relies on empirical evidence to settle such disputes, and almost all empirical scientists believe that the preponderance of empirical evidence on evolution supports some version of the theory of evolution. True, the evidence is incomplete, and science has no explanation for the ultimate beginning of everything, and there is always the possibility that scientists are collectively fooling themselves—they have done so before. Scientists admit to this possibility because good science requires them always to be skeptical even about issues they think they know; but what will convince them is contradictory empirical evidence, not arguments about the limitations of human knowledge.

Whereas good scientists are always on the lookout for contradictory evidence, good religious people are not. Almost all religions, and certainly the Christian religion, require people to accept things on faith. Religious beliefs are supposed to be held regardless of the empirical evidence—the more the empirical evidence contradicts the foundation of faith, the stronger the faith must be. This means that the two sides do not have a common method of resolving the debate.

Whether scientists should have a more open mind to additional hypotheses that complement or are in addition to evolution, but do not contradict it—such as the hypothesis that there is an intelligent design underlying the evolutionary process—is an open question. The problem with these hypotheses is that it is difficult, and perhaps impossible, to find empirical evidence that would lead us to choose one hypothesis over another. Other than the fact that we exist, and that our existence may have some cause, there seems to be no test of the intelligent design hypothesis. Thus, most scientists tend to find the arguments made by Ben Stein in his documentary, "Expelled: No Intelligence Allowed," as primarily propaganda for a particular faith rather than an argument for a serious scientific addition or alternative to the theory of evolution. That said, the close-mindedness and unwillingness of some scientists to even address the issue, or to allow people to put their ideas forward, goes against the openness that is essential to scientific inquiry. Lastly, science has no explanation for existence; evolution is a theory of change, not a theory of existence.

these moths is known to result from a dominant allele, or a pair of dominant alleles for dark color, and a pair of recessive alleles for light color.

Human characteristics result from this same combination of dominant and recessive alleles. In the case of eye color, brown eyes are dominant and blue eyes are recessive. A person must have two recessive alleles to have the recessive characteristics; otherwise, the dominant characteristics prevail.

The first human beings, or their humanlike precursors, probably evolved in tropical regions where survival was possible without clothing. It is likely that they had very dark skin because light skin would have given little protection against the burning rays of the sun. There is debate about whether these people spread into other parts of the world or, instead, whether people developed independently in various parts of the world. Whichever the case, it is believed that in time they became capable of spreading out from Africa, eventually to most of the world. This was probably because their physical characteristics changed. For instance, early hominids probably did not walk upright, but when they developed that ability, they could travel more efficiently. More important, perhaps, was their development of tool making. With tools, they could hunt or scavenge other animals, so they could consume more protein and fat than their low-energy vegetarian diet would have provided. Not only their bodies but also their brains would have been changed with more energy. The brain needs lots of energy to grow. As their diet expanded, hominids could physically and intellectually expand their territory.

Although all early hominids were probably dark-skinned, as they moved, that changed. In the most northern of the territories into which they expanded, the sun was very weak, especially in the long winters, and was often hidden by clouds or fog. Dark skin, which had been an advantage in warm, sunny climates, became a disadvantage because the sun's rays, by penetrating human skin, help produce vitamin D, which is an essential element in nutrition. Populations that remained in these colder regions for very long periods of time—perhaps 100,000 years or more—seem gradually, through gene mutations and the process of natural selection, to have developed much lighter shades of skin.

Limitations of Natural Selection.   Natural selection does not completely account for all evolutionary changes. In small groups, some such changes may result from gene mutations that are harmless but do not create characteristics that contribute to survival. But other characteristics developed by such groups may increase their chances of survival, and so they grow in number and spread over wider areas. Natural selection may explain the dark skins of black Africans and the lighter skins of northern Europeans, but it is not an obvious explanation of some other group characteristics, such as the different construction of the eyes in Asian and Occidental people, nor does it account for as much similarity as exists. Therefore, work in this area will likely continue.

Recent Developments in Genetics

In recent years, scientists have significantly extended our knowledge of genetics. Whereas once it was thought that genes were the building blocks of life, today scientists have unraveled the gene and discovered a small building block, **DNA,** or deoxyribonucleic acid, the basic chemical building block of genes. Scientists had known for a long time that DNA existed, but it was only in 1953 that James Watson and Francis Crick unraveled its double helix structure, discovering that DNA resembled a spiral staircase. They found that each of the steps serves as a code word and determines how amino acids are linked into the proteins of which all living things are made. It was like discovering the blueprint for life (but not how life was originally created or what force had drawn the blueprint).

Once DNA was reasonably understood, the next step for scientists involved gene-splicing, and changing the blueprint. This opened up a whole new field. If scientists could change a gene, they could exercise some control over living organisms by cloning—that

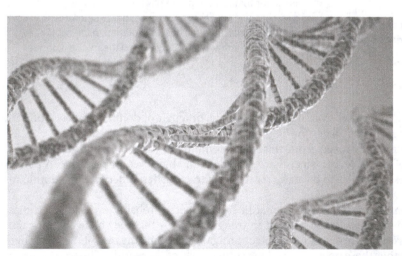

© Alamy

is, duplicating—existing forms and possibly building new ones. This process is called **genetic engineering,** rearranging genetic material to create new, human-made life forms or to change existing ones. By 2001, scientists had identified all the human genes, which meant they had the beginning of the set of directions to what makes us biologically what we are. Researchers found that humans had only about 25,000 genes, about 6,000 more than a worm, and that humans share many genes with a wide variety of animals.

As scientists have studied DNA and evolution they have found that the evolutionary process is more complex than they originally thought. Specifically they are discovering that there is another protein, RNA (ribonucleic acid), that acts as a messenger and determines or expresses how DNA combines in the reproduction process. This discovery is important for two reasons. The first is that it makes the study of reproduction much more complicated than it would be if DNA alone controlled the evolutionary process. The second is that it allows for epigenetic influences on reproduction which means that nurture can affect nature. **Epigenetics** is the study of environmental influences on reproduction. For example, if living organisms are stressed, the genes of their children will encode some of their responses to stress, such as becoming smaller than usual. This feedback from nurture to nature is a path for much faster evolutionary changes to occur than would be predicted by mutation-based natural selection mechanisms. The environment not only selects for changes that fit the environment, it also influences which genes combine so that learned and environmentally determined traits can become inheritable.

This genetic map, combined with gene-splicing technology, has given us a much better understanding of the biological causes of differences among people and what can cause changes in people. Scientific research using this enormous amount of raw information has taken off in many directions and will likely have to be complemented by a study of the many proteins that are the building blocks of cells. Thus, a new applied science—proteomics—is building on the genome project. This study is still in its early stages, although some scientists believe that soon they will be able to combine the nonliving chemicals that make up DNA, and by combining them in the right proportions, be able to turn those chemicals into something living. The major breakthroughs from genetic engineering for medicine are, however, probably decades away.

Having our genetic codes presents many social and ethical dilemmas. Can we extend life spans by one hundred years? If we can, should we? Can we create new life forms? If so, what rights would they have?

The Multi-Level Group Selection Debate. Another debate that is ongoing among sociobiologists concerns the existence of what is called **multi-level group selection**—the theory that natural selection takes place not only at the individual level, but also at various group levels. The standard theory of natural selection that Darwin used involved selection only at the individual level. In it individuals are selected for their fitness to the environment, so that when the environment changes, those individuals with characteristics that fit that environment change because it increases their likelihood of survival: there is survival of the fittest individuals.

Using standard natural selection theory one would not expect altruistic behavior toward a group, because that would not increase the likelihood of the individual's survival. But if the selection is at the group level, then one would expect prosocial altruistic behavior toward a group to survive since it increases the likelihood of the group's survival. With multi-level group selection, the possibilities are much greater. All types of prosocial and altruistic behavior will be consistent with evolutionary theory.

Some social scientists have even argued that we can see groups as a type of emergent sentience, and that our feelings about what is right or wrong are part of a larger sentient reality that is in the process of emerging. If this is true, it is best to think of individuals as made up of components which have come together in a way that allows a collective sentience that manifests itself within the individual. But just as we are made up of components that work for the good of the collective, so too are we components of a larger collective sentience, which is far beyond our individual understanding, but which we feel instinctually when we feel what is right or wrong. The strong role that religion has played within human societies is a manifestation of this instinctual push to play our role as part of the collective sentience, which we as individuals are unable to sense, but which may exist at some higher level of being.

Multi-level natural selection is particularly relevant for humans and culture since it suggests that cooperation and prosocial behavior, rather than selfishness, could be one of the traits that individuals are selected for, and that analysis treating individuals as selfish and rational is missing an important element of human society.

Some Implications of Recent Developments

Changes in technology present society with extraordinarily difficult questions. If, for instance, parents can choose characteristics for their children, what characteristics will they choose, and how will their decisions affect the overall population? Will a line be drawn forbidding cloning of human beings but permitting genetic alteration and possibly control of existing human beings? Who would draw such a line and how would its boundaries be enforced? The information gathered by researchers might be used in unforeseen and possibly undesirable ways. For instance, a government might collect knowledge about its citizens and use it to manipulate them. Or pension systems might use it to identify potentially long-lived people and charge them more for pensions. Or insurance companies might use the information to deny medical coverage to individuals predisposed to certain diseases. We can expect significant social repercussions from this scientific enterprise throughout the twenty-first century.

Moral, political, religious, scientific, and governmental forces will undoubtedly mobilize on an international scale for debates on these issues. Thinking about them gives you a sense of how new discoveries can have profound effects on the social system in which we live. In short, our future social evolution will likely be substantially influenced by the information we have about our human evolution. What we know will change what we are.

Should the Species Be Regrouped?   As our knowledge of biology has progressed and we have developed far more information about the genetic makeup of life forms, our abilities to differentiate species and to place them in orders of progression have changed enormously. The divisions of the species that we currently use were created by Carolus Linnaeus (1707–1778). His divisions were determined primarily by physical traits. As our knowledge of genetic makeup has improved, we have come to realize that physical similarities do not necessarily imply genetic similarity, and vice versa. Given the importance of genetic makeup, it would seem logical to organize species by genetic components. However, division by physical characteristics is still the dominant division used. This is an example of the inertia in any system of knowledge and terminology. They evolve slowly.

Sociobiology

The study of genetics is not the only evolution-related field to experience progress; the study of evolution itself has progressed, and on one front it has been extended.

A group of scientists called *sociobiologists* has argued that human behavior evolves in the same direction that anatomy and body chemistry do: to increase the chances of survival of the species. Behavior that does not increase chances of survival will eventually lead to destruction. **Sociobiology** is a combination of sociological and biological reflections that theorize a genetic basis for human behavior.

A leader in sociobiology, Harvard entomologist (one who studies insects) Edward O. Wilson has provided an example that may help clarify the reasoning sociobiologists use. People are born with an inherent fear of strangers. This fear is a necessary genetic trait; it is a

"It'll never work out. She's patented, he isn't."

form of "prepared learning" that can be seen in infants less than a year old. If infants did not have this fear, they would be more susceptible to attack and thus less likely to survive. Over generations, more individuals who exhibit this trait generally will survive than individuals who do not, and eventually the genetic trait will become inherent in the species.

The argument may seem simple and of little consequence, but if we replace "strangers" with "persons of another race," the argument becomes more problematic and conflicts with our society's views on equity. People can justify or at least rationalize any behavior as being "in their genes." Therefore, sociobiology has provoked strong attacks that it "justifies racism." In response, sociobiologists point out that their argument is not that genes directly control behavior, but rather that genes play a role. Wilson states, "We're suggesting that there is a mechanism which one sees during evolution continuously around the circuit: genetic change, cultural change, genetic change, and so on." The issues raised are highly controversial and are reminiscent of the free will–determinism issue early Christian philosophers debated. Do we do what we do because we are programmed to do it, or do we do it by choice? We suspect the debate will continue for some time.

The concerns about the almost singular focus of sociobiology on genetic natural selection have led to the development of a new field of psychology—evolutionary social psychology. This field accepts that biological and genetic factors play a role in explaining behavior but argues that other factors are also important.

Punctuated Equilibrium versus Gradual Change

Evolution theory is also being challenged on another front. Darwin saw evolution as a gradual process of natural selection and survival of the fittest as the most likely phenomenon. Now evolutionists such as paleontologist Niles Eldredge and polymath[2] Stephen Jay Gould argue that evolution is characterized by long periods of relative stability that are punctuated by sudden changes, followed by more stability, followed by more changes, and so on. One hypothesis why this occurs is that changes in environment cause species to diversify and specialize into several new niches, creating new lineages. In Gould's theory, a species will be unchanged for thousands or hundreds of thousands of years and then suddenly something will happen that will change it (perhaps gene-splicing?) or even wipe it out. Gould's theory can be thought of as macroevolution—periodic sudden large changes, and the normal concept of gradual evolution can be thought of as microevolution—a continuous, almost unnoticeable succession of small changes.

The debate centers on fossil evidence from millions of years ago that paleoanthropologists find in their digs. In the study of evolution, archaeologists have found fossils that demonstrate the changes various species such as humans have undergone. However, large gaps that scientists expected to fill eventually somehow remain. It is here that Gould's theory enters. Gould's **punctuated equilibrium** theory holds that evolution is a stop/go process of sudden change, with long intervening periods of no change.

---

[2] A *polymath* is a person of encyclopedic learning, and the term has been applied to Gould because he was a biologist, geologist, and historian; he was also a leading theorist on large-scale patterns in evolution and an informative writer.

The difference between punctuated equilibrium and gradual evolution can be seen in Figure 2.1. The straight upward-sloping line represents the traditional view, and the new view, punctuated equilibrium, is depicted by the horizontal lines with sudden upward jumps or stages every million or so years. An example of sudden jumps has been found in snail fossils at Lake Turkana in Kenya by Harvard archaeologist Peter Williamson. He discovered that, over a 2-million-year period, there were two sudden changes in which major evolutionary changes occurred, and in between almost no change occurred. Thus, in Gould's view, evolution is merely a series of revolutions interspersed with long periods of calm. The punctuated

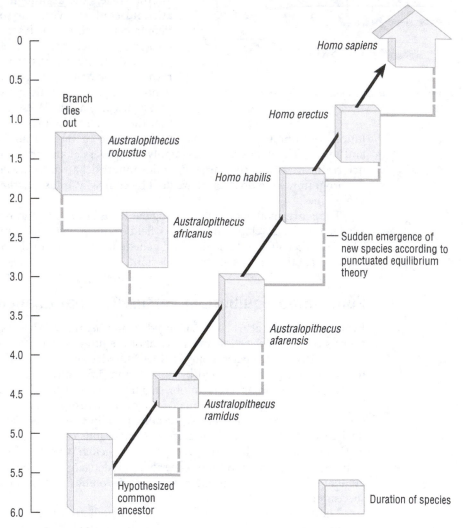

Figure 2.1

A possible theory of evolution. In the traditional view, evolution is represented by the straight, upward-sloping line. In an alternative view that has been advanced in recent years, equilibrium is represented by the horizontal lines with sudden upward jumps at intervals of thousands or hundreds of thousands of years. Note that the lengths of the time periods on the vertical axis are the estimates of some authorities. Other authorities give other lengths of time, but all authorities agree that the time periods are very, very long. In the interest of simplicity, the graph does not show all the species that are now extinct but are thought to have existed at various periods along the way to Homo sapiens.

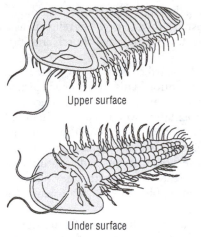

Upper surface

Under surface

Figure 2.2

Trilobites. Trilobites *resembled mod-*
ern wood lice. The discovery of their
fossils challenged Gould's theory of
punctuated equilibrium.

equilibrium theory of evolution has attracted interest because it explains parts of the phenomenon that the old theory could not. For example, his theory could explain the sudden disappearance of dinosaurs millions of years ago. If evolution were a continual process, they would have died off slowly.

Gould's punctuated equilibrium theory was challenged by Peter Sheldon. Researchers before Gould had noted a significant gap in a set of crab-related creatures called trilobites (see Figure 2.2). In the evolution of these trilobites, it appeared that there was a sudden stop, and then the set of trilobites picked up again but with some different characteristics, especially in the number of ribs they had. The absence of trilobites that would have filled the gap with a steadily changing number of ribs had been cited as supporting Gould's theory. However, through painstaking work, Sheldon found specimens that filled in the gaps, showing that the average number of ribs the trilobites contained changed slowly over time. Sheldon's findings generated much debate, and the general feeling was that both sides were in some way correct and that some changes may be punctuated and others may be gradual. But these views are evolving and more evidence is likely to be found in years to come.

*T*he Evolution of Human Beings

Much of what happens in abstract scientific theory does not make news, except for articles in such periodicals as *National Geographic* and *Scientific American.* However, because it has seemed to some people to go against the Bible's version of creation, evolution has stirred popular press controversy from Darwin's time to ours, especially on the part of fundamentalists who believe in literal interpretations of the Bible.

Science, Faith, and Controversy

Just how much controversy evolution has caused can be seen in some famous court trials that have dealt with the issue. In 1925, for example, a Tennessee high school biology teacher, John Scopes, was prosecuted for and found guilty of breaking a state law forbidding the teaching of evolution in the public schools. The law and others like it in several neighboring states were not repealed until the late 1960s. In recent years, evolution has again made headlines, this time over attacks by a group called scientific creationists. **Scientific creationism** is not a science, but rather the belief that all present life forms were spontaneously created at one point in time. Proponents have helped pass statutes in a number of states requiring the teaching of what is actually religious objections to evolution wherever the latter is presented in public school classes and textbooks. In response, publishers have suggested to their authors that they tone down the discussion of evolution in textbooks so that it is acceptable to the scientific creationists. The result has been that some textbooks have devoted only minimal discussion to evolution. Many educators have complained, and in 1985 California did something about those complaints. It informed publishers that unless their books dealt with the issue head on, their books would be dropped from public school purchases in California.

To put the matter bluntly, no organization of U.S. professional scientists has given any scientific support to creationism. In fact, almost all recognized scientific authorities strongly reject such assaults on academic freedom, the traditional scientific method, and the American principle of separation of church and state. A 1982 federal court decision endorsed the scientists' view by throwing out an Arkansas law mandating the study of scientific creationism in the state's public schools on the grounds that creationism is not a science but religion, as it rests on a spiritual, not objective, premise and thus violates the separation of church and state principle that is part of the U.S. approach to government.

At the close of the twentieth century, the Kansas State Board of Education decided that individual school boards could choose whether to teach evolution. This step evoked spirited discussion throughout the country and does not represent a major trend in U.S. education. One of the objections to the provision was that its implementation would place graduates of Kansas school systems outside the mainstream of U.S. scientific theory and thus at a disadvantage in many future careers. Few Kansas school boards chose to discontinue the teaching of evolution, and in the state elections of 2000, several proponents of discontinuance who were running for reelection to the state board were defeated. The controversy has continued, and a number of state governments are still debating bills to limit the teaching of evolution.

These debates are relevant here because scientific creationists have used Gould's evolutionary theory of sudden rather than gradual evolutionary changes as scientific evidence to support their position. They say that the physical evidence of earth's multibillion-year existence can be explained by a series of creations, each one replacing the one before it. But as Gould explained, his theory is not anti-evolutionary; it merely challenges the *process* whereby evolution occurs.

The actual issues of what should be taught in classrooms are too complex to be addressed here. However, it must be stressed that although there have been sound professional scientific criticisms from time to time of the specifics of evolution, responsible scientists have not denied its basic point. The phrase *scientific creationism* is in many ways a contradiction in terms. Creationism begins and ends with a belief that life sprang from a sudden act of divine power and has not appreciably changed. This is an essentially religious version of natural origins. Science studies cause and effect and thus looks for continuity. This is not to say that religious faith cannot coexist with science. Ultimately, "existence" or "being" must be explained, and no scientific theory can yet explain how something was created out of nothing.[3]

In the mid-1990s, a more acceptable but still controversial method of integrating religion into science developed. It was called **intelligent design** and it was the center of a fight about a textbook entitled *Of Pandas and People.* The central thesis of intelligent design is that the world is too complex to have developed on its own and that it can only be explained with some concept of initial intelligence. This is different from scientific creationism in that it does not challenge evolutionary evidence. It simply adds to it a theory of what is behind evolution. Critics see it as a sneaky way to introduce creationism into schools, while supporters see it as an acceptable hypothesis because it discusses issues that science and empirical evidence do not contradict.

Let me be clear, social science does not deny the importance of religion, and of the possibility that we are part of a larger sentience, as we discussed in the consideration of group selection. But social science does hold that our understanding of that larger sentience needs to be consistent with our understanding of evolution, and that, if a theory is to be considered potentially scientifically true, it be specified in a way that is empirically testable, and that until it is empirically tested, it be acknowledged as being based on faith.

Predecessors of Modern Humans

Some of the most interesting studies of evolution have concerned the evolution of humans. Though humans are closely related to the other primates, we are not certain how they evolved.

---

[3] Most religions solve this problem by postulating a god who created all, but as many Sunday school students have pondered, that still leaves open the question of who created God. At some point, faith must still play a role, and when an explanation relies on faith rather than reason, it becomes a religious explanation. Even the "big bang" cosmological theory has no explanation of what "banged."

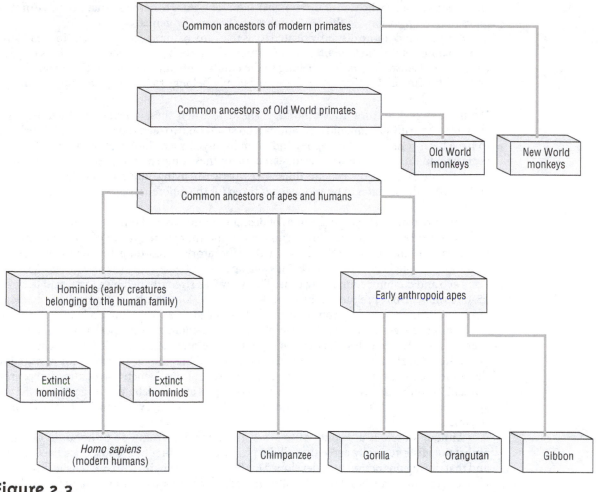

Figure 2.3

Possible lines of descent of humans and other higher primates from their common ancestral type.

New work in genetics, combined with continual finds of paleoanthropologists, is improving our understanding, and with allowance for oversimplification, a basic outline can be drawn.

The origin of life is thought to have occurred billions of years ago as one-celled organisms arose from the primordial ooze. Over the millennia, the organisms evolved into a wide variety of life forms. **Primates,** from which humans developed, evolved some 65 to 70 million years ago, and a monkey-apelike creature from which the human species evolved is thought to have appeared somewhere between 22 and 38 million years ago. This apelike species is considered the common ancestor of modern apes and humans. Figure 2.3 gives you a general sense of that evolution. Each box in it represents a different species.

First let us explain that a **species** is a broad category of individuals who look alike and can mate with each other to produce fertile offspring. Today's humans are the only members of the species *Homo sapiens* (reasoning man).[4] They are also the only surviving human species. At least two other human species, *Homo habilis* (man with tool-making ability) and

---

[4] To distinguish early modern humans from contemporary modern humans, some authorities use the term *Homo sapiens sapiens* for the latest humans. In simplifying, we have not made this distinction, but it is useful to know that the term exists and what it means.

Homo erectus (man who stands up straight), have long since become extinct. All three of these types of humans belong to the same umbrella category, or genus.

A human type more distantly related to us than any of the species just mentioned belongs to a separate genus, *Australopithecus,* creatures who have been extinct for millions of years. Humans and *Australopithecines* belong to the family *Hominidae,* along with several kinds of apes, both living and extinct. And the whole family belongs to the larger group of primates.

From Apelike Creature to Hominid. The date when these apelike creatures began to change to **hominids,** humanlike creatures who stood on two feet, is unclear, but it is believed to have been somewhere between 6 and 10 million years ago in Africa, and several million years later in Europe and Asia. The fossil record for these time spans is poor or nonexistent, so the estimate is based on genetic differences between living humans and living primates combined with estimates of how long it has taken for the differences among these creatures to occur.

Much debate exists about the lines of descent of humans and other primates. In trying to resolve this debate, researchers are turning more and more to the realm of molecular biology and chemical analysis of DNA done in the laboratory. According to fossil evidence, the evolutionary split between human beings and apes might have occurred as early as 25 million years ago and continued for a long time. This view was strengthened by a fossil said to be of a 15-million-year-old prehuman jawbone found in 1991 in southern Africa. This evidence, however, is contradicted by comparison of blood substances from human beings with those from chimpanzees, indicating the divergence was far more recent—perhaps only 7 million years ago. The DNA analysis has tended to support the later dating, and, in fact, recent work by David Reich of Harvard has suggested that chimps and humanoids interbred for hundreds of thousands, or even millions, of years. Even today, chimps' genetic structure differs from humans' by only 1.2 percent. While Reich's hypotheses are still debated, the general belief that genetic analysis will provide important clues about human evolution is shared by most scientists.

Although there is a dispute as to when the transition from ape to hominid occurred, anthropologists generally agree that all the primates, including hominids, once lived in trees and that during this period they developed limbs of great strength, with prehensile fingers and toes for grasping branches. Most primates, including the gibbon and the orangutan, still live in trees, but gorillas, like humans, live on the ground. Chimpanzees sleep in tree nests but spend much of the daytime on the ground. Apparently, one reason for this descent to the ground was their increase in size. Gorillas typically weigh from 400 to 600 pounds and are far too heavy for life in the trees. Even chimpanzees are too heavy to swing about through the branches unless they choose them with care. The great apes can walk on two legs but they have not achieved the human's erect posture and normally walk on all fours.

Perhaps the most important physical difference between human beings and apes is in the size and complexity of the brain. Between various animal species, there seems as a rule to be some relationship between intelligence and the weight of the brain, especially its weight in relation to the body. But the most important factor is the organization of the brain. The chief advantage of large size seems to be that it provides space for additional cells and for more complex mechanisms. On average, chimpanzees are smaller than humans, but some weigh as much as 120 or 130 pounds. The brain of a small human typically weighs about three times that of a chimpanzee of the same body weight, and a normal human cerebral cortex, the part of the brain most concerned with memory and thought, may have ten times as many cells as the cerebral cortex of a typical ape. Today, there seems little doubt that this complex brain is an essential basis of the human power to acquire a vast store of memories, to use word symbols, and to carry on abstract thought.

With respect to behavior, there are both striking similarities and striking differences between apes and human beings. Like humans, apes have family life and care for their young. They have emotional responses, can express gratitude and shame, and often are sociable and

This eighteenth-century drawing from Diderot's Encyclopédie *shows what some people at that time imagined early humanlike creatures to have looked like.*

cooperative. On occasion, they compete with one another, and sometimes they engage in play. Certain chimpanzees have responded well to training in various types of behavior such as smoking, riding a bicycle, eating with a knife and fork, and drinking from a bottle. They have also shown ability to solve problems requiring reasoned judgment. But to all these accomplishments, there are limits that argue unmistakably for the superior intellectual qualities of human beings.

The problem for physical anthropologists is to fill in the gaps of precisely how humans evolved and, if the evolutionary theory of punctuated equilibrium discussed earlier is true, to explain why the changes occurred when they did. In the last century, and especially since the 1930s, anthropologists have made tremendous strides in solving the puzzle. Archaeological finds date our ancestors back about 6 million years, and a wide variety of early hominid fossils have been given forbidding names such as *Africanus ramidus, Zinjanthropus,* and *Orrorin Tugenesis.* Fossil finds are still occurring. In 2014 researchers in South Africa found a subterranean bone yard with over 1,500 bone fragments of an offshoot of early hominids.

A key element in determining when to date the start of modern human history is when these early hominids began using tools. Discoveries of tools with skeletons have been dated from 3.3 million years ago. This group of hominids is called *Homo habilis* because *habilis* means "maker."

DNA Evidence and the Descent of Humans

Until recently, the story of human prehistory was told through the discovery of fossils, which, by careful analysis, were compared with other fossils for similarities. Based on differences among those fossils, physical anthropologists would piece together a story of human prehistory. Since fossils were highly limited, it was a bit like telling a story from a hundred-page book with only quarter-inch scraps of a few pages. The stories required an imaginative mind to make them complete, and, to be quite honest, much of the stories involved significant conjecture.

In the last decade, the nature of prehistory storytelling has changed somewhat. Using what is called "high-throughput DNA sequencing", scientists have a new window into that prehistory. They can now analyze how the genes of humans and prehumans have changed, and compare them with what they are currently. The result is a more accurate (and sometimes quite different) story of that prehistory. What they are finding by studying the DNA of ancient fossils is that there was much more movement among prehistoric humans than previously thought, and that almost no one anywhere on the planet has a linear heritage that does not involve interchange with multiple groups of human ancestors. Humans and prehumans have been moving around and blending together from the beginning of history.

Remaining Gaps.   Despite advances in fossil discoveries and DNA analysis, significant gaps remain in our knowledge of our ancestors, even among experts with their detailed and technical grasp of the subject. For instance, what happened during the intervening years? Were these apelike beings the predecessors of modern humans or only of apes? Did humans start out in a number of places or in only one, from which they dispersed throughout the world? These questions still are unanswered and probably always will be. However, genetic studies are leading to more specific answers.

The latest genetic data suggest that all humans descended from Africa and spread throughout the world along the lines shown in Figure 2.4.

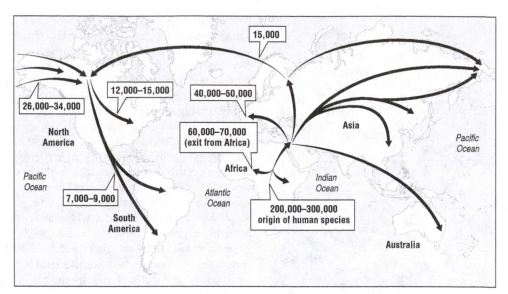

Figure 2.4

Early human migration.

From Hominids to Homo Sapiens. The earliest known species of *Homo* (human), **Homo habilis,** emerged from these early ancestors. *Homo habilis* had a larger brain but smaller teeth than these early ancestors and probably produced stone tools and other stone objects.

As we move closer to our own century, our information increases somewhat, but despite substantial progress, it is still sketchy and incomplete. An important find occurred in 1891 in Java when a Dutch surgeon, Dr. Eugene Dubois, unearthed another piece of the puzzle: **Homo erectus**. *Homo erectus* lived from about 1.8 million years ago to possibly as recently as 250,000 years ago and was a hunter who knew how to use fire.

It is believed that about 1.8 million years ago in Africa, *Homo erectus* developed from *Homo habilis* and then dispersed to Europe and Asia about a million years ago. *Homo erectus*'s brain was even larger and the teeth even smaller than *Homo habilis*'s. The lessening of tooth size indicates that dependence on hard food such as nuts and seeds, which requires powerful teeth and jaws, was decreasing as human diet veered toward softer foods such as fruit and, increasingly, meat. *Homo erectus* seems to have been very strong—which would have facilitated hunting.

Among *Homo erectus*'s nonbiodegradable waste are found more sophisticated objects than *Homo habilis* made, such as axes, and there is evidence, from ashes and charred material, that toward the end of *Homo erectus*'s existence, *Homo erectus* learned to use fire.

In 1997 two Spanish paleontologists, José María Bermúdez de Castro and Juan Luis Arsuaga, announced that their study of 800,000-year-old fossils found in Spain had led them to believe that **Homo antecessor** (man who goes before) was a separate species who was a possible common ancestor of Neanderthals and *Homo sapiens* (discussed next). They speculated that the fossils they found in northern Spain represent emigrants from Africa.

Homo erectus seems to have become extinct nearly 500,000 years ago. The reasons are not at all clear. Artifacts of *Homo erectus,* although more sophisticated than those of their predecessors, do not show much change over more than a million years. Thus, one theory holds that *Homo erectus* may have been too conservative and inflexible to adapt to changing conditions.

Another theory is that *Homo erectus* did change, separating into two branches. One branch was the Neanderthals and the other was the modern human, *Homo sapiens*. **Homo sapiens** is a group of hominids who began to differ from their predecessors by their larger brains and by the better-quality tools they made. *Homo sapiens* (reasoning man) was a species composed of people more highly developed than *Homo erectus*. Early *Homo sapiens*, however, shared many characteristics with *Homo erectus*. They seem to have been unable, for instance, to adapt to harsh climates, or to find food more easily than did *Homo erectus*.

Homo sapiens first appeared in Africa and Europe about the same time that *Homo erectus* was disappearing. Once again, we see the new people displaying larger brains than the people they were replacing, and they differed so much from *Homo erectus* that they were assigned to a new species. It is the species to which all modern human beings belong today. European and African sites have yielded some fossils of these human ancestors ranging roughly from 200,000 to 300,000 years old, but according to genetic evidence, they may have existed as long ago as 800,000 years—earlier than the fossil record. A 2003 fossil find of modern man in Ethiopia fits with recent genetic studies of the time and place of the emergence of humankind. These support the replacement theory—"Out of Africa"—that a late migration of humans eventually supplanted most other humanlike species around the world at the time, such as Neanderthals.

There are continually new discoveries. When these new discoveries are combined with advances in fossil dating techniques, our understanding of the history is continually being modified. For example, in 2017, a new fossil find in Morocco suggested that *homo sapiens* lived around 100,000 years earlier than previously thought. These finds suggest that *homo sapiens* first spread all through Africa over an extended period, rather than only in East Africa as had been thought before. This suggests that *homo sapiens*'s genetic makeup is significantly more diverse than previously thought.

Neanderthals.   Remains from periods longer than 100,000 years ago are few. We do know, however, that the evolutionary network produced the **Neanderthals,** who bore a close resemblance to modern human beings, about 100,000 years ago. Despite this close resemblance, the recent fossil evidence and genetic studies strongly suggest that the Neanderthals were not our ancestors. Instead, they probably shared a common ancestor with modern humans. If modern features already existed in Africa 160,000 years ago, we could not have descended from a species like the Neanderthals.

Neanderthals get their name from the Neander Valley in Germany, where in 1856 the first evidence of their existence was found. They lived in Europe and spread to Asia, although a few researchers believe they developed independently in Asia. Physically, they differ from all other people, modern or extinct, in the shape of their heads and, strangely, in the length of their thumbs, which were about as long as their other fingers.

It used to be thought that Neanderthals were dim-witted, slouching cavemen completely covered with hair. But this reputation is based on just one fossil, which modern scholarship has proved happens to be that of an old, diseased, and injured man. He was approximately 40 or 45 years old when he died—very old for people at that time. Healthy Neanderthals probably walked erect. Objects found at Neanderthal sites show that Neanderthals could make complex tools. The characteristics of their skulls suggest that they probably could speak, although perhaps not with the full range of sounds that modern humans make. Sites also show that they did not necessarily live in caves, but, if they did, they likely altered the caves to make them more livable. Sometimes they built shelters rather than settled in caves. In 1996, scientists digging at a Neanderthal site in Slovenia announced they had found what appeared to be a musical instrument, a flute made from a bear bone.

As we will discuss in later chapters, the development of language capability was a major evolutionary step. (See the box on the uniqueness of the human species.) It allowed the species much greater interaction and hence social development than could occur in nonspeaking species. In doing so, it made the passing on of learned knowledge about the environment

Is the Human Species Unique?

There is an ongoing debate among social scientists about whether the human species is unique. The argument that human beings are unique emphasizes that (1) only humans can think and reason, (2) only humans can communicate with others by means of language, and (3) only humans can use tools. Each of these points is debatable. Social scientists who argue that human beings are not unique point out that animals have solved enormously complex problems, some better than humans have.

Certain social scientists argue that language is not limited to humans and have shown that chimpanzees can communicate by sign language and by touching geometric symbols. One chimp has learned more than 150 different signs, and a psychologist has taught a gorilla, Koko, more than 500 words. In addition, Koko can express emotion: When her pet cat was killed in a traffic accident, she mourned its death. After a time, she "asked" to be given another cat to care for and love. Moreover, the gorilla specifically asked that it be replaced with a Manx cat (a highly unusual breed remarkable for having no tail).

The ability to use tools, disputants hold, is another characteristic not unique to human beings. Yes, humans have a greater ability to devise and use tools, and that ability has given them power over other creatures, but power is not necessarily differentiation, and animals use a variety of tools and social structures. For example, the cattle-tending ant gets honeydew by cultivating aphids and other insects who secrete it, and it even constructs shelters, such as underground galleries, in which to herd its aphids.

To counter these arguments, supporters of human uniqueness assert that the power of the human mind to solve complex problems goes far beyond that of animals and that although animals can learn words, they cannot learn syntax, an important aspect of language. As the linguist Noam Chomsky put it, to say that animals can communicate with each other by language is like saying that because people can rise into the air by jumping they can fly like birds, only not as well.

What difference does it make whether human beings are unique? A lot. Consider the following questions: Is it morally wrong to use animals in experiments? Should we eat meat? If you believe that human beings are unique, it is relatively easy to argue that animals can and should be used by human beings. If human beings are not unique, then it is much harder (but not impossible) to argue in favor of using animals in ways that we would not use human beings.

In the space between these two views on the morality of killing living creatures, we find a number of places where we can draw a line. It may, for example, be okay to kill a cockroach, but not a dog, a cow, or a pig. Precisely where to draw that line is the problem, however, and some radical thinkers have even argued that not only is there nothing distinctive about human beings, but that it is moral for society to eliminate individuals whose lives are no longer worth living—for instance, people with brain damage or individuals who have lived out their "useful" lives and are no longer able to care for themselves.

Do not expect any of these debates to be settled any time soon; rather, we ask you to acknowledge here, and throughout this book, that recognizing the arguments of many sides, considering them thoroughly and objectively, and coming to a conclusion that does not stubbornly exclude every other theory are the essential qualities of a good social scientist.

Many believe that gorillas can communicate and express emotion.

© olga_gl/iStock

much more efficient. It also allowed the species to develop concepts of time, space, and quantity, thereby creating the potential for symbolic interaction.

The Neanderthals were powerfully built but somewhat shorter—about five feet four inches—than present-day humans. They had sloping foreheads, heavy ridges over the eyes, large wide noses, and protruding jaws, and the Neanderthal brain was larger than that of the average modern person. A tribute to their humanity is the fact that among the buried remains are people who were handicapped or aged, which means that Neanderthals cared enough and were organized enough to provide for these economically unproductive members of their communities.

To date, few Neanderthal sites have been found from the period 35,000–60,000 years ago. Because this is also the period in which they seem to have disappeared, there is little or no evidence of why they disappeared. Theories of what happened include the following: (1) they interbred with another group, Cro-Magnons (discussed below), and eventually Neanderthal characteristics were completely absorbed into Cro-Magnons; (2) they battled with Cro-Magnons in a struggle and were annihilated; and (3) they wandered away into regions that were too environmentally inhospitable for survival. Recent genetic testing seems to confirm, at least in Europe, that Neanderthals were replaced by, rather than absorbed into, the Cro-Magnon gene pool.

Cro-Magnons.   Another group of people, whose origins are uncertain but who may have been the immediate precursors of *Homo sapiens,* were **Cro-Magnons.** The name comes from the French village near which the first specimens were found in 1868. Cro-Magnons were anatomically modern, tall, well-built people with skull capacity comparable to that of present-day humans. They and other early anatomically modern sapiens existed before Neanderthals disappeared.

In western Europe, no Cro-Magnon skeletons have been found older than 30,000 years, but 40,000-year-old tools that archaeologists believe must have been made by modern people have been found at a number of western European locations. Cro-Magnons appear to have flourished only beginning about 35,000 years ago. Their remains have been found at various European sites and, in smaller numbers, in the Near East, China, Indonesia, Australia, and Africa. The remains indicate that they were not as strong as Neanderthals, probably because they did not need to be. Less strength, for instance, means that less food was necessary, so the same total amount of food could support a larger population.

Conclusion

Modern people are distinguished from their ancestors by more than physical characteristics. By about 35,000 years ago, they were exhibiting cultural sophistication, for example, in the cave paintings that can still be seen, especially in southern France and northern Spain. The closer we come to our own times, the more evidence we find of strategies such as coping with cold climates by the making and use of clothing and the building of shelters. There is also evidence of increasingly complex social organization and even some limited trade with groups as much as ninety miles apart.

As is true of much anthropological theory, there is debate about these findings. For instance, one method of dating was a controversial technique that relates the age of the human remains to the detection of when the artifacts discovered with the human remains were last heated. There are innumerable unanswered questions about the development of human beings. For example, what in the theory of natural selection explains the various emergences of human behavior? And did most sophisticated behavior appear at roughly the same time, or were there successive advances? Because work continues in this fascinating field, it is likely that the answers to at least some of these questions, and to other questions you might think of, will one day be discovered, or at least be deduced.

The Cro-Magnons, like the Neanderthals, were hunters and gatherers; they roamed from place to place in search of food and survivable weather. As we see in the next chapter, about 11,000 years ago that changed. The change was due to a technological development.

At this point, we stop our consideration of the origins of human beings, leaving the development in what anthropologists call the Stone Age, a period beginning more than 600,000 years ago and lasting to about 10,000 B.C. We make this break not because Stone Age humans were physically different from modern human beings, but because of the technological developments of the Stone Age, which significantly modified the way individuals interrelate. We leave you with the question: What were those technological developments?

 Study and **Review**

Key Points

- Darwin's theory of evolution centers on the survival of the fittest or natural selection; beneficial mutation makes evolution possible.
- Genes contain DNA, the building block of living organisms. DNA contains the codes that determine an organism's development.
- Sociobiologists argue that behavior that decreases chances of survival will eventually be eliminated from human behavior.
- Whether evolution is punctuated or continuous is still much in debate.

- The evolutionary split between human beings and apes occurred more than 25 million years ago.
- DNA evidence is adding enormous insight into the decent of humans.
- The search for human origins has led to many fossil finds but not to a definitive statement: "This is where human beings began."
- Cro-Magnons may have been the immediate precursors of *Homo sapiens*.

Some Important Terms

alleles (28)
Cro-Magnons (43)
DNA (30)
dominant allele (28)
epigenetics (31)
evolution (27)
genes (28)
genetic engineering (31)
genetics (28)

hominids (38)
Homo antecessor (40)
Homo erectus (40)
Homo habilis (40)
Homo sapiens (41)
intelligent design (36)
multi-level group selection (31)
mutation (28)
natural selection (28)

Neanderthals (41)
primates (37)
punctuated equilibrium (33)
recessive allele (28)
scientific creationism (35)
sociobiology (32)
species (37)

Questions for Review and Discussion

General Questions

1. Why do we say the human being is a social creature?
2. Why are humans, apes, and monkeys all placed in the biological order of primates?

3. Explain Darwin's theory of evolution.
4. How do epigenetics and multi-level group selection modify Darwin's theory of how evolution works?
5. Can scientists create life? What possibilities can you see in genetic engineering?

6. How does sociobiology explain the development of human behavior?

7. What is the theory of punctuated equilibrium, and why is it important?

8. Should scientific creationism be taught in schools? Why or why not?

9. How long ago do you think humanlike creatures appeared on earth? Why is it so hard to determine the date, and why do you think we keep trying?

10. Who are some of the earliest precursors of human beings? What makes them like us? What makes them unlike us?

11. What three abilities gave humans advantages over all other creatures? Are humans unique?

Internet Questions

1. Read the short article at https://www.sfgate.com/news/article/Theory-still-rocks-scientists-equilibrium-2817468.php. What are some of the examples given as evidence for punctuated equilibrium? Is one mechanism of evolution singled out for these cases?

2. Pick one of the articles about a recent discovery in paleoanthropology listed on http://www.sci-news.com/news/othersciences/anthropology/paleoanthropology. What was found? Where was it found? Why is this discovery important?

3. Go to https://www.youtube.com/watch?v=xp4Vsq4jRFY and watch the video. What are homologous structures? What are vestigial organs?

4. According to the information at http://discovermagazine.com/2006/apr/chimp-genome, even though humans and chimps share 98.7 percent of their genes, what makes them so different?

5. Go to https://www.youtube.com/watch?v=S5UsRpd0IPc and watch the trailer to Ben Stein's documentary, "Expelled: No Intelligence Allowed" on Darwinism and what he considers the suppression of intelligence design. Is it an alternative to the theory of evolution, and how does the scientific community explain their dislike of this theory?

*F*or Further Study

Books to Explore

Begun, David R, *The Real Planet of the Apes: A New Story of Human Origins*, New Jersey: Princeton, 2016.

Darwin, Charles, *On the Origin of Species*, Irvine, Charlotte, and William Irvine, eds., New York: Ungar, 1959 (first published in 1859).

Doudna, Jennifer, and Samuel Sternberg, *A Crack in Creation: Gene Editing and the Unthinkable Power to Control Evolution*, New York: Houghton Mifflin Harcourt, 2017.

Gottschall, Jonathan, *The Storytelling Animal: How Stories Make Us Human*, Boston, MA: Mariner Books, 2013.

Gurche, John, *Shaping Humanity: How Science, Art, and Imagination Help Us Understand Our Origins*, New Haven, CT, Yale University Press, 2013.

Harari, Yuval Noah, *Sapiens: A Brief History of Humankind*, New York: Harper Collins, 2015.

Hess, Elizabeth, *Nim Chimpsky: The Chimp Who Would Be Human*, New York: Bantam, 2008.

Johanson, Donald, and Kate Wong, *Lucy's Legacy: The Quest for Human Origins*, New York: Broadway, 2010.

Marks, Jonathan, *What It Means to Be 98% Chimpanzee: Apes, People, and Their Genes*, Berkeley, CA: University of California Press, 2003.

Meredith, Martin, *Born in Africa: The Quest for the Origins of Human Life*, New York: Public Affairs, 2011.

Pyne, Lydia, *Seven Skeletons: The Evolution of the World's Most Famous Human Fossils*, New York: Viking, 2016.

Stringer, Chris, *Lone Survivors: How We Came to Be the Only Humans on Earth*, New York: Times Books, 2012.

Tattersall, Ian, *Masters of the Planet: The Search for Our Human Origins*, New York: Macmillan, 2012.

Tattersall, Ian, *The Strange Case of Rickety Cossack*, Palgrave Macmillan, 2015.

Internet Sites to Explore

"http://www.actionbioscience.org" Action Bioscience.

"http://www.talkorigins.org" Creation/Evolution Newsgroup Archive.

"http://www.genengnews.com" Genetic Engineering News.

http://www.greenpeace.org/international_en/campaigns/intro?campaign_id=3942.

"http://genomics.energy.gov/" Human Genome Project.

"http://webspace.ship.edu/cgboer/sociobiology.html" Sociobiology.

Origins of Western Society

chapter 3

After reading this chapter, you should be able to:

- Explain why the domestication of animals and control of land were central developments that created society as we know it today
- Trace the development of modern civilization from Mesopotamia and Egypt to today
- Explain the Greek and Roman origins of modern civilization
- Distinguish three periods of the Middle Ages
- Explain the importance of the Renaissance to modern civilization
- Define the Age of Revolutions

Time is a river of passing events, and its current is strong. No sooner is a thing brought to sight than it is swept by and another takes its place—and this too will be swept away.

—Marcus Aurelius

Throughout most of the remainder of this book, we look at and contrast the origins, development, and operation of societies' cultures so that we can better understand modern problems. At this point, however, it seems advantageous to take a whirlwind tour of history and the development of Western culture. On this tour, you will see some of the influences that have led to the formation of the types of societies we have, and although what we can cover in a chapter is severely limited, we can at least introduce you to some of the terminology we use when we describe historical periods. The chief purpose of our tour, though, is to gain some historical perspective and use it to find continuity and similarities among periods and developments that, if we glance at them casually and individually, seem different from one another.

In the next section, we take you on that whirlwind tour, covering millennia in half pages. In doing so, we consider the origins of Western culture as embodied in the social, political, and economic institutions that shape our modern society.

From the Stone Age to the Agricultural Age

We ended the last chapter with a cliffhanger, saying some technological development significantly changed the nature of humankind and society, and asking if you could guess what technological developments appeared in the Stone Age. If you guessed the bow and arrow, you were right in guessing that it was developed by humans in the Stone Age, but wrong if you were thinking it was the development that caused the major change in society. The bow and arrow improved Stone Age humans' ability to hunt but did not change the basics of their daily lives.

Another technological development, however, *did* fundamentally change society. A central development that created society as we know it today occurred when human beings learned that they could exercise control over the land (through cultivation by hoe) and animals (through domestication for carrying, riding, pulling, and the systematic practice of egg gathering and milking). This development moved human beings from the Stone Age to what we call the **Age of Agriculture,** a period beginning about 11,000 years ago and characterized at first by the storing of wild crops and then by the cultivation of land, domestication of animals, and creation of permanent communities. The Age of Agriculture changed the habits of most human beings from those of roving hunters to those of people living in a more or less fixed community.

The importance of this development for society cannot be overemphasized. People could live in one place; they could accumulate more physical items and pass those on to their children. Moreover, once they could be assured of food, they could devote time to other aspects of life. During the Age of Agriculture, pottery was invented, making it easier to store surplus liquids; it was discovered how to make cloth from both flax (linen) and wool. Moreover, because agriculture and domesticated animals required constant care, people built permanent buildings, usually in clusters. Thus began villages.

The agricultural revolution produced significant population growth in what is now the Middle East and Europe, although village living fostered disease because there was little or no understanding of the need for sanitation. Moreover, the same technological developments that made farming possible also made warfare more effective. Horses provided better transportation, and bows and arrows provided better attack mechanisms. Archaeological excavation has revealed various weapons from this period. Although many could be used in hunting, they are also suitable for attacking and for holding off attackers. Conflict and the lack of sanitation kept the level of population from exploding.

*E*arly Civilizations

Slowly during this period people addressed two issues that are crucial to the preservation and extension of the human life span: sanitation and warfare. They learned how better sanitation led to longer lives, and they began to try to solve the problem of constant fighting. These developments were most pronounced in the Middle East. In approximately 4000 B.C., large numbers of people began moving into the lowlands of Mesopotamia (modern-day Iraq) and Egypt. During this time, writing developed (about 3000 B.C.), and with it began what we call recorded history. Because of that development, we have a much better knowledge of this period than of prerecorded history.

The Cradle of Modern Civilization: Mesopotamia and Egypt

Although we do not know the reason for the development of cities in the Middle East, we can deduce that it was made possible by improved methods of cultivation, which created a surplus of food, and improved sanitation conditions. Once in existence, cities took on the purposes of administration, commerce, and entertainment. It seems likely that in order to protect themselves from constant warfare, individuals submitted to a powerful leader, and for that protection they had to pay a certain percentage of their farm output. Thus began our basic political institution, which is the gathering of people into spatially and ethnically defined units organized and run by a small group. This group's efforts provide the stability within which individuals in the units can work, play, buy, sell, and plan because they are willing to recognize and pay administrators to enforce accommodation among the members of the units and defend the peace against outsiders.

Agricultural surpluses, as well as defense, probably contributed to fighting between groups, as it created questions about the division of the surplus and the opportunity for other

Some Milestones of Civilization

Stone Age	3,300,000–10,000 B.C.*
Humans appear in China	25,000 B.C.
Age of Agriculture	9000 B.C.
Copper Age	6500 B.C.
Egyptian civilization	5000 B.C.
Near Eastern (Mesopotamian) civilization	4000 B.C.
Bronze Age	3800 B.C.
Indian civilization	3000 B.C.
Chinese civilization	1800 B.C.
Iron Age	1000 B.C.
Greek civilization (at its height)	700 B.C. –500 B.C.
Roman civilization	753 B.C. – A.D. 476
Japanese civilization	A.D. 57
Middle Ages	A.D. 476–A.D. 1453
Crusades	A.D. 1095–A.D. 1291
Renaissance	A.D. 1400–A.D. 1600
Reformation	A.D. 1517–A.D. 1690
Voyages of discovery	A.D. 1450–A.D. 1600
Age of Revolutions	A.D. 1750–A.D. 1850
Victorian era	A.D. 1837–A.D. 1901
Edwardian era	A.D. 1901–A.D. 1914
World War I	A.D. 1914–A.D. 1918
World War II	A.D. 1939–A.D. 1945
American world domination (Pax Americana)	A.D. 1900–
Emerging East Asian century	A.D. 2015–

*Many of these dates are estimates and are subject to debate.

groups to take it away. Because of constant disputes among various localities, it probably became obvious to people that some method of stopping the fighting, either by one group winning over all the others or by groups coming to an agreement, would make everyone better off. To further these ends, small localities coalesced into more or less unified kingdoms.

As the size of a kingdom increased, the leader of the kingdom likely became more and more removed from the ordinary inhabitants. As this happened, the leader became closely identified with divinity, either as a god or as a delegate of a god, and a feature of these early Middle Eastern countries was the king-god. The king-gods, in turn, appointed priests, and thus began pagan religious institutions.

We see in this process the organization of society into a military aristocracy, a priesthood, and, finally, a laboring class of landless peasants. As the kings gained power, they also gained control of the ownership of land, which was gradually transferred from individuals who farmed the land to the nobility who protected the land. Wars created the lowest class; the captured losers in a war became slaves. By about 3000 B.C., this organization had become stable; within it, people, freed from the basic struggle merely to live another day, could begin to trust, create, and provide for the future. If we name the result *civilization*, we may say that by about 3800 B.C., a group called the Sumerians had civilized the Mesopotamian area, which is in modern-day Iraq.

To have an organization requires codifying its rules. To do that, one must recognize that what has been going on has in fact been going on and that a certain order exists in those activities. For example, when a child was murdered, the parents probably became angry and

Code of Hammurabi statue.

© Jake Lyell/Alamy Stock Photo

attempted some type of revenge, which brought on revenge for revenge in a cycle of individual retribution. If rules that incorporated the revenge could somehow be established, impulsive killing could be reduced. To do that, someone had to record those rules so that they could be known and followed, by both the leaders and the subjects.

The **Code of Hammurabi** is an early collection of rules, or laws, set up by King Hammurabi of Mesopotamia about 4,000 years ago. The code set up an "eye for an eye" system of retribution, combined with humanitarian rules such as prohibitions against defrauding the helpless.

The Mesopotamian political organization did not last; another group of individuals, less civilized and more warlike, soon overran the Sumerians. This group was the Semites. Even though the Semites won their war, they did not win the cultural competition, and their culture was soon absorbed into the Sumerian culture.

As the Semites were absorbed into the Mesopotamian culture, another culture, similar to the Mesopotamian, was flourishing in Egypt. Like Mesopotamian society, Egyptian society was ruled by a king-god. Because of the geography of the area, Egypt was free of hostile invasions (the sea and the desert made it difficult for attackers to menace Egypt). This freedom from invasion combined with the warm, predictable climate and the fertile farmland of the Nile led to an extremely productive society that generated significant agricultural surpluses. The pyramids, great funerary temples, and rock-cut tombs in which the kings and queens of Egypt were laid to an uneasy rest are evidence both of the power of the king-gods and of the enormous surpluses generated by that culture.[1]

Development of Greek Civilization

Throughout southern Europe, parallel developments to those in Mesopotamia were taking place, although they did not reach into most of those regions until much later. In Crete, part of ancient Greece, pictographic writing was known as early as 3000 B.C., but what we have

---

[1] Almost every known burial site has been shorn of its contents, whether by ancient marauders or modern archaeologists.

defined as the civilizing process did not flourish until later—its heyday there was from about 2000 B.C. to about 1200 B.C., when physical Cretan civilization was suddenly destroyed, probably by an earthquake, tidal wave, volcanic eruption, some combination of these disasters, or even an invasion by the Doric tribes of the north. What exactly happened cannot be determined, simply because of the sheer finality of whatever it was that destroyed human constructs.

From about 700 B.C. to 500 B.C., a new Greek civilization emerged, and many of the roots of Western civilization and institutions are to be found here. For example, Western political organizations have their foundations in the Greek **polis,** or political community. The Greek polis was originally an agricultural village. These villages or cities were also independent political units. The two most famous are Sparta and Athens (today Sparta is a town of about 16,000 inhabitants, whereas Athens bustles with close to 5 million people and is the capital of modern Greece). The citizens of such a unit were seen as relatives of each other, theoretically descended from a common ancestor. The Greek philosopher Aristotle argued that the polis was a natural outgrowth of the human being's nature. He felt that without law and justice the human being was the worst of animals, but with law and justice, the best.

The concept of the polis and its increasingly skillful and sophisticated implementation resulted in the growth of such cities and in the growth of their contacts with each other and with other civilizations. With the development of trade, industry, and colonization, a new class of people, the merchants, became wealthy and important. This change caused trouble for the polis: division within the ruling aristocracy and the establishment of tyranny, or rule by a tyrant, a monarch or leader who had gained power in an unregulated but not necessarily wicked way and who governed through one-man rule. This is one example among many in the history of economic changes and shifts in the distribution of wealth leading to changes in both politics and the social relations among people. Although the concept of "tyrant" was antithetical to the polis, and the custom of rule by tyrant lasted only about a hundred years, tyrants played a role in reducing civil wars among the poleis and in encouraging economic and social change necessary for the development of technology, the arts, and literature; reducing the grip of the aristocracy; and, paradoxically, giving more people the potential for roles in government.

The Persian Empire

In the fifth century B.C., the Persian Empire arose in lower Mesopotamia, and in the fourth century B.C. the Macedonians conquered the various city-states that made up the world of Greece. The Macedonians had no polis and were ruled loosely by a king. A council of aristocracy served as a check on the king's power, and by 338 B.C. one of these kings, King Philip II, had conquered Athens and other Greek city-states. Philip was assassinated in 336 B.C., and his rule was assumed by his son, Alexander the Great, who was not yet 20 years old. By the time Alexander died, overcome by a sudden and unidentified disease when he was only 33 years old, he had solidified his father's conquest of Greece and then gone on to conquer Egypt, almost all of what we now call the Middle East, and the greater part of India. To Alexander is attributed the demand "Bring me more worlds to conquer."

Greek Civilization in the Persian Empire.   Notice that in contrast to the previous sections, we titled the last section "The Persian Empire," not "The Development of the Persian Civilization." The reason is that the Persian legacy was not cultural; its legacy was primarily the creation of an empire. Alexander's empire did not end the cultures and civilizations that made up the Persian Empire, and, although conquered militarily, Greek culture won out over the Persian culture. Even the Persian Empire did not last long. After Alexander's sudden death in 323 B.C., the empire quickly collapsed. It is the Greek, not the Persian, cultural legacy that most strongly influenced modern society.

The Eastern Connection

In this chapter and throughout this book, we have concentrated on Western culture, institutions, and history. We have done so because we have to stop somewhere; to include the East we would have to make the book twice as long. However, it would be inappropriate not to mention some of the multitudinous ideas in Western culture that first developed in the East.

In terms of beginnings of civilizations, the East developed slightly later than the West, but once developed, it quickly surpassed the West in political and economic organization, in technology, and in sophisticated philosophy.

Language—India, five or six thousand years ago. The language is Indo-European, and today half the world's population speaks languages derived from it. These include Hindi, Lithuanian, Russian, Greek, Gaelic, Latin, German, all the Scandinavian languages, English, Italian, French, Spanish, Portuguese, and Romanian.

History—India dates the beginning of the modern era at 3102 B.C.

Bronze casting—China, 1600 B.C.

Monotheism (only one god, not multiple gods)—Iran, sixth century B.C.

Sanskrit grammar, with 3,873 rules—India, 500 B.C.

Kite—China, 400 B.C.

Great Wall of China—begun in 209 B.C.

Cable suspension bridge—China, 100 B.C.

Sophisticated eye surgery, including cataract removal—India, before A.D. 33

Trade—by the second century A.D., China was trading with Rome

Wheelbarrow—China, A.D. 231

A centralized nation-state—as early as the sixth century A.D., Japan had a system of centralized government (borrowed from China)

Paper money—China, A.D. 811 (it was called flying cash because it could be transported so much more easily than silver or copper coins)

Arabic numerals (0, 1, 2, 3, 4, etc.)—India, ninth century A.D.

Movable type (made of clay)—China, A.D. 1045

Movable type (made of metal)—Korea, A.D. 1302

Many Greek ideas and institutions were revived almost 1,800 years later in what became known as the Renaissance. (*Renaissance* can be translated as "rebirth," and Greek ideas were some of the concepts that were reborn.) Because of their predominance in the Renaissance, the ideas of Greek society played a central role in the subsequent history of Western civilization.

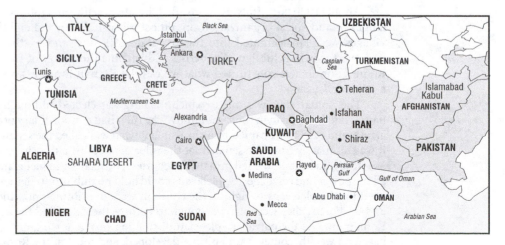

The Persian Empire (shown in the shaded area) at its height.

How the Greeks Tried Laughing All the Way to the Peace Talks

In 413 B.C., Athens suffered a terrifying defeat: Its navy was destroyed. The opposing army, the Spartans, was nearby and well equipped. Allies not only deserted Athens but also joined the enemy. Aristophanes, a famous comic writer, chose to face this despair by writing a play.

Lysistrata is about a unique way to enforce peace. The plot is simple: The heroine, Lysistrata, organizes the women of both sides to refuse sex with their husbands and lovers until the men agree to end the war.

Initially, most of the women are unwilling to give up sex. Lysistrata convinces them by rational arguments that her plan will work. She persuades the older women to join, giving them a vital task—guarding the public treasury so that no money can be disbursed for the war. She holds them together when they waver after suffering without men for a long period (well, five days—but it's clear Aristophanes thought that was a long time). She knows, and she makes them realize, that if they stick together, and if they can endure longer than the men can

endure, they will win. When the men debate with her, she wins every point.

The men give in first. And their reward is even more than they hoped, because the women remind them that both sides worship the same gods, both sides have in the past done noble deeds in aid of the other, and in this quarrel surely they can compromise. After a little bickering, the opposing armies do come to an agreement, after which both sides join in a satisfying feast of all domestic joys (including, but not limited to, eating and drinking).

As you can see, the play is far more complex than it may have seemed at first. It is about sex, money, reason, greed, graft, war, politics, organization, cunning, religion, prejudice, psychology, folly, resolve, accommodation, denial, and triumph. It is even about love. In short, it is about the issues of social science.

P.S. *Lysistrata* is a play. In real life, the Spartans did not attack Athens immediately, and while they hesitated, the Athenians were able to build a whole new navy, defend their city, and win an honorable peace. What part the women of Athens played in the real peace must be left to your imagination.

Roman Civilization

As we mentioned earlier, individuals were organizing into social groups throughout southern and middle Europe in a period beginning about 4000 B.C. If we had thousands of pages to explain and you had hundreds of years to study, we could recount the history and interaction of these groups. We are forced to be selective, however, and the next civilization that we have time and room for is the Roman civilization, which developed in what is now Italy. It developed later than many of the others, and as late as 1000 B.C. it remained a collection of unorganized tribes.

About 1000 B.C., Italy was invaded by its warlike neighbors, who imposed their language and social organization on almost all of Italy. In the eighth century B.C., small villages were amalgamated into the city-state of Rome, and by the sixth century B.C., it had overthrown its foreign conquerors and become the center of Italy and Italian culture. Rome's dominance constituted what we call the Roman Empire, and it was to last almost a thousand years.

The Roman state was one in which the king was elected, although the office appears to have tended to remain in the same family. The ruler had extraordinary powers and could make arrests and even order capital punishment, but what was called the senate had veto power, and it was ultimately from the senate that the ruler derived his authority.

Individuals in Rome fell into two categories: patricians and plebeians. The patricians had all the power and privilege; the plebeians could hold no public or religious office. However, the need for the plebeians to fight in the constant wars that Rome undertook gave them power, and by 450 B.C. they were strong enough to enforce their demand for a major codification of Roman law. As the patrician–plebeian distinction broke down, another class distinction— based on wealth, contacts, and birth—developed, and most of the Roman leaders came only from the few families in this new aristocracy.

Ruins of the Roman Forum.

© pavel068/Shutterstock

Roman civilization endured until the fifth century A.D., but it did not remain static. The Roman republic was transformed into the Roman Empire, and pagan religion gave way to Christianity; by the fourth century A.D., Christianity was the state religion.

The Romans exercised their power for centuries, and their influence pervades Western civilization today. They overran Greek civilization and incorporated it into their own, so that when Roman influence is transmitted to us, Greek influence is transmitted to us. Here are some of the things that reflect our Roman heritage.

- The dominance of the family
- The custom of women to rule in household matters and to have certain legal property rights
- Political patronage
- The "network" system of contacts for social and professional advancement
- Ingenuity in solving technical problems
- Reliance on and practice of all manner of engineering and inventive art
- The concept of empire
- Existence of a military-industrial complex
- Second homes and resorts
- Large agricultural holdings
- The lure of city life
- A flexible legal system that is constantly changing to suit circumstances, relying on a body of precedents to interpret and modify statutes
- The names of all of our months and the organization of our calendar

From the four phenomena that are the most striking in Roman history—military undertakings, engineering, law, and political administration—we choose the last as being basic to all the rest. Roman political administration was efficient, reasonable, flexible, realistic, and humane. Because the government was so well organized, Rome was able to devote its ample excess energies to building, manufacture, agriculture, literature, trade, moral philosophy, and world conquest. Rome also had the leisure and Latin language to develop, refine, and express its thoughts, principles, discoveries, speculations, and decrees. Today, Latin forms the basis of hundreds of thousands of words in the English language, although essentially English is a Germanic language.

Rome's success, however, also had its negative side: Along with the benefits came complacency, ambition, greed, arrogance, and tyranny. Because these traits are more dramatic than the steady march of its well-ordered society, today we often think of ancient Rome in terms of the religious conflict, savage combat, extravagant public carnivals, graft, brutal suppression of opposition, and dissolution that eventually weakened control over its enormous territory[2] and caused popular uprisings, financial collapse, and military defeat—in short, the fall of the **Roman Empire,** the territory encompassing Great Britain, most of Europe, northern Africa, and the Middle East administered by the Romans.

Rome was attacked by other groups from both the north and the south, and by about A.D. 500 the population of the empire had declined from an estimated 1.5 million to about 300,000, and Rome, as a civilization, ended. Why did it end? It is hard to say, and maybe that is not even the right question. Edward Gibbon argues in *The Decline and Fall of the Roman Empire* that perhaps the question should not be Why did Rome fall?, but Why did it last so long?

The Middle Ages (A.D. 476–1453)

With the fall of Rome came the advent of a period we now call the **Middle Ages,** from about A.D. 476 to A.D. 1453, between Roman civilization and modern civilization.

The Middle Ages began in A.D. 476 with the defeat of the Roman Empire by wandering tribes that roamed over much of what is now northern and central Europe.[3] Even though the northern tribes had conquered Rome, Roman culture at least partially conquered the northern tribal culture. The tribes began to adopt some of the technological, social, religious, and political structures that the Roman Empire had developed.

As Roman culture spread north, Muslim culture spread across North Africa and into all of Spain and Portugal. Muslim armies, formed of warriors known as Moors, attacked Europe, spread into Spain, and then moved into France. In A.D. 732, they lost a major battle against the Franks, but their influence remained strong in Spain and Portugal.

Because Muslims controlled the Mediterranean Sea and Europe's contacts with the Orient were curtailed, Europe was forced into a kind of isolation. The coastal cities became less prosperous, and workers were displaced from seagoing occupations to agriculture. Wandering decreased, agricultural activity increased, and life became centered on a manor, or **feudal estate**—an area ruled by a lord. The land on the feudal estate was worked by **serfs,** peasants who were bound to a particular manor and subject to their feudal lord's will. Christianity, which had been flourishing in the Roman Empire, retained and strengthened its influence partly because it had modeled its administrative structure on the efficient civil Roman organization.

The church consolidated its political and military power by asserting its independence from civilian rulers and by fending off attempts by the Muslims to encroach further on Europe. It also had the time and energy to fight bitter quarrels within its own ranks on matters of religious doctrine. Meanwhile the holders of large manors quarreled, reconciled, and rearranged their allegiances among themselves and the various kings and civil

---

[2] The empire was constantly conquering, annexing, and losing pieces of territory, but at its largest, about A.D. 200, it included what we call today the Middle East, North Africa, Spain, Great Britain, and most of present-day Europe.

[3] The Eastern Empire, which had been officially divided from the Western Roman Empire in A.D. 395, survived until 1453, when the Turks conquered its capital, Constantinople. Today, Constantinople is the Turkish city of Istanbul.

Origins of Pakistani Society

Although there isn't space here to discuss the origins of Eastern society, it is so important that you have some sense of Eastern culture that we offer brief insights into other countries' social, cultural, political, and economic institutions throughout the book. Here, Pakistan will be our example.

As a nation-state, Pakistan has been around for about seventy years, but it has origins that predate the birth of Islam (A.D. 622), the religion today of the majority of its inhabitants. By 5000 B.C., a civilization was already flourishing in the Indus Valley, then still a part of India. Excavations of its two greatest cities, Mohenjo Daro and Harappa, show that it had an extensive system of civic administration as well as sewage, drainage, and irrigation systems.

About 1500 B.C., this civilization was supplanted by a group of Indo-European tribes from central Asia who established their own rule over India and instituted a caste system to maintain a permanent hold over the conquered people, from whom, however, they assimilated many things. In the fourth century B.C., when Alexander the Great advanced up the Indus River, a group called Mauryas was already laying the foundations of the first Indian Empire, which saw the growth of economics, learning, and Sanskrit (one of the earliest languages, the mother of dozens of the world's modern languages). The Mauryas's religion was Buddhism, different from the Hinduism of the conquered people. Then in the eighth century A.D., the Arabs invaded north India and fostered the religion of Islam there.

The Indian Empire was united by a Turkish dynasty, the Mughals, the greatest of whom was Akbar (1542–1605). He gave administrative unity to the country; advanced the notion of secular as opposed to religious rule; promoted the concept of Indian indivisibility; encouraged tolerance among all races and religions; raised splendid monuments and cities; married Hindu princesses to solidify alliances; and patronized poets, painters, and scholars. Akbar was a Muslim, and under his rule much of India converted to Islam.

In 1757, India was conquered by the British, who originally came as traders but who exploited internal dissensions to take over the country. In 1947 British rule ended. At that time, Pakistan was created, but the new country was physically divided by a portion of north India that lay between Pakistan's eastern and western sections. This situation proved unworkable, and in 1971 the eastern section broke away to become the independent state of Bangladesh.

Today, Pakistan is an independent, unitary country located on the northwest border of India. Its other bordering neighbors are Afghanistan, Iran, and China.

administrators. The local lords, the kings, and the church constantly jockeyed for power, wealth, and land as they all struggled to control these available resources and seize them from one another.

Manor life in the early Middle Ages was relatively straightforward: You were born; you lived a life similar to that of your parents in the same place that they lived; and you died, leaving your children to continue the process. The manor estate was owned by the feudal lord, although ownership was not defined in the way we define it today. Land was not thought of as something that could be bought and sold, but rather as something that belonged to the lord because it belonged to the lord. The peasants, or serfs, did the work on the farm and in return received protection from the lord and enough food to live. The lord provided some security from attack.

What is simple has a tendency to become complex. As the lords became accustomed to managing the land, they began to feel like real owners and to act like owners. Toward the end of the tenth century, the concept of land ownership gained acceptance. This was logically followed by preoccupation with acquiring more and more land while concern for preserving the old feudal way of life faded.

At the end of the tenth century, a series of strong rulers in what is now the countries of France and Germany succeeded in imposing centralized government on parts of Europe. Administrative systems developed in which the interests of the various classes—the lords, the church, the peasants, and the townspeople—were represented. The decline of the feudal manor meant that many of the workers who had been attached to those manors went back into the towns looking for other kinds of jobs. Because of technological improvements having to do with methods of plowing and rotating crops, it took fewer agricultural workers to provide needed food. As the towns grew, their economies grew, too. People bought and sold within the town, towns traded with each other, regions had an interest in keeping the peace in order to protect trade, and Europe became strong enough even to venture into the Mediterranean Sea.

Two motives interacted to begin the end of Europe's isolation: religion and commerce. In the Middle Ages, religion played a central role in all individuals' lives. In fact, the Catholic Church was the primary institution for people outside of the manor. It controlled education and knowledge, and it told people how they should live their lives. Moreover, the church owned enormous amounts of land and had significant economic and political power. That power was demonstrated by the **Crusades,** a series of religious wars between the eleventh and thirteenth centuries that, the church said, were necessary to recover Jerusalem (in modern-day Israel) from the infidels.

The contacts the Crusaders made with Arab culture introduced new products to Europe, taught the Europeans what Arabs had learned about science and mathematics, and revived interest in Greek culture. The Crusades stimulated trade and made the merchants of Venice, Pisa, and Genoa rich. This new merchant class changed the internal structure of the society of the Middle Ages because most merchants had been formerly landless adventurers. Its growth and the growth of the cities in which trade prospered changed the nature of the social system.

Whereas life on the manor was structured and individuals' roles were well defined, in the cities there was ambiguity about roles, and individuals had the freedom to choose what they could be. Although by modern standards the cities were merely small towns, they offered the opportunity for wealth and the amusements and intellectual variety that we associate with cities. The freedom of the cities had attracted many serfs and peasants, especially those whom new agricultural technology had dispossessed from manor lands. When this occurred, the landed nobility lost power and in their weakened state were taken advantage of by the merchants, who sided with the kings. The loose associations that had previously existed were solidified into modern **nation-states,** separate countries with defined borders and populations with the same language and more or less the same interests, administered by rulers who sought to foster the particular nation-state's economic, political, social, and cultural growth.

As Europe grew richer, the nation-states and the church had more to fight about. All were rich and wished to be richer, were powerful and wished to be more powerful. The worst fight was between the English and the French and was called the Hundred Years' War. It raged from 1337 until 1453, more than a hundred years, but there were periods of peace, or at least periods of exhaustion when both sides rested. What was it about? It was about whether the French should rule in England or the English should rule in France. It was about prestige, about who was smarter and stronger, about boundaries and national identity. It was about what all wars are about.

Worse even than the Hundred Years' War was the **Black Death,** or bubonic plague, a disease transmitted by rats. In the 1290s, bubonic plague arrived in Sicily, carried there by infected rats from ships in the Middle Eastern trade. The plague was carried from country to country by commercial routes, attacking all of Europe as far as Norway, where it died out about 1350. It had probably just run out of victims. There are all kinds of estimates of how many people died, but a generally accepted figure is 40 percent of Europe. Population levels did not recover for 200 years.

This population change had enormous social and economic consequences. For example, so many people were killed by the plague that the surviving workers were able to command much higher wages. Cities grew wealthier. Even the Catholic Church profited because it received so many inheritances and religious fees. Landholders, on the other hand, suffered because their workers died off, the demand for food dropped (fewer people to eat it), and they had to pay higher prices for the things they bought.

Struggles within the church went on all during this period. One of the questions was: Shall policy be set by the pope or by the individual churches? The papacy was weakened by

*I*s a Modern Plague Possible?

It was trade that made the West rich, but it was also trade that brought the bubonic plague to Europe. Can such a calamity happen again? The answer is yes. One indication that it can happen again was seen in 2003 when SARS, which killed approximately 10 percent of its victims, spread from China around the world. SARS had no cure, and it spread like the common cold.

With the increased interconnections among countries that occur with globalization, it is becoming increasingly difficult to keep an illness geographically constrained. SARS was quickly contained, but that did not allay fears. New concerns quickly developed that a bird flu pandemic could spread throughout the world. In 2009, the rapid spread of the H1N1 virus—commonly known as swine flu—from Mexico to more than seventy countries led the World Health Organization (WHO) to declare a global pandemic, demonstrating how easily a deadly disease can circle the world. So, in response to the question "Is a modern-day worldwide plague possible?"—the answer is yes.

An engraving depicting victims of the plague.

these quarrels, and monarchs moved into the power vacuum. Religious life became subject to civil control. Although the papacy still had a stronghold in Rome, its power base shrank and it lost much of its unquestioned authority over the rest of Europe. Religious debates had fostered new ways of looking at the world, and intellectual Europe was ready for new ideas.

New ideas were about to arrive. In 1453, Constantinople, which was under Christian control, fell to the Turks, who were Muslims. Among the refugees who escaped to Europe were Greek scholars, who brought with them learning and traditions that fueled the Renaissance.

*T*he Renaissance

The Middle Ages ended sometime in the fifteenth century, when scholars of the time decided that they were embarking on a "new beginning." They called the new beginning the Renaissance. **Renaissance** means "rebirth," and it occurred after the Middle Ages, when the knowledge of the ancient Greeks and Romans was reestablished and reason, critical thinking, and the arts flourished. Architecture, sculpture, painting, and even engineering and critical investigation were created by artists such as Leonardo da Vinci, Raphael, Michelangelo, and Donatello. The Renaissance encouraged critical thinking, and people no longer necessarily accepted the dictates of the church elders on all topics under the sun.

Marco Polo's Travels

One of the ways in which the West learned about the culture of the East was through the tales of explorers. One of the most famous was Marco Polo, who traveled throughout the East. The map traces Marco Polo's travels. His description of where he went is not always easy to identify on modern maps, but he followed this plan more or less. He was one of the earliest travelers from West to East. He reached Beijing on a trading mission in 1275 and remained in China for seventeen years. As late as the nineteenth century, the book he wrote about his travels continued to be almost the only source of information the West had about the remote areas of central Asia. Some of the things the West learned about from Marco Polo were tattooing, coal, condensed milk, paper money, and fuel oil.

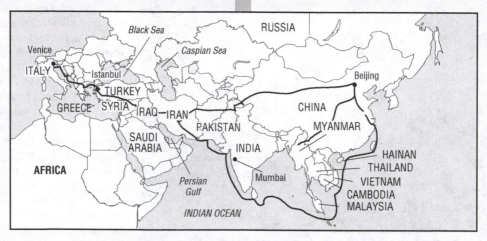

In 1517, such critical thinking put in motion a set of events that came to be known as the Protestant Reformation, when a German Augustinian friar by the name of Martin Luther posted ninety-five theses against indulgences on the door of the castle church of Wittenberg. Indulgences are reductions in, or even elimination of, the time a sinner would otherwise have to spend being punished in purgatory. They are granted by the Catholic Church to sinners in return for actions such as saying certain prayers or visiting certain holy shrines. In Luther's day, the practice had been corrupted because the church sold indulgences for profit. Luther was outraged by this practice. He believed that human beings must be saved not by indulgences but by faith alone. Luther's posting of the theses was a direct challenge to the pope's absolute authority. With this challenge, Luther and other Protestant theologians began a forced retrenchment of church power and created a complex of hostilities between groups that can still be seen today, for example, in the antagonisms between Protestants and Catholics in Northern Ireland.

The importance of free thinking and rationality to the events that shaped our world can be seen in the popular saying to the effect that the philosopher Erasmus (1466–1536), who was one of the strongest advocates of rationality, "laid the egg that Luther hatched." Nevertheless, throughout the Renaissance, the influence of religion remained strong. The Protestant Reformation challenged only those aspects of the Renaissance that paid obeisance to traditional religion. The Reformation replaced it with a religion that gave a stronger role to the individual. Other Renaissance values, such as the importance of education, religion, and obedience to God, were maintained.

As we discussed earlier, until the latter part of the Middle Ages the individual feudal lords had strong powers, and although they were tied together into loose confederations with a king or monarch, often the individual lords had more power than the monarch. The expansion of trade, the development of cities, and the creation of a new merchant class led to a new set of

Martin Luther discarding the Pope's Bill.

© SuperStock/Alamy Stock Photo

alliances that made possible the development of the modern state. The Renaissance solidified that development. The states continued to develop throughout the 1700s, and by the end of that century, most of the states of Europe that we are now familiar with had been formed as monarchies.

Throughout this period, the middle class, consisting of merchants and wealthier peasants, continued to grow, but the focus on traditional life remained. Change was considered bad, and tradition remained the important focal point, governing the direction of society.

The Development of Modern Economic and Political Institutions

During the Middle Ages and under the feudal system, markets existed, but they were not the chief ways by which individuals acquired the goods they needed for existence. Markets and trade did, however, provide luxuries and a variety of goods, and throughout the Middle Ages a set of fairs developed during which individuals bartered these goods. Merchants acquired more and more income from the trade at these fairs and gradually became strong enough to join with the king in reducing the rights of the lords. These changes occurred simultaneously with the Renaissance.

In the Middle Ages, people looked at the economy quite differently than we do today. Economic activity was not necessarily good in itself; tradition, rather than the profit motive, guided people's actions. Everyone knew their place, and roles were well defined. There were a few free individuals, such as the merchants, and as a by-product of their traveling from place to place, a variety of cities or marketplaces sprang up where individuals from the manors could go to trade with the merchants. But all of these events would not have brought much change were it not for the Crusades, which sped up and significantly increased the breakdown of the manorial system.

If You Hated Inquisition I, Wait until You See Inquisition II

The phenomenon known as the Inquisition was not exclusively medieval and did not occur just once.

Inquisition I: The Medieval Inquisition

The medieval Inquisition began in about 1200, when the Roman Catholic pope replaced local bishops with his own appointees. Their duty was to inquire into heresy (theories of religion that differed from the official Roman Catholic version). The inquisitors would give notice that they were coming to a locality and why. People would have a month to come forward voluntarily and swear they were not heretics. Usually the inquisitors believed them and that was that. But some people did not come forward.

It was not until the 1800s that the custom was abolished. Until then it was a fact of life in France, Italy, and Germany. In every age and country, there were bunches of nosy neighbors who were willing to denounce this or that person to the inquisitors. Then the inquisitors would hold a trial. The accused could have legal counsel and could appeal to the pope if the decision was adverse. However, the accused could not find out who had accused him or her. (On the other hand, the accused could give the inquisitors a list of his or her enemies, and if an enemy's name was the same as an accuser's name, the accusation of that enemy was thrown out.)

Generally the pope's appointees were willing to believe heretics who swore that they would give up their heresy and be good. But if people were found guilty, they were turned over to the local ruler for punishment. The most common punishment was imprisonment, although once in a while one of these unfortunate people was burned alive at the stake.

Inquisition II: The Spanish Inquisition

The second inquisition, known as the Spanish Inquisition, was much worse than Inquisition I. It was established by the Spanish rulers Ferdinand and Isabella, the same folks who brought you Christopher Columbus, the New World, and America. (No one is all bad; but no one is all good, either.) Inquisition II was harsher and tried many more people than the medieval Inquisition. It is the Inquisition that is famous for torturing both the accused and the unlucky witnesses, for handing out guilty verdicts right and left, and for using the preferred punishment of burning at the stake. Because Inquisition II was run by the Spanish kings and queens, the Roman Catholic pope did not really approve of it, but papal authority did not succeed in abolishing it until 1820.

People were usually heavily drugged before they were burned at the stake. Sometimes, though, the authorities were mean and nasty, and if they thought the accused was especially wicked, the drugs were omitted.

From Serfdom to Mercantilism

During this time, there was a gradual transition from the system of **serfdom,** feudal obligations owed by vassals to their lords based on a percentage of their agricultural output or days of labor, into payments of money due for rent owed. The central economy shifted from a system of traditional obligations to a system based on the exchange of products and services for money. The lords were in favor of this movement because the expanding trade required them to have money in order to deal with the merchants. The expanded wants generated by this trade left many lords impoverished, and the merchants had incomes significantly exceeding those of the richest lords.

At that point, the landed aristocracy began to view their ancestral manors not just as something that belonged to them but as possible sources of cash, and when sheep became profitable, they began to enclose the land that had been previously held in common, so that the sheep could graze on it. This made it more and more difficult for the tenants to support themselves. Enclosure dispossessed many tenants and created a new type of labor force—individuals without land who moved into the cities and led a marginal existence or wandered from place to place.

Although serfdom was not formally abolished in France until 1789 and in Germany until the 1850s, by the 1700s the market economy was definitely emerging, but it had yet to receive full legal and political status. The new economic order was **mercantilism,** an early phase of capitalism in which private ownership and profits were important, but in which there was significant state control. In a mercantilist system, the king granted rights for individuals to

A Ripple from the Third Crusade

When returning to England from the Third Crusade at the end of the twelfth century, King Richard the Lionheart was taken captive by Henry VI of France, and the English were forced to pay a large ransom for him. In order to pay that ransom, Richard's younger brother, John, who was ruling England in Richard's absence, had to establish high taxes, which did not decline after Richard's release.

The high taxes, together with John's military and administrative failures, caused a revolt against the English monarchy. The English nobles, backed by the church and by solid citizens of the towns, forced John, who had come to the throne after Richard's death, to accept the Magna Carta. The **Magna Carta,** "the great charter," forced the king to agree that free men had rights and liberties that could not be trampled on.

We quote from the Magna Carta to show how bad the conditions must have been that forced the revolt, and to show you why the Magna Carta is said to be the basis of some of the rights we ourselves take for granted today:

No constable ... shall take anyone's ... chattels without ... paying for them in money.

No sheriff ... shall take horses or wagons ... except on permission.

We ... will not take the wood of another man ... except by permission of him to whom the wood belongs.

No free man shall be taken, or imprisoned, or dispossessed, or outlawed, or banished ... except by the legal judgment of his peers, or by the law of the land.

To no one will we sell, to no one will we deny or delay, right or justice.

conduct a variety of trades, the state was intricately involved in all aspects of commerce and business, and countries all tried to export more goods than they imported and to build up their gold reserves. Technological developments continued throughout this time, but in the 1700s, technological changes themselves fundamentally altered the methods of, and needs for, labor.

The Emergence of Nation-States

As the individual states grew and trade picked up, the monarchs attempted to consolidate and broaden their power by supporting the merchants in voyages to Africa (in search of gold) and

King John signing the Magna Carta.
© GL Archive/Alamy Stock Photo

India (in search of spices). Such voyages avoided the Arab land routes by which gold had been making its way to Europe and the long, arduous overland route between western Europe and India through which pepper, cloves, and other spices came. Thus we have a variety of voyages of discovery such as Columbus's that tremendously broadened possibilities for society. It was through these voyages in search of still better routes to India that what became the United States enters the picture of Western development.

The emergence of nation-states led to numerous wars both within and among nations. These included the French Wars of Religion (1562–1598), the Thirty Years' War (1618–1648), the Glorious Revolution in England (1688), the Great Northern War between Sweden and Russia (1700–1721), the War of the Spanish Succession (1701–1714), and many others. Such wars were present throughout much of history; and both conflict and the threat of conflict are still the most important problems facing the modern world.

The Industrial and Political Revolutions of the 1750s to the 1850s

The period of time from 1750 to 1850 is often called the **Age of Revolutions** because of the enormous economic and political changes that occurred during that time.

In the 1750s, once again technological changes had enormous influence on all parts of society. These technological changes were so important that the next significant period is called the **Industrial Revolution,** a period from 1750 to about 1900 characterized by the invention of machines that had the effect of greatly increasing total output and reorganizing work patterns and social relationships. Although the Industrial Revolution began in England, its influence soon spread throughout the world. The revolution was spurred by technological developments such as John Kay's flying shuttle[4] (1733), James Hargreaves's spinning jenny (1765), James Watt's steam engine (1769), and Richard Arkwright's power loom (1769). These inventions made it possible to produce much more output than had hitherto been possible, and in doing so created the need to reorganize the types of work that individuals did.

In order to produce these machines and use the technology, individuals were needed in cities to work in factories. Thus people leaving the rural manors had an alternative. Because pay was often initially higher in factories than on the farm, a migration began into the cities, where people hoped to get jobs. The Industrial Revolution further strengthened the power of the merchants, who had allied themselves with the monarchy.

On the political front, this period witnessed both the American and French Revolutions. In 1776, the American Revolution began, weakening the British empire and establishing the rights of individuals relative to the state and ruler. The pressures that had erupted in the American Revolution were founded in the same conditions as those that later caused the French Revolution. Because of the wars that had marked much of the 1700s, governments had significant debts on which they continually had to pay high interest. On the eve of the French Revolution (1789), the interest paid on the French debt was more than half of France's total budget. As the merchants grew tired of paying this debt, the middle class aligned itself with some members of the aristocracy, leading to a revolution in the way societies were organized. The power of the king was eliminated, and there was a declaration of the rights of man and citizenship. The French Revolution, embodying the ideas of the emerging social sciences, changed the political and economic organization of society.

---

[4] This was a technological advance but not, like the U.S. shuttle, a space vehicle. It was an improvement to looms that enabled weavers to weave faster. The invention of the flying shuttle frustrated the textile industry because it enabled workers to weave so much cloth that the spinners of thread from which it was woven could not keep up; it was a challenge to the textile industry that was met by offering a prize to anyone who could invent something to increase the threadspinners' productivity. The prize was won when the spinning jenny was invented.

Drawing of early Industrial Revolution factory, from Diderot's Encyclopédie.

The Industrial Revolution took hold in the 1800s. The middle class grew enormously and, with its newfound political power, pursued an increasingly important role in running the economy. During this time, significant social experimentation took place as the state and the organization of society went through the process of reform and of throwing off tradition. Throughout this period, societies and individual countries became more clearly defined, and by 1850 in western Europe, the concept of a nation-state with parliamentary government ruled the day.

But these nation-states had to learn to live together, and their failure to do so and to discover a way to negotiate settlements of disputes among them led to continued warfare and significantly changed the boundaries separating nation-states. As a result of wars, many new nation-states have sprung into being, whereas from time to time old ones have died out. During the nineteenth century, Turkish authority was expelled from most of Europe, and new states took its place on the Balkan Peninsula: Greece, Bulgaria, Serbia, Romania, Albania, and Montenegro. Approximately twenty new states were formed from the old holdings of Spain and Portugal in the New World. About the middle of the nineteenth century, China and Japan opened their doors to Western trade. They, too, entered the community of nation-states, in 1842 and 1854, respectively.

Learning to Live Together

World War I was a war between Germany, Austria-Hungary, and Turkey on one side and Britain, France, Belgium, Italy, Luxembourg, Bulgaria, parts of Yugoslavia, Russia, Japan, and the United States on the other side. It lasted from 1914 to late in 1918. It tore down the old multinational states of Austria-Hungary and Estonia, and redrew other parts of the European map. Lasting from 1939 to 1945, **World War II** was a much more international war and was fought between Germany, Japan, and Italy on one side, and the United States, Canada, the British Empire, most of Europe, much of Asia including China, many of the Western Pacific countries, and the Union of Soviet Socialist Republics (USSR) on the other side. It led directly to the establishment of Israel, and the divisions of Korea and Germany. After World War II, a surge of nationalism took place in the colonial areas of Africa and

Asia, and in the 1960s a number of African and Asian states emerged from the British and French empires.

Beginning in the late 1980s, additional dramatic changes took place. The USSR broke up, and political subdivisions within the USSR, such as Russia, Georgia, Uzbekistan, and Ukraine, all became independent countries. The wall between East and West Berlin was torn down, and East and West Germany reunited to become one Germany. Other Eastern European countries broke from Russia and became part of an expanded European Union, tying themselves with the West. In the late 1900s, these changes made the United States the world's sole superpower, but that period was short-lived. As the European economies grew, the European Union increasingly exerted its independent power, and China and India emerged as future economic and likely political superpowers. These factors—combined with the reawakening of Islamic countries, and significant changes in government in Arab countries such as Iraq, Egypt, and Libya—indicate that the world in the early decades of the twenty-first century is likely to be one of difficult change and shared power.

Conclusion

That's it: the history of Western civilization in a chapter—not the most thorough or complete history, but one that will give you some sense of the origins of our society and the institutions we consider throughout much of the rest of the book.

 Study and **Review**

Key Points

- The development of agriculture and the domestication of animals played key roles in the establishment of fixed communities, which were essential to modern civilization.
- Egypt and Mesopotamia formed the cradle of modern civilization.
- The Greek civilization that significantly influenced our own emerged from about 700 B.C. to 500 B.C.

- In the fifth century B.C., Roman civilization emerged and remained dominant until the fifth century A.D.
- In the Middle Ages, the church dominated life.
- The Renaissance was a period when the arts flourished and people were encouraged to question some church dictates.
- The Age of Revolutions, from about 1750 to 1850, led to the emergence of our modern economic and governmental systems.

Some Important Terms

Age of Agriculture (47)
Age of Revolutions (62)
Black Death (56)
Code of Hammurabi (49)
Crusades (56)
feudal estate (54)

Industrial Revolution (62)
Magna Carta (61)
mercantilism (60)
Middle Ages (54)
nation-states (56)
polis (50)

Renaissance (57)
Roman Empire (54)
serfdom (60)
serfs (54)
World War I (63)
World War II (63)

Questions for Review and Discussion

General Questions

1. What are some of the developments that changed human beings from roving hunters to people living in fixed communities? What responsibilities and functions did the towns grow to provide?

2. What are some of the legal systems that have existed in Western society? Do you think any of their provisions have relevance today?

3. What conditions enabled certain classes of society to grow wealthy? Do you think concentrations of wealth were a positive or a negative factor for the nature of society?

4. Name some human characteristics that have persisted over time in the development of Western society.

5. In thinking about your life today, can you identify any ideas that may have come from the Greeks? From the Romans? From the Middle Ages? If so, what are they? (If you prefer, choose some of the other periods discussed, such as the Reformation and the Industrial Revolution.)

6. How did the Arab world influence the development of Western society in the Middle Ages? Do you see any parallels with the situation in the Middle East today?

7. What did the peasant get from the feudal lord, and what did the feudal lord get in return? Do you think it was a fair exchange?

8. How did the church affect life in the Middle Ages? Did its influence change in the Renaissance?

9. How did trade and commerce develop? What do you think your life would be like today if the only things you could buy were those that were grown or manufactured within ten miles of your house?

10. What was revolutionized by the Industrial Revolution?

11. Name some of the wars that altered the course of Western society. Why do you think they led to change?

12. Identify some of the institutions that have grown up in Western society. How are they changing society today?

13. What is the most important problem facing Western society today? What solutions can you think of?

14. Throughout the chapter, the influence of the Muslim world has been brought into the discussion. How do you think this influence will play out during the next fifty years?

Internet Questions

1. According to Matthew Gabriele (https://www.washingtonpost.com/opinions/5-myths-about-the-middle-ages/2016/09/22/e56c4150-7f50-11e6-9070-5c4905bf40dc_story.html?utm_term=.3a93ddba8f6b) what are five myths of the middle ages?

2. Go to http://industrialrevolution.sea.ca/impact.html and read about the Industrial Revolution. How did the social structure change during the Industrial Revolution?

3. Read about the Black Death at http://www.eyewitnesstohistory.com/plague.htm. What were the symptoms? How did people try to avoid the disease?

4. Go to http://www.thenagain.info/WebChron/WestEurope/AgeRevs.html. What are the five major groupings in the Age of Revolutions (1763–1848)? Pick one and list the important events.

5. Go to https://classicalwisdom.com/politics/empires/the-rise-the-fall-and-the-mystery-of-the-mycenaeans/. Read about the ancient Greek civilization of the Myceneans. How did this civilization fall?

For Further Study

Books to Explore

Acemoglu, Daron, and James Robinson, *Why Nations Fail: The Origins of Power, Prosperity, and Poverty*, New York: Crowne Business, 2012.

Blundell, Sue, *The Origins of Civilization in Greek and Roman Thought*, Routledge, 2015.

Bowden, Jonathan Et, *Western Civilization Bites Back*, San Francisco: Counter-Currents Publishing, 2014.

Daly, Jonathan, *Historians Debate the Rise of the West*, New York: Routledge, 2014.

Diamond, Jared, *Collapse: How Societies Choose to Fail or Succeed*, New York: Viking, 2005.

Diamond, Jared, *Guns, Germs, and Steel: The Fates of Human Societies*, New York: Norton, 1997.

Dorling Kindersley Publishing Staff, *Big History*, New York: Penguin Random House, 2013.

Harris, Lee, *Civilization and Its Enemies: The Next Stage of History*, New York: Free Press, 2004.

Heilbroner, R., *The Worldly Philosophers*, rev. ed., New York: Simon & Schuster, 1980.

Kelly, John, *The Great Mortality: An Intimate History of the Black Death, the Most Devastating Plague of All Time*, New York: HarperCollins, 2005.

Larner, John, *Marco Polo and the Discovery of the World*, New Haven, CT: Yale University Press, 1999.

Lewis, Peter, *The Middle Ages*, Munich; Verlag C. H. Beck o HG, 2015.

Margolis, Howard, *It Started with Copernicus: How Turning the World Inside Out Led to the Scientific Revolution*, New York: McGraw-Hill, 2002.

Morris, Ian, *Why the West Rules—For Now: The Patterns of History, and What They Reveal About the Future*, New York: Farrar, Straus & Giroux, 2011.

Internet Sites to Explore

"http://www.medievalcrusades.com" Medieval Crusades.

"http://www.history.com/topics/middle-ages" Middle Ages.

"http://www.ancient.eu/Stone_Age" Stone Age.

"http://www.ancient-greece.org/resources/timeline.html" Timeline of Ancient Greece.

"http://www.exovedate.com/ancient_timeline_one.html" Timeline of Ancient Rome.

Society, Culture, and Cultural Change

chapter 4

After reading this chapter, you should be able to:

- Explain why culture is necessary to hold society together
- List some important elements of culture
- Summarize briefly three popular theories of cultural change
- List five factors that cause culture to change
- List three factors stabilizing culture
- Discuss the cultural lag theory and its limitations
- Explain the doctrine of cultural relativism

Culture is the sum of all the forms of art, of love, and of thought, which, in the course of centuries, have enabled man to be less enslaved.

—André Malraux

Human beings are social beings. We cannot understand our nature independently of our social environment. That is why we call our discipline *social science*.

To understand human beings' role as social beings, we must understand culture. To understand culture and its key role in social science, it is helpful to consider an analogy to physics. When the authors studied physics in high school, we were taught that there are electrons, protons, and neutrons. Together, these made up atoms, atoms made up elements, and elements made up matter. Since that time, learning physics has become much more difficult. Physicists have discovered even smaller particles, which they tell us are the building blocks of all matter. These building blocks include quarks, leptons, and ghostly particles called gluons, whose existence is assumed by physicists because something has to hold matter together. Quarks and leptons make up matter; gluons hold matter together.

Why are quarks, leptons, and gluons relevant to social science? Because just as physicists need to assume the existence of gluons to hold matter together, social scientists must assume the existence of a force that holds society together. Without gluons, quarks and leptons would fall apart and the world as we know it would not exist. Society has a similar force holding it together. Why don't you just haul off and clobber your neighbor when he or she does something wrong? Why don't countries always enter into war to get what they want? What sensibility makes it possible for society to continue to exist and to coordinate the individual wills of some 7.4 billion individuals? The answer is culture, and the social science equivalent to the gluon is culture, embodied in social institutions, mores, conventions, and laws.

Culture and Multiculturalism

Culture is the total pattern of human behavior and its products, embodied in thought, speech, action, and artifacts. It is the way of thinking and doing that is passed on from adults to children in their upbringing and can be thought of as the shared language, norms, and values of a society. Culture is dependent on the capacity for learning through the use of tools, language, and systems of abstract thought. It includes not only patterns of behavior but also the attitudes and beliefs that motivate behavior. Culture creates human beings and human societies. Reciprocally, by slow accumulation over many generations, culture is the product of human societies and of the individuals who compose them.

Cultures as we know them have evolved through a long process of change. **Cultural evolution** is the name given to this gradual, accumulative process. Any modern culture is largely the product of the originality and initiative of great numbers of individuals in times past, though in most cases the contribution of any one person has been so small that it cannot even be identified.

Because culture is learned by association with other human beings, the character and personality of all human beings are in large part reflections of the society in which they live. Individuals acquire their knowledge, skills, customs, ideals, religion, and morals from their social environment. This is made possible through socialization. **Socialization** is the process that shapes the personality of individuals so that they can adjust to and become members of society. In the United States, most of us feel, think, and act like U.S. citizens because we have spent all our lives in a mainstream U.S. social environment. If, from earliest childhood, we had associated only with a group of Inuits who never had any contact with mainstream U.S. culture, we probably would neither understand nor feel comfortable with that culture.

This does not mean that all people in a culture are alike in their personalities. Significant differences exist in our family backgrounds and in many other aspects of our personal social environment. To develop human nature, we must be human beings and inherit human potentialities, but no two people will ever react to the same environment in exactly the same way. Biologically inherited differences affect the intelligence and temperament of every person and therefore affect thinking and behavior. In any given individual, social inheritance and biological inheritance are so closely bound together that we can never be sure of the relative influence of each. However, for nearly all of us the general pattern of life is largely determined by our social environment. Almost everything we believe or know or do, we learn from observing other people, from listening to other people, or from reading and thinking about what other people have written.

Multiculturalism

The United States does not have a single culture, but instead has a blend of overlapping subcultures. For example, black culture is different from Hispanic culture, which is different from Jewish culture, which is different from rural Midwestern culture, and so on. The blending of these various cultures is not always smooth, and at times is disruptive. Hip-hop, classical, and country music do not a symphony make. Nonetheless, the similarities of the various U.S. subcultures hold together, and allow us to speak of a single U.S. culture, which actually is a composite of various subcultures.

Political debates about culture often focus on whether the government should support monoculturalism or multi-culturalism. Technically, monoculturalism emphasizes the shared aspects of subcultures, whereas **multiculturalism** emphasizes the differences among subcultures. However, the term *multiculturalism* has developed a somewhat different

© Cineberg/iStock

The European Migrant Crisis

Conflicting cultures often lead to crises. In 2015 and 2016 the European Union faced a migrant crisis as millions of people fled to Europe both to seek better jobs and lives and to escape war-torn countries such as Syria. A large majority of these migrants were Muslim, and their culture reflected that heritage. A large majority of European countries, where they were immigrating to, were Christian and their culture reflected that heritage. That difference created a culture clash.

While a small number of immigrants can be assimilated into a pluralistic culture, which most Europeans saw themselves as having, a large number of immigrants in a short period of time makes assimilation difficult and perhaps impossible. Instead of adjusting slowly, and solving problems through discussion and good will on both sides, tension leads to anger, riots, and a hardening of positions. Pluralism is undermined as each side tries to protect its cultural heritage. Europe's migrant crisis was precipitated by too many migrants in too short a period of time.

In post-World War II Europe, because of its experience with displaced people during the war, Europe developed a legal structure that welcomed all people displaced by conflict and political turmoil. This legal structure led to the large influx of migrants, as more and more individuals in war-torn and economically depressed countries headed to Europe to find better lives. Europe was overwhelmed. Those laws are now in the process of changing, but, in the short term, the prospect of change brought even more migrants to Europe, as they attempted to immigrate before the laws changed.

This issue is likely to continue influencing policy choices in Europe for some time, but precisely how is unclear. In 2017, for the first time since the beginning of the migrant crisis, the number of refugees arriving in Southern Europe decreased as Europeans helped North African naval forces to turn back refugees before they had the chance to cross the Mediterranean Sea.

meaning. Specifically, the term was used in the 1980s as a way to emphasize that most university curricula reflected a Eurocentric bias at the expense of other U.S. subcultures. Thus, to support multiculturalism was to be against the Eurocentric bias in university curriculums. As often happens when terms become part of a political debate, monoculturalism and multiculturalism were seen as opposites. We don't see it that way. We see both as supportable. Specifically, if the U.S. monoculture were understood as being committed to **pluralism**—the value that cultural diversity is good—there would be no contradiction between the two. The debate is simply about getting the right mix. The advantage of monoculturalism is that shared culture tends to hold society together; the advantage of multiculturalism is that it incorporates diversity and lets subgroups revere their own history and view that history as a strong building block of the larger culture.

The Shared Beliefs in Culture

Culture is an enormously vague concept that is difficult to grasp. Perhaps the easiest way to understand culture is to answer a few questions:

1. Should children, age 11 to 15, sleep in the same beds as their parents?
2. Should women be allowed to drive?
3. Should females be circumcised?
4. Should people wear swimming suits on public beaches?

Most of you from the United States, we suspect, answered the questions (1) no, (2) yes, (3) no, and (4) yes. Why do we suspect that? Because you come from a shared culture. But if you were from another country, or a part of the United States that is not affected by mainstream U.S. culture, your answers would likely be different. For example, according to Richard Shweder in his book, *Why Do Men Barbecue? Recipes for Cultural Diversity,* in Mali and Somalia many women are repulsed by the idea of not circumcising women. Similarly, in Saudi Arabia some women see it as simply inappropriate for a woman to drive. However, the number of women and men who hold this view has been falling and in 2017, the Saudi Arabian government overturned the law prohibiting women from driving. Many more examples could be provided, but these should be sufficient to give you a sense of how culture is the shared beliefs of a society.

Culture and the Nature of Society

Even though the personality of each individual is in large measure molded by society, it is clear that society can have no existence apart from the people who constitute it. **Society** is a group of individuals living as members of a community. The characteristics of every society are gradually shaped and changed over succeeding generations by innovations introduced by the people who belong to it. The influence of any one individual may be small, but the contributions of many individuals over long periods of time can be great.

It is important to pay close attention to our definition of society. Though the basis of any society is a group of individuals, equally important to its establishment is the continued existence of the group over a period of time. A crowd brought together for a football game is an aggregate, but it is not a society. Its members are physically close together, and for the moment are united by a common interest. However, any sense of unity they may have is superficial and temporary. When the game is over, they disperse. They are not together long enough to organize into a society. But if the same people were marooned for a year on an uninhabited island, they would be forced to organize themselves into a society.[1] They would develop common ideas, interests, and techniques for living and working together. It is the sense of living together as a community that distinguishes a society.

Culture and Its Role in Human Societies

There is a problem in precisely defining culture because it has a variety of aspects. But our earlier definition of it is probably the best. Culture is the way of life that the people of a society follow. It includes all knowledge, beliefs, art, morals, laws, customs, and any other capabilities acquired by a human being as a member of society.

In short, culture is the total pattern of human behavior and its products embodied in thought, speech, action, and artifacts. Culture is also dependent on the capacity for learning through the use of tools, language, and systems of abstract thought.

As you can see, the culture of a society includes everything of human origin in the lives of its members—that is, everything they learn through their direct or indirect contacts with other people. It includes the customary ways of behaving in everyday life, religious beliefs, moral standards, the way family life is organized, the methods used to provide food and shelter, language, government, and forms of artistic expression.

The Elements of Culture

Culture develops only through the association of human beings and thus presupposes society; at the same time, culture is what makes a human society possible. Only when people develop in some degree a common culture can they function as an organized group, for only then do they know what to expect of one another and how to behave to meet the requirements of the group. A society can exist because human beings have the capacity for creating culture and, what is equally important, for sharing it with their contemporaries and transmitting it to succeeding

---

[1] The television program *Survivor* assembles a small group of people on an uninhabited island. The basic purpose is to allow viewers to watch the difficulties this group has in making decisions. Were there truly no hope of rescue, and no need to "eliminate" individuals periodically, the group would probably organize and cooperate in a more socially beneficial manner than they do on the show.

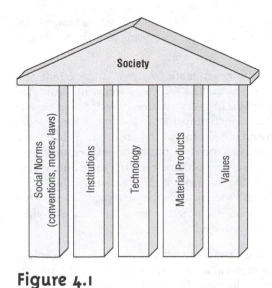

Figure 4.1

The elements of culture.

generations. Culture creates societies and societies depend on culture. In short, culture embodies social norms (its conventions, mores, and laws) and institutions, together with a society's technology, its material products, and its values. Figure 4.1 presents the elements of culture upon which society rests. Let us consider briefly some of the elements of culture.

Social Norms: Conventions, Mores, and Laws.   Conventions are the simple, everyday customs of a group that represent the usual ways of behaving. Conventions change slowly, and many of them are very persistent. In our society, it is customary or conventional to sleep on a bed; to eat at a table; to handle our food with knives, forks, and spoons; and to greet an acquaintance on the street. All these are **conventions.** Conventions are established customs to which we attach little moral significance. We may think that people whose conventions are different from ours are themselves different, but we try to understand those differences, not ostracize people because of their differences. For example, we will probably wonder about a woman who shaves her head, but our social practice will be to try to act as if we notice nothing unusual.

Mores (pronounced mor-rays) are conventions that would have serious consequences if they were violated. They include those customs that must generally be observed by all members of a society for the culture to survive. People who disregard mores are usually seen as more than slightly odd or eccentric—their character definitions are beyond weird. Although a violation of a society's mores would not necessarily land a person in jail, it would incur social punishment in the form of peer disapproval. For example, a claims adjuster who showed up at the insurance office and completely disrobed would have violated one of society's mores and, even if not arrested for indecent exposure, would nevertheless face informal punishment. On the other hand, a person who wears informal clothing to a wedding reception is merely violating a convention.

In contrast to mores and conventions, which are merely customs taken as understood in governing the conduct of the group, laws are more exact, and are generally recorded, codified, and enforced as a means of securing public obedience. **Laws** are the principles and regulations established in a community by some authority and applicable to its people, whether in the form of legislation or of policies recognized and enforced by judicial decision. Violations of laws may carry severe punishments and/or ramifications for the offender. Being caught speeding results in a small fine, whereas premeditated murder may be punishable, at least in some states, by death. What is against the law and the punishment for violation of laws vary in different societies. For example, in some Islamic societies it may be against the law for a woman to appear in public with her face uncovered, and stealing may be punished by the loss of one's hand. In the United States, there are no laws about covering one's face, and stealing results in a jail sentence at most.

Social Institutions.   A **social institution** is an established complex pattern of behavior in which a number of persons participate in order to further important group interests. Institutions are usually organized around some central interest or need. The government, for example, provides the necessary order and coordination among individuals. The school provides for formal education of the young, while the family, one of the most basic of all social institutions, helps meet many of the needs of daily life, such as those for shelter, food, close companionship, and affection. The church, temple, mosque, and synagogue are the institutions that enable people to express their religious beliefs by joining others in worshipping a deity or deities in established rituals. Social institutions not only provide order and coordination, but they also provide for social change. For example, religious groups played a significant role in the civil rights movement in the United States, a movement that forced U.S. society to treat African Americans more equitably and to remove some of its blatantly discriminatory laws.

Material Products.   Strictly speaking, culture is never material. It is in the minds and personalities of people. It is what they have learned from their social environment—attitudes, beliefs, knowledge, and ways of behaving. However, in every culture, knowledge of how to produce and use a variety of material products, including food, clothing, houses, tools, machines, and works of art, is important. **Cultural objects (artifacts)** are products of human skill and effort that are essential to the functioning of a society. Cultural objects are more than mere expressions of the culture that produces them; they become essential to its functioning because without them people could not carry on the necessary activities of daily life. This is strikingly true in a modern industrial society. Such a society would be paralyzed if it could not use computers, airplanes, cars and trucks, telephones, power plants, factories and their machines, supermarkets, and fast-food outlets, to name a few.

Language.   **Language** is a body of words and the system for their use common to a people of the same community or nation, the same geographical area, or the same cultural tradition. Language is intrinsic in the societies and cultures of humans. Benjamin Lee Whorf argued that each particular language embodies and propagates a worldview. Groups of people speaking the same language, therefore, communicate in the same cultural tone. Cultural assumptions and observations are locked into a society's language. For instance, communication between multilingual people transmits cultural differences between societies.

Language plays a central role in the development and transmission of culture. It allows communication, which is essential for the coordination of activities. It allows cultures to save and transmit a knowledge of their history. Writing allows many further uses of language, widening its ability to store and accumulate knowledge. Writing allows cultures to be preserved and passed on in expanded ways. But language also creates limitations. The structure of the language influences the way individuals look at issues and can therefore incorporate many hidden biases.

---

*F*WIW :-)

Text messaging by email, phone, and instant messenger programs is becoming more and more common—so much so that a new language is developing, both with abbreviations and acronyms, and with emoticons—symbols that add emotion. Below is a sampling of some of these abbreviations and emoticons. Younger students will likely know them all, and more. Older students and professors can find many more by searching the Internet. (The meanings often change slightly over time, as do the specific emoticons. For example, my student proofreader told me that :-P meant tongue sticking out, not the wry smile I thought it meant.) t(-__-t)

143	I love you
BTW	By the way
IMO	In my opinion
NVM	Never mind

TBH	To be honest
TTYL	Talk to you later
FWIW	For what it's worth
LOL	Laughing out loud
:-)	smiley face/happy
;-)	wink
:-(	frown/sad
:-@	scream
:-|	indifference
:-/	perplexed
;-}	leer
d[-_-]b	wearing headphones
:->	devilish grin
:-D	shock or surprise
:-P	tongue sticking out
>:-(	angry
:-&	tongue tied
:-s	worried
(╯°□°)╯︵ ┻━┻	table-flip (frustration)

Social Values. Social values are the motivating power that makes institutions function effectively. They are the things that a given society considers desirable because they are believed to contribute to a good life and the general welfare. In our cultural environment, honesty, courage, justice, and respect for law and for the rights of others are highly regarded social values. So also, on a somewhat different level, are financial success, health, and education.

Individuals' desires tend to reflect the values stressed in the societies to which they belong. Society in the United States is often said to be materialistic. This may not be a wholly correct characterization; yet it contains an element of truth. In our modern United States, we have great respect for success in business, entertainment, and sports, and we place great emphasis on the importance of raising standards of living and abolishing poverty. Because we put such a high value on material welfare, many of our people have come to regard the earning of more and more money as their major life objective. Others, of course, look on money merely as a means to achieve more important objectives. These more important objectives may involve such "higher" social values as the education of one's children; charity; the appreciation and encouragement of art, science, and religion; and the rendering of public service.

Social values make institutions function effectively. The church, temple, mosque, or synagogue, for instance, will be a dynamic force in society only as long as a large portion of their members firmly believe in a supreme being or spiritual guide and have faith that their religious organization is an essential instrument for the growth of the soul and the creation of a good society. Where religion has a strong hold on a society, it is usually a conservative force tending to preserve established moral values.

Social values are relative rather than absolute. They often vary widely from one culture to another, and each individual acquires from his or her own culture ideas of what is desirable or undesirable, good or bad, right or wrong. In some societies, sexual relations before marriage are regarded as a cardinal sin; in others, they are permitted or even expected. In some societies, women must be very plump to be regarded as beautiful; in others, they must be rather slim. In most if not in all modern societies, the killing of infants is regarded with horror, but a few tribal societies see it as commendable under certain circumstances—for instance, if the infants have physical disabilities.

Cultural Integration

Cultures or societies contain certain aspects that are similar among all cultures. These aspects or traits are called universals. A **cultural universal** is an aspect of culture that is found in all cultures. Religion, for example, is a cultural universal, as is the existence of some form of government, family life, and national ideals. **Cultural alternatives** are those cultural characteristics not necessarily shared by other cultures. For example, some cultures might place the elderly in a subordinate role, whereas others might place them in an exalted role. Therefore, exalting old age is a cultural alternative; not all societies do it.

Traits differ not only among cultures; they also differ within cultures. **Cultural integration** is the degree to which a culture is internally consistent and homogeneous. In large, complex modern cultures such as the United States, there tends to be more diversity. In small, preliterate cultures such as that of the indigenous Yahma tribe that lives in the Amazon, there tends to be less diversity. Thus, these cultures are more unified.

In U.S. culture, which greatly values freedom of choice with respect to both ideas and commodities, life is more complex and stressful. Many social problems such as crime, teenage rebellion, alcohol and drug abuse, and emotional disorders result from our greater ability to choose options. For example, if culture determined what job you would have when you graduate, your life would probably be less stressful. Even cultures that place a high value on freedom must achieve some measure of balance between shared cultural traits and the potentially disintegrative forces of nonshared traits. Since about 1960, we have seen in the United States a decline in the social behavioral consensus that was more typical of the earlier years of the twentieth century. Some social scientists believe that this flexible value system could cause serious trouble for our society. Whether they are right, and whether our society will move toward more shared cultural traits, remains to be seen.

As you can see, culture is the glue that holds society together, but like glue it can also cause difficulties for society. The reason is that societies are in constant transition, and to be successful a society must adjust to new technologies and relations with other societies. The glue that really held society together in one time period may be the sticky mess that in another time period entraps some members of society. Therefore, to understand the role of culture in society, we must consider the process of social change, the factors that contribute to that change, and the effect that change has on culture.

Culture, Society, and Social Change

The culture of a society is constantly evolving to fit new situations. For instance, wars can create almost instantaneous change and can focus a society's interest, money, and energy on a single goal—winning. Total emphasis is placed on war-related activities rather than on a more diverse range of activities. Whether a country wins or loses, the postwar society will substantively differ from the prewar society. Some of these changes will be the result of an opponent's war effort, and others will be the result of interaction with members of other societies.

The rate of social change has gradually gained momentum through the course of human social development. In early times, it started slowly. Many thousands of years ago, all human beings belonged to small, preliterate groups. Though the groups varied greatly in the nature and complexity of their cultures, as a rule the customs and traditions of each were so firmly established that its members tended to follow much the same way of life over a great many generations. Then the rate of social change increased. In effect, social change has behaved much like a snowball rolling down a hill. First, it starts out small and moves slowly; then, as it picks up more snow and gets larger, it gains momentum.

Certain factors have been especially important in contributing to an increased rate of change. Outstanding among these is the development of agriculture. The growing of crops allowed people to live in permanent dwellings, abandoning their former nomadic lifestyle. Increasing the food supply through storage brought about an increase in population and, gradually, the growth of towns and cities. Another important factor is the invention of writing, which made it possible to record human knowledge and to transmit it to future generations more adequately than ever before. As the sum total of human knowledge increased, the rate of its accumulation accelerated.

Later developments that did much to speed up the rate of social change include the invention of printing, the rise of modern science, and the Industrial Revolution, which began in Britain in the mid-1700s. The Industrial Revolution represented a shift in the methods of production; it entailed the replacement of hand tools by machines and power tools, and initiated the movement away from small-scale agriculture to the development of large-scale industry. This necessitated enormous numbers of workers

'We're playing I'm a mummy with lots of different daddies!'

The structure of social institutions change over time.

© Cartoon Stock

for the factories, fewer workers in the fields, and therefore facilitated urbanization—the movement of people from rural to urban areas. A more recent factor of great importance in accelerating change has been the annihilation of distance through the development of rapid transportation and communication. Today, we can use satellite transmission to simulcast events and ideas all around the world while they are actually happening or being formulated.

Not only is the rate of technological change increasing, but so is the interaction among cultures. This is especially true in developing countries. Western science and technology are now spreading throughout the world at an accelerating pace, and further Westernization is a likely prospect for many developing countries. The **Internet**—an interconnected set of computers through which people can communicate and transfer information—has transformed communication among individuals and is in the process of making our world one enormous community. With social interaction through Internet portals such as Facebook, Snapchat, Twitter, and LinkedIn, people are interacting with others in ways that were previously impossible, changing what determines and constitutes a community. (Older people often have a much harder time adapting to the avenues of social interaction, which the new technology allows, than do younger people.)

One result of increasingly close contacts with distant lands is that the peoples of the world are becoming more and more alike in their customs, the products they use, and the ways they earn a living. Wide cultural differences among peoples can still be found and may never completely disappear. Today, bitter enmities seem ineradicable within countries such as Nigeria and between countries such as India and Pakistan. However, cultural differences are, on the whole, diminishing, and at a more rapid rate than ever before.

We would be wrong, however, to see the diffusion of cultural traits as a one-way street. Styles of dress, food specialties, art forms, and modes of thought in other continents and societies are bringing changes to our own culture. Change in itself is not necessarily good or bad. It only means that old situations are replaced with new ones. Evolution has more definite implications than change. Evolution implies a gradual development from simpler forms of life, art, technology, or social organization to more complex forms. **Social evolution** is the long and complex process of change and interaction by which cultures gradually develop. Whether this change is desirable is debatable. From a Western, ethnocentric perspective, we often think of change as progress, but from a broader perspective, change is not necessarily progress—it may be regressive change. Change cannot be seen as progress unless we know what the life goals are and how those changes help us meet those goals. Views of what life goals should be differ; hence, views of whether social evolution is progressive differ.

Popular Theories of Social Change

Human beings have a tendency to glorify the past. Some become firmly convinced that the good old days of their youth and childhood were far superior to the present. One of the earliest theories of social change was held by certain Greek philosophers who believed that humankind once lived in an ideal golden age. From this, we gradually descended to a silver, then a bronze, and finally an iron age.

A quite opposite theory of social change has been popular in Europe and the United States in the last century or two. This is the doctrine of inevitable progress, the belief that the world is getting better and better. Not even two world wars and a multitude of smaller wars have been able to shake the faith of those who firmly hold this doctrine.

Another theory of social change, popularized by Oswald Spengler and Arnold Toynbee, is that such change runs in cycles. According to their theory, institutions, societies, and civilizations pass through cycles of growth, climax, and decline. Modern civilization is no exception and is bound ultimately to disintegrate. This cycle theory of social change is based on the idea that history repeats itself. Some cycle theorists maintain that modern civilization is now on the verge of a decline, and to support this contention they point to the fate of certain past civilizations, including ancient Greece and the Roman Empire. Cycle theories vary considerably, but they all tend to support the thesis that civilizations first advance, ultimately reach a peak, and finally decline.

Other attempts to explain social change have relied on the supernatural, racial characteristics, economic conditions, cultural diffusion, or invention. Any given culture, however, is the result of too many factors to be explained adequately by any simple formula. Yet one thing is sure: Change is inevitable. Humans' relationship to their environment is dynamic, no matter where they live, and this dynamic relationship produces change.

Factors Causing Cultural Change

We now look at some of the most important social forces that cause cultural change, together with the problems that change has brought about. We begin with a discussion of technological development; then we examine the role of religion, ideologies, cultural diffusion, wars, planned group action, geography, and climate.

Technological Development. Technological development begins with discovery and invention. A **discovery** is something learned about the physical or social environment that was not known before. In the past, explorers have discovered new islands and continents, astronomers have discovered laws that regulate the motions of the heavenly bodies, and anthropologists have discovered many interesting differences between the cultures of preliterate peoples. Discoveries about the natural world often furnish the basis for inventions. For example, the discoveries about electricity from some of the great scientists made it possible for Thomas Edison to invent the incandescent electric lightbulb and other useful devices.

An **invention** is a new way of doing something or a new object or mechanical device developed to serve some specific purpose. It is a cultural innovation devised by one or several individual members of a social group. Inventions may be either material or nonmaterial. Familiar machines such as the lawn tractor and the airplane are material inventions. Old-age insurance and crop rotation are examples of nonmaterial inventions. One of the greatest of all nonmaterial inventions was the Latin alphabet, which made possible our present system of writing and printing.

An invention is really a special kind of discovery, and hence no sharp line can be drawn between the two. We can call the making of fire by striking together flint stones either a discovery or an invention. All mechanical inventions involve the discovery that materials combined and used in certain ways will produce certain desired results. Inventions bring about changes in technology, and in modern societies technological change has been a powerful force behind social change.

A good example is the computer, which is changing our lifestyle and culture in many ways. Computerized robots are replacing workers in many jobs, tiny robots are being developed for medical uses, and the Internet is changing the way we shop and communicate with others. Similarly, developments in biotechnology are changing our lives and soon may make it possible for us to choose characteristics for our children and to influence medical treatment.

In fact, some would argue that technology and the information age are not just changing our culture, but are creating a new culture entirely. The Internet has enabled the birth of an autonomous society, where people all over the world interact to form the social norms and conventions of a digital world. Instead of being based on geographical proximity, this online culture is united by a unique vocabulary, anchoring institutions, a common history, and shared values. The community fostered online every day between billions of people regardless of nationality is changing the way that we see the role of culture in our increasingly globalized world.

Technological change has become so important to understanding society that we devote an entire chapter, Chapter 6, to a deeper consideration of the issues.

Cultural Diffusion.   Once a new cultural element is well established in one society, it may spread to others. **Cultural diffusion** is the name given to the spread of cultural traits from one social group to another. In other words, not all the elements found in the culture of a given group were invented or developed within that group. In most cases, the greater part of the content of any culture has been borrowed from other cultures. In most societies, cultural diffusion is an extremely important factor in social change. Societies isolated from outside contacts tend to be static, whereas those that can readily communicate with other groups constantly acquire new cultural elements. However, contact does not always lead to cultural diffusion. For example, the Amish society in the United States has significant contact with mainstream U.S. culture. Despite this contact, Amish society has maintained its separate cultural identity through deliberate delineation and has shunned many modern technological developments.

Cultural diffusion, more than any other factor, has been responsible for the development of Western civilization. Western civilization was nurtured in Europe, and its center is still there. Yet most of the basic elements of this civilization did not originate in Europe but were borrowed from other peoples in other parts of the world. Our modern number system, so much more flexible than that of the Romans, was borrowed from the Arabs, who in turn borrowed it from the Hindus in India. Without this number system or a good substitute, it would be almost impossible for us to carry on the mathematical calculations now required by both business and science. Again, our alphabet, which with modifications is used for writing and printing all European languages, was borrowed originally from the Phoenicians of Africa. It seems probable that they, or a neighboring people speaking a similar Semitic language, were the original inventors.[2]

Ideas and Ideologies.   Social change may also be initiated by new ideas. Relatively simple, practical ideas may result in inventions that soon are accepted and become a recognized part of the cultural pattern—a new type of dance, a new kind of business corporation, or a new mechanical gadget. However, not all new ideas are of this type. Some represent important changes in social attitudes and basic social values. Such ideas may in time gain a powerful hold on minds, as did the concepts of "liberty, equality, and fraternity" of the French Revolution, or the civil rights movement in the United States in the 1960s. Often they come to represent hopes and aspirations that, though they can never be fully realized, can be approached in a variety of ways. Once ideas of this kind become well established in any society, they become a powerful force for continuing social change in directions that are thought to lead toward their realization. Religions, which embody people's conception of what is good and what is bad, often are vital forces for social change. For example, as we stated earlier, religious groups played an important role in the civil rights movement, and in the early 2000s some Evangelical Christian churches were exerting pressure on the government on issues as diverse as abortion and foreign policy.

Even in the modern world, it usually takes considerable time for major new ideas to gain a firm foothold. Various writers have maintained that social change is always motivated by the discoveries or theories of great thinkers of a past generation. Karl Marx, for example, had little effect on society during his lifetime; British economist John Maynard Keynes's economic

Ideologies are systems of values that are fervently held.

---

[2] The Phoenician alphabet contained only consonants. The Greeks, who were the first Europeans to appropriate this alphabet, added vowels.

ideas of the 1930s did not have any great impact on the public or on government policies until the 1960s.

An **ideology** is an organized system of ideas for remodeling society to bring it "nearer to the heart's desire." We may regard it as a composite of ideas, values, and emotions. Those who believe in an ideology often support it with religious fervor. Fascism, communism, socialism, and democracy are all ideologies. Each has its system of values, and each would organize society—supposedly to further the common good—according to a somewhat different pattern. No ideology ever achieves the ideal society that its adherents envision. We regard our U.S. society as democratic, but we often are keenly aware that we fall short of the democratic ideal in many ways.

Collective Action.   Most social changes take place gradually and are not planned and carried out by a central agency. At times, however, social changes of importance are brought about more or less rapidly by planned group action. Group action by an entire society, such as a modern nation, usually means government action, because the government is the only agency that can make and enforce rules that in theory apply to the whole social group.

Japan is a nation that has experienced a great social transformation within the past 150 years. It has changed from a feudal society to a modern, highly industrialized democracy. Much of this change has been brought about by government policies that were specifically designed to bring Japan into the modern world.

The outstanding twentieth-century examples of drastic and far-reaching social changes carried out by governments on a vast scale are found in the former Soviet Union and in China. There, in two of the largest and most populous countries of the world, when the communist leaders came into power, they completely changed in a relatively short time many basic aspects of the political, social, and economic structure. In an attempt to create societies based on the communist ideology of Karl Marx, the state seized vast amounts of property from the middle- and upper-class owners, uprooted millions of peasants from their holdings and put them to work on collective farms or communes, and took over the operation and expansion of practically all productive enterprises. But the achievement of such broad and rapid changes was possible only through the establishment of powerful dictatorships that had small regard for the rights and freedoms of individuals.

In the 1990s, many of these communist dictatorships ended. Eastern Europe went through dramatic upheavals. Several communist systems were overthrown; the Soviet Union broke up into various countries; and all of these countries experienced enormous political, social, and economic change. In 2011, it was the Middle East that went through violent social upheavals in what became known as the Arab Spring. People revolted against strong dictatorships, which the Arab people had accepted for decades, and demanded new forms of government. The result was quite different than the result most people hoped for. War broke out in some countries and others returned to repressive governmental regimes. Only Tunisia, the origin of the Arab Spring movement, successfully transitioned to a democracy in the wake of the unrest. But even it struggled with instability. As of 2018, the region was chaotic and volatile.

Important social changes can also be brought about in democratic countries through planned government action, but only if the action has popular support. However, such changes are implemented more slowly and are much less drastic than those that can be made by a dictatorship that has strong control over the press.

Even dictatorships must, however, have some support from the people, as was demonstrated by the Arab Spring. To be effective in promoting social change in a democracy, government action must either reflect the established beliefs of the people or change those beliefs relatively quickly. If legislation violates what the majority of citizens believe to be their just rights and privileges, it has little chance of success. For instance, the Prohibition amendment to the U.S. Constitution, legally in force from 1919 to 1932, failed and was finally repealed because the majority of Americans felt that outlawing the sale of liquor was an unreasonable violation of their personal liberties.

Technology is changing the way people organize, and thereby affecting the nature of social change. For example, in 2012, when a neighborhood watch volunteer killed an unarmed black teenager and was not charged with a crime, within days, millions of people quickly signed a petition demanding that the person be arrested. He was. Before the Internet and social networking, such a quick, spontaneous movement would have been impossible.

Geography and Climate.   When people live in a given region over a long period of time, they become adjusted to local conditions of geography and climate. A society, for example, set on the edge of an ocean would be more prone to utilize marine resources—fish for food, shells as jewelry, and perhaps greater trade owing to the oceanic access—than would a landlocked society. Changes in the natural environment can and do occur. In extreme cases, droughts, earthquakes, the exhaustion of important natural resources, changes in climate, and the like may require radical cultural adjustments.

Geography and climate are also important factors in social change when people migrate from one region to another. The European settlers who emigrated to the Americas, Africa, Australia, and New Zealand found many differences of climate, topography, and natural changes, especially in food, clothing, houses, and ways of earning a living. We consider these issues in more detail in Chapter 5.

Language and Cultural Change

Social change takes place over long periods of time and often is difficult to discern. Because our perceptions of the past are imperfect, our knowledge of the past is also limited and imperfect. We don't know what was; we only know what is. One way to get an idea of the change that takes place is to consider the evolution of languages. Some social scientists believe that all modern languages sprang from a single root—spoken by a tiny population that probably lived in Africa or Asia about twenty thousand years ago.

How much a language can evolve can be seen by comparing the Old English phrase for "How are you?" in a book like *Beowulf* (eighth century A.D.): "Hal! Geard weallas!" (it reads like a foreign language) to that same phrase in Shakespeare (sixteenth–seventeenth century A.D.): "How art thou?" to a modern variant: "How ya doin'?" Given how much languages can change without our noticing, we should not be surprised by how much cultures can change and how different cultures can be from one another.

Factors Stabilizing Culture

The various factors of social change lead to a dynamic, continually altering society. Change and culture will often conflict, with culture providing strong resistance to social change. In the present-day United States, underlying the many changes constantly taking place in our culture is a great body of stabilizing elements that give continuity to our way of life.

Stability of Social Norms.   In spite of the high value that some industrial societies place on so-called progress, human beings appear basically conservative. The human mind and personality are so constituted that once people acquire certain beliefs, attitudes, and patterns of behavior, they have difficulty changing them. This is especially true of the basic elements in our culture that we acquire unconsciously in the impressionable years of early childhood. Our beliefs and attitudes may include some approval of change—for example, changes in fashions—but only within limits. The mores, the principal institutions of our society, and even many of its conventions are so firmly impressed on us that they become an essential part of our own personalities. For example, the tradition that women need to be protected from the harsh realities of commercial competition, the rough and tumble of military life, and the demands of heavy physical labor played a role in the failure of the passage of the Equal Rights Amendment to the U.S. Constitution in the 1970s.

Habit.   A chief reason for the persistence of conventions, mores, and social institutions is that they become largely habitual for all members of the social group. **Habits** are ways of behaving that have been learned so well that they can be carried on without conscious attention. Once acquired, however, they are difficult to change because they become a part of the individual's personality.

Value Attachment.   Another reason for the persistence of conventions, mores, and institutions is that we and our group attach values to them. In the case of conventions, these values may be small, but in the case of mores and certain basic institutions they are great. When we believe that established patterns of behavior have high moral value and when, in addition, they arouse in us strong emotions, these patterns become resistant to change.

Social changes of any importance, even though favored by the majority, are likely to meet opposition from many individuals and groups who have vested interests. A **vested interest** is a privilege or advantage that an individual enjoys because of the status quo, which is the existing state of affairs. A skilled plasterer has a vested interest in the plastering trade, and is not likely to favor substituting wallboard for plaster. Various unions in the building industry, in order to protect the jobs of their members, have fought against prefabricated housing and have insisted on retention of slower, more expensive, on-the-spot building methods.

Industry and labor are not alone in opposing, for selfish reasons, the introduction of new elements into our culture. Many people stand to lose by changes in the status quo, not only materially but also in power or prestige. Theologians, philosophers, and scientists have again and again opposed new ideas and new knowledge for fear that their own established beliefs and theories would be discredited.

Social Change versus Social Stability

Many of the things we value in our modern society—for example, our relatively high standards of living—could not have been brought about without a receptive attitude toward social change, because all change produces new situations. However, if change occurs rapidly, it may create new problems for which we are unprepared. Instead of introducing a better world, it can bring on periodic crises and give people a constant sense of uncertainty and insecurity. Every social group feels the need for some degree of stability. If this stability is to be maintained, change in our basic institutions must be gradual. It must take place by evolution rather than by revolution.

For any large modern society to meet the needs of its people requires a remarkably complex organization; the organization can be challenged, it can be adapted, it can be changed, but any belief that it can be destroyed and quickly replaced with something better is unrealistic. Social revolutions are never complete, and they bring few of the results that were envisioned. The communist revolution in Russia, after years of struggle and confusion, produced Stalin; and the National Socialist revolution in Germany produced Hitler.

Social Change and Social Problems

Although not all social scientists would agree on the exact nature of a social problem, for our purposes the following definition suffices. For a social problem to exist, two conditions must be fulfilled. First, there must be wide recognition of some condition that adversely affects the welfare of a significant number of people. Second, there must be a belief that this condition can and should be changed. In other words, a **social problem** is a situation that has been recognized as adversely affecting the welfare of large numbers of people and for which it is believed a solution exists. To admit the existence of a social problem clearly implies the possibility of change, for no matter how undesirable a situation may be, it is not a problem unless we believe there is a way to change it. In primitive societies, drought, famine, and pestilence may not have been regarded as problems because nothing could be done about them. They were simply accepted. However, they became problems if it was believed there were ways to avert them—for instance, by making adequate sacrifices to the gods.

In a sense, social problems are always individual problems, for it is individuals who experience their adverse effects. We call them social problems for two reasons: first, because they affect such a significant proportion of people as to constitute a threat to the welfare or safety of the whole group; and second, because they cannot be adequately met by individuals. If they are to be solved at all, it must be by some kind of group action. This becomes clear when we consider such major social problems as widespread poverty, disease, recurrent periods of mass unemployment, crime, family disorganization, and war.

As would be expected, a large modern society is much more likely to possess complex social problems than a smaller society. Larger societies often contain important subgroups with differing cultural patterns, and these subgroups are likely to be subject to inconsistencies, strains, and conflicts that speed up social change and often are intensified by it.

When we attempt to define and study any particular social problem, we encounter certain difficulties. For one thing, every social problem is closely related to a number of other social problems and is therefore highly complex. To fully understand one problem, we must know something about the others. Thus, to understand fully the problem of family disorganization and divorce, we may, for example, need to know something about poor housing, unemployment, and social classes.

There is seldom any simple or complete solution for a major social problem. The causes are always complex, and practical remedies are difficult to find or implement. Moreover, the action necessary to solve or mitigate a social problem may be effectively blocked by public indifference and ignorance and by the opposition of vested interests. This does not mean that all attempts at social improvement are useless. It does mean, however, that a number of our major social problems are likely to remain with us in some form or degree for the indefinite future.

"This 'reclaiming' of pejorative terms has gone too far."

© Cartoon Stock

Cultural Lag and Social Problems

Though some elements in culture may change while others remain relatively constant, the various aspects of a given culture are by no means entirely independent of one another. To illustrate, religion may have a substantial influence on technological change. On the one hand, it may encourage technological change by teaching that material progress is in accord with the divine will; on the other hand, it may discourage such change by teaching that mechanical innovations are works of the devil.

The late eminent sociologist William F. Ogburn assigned great importance to what he called *cultural lag* as a source of social disorganization. According to his theory, the culture of any society constitutes a pattern of interrelated elements. Once integration and stability have been achieved, a change in any one part of the pattern may create strains and disturbances in the closely related parts. Eventually, adjustments will be made to restore harmony, but meanwhile there may be a considerable time lag during which tension persists. In modern industrial societies, it is technological change that sets the pace. According to Ogburn's

*A*re You PC?

Social change affects our everyday life. A recent example of this is the PC phenomenon, which has been much in debate on college campuses and elsewhere since the early 1990s. PC stands for "politically correct." To be PC is to be attuned to an unstated but nonetheless strong and reasonably well-defined set of social norms emphasizing minority rights, women's rights, social justice, and environmentalism. It is a derogatory term that was adopted in use in response to the social pressure on individuals to meet those norms.

In the early 1980s, the pressures on many college campuses for individuals to be PC were rather strong, but the phrase did not exist. New courses, course requirements, and departments were instituted at many schools in women's studies, ethnic studies, and the environment.

The underlying philosophy of some of these pressures went against the grain of some individuals, as did the sometimes strong-arm tactics (such as sit-ins and taking over buildings) supporters used to implement and demand change. Supporters justified these strong-arm tactics on the grounds that ours is a repressive society and, given that repression, the ends justify the means. This justification went against the grain of another Western social norm—toleration and respect for others' rights—leading a number of people, including some who supported the social norms that the strong-arm tactics were meant to achieve, to repudiate the movement. It also led to the adoption of the term PC, which was used by Nazis to describe individuals who believed that the white Aryan race was superior to all others. The Nazi association brought out the dissonance between the strong-arm tactics used by some PC supporters and the norms of toleration and respect for individual rights.

The debate between PC supporters and opponents concerns conflicting social norms—toleration versus social justice. PC supporters argue that one should not be tolerant of injustice, and that if our society were truly tolerant and maintained respect for all others, the movement wouldn't be needed. But because our society isn't, it is necessary to be intolerant of injustice and intolerance.

Recently, tensions surrounding PC culture on college campuses have risen, with students who believe that colleges should prevent certain speakers whose views they find reprehensible and demeaning clashing with students who believe that the college, not any one group of students, should make decisions as to what speaker to allow or not to allow, and that in making those decisions colleges should lean toward the side of free speech. They argue that disrupting and physically preventing speakers who have been invited by the college is wrong. This tension has resulted in numerous instances of controversial speakers being uninvited for fear of physically disruptive protests, provoking a reaction from those who see free speech, especially on college campuses, as a foundation of our society.

Social science doesn't tell us whether the PC movement is right or wrong, but it does help us put it in perspective and have a better appreciation for the inevitable tensions that social change brings about.

theory, technological progress produces rapid changes in the material aspects of our culture, but the nonmaterial aspects fail to adjust, or they do so only after an excessive time lag. As a result, many troublesome social problems are created.

Cultural lag is the discrepancy between the rate of change of one part of a culture in relation to another, resulting in a maladjustment within society. A frequently cited cultural lag is the failure of political organizations to adjust to advances in transportation. To illustrate, the present system of counties and county governments in the United States was established when the only way to travel to the county seat was by horse and buggy. Because twenty miles or so was the practical limit of a day's travel, larger units of local government would have been difficult to administer. Today there is no such restriction on travel, but there has been little change in existing lines of local government.

Limitations of the Cultural Lag Theory

The cultural lag theory is useful, provided we clearly understand its meaning and its limitations. In the first place, we must not assume that changes in the material aspects of culture always precede changes in the nonmaterial aspects. There is a constant interaction between the two, and in the long run technological progress itself is largely dependent on certain nonmaterial factors such as social attitudes and forms of social organization. Most, if not all, of the material products of culture originate in the human mind, and new material devices will not be invented and put to use unless the nonmaterial cultural atmosphere is favorable. The rapid material progress characteristic of present-day society is itself the result of earlier changes in our nonmaterial culture, changes that made possible the development of modern machine technology. We have already called attention to some of these earlier developments. One was the increased receptivity to change that was brought about by historical movements such as the Renaissance, the Reformation, and the great voyages of discovery. Another closely related factor was the development of mental attitudes that made it possible to apply the scientific method to the search for truth.

In the second place, when changes occur in the material culture we may sometimes have difficulty in agreeing on the kinds of adjustments needed in the nonmaterial culture. Consider, for example, the invention of the automobile and its widespread adoption as a means of transportation. The automobile brought about many social changes, including changes in the customs of courtship and dating. One of its effects was to enable dating couples to escape, to some degree, the close supervision of their elders. Did this represent an unsatisfactory adjustment of our nonmaterial culture to the automobile? Some observers maintained that it did. They considered it an example of cultural lag and argued that new ways of supervising dating couples had to be devised to maintain moral standards. Others, however, regarded greater freedom in the relations between the sexes not as a problem but as a development that represented social progress.

But even if there is general agreement that the nonmaterial culture has not satisfactorily adjusted to changes in the material culture, making the desired adjustments may be difficult or, conceivably, impossible. The word *lag* implies optimistically that the satisfactory solution of social problems resulting from technological change is merely a matter of time, but in some cases this time may never come. Our society's increased medical knowledge of fetal abortive processes has only added to the social conflict surrounding that issue, for instance.

Contrasts among Cultures

The interaction between culture and social change leads not only to social problems within a society but also to problems among various societies. The reason is that different cultures often evolve along quite different paths. For example, in our culture women and men are considered equal, even if they are not always treated that way. In certain other cultures, a woman's role is fundamentally different from a man's role. (For example, in some Islamic societies a man may divorce his wife simply by saying or writing the words: I divorce you. (Women don't have the same option.)

Archaic tribal societies often differ from one another greatly, but unless they are brought into contact with powerful outside influences, they tend to be relatively stable. Industrial societies are much more subject to change. In them people's wants tend to multiply rapidly, as do the products with which to satisfy them. From one culture to another, family relations, economic activities, government, religion, and art take on an endless variety of forms.

The Interaction of Humans and Society

Though we are all, in part, products of our cultural environment, no two persons will have exactly the same personal experiences. Furthermore, they will not inherit biologically the same physical and mental constitutions, and these inherited differences will cause them to react differently to many of the elements in their cultural environment.

Thus, the study of humankind is a complicated one that moves from unique traits of individuals to general aspects of society and back again to unique aspects of individuals. Therefore, such a study must encompass a wide range of issues.

Cultural Relativism

The doctrine of **cultural relativism** asserts that all cultures are for the most part equally valid. That is, cultures develop in a way that best suits the population's needs, and the cultural traits within a culture have a specific purpose. Thus, we can't say that one culture is better than another without taking into account its full history.

Today, few students of society would question the proposition that any culture that has enabled a group to meet its basic needs, and to survive over a long period of time, is worthy of respect, as are the individuals who practice its customs and follow its moral precepts. Cultures are not as a whole good, bad, right, or wrong; they simply exist and must be judged relative to their own value system. Therefore, to understand other cultures, we must try to look at them through the eyes of those who have been brought up under their influence rather than through our own eyes. If we do this, we may find that these cultures meet needs we have failed to recognize. For example, nineteenth-century missionaries to certain South Sea islands were shocked to find that the native women wore no clothing above the waist. Part of their mission was to convert the women to wearing Mother Hubbards, shapeless dresses that kept their bodies well covered. To the missionaries, this seemed a great gain. But from a health standpoint, it may have been unfortunate. In the tropical rainy climate of the islands, the Mother Hubbards were wet much of the time, and they may have contributed to poor health.

Ethnocentrism is the tendency to judge other cultures by one's own culture and its standards, and the belief that one's own people and their way of life are superior to all others. An extreme example in the twentieth century was the Nazi doctrine that the Germans were a super race. In modern societies, feelings of ethnocentrism and chauvinism increase during times of insecurity or economic depression. Pre-Nazi Germany was in a severe depression, which many believe enabled Adolf Hitler to rise to power. In the late twentieth century, we saw, or were forced to recognize, the power of religion as a divisive force. In countries such as Northern Ireland, Nigeria, Pakistan, and the former Yugoslavia, opposing religious groups have fought bitterly with each other within their own borders, and their internal differences can affect their relations with foreign countries as they sometimes attempt to influence beliefs in other nations. Frequently, these religious convictions are mixed with political problems, making the cultural issues complex and recalcitrant.

At one time, ethnocentrism may have had a survival value for some nonliterate tribal societies by giving them confidence in the superiority of their own people and own way of life.

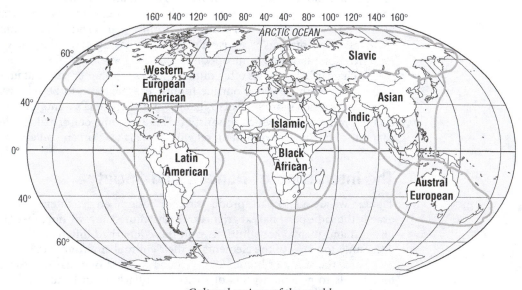

Cultural regions of the world.

But nowadays, although ethnocentrism still contributes to the cohesion of a society, survival is likely to depend on achieving understanding and cooperation among races, peoples, and nations. Although some ethnocentrism is necessary to hold a society together, the conscious cultivation of ethnocentrism generally results in misunderstanding, prejudice, ill feeling, and conflict.

Approach to the Study of Society

In this book we are primarily concerned with the nature of modern U.S. society. Most of the discussion is therefore centered on our own culture and its basic values and on the problems that arise in connection with efforts to achieve these values. However, we can understand our own society better if we see it in perspective. Hence, throughout the book we call attention to other societies and cultures, to the characteristics common to all cultures, and to the differences that distinguish them.

Because it is not the function of science to determine social values, we simply assume for the most part the validity of the basic ideals of our own democratic society, and occasionally we attempt to clarify these ideals. But our principal efforts are concerned with giving a picture of the general character of U.S. society. We explain its values and its social institutions. We also discuss its failures to achieve its goals and the frustration and conflict that are sometimes the result, and we consider the nature of its major problems and explore the possibilities of solving them through social action.

 Study and **Review**

Key Points

- Culture holds society together.
- Important elements of culture include social norms, social institutions, material products, language, and social values.
- Three popular theories of cultural change include the "good-old days" theory, "the world is getting better" theory, and the "change runs in cycles" theory.
- Five factors that cause culture to change are technology, cultural diffusion, ideas and ideologies, collective action, and geography and climate.

- Three factors stabilizing culture are stability of social norms, habit, and value attachment.
- The cultural lag theory states that a change in any one part of culture may create strains and disturbances in the closely related parts.
- The doctrine of cultural relativism states that all cultures are for the most part equally valid.

Some Important Terms

conventions (71)
cultural alternatives (73)
cultural diffusion (77)
cultural evolution (68)
cultural integration (73)
cultural lag (82)
cultural objects (artifacts) (72)
cultural relativism (84)
cultural universal (73)
culture (68)

discovery (76)
ethnocentrism (84)
habits (80)
ideology (78)
Internet (75)
invention (76)
language (72)
laws (71)
mores (71)
multiculturalism (68)

pluralism (69)
social evolution (75)
social institution (71)
socialization (68)
social problem (80)
social values (73)
society (70)
vested interest (80)

Questions for Review and Discussion

General Questions

1. What is the definition of culture given in the text?
2. What is cultural evolution?
3. Do the authors see monoculturalism and multi-culturalism as opposites? Why or why not?
4. What are some examples of conventions, mores, and laws found in U.S. society?
5. What are social institutions?
6. What are social values? Give some examples. Do you think Americans could ever accept infanticide as a positive social value? Why or why not?
7. Why are the cultures of primitive societies more integrated than the cultures of modern industrial societies?
8. Explain the relationship between culture and society.
9. What developments of the last five or six centuries do you think have been of greatest importance in speeding up the rate of social change? Explain why in each case.
10. Distinguish between the concepts of social evolution and social change.
11. How is the Internet changing the way cultural diffusion takes place?
12. Why does social change usually encounter strong resistance? Is this fortunate or unfortunate? Explain.
13. What is a social problem? Why is a particular social problem often difficult to define or isolate?
14. State the theory of cultural lag and discuss its limitations.
15. What is cultural relativism? How does this concept relate to ethnocentrism?
16. Of today's major social problems, which three seem to you most critical? Defend your choices.
17. Sometimes we are dissatisfied with aspects of our social system. Should we therefore dismantle it completely and start over? Why or why not?

Internet Questions

1. The site http://www.toolpack.com/culture.html discusses cultural change at the organizational (business) level. What is organizational culture? Name the four companies used as examples of successful cultures.
2. Look through the website for the United States Golf Association http://www.usga.org/. Is the USGA a social institution? Do golfers comprise a society?
3. Go to https://www.youtube.com/watch?v= FOe-x1-aUP2o and the video about Indian boarding schools. What resulted from the interaction of Anglo-American and Native Navajo cultures? What term from this chapter best illustrates the views of Civil War general William Sherman and How was General Pratt's comment, "Kill the Indian, save the man" reflected in the actions of the U.S. government concerning the education of Native Navajo children?
4. Go to http://www.phrases.org.uk/meanings/french-phrases.html and read some of the French phrases that have become commonly used in English. Do you think this is an example of cultural diffusion? Give your own example of cultural diffusion.
5. Read the article at http://www.irespect.net/Untold%20Stories/Chinese/Chinese%20Values.htm on Chinese social values. Whose teachings largely influence these values? Are there values that Chinese and American cultures share?

For Further Study

Books to Explore

Bloom, Paul, *Against Empathy: The Case for Rational Compassion*, New York: Harper Collins, 2016.

Bronson, Po, and Ashley Merryman, *NurtureShock: New Thinking About Children*, New York: Grand Central Publishing, 2009.

Henig, Robin Marantz, *Pandora's Baby: How the First Test-Tube Babies Sparked the Reproductive Revolution*, New York: Houghton Mifflin, 2004.

Hoffman, Andrew J., *How Culture Shapes the Climate Change Debate*, Stanford, CA: Stanford Briefs, 2015.

Mead, Margaret, *Continuities in Cultural Evolution*, New Haven, CT: Yale University Press, 1964.

O'Keefe, Kevin, *The Average American: The Extraordinary Search for the Nation's Most Ordinary Citizen*, New York: Public Affairs, 2005.

Sapolsky, Robert, *Behave: The Biology of Humans at Our Best and Worst*, New York: Penguin Press, 2017.

Scalia, Maureen, *Scalia Speaks: Reflections on Law, Faith, and Life Well Lived*, New York: Penguin Publishers, 2017.

Schlosser, Eric, *Fast Food Nation*, New York: Perennial/HarperCollins, 2004.

Schwartz, Howard S., *Political Correctness and the Destruction of Social Order: Chronicling the Rise of the Pristine Self*, Basel: Palgrave Macmillan, 2016.

Shweder, Richard, *Why Do Men Barbecue? Recipes for Cultural Diversity*, Cambridge, MA: Harvard University Press, 2003.

Weinstein, Jay, *Social Change*, Lanham, MD: Rowman & Littlefield, 2010.

Zeigler, Alexis, *Conscious Cultural Evolution: Understanding Our Past, Choosing Our Future*, Charlottesville, VA: Ecodem Press, 2000.

Internet Sites to Explore

"http://www.quantonics.com/Famous_CRites.html" Adherents of Cultural Relativism.

"https://www.worldbusinessculture.com/topic/culture/" Business Culture Guide by Country.

"http://www.cal.org/" Center for Applied Linguistics.

"http://www.pitt.edu/~dash/folktexts.html" Folklore and Mythology Electronic Texts.

"http://www.isoc.org" Internet Society.

Geography, Demography, Ecology, and Society

chapter 5

After reading this chapter, you should be able to:

- Identify the major countries on a map of the world
- Explain why many people believe population growth is a problem
- State the Malthusian theory and explain how technology can affect its predictions
- Explain how culture and environment interact
- Explain how geography, population, culture, and the natural environment interact—and affect the ecological balance

Ecology is rather like sex—every new generation likes to think they were the first to discover it.

—Michael Allaby

In the last chapter, we discussed culture, the glue that holds society together. In this chapter, we look at society from three slightly different perspectives—geographic, demographic, and ecological—discussing each in terms of its interrelationships with culture. Each of these perspectives highlights certain problems that societies face and provides a foundation for a better understanding of those problems.

Geography

In 1988, the National Geographic Society commissioned a study called "Geography: An International Gallup Survey." It tested 10,820 people in nine countries on their ability to identify sixteen spots on a map of the world. Citizens of the United States could identify about half the places, but citizens aged 18 to 24 could identify fewer than seven. People in Sweden did the best. In the early 2000s, the situation hadn't changed; as a follow-up, National Geographic-Roper conducted a survey on geographic literacy among young adults and found that only 37 percent could find Iraq on a map, and less than half of U.S. citizens could identify France or Japan; just one-half could find the state of New York. The survey also looked at the world's cultural, economic, and natural resources. United States citizens were least likely to know that the Taliban was based in Afghanistan, and over one-third estimated the population of the United States to be ten times the actual number. (An online version of the Roper test is available, which can be located through a search on Google or another search engine.)

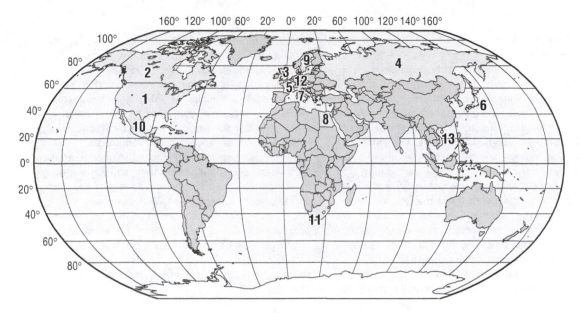

A geography quiz. Can you name the countries numbered on this map? Be careful—countries sometimes change their names suddenly. Within the past twenty years, Burma renamed itself Myanmar, Kampuchea changed its name back to Cambodia, and Zaire changed its name to the Democratic Republic of the Congo (its name before it was called "Zaire" was "The Congo"). The answers to our quiz follow (they're printed upside down).

1. United States; 2. Canada; 3. United Kingdom; 4. Russia; 5. France; 6. Japan; 7. Italy; 8. Egypt; 9. Sweden; 10. Mexico; 11. South Africa; 12. Germany; 13. Vietnam

Above, you'll find a map of the world. To keep our quiz easy, we are asking you to identify only thirteen countries (leaving out the other three spots the National Geographic asked about). The countries we ask you to name are numbered. Let's hope you're as smart as the Swedes (who scored about 75 percent).

Even if you scored 100 percent, you do not necessarily know geography.[1] Geography is far more than the knowledge of where places are. **Geography** is a social science that focuses on the spatial interaction of human beings with each other and with their physical environment. Geography considers questions such as why cities are located where they are, how the environment shapes society's culture, and why some areas develop while others don't. For example, one explanation why central Africa was little touched by Western culture before twentieth-century technological advances in transportation is that most of its rivers are too difficult to navigate—it was just too expensive and difficult to get a boat up the rivers into the interior of the continent.

Where does such knowledge fit into the social sciences? As we emphasized in Chapter 1, enormous overlap exists among the social sciences. Therefore, it is not only geographers who have considered the location of cities, the effect of environment on culture, and why some areas develop rather than others. Sociologists have considered these issues too. In fact, sociologists and some social scientists other than geographers were the first to raise many of the issues we discuss in this chapter. When geographers are asked about this, they say that sociologists actually are geographers. That claim seems to be a bit of social science equivocation, but it is less important to know which social science has had a particular idea than it is to know the idea itself.

---

[1] If you think you did well on our little quiz, remember that the places we chose were some of the most obvious. If we had asked you for cities, rivers, and oceans, the quiz would have been more difficult.

GIS Method

Sometimes the tools social scientists use differentiate them. For example, economists tend to use more math and statistics than sociologists, while anthropologists tend to use more case studies. For geographers, the latest tool of choice is the geographic information system (GIS). This is a computer program designed to "capture, store, manipulate, analyze, manage, and present all types of geographically referenced data." It merges cartography, statistical analysis, and database technology, and allows the geographer to manipulate the spatial area for expositional and analytic purposes. Examples of its use include an application that allows emergency planners to calculate emergency response times and one that allows development of protection strategies for pollution.

The adoption of this tool as a central tool of many geographers has made many geographers take a more technical approach than do sociologists studying the same issues, and has led to much discussion of the advantages and disadvantages of various methods. Some sociologists see the method as one that can be expanded into a sociological information system that would integrate, store, edit, analyze, share, and display all quantifiable sociological, geographical, and other information for decision makers. Various GIS applications allow users to create interactive queries; analyze both textual and spatial information; edit visual displays of user-created searches, as well as of data and maps; and to present the results of all these operations. Sociological information systems would do likewise for a broader set of data and information. For example, some sociologists are using information systems to study how social networks influence events—how, by changing the social network, the way in which an event occurs can be changed.

Demography

Societies are made up of people. Whereas geography approaches the study of society by means of a spatial dimension, demography approaches it through a people dimension.

Demography is the study of the number and characteristics of a population. It is concerned not only with the number of people in an area but also with the factors that may be causing their number to increase or decrease. These include matters such as the state of health care and sanitation, the extent to which birth control is practiced, and the availability of food and other resources. Further, demography concerns the distribution of people among countries and regions and the different kinds of people who make up any given population, including their physical, mental, and cultural characteristics. Demographers classify and count people on the basis of characteristics such as age, gender, marital status, occupation, income, nationality, and race.

Population Estimates

When we add up the population statistics for all countries, we conclude that there were slightly more than 7.5 billion people in 2018. Population is divided up unevenly among countries and regions (see Figure 5.1). China has the largest population of any country, with more than 1.3 billion people; and Asia, with more than 4 billion people, has the largest population of any region.

Determinants of Population Growth

Because two key determinants of the population of any country are its death rate and its birthrate, these deserve special consideration. Figure 5.2 shows the U.S. birthrates and death rates since 1960.

The current world death rate is considerably lower than in the distant past. How much further the death rate will drop in coming years will depend both on changes in the age composition of the world population and on the rate of advance in medical science.

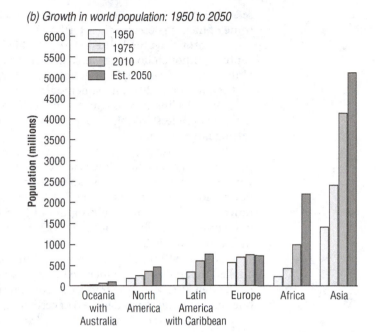

(a) The twenty most populous countries in 2018 (in millions) (estimated)

Rank	Country	Population
1.	China	1,379,302,784
2.	India	1,281,935,872
3.	United States of America	326,625,792
4.	Indonesia	260,580,736
5.	Brazil	207,353,392
6.	Pakistan	204,924,864
7.	Nigeria	190,632,256
8.	Bangladesh	157,826,576
9.	Russia	142,257,520
10.	Japan	126,451,400
11.	Mexico	124,574,792
12.	Ethiopia	105,350,016
13.	Philippines	104,256,080
14.	Egypt	97,041,072
15.	Vietnam	96,160,160
16.	Democratic Republic of the Congo	83,301,152
17.	Iran	82,021,568
18.	Turkey	80,845,216
19.	Germany	80,594,016
20.	Thailand	68,414,136

(b) Growth in world population: 1950 to 2050

Figure 5.1

World population. The populations of the twenty largest countries are listed in (a). In (b), distribution of the world's population by regions is given for 1950, 1975, 2010, and estimates for 2050. (Some of the changes are due to changes in which region countries are included.) (Sources: http://www.geoba.se/population.php?pc=world and Population Division of the Department of Economic and Social Affairs of the United Nations Secretariat)

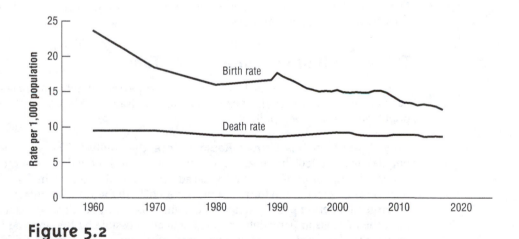

Figure 5.2

U.S. birth and death rates, 1960 to 2017. (Source: World Bank Indicators https://data.worldbank.org/indicator/SP.DYN.CDRT.IN?locations=US)

Although some further reduction in the death rate can be predicted, unless we make great advances in controlling degenerative diseases and the aging process itself, the future of population growth will depend largely on the trend of the birthrate. As death rates decline, the world population will increase unless birthrates also fall. Developing countries have already seen their populations increase because of their declining death rates, despite the efforts of some of them to decrease their birthrates.

In Europe and the United States, the birthrate has been declining since the nineteenth century, although upswings have occurred periodically in one country or another. In the United States, for example, although the birthrate rose slightly in the beginning of the 1990s, and again around 2015, most demographers believe these were temporary trends, and the long-term decline of the birthrate will likely continue due to social and economic forces that make people less willing to accept the trouble, expense, and responsibility involved in raising large families.

Birth control has been so effective in the United States, Japan, and Europe that their population growth has slowed to a crawl or even begun to decline. In less developed countries where children play an important economic as well as social role in the family, population growth has continued at a high rate despite governmental attempts to slow it down. In India, a state-run program of forced sterilization was a factor in the fall of the government of Indira Gandhi in 1977. She was later reelected and the program was significantly modified.

Until recently in China, strong social and economic pressures to have only one child were applied to families. These included peer pressure (families deciding to have more than one child often were socially ostracized), economic pressure (families deciding to have more than one child were fined and deprived of certain rights to housing, whereas those agreeing to have only one child were financially rewarded), and counseling (the party leaders visited and explained the reasons and need for birth control). The one-child program was not as effective as some expected, and despite official pressures and even fines of as much as $1,000 for families having more than one child, many couples chose to have more children. In 2016, faced with the possibility of having a workforce too small to support its elderly population, China ended its one-child policy and replaced it with a two-child policy.

Probably the most original approach to reducing the birthrate existed in Thailand, where the head of the family planning services used a condom as his calling card. There, rather than university names or slogans on T-shirts, many wore T-shirts with the message, "A Condom a Day Keeps the Doctor Away." Contraceptive information was printed on things such as bottle caps, towels, and ice cream sticks.

The Growth of Population over Time

The past history of population has been one of significant but not continual growth. Instead, it has been marked by periods of expansion and contraction. Since 1800, however, the world population has grown rapidly.

Why Population Has Grown Rapidly since the 1800s. The great increase in world population since 1800 has resulted directly from a continuing decline of the death rate. Two factors are responsible for this: first, great advances in sanitation and health care, and second, a relatively rapid increase in the per capita output of both food and manufactured goods, so that for large numbers of people standards of living rose substantially above subsistence level. In part, the increase in per capita output was made possible by the opening up for trade and settlement of some of the undeveloped areas of the world. Principally, however, the increase was a result of the Industrial Revolution. The great advances of science and technology in the nineteenth and twentieth centuries made it possible for the world to support a rapidly rising population.

Unequal Population Growth since the Late 1800s. In the latter part of the nineteenth century, some of the less developed parts of the world began to experience some of the benefits of modern science, industry, and transportation. Sanitation and improved health care began to reduce the death rate and to increase the rate of population growth. Some of the less developed regions of the world, such as Asia and Latin America, made substantially greater gains in population than Europe, the United States, and Canada.

However, increases in population in the developing areas of the world often occurred at the expense of standards of living. Birthrates remained high and production expanded slowly. If an increase in the food supply temporarily put off famine or relieved malnutrition, it was soon matched by a further increase in population. Since 1900, the population of Asia has increased fivefold; today, more than 60 percent of the people of the world are found there.

As you can see in Figure 5.3, demographers believe that world population will grow more and more slowly. They see the net gains in population decreasing at the beginning of the twenty-first century and almost ending by the beginning of the twenty-second century. Even then, it is unlikely that all countries will have the same population growth rate. Instead, regions with faster growing populations will be balanced by those where the population is stable or even shrinking.

The Problem of Counting

The population figures given in this chapter are *estimates*; some are not very good estimates. In fact, we have practically no population figures based on an actual census except for those of relatively recent years. A **census** is an official, systematic count of the number of people who live in a given area. Usually, when people are counted, other kinds of information about them, such as age and gender, are also gathered. Lacking any census figures, we can make only rough guesses about populations and population changes that occurred before the latter part of the eighteenth century.

The first reliable census of a European country was taken by Sweden in 1749. In the United States, the first census was taken in 1790. About that time, several other European countries began to take censuses, and by 1850 reasonably accurate figures were available for western Europe, the United States, and some countries in other parts of the world. Today, we

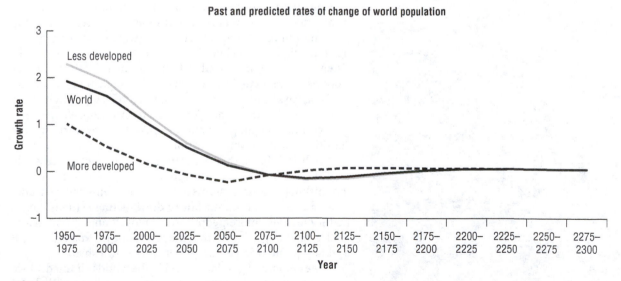

Figure 5.3

The future population growth rate is expected to decline significantly, especially in less developed regions until about 2075. Then it is expected to level off. (*Source: United Nations,* World Population to 2300)

have fairly dependable population statistics for most countries; yet even the simplest numbers, such as how many people there are in a country, often are subject to debate. Although U.S. census figures are about the best in the world, there are still debates about how many people were missed. For example, in the 1990 Census, the Census Bureau accepted that it actually missed about 10 million people in its count and that it double counted about 11.2 million people. Final compilation of the U.S. census of 2010 shows the total U.S. population at 308,745,538. This means that 27 million people were added to the total population from 2000 to 2010.

Why are the statistics not better? Ask yourself how you would work out a system to count more than 300 million people constantly on the move, including homeless and undocumented people, and you'll quickly see why. There is a significant debate about whether sampling techniques should be used to "fill in" for the numbers of people who are missed when they are not individually counted. The issue is politically charged because allocation of federal grants is often dependent on formal census counts. The moral of this story is that social scientists use census data, but they use them carefully. They use their own estimates of the future even more carefully.

The Malthusian Theory

For more than a century, most discussions of the population problem have started from the theory of Thomas Robert Malthus concerning the relationship of population to the means of human subsistence. Malthus was a Church of England clergyman and an early English economist. In 1798, he published a short treatise called "An Essay on the Principle of Population as It Affects the Future Improvement of Society."

Reduced to its simplest terms, the **Malthusian theory** is the belief that a population tends to outrun the means of subsistence. This was not a new idea, but Malthus developed it with

such clarity and force that his treatise attracted wide attention. He contended that people are impelled to increase their numbers by a powerful natural urge, the attraction between male and female. As a result, if there are no obstacles, population will increase rapidly and without limit. Furthermore, it will increase in geometric ratio—that is, by multiplication. By this Malthus meant that if a population could double in, say, twenty-five years, it would double again in the next twenty-five years, and so on indefinitely. He believed, however, that the means of subsistence could be increased only in arithmetic ratio—in other words, slowly and to a limited extent. Consequently, population would always tend to press against the food supply. When the food supply became inadequate to support more people, any further increase in population would be prevented by the "positive" checks of malnutrition, famine, disease, and war.

Malthus's belief that population growth would necessarily tend to outrun means of subsistence was based on the law of diminishing returns. In terms of the relationships between land, labor, and food output, the **law of diminishing returns** means that if more and more people are employed on a given area of land, even though total output may continue to expand, beyond a certain point average output per worker will shrink.

The amount of good farmland in the world is limited. Once all the undeveloped regions of the earth have been settled and cultivated more or less intensively, further attempts to increase food production will become less and less effective because they will bring into operation the law of diminishing returns. It will

Crowded street in New Delhi, India.

still be possible to increase output by employing more workers on the land already cultivated or by cultivating land that is less fertile. However, assuming no advances in agricultural technology, this will bring about a decrease in the average output per worker, a decrease that will become greater and greater as attempts are made to raise production to higher and higher levels. It is possible that advances in agricultural technology might, for a long time, more than offset this tendency toward diminishing returns, but they could not do so indefinitely if population continued to grow. Sooner or later, the amount of land per person would become impossibly small.

Malthus recognized that certain preventive checks might conceivably slow population growth by reducing the birthrate. These preventive checks he summarized under the general heading of "moral restraint." By this term he apparently referred to premarital chastity and late marriage. However, he did not believe that these preventive checks were likely to be practiced sufficiently to have much effect in keeping down births. Malthus apparently opposed both postmarital abstinence and contraception. He thought that marriage and its sexual satisfaction should carry with them the risks of bringing children into the world along with the responsibility to support them. Otherwise, people would get something for nothing and be deprived of their main incentive for economic improvement.

Because Malthus had little hope that the preventive checks would be effective in keeping population from exerting pressure on the means of subsistence, he was pessimistic about the chances of greatly improving the economic condition of most people. However, in the final edition of his essay, he recognized that conditions in Europe were slowly improving in spite of the growth of population, and he expressed the hope that some way might yet be found to make possible the "gradual and progressive improvement" of human society.

The Concept of Optimal Population

Given the level of technological development, in any country growth of population beyond a certain point would mean lower standards of living. Relative shortages of farmlands, fuels, timber, metals, and other resources would develop. On the other hand, a very small population would also have disadvantages. In thinly populated areas, it is often difficult to maintain law and order, to provide medical and hospital services, or to provide schools. Also, there are not enough people to build adequate roads or to make it worthwhile to operate public transportation services. The **optimal population** is the population that would maximize welfare for its members. What, then, is the optimum, or best, size of population from the standpoint of maximizing welfare?

Actually, there is no way of determining with even approximate accuracy what the optimal population of a country would be at any given stage in its development. Yet for any country, there is likely a point beyond which an increase in population would strain its resources and reduce average output per worker, and hence reduce standards of living.

This view, however, is disputed by Julian Simon, author of *The Ultimate Resource*, who argued that people are the ultimate resource and that there can be no such thing as too many people. People create ideas, and as they do they create the technology by which the world can support an ever-larger population.

Most demographers do not share Simon's optimism. They believe that India, Pakistan, and China have already exceeded their optimal quantity and that the United States and western Europe have reached theirs. But such views are primarily held by demographers from the United States and western Europe who have a Western cultural bias, and any statements about optimal population are inevitably culturally determined.

Poor, under-developed nations, for example, lay the blame for shortages of resources and other goods on the excessively wasteful policies of developed countries, with their emphasis on consumption rather than conservation. Some critics claim that Western nations are using the population issue and the need for reduced birthrates in countries with high birthrates as another form of imperialist control over these areas, which were so recently freed from colonialism.

The Question of Population Quality

In the past, some students of human society have been concerned about the possibility that social forces would bring about a serious deterioration of the biological quality of human populations. They feared that the danger would be greatest in the countries that have made the most social and economic progress. This deterioration, they felt, might take two forms: (1) a decline of the physical quality and stamina of individuals, with an increasing incidence of physical defects, and (2) a decline of native intelligence—that is, the capacity for mental development.

Their arguments as to why this might happen were varied. One was that the advances we have made in medicine and science have meant, among other results, that it is easier for children who are weak or have physical disabilities to survive, grow to maturity, and have children of their own. Modern medicine makes the principle of the survival of the fittest inoperative, or greatly weakened. In short, they argue that, in a worst-case scenario, humanitarianism and science, instead of saving the human race, will ultimately destroy it.

A second argument being made today is a socioeconomic one. It goes as follows: With the development of the two-income family, intelligent individuals will choose careers over marriage and family and will have few children, leaving the less advantaged and less educated to bear the majority of the children. To support this view, they usually point to the difference in the birthrate between the upper and middle classes on the one hand and the less advantaged classes on the other.

No one can be certain to what extent economic and social success results from inborn qualities that the upper classes possess in greater measure than the other classes. We know that individual success depends on both social environment and biological inheritance.

There is always an interplay between the two. But to move from this obvious fact to a belief that we can determine whether society will be better or worse off when one socio-economic group has children while another does not is a difficult step that few are willing to take. Moreover, most people are unwilling even to consider the social measures required to ensure that only certain groups have reproductive rights.

Given modern developments in genetic engineering, these issues are likely to become more and more discussed. For example, it is now possible with amniocentesis to check a fetus

*T*he Missing Girls

One of the most significant technologies to affect the demography of developing countries is inexpensive ultrasound, which lets families determine the sex of their unborn child. In countries such as India and China, where having sons is sociologically preferred and abortion is acceptable, the ultrasound has led to a decrease in the number of female babies being born, with the gender ratio changing from near equality to ratios approaching 45 percent women and 55 percent men in some areas. This gender inequality has created a mismatch when it comes time to marry and means that some men, especially poorer men, are having a difficult time finding brides.

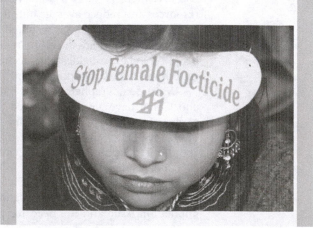

for gender and for some birth defects long before it is born. Eggs from one woman can be transplanted into another, and sperm can be frozen to be used for artificial insemination. Sometime in this century, it may be possible to change the genetic characteristics of sperm and eggs so that children's characteristics can be controlled. In principle, couples might go to a genetic engineering company and order the type of child they want ("girl who will grow up to be 5 feet 7 inches tall and weigh 128 pounds, with an IQ of 217," and so forth). Because of these possibilities, society faces a couple difficult questions: Should such technological advances be allowed to continue? And if they are, who gets to determine which modifications are acceptable and which ones go too far?

Some societies have taken an active role in trying to control the genetic qualities of their population. For instance, Singapore, whose government has successfully administered severe laws against drug dealing, pornography, and littering, in the 1980s instituted a program whereby extra privileges were promised to female university graduates who married and had children. Bonuses of $5,000 were awarded to less educated mothers who submitted to sterilization. The government's stated reasons for these laws were that uneducated women were having twice the number of children as college graduates were, and the prime minister claimed that this would "deplete the talent pool" and that the "level of competence would decline." However, many segments of the population had strong objections to the program: both women and men perceived the program as unfair; scientists questioned the assumptions on which it was based; less educated women did not want to be sterilized, even for $5,000; and women did not want to be treated as breeding stock. The experiment was withdrawn after about a year and a half.

*E*cology: The Interaction of Geography, Demography, and Environment

Geography and demography come together in a consideration of environmental issues and ecology. The **environment** is the sum of all the external influences that impinge on the human organism. These influences exert their effects through physical stimuli that produce sights, sounds, tastes, smells, and other bodily sensations. These sensations make us aware of our environment, and through them we are able to interpret our environment and react to it.

The **social environment** is composed of the elements in our surroundings that are human or of human origin. The **natural environment** is composed of the nonhuman elements in our surroundings. The general character of our social environment depends chiefly on the culture of the group to which we belong. The character of our natural environment depends primarily on the climate, water resources, soil, topography, plant and animal life, and mineral resources of the part of the world in which we live. However, once human beings have lived in an area for a long time, they are certain to have made changes, for better or worse, in their environment. It then becomes difficult to draw a sharp line between the constructed physical environment and some aspects of the natural environment.

The Ecological Balance

Ecology is the science concerned with the interactions between living things and their environment. The environment of each species of organism includes not only the inanimate world but also all other living species that affect it directly or indirectly. It includes the population density of its own members and the character of their behavior.

Human ecology is the part of ecology that deals with the way in which human societies adjust to their environments. It considers the processes by which populations adapt to their surroundings, taking into account the technology and the types of social organization by

"Frankly, I think we'll regret introducing these organisms into the environment."

which adjustment is achieved. Human ecology applies some of the findings of the biological sciences to problems dealt with by the social sciences.

In the world of nature, there is normally a movement toward ecological balance. **Ecological balance** is the term applied to the state achieved when each plant or animal species, with its own characteristics and needs, has adjusted to its environment and survived, and when other species, which have likewise adjusted to the environment, prevent it from expanding indefinitely and from crowding them out. Most species depend on other species for food or for meeting other needs. Though the natural ecological balance is not absolutely static, normally it changes slowly over long periods of time. New species that can make superior adjustments to their environment evolve and may destroy or crowd out old species and render the latter extinct, or changes in climate may occur such that some species cannot survive.

Modern times have brought about rapid changes in the ecological balance in many parts of the world. Sometimes, the results have been good from the human point of view, but sometimes they have been almost disastrous. When rabbits were introduced into Australia, where they had no natural enemies and multiplied by the millions, they became a national problem. By building the St. Lawrence Seaway, engineers allowed lampreys to enter the Great Lakes, where they almost completely destroyed the whitefish. People have caused the introduction of insect pests from one part of the world to another, often with disastrous results. After World War II, the nearly worldwide use of an insecticide called DDT did indeed control or eliminate undesirable insects, but it also destroyed or damaged other forms of animal life and even human health.

Examples of threats to the ecological balance are many: global warming, industrial pollution, smokestack emissions, acid rain, depletion of water tables, and paving over of fertile soil and plant and animal habitats. These by no means exhaust the list, and we have not even attempted to describe ecological catastrophes on whole continents, such as Africa. Since the 1970s, the United States has had to face the fact that many industrial, military, and agricultural chemicals are not only lethally affecting animal life but are also exercising long-term effects on human health. The cost of eliminating these chemicals and repairing their ravages (where possible) is astronomical. These costs include the policing of hazardous waste disposal, discovering and salvaging previously used sites, finding alternative chemicals to those that have caused trouble, and devising ecologically safe methods for disposal of waste from indispensable activities such as radioactive medical technology. Today, given snowballing technological growth, the possibility of irreversible change is enormous. For example, the explosion in worldwide commerce and travel has already meant that plants, animals, and insects have traveled outside their natural habitats and are crowding out or eliminating plants and animals in the localities to which they emigrate. Some scientists predict that, in that same way, the migration of viruses will spread nearly untreatable diseases far from the sites to which such viruses were formerly confined.

Pollution

A major concern of ecologists is **pollution**—the destruction of our natural resource base by the productive process. Over the past fifty years, there has been extensive pollution of rivers, lakes, and forests by sewage and industrial wastes. Pure air also has become scarce

A man disposes of a fish at a toxic waste disposal site.

© PhotoAlto/Alamy Stock Photo

in many of our urban centers, where the inhabitants often must breathe a mixture of air combined with auto fumes, dust, and various waste products from trash fires, incinerators, and the smokestacks and flares of industrial plants. Improperly disposed toxic chemicals and various noxious waste products have invaded the soil in some areas, and sometimes whole communities must be moved while the sites of their former homes are cleaned up. In other communities, people suspect that various illnesses are caused by this kind of problem, but no cleanup seems immediately practical. In the United States, a federal law enacted near the end of the twentieth century mandated that by 2000 nuclear waste must be safely disposed of in sites where no leakage will occur for "thousands of years." This mandate proved impossible to implement, partly because it was seemingly beyond current technology, but principally because people did not want such a site anywhere near where they lived. We are seeing much vigorous disagreement as localities all strive to avoid being chosen. NIMBY (Not In My Back Yard) has become a watchword of modern times.

Some pollution is an inevitable consequence of production, presenting society with a trade-off: do we want more material things, or do we want a more pristine environment? In making that decision, both the costs and benefits must be considered.

Although people can agree on the need for conservation and strong anti-pollution efforts when costs are not considered, when costs are considered there is significantly less agreement. Let's consider some of these costs. They involve restrictions on individual actions, relocation of industry and jobs, new bureaucracy, and the development of expensive new technology. In assessing the issue of pollution, the costs as well as the benefits must be considered. Therefore, it is unlikely that we will decide to institute a "no pollution" policy; that would be impossible to implement. And even approaching a standard of "little" pollution, for many, would be too expensive. Instead we are likely to choose an "optimal level" of pollution.

Since the 1960s, the United States has made considerable gains in fighting pollution, but it has not been easy. The central problem is what is called the "tragedy of the commons." Because the environment belongs to society as a whole, and not to specific individuals, no individual has the incentive to care for it. A number of governmental anti-pollution agencies have been established. The **Environmental Protection Agency (EPA)** is the most important government anti-pollution agency; it directs antipollution efforts and monitors environmental problems. Some of its gains have been impressive. In the early 1950s, Lake Erie was so polluted by untreated sewage from surrounding areas that many forms of animal life could not inhabit it. Today, it is well on the way to recovery. Sewage treatment plants were mandated, and firms were prevented from dumping industrial waste into the lake.

To reduce pollution from oil, laws were passed dealing with oil spills so that companies responsible for the spillage are responsible for cleaning them up. Similar laws have been passed concerning other types of pollution.

Many environmental issues have international dimensions. An example is climate change and the associated global warming. Climate scientists have determined that this global warming is caused, to a large degree, by greenhouse gas and carbon dioxide emissions associated with the burning of fossil fuel, and that unless something changes, there will be significant rises in ocean levels. The result will be that low lying areas will be flooded, and extreme weather events will increase in frequency and severity. The effects will be worldwide, regardless of where the emission takes place. So it is a global problem, not an individual state problem, which if it is to be dealt with effectively, will have to be dealt with globally.

Concerns about the effects of climate change led countries to try to organize collective action to prevent or slow global warming, starting with a 1997 meeting in Japan that led to the **Kyoto Protocol**, in which industrialized countries agreed to cut emissions of greenhouse gases, especially carbon dioxide.

Some in the United States were upset that only industrial countries would be required to reduce emissions and that developing countries such as China and India would not have to comply. The exception of developing countries was justified by the argument that they began emitting later than industrial countries, and they need to "catch up" economically. The Kyoto Protocol set 2000 as the date for its accomplishment. The United States refused to sign and no industrial nation met that deadline. By 2000, U.S. emissions were about 13 percent above 1990 levels. The problems of the protocol, which had no enforcement mechanism, were "dealt" with by setting the deadline further and further ahead.

The United States justified not signing the protocol by arguing that the agreement would be bad for the U.S. economy and, moreover, would not work even if attempted. Four years later, when President George W. Bush entered office in 2001, he declared the protocol fatally flawed and instead proposed his own plan to address climate change. Called the Clear Skies Initiative, it was a plan to combat global warming through voluntary measures, with a cap-and-trade approach that rewards industries that reduce pollution. In a cap-and-trade approach, a total amount of pollution is determined (the cap), and new sources of pollution must buy the rights to pollute from existing polluters who agree to lower their pollution by an offsetting amount so that total pollution does not increase above the set limit (the trade).

With the election of President Barack Obama, the United States demonstrated a willingness to work with other countries in the world to attempt to arrive at a world climate policy that would slow global warming. The United States played an active role in the Copenhagen Climate Conference in 2009. Nonetheless, the political problems of achieving a meaningful climate change policy acceptable to all countries were immense, and there were significant disagreements in Copenhagen between developed and developing countries about who should pay the enormous costs to combat global warming. So, even with a United States seemingly committed to the goal of fighting global warming, it is unclear whether the actual policies seen as politically feasible will be sufficient to do the job or whether they are just "feel-good, window-dressing" policies. In late 2015 the countries met again in Paris. This time the results were more positive, and the countries arrived at the **Paris Accord**, in which almost all countries made pledges to reduce emissions.

In 2016, following his election win, President Donald Trump stated that the Paris Accord was unfair to the United States and that, following his America First policy, the United States was withdrawing from the Accord because it required much more reduction in the United States than he found acceptable. This upset many environmentalists, but others pointed out that the withdrawal was mostly symbolic, since the Accord was voluntary, and the United States was making many of the changes it promised to make regardless of whether it was in the Accord or not. Moreover, many U.S. states and companies said they were going to stay with the Accord regardless of what Trump did.

Conservation and the Price of Gasoline and Oil

Economists point out that, while voluntary reductions of emissions are great, the real driver of an effective policy will likely be changes in incentives to use fossil fuels, which comes from changes in price. Initially, many environmentalists believed that oil was becoming scarcer and that we were overusing our resources. Economists pointed out that if that were the case, the problem would solve itself: as oil became scarcer the price of oil would rise. As it did people would economize on their use of oil and gas, driving fuel-efficient cars, using new technologies that use less oil such as electric cars or hydrogen based fuel cell cars.

The price of oil didn't rise to anywhere near the level that was needed to change behavior, in large part because oil wasn't that scarce. New technologies to find and extract oil were developed, such as fracking, which increased the amount of available oil for the next fifty years enormously, and held down the price. Rather than rising to $5 or $10 a gallon, prices that would have ended the U.S. consumer's love of SUVs, gas prices stayed at about $3. If other technologies were to be used, they would have to provide energy at prices cheaper than that. To encourage that, these other technologies can be subsidized, which states and the federal government did, or oil and gas use would have to be significantly taxed. (Economists have suggested a $3 or $4 per gallon tax, which would mean the price of gas would rise to $6 per gallon.)

What has made the possibility of change more likely are technological advances in energy storage capabilities, and in solar and wind technologies. These are lowering the price of "green" energy making it competitive with fossil fuel technology without the large subsidies that have made them competitive to date.

Conclusion

This chapter has reviewed geographic, demographic, and ecological problems that society faces and has shown some of the ways society meets them. Of the three types, the geographic problems are the most static, but with new technologies even these can change. The Internet, for example, has made it possible for more individuals to work in more rural areas and has increased the range of areas where businesses can operate.

Demographic problems are constantly changing: As societies become richer, their population growth generally decreases on its own. Nonetheless, population problems play central roles in many countries' social problems. Whereas demographic problems generally improve as a country gets richer, ecological problems often become more severe. But the wealth of society also gives it the means to deal with those ecological problems. Whether it actually does deal with them is a political issue; often, even though the means are there, the political will is not.

Social scientists study such problems and work on alternative solutions that circumvent the political problems. Finding an acceptable alternative is seldom easy, but that work generally leads to a better understanding of the problem and of alternative solutions.

 Study and **Review**

Key Points

- Knowing the geography of the world is an important skill.
- The birthrate and the death rate interact to determine population growth.
- The world population has fluctuated over time, but since the 1800s it has grown substantially.
- The Malthusian theory is the belief that population tends to outrun the means of subsistence.
- The law of diminishing marginal returns: If more and more people are employed on a given area of land, beyond a certain point—even though the total output may continue to expand—average output per worker will shrink.
- The ecology of our world is affected by human action, the life and death of species, climate changes, productive changes that result in pollution, and conservation measures.
- There is often a trade-off between economic production goals and environmental goals.

Some Important Terms

census (93)
demography (90)
ecological balance (98)
ecology (97)
environment (97)

Environmental Protection Agency
   (EPA) (99)
geography (89)
human ecology (97)
Kyoto Protocol (100)
law of diminishing returns (94)

Malthusian theory (94)
natural environment (97)
optimal population (95)
Paris Accord (100)
pollution (98)
social environment (97)

Questions for Review and Discussion

General Questions

1. What are some of the questions that geography is concerned with?
2. What is the GIS, and how might it be used in social science research?
3. How does geography interact with sociology?
4. How many people are there in the world?
5. What is the world's most populous country? Explain some of the problems that a country faces in trying to limit its population growth, including the problems it will have if it is successful.
6. What is the Malthusian doctrine? Have the predictions of Thomas Malthus come true?
7. Identify some of the reasons why the world population has grown in the past 200 years.
8. What are some possible ways to limit population? Mention natural causes as well as those encouraged by government or other policies.
9. In practice, are all policies for limitation of population growth acceptable? If not, which ones would you argue against?
10. What are some of the costs of pollution? What are some of the gains from pollution? It is very expensive to clean up areas that have been polluted. What are some ways you can think of to pay for such cleanups?
11. You are a government planner in the country of Growthlandia. You would like to know where to build new schools, where to close schools, and whether it makes sense to embark on an ambitious program to expand the number of job opportunities. What would you like to know about the composition of Growthlandia's population now and how that population is likely to change in the next fifteen years?
12. How would your life be different if gas cost $10 per gallon?

Internet Questions

1. Go to an atlas site (for example http://www.atlapedia.com/) and look at a country or region. Look at its physical and political map. What borders it? Which borders are natural?
2. Do an Internet search for kudzu. What is it? What are its benefits and what are its harms to the southeastern United States?
3. What does the UN see as a significant constraint on women's rights in its Progress of the World's Women Report at http://progress.unwomen.org/?
4. Go to "http://www.pewresearch.org/fact-tank/2015/08/14/why-the-former-ussr-has-far-fewer-men-than-women/. What two countries have the highest percentage of females? Of males?
5. What is the ozone layer according to the EPA, https://www.epa.gov/ozone-layer-protection/basic-ozone-layer-science? What is today's UV index value for your zip code (http://www.epa.gov/sunwise/uvindex.html)?

For Further Study

Books to Explore

Connelly, Matthew, *Fatal Misconception: The Struggle to Control World Population*, Cambridge, MA: Harvard University Press, 2010.

Current Population Reports, Washington DC: U.S. Bureau of the Census. Population estimates for the United States issued monthly; special reports from time to time.

Fong, Mei, *One Child: The Story of China's Most Radical Experiment*, Boston, MA: Houghton Mifflin Harcourt, 2016.

Friedman, Thomas L., *The World Is Flat: A Brief History of the Twenty-First Century*, New York: Farrar, Straus, & Giroux, 2005.

Friedman, Thomas L., *Hot, Flat, and Crowded*, New York: Farrar, Straus, & Giroux, 2008.

Goodell, Jeff, *The Water Will Come: Rising Seas, Sinking Cities and the Remaking of the Civilized World*, New York: Little Brown and Co., 2017.

Hanski, Ilkka, *Messages from Islands: A Global Biodiversity Tour*, Chicago: University of Chicago Press, 2016.

Kolbert, Elizabeth, *Field Notes from a Catastrophe: Man, Nature, and Climate Change*, New York: Bloomsbury, 2006.

Malthus, Thomas, *An Essay on the Principle of Population, or, A View of its Past and Present Effects on Human Happiness*, New York: Cambridge University Press, 1992 (first published in 1798).

Marshall, Tim, *Prisoner of Geography: 10 Maps that Explain Everything about the World*, New York: Scribner, 2015.

Mead, Margaret, ed., *Cultural Patterns and Technical Change*, New York: New American Library/Mentor, 1955.

Pearce, Fred, *The Coming Population Crash and Our Planet's Surprising Future*, Boston, MA: Beacon Press, 2011.

Simon, Julian, *The Ultimate Resource*, Princeton, NJ: Princeton University Press, 1981.

Statistical Abstract of the United States, Washington DC: U.S. Bureau of the Census. Issued annually.

Internet Sites to Explore

"http://ecology.com/index.php" Ecology Global Network.

"http://www.epa.gov" The Environmental Protection Agency.

"http://www.cleanairprogress.org/" Foundation for Clean Air Progress.

"http://maps.nationalgeographic.com/maps/" National Geographic Maps.

"http://www.lizardpoint.com/fun/geoquiz/" Test your Geographic Knowledge.

"https://news.nationalgeographic.com/2016/09/survey-geography-foreign-relations-americans-students/" 2016 Geographic Literacy Study.

"http://www.un.org" The United Nations.

"http://www.census.gov" The U.S. Bureau of the Census.

Technology and Society

After reading this chapter, you should be able to:

- Define technology and explain its importance
- Discuss the role that technology plays in social change
- Explain how the Industrial Revolution significantly changed all aspects of society
- Explain the relationship between technology and natural resources
- Distinguish the Industrial Revolution from the Information Revolution
- Speculate on how technological developments in the future will change society

Political activity is shadowplay . . .; technology is the underlying reality. Engineers, not poets, are the secret legislators of the world.

—David Warsh

On May 23, 2017, a momentous event occurred. Google's AlphaGo beat the best human Go player in the world. Why was this momentous? After all, computer algorithms had already won in Jeopardy and Chess. Why was winning in Go different? The reason is that Go is a highly intuitive game at which it was believed that humans were uniquely adapted; Go requires intuition and imagination, as well as rote computing power. If computer algorithms can win at Go, they can do just about any of the mental work that people do, only quicker and better. Soon, computers can also likely do art better, music better, emotional counselling better . . . Bottom line: To do what humans have traditionally done, changes in technology are making humans obsolete.

In this chapter we discuss these issues. First, we discuss the broad question of the relations between technology and social change, giving some case studies to make the process a bit more real. Then we discuss the traditional Industrial Revolution, providing some examples of how it progressed and the social change it brought about. We next turn to the new Information Revolution that is currently in its early stages. That revolution is likely to have similarly large-scale effects on our culture, although precisely what those effects will be is not yet known.

Technology and Social Change

Technology is the universe of tools, means, and methods through which we interact with our environment. The better the tools, the less we need human activity to accomplish the same result. We devote a separate chapter to technology because it is an integral cog in social and cultural change.

The social effects of technology can be seen all around us. Geography used to define our social destiny; it no longer does. Friends used to be determined by who lived near us; they no longer are. Today, friends are the people we include in our social network, which, because of changes in technology, can extend throughout the world. Today, we text; we don't talk. We shop online, not at our local stores. We attend more and more classes online, not in a specific room. And the social networking element of modern technology is only the beginning. In twenty years, there may well be implants with direct connections to our close friends embedded in our brains. Why waste effort calling—simply think of a person, and presto, you communicate.

With recent developments in **artificial intelligence**—algorithms (computer programs) that process information at the same level that human's process information—and **deep learning**—computer pattern-finding algorithms that discover hidden patterns in communications, we can expect enormous social change in the coming decades. Algorithms will be doing not just games—Chess, Go, Jeopardy—better than humans, they will also do all types of jobs that require mental effort—diagnosing a patient with a sickness, driving, deciding what to invest in, the list goes on and on—more cheaply and efficiently than humans. In the future the heavy mental work will be done by computers assisted by humans rather than by humans assisted by computer. These changes have profound implications for society and culture as we will discuss later in the chapter.

A good background for thinking about those future changes is to consider the history of some past changes. In our brief Chapter 2 overview of civilization's history, we saw the importance of technology to society and culture—in the initial establishment of cities, made possible by crop cultivation; in the spread of population to overcome environmental limitation, through the use of fire; and in the evolution of our thinking about society, by means of printing. That evolution is continuing. And as it does it will change our society, presenting us with new problems and new horizons. Exactly how that technology will affect society is hard to predict, but it is certain that it will. To see the connection between technology and social change, let's consider the story of one small change—the canning of food.

The process of canning food was developed in 1810 by an enterprising Frenchman, Nicolas Appert. The stimulus for this invention came from Napoleon Bonaparte. As early as 1800, Emperor Napoleon recognized the importance of preserving food after nearly losing the Battle of Marengo because of a lack of provisions. The emperor realized that a reliable method of food preservation would enhance his chances of military success. Therefore, Napoleon offered a set of prizes for technological improvements, including food preservation, believing that France lagged behind its rival, Great Britain, in technology.

When Appert, a cook who had worked in a wine cellar as a champagne bottler, heard about the prizes, he began work on a method to preserve food. It was many years before he perfected his process. Drawing on his experience as a cook and a bottler, Appert had an idea that he might be able to preserve food in champagne bottles by filling them with food, sealing them, and boiling the bottles. Although he did not know why the food in the bottles did not spoil (we now know it was because he had sterilized the contents of the bottles), still he was successful, and soon bottled food (and, later, canned food) allowed individuals to eat vegetables in winter and to preserve meat over long periods. The desired result— better provisioning of armies—was accomplished, along with the far more widespread benefits that preserved food meant for public health.

Canned food was important in the early 1800s because mechanical refrigerators did not exist. At that time, the only way to refrigerate food was by storing ice, which was cut from ponds in the winter and kept till the next winter, insulated by hay in windowless structures known as icehouses. In the United States, some southern states imported ice all year round from these icehouses. (As you can imagine, much of it

Canned food changed what people ate.

melted, and one year in Apalachicola, Florida, the price rose to $1.25 per pound—about $50 in today's dollars.)

John Gorrie, a doctor trying to solve the problem of malaria, which was rampant in Florida at the time, discovered that the disease occurred more frequently in hot, humid weather. He felt he could reduce its incidence if he could lower the temperature of his hospital wards. At first he did this by blowing fans over blocks of ice, but when an ice shortage pushed the price to high levels, he decided there must be a better way. He was aware of some recent discoveries in chemistry—specifically, that compressed gases, when expanding rapidly, will absorb heat from their surroundings. He constructed a steam engine that would compress air (a gas) in a cylinder. As the piston withdrew, it would allow the air to escape and expand into another cylinder. Gorrie put a brine solution around this cylinder and found that it would get cold because the air inside the cylinder was cold. By pumping this cold air into his hospital wards, he invented the first air conditioner.

Gorrie also discovered that by placing water around the brine solution, he could draw heat from the water to such an extent that the water turned to ice. Gorrie realized the enormous possibilities of the ice-making machine and tried to market it but could not find any financial backing; he died a poor and broken man. For the next twenty years, people tried to perfect the invention, but with only moderate success. By the early 1900s, however, the process was sufficiently developed, and refrigerators became a commercial reality.

The social effects of refrigerators were also enormous. People could buy larger quantities of food at lower prices. They no longer had to make as many trips to the store, which meant that neighborhoods provided fewer social and commercial contacts. Eventually, refrigerators played an important role in destroying the basis for neighborhood stores and replacing them with the modern supermarket and modern advertising, both of which created profound changes in urban, suburban, and rural society. Changes in refrigeration technology are ongoing. Thermal acoustic methods of cooling—in which sound waves are used to do the cooling—and magnetic field cooling are being explored as more efficient and less harmful methods of achieving refrigeration.

We recount these stories of the development of the food canning process and of refrigerators not because these inventions are unique—we could have chosen numerous other examples—but because seeing a particular instance gives us a better sense of the tremendous and far-reaching influence that even seemingly minor technological developments can have on society.

The Industrial Revolution

The **Industrial Revolution** is the name given to the sum of all the changes in economic and social organization characterized by the replacement of hand tools with power-driven machines and by the concentration of industry in large establishments. It had its beginnings in Britain around 1760. There, for the first time, people began to employ power machines for industrial production and to build factories to house them. By 1800, this movement had made substantial progress.

The British Industrial Revolution was brought about by an accumulation of inventions. A new invention in one industry was followed by improvements and inventions in related industries. This is well illustrated by the textile inventions of the eighteenth century. These inventions were first employed in the cotton goods industry, which was relatively small and new, and the machinery was operated by water power. When James Watt devised a greatly improved steam engine, the revolution really took off. Machinery for producing cotton textiles was modified and applied to the production of woollen cloth, the output of which expanded by leaps and bounds. Costs and prices were so reduced that a great new demand developed for both wool and cotton products.

The interior of a nineteenth-century cotton factory.

The developments just described gave Britain an advantage over its competitors. Because Britain was able to mechanize its industries so much sooner than other countries, it was for many years the workshop of the world. Its production, trade, and wealth rose to what was then regarded as high levels. But in time industrialism began to spread to other nations.

The Development of Industrialism in the United States

In the early nineteenth century, the machine industry and factory system began to develop in the United States. The Napoleonic Wars (1803–1815) and the War of 1812 gave U.S. industrialization a strong push because they made it difficult for the United States to import British textiles. To make up for the resulting shortage, many new textile factories were established in this country. Employers had to pay higher wages than their counterparts in the British factories, but as long as British textiles were not available, they could operate profitably. When peace came to Europe and normal trade was reestablished, many of these new factories were forced to close down. Others, however, survived, and from that time on the United States gradually became more and more industrialized.

In some respects, conditions in the United States favored industrialization. First, our domestic market was rapidly growing. Second, raw materials were plentiful. Third, labor was relatively scarce and wages were higher than in Europe, partly because workers kept leaving their jobs to settle on free or cheap land along the frontier. Although this raised costs of production, it also put a premium on the introduction of labor-saving machines. To reduce costs, as many operations as possible were shifted to power machines. As a result, production increased much faster than the number of workers, standards of living gradually rose, and wealth began to accumulate.

Standardization, Interchangeability, and Mass Production

Early machines were crude by our standards. Because their parts did not fit together perfectly, they ran with a great deal of noise and clatter and frequently broke down. Often their products were imperfect, so that further work had to be done on them by hand to make them acceptable. One of the greater advances in industrial technology was the gradual development of precision machines that would run smoothly and that could also turn out standardized, accurately made, and hence interchangeable parts for more or less complex finished products such as watches, guns, washing machines, and automobiles. This development made it physically possible for a machine to produce thousands of units of a given part, all so nearly alike that they could be freely substituted for one another. **Standardization**—the production of uniform, substitutable parts—was made possible by a humble but far-reaching development, the improvement of measurement devices. Similar small improvements have played large roles in shaping our society, so it is worth describing this one in detail to give you a sense of the mundane aspect of technological development.

To understand the problem of standardization, think of a car. If you blow a piston, you go out and buy a new one. Getting the new piston is not cheap, but it is a lot cheaper than if you had to have a machinist make a new piston to fit your individual engine. It would probably cost twenty or thirty times as much. Extending this analogy to other areas, much of the machinery—for example, dishwashers, tractors, and photocopiers—we use today relies on **interchangeability**, the ability to substitute one part for another. Without it, there would be far fewer goods than we now have, and those that we do have would be more expensive.

So interchangeability is important; that's obvious. But if it is obvious that interchangeability has so many advantages, why weren't early machines built with interchangeable parts? The reason is a technical one: To achieve interchangeability in machines, tolerances (variations in size and shape) must be less than one-thousandth of an inch. With the tools available in the 1700s and early 1800s, even the best, most skilled machinist could not approach such tolerances, so interchangeability was only a dream until some method of achieving those tolerances could be found.

As has happened with many inventions, the strongest impetus for standardization came from the armed forces. Before and during the Civil War (1861–1865), each rifle had to be produced separately. If one broke, a skilled machinist or gunsmith was needed to repair it. These craftsmen, using a variety of tools, would fashion a musket or even a rifle. Each musket had to be built precisely; that is, all the parts, such as the stock, barrel, and lock, had to fit together and work as a coordinated whole (hence the phrase, "lock, stock, and barrel"). But precision did not mean interchangeability. A gunsmith would work the individual components until they fitted together, but as he modified each part to fit the others, he made it specific to that weapon; the part worked in no other. To repair rifles, armies had to have their own musket makers who would fix individual muskets that had broken in the field. Armies would also keep armories, where they made individual weapons, and armories were an important part of the defense capacity of any country.[1]

In about 1820, one of the skilled musket makers, John Hall, argued that this procedure was inefficient and that armies would have a tremendous advantage if their muskets had interchangeable parts. An army would only have to carry spare parts, which could easily be used to repair a broken weapon. It would not only be cheaper, but it would also be far more efficient. As we stated earlier, technological requirements for interchangeable parts were enormous because, if all parts were to be interchangeable, each musket had to fit together precisely and be identical to every other in a way that two individuals each producing an entire musket could not accomplish.

To meet the problem, Hall developed a method of precision machine production. The movement to precision machine production required a number of small but extremely important technological breakthroughs, which included measuring from a standard pattern rather than from each piece and the development of dies by which individual parts were compared and tested. With these developments, machines could reach a level of precision and consistency necessary for interchangeability, a level much higher than even the most skilled worker could achieve.

---

[1] In a later chapter we discuss the modern military-industrial complex (the interconnection between the military and business) and its implications for society. It is important to remember that the military-industrial complex is not a new phenomenon but has existed for as long as societies themselves have existed.

Rather than a machinist measuring each part, a machinist could make an initial part, or die, and then a machine employing a micrometer could produce a duplicate, using a process similar to the one hardware stores use today to duplicate keys. The machine traces the original and fashions the new part to conform. By means of this process, each part is sufficiently identical so that interchangeability is possible. There are, of course, some minute variations, but by making each part and measuring it relative to the original with a micrometer, a skilled machinist can keep the variations between the individual pieces at an acceptable level for interchangeability.

Social and Economic Effects of Interchangeability

Once interchangeability was introduced, the production process quickly changed and the pace of the Industrial Revolution quickened. In the early 1900s, Henry Ford carried through this development with the introduction of the **assembly line**, a production technique in which each worker in a factory performs a single operation on an item as it is passed along. Because of this innovation, the price of a car was lowered in the 1920s from about $1,600 to $300.

With standardization and machine production, while one machine was making one part, other machines could be making other parts, and by using an assembly line great quantities of the finished product could be turned out by merely assembling the proper parts. Thus standardization led to **mass production**, the use of standardized parts to construct great quantities of a product on an assembly line.

Naturally, it does not pay to make large amounts of a product if that product cannot be sold. But when the market is large enough, the use of standard interchangeable parts makes mass production possible and substantially reduces costs. To construct an expensive machine to make a standardized part would not pay if the machine could be used to produce only a few units of output, because the sale of these few units would have to cover the entire cost of the machine. But if mass production is possible and a machine can be employed to produce thousands or hundreds of thousands of units, the portion of the cost that must be charged to each unit becomes small or even negligible. It then pays to use a machine in place of human labor whenever one can be devised to perform a necessary operation. When standardized parts made by machines are combined into a finished product on a modern assembly line, as in the automobile industry, mass production reaches a high level of efficiency.

The effects on society of interchangeability and mass production were enormous. Individual skilled workers were no longer held in high esteem; their pay fell, their social position fell, and the skill level necessary to produce goods fell. In response, they led movements against the use of new machines. As the status of skilled workers fell, the status of the owners of machines rose. Fortunes were built by industrialists, and high society had to make room for these newly rich. Business provided a way to move up the social ladder, and as businesspeople

YOU KNOW, IF IT WASN'T FOR THE BORING
REPETITION, THIS JOB WOULD BE THE PITS!

moved up, they brought their own values and worldview. Armies and arms became less costly; war and killing increased.

As the interchangeable-parts approach to production spread, these effects were multiplied. With the development of low-priced cars, the limitations geography placed on society changed, and the nature of cities changed. Low-priced tractors increased productivity in farming, lowering food prices and forcing more and more people off the farms. None of these changes would have occurred as early as they did if Hall, or someone else, had not figured out a way to machine-tool more exactly.

The Cultural and Social Basis for Technological Progress

The historical examples discussed above provide you with some sense of the effects of technical change on culture. But culture also plays an important role in technology. So the connection is reciprocal, not unidirectional. For example, because of the extensive social changes new technological developments involve, technological developments may never come about, even though they are possible. Technological progress occurs only as long as social conditions encourage it.

Many factors might, in the long run, greatly slow our technological progress. The costs of the research and equipment necessary for developing new technologies are likely to be resisted by many corporations and also, where government is directly involved, by many taxpayers. Technological progress also tends to be slowed by organized pressure groups that have an interest in limiting the output of certain products and in opposing the introduction of new methods or products in order to maintain the demand and the prices for the things they sell. For example, labor unions often oppose the introduction of methods or materials that might reduce the jobs available to their members, and producers of building materials sometimes seek to discourage the introduction of substitutes for their products, even though these may be better and cheaper and may use materials that are more plentiful. Similarly, existing taxi drivers oppose Uber because it undermines their livelihood, and farmers demand that the government take measures to reduce farm output in order to raise farm prices and incomes. As teaching machines are developed, we can expect that existing teachers will work to see that they are not replaced.

A more subtle influence that might slow up technological change would be a less receptive attitude of society toward change. This might result not only from a lack of interest in consuming more goods but also from a feeling of indifference toward improving both the quality of goods and the quality of the environment; or it might result from a gradual dilution of the spirit of adventure and from an increasing emphasis on the potential harmful effects of change. Change often seems dangerous and disturbing. It puts some people out of jobs and forces them to seek types of employment not to their liking. It causes some business enterprises to fail, even though others may be expanding rapidly. A society that puts

The information revolution has been based on miniaturization of electronic components, allowing the compression of complex and messy connections such as seen here into a quarter inch chip.

its whole emphasis on stability and security is not likely to look with favor on major technological innovations.

The Technological Foundation of Globalization

One of the political forces that has encouraged the development of technology has been the openness to trade and globalization of the economy. The reason is that the development of technology is generally associated with specialization and increased trade; trade allows individuals and companies experiencing a technological change to become better at what they do, in a process called learning by doing. As companies learn, they can produce more products at lower cost. Additionally, trade allows companies to take advantage of economies of scale—the bigger a firm's production facilities, the lower its per-unit costs of the good. For example, making one car is extremely expensive; making many cars has a much lower per-car cost.

If a company can produce something more cheaply, it can out-compete other firms and hence make enormous profits. With those profits, it can spend more on research and development and gain even more of the market, as long as other firms cannot duplicate that technology quickly. **Globalization**—the integration of world economies—increases the speed of technological change. Globalization spreads technological change and creates strong incentives to introduce more change, since it creates a much bigger market within which a company can gain from a technological development.

Globalization has been occurring at a fast rate in recent years. It has both encouraged technological change and been spurred on by it. Technological development has allowed companies to communicate cheaply over the entire world and ship goods cheaply as well. In recent years, enormous amounts of manufacturing activity in the United States were transferred to countries such as India and China, with profound effects on their economies and culture. It has made them better off materially, but has also introduced large income inequalities and Westernization of their culture, which many people consider a loss. For the United States it has exacerbated income inequalities, lowering the pay of those whose jobs could be sent abroad, and increasing the pay for those who introduced the new technologies.

*T*echnology and Social Change Revisited

As you can see from our discussion of the Industrial Revolution, technology plays an important role in determining a society's culture. Changing technology allows enormous increases in living standards but it also creates social problems. Work in the first factories took people away from their homes all day and disrupted the established pattern of domestic life. It also forced large numbers of people to live close to their new places of work, which in turn resulted in crowded industrial towns and cities. On the other hand, there is evidence that even the early factories gave the masses more opportunities to earn and a better chance of survival. Indications of this are the fall in the death rate and the increase in the rate of population growth that have occurred over time.

The effects of technology on society are so pervasive that some social scientists claim that technology is the primary determinant of social and cultural relations. These social scientists argue that mass production and the assembly line, where each individual does one task repeatedly, developed not because they were more technically efficient, inasmuch as you can get more output from a certain amount of work, but because they established and fortified social divisions. For example, suppose two kinds of a machine can produce widgets. One requires each individual to work on a part of the widget with no one supervising; the other requires a supervisor directing individuals to perform specific tasks. Even if the first kind of machine provides a cheaper way to produce a widget, if the decision were left to the supervisor, he or she would be highly unlikely to choose the one that eliminated the supervisor's job.

Qwerty

When considering the interrelationships between technology and social institutions, it is instructive to think about the keyboard. Note that the first six letters on the top of the keyboard spell QWERTY. When you learned keyboarding, you learned to memorize the positions of these keys, and eventually you learned to type anywhere from 5 to 150 words per minute. You might wonder how the letters were given those positions, instead of being arranged some other way. They were put there on purpose by an inventor, Christopher L. Sholes.

Initially, typewriters were built with letters in serial fashion, but it was found that some people typed too fast on such a keyboard, and often the keys would lock together when pressed in succession too quickly. Sholes developed the QWERTY keyboard to minimize the occurrence of such stickiness by slowing down how fast people could type. Of course, the problem of keys sticking was relevant only for the earliest typewriters. The "golf ball" typewriters developed in the 1960s and the electronic typewriters that followed had no such problem at all, and neither do computer keyboards. Yet QWERTY, the innovation devised for a specific purpose at an earlier time, remains standard for all of these keyboards. Redesigning the keyboard would mean that teachers must retrain and experienced typists must relearn how to move their fingers, so it seems unlikely that such a change will take place.

Precisely the same set of issues is relevant to a variety of existing technologies and social institutions. Although they may have had a purpose at one time, they might be limiting now. The mere fact that they are limiting does not mean they will be changed.

QWERTY Keyboard.

Social scientists who use this line of reasoning argue that the social class structure of capitalism is inevitable with the capitalist means of production. They argue that even communist countries, which in theory attempted to avoid class divisions, nevertheless maintained the class divisions of capitalist society and they will maintain it as long as they continue to use capitalist technology and capitalist modes of production. When a technology is designed for a boss and a worker, unless these divisions are maintained, the technology cannot be effective. According to these social scientists, communism self-destructed because it did not develop its own technology. Only by developing an alternative technology, one not designed to hold workers down, can any society divest itself of class structure.

This argument is subject to much criticism, but the fact remains that capitalist technologies have inevitably led to capitalist countries developing a class system. (But so too have precapitalist and noncapitalist countries developed a class structure as well.) Concern about this effect of technology initially kept China from encouraging Western technology. Through much of Mao Zedong's Cultural Revolution of the 1960s and well into the 1970s, China attempted to purge many of those Western technologies. However, under new leadership in the late 1970s and early 1980s, China reversed its position and began the conscious introduction of Western technology into its system, with the intention of pushing economic development. The debate, however, continues, especially because the recent growth in formerly socialist societies has been marked by increasing inequality.

Technology, Income Distribution, and Jobs

A widely held belief is that new technological developments destroy jobs and create unemployment. On an individual job level that is obviously true—technology eliminates specific jobs. For example, after the introduction of the power loom in Britain in the eighteenth century, the price of cloth dropped so sharply that skilled hand weavers could no longer make a living at their trade—they lost their job. On the aggregate level, the argument is not true, or at least it has not been true in the past. The number of jobs in the US has been increasing significantly each year, roughly keeping pace with the increase in population looking for jobs. So even though technology has increased enormously, employment has also increased enormously. What this history suggests that when new technologies are introduced, new jobs in different areas are created and they replace the old jobs.

A more supportable argument about the effect of technology on jobs involves not the total number of jobs, but the distribution of jobs and the income associated with those jobs. Technology changes the distribution of jobs available to people and hence the distribution of income. For example, the Industrial Revolution lowered income of skilled craftspeople since machines could do what they did faster and cheaper. It raised the income of a large number of unskilled workers by a small, but definitely perceptible amount, and the income of a small number of entrepreneurs who introduced the new technology a lot. On average the result was that income in society was made more equal. Since it raised the standard of living of the large proportion of the population, whose work was heavy and hours long, most observers saw this redistribution as a good outcome.

But technology doesn't always make income distribution more equal. It can also make it less equal, especially within a particular country such as the United States. For example, more recently, new technologies have played an important role in increasing income inequality within the United States. By making globalization much easier, technology has channelled large amounts of income to a small number of people who were either first in developing the technology, and thus have what economist call first mover advantage, or who have acquired patents and other legal protections that prevent others from competing with them, and therefore not forcing them to lower their prices, and income, which they would have had to do if they didn't have the patents.

© DanielVilleneuve/iStock

Let's consider an extreme case to make the argument clear. Say that a new technology replaces an old technology because it is 30 percent more efficient, and that one person has a patent on that technology so no one else can use it unless they pay him to do so. Judged only by the total output that it is possible to produce society is better off. There is more output to go around. But is society better off? Say, for example, that under the old technology there was a relatively equal distribution of income and that we had social stability because of it. With the new technology controlled by the single person, the income distribution will be highly unequal. So while there is more total output, it is not spread out throughout society in the way that many would like it to be spread out. Whether we consider the new technology a gain to society depends on how much we value equality and, if we do value equality, on how easy it is for society to figure out a way to transfer money from the one person who gained to others who lost. In our current society we don't have good ways of doing that, and thus new technologies are creating social and political problems.

As we will discuss below, recent technological changes are tending to make the income distribution less equal. Given our current institutional structure, the new technology is providing enormous income for a few who are in at the ground floor of the Information Revolution and for those who are trained in information processing and have high-level jobs, while undermining the income of the modern version of skilled artisans—professionals. In doing so, it is putting pressure on the social stability of our society—a social stability built on the belief that, if you work hard, you will receive an income adequate to have a lifestyle that meets or exceeds that of your parents.

Society is responding to the income distribution and jobs problems in a variety of ways. The push for a higher minimum wage is one way. But that push, while it might temporarily help, will likely further exacerbate the problem by encouraging even more replacement of semi-skilled jobs by computers and smart technology. Another way society is responding is by the government providing more and more support for lower- and middle-class workers in the form of subsidies and programs that provide them with income. Social security, food stamps, Medicare, and subsidized medical care insurance are examples. But that government support has problems as well. One of the pleasures of being human is doing things on one's own, solving problems. Living off a dole from parents, or the government, doesn't provide those pleasures, and inevitably results in whoever is doing the funding to also want to control. Moreover, those government programs require increasing taxes significantly—something society has not been willing to do.

A more fundamental way of dealing with the unequal income distribution caused by technological change would involve providing less legal support for the intellectual property rights such as patents, trademarks, and copyrights. These rights prevent others without those rights from competing with those who managed to get into the market first. Eliminating, or at least reducing the length of patents and copyrights, would create more competition and lower prices, spreading the benefits of gains from new technologies to a wider group of people.

Opponents of this idea rightly point out that such changes might slow the pace of change. Supporters argue that it would only slightly slow that pace, and that spreading the benefits more widely would help avoid major social conflict. They argue that the goal of social policy should not be to produce as much "stuff" as possible. The goal is to design an institutional system in which the greatest number of individuals can have the most fulfilling and meaningful lives, so that at the end of people's lives they can look back and say, that was a life well lived. Achieving such a fulfilling life often includes overcoming adversity on our own, which means that if the adversity is removed, one has to add it back in some other way. Debates about these issues are ongoing, and can be expected to continue into the coming decades.

Natural Resources, Economics, and Technology

Another effect of technological change is on the ecosystem, and one of the debates that often surfaces among social scientists concerns whether there are sufficient resources for society to continue to grow, and whether we will someday reach a limit to growth. It is relevant to our discussion here because technology provides a necessary link between resources and the economy. To see this link, we need to consider the nature of economic activities, natural resources, and technology.

Economic activities are those activities concerned with making a living, and they necessarily play a major role in every culture. Their character is largely determined by three factors. First, all human beings have wants for many kinds of scarce goods. **Scarce goods** are goods that exist in limited quantities and that we can obtain only if we produce them or if we offer something valuable in exchange for them. The desire to satisfy specific wants is the motive behind much economic activity. Society's ability to meet those wants depends on what

*B*ottom Up Manufacturing and Nanotechnology

Standard manufacturing requires finding and processing raw materials and then manufacturing those raw materials into products we want. For example, we mine iron ore, process it into steel through chemical processes, and then, using the steel ingots we produce, we manufacture the parts we use for building cars and automobiles. The process is one of discovering and mining raw materials and then changing them into a form that we find useful. Scientists are now working on a different bottom-up manufacturing process, one in which we build up what we want from the basic building blocks of matter, which can even be at the atomic level. The bottom-up manufacturing process is called nanomanufacturing and it operates in a similar fashion to biomanufacturing. Both use a process of atomic and/or genetic and molecular self-assembly of parts where the parts self-assemble into the desired product.

The foundation of nanomanufacturing is *nanotechnology*. (A nanometer is one billionth of a meter.) If we can master nanotechnology, all manufacturing will be fundamentally changed. With nanotechnology if one wants a bike, one will simply direct the atoms to form themselves so that they grow into a bike. No mining of raw materials, or manufacturing from those processed raw materials. The process is done much more simply using atomic building blocks.

Similar bottom-up processes can work with living things, and the parallel to nanomanufacturing is biomanufacturing, which involves manipulating genetic material at the molecular level. If these predictions about biomanufacturing are correct, we will no longer have to raise animals, and kill and slaughter them if we want meat. We will simply grow the meat we want—if we want a chicken breast, we direct the genes to create molecules that grow into a chicken breast, preferably without the feathers. If we want a steak, we simply get a steak genome, put it in the genome processor and out comes a marbled rib eye. Needless to say, these are currently highly fanciful ideas, and a lot of work is still needed before any of this becomes reality, but the changes are possible, and if they take place, humans can have a much smaller footprint on nature than we currently have.

In the near-term future, baby steps toward this new bottom-up technology can be seen in **personal fabrication technology**—technology that allows you to "print" an object that you design. Like the current two-dimensional printers on which you can print what you type, the new three-dimensional printers allow you to design an object and then "print" it. These 3D printers (called "fabbers") are available on the Internet now—the cheapest we found was $1,500, but, like regular computer printers, their costs will likely fall significantly in the future, just as what they can "print" will likely expand. For example, MIT technology researchers are exploring how to print using proteins; they hope that someday this technology may be available to print a new arm or leg for you, should you lose one.

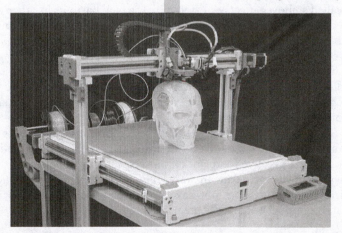

A 3D printer.

resources are available. Economic goods such as food, clothing, housing, and weapons cannot be created out of nothing. Given current technologies, if people are to have goods, they must find the raw materials to produce them in nature—natural resources—and then process those raw materials.

What, and how many, raw materials are needed to satisfy wants depends on technology. In fact, the concept, natural resources, has meaning only in reference to technology. As technology changes, what we consider valuable natural resources changes. For example, before we knew how to process oil and use it for generating power, oil was seen as black gooey stuff that made land unusable. Once we could refine it, it became a valuable natural resource. Alternatively, if a technology develops that can turn sand into a steel-like substance cheaply, then there will be an almost unlimited amount of building material. Other previously valuable building materials will lose much of their value. One technological change that is currently in its infancy has the potential to fundamentally change what we consider to be a natural resource. That technology is nanotechnology. **Nanotechnology**—technologies that manipulate matter on the atomic level—allows us to create products directly from atoms. Using nanotechnology we don't have to transform already formed natural raw materials to create the products and goods we want. We can create them directly from atoms with a minimal ecological footprint.

Natural Resources, Technology, and Climate Change

Concern about future availability of resources reached a high point in the 1970s as some ecologists argued that we were headed for doom. Their argument was twofold: Either we were going to run out of natural resources, or the pollution resulting from production was going to destroy us.

Most economists believed that much of the ecological concern at that time was overdone. The basis of this view is that technology changes, and as it does what we consider "natural resources" change. The fear that we were running out of oil that was rampant in the 1970s has been replaced with a fear that we have too much oil. One reason for the change of view is that the natural forces of supply and demand tend to ameliorate the problems of shortage. As a resource becomes scarcer, its price rises. Because of that price increase, we use less of it and individuals devote more resources to designing new technologies to achieve the same result without using that resource. Thus, in response to higher prices for oil, cars became more fuel efficient, and new sources of oil were developed.

Today, the concern about oil is not that we are running out of it but that its use has what are called spillover effects or externalities, which harm us in other ways. For example, one of the ecological effects of the heavy use of oil to generate power is **climate change**—the effect on earth's climate (such as global warming) caused by human activities such as the burning of oil and other fossil fuels. Scientists have determined that climate change is taking place and that the average surface temperature of the earth is higher than it was a hundred years ago. They predict it will continue to rise at a fast rate. That rise in temperature will likely have significant effects on society, making formerly habitable areas uninhabitable, and changing the weather for other parts of the world.

Some social scientists argue that the spillover effects of using oil and other fossil fuels means that we should move back to a simpler, less technologically advanced society, so that we have less of a negative footprint on our ecosystem. Others argue that it is advances in technology that will provide our answers to climate change. What direction our society chooses is a social question that does not have a right or wrong answer; social science highlights the questions; it does not answer them.

The Anthropocene Age

Geologists divide the earth's formation into "ages" or epochs. For example, the Holocene Age generally begins with the end of the Ice Age and comprises the last 12,000 years or so. Recently, however, a number of geologists have been calling for the creation of a new age—the **Anthropocene Age** (the age of man). They argue that this Anthropocene Age category, which begins with the Industrial Revolution, is needed to reflect the significant feedback of humans' actions on the geology of the world.

Others argue that such feedback has always been important and that if one is to use the term *Anthropocene*, one should extend it back more than 12,000 years, making the term *Anthropocene* synonymous with *Holocene,* which in Greek means "entirely recent." In our view, the terms themselves are not important, but the debate about them is. It reflects the debate among scientists about how much importance should be given to humans' influence on the environment.

Technology and Social Change in the Future

Technology is continually surprising us but that doesn't stop social scientists from trying to find broad trends and to relate those trends to the future. In this last part of the chapter, that is what we attempt to do. The biggest change in technology's effect on society involves the nature of the changing technology. Instead of technological changes that replace physical activities, the upcoming changes in technology are replacing mental activities.

The Industrial Revolution fundamentally changed physical labor. It replaced much of the physical labor done by humans with machine labor. Instead of plowing the land with a hand plow, one plowed it with the tractor. Labor power based on strength became less important; it was replaced by skill-based labor power. That led us to think of technology in terms of physical labor and output. But technology affects more than just physical labor and the latest developments in technology are having their greatest effects on what might be called mental labor.

The One-Second Essay Writer

Technology is central to social science because it changes the value of various types of skills, and thereby changes the power structure in society. For example, before the Industrial Revolution, being physically strong was an extremely useful characteristic. Physically strong people gained relative power and physically weaker people lost relative power. The Industrial Revolution has, over centuries, decreased the value of physical strength. Machines designed by mentally strong people, which could do replicable physical work faster, kept developing and reducing the need for physical strength. Mentally strong people gained relative power, and physically strong people lost power. (There was still a need for some physically strong people, and the superstrong (professional athletes) were in high demand for entertainment.)

The Information Revolution is now doing to mentally strong people what the Industrial Revolution did to physically strong people. Replicable mental work is increasingly being done more quickly, cheaply, and easily, by computers. For example, many small newspapers are now having computers write some of their articles about local sports activity. Someone at the game fills in a questionnaire with information about what happened, and then the computer writes the article. Similarly, the Associated Press is moving toward computer-written stories in finance. See http://www.the verge.com/2015/1/29/7939067/ap-journalism-automation-robots-financial-reporting.

Computers are also doing more of the grading for teachers, even when the test being graded is an essay test. Today, computers can almost instantaneously grade papers on technical structure—i.e. seeing that papers avoid grammatical and spelling mistakes, and use appropriate sentence structure and vocabulary. They can assign a grade to papers thousands of times faster than humans. Moreover, since solid content often correlates well with technical proficiency, the grades are close to what humans give them.

What computers cannot yet do is judge content directly. A paper might be technically well written, but might say nothing. (I suspect you know when you have written such a paper.) To show the problem with online grading of essays, an MIT professor developed a computer program that would write an essay about anything. He called it the "one-second essay writer." You put in a few key words and it writes an essay on the subject. This essay writer was able to get top grades for essays it wrote for an online grading system. (You can see a story about it at http://www.marketplace.org/topics/tech/education/computer-program-write-your-essays.) The problem was that the content of the essays was essentially garbage—the essays had some big words thrown together that sounded impressive, but were meaningless. In a future edition, I suspect that the computer will be writing much of this book. For me, that's scary.

The Information Revolution

The technological changes go under the name the **Information Revolution**—the replacement of human processing of information with computer processing of information.

More and more mental activities can be done more quickly, efficiently, and precisely by computers. Some such activities you are familiar with. Math and word processing are done much more effectively by computers. Similarly, driving will soon be done more effectively by computers than by humans, and instead of driving where you want to go, you will be driven by a smart car—which drives itself. Writing a paper for a class will soon be done by computers, and possibly even writing a textbook. Just click on the paper writing app, or the social science textbook writing app. As you can see in the accompanying box, we are not there yet. But with new developments in artificial intelligence and deep learning, we need to start to think of computers as being creative and intelligent. That has profound implications for society and out culture.

The process that underlies many of these developments is how computers are configured. Initially they were designed to provide specific answers and deal with well-defined questions. They can calculate prime numbers much better than we can. They couldn't deal with imperfect data and could not be imaginative. The new computers are designed more like our brains are designed, as a neural net, which are meant to deal with ambiguous questions and integrate imagination into the reasoning process. They find patterns in the data and draw implications from those patterns. That's what we call intelligence and is why we describe the new computers as exhibiting *artificial intelligence*, although it would better be called nonhuman intelligence. Because they can precisely process much more information than can our brains, these computer neural networks can find patterns that we cannot find—that's what we call *deep learning*, and thus can out-do humans in dealing with not only precise information, but also with ambiguous information using what we used to call human intuition, but which is probably better called human deep learning. It's a brave new world out there.

It was these developments in deep learning and artificial intelligence that led me to begin the chapter with the discussion of a computer beating a human in Go. That story was meant to convey the point that as computers learn to do what humans have traditionally done, humans are becoming obsolete and are being replaced by algorithms.

The implications for society of this Information Revolution are huge. The nature of all types of professional jobs will change—reducing the demand for general purpose thinking, and increasing the demand for niche technicians who assist a computer based algorithmic process. Professional jobs, such as teacher, doctor, or lawyer, which were previously seen as playing an important role in society, and were therefore pleasing to many, will lose much of their fulfilling nature. Life fulfilment will have to come from something else.

For example, consider a doctor, whose job is to meet with a patient, make a diagnosis, and prescribe a treatment, perhaps to take a medicine, or to have a certain type of operation. Now let's see the future. The patient opens an app which does an initial diagnosis and advises him or her whether to go to a diagnostic clinic for a body scan. Using the information from the app and the scan, together with your complete medical history of the patient, which it accessed on the internet, a computer algorithm provides a diagnosis: you have the flu, and should (or should not), take an antiviral. No doctor needed. There might be a technician there to reassure you that the diagnosis makes sense, and to comfort you, but he too might be replaced by a comfort robot, who cuddles up to you, telling you it's ok; you'll feel better in a couple of days, and advises you to have some chicken soup. It could, of course, be something more serious; say you need an operation. The computer algorithm will schedule one, and that too would be done by a robot guided by an algorithm.

These changes are not happening immediately. The algorithmic component of the Information Revolution will take decades, even centuries to implement. The evolution will likely go something like this. There will be an increasing number of Specific Job Algorithms (SJA's) designed to replace humans in just specific facets of production. These algorithms will likely be designated by names. For example, General Physicians will be replaced by Algorithm

*T*imeline: The Future

2025	Breakthrough in medicine; method delays aging process and extends average life expectancy by ten years (world population increases; causes Social Security programs to fail).
2030	Developments with buckyballs redefine matter; diamonds and metals no longer scarce.
2035	Fusion reactor created that makes energy "too cheap to meter"; oil companies go broke; gas stations are eliminated.
2040	Genetic engineering means fabricated human replacement organs roll off assembly line. Amputated limbs can be regrown.
2045	Human cloning perfected; all parts of body can now regenerate themselves.
2050	Computer chips developed to place in the human head; eliminates the need for teaching.

2110	Temperature rise on earth means snow and ice at the poles melt and oceans flood all low-lying areas. Miami is no more.
2160	Various complicated life forms reproduced from organic chemicals create significant debate about morality and the meaning of life.
2190	Major viral outbreak from genetic engineering experiment; half the world population dies.
2210	Instant transportation created; old-fashioned means of transportation—cars, legs, and so forth—no longer needed.
2240	Human body shapes modified to eliminate useless appendages.
2270	Life forms discovered in different galaxies now reachable with instant transportation.
2280	The starship *Enterprise* returns safely to home base.

Doc-1; Surgeons by Algorithm Doc-97 and Life Coaches specializing in males 35–40 by Algorithm-LC-M35-40. Simultaneously, general-purpose algorithms will be created that can do multiple types of jobs—overall planning and supervision—and they will control and coordinate the specific algorithms. Individuals will assist the apps handling small issues for which it hasn't yet been worth designing an app.

Don't Hold your Breath Expecting Immediate Change

Once we've developed all these, the question is what role will there be for humans—won't all jobs disappear? As we discussed above, that is unlikely to be the case. Based on past experience, there will be jobs for everyone. The question is: Will the jobs be good jobs at pay levels that people, and society as a whole, are willing to accept? That is far from clear. The Information Revolution is creating a small number of very highly paid mental jobs, and a large number of relatively low-paid and not especially intellectually fulfilling, mental jobs.

So the deeper problem facing society is not economic, but rather psychological and spiritual. The sense of need and fulfilment that comes from feeling needed—doing something that one senses is worthwhile and helpful—will be slipping away from many of us. It is such feelings that generate interest in religion that ask the bigger questions of life: What is its purpose, and why are we here? So while many see technology as anti-religious, modern developments in technology may well be pushing people toward religious reflection.

*C*onclusion: Speculating About the Future

In considering the effects of technology on the future, you will quickly see that predicting the future is one of the most difficult but enjoyable activities of social science; it allows the imagination to roam. Will spaceships like the *Enterprise* develop out of our exploration of space efforts? Will we find new technologies that totally change our lives, such as instant transportation or intelligence transfers? The possibilities are endless and not always pleasant for specific individuals. The point of this speculation is to bring home to you the fact that life in 2050 will be significantly different from life in 2020, and that social institutions will have to change to fit the technology.

The technology of the future will probably involve changes that are much more imaginative than those we have just speculated on. Some imaginative technological changes and their potential effects are listed in the Timeline: the Future box. Each of these ideas is fanciful, but each has been advanced by futurists at one time or another. They are placed here, not because we expect them to materialize, but to make us reflect and think about their implications for society and culture. Each would have social, economic, and cultural consequences that in turn would affect society's ability to use that technology to its advantage and not to its detriment. Seeing that society uses technology for good rather than evil is what social science is all about.

 Study and **Review**

Key Points

- Technology comprises the tools, means, and methods through which we interact with our environment.
- Technology influences culture, and culture influences technology.
- The Industrial Revolution significantly changed all aspects of society through its introduction of interchangeability and mass production of material products.

- Technology does not decrease the total number of jobs, but it changes the composition and relative pay of the jobs provided.
- As technology changes, what we consider a natural resource changes.
- The Information Revolution is doing to mental work what the Industrial Revolution did to physical work.
- Potential technological developments in the future are limited only by the imagination.

Some Important Terms

artificial intelligence (105)
Anthropocene Age (116)
assembly line (109)
climate change (116)
deep learning (105)
economic activities (114)

globalization (111)
Industrial Revolution (106)
Information Revolution (117)
interchangeability (108)
mass production (109)
nanotechnology (115)

personal fabrication
   technology (115)
scarce goods (114)
Standardization (108)
technology (104)

Questions for Review and Discussion

General Questions

1. Why was AlphaGo's win over a top human Go player so important an event?
2. Name some technological change that took place in the past and explain how you think it has changed conditions ever since.
3. What was the Industrial Revolution? What are some of the reasons it was successful in the United States?
4. Why are standardization and interchangeability so important to mass production?
5. When it became possible for machines to make products formerly made by hand, what effects did this have on the number of people employed?

On the level of wages? On the profit of employers? On the quality of the products?
6. Explain how the technology of the assembly line led to other technological and cultural changes.
7. Does technological change reduce the number of jobs in society?
8. Does reducing the length of patents make sense as a policy?
9. In what way do natural resources only have meaning in relation to technology?
10. Does the argument that the world is going to run out of natural resources make sense?
11. What is meant by the Anthropocene Age?

12. How does the Information Revolution differ from the Industrial Revolution?

13. Are there any technological changes you think should not be made? What are they? If you oppose a particular technological change, what alternative solution do you have for the problem that change was meant to address?

14. Try your hand at predicting a technological change that may occur in the future. What effects on society might that change produce?

Internet Questions

1. Using the website http://www.eyewitnesstohistory.com/brooklynbridge.htm and learn about the technical problems faced in constructing the Brooklyn Bridge. How did the builders overcome these difficulties?

2. Go to http://www.usbr.gov/projects and look up the Hoover Dam. How large is the structure? Where is it located and when was it built?

3. Go to http://www.npr.org/templates/story/story.php?storyId=19174580 and either read the article or listen to it. Who makes Blu-ray discs? What new technology may make Blu-ray discs obsolete? What earlier formatting war is mentioned in the article, and which brand came out on top then?

4. Go to https://www.livescience.com/18801-greatest-inventions.html and take the quiz. How do you score?

5. Go to https://www.weforum.org/agenda/2015/07/countries-emitting-most-greenhouse-gas/. What are some of the consequences of climate change?

*F*or Further Study

Books to Explore

Brown, David E., ed., *Inventing Modern America: From the Microwave to the Mouse*, Cambridge, MA: MIT Press, 2002.

Brynjolfsson, Erik, and Andrew McAfee, *The Second Machine Age*, New York: Norton, 2015.

Carr, Nicholas, *The Glass Cage: How Our Computers Are Changing Us*, New York: W. W. Norton & Company, 2015.

Essinger, James, *Jacquard's Web: How a Hand Loom Led to the Birth of the Information Age*, Oxford: Oxford University Press, 2004.

Freeman, Joshua, *Behemoth: A History of the Factory and the Making of the Modern World*, New York: W. W. Norton, 2018.

Husain, Amir, *The Sentiment Machine: The Coming Age of Artificial Intelligence*, New York, Simon and Schuster, 2017.

Kotler, Steven, *Tomorrowland: Our Journey from Science Fiction to Science Fact*, Seattle, WA: Amazon Publishing, 2015.

Mead, Margaret, ed., *Cultural Patterns and Technical Change*, New York: New American Library/Mentor, 1956.

Millett, David, *Anthropocene: The Age of Man*, CreateSpace Independent Publishing, 2015.

Ridley, Matt, *The Evolution of Everything: How New Ideas Emerge*, New York: Harper, 2015.

Schwab, Klaus, *The Fourth Industrial Revolution*, New York: Penguin Random House, 2016.

Shreeve, James, *The Genome War: How Craig Ventner Tried to Capture the Code of Life and Save the World*, New York: Knopf, 2004.

Toffler, Alvin, *Future Shock*, New York: Bantam, 1971.

Turkle, Sherry, *Alone Together: Why We Expect More from Technology and Less from Each Other*, New York: Basic Books, 2011.

Warschauer, Mark, *Technology and Social Inclusion: Rethinking the Digital Divide*, Cambridge, MA: MIT Press, 2003.

Weinersmith, Kelly and Zach Weinersmith. *Soonish: Ten Emerging Technologies That'll Improve and/or Ruin Everything*. New York: Penguin Random House, 2017.

Internet Sites to Explore

"http://www.asci.org" Arts and Science Collaborations, Inc.

"http://www.cdt.org" The Center for Democracy and Technology.

"http://www.epa.gov/climatechange/" EPA, Climate Change.

"http://www.nist.gov/index.html" National Institute of Science and Technology.

"http://www.avs.org/" Science and Technology.

"http://www.sierraclub.org/" Sierra Club.

"http://www.npr.org/sections/money/2015/05/20/406484294/an-npr-reporter-raced-a-machine-to-write-a-news-story-who-won" NPR, An NPR Reporter Raced A Machine To Write A News Story. Who Won?

"https://waitbutwhy.com/2017/04/neuralink.html" Wait But Why, Neuralink and the Brain's Magical Future.

"https://stateimpact.npr.org/florida/2014/03/25/why-computer-scored-essays-could-eliminate-the-need-for-writing-tests/" StateImpact, Why Computer-Scored Essays Could Eliminate The Need For Writing Tests.

"http://www.ted.com/talks/matt_ridley_when_ideas_have_sex?language=en" TED, When Ideas Have Sex.

"http://wptt.org/" World Peace Through Technology

Psychology, Society, and Culture

chapter 7

After reading this chapter, you should be able to:

- Explain how culture and personality are related
- Summarize the nature/nurture debate
- State the importance of positive and negative reinforcement
- Discuss Maslow's hierarchy
- Differentiate the id, ego, and superego
- Explain how IQ is calculated and the problems with its use
- Define *deviance* and name five sociological theories about deviance

If I am not for myself,
who will be?
And if I am only for myself,
who am I?
And if not now, when?

—Rabbi Hillel

Culture is created by the individuals within that culture, but individuals' personalities are shaped and molded by culture. In this chapter, we take a social psychology perspective and consider the relationship between the individual and society. Much of our discussion will center on personality. **Personality** is the total organization of the inherited and acquired characteristics of an individual as evidenced by the individual's behavior. Culture's role in shaping individual personality is major, whereas each individual's influence on culture is usually slight. As individuals, people must accept their culture much as they find it, and if they hope to lead satisfactory lives as human beings, they must adjust to it.

This dependence of the individual on culture sometimes makes culture appear to be an independent entity, something that has an existence and continuity regardless of the people who are its carriers. This impression is strengthened when we view culture historically and note that many of its basic elements persist generation after generation. Two hundred years ago, the English language in its essential characteristics was not very different from what it is today. Yet, of all those who spoke English then, not a single person is now alive.

For some purposes, it is convenient to think of culture as if it had an independent, objective existence. In the final analysis, however, this is untrue. All cultures have been created by people. When we analyze culture closely, we find only a series of patterned reactions characteristic of the individuals who belong to a given group. It is people who hold beliefs, have attitudes, practice customs, and behave in conformity with patterns accepted by the group. Cultures are built up so slowly and gradually that it is seldom possible to isolate the contributions made by particular individuals. In a large society, the individual is only one among millions. Furthermore, most individuals accept the social situation in which they find themselves and make little attempt to change it.

The fact that people as individuals are shaped by their culture does not mean that they are deprived of all freedom to control their behavior, to choose their mode of life, or even to affect the conditions that surround them. Any general cultural pattern is flexible to a degree and permits some variations from the norms. In simple primitive societies, the permissible variations may be rather limited, but in modern complex societies they are great. However, in any society the average individual is seldom aware of the extent to which culture restricts freedom. Culture becomes so internalized—so much a basic part of personality—that most of the time people do not wish to behave in ways other than those culturally approved. Only in special situations do they become keenly aware of conflicts between their own desires and the kind of conduct that is socially permissible.

Socialization of the Individual

Socialization plays a major role in the development of human personality. This does not mean that a child's personality may not be greatly influenced by its biological inheritance and by contacts with the physical environment. For the most part, however, a child learns from people the patterns of behavior and the attitudes, beliefs, and expectations that motivate behavior. All of these are largely cultural in origin, and, therefore, as a child grows and develops, his or her behavior reflects to an ever-greater degree the culture of the society into which he or she was born.

Significance of the Early Years of Childhood

The experiences of the young child within the family group seem to have the greatest influence on the development of human personality. Very early a normal baby begins to recognize familiar faces, sense approval and disapproval, seek attention, and in other ways react to the social environment.

Our personalities develop in this early childhood. Although tremendous gaps exist in our knowledge, we have discovered some of the ways in which children learn. One of the leaders in this discovery was noted psychologist Jean Piaget who developed several widely accepted theories on the development of children. His first point is obvious: Very young children think differently from adults. For example, many children think their shadow is a living entity that follows them wherever they go. Similarly, imaginary friends fly around the room at night, and inanimate objects, from marbles to vacuum cleaners, have very human characteristics. Reality for them blends in with imagination. As we grow older, most of us learn to separate reality from imagination. If, however, an individual lacks the right environment, he or she will not be able to do so and may go through an entire lifetime living in a semifantasy world.

Piaget finds it useful to divide a child's life into four stages (shown in Figure 7.1). From birth to two years, a child is primarily concerned with learning about physical objects. From two to six or seven years, the youngster learns about symbols in language, dreams, and fantasy. Next, he or she begins to learn about abstract concepts such as numbers and the relationships between them. Finally, from ages twelve to fifteen, the child masters purely logical thought and learns to understand nuanced messages, such as irony and double entendres.

In order to develop normally both emotionally and mentally, a child must be accepted and receive affection, but overprotection and overaffection are not desirable, for they tend to lead to dependency and immaturity. At the other extreme, parental

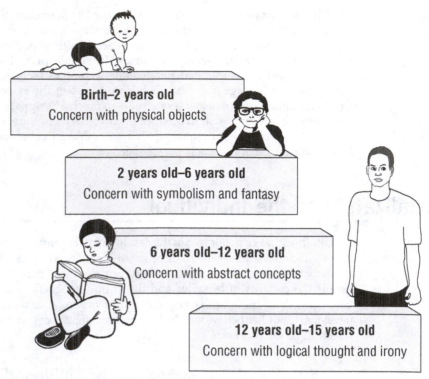

Birth–2 years old
Concern with physical objects

2 years old–6 years old
Concern with symbolism and fantasy

6 years old–12 years old
Concern with abstract concepts

12 years old–15 years old
Concern with logical thought and irony

Figure 7.1

Piaget's four stages.

rejection and lack of affection create feelings of insecurity and inferiority and often bring on compensatory reactions such as aggressive, rebellious, or domineering behavior.

As young children grow, they come into contact not only with parents, brothers and sisters, and other members of the household, but also with outsiders such as neighbors and playmates. They acquire greater physical competence and greater skill in the use of language and continually make adjustments to new people and new situations. These early experiences leave nearly indelible impressions and influence the "set" of each one's personality.

Significance of Differences in Individual Environment

It is questionable whether any two individuals have precisely the same hereditary characteristics, though in the case of identical twins there is a close approximation to this situation. Certainly, no two individuals have exactly the same social environment. Some of the differences in individual environments are obvious to the most casual observer, but other differences are not so easy to see.

We are all aware that in a country such as the United States people often grow up in social environments that differ widely. To begin with, there are noticeable differences in the language, attitudes, and customs of the people in different regions. Also, even in the same region there are differences between rural life and city life; and in a city of even moderate size there can be found a great variety of more or less distinct social groups. Among the more important of these groups are those set off from one another by differences in income, social prestige, religion, nationality, or race. But differences in individual social environment go further than this. In any given social group, families are likely to differ significantly from one another in their modes of life, so that a child brought up in one family may have a quite different environment from that of a child reared in another.

All these differences are fairly obvious. It is not quite so obvious, but nonetheless true, that two children brought up in the same family at the same time may have quite dissimilar environments. This is because social environment depends not only on people, but also on the nature of personal relations with them. One child in a family may be loved by the parents, given every advantage, perhaps be overindulged, whereas another child may be disliked, neglected, even mistreated. Clearly, such children do not have at all the same environment, and the differences are likely to have deep and lasting effects on their mental and emotional development, on their personalities, and on their relations with other people in later years.

Effects of Extreme Isolation on Children

The study of children who have been largely isolated from social contacts demonstrates the importance of socialization by showing what happens in its absence. It also considers the possibility of compensating in later years for development that failed to take place earlier at the normal time.

It is impossible to find children who have been completely isolated from other human beings from the time of birth. The reason is simple. The human infant is so helpless that it cannot possibly survive without receiving some care from older people who understand its needs. However, cases have been reported of children who, in early life, have been partially or completely isolated from human contact over considerable periods. These reports are of two types: (1) cases of **feral children**—children who have lived in a wild or untamed state with animals—and (2) cases of children kept isolated in a room, basement, or attic and given little attention except for being provided with food and drink. (Less extreme examples of isolation occur with children who are merely neglected, or who are cared for, more or less impersonally, in institutions.)

Stories of feral children appeal to the imagination. They are stories that have been told in all ages about children believed to have been cared for when very young by boars, wolves, bears, or other animals. These stories have nearly always been spread by hearsay, and it is doubtful whether any of them are based on fact. Perhaps the oldest of such tales is about the legendary founders of Rome, the twins Romulus and Remus, who are said to have been abandoned as infants and suckled by a wolf. As you might have noticed, our history of the world skipped these legendary twins.

The one report that has some credibility is of two children found in a wolf den in India. They could not talk, and they are reported to have run on all fours and in other respects to have exhibited animal-like behavior. Under human care, they responded very little to the attempts

According to legend, the founders of Rome were human twins, Romulus and Remus, who were nurtured by a wolf.

made to socialize and educate them, and both died at an early age. Most psychologists believe that they most likely suffered from **infantile autism,** a condition in which a child is unable to respond emotionally to others. Most psychologists believe these children, not very long before they were found, had been abandoned because they were autistic.

Though stories of feral children should be regarded with skepticism, there appear to be well-authenticated cases of children who for considerable periods of time have been locked in basements, attics, or upstairs rooms and isolated from almost all normal human contacts. One case involved a girl named Isabelle, who, because she was illegitimate, was kept secluded in a dark room with her deaf-mute mother until she was six and a half years old. In another case, a girl named Anna was kept in a room alone until she was about six.

In each of these cases, when the girl was discovered, her behavior in many respects resembled that of an infant or a wild animal. But Isabelle, when placed in a normal social environment and given special training, caught up rapidly. In a few years, she was making good progress in school and gave the impression of a bright, cheerful, energetic little girl. However, when Anna was placed in a normal environment, she made much less progress, and she was still considered mentally disabled when she died at the age of ten and a half.

We have no way of knowing why Anna failed to develop as much as Isabelle. Perhaps Isabelle's close contact with her deaf-mute mother gave her a sense of being loved and secure, and thus she enjoyed a great advantage over Anna in her emotional development, or it may be that she received more expert attention after she was removed from isolation. It is also possible that Isabelle's biological inheritance was superior to Anna's.

In 1970, a thirteen-year-old girl, who was given the name Genie, was found. She had been tied up and kept in a room without human contact by her elderly parents, who were psychologically disturbed. She had been fed only milk and baby food and was never spoken to. She was incontinent, could not speak, and weighed only fifty-seven pounds. After she was brought to a hospital, she learned to communicate, but, although her mother said that she had been normal at birth, Genie's IQ was only seventy-four and her language ability never fully developed.

Personality and Its Development

To have a full understanding of the relationship between individuals and society, it is helpful to have a clear concept of the meaning of personality. It has been said that every human being is in some respects like all others, in some respects like some others, and in some respects like no others.

As we mentioned earlier, personality may be defined as the total organization of the inherited and acquired characteristics of an individual as evidenced by the individual's behavior. It is the product of the interaction between an individual's original biological nature and his or her social and natural environment. Therefore, it bears the imprint of four things:

1. The inherited potentialities of the individual
2. Natural environment
3. The culture of the individual's society
4. Unique personal experiences

However, once personality has begun to form, it becomes an independent force that may play a dominant part in its own future development and in the adjustment of the individual to the total environment.

The Nature/Nurture Debate

The human baby is a helpless creature at birth. It cannot walk; it cannot talk; it cannot even sit up, turn itself over, or grasp an object it is offered. It is not equipped, as are most animals, with a large number of hereditary **instincts**—inherited complex patterns of behavior that do not have to be learned. Instincts enable animals to satisfy needs that arise at various stages of their development. A good example is the nest-building instinct of birds.

Human babies at birth have instincts, but they also have an innate capacity for growth and development. Gradually, a baby learns to adjust to its environment, and in the process it slowly becomes conscious of itself as a person, separate from its environment. As it develops physically, its power to learn keeps increasing, but all the patterns of behavior that will later characterize it as a normal human being must be learned, and the learning process is not always easy.

The drives that a baby inherits are urges to satisfy basic needs such as those for sleep or food. When these are not satisfied, they are felt as tension or discomfort. These drives provide the stimulus for learning. One of the most powerful of human drives is hunger. To satisfy hunger, a baby depends on its mother's breast or a bottle. But when it becomes hungry, nourishment is not always present, and as its discomfort increases, the baby cries. This may bring the breast or the bottle and with it the pleasure that is felt as hunger is satisfied. Before long, the baby associates crying with the appearance of the nourishment, and so it cries as soon as hunger begins in order to bring the satisfaction. This illustrates the beginning of the learning process and perhaps also the beginning of the development of personality.

B. F. Skinner, a psychologist who did extensive research in this area, strongly emphasized the influence of society on the individual. He saw individuals' personalities shaped in large part by conditioning. He believed that individuals' behaviors could be changed by **operant conditioning**—altering individuals' habits by behaviors (operants) that themselves have an observable effect on the environment affecting an individual. Operant conditioning often is discussed in terms of **positive reinforcement, negative reinforcement,** and **punishment.** Procedures that strengthen behavior are called reinforcement; those that suppress behavior are called punishment. There are two types of reinforcement and two types of punishment, as outlined in Table 7.1.

It is important to note that punishment is not the same as negative reinforcement. If you speed and get a speeding ticket, you experience a positive punishment. If, however, the judge offers you the choice of attending a driver education class or losing your license, that's an example of negative reinforcement. You attend the class to avoid a worse alternative—losing your license. To summarize, positive and negative reinforcement are both procedures that strengthen behavior. Positive and negative punishment are both procedures that weaken behavior.

The effects of reinforcement and punishment on personality leave individuals with some hard choices. For example, should parents console or ignore a crying child? Consoling can

Table 7.1

Types of Punishments and Reinforcements

PROCEDURE	STIMULUS EVENT	EFFECTS	EXAMPLES
Positive reinforcement	Applying a desirable stimulus	Strengthens responses that precede occurrence of stimulus	Praise
Negative reinforcement	Loss of an undesirable stimulus	Strengthens responses that allow escape from stimulus	Getting out of jail for good behavior
Positive punishment	Applying an undesirable stimulus	Weakens responses that precede occurrence of stimulus	Speeding ticket
Negative punishment	Loss of a desirable stimulus	Weakens responses that lead to loss of stimulus	"Time-out"

© Science History Images / Alamy Stock Photo

reinforce undesirable crying behavior; on the other hand, ignoring might make the child feel unloved and have a undesirable influence on the child's development.

Skinner did extensive work with laboratory animals such as rats and rabbits to test his theories. He and his adherents have shown that animals can be taught to do things such as push on a bar to receive food or water. Such laboratory work is, on the whole, noncontroversial (except when the experiments directly harm animals). But when Skinner's theories are extended to humans and to the way humans learn, they can be controversial.

Some researchers have emphasized the influence of punishment and reinforcement so strongly that little room remains in their theories for any other determinants of personality. Moreover, they have derived from these theories a number of proposals for education and controversial rehabilitation programs. For example, Skinnerians developed programmed texts that provide fast positive reinforcement for students. Also, some sex criminals may submit themselves to a rehabilitation program in which whenever they are shown sexually arousing pictures, they experience an electric shock (positive punishment) designed to modify their behavior.

Skinner's emphasis on the environment's role in shaping personality is disputed by many psychologists who emphasize instead the role of **heredity,** the genetic transmission of characteristics from parent to offspring. The debate between the two sides has often been called the nature/nurture debate. The **nature/nurture debate** focuses on whether heredity or environment is more important in determining the personality and the success in the life of an individual. It is like asking, "Which is more important in making an automobile run— the gasoline or the engine?" Quite obviously, if the car is to run at all, both gasoline and an engine must be provided. Likewise, if a baby is to develop normally, it must have both a reasonably adequate biological inheritance and a reasonably adequate social environment.

If we could somehow take two identical individuals and place them in different environments, we could answer the question. However, no two people are physiologically identical (even identical twins have some slight differences), and no two people have the same environmental background. Instead, researchers must concentrate on groups of people to determine whether heredity or environment is more important.

There have, however, been attempts to determine the relative importance of heredity and environment. An example of the research involved people's sexual choices. Researchers have attempted to determine whether people's choices are determined by nature or nurture by studying the choices of identical twins, who have the same genetic makeup, and fraternal twins, who do not. These studies have all found that these choices stem from both nature and nurture; generally the researchers have attributed roughly one-third of the causation to genetics and two-thirds to environment. Researchers caution, however, that these results are still preliminary, and most researchers see the two as inextricably linked, with nature setting the scene for nurture. There are other studies as well. Anthony Bogaert of Brock University found that boys with older brothers had a higher probability of being gay than those without, and that the more brothers one had, the higher the probability of being gay. That was not the case for stepbrothers, however, so the reason is more likely nature than nurture. He hypothesized that it had something to do with antibodies developed by the mother of boys that affect the sexual orientation of future children.

Recently, a test of the nature/nurture question was conducted with respect to obesity. The population studied consisted of adopted children, and the question posed was: Would the children resemble their biological (nature) or their adoptive (nurture) parents? In this study, it was found that children of obese biological parents tended to be obese. The obesity of the adopted parents had little effect. In this case, nature seems more important than nurture.

Recent discussions of the nature/nurture debate have tended to emphasize the complex interaction between the two. For example, measures of the inheritability of intelligence rise with age, from 40 percent in childhood to 60 percent in adulthood. James Flynn, a psychologist in New Zealand, suggests the reason is that a slight difference in intelligence at birth leads caregivers to treat children differently, with the seemingly brighter child being more strongly reinforced in learning, while the seemingly less bright child receives negative reinforcement. As we discussed in Chapter 2, recent work in the field of **epigenetics**—the study of modification in gene functions caused by the expression of genes, not the genes themselves—allows nurture to feed back into what was previously considered nature. The bottom line: nurture and nature are so intricately interconnected that there is little hope in definitively distinguishing the two.

Explanations of Behavior

The nature/nurture debate is part of a larger debate in psychology about how best to understand behavior. We distinguish four general approaches:

1. The **cognitive approach** focuses on nature; it sees thought as the initiator and determinant of behavior. In this approach, human actions represent reactions to physical processes in the brain, and **cognitive science**—the scientific study of the mind—is looked to for explanations of behavior.

2. The **psychoanalytic approach** also focuses on nature, but it does not look to cognitive science. Rather, it takes a more mystical approach, focusing on certain innate tendencies of people. The most well-known of the psychoanalytic approaches is Freud's, which we discuss later in this chapter. Freud's approach focuses on the unconscious and its relation to conscious thoughts and actions. The psychoanalytic approach has produced a variety of therapeutic approaches besides that of Freud, one of which is Albert Ellis's "rational emotive therapy," also discussed later.

3. The **behavioralist approach** focuses on actions, not thoughts. B. F. Skinner was an advocate of this approach. The behavioralist approach has a recent addition—what might be called the biopsychological approach. Flowing from biology as much as it does from psychology, this approach views behavior simply as responses to chemical stimuli in the body (although its basis often is not put so bluntly). In this approach, one's genetic structure is believed to determine the ranges of behavior one will display; the chemical messengers determine specific behaviors within that general range. The mind is seen as just another part of the physical world.

4. The **humanist approach** emphasizes the entire person and his or her interrelationship with culture. Abraham Maslow's work, discussed later, is an example of this humanist approach.

These approaches are not mutually inconsistent, and recently a group of therapists emphasizing a combination approach—a cognitive behavioralist approach—have been gaining ground. The cognitive behavioralist approach emphasizes that thoughts can be "operants of the mind." Thus, cognitive approaches focusing on thought are opened up to behavioralist analyses focusing on behavior.

Before we move on to discuss how these different approaches lead to different treatments of maladjustment, let us briefly consider Abraham Maslow's theory of the well-adjusted individual

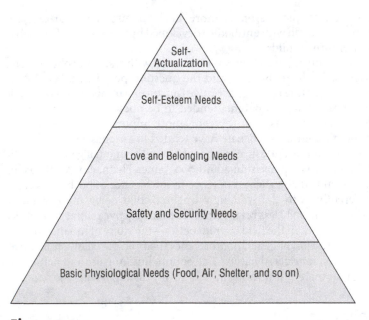

Figure 7.2

Abraham Maslow's hierarchy.

and Freud's conception of the personality to give you a little better idea of the differences to which varying approaches can lead.

The Well-Adjusted Individual

Probably the most famous theory of the development of a healthy personality is that of Abraham Maslow, known as Maslow's hierarchy. **Maslow's hierarchy** states that there are five levels of human achievement, each of which must be satisfied before the next is attempted. They are shown in Figure 7.2.

Self-actualization, the level of human achievement in which one is well adjusted to one's reality, is the highest level one can reach, according to Maslow. A person need not be famous, or the best in the field, in order to be self-actualized. Rather, we are self-actualized when content with life and capable of handling the problems that all of us must face. Because each level of the hierarchy must be satisfied before the next can be attempted, few of us reach self-actualization; even for those few who attain that highest level, it is a constant effort to stay there and not slide back down.

What do we mean by good social adjustment? There are dangers in setting up social adjustment as an ideal to be sought. If an individual were perfectly adjusted to the environment in the sense of having no problems or tensions and not wishing that anything were different, that person would stagnate. On the other hand, if we mean by a well-adjusted person, someone who loves life and finds it interesting and stimulating, that person must have dissatisfactions, problems to be dealt with, and goals to be achieved. Good adjustment must be a dynamic concept, and there is no simple formula for it that will apply equally well to everyone.

The truly well-adjusted person has developed a strong and balanced personality that can suffer misfortunes and recover from them. It should be emphasized that disappointment, pain, and grief are common experiences of life that come to all of us from time to time. The well-adjusted person can deal with these without being crushed.

Much research has gone into studying the genetic component of adjustment. In one study, psychologists David Lykken and Auke Tellegen surveyed 732 pairs of identical twins and found that their level of happiness was the same regardless of their surroundings. Another study reinforced this finding and discovered that the actual circumstances a person experiences have little to do with the satisfaction that person experiences. For example, people in China were happier in measures of subjective well-being than people in Japan, even though people in Japan were ten times richer.

In a book that attempted to pull all these ideas together, University of Pennsylvania psychologist Martin Seligman tried to explain what these findings meant for people searching for the "good life." One of his suggestions gives a sense of the ideas he raises. Specifically, he suggests: Keep your illusions. For example, he argues that happy couples—the couples who stay together happily—are ones who do not see their partner objectively, but instead see him or her through rose-colored glasses and think that the partner is better than he or she actually is. Other research, however, leads to different views. For example, research comparing people who have pessimistic personalities with people who have optimistic personalities found that those with pessimistic personalities are more attuned to reality and less stressed than people with optimistic personalities. We leave a consideration of these ideas to you as an optional research project; and we're sure that you will do the research (even though deep down we have our doubts) because, although we have underlying pessimistic personalities, we are trying to be optimists, which is another of Seligman's suggestions of how to have the good life.

Adjustment and Normality

Good adjustment and normality do not have precisely the same meaning when applied to personality, but their relationship is close. Conversely, a normal person in any society is necessarily a reasonably well-adjusted person. In cultural terms, a **normal person** is one who has acquired the basic attitudes and behavior patterns of the culture sufficiently well to be accepted and approved by the group. In any society, a well-adjusted person is likely to be recognized as a normal person. This normal person may not in all respects represent the typical person in the group, or the statistical average, but the normal person's behavior must not deviate too far from what is acceptable. Cultural norms are determined by the group. Types of behavior that in one culture would be quite normal might in another culture be regarded as wholly abnormal.

The Freudian Concept of Personality

Probably the best-known name in psychology is Sigmund Freud, who lived from 1856 to 1939 and spent most of his life in Vienna, Austria. He was trained as a physician but specialized in neurology, and in those days this meant that most of his patients were people with emotional problems.

Freud became famous as the originator of the system of psychotherapy known as **psychoanalysis,** a method of analysis based on the exploration of unconscious mental processes as manifested in dreams and disturbed relationships with others. Essentially, the method of psychoanalysis is that of free association. A patient is induced to express anything that comes to mind in the hope of uncovering memories or ideas of which the patient is unaware but that may be causing mental and emotional conflicts. For example, perhaps a terrifying experience in early childhood has been repressed below the level of consciousness. The psychoanalyst believes that if the patient can be helped to recall such an experience, the patient will be able to deal with it realistically, so that the mental disturbances it has been causing will disappear. But to bring unconscious mental processes to the level of consciousness takes time and persistence on the part of both the psychoanalyst and the patient.

In time, Freud became recognized as one of the great original thinkers in the field of psychology, and today most psychologists believe he made important contributions to our understanding of the human personality. But his theories have been the center of much controversy.

The Id, Ego, and Superego. To Freud, personality consisted of three major systems or "structures," which he called the id, the ego, and the superego. In the normal person, these three personality systems cooperate to enable the individual to satisfy basic needs and desires within an environmental setting, but when they are in serious conflict with one another, various mental disorders will result.

According to Freud, the **id** is the part of our personality controlled by the pleasure principle. It is driven by the goals to seek pleasure and avoid pain. It is the immature, selfish side of our personalities. Its counterpart, the **superego,** is our primitive conscience, which develops as we grow older and is guided solely by our morals. The third major structure of the personality is the **ego**—the personality component that most immediately controls behavior and is most in touch with external reality—which plays referee between the other two systems, sometimes allowing us to seek pleasure, at other times allowing the superego to guide us to more restrictive behavior. The id, ego, and superego are, of course, not independent entities. Rather, they are convenient terms to designate different groups of forces that interact within the human personality.

Defense Mechanisms. Among the many elements of Freud's psychology are **defense mechanisms**—behaviors that individuals use to avoid facing issues. These include:

- Displacement, in which one redirects one's anger away from the real target and toward an innocent target. For example, a frustrated worker kicks his dog.
- Reaction formation, in which an individual connects an anxiety-causing impulse with an overemphasized opposite. For example, people who are unconsciously attracted to the same sex may develop an intense hatred of gays.
- Projection, in which unacceptable urges in oneself are attributed to others. For example, a spouse tempted to have an affair becomes unduly suspicious of his or her partner.
- Rationalization, in which one gives excuses for one's shortcomings. For example, after you fail an exam and flunk out of school, you say it was all boring anyhow, and you prefer doing active, not mental, work.
- Fantasy, in which one avoids one's real worries by living in a fantasy world. For example, you don't study but rather spend all daydreaming of the great job you will never get because you didn't study.
- Sublimation, in which one transforms an unacceptable need into an acceptable ambition. You study hard because you hate the textbook author's stupid sense of humor.

Defense mechanisms include other behaviors that we all follow to varying degrees, but this list should give you a good idea of what is meant by defense mechanisms.

The Oedipus Complex. Probably the best-known aspect of Freud's work is the **Oedipus complex**—a child's sexual attraction to the parent of the opposite sex—so called because of its analogy to the Greek myth about Oedipus, the man who unknowingly killed his father and married his mother. Freud's formulation of the Oedipus complex grew out of the fact that rather early in his career he believed he had uncovered, in the unconscious mental processes of his neurotic patients, fantasies of sexual relations with the parent of the opposite sex, combined with jealous anger against the parent of the same sex. Later he came to believe that a strong sexual attraction to the parent of the opposite sex, along with jealousy of the other parent, is a universal experience of childhood in the years before the age of five. After this period, the Oedipus complex is repressed and disappears from the conscious mind because of recognition of the impossibility of fulfilling the sexual wishes; also, in the case of a boy, because of fear of retaliation from the father. At this stage, the child begins to identify with the parent of the same sex. Freud believed that the Oedipus complex was an essential factor in the development of every child's personality and hence in determining the nature of all human societies.

The Oedipus complex received much publicity and aroused widespread opposition. Many people found it difficult to accept in the form in which Freud presented it. He made it clear that the Oedipus complex referred to a definite desire of the child for sexual relations with the parent of the opposite sex, and to jealousy of the other parent because of the sexual relationship, but in our society it seems doubtful that most very young children have even a

Perfection Blueprint and the 12 Rules of Life

If the perfect child will make the perfect adult, the early 1980s produced a recipe to satisfy society's appetite for good adjustment. Judith Martin wrote two no-nonsense books that explained how to perfect the child. Briefly stated, her rules are for parents to nag, to start early, to set a good example, and to keep at it. She based her system on the belief that if the child acts perfect, the child is perfect.

She has no patience with uncertainties such as, "Who is to decide what is right and wrong, what is proper and improper?" and "What difference does it make which spoon you choose for the soup?" If you teach your child to sit up straight and your child learns to do that, then, Martin believes, your child will look nice, will seem to be paying attention in school, will be paying attention in school, will be learning lessons, and will be on the road to success and perfection.

She advocates advancing by increments, or steps. Say please and thank you to the baby; withhold the candy until the toddler says please; give the child a place at the dinner table when she no longer spits spinach around the kitchen; let the kid eat in a restaurant when he has learned not to interrupt adults' conversation; send the eighth-grader off to buy her own clothes when she has learned to polish her own shoes and press her shirt before starting out for school.

There are old-fashioned sayings that summarize these ideas, such as "Manners maketh the man" and "Handsome is as handsome does" and even "Go along to get along." Social scientists call this process socializing. Or it could be called civilizing. Whatever you may think of her methods, Martin has hold of a basic principle. If individuals can be molded to a standard set by the society in which chance has deposited those individuals, the standards will be preserved, the people will get along with each other, everyone will know what to expect, there will be no surprises, and the world will run smoothly.

These ideas about tough love are to be found in folk wisdom—what above we called phronesis—and it is not surprising that variations of them occur sporadically. Most recently, they can be found in Jordan Peterson's YouTube videos (e.g. https://www.youtube.com/watch?v=taNqLH2kLXM) and his book *12 Rules of Life*. Peterson's work is highly interdisciplinary and he has provocative things to say about politics, and culture. Although, and perhaps because, much of it borders on pop psychology it is influencing public debate and capturing the same types of sensibilities that led to Donald Trump's election—a guttural dissatisfaction of world views that don't center on personal responsibility.

Dr. Phil provides entertainment by discussing people's psychological problems.

vague concept of the existence or nature of sexual relations. Certainly many do not, and in that case it is hard to see how they can desire sexual relations or be jealous on account of them. Numerous psychoanalysts who subscribe to most of Freud's theories question or reject Freud's theory of the Oedipus complex.

Pop Psychologies

Modern scientific psychology is supplemented by what might be called pop psychology, in which the more scientific theories are translated and digested, making them available for popular consumption. One such translation is transactional analysis, or TA, which in some respects is similar to Freud's theories. It was made famous by Thomas A. Harris's best-selling book *I'm O.K., You're O.K.*, and it breaks down the human personality into three "parts"—parent, adult, and child—which roughly coincide with the superego, ego, and id of Freud. According to TA, when two people interact, they must be using the same mode of personality (preferably the adult voice). When one person's parent mode attempts to address another person's child mode, but the receiver is thinking in the adult voice, confusion of the message and frustration result.

Other pop theories include ESP (extrasensory perception), scream theory, and channeling. More recently, pop psychologists have become famous on TV, with shows bringing in people with problems, and then the psychologist working with them to "solve" the problems. The TV notable, Dr. Phil, is an example. Critics claim that his advice is at best simplistic, and at worse, ineffective. Whichever it is, he "retired" his psychology license once the show became famous in order to make it very clear that the show involves "entertainment" rather than serious psychology.

Intelligence, Personal Adjustment, and Normality

Before we move on to discuss some of the approaches various psychological theories lead to, let us consider the issue of intelligence and its role in determining personal adjustment and normality. Although this subject is not directly related to personal adjustment, it is an important topic that often causes confusion.

In every human society, individuals have varied **intelligence,** which is the ability of a person to understand the situations that confront him or her and to make satisfactory adjustments to them insofar as such adjustments depend on learning and thinking. Low intelligence has prevented some people from making an adequate adjustment to their environment. But only in recent decades have systematic efforts been made to define and measure intelligence or other mental qualities.

Mental Tests

Mental tests are intended to discover or to measure the mental characteristics of an individual. One of the earliest mental tests is described in Greek mythology. During the Trojan War, according to the story, a Greek named Ulysses paid no attention to the government's call to arms. The authorities visited him and found him plowing up the beach and sowing salt. Determined to see whether he was pretending to be insane, they placed Ulysses's only son in the plow's path. Ulysses quickly turned aside, and the test was deemed conclusive proof that he was sane.

Modern mental tests are based on the assumption that we can predict the reactions of an individual in various situations by giving specially designed tests in which similar conditions are involved. Furthermore, we assume that by presenting an individual with a large variety of sample situations, we can estimate how that person's abilities compare with those of other people.

Psychologists employ various types of tests to determine the characteristics of an individual. One type attempts to measure general intellectual ability; this is known as an intelligence test. Another type explores the individual's basic interests by presenting various hypothetical choices and asking the subject to express preferences. A third type is intended to measure aptitudes for certain kinds of work. A fourth is known as a test of achievement and is essentially a test of how well certain skills have been learned or certain kinds of knowledge have been assimilated. A fifth is intended to discover special abilities or disabilities and is generally given to children or adults with disabilities. Finally, a sixth type of test used by psychologists tries to determine the individual's personality structure and basic emotional needs. This type of test is known as a personality, or emotional adjustment, test.

All these tests are used by clinical psychologists to diagnose the power and potentialities of the individual as they exist at any given stage of development. On the basis of such tests, psychologists are able to learn something about the mental difficulties of an individual and judge the possibilities of helping the individual to overcome them.

Mental Age and the IQ.   The best-known psychological test is the IQ, or general intelligence test, which attempts to reduce the many dimensions of intelligence to a single number that estimates a person's mental age. To do this, researchers devised a wide variety of test items, from the simple to the complex, and arranged them in order of difficulty. They then tried these items out on a large number of children at various grade levels. On the basis of this experience, they assigned a mental-age value to each item. Their procedure in assigning questions or problems to various ages was as follows: If a certain item was responded to correctly by as many as 65 to 75 percent of the children whose age was, say, eight years, but by a smaller percentage of children below that age, it was considered a test of eight-year-old intelligence. They then grouped several items of appropriate difficulty, usually five, to test children of each age. If a child could answer the questions for all levels up through those for eight-year-olds, but none of those for the years above that, mental age was considered to be eight regardless of actual or chronological age. But the child received proportionate credit for any questions actually answered. For example, if the child could answer all the questions for eight-year-olds, and three out of five of those for nine-year-olds, mental age was considered 8.6. If the child could also answer two out of five of the questions for age ten, a mental age of nine was assigned.

Later, other psychologists refined the technique so that each mental year consisted of twelve mental months. For example, each test item might represent two mental months, in which case six items would represent a mental year. Each person tested would then receive two months' credit toward a mental age for each item answered correctly.

Once the concept of mental age was developed, it was only a step to the notion of expressing a ratio between the mental age and the chronological age of an individual. This ratio was called the **IQ, or intelligence quotient**—an index of an individual's tested mental ability as compared to the rest of the population. IQ is calculated by dividing mental age by actual age and multiplying the resulting fraction by 100. Multiplying by 100 expresses the ratio or fraction as a percentage, but it is not customary to write "percent" after the number expressing IQ. The formula for finding IQ may be written as follows:

IQ $=$ Mental Age/Chronological Age $\times$ 100.

Let us see how this formula works in practice. A child eight years old having a mental age of eight is an average child. IQ would be $8/8 \times 100 = 100$. It is apparent, therefore, that an IQ of 100 represents average intelligence. If a child eight years old had a mental age of twelve, as indicated by an intelligence test, that eight-year-old would obviously be very bright. This would be indicated by IQ, which would be $12/8 \times 100 = 150$.

Today it is often the practice to assign an individual a percentile rank rather than an IQ. **Percentile rank** is a ranking of an individual with reference to other individuals in a certain group when all individuals in the group are ranked in order from the most capable to the least capable. The hundredth percentile consists of the 1 percent of the group who have made the highest scores. The first percentile consists of the 1 percent who have made the lowest scores. Similarly, the 50th and 51st percentiles consist of those who have made average scores. Figure 7.3 shows the IQ rankings for society.

Mental tests indicate that great differences exist in intelligence in our population. This fact has long been known, but tests have made our knowledge more definite. Though these and other psychological tests are used more widely than ever before in schools, in government, and in business, they are also subjected to increasing criticism because of cultural biases in the tests. Nevertheless, mental tests are probably the best means we have for comparing the mental powers of large numbers of individuals.

Limitations of IQ and Other Tests. Many of the early experimenters believed they had devised tests that did not depend on acquired knowledge but were essentially a measure of innate or inherited mental ability. Hence, they thought the scores of individuals on such tests could not be affected by any ordinary differences in environment. However, various studies and experiments have demonstrated beyond a reasonable doubt that factors such as

IQ Score	Category		Percentage
20		PROFOUND	
30			
40	Retarded	SEVERE	0.4%
50			
60		MODERATE	
70	Mildly Retarded		2%
80	Borderline		7%
90	Dull Normal		17%
100	Normal		25%
110			25%
120	Bright Normal		17%
130	Superior		7%
140			2%
150			
160			
170	Very Superior		0.4%
180			
185			
200			

Figure 7.3

Percentage of children at different IQ groupings.

differences in family environment and schooling may have a substantial effect on the scores individuals make on standard intelligence tests. For example, when identical twins are separated early and reared in different types of homes, the twin reared by parents of superior social, economic, and educational status almost invariably does better on an intelligence test than the other member of the pair, and sometimes the difference is fairly substantial.

Another example is that people who take the same test thirty years after entering high school will score in direct relation to how much education they have received in that span of time. Yet another chink in the armor of IQ test infallibility comes from Robert Rosenthal of Harvard University and Lenore Jacobsen, an elementary school principal in San Francisco, who successfully convinced a group of teachers that certain students were gifted. According to *Pygmalion in the Classroom,* in which the study is published, the students, who actually were chosen at random, surpassed their classmates and became high-level achievers. These "brighter" students scored an average of 12.22 points improvement on achievement tests administered at the beginning and end of the year, compared with only an 8.42 point improvement from their classmates. The only difference between the two groups was in how the teachers responded to their learning needs.

Another indication of the limitation of the IQ test is the fact that scores on the same test have been increasing over time. Because it is almost impossible that intelligence is rising that fast, this suggests that there are sociological aspects to the test and that the test reflects those sociological aspects.

In recent years, some social scientists have argued that standardized intelligence tests are racially biased as well. Again, this relates to the environment in which the child is raised. A black child raised in a low-income area may not know what the capital of Greece is, but the lack of that one bit of information does not indicate less learning ability than a child from a high-income background enjoys. Others disagree, arguing that it is not "white information" that is tested.

The conclusion we can draw from such studies is that the scores people make on intelligence tests are a result of their previous experiences as well as of their inherited mental aptitudes. Where conditions of environment have been similar, differences in scores may be a rough indication of differences of innate mental aptitude. However, we must be cautious in assuming that any two given individuals have really had the same, or nearly the same, environment.

Some educators say that these intelligence tests are knowledge tests, not necessarily tests of intelligence. Currently there is a trend to use different kinds of tests, such as assessing a portfolio of a student's work or testing on a computer where the computer selects the next question based on how the test-taker has answered the preceding questions. However, it is expensive to develop new tests, to persuade schools to adopt them, and to train educators to administer and grade them. The standard IQ tests currently employed will probably continue to be widely used for many years.

Intelligence Is Far More than Mental Manipulation.   All tests are useful only if we recognize their limitations. IQ tests tell us something about the probable intelligence of an individual at the time a test is taken, but they do not and cannot measure innate or inherited mental potentialities. A possibly more serious limitation grows out of the difficulty of defining intelligence in such a way that all the elements that enter into it can be correctly rated by a test. It is doubtful whether the concept can be defined with much precision and whether the relative intelligence of different individuals, especially at the higher levels, can be determined with much accuracy. Defining intelligence is problematic, but our earlier definition—that intelligence is the ability of a person to understand the situations that confront him or her and to make satisfactory adjustments to them insofar as such adjustments depend on learning and thinking—is probably the best we can do.

The more intelligent a person is, the better able he or she is to do the following:

- Perceive a situation as a whole rather than partially or incompletely
- Learn quickly
- Concentrate thought and learning in a desired direction
- Find satisfactory solutions, either with or without help from others

High intelligence probably requires considerable imagination and originality, since in order to solve a difficult problem we generally need to think of and evaluate a number of novel approaches.

When we assume that a so-called mental test measures intelligence, we are assuming that the mental abilities required for correct answers to its questions are the same as those needed for solving the sometimes complex problems encountered in real life. This is not always true, since mental tests have many limitations. For example, they must be completed within a limited period of time on the theory that this makes the scores of individuals more comparable. But some of the world's greatest achievements have been made by people who have acquired the habit of thinking through difficult problems slowly, checking at every step to avoid missing some important consideration. Furthermore, to allow one's mind and imagination to wander with a purpose, to take time to search for the unusual or unlikely aspects of a situation, is one kind of intelligent behavior. It is also an important ingredient in originality or creativity. IQ tests do not measure such abilities. Much research has been done on multiple intelligence models, which assume that there are several different dimensions of intelligence, and that these dimensions cannot be reduced to a single meaningful number such as is attempted with IQ. Researchers have yet, however, to come up with an acceptable alternative.

Your IQ Is 132? So What?

Is the intelligence level of people in the United States falling? If it is, why?

Charles Murray, an author who explores various social and political issues, thinks the intelligence level in the United States is falling and that he has found out why. He explained his theories in a book called *The Bell Curve* (written with co-author Bruce Herrnstein).

In that book, he concludes that the average level of U.S. intelligence is falling because some large groups of nonwhite Americans and some large groups of nonwhite immigrants to the United States have lower IQs than large groups of whites (but East Asians, he says, have higher IQs than whites). He reaches this conclusion because of the results of his research on IQs (the average IQ of some groups is lower than that of others) and because he takes the further step of treating IQ as the measure of intelligence.

Many social scientists consider Murray's arguments wrong and prejudiced. Murray insists they are not.

He points out that although large groups may exhibit a particular average test score level, individuals in any of the groups may vary widely in intelligence, and no assumptions should be made about any individual's intelligence based on the overall scores for a particular group. Murray explains that his position is that one group is not inferior to another, just different.

Whether Murray's research is prejudiced against or toward any particular group or individual, he is open to criticism just because he equates IQ with intelligence. The book claims that IQ measures intelligence and that IQ/intelligence depends primarily on what you're born with, rather than what you get from living. But although IQ scores are definitely measurable, and one group or another does on average score higher or lower than others, there is a lot of doubt among social scientists as to what an IQ score means. So Murray's work is widely criticized. Still, Murray's controversial books on social policy topics are useful to consider; they make for spirited and challenging discussion, whatever their effect on the real world of politics and social interaction may be.

Intelligence and Personal Adjustment

Intelligence, especially if we mean intelligence measured by IQ tests, has little relation to one's ability to adjust except at the highest IQ levels (above 150) and lowest IQ levels (below 60). Both of these extreme groups often have a harder time adjusting to society than do people in the middle ranges. The reason that IQ generally is not important is that personal adjustment has more to do with emotional stability and coming to terms with what one is as a person than it does with one's ability to score high on a test.

Even if IQ tests did measure intelligence accurately, it should be pointed out that intelligence and success are not synonymous. Many high-IQ individuals have difficulty coping with life; they might be able to solve a complicated mathematical problem, but they haven't the faintest idea how to interrelate with other people. Business leaders generally fall in the average

Who Stands Stress Better: Men or Women?

It used to be thought that women were more emotionally and psychiatrically disabled and had more symptoms of stress than men. However, in 1984 the National Institute of Mental Health (NIMH) completed a six-year study of psychiatric ailments and concluded that although women tend to suffer more than men from phobias and depression, men suffer more than women from alcohol abuse, dependence on drugs, and long-term antisocial behavior. Taking all psychiatric disorders into account, the NIMH study found that although both men and women are about equally likely to be affected, women

have often continued to be perceived as more subject to psychiatric problems because, as the study also showed, they seek professional help twice as often as men do. In fact, it could be argued that women have a healthier attitude than men because they do seek help, whereas, according to the study, men tend to mask their depression with alcohol.

You can probably see the tendencies in your own life. Women talk with other women; they discuss their problems, and they expose and examine their weaknesses. Men generally hide them and are far less likely to have close male friends with whom they discuss personal problems. Instead, male friends do things together. It is the "macho" thing to do.

(normal and bright normal) IQ category, not the superior or very superior categories. They have qualities such as internal fortitude, drive, ambition, ability to work with others, and imagination, which are necessary and probably more important than superior intelligence for business success. We can speak from experience; being at a university we're around people with high IQs all the time and, quite frankly, many of them can be real pains.

Conclusion

As you can see from the discussion in this chapter, and as you probably know from your own life, adjusting personality to fit society and adjusting society to fit personality are not easy. These adjustments involve a continual effort extending from birth to death. For many of us, it will seem an almost insurmountable effort in which the cards are stacked against us. It is precisely this feeling that leads so many into pop psychology.

This chapter presents a variety of theories and therapies, and almost all of them have some value. Perhaps the most useful lesson here is not so much what the theories are (although this knowledge is necessary) as it is that psychological problems are prevalent among most members of society. It is all too easy to see ourselves as out of step and others as well adjusted (or vice versa).

In terms of the course, the important lesson is to understand the processes by which individuals and societies interrelate. Society is composed of individuals, but society as a whole is much more than the sum of those individuals. Thus, individual development and societal development make up a two-way street.

 Study and **Review**

Key Points

- Culture is created by the individuals within that culture, and individuals' personalities are in turn shaped and molded by culture.
- Both nature and nurture affect personality and individual development.
- Positive and negative reinforcement help shape an individual's personality.

- Self-actualization is the highest level of Maslow's hierarchy of needs.
- Freud saw personality as consisting of three major systems: the id, the ego, and the superego.
- Defense mechanisms are behaviors that individuals use to avoid facing issues.
- IQ tests can be useful, but only if their limitations are kept in perspective.

Some Important Terms

behavioralist approach (129)
cognitive approach (129)
cognitive science (129)
defense mechanism (132)
ego (132)
epigenetics (129)
feral children (125)
heredity (128)
humanist approach (129)
id (132)

infantile autism (126)
instincts (127)
intelligence (134)
IQ (intelligence quotient) (135)
Maslow's hierarchy (130)
nature/nurture debate (128)
negative reinforcement (127)
normal person (131)
Oedipus complex (132)
operant conditioning (127)

percentile rank (135)
personality (122)
positive reinforcement (127)
psychoanalysis (131)
psychoanalytic approach (129)
punishment (127)
self-actualization (130)
superego (132)

Questions for Review and Discussion

General Questions

1. Does culture control people or do people control culture? Explain the relationship between the two.

2. How do the effects of isolation on children support the importance of socialization?

3. Some outstanding individuals have made significant contributions to our culture. Name someone who you think has done this, and discuss that person's contribution.

4. Discuss some of the factors in childhood that influence an individual's personality.

5. Explain how, according to Skinner, operant conditioning shapes personality.

6. What do "positive" and "negative" mean in the context of operant conditioning?

7. Which is more important in the development of personality: environment or heredity? Explain the relationship between the two.

8. Contrast the four approaches to the determination of behavior: cognitive, psychoanalytic, behavioralist, and humanist.

9. According to Maslow, what are the five levels of human achievement?

10. What are some of the characteristics of a well-adjusted individual?

11. What does Martin Seligman suggest one must do in order to "have the good life?" Do you agree?

12. Explain some of the contributions that Sigmund Freud made to the understanding of human personality.

13. Explain the IQ test and what it tries to measure.

Internet Questions

1. Jung was a psychologist and a peer of Freud. The site http://www.terrapsych.com/jungdefs.html has a glossary of Jungian terms. What is an Electra complex?

2. Go to http://files.eric.ed.gov/fulltext/ED353079. pdf. According to Stough's research, does home schooling limit socialization?

3. Go to http://www.nytimes.com/2005/07/05/health/ explaining-differences-in-twins.html to answer the question: As twins grow older, do they become less similar to one another?

4. Take a free IQ test, such as that found at http://www.intelligencetest.com. What aspect of intelligence do you believe the test is designed to evaluate? What other aspects of knowledge are there?

5. Pick a child from the list on http://archive.is/ 6LohO. What or who was the caregiver? Do you believe the story? For all the children listed, what was the most common caregiver? Where would the child usually be from?

For Further Study

Books to Explore

Alford, Henry, *How To Live: A Search for Wisdom from Old People (While They Are Still on This Earth)*, New York: Twelve Publishers, 2009.

Dalio, Ray, *Principles: Life and Work*, New York: Simon and Schuster, 2017.

Haidt, Jonathan, *The Righteous Mind: Why Good People Are Divided by Politics and Religion*, New York: Pantheon, 2012.

Johnson, Steven, *Mind Wide Open: Your Brain and the Neuroscience of Everyday Life*, New York: Scribner, 2004.

Justman, Stewart, *Fool's Paradise: The Unreal World of Pop Psychology*, Chicago, IL: Ivan R. Dee, 2005.

Kahneman, Daniel, *Thinking Fast and Slow*, New York: Farrar, Straus and Giroux, 2011.

Lilienfeld, Scott, Steven Jay Lynn, John Ruscio, and Barry L. Beyerstein, *50 Great Myths of Popular Psychology: Shattering Widespread Misconceptions about Human Behavior*, New York: Wiley-Blackwell, 2009.

Martin, Judith, *Miss Manners' Guide to Rearing Perfect Children*, New York: Atheneum, 1984.

Maslow, A. H., *Psychology of Science: A Reconnaissance*, Chicago, IL: Regnery-Gateway, 1969.

McGuire, Kevin John, *Maslow's Hierarchy of Needs: An Introduction*, GRIN Verlag GmbH, 2015.

Peterson, Jordan, *12 Rules for Life*, Toronto: Random House, 2018.

Pink, Daniel, *Drive: The Surprising Truth About What Motivates Us*, New York: Penguin, 2009.

Pinker, Steven, *The Blank Slate: The Modern Denial of Human Nature*, New York: Penguin, 2003.

Slater, Lauren, *Opening Skinner's Box: Great Psychological Experiments of the Twentieth Century*, New York: Norton, 2004.

Simler, Kevin and Robin Hanson, *The Elephant in the Brain*, New York: Oxford University Press, 2018.

Small, Meredith F., *Kids: How Biology and Culture Shape the Way We Raise Our Children*, New York: Doubleday, 2001.

Internet Sites to Explore

"http://www.bfskinner.org" B.F. Skinner Foundation.

"http://www.piaget.org" The Jean Piaget Society.

"http://www.loc.gov/exhibits/freud" Library of Congress, Freud: Conflict and Culture.

"https://www.verywellmind.com/what-is-maslows-hierarchy-of-needs-4136760" Maslow's Hierarchy of Needs.

"https://www.mayoclinic.org/diseases-conditions/personality-disorders/symptoms-causes/syc-20354463" Mayo Clinic Personality Disorders.

"http://www.socialpsychology.org" Social Psychology Network.

Deviance, Crime, and Society

After reading this chapter you should be able to:

- Explain why social scientists emphasize the relativity of norms
- Name various social science theories of deviance
- Define deviance and distinguish it from crime
- List three interrelated problems with the U.S. justice system
- Explain how legalizing the use of recreational drugs could reduce crime
- Distinguish between the guidance and the punishment purpose of the criminal justice system

> The only power any government has is the power to crack down on criminals. Well, when there aren't enough criminals, one makes them. One declares so many things to be a crime that it becomes impossible for men to live without breaking laws.
>
> —Ayn Rand

On July 22, 2011, Anders Behring Breivik went to a summer youth camp and killed 69 students. He was caught and sentenced to twenty-one years in prison. His accommodations are better than most college dorm rooms; his room is part of a three-cell suite of rooms equipped with exercise equipment, a television, and a laptop. In 1996, Timothy Jackson shoplifted a $159 jacket. He was caught and sentenced to life in prison. He lives in a small, spartan cell with a toilet and a bed. Why the different results? Because Anders committed his crime in Norway, while Timothy committed his crime in the United States.

In this chapter, we consider how society deals with **deviance**—actions that society finds inappropriate—and how social science thinking about such issues might be useful in thinking about reforms in our criminal justice system. There has been extensive theorizing by social scientists about these issues. Most of that theorizing quickly gets too complicated for a general social science course, so in the first part of the chapter we provide a general discussion of deviance, crime, and society, avoiding the social science jargon. Then, in the second part we provide you with a brief summary of academic discussions of the issues. Finally, in the third part of the chapter we discuss some problems with the U.S. system of justice and some proposals that have been put forward for changing it.

Deviance and Norms

Any society must coordinate the actions of large numbers of individuals so that they fit together. One way in which society does so is to develop **norms**—expectations about what constitutes appropriate or acceptable behavior—and to develop methods by which individuals adopt those norms to guide their behavior. All of our actions are significantly influenced by norms, even though we seldom think about them specifically. Individuals often think they are independent free-thinkers, but in fact, their views are significantly shaped by their environment.

By definition, most people follow society's norms, but specifying precisely what those norms are is often difficult. One reason it is difficult is that norms can include a norm which encourages some deviation from other norms. Society supports diversity, but not too much diversity. Individuals' actions are called *deviant* when those actions conflict with society's norms.

A number of aspects should be noted about the concept of deviance. The first is that it is a relative concept. An action can only be considered deviant relative to a norm. An action could be deviant relative to one set of norms, but quite acceptable relative to other norms. For example, picking one's nose in public and wiping the result on one's hair would be considered deviant in the United States. In the Yanomamö tribe in South America, that is the norm; not following that norm is the deviant behavior. Another example is cheating on exams. In some societies, a certain amount of cheating is the norm; it is expected. Teachers even leave the room to facilitate it. In the United States, that is far less the case. To make this relativity of norms clear, sociologists emphasize that it is society's reaction to the action, not the action itself, that makes an action deviant.

Policy in society doesn't choose norms, but it does influence them, and many of the debates about policy are actually debates about the set of norms people believe are best for society. Should the norm of society be that everyone gets married and has two children, with the "good woman" staying home and taking care of the kids? Or should the norm of society be one in which both spouses work, share child-rearing responsibility, and cringe at even the use of the term "good woman"? Or should it be one in which people don't get married or even live together, with the male just contributing his sperm to reproduction, and otherwise taking little part in the rearing of children?

These are not questions people normally ask. Norms are usually unstated; people know them intuitively, but if they are asked to explain what they are, or why they are the norms society should have, they can't do so. What makes it even harder is that norms evolve over time, and they evolve differently for different geographic areas and social groups. So, actually, society's norms reflect a combination of the norms of the subgroups of a society. Often, conflict among subgroups in society is rooted in conflicting norms. A subset of norms is **mores** (pronounced mor-rays). Mores are norms that have great moral significance. A deviation from mores is more significant than a deviation from norms. An example of mores would be views of homosexuality and whether society condones it.

Conflicting Norms and Tension

Conflicting norms and mores can cause social tension, so society needs institutions that resolve or at least limit those conflicts. One of the effects of the U. S. college education system, which brings together students from different backgrounds and geographic areas, is a homogenization of society's norms. College does more than educate you. It also transforms you—the person graduating from college will not be the same person who started college. One of the goals of a social science course is to get you thinking about that transformative process—to get you to watch yourself being changed, and thereby help you determine who you are: the person watching, the person being changed, or someone in between. To be honest with you, I am attempting to change you right now by imbuing you with the norms of tolerance and thoughtful deliberation. The goal is to make you more tolerant, even while you retain your personal normative views of right and wrong.

In an earlier chapter, I said that one of the goals of this course was to provide you with an introduction of "book smarts" so that you are tuned in to reading the societal norms of your surroundings. That "being tuned in" skill, often more than any specific skill, is central to succeeding in life. To be tuned in doesn't mean that you have to agree with and/or follow all of

Physical punishment of children is no longer found acceptable in much of the United States, especially among the elite part of the population.

© PhotoAlto/Sandro Di Carlo Darsa/Getty

society's norms. In fact, as I stated above, society values a certain amount of deviance. But it does mean that you should be aware when you are challenging the norms of the group you are interacting with, that you do so by choice, not by accident, and that you are aware of and prepared for the consequences. As country singer Kenny Rogers put it, "You have to know when to hold 'em, and know when to fold 'em."

Some norms are almost universal—a norm against killing others for example. But even such universal norms allow for deviations. For example in gang culture, if someone disses a gang or violates its turf, members of the gang may be expected to kill the violator. In other cultures, if a woman has relations with a man before marriage, her family is expected to kill her for violating the family's honor. Abortion is another act that is seen differently according to different norms. Some groups in our society see it as killing; others see it as simply allowing the mother to have a choice of whether to have a child or not.

Another type of killing that is seen differently by different groups is capital punishment, where the state punishes a person by putting him or her to death. Some societies see this as allowable; others see it as unallowable killing by the state—a violation of a fundamental norm.

Other norms, such as the norm about homosexuality, are less universal. Most African countries see homosexuality as deviant behavior, whereas European and North American societies increasingly see homosexuality as normal behavior. The goal of a social science course is not to tell you what set of norms are the right ones; the goal is to make you aware of the differing norms, and to recognize that society has to find ways of blending those different norms into a social policy that respects individual rights, but that also tempers and blends those individual rights into society's norms. Ideally, understanding that process makes you more tolerant and less likely to impose your norms on others.

This relativity of norms is more pronounced the greater the heterogeneity of the society. An example involves the norms surrounding parental punishment for children. In some subsections of society, it is the norm to use physical punishment—say, spanking the child with a belt when the child has misbehaved. NFL running back Adrian Peterson punished his child in this manner, because he had been physically punished when he was a child and he felt the physical punishment made him a better person.

Such actions used to be acceptable within broader U.S. society and still are in parts of the United States. The old saying "spare the rod; spoil the child" reflects this view. But physical punishment of children is no longer found acceptable in much of the United States, especially among the elite part of the population. The norm against such physical punishment has become so widespread that it has been built into the law and made into a crime. Adrian Peterson found that out when he was convicted of a crime for doing what he thought was part of being a good parent.

As the above discussion should make clear, there is a certain arbitrariness to norms, what is considered deviant behavior, and what is considered a crime. Since norms are seldom clear-cut, an important skill that individuals need to function well in society is to be able to sense the norms of the society they are in and to fit their actions into those acceptable norms.

Norms, Crime, and the Rule of Law

To move from norms to crime, we must integrate government and the rule of law into the discussion. Although we will discuss government specifically in a later chapter, let us present a brief summary of a standard political science explanation of government and the law: In political theory, government is an institution that has been established by people to help coordinate their actions and translate vaguely understood norms into precise laws, which "control" people's behavior. In the absence of government, there would be chaos and continual war. Government involves an agreement among people to follow the laws that government establishes to achieve a better life for all. To do so, governments establish laws that specify which deviant behavior is a punishable crime, which deviant behavior is not approved but is not a crime, and what the punishments for "crimes" are.

While governments are necessary, government needs to be limited since it has such strong powers—the power to tax, the power to restrict individual actions, and the power to punish individuals. To prevent governments from becoming too oppressive, governments establish laws that restrict not only what individuals do, but also what governments do. Specifically, governments are limited by what is called the rule of law. The **rule of law** means that decisions about whether something is, or is not, a crime are not made on a case-by-case basis, but are instead codified into the law of the land. This allows an individual to know whether he or she is undertaking an action that is legal, even if that action might not be liked by most of society or by the current government.

The "rule of law" limitation on government is designed to see that decisions about specific issues are not made arbitrarily by the current government but are made according to legal precedents that have somehow been codified into law. The U.S. Bill of Rights is an example of limits on government created by the rule of law: it embodies limitations on what government can do and what government is required to do so that it does not violate an individual's rights. In principle, the U.S. government cannot throw someone into jail because it doesn't like his or her beliefs or because it doesn't like his or her attitude. That's at least the way it is supposed to work in theory. The way it works in practice is much more complicated, messy, and differs in different societies.

Most observers find the United States' theoretical legal structure admirable. They see the way it works out in practice as far less admirable. Consider the question "Can a citizen be expected to be treated fairly and consistently in the United States, given all the heterogeneous norms in U.S. society?" The answer that many people come to is "No, large segments of the U.S. population are not treated fairly or consistently. The U.S. isn't the worst system, but it is far from the best." You can see this in a ranking done by the World Justice Project. In that

Differing Legal Traditions

There are different ways in which the rule of law can be imposed, and different societies have chosen different approaches. Each leads to a different type of legal system that differs on the basis of how much emphasis the system gives to "past precedents," and how much to "reasonable judgment" of the judicial system. Three different traditions of legal systems can be found:

- *Common law tradition.* The common law tradition makes past precedents developed in previous judicial decisions the primary guide for future decisions. In the common law tradition, previous judgments play a central role in how current judgments are made. England, the United States, and countries that base their legal systems on the American or British systems, follow a common law tradition.

- *Civil law tradition.* The civil law tradition focuses less on previous case law, and more on core principles that have been codified into a referential system. Generalized abstract codes guide decisions. In the civil law tradition, judges have more flexibility to interpret the laws than they do in the common law tradition. Many European countries, such as France, and countries that have based their legal systems on the French system, follow this tradition.

- *Socialist law tradition.* The socialist law tradition is a newer tradition that China is creating. This tradition makes the Communist Party's views a guiding feature of the law. While this tradition accepts that there are both past precedents and civil law, it holds that the final arbiter of the law is the Communist Party, which the socialist law tradition sees as the defender of the people.

ranking, the United States ranked nineteenth out of 102 countries; China came out seventy-first (see http://data.worldjusticeproject.org/#table).

When Norms Conflict: *Straight Outta Compton*

Let's consider an area in which the U.S. justice system falls short—the treatment of low-income blacks—and the differing views of how to try to improve the situation.

In a large society, such as the United States, there are many subsets of society, each with its own norms but not with its own laws. That means that one can be following a norm of one subset of society and be deviant in relation to the broader society's set of norms and laws. An innocuous example is the following: A waitress calling a customer "honey" is normal in some geographic areas, but inappropriate in others. Dress codes also vary significantly. When society is not homogeneous, different norms for subsets can cause problems for society. A less innocuous example is when a norm says that if someone has dissed you, you have to physically punish that person. In some parts of society that is the norm, but the broader U.S. norm embodied in the law says that is inappropriate and illegal.

Differing norms and laws can make a subset of society both deviant and criminal in the eyes of broader society, even though the people in that subset are simply following the norms of that subset. In that case, the result can be a clash of cultures, violence, and loss of respect for the law. Many believe that has happened in the United States as low-income areas, especially those that are black, have developed different norms than those that the broader society follows.

Gangsta rap is an example, and the movie *Straight Outta Compton* recounts the history of the group NWA or Niggaz with Attitude. Their work was seen by many as promoting violence, murder, misogyny, profanity, sex addiction, homophobia, racism, promiscuity, rape, vandalism, and thievery—actions that most in society find reprehensible. Their songs reveled in the violation of norms, and that violation made their work popular among youth, who have a natural tendency to want to rebel against society's norms in an acceptable way. This acceptance of gangsta rap among the youth provoked two reactions in mainstream society.

NWA or Niggaz with Attitude.

© Lynn Goldsmith/Corbis

Progressive liberals justified the lyrics of gangsta rap as an expression of legitimate outrage at the injustices faced by blacks in U.S. society; they saw it as an acceptable violation of norms. Even though progressives found the actions glorified by NWA repugnant, they nonetheless supported NWA. They argued that NWA wasn't really arguing for the norms conveyed in the lyrics; it was simply venting about the oppression poor blacks face.

Conservatives saw gangsta rap as an unacceptable violation of norms—if it was venting, it was inappropriate venting that should not be glorified. Conservative social scientists, such as Thomas Sowell, argued that glorifying gangsta rap hurts young blacks because it encourages them to express the same cocky attitude of NWA, an attitude that conflicted with mainstream norms. By doing so, it undermined young black people's ability to fit into existing mainstream society.

Yes, Sowell agreed, young black males are discriminated against—he is black and when he was young and poor, he was discriminated against. But he further argued that some of that discrimination is a response to an attitude that would be objected to regardless of who exhibited it in society. He tells how he learned the norms of broader society, and how because of luck, help from

*T*he Fine Line of Acceptable Behavior

The NWA example in the text exploring the fine line of conflicting norms is one of many examples of subgroups in society adopting a behavior as a norm that they know is in conflict with broader society's norms. Adopting a conflicting norm helps the subgroup create cohesion within the subgroup and gives the subgroup an identity. It is much like children sharing a secret among themselves. Doing so makes them feel special and provides a bond of friendship for them.

A less incendiary example of such a violation of norms involved the Ohio State University Band, which was a highly successful band famous for its elaborate choreographed marching (see, for example, https://www.youtube.com/watch?v=GTca2nrln4U).

It takes a lot of work and cohesion to attain the precision the marching band achieved. One way the band created that esprit de corps was to provide band members with a secret songbook. How it was provided was unclear, but all members of the band who received it were told that it was to be kept confidential. The problem was that this songbook included significant anti-gay and anti-Jewish lyrics, going so far as to mock Holocaust victims. The lyrics were far less incendiary than those found in a NWA rap, but they definitely crossed society's line of acceptability.

Ohio State marching band.

© Mark Davison/Icon Sportswire/Corbis

Just about anyone would recognize that these songs violated societal norms, and it was that violation that made them special to the band. The songs were part of its history, and they helped bond the band members together. The band's director knew of the book and officially "banned" it, but it continued to be used, which to many meant that it was likely a "wink and a nod" ban, not an actual ban. In 2015, the book became public to much outcry in the press. The band's director was fired, and the band received significant negative publicity for violating society's norms. So rather than becoming rich as some gangsta rappers did, the people involved in this incident lost their jobs.

The existence of these songs does not suggest that the members of the band were anti-gay or anti-Jewish—the band included both gays and Jews. Band members agreed that if the lyrics had been made available to a broader audience, and were not kept just for the band, they would be unacceptable. So, unlike gangsta rap, it was not meant to be publicly aired. But, band members argued that individuals should be given some freedom to joke about things in private that society does not find acceptable to joke about in public. It happens all the time. One former band member stated, "I don't think you are going to find many 19-year-olds who don't joke about those things."

The lesson to be drawn from this incident is that there is ambiguity about norms—and that norms can conflict. One norm is that it is okay to use offensive language that violates broad societal norms within a small group, as long as one recognizes that it is done as a parody, not as a belief. Another is that some matters are not acceptable for joking about, even among friends. Norms inevitably involve gray lines that society is continually exploring.

So let me end this box with a warning to students: With today's communication technology, statements, pictures, and views can quickly go public, and social media will often amplify something you post way out of proportion. So beware of what you post—treat any post as something that will be seen by all and that will be used to judge you. Recognize that the norms of your immediate group may well violate norms of that part of mainstream society that does the hiring. Them got the power, and that ain't goin' to change soon.

---

mentors and individuals, and hard work on his part, he was accepted by mainstream society and had a much more productive and fulfilling life than he otherwise would have. He argues that most black youths would be better off if they followed a similar path. Encouraging young black males to flaunt a cocky, defiant, and in-your-face attitude, even if that attitude may be justified, undermines their chances to succeed in mainstream society.

What gangsta rappers saw their work as is unclear. Initially gangsta rappers may have been advocating the norms expressed in their lyrics; such norms were prevalent in gang culture. But as NWA became more successful (gangsta rap became a highly lucrative art form that made a number of rappers rich), they started to "explain" their lyrics in ways that fit the liberal justification—as necessary outrage to highlight the problems in U.S. society that were not being addressed. They presented their work as a vehicle that gets society to discuss issues it would rather avoid.

NWA's recent justification and phraseology shows that it has learned society's norms— the justification it provides accepts that the lyrics in their songs violate society's broader norms, but justifies that violation by another norm of society—the norm of being tolerant of people who have been oppressed by society. That tolerance norm allows that certain norms can be violated—at least verbally—if the goal is a higher purpose: to change society for the better.

Liberals see such justification as acceptable—oppressed subgroups should be allowed more leeway than others in society. Conservatives see such justifications as just a lot of double-talk designed to justify actions and song lyrics that are unjustifiable. They argue that encouraging expression of such misanthropic views is highly detrimental to precisely the oppressed subgroup that liberals want to help; it undermines the establishment of norms that would advance young black men's future.

The goal of this book is not to argue that the liberal or conservative view is correct. Instead it is to let you know that such methods of justification exist, and that they potentially contain some elements of truth to them. Whether such justifications are reasonable, or whether they are simply a social science papering-over of the glorification of actions that almost all educated people condemn, not glorify, is something that you will have to decide for yourself.

Major Theories on Deviance

Now that we've discussed the importance and ambiguity of norms in real life, let's now turn to a more academic presentation, and consider the major social science theories of deviance. All of us exhibit some deviant behavior. Every so often, any well-adjusted person says, "Phooey on the norms!" and lets go, blowing off steam to release tension. Such limited deviant behavior is often condoned and even admired by society. It gives the person an identity, a personality. However, there is a line, and if one crosses it, one's individuality becomes too much for society. Society wants you to be different, but not too different.

There are a variety of perspectives on deviance and explanations of why people step over the line. Psychologists tend to look within individuals—into their upbringing or into their genetic makeup. Sociologists, by contrast, tend to look for factors outside individuals—such as social conditions within society. As soon as these explanations are explored more carefully, one quickly gets caught up in competing perspectives, each of which has its own terminology and theoretical nuances. We'll leave those issues for a sociology or psychology course, and simply try here to introduce you briefly to some of the terminology, major perspectives, and theories.

Psychological and Biological Explanations of Deviance. We do what we do because certain chemicals are released in the brain. These chemicals tell us what actions to perform. The chemicals that are released are themselves determined by a combination of what we eat, our genetic makeup, and the way we are brought up. Psychological and biological explanations of deviance focus on such biological or physiological explanations of criminal behavior. Some of the psychological explanations of deviance focus on **personality disorders,** abnormalities in individual personalities caused by hereditary factors or by upbringing. These disorders might result, for example, from emotional deprivation—lack of love—in childhood or from being brainwashed by television programs in which crime is glorified. Or, alternatively, these explanations focus more on neurological and biological issues resulting from heredity or psychological causes. Let's consider one of those subissues: the issue of genetic and biological predisposition to deviance and crime.

Genetic and Biological Predisposition to Deviance.   The idea that there is a criminal type has long been a popular belief among laypeople and among some criminologists. For example, in the late nineteenth century, noted Italian criminologist Cesare Lombroso claimed that criminals are less sensitive to pain and more subject to epilepsy than normal individuals. He found criminals to have heads higher at the rear than at the forehead, longer lower jaws, flattened noses, scanty beards, long ears, and other physical peculiarities. He explained these peculiarities as atavistic reversions to the characteristics of early savage ancestors. Later studies have totally discredited Lombroso's theory.

Modern approaches have not concentrated on body type but rather on genetic structure. Some studies have argued that a causal link exists between the presence in some males of an extra Y or "male-producing" chromosome (designated the XYY syndrome) and criminal behavior. Much of this work has also been discredited. But new work is continually coming forward that makes the case that some aspects of deviant behavior are genetically determined. Ultimately, genes guide behavior, so there is likely a genetic predisposition to certain types of deviant behavior. But that genetic predisposition is also likely to be a predisposition to other behaviors that are seen by society as positive: being an entrepreneur, or a leader. Leaders also violate society's norms. Social science doesn't argue against all genetic predisposition theories. What it does argue against is letting those theories mask inherent prejudices that foster stereotyping of individuals.

Sociobiology and Deviance

The advent of sociobiology has brought another resurgence of biological explanations of deviant behavior. Sophisticated studies, such as one by Sarnoff Mednick and Karl Christiansen, have suggested some biological predisposition to criminal activity. They found that boys adopted at birth whose biological parents were criminals were more likely to be criminals than those with noncriminal parents, even though neither group knew about their parents. Yet another attempt to establish a biological basis for crime was the work of James Q. Wilson of Harvard and Richard Herrnstein of the University of California.

They argued that crime is a matter of relating costs (getting caught and punished) with the benefits of crime. The authors hold that for certain types of individuals, such as those with athletic builds and slightly lower than average IQ (92), immediate benefits outweigh the future costs; that is, punishment for crime occurs with a lag, whereas the benefits of crime are instantaneous. They propose that this means individuals' time preference (how much they value the present relative to the future) plays an important role in determining whether a person is predisposed to crime. As with most theories that focus on a biological basis for crime, these theories are much in debate.

Sociological Explanations of Deviance

The group of social scientists that has had the most to say about deviance and crime is sociologists. To introduce you to the sociologists' perspective, we will briefly discuss differential association theory, labeling theory, control theory, strain theory, and illegitimate opportunity theory. These theories are part of two broad sociological perspectives: (1) a **symbolic interactionist perspective,** which sees individuals interpreting social life through symbols that we learn from the groups to which we belong, and (2) a **functionalist perspective,** which sees all activities in society as having a function. Differential association theory, labeling theory, and control theory fall within the symbolic interactionist perspective. Strain theory and illegitimate opportunity theory fall within the functionalist perspective.

Differential Association Theory.   **Differential association theory** argues that deviant behavior often is simply behavior that is conforming to norms. The difference is that they

Cesare Lombroso's (1835–1909) characteristics of a criminal: Excessive wrinkles on skin, excessive cheekbones, a twisted nose, long arms, large jaw, and large chin.

© Mary Evans Picture Library/Alamy Stock Photo

are deviant norms. For example, some groups develop a different set of values or norms—such as toughness and the propensity to take risks—considered deviant from the dominant norms.

This theory, put forward by sociologist Edwin Sutherland, argues that whether people deviate or conform is most influenced by the groups with whom they associate. Because different groups have different forms of deviant behavior, people who associate with different groups experience an "excess of definition" and in some groups seem deviant. For example, street gangs can require individuals to "stand up" to an insult, and if one is insulted, one is expected to respond by defending one's honor with physical violence.

Differential association theory comes more into play when significantly different cultures interact. In the Hmong culture of Southeast Asia, one of the ways one finds a wife is to "capture" her and forcibly have sex with her. In the United States, that is called kidnapping and rape, both of which are serious crimes.

Most people will agree that differential association theory explains some deviant behavior, but most also argue that it should not be used to condone it. Society must have norms, and individuals must learn to conform to those norms and abide by those that have been codified into law.

Labeling Theory.

Labeling theory focuses on the significance of labels given to people (such as names and reputational labels). These labels assigned by society to groups can tend to make the actions of certain groups criminal and the actions of certain other groups non-criminal. A classic study of the effects of labeling was done by sociologist William Chambliss. He studied two groups of adolescent lawbreakers in a high school. He labeled one group "the Saints" and the other group "the Roughnecks." Both groups were wild and were into drinking, truancy, vandalism, and theft, but the Saints were seen by their teachers as headed for success whereas the Roughnecks were seen as headed for trouble.

The cause of this distinction was family background and social class. The Saints came from respectable, middle-class families. The Roughnecks came from working-class families. This led to a number of differences: The Saints had cars, so their debauchery was spread over the entire town and was less conspicuous; the Roughnecks did not have cars, and their actions, taking place in the same area day after day, made them conspicuous and drew the attention of the police. They also had different "styles of interaction" when caught by police. The Saints were seemingly apologetic and penitent; they showed a seeming respect for the police and generally were let go with warnings. The Roughnecks showed contempt and consistently had the book thrown at them. The results were predictable: The Saints became doctors and lawyers while the Roughnecks became criminals. The issues here are obviously more complicated than can be captured by this brief discussion of Chambliss's study, but the idea should be clear: Labels make a difference in how people are treated and in many cases can become self-fulfilling.

Control Theory.

Control theory argues that the desire to rebel is more akin to our natural desires but that certain forces prevent us from doing so. Control theory argues that the question is not, "Why do people deviate from society's norms?" Rather, the question is, "Why don't we deviate more than we do?" To prevent such deviation, society has developed norms and institutions that subtly control us and our actions. Much of the subtle control is instilled by parents during our childhood, and thus, the type of family we come from and the type of friends we have in early childhood play major roles in determining how much deviance we will exhibit.

Strain Theory.

Strain theory falls within the functionalist sociological perspective. Functionalists argue that deviance is a necessary part of a society; it clarifies moral boundaries and affirms norms; and it promotes social unity and brings about necessary social change. Successful industrialized societies must arouse discontent in people to instill within them the desire to advance and better themselves. **Strain theory,** which was developed by sociologist Robert Merton and other functionalists, argues that when the social structure does not provide equal access for economic success but instills in all people a functional striving for economic success, the result is a social strain. This social strain can result in a variety of reactions, one of which is crime. Notice the difference between strain theory and the psychological theories. Strain theory sees deviance as a product of society, not of individuals. In strain theory society creates crime and criminals.

Illegitimate Opportunity Theory.

A slightly different take on the functionalist perspective on crime is the illegitimate opportunity theory, put forward by sociologists Richard Cloward and Lloyd Ohlin. This theory argues that crime is all around us but that different social classes have distinct styles of crime. All individuals are imbued with the desire to achieve material success, but the lower social classes have significant barriers to achieving that success legally. They are, however, presented with **illegitimate opportunity structures**—opportunities to make larger amounts of money through "hustles" such as drug dealing, pimping, and gambling. Society sees all these as crimes. The more privileged class does not face the barriers and its crimes are "white-collar crimes" such as tax evasion and false advertising, which are not prosecuted as much and are not so widely seen as crimes.

Economic Explanations of Deviance

Economists tend to see all issues through a prism of costs and benefits. Thus, their explanation for crime and deviance is that the benefits of crime exceed the costs and that the way to decrease crime and deviance is to increase its costs. For example, the death penalty increases the cost of a crime to an individual, and economists argue that having the death penalty helps prevent killings. Critics of such economic explanations argue that killing generally is an irrational act—a crime of passion in which the penalty plays only a very small role; thus, having the death penalty will not significantly reduce killings. Who's right? That's unclear; both sides are still debating the empirical evidence.

Another implication of the economist's approach is the proposition that lower-income individuals are more likely to commit an "equal payoff" crime than are high-income individuals because the cost to the higher-income individuals of going to jail is higher. Similarly, a rich person is less likely to be deterred by a fine than a poorer person because the same fine has less meaning to the rich person. (Finland has an interesting application of this view. It makes all traffic fines income-sensitive, so that a rich person pays a much higher fine than a poor person. Thus, a really rich person might have to pay $200,000 if caught speeding.)

Even economists admit that much is left out of their cost–benefit approach to crime (and to many issues). But they argue that its simplicity and clear statement often shed some light on the issues missed by other social science approaches.

Summary of Various Perspectives on Deviance

Our discussion has only touched on the various theories of deviance. Many, we are sure, have led to reactions from you such as "But how about. . . ?" To really get into those issues, you'll have to take a psychology or sociology course on deviance. What you should get out of this course is the knowledge that there are many theories of deviance, and not a lot of agreement. Before we move on, however, let us point out that the theories are not mutually exclusive, and our brief overview of them has not done them justice. Deviance is not a simple issue, and truly understanding that issue requires study beyond that which can be presented in an overview course such as this.

Crime, Law, and Order

Deviance is of scholarly interest. Most laypeople are less interested in the scholarly concept of deviance, and more interested in the narrower concept of a certain type of deviance: crime. So now that we've been through the major academic theories of deviance, let's relate that theory to policy and discuss crime. A **crime** can be defined as deviant behavior that violates society's norms that have been codified into the law. Deviance becomes crime when the government passes a law that makes deviant behavior illegal. This means that crime is highly dependent on the way in which a society relates deviant behavior to crime. Other things being equal, the more tolerant the society is to deviant behavior, the less crime a society will have.

Above, in our discussion of the law, we stated that the United States did not come out well in many international rankings of the success of its system of justice. Why did the United States not do so well? Most observers believe that the problem with the U.S. system of justice is not so much with the general structure of the legal tradition, but with its implementation. In theory the U.S. system of justice sounds great; in practice it leaves much to be desired.

We will focus our discussion on three interrelated problems with the U.S. system of justice.

- The first is that it may be trying to do too much—to control its population in ways that the population does not want to be controlled.
- The second is that there is an unequal application of the implementation of justice.
- The third is that the United States focus on punishing crime, rather than on providing guidance, is both unfair and outrageously expensive. Punishment, not guidance, has become pervasive in the U.S. criminal justice system. It is even built into its system of policing.

These three problems combine to bring about outcomes, such as those listed below, that most people don't like.

- There are too many people in U.S. jails and prisons—ten times as many per capita than most other countries. The United States makes up 5 percent of the world population, but has 25 percent of the world's jailed prisoners.
- Far too many of those imprisoned are young black men. Sixty percent of the prison population is black or an ethnic minority, even though that group makes up a much smaller percentage of the population. One in three black men can be expected to spend some time in prison over their lifetime.
- Many poor and minority groups, especially blacks, have lost faith in the U.S. policing and justice system; they believe that they will be treated unequally and unfairly, and therefore, they do not cooperate with it.

So what should the United States do? Let's explore that question by considering the three problems and how they relate to outcomes.

Problem 1: Is the United States Trying to Exert Too Much Control over Individuals?

The more laws a society has restricting behavior, the more people are going to violate the laws. Crime and the number of people in prison increased in the United States significantly in the 1980s, precisely the time that the United States instituted a war on drugs. Making something illegal that was previously not illegal, and strictly enforcing laws that previously were not strictly enforced increase crime almost by definition. Actions that previously were not crimes now are crimes.

You can see the effect of the war on drugs, which began in the 1970s and started in earnest in the 1980s, by looking at what happened to people in prison when it was introduced. In Figure 8.1, which shows the number of people in jail or prison from 1925 to 2016, we do so. (Jail refers to places of local incarceration for less than one year—a county or a city will have jails. Prisons refer to places of incarceration for longer than a year. States and the federal government have prisons.)

The United States had previously tried to deter people from an action that it considered bad for people back in the 1920s with **Prohibition**, laws that banned the sale and drinking of alcohol. People did not follow the Prohibition laws, and "crime" increased—not because people were doing something different than before, but because actions that previously had

U.S. state and federal prison population, 1925–2016

Figure 8.1

The increase in prisoners in the United States. (Source: Bureau of Justice statistics)

not been a crime were made a crime by the law. The bottom line is that if society has fewer laws restricting action, society will have less crime and fewer people in prison.

Classifying Crimes.   To say that the United States should take a looser view of drug use is not to say that government should not see drug use as deviant, or even as a crime. It is simply to say that it might be best not to deal with it by putting people in jail. Society can think of drug use as stupid and something that should be strongly discouraged and still believe that it should not be treated as a crime. This differentiation between actions society discourages and actions society treats as crime leads to an alternative way of dealing with the drug crisis. Society can keep drug use as an action it attempts to discourage, but it can discourage it by advertisements and high taxes, not by arresting people. Even if society wants to keep drug use a crime, the degree of seriousness of that crime could be reduced.

To see how this would be done, you need to know that in the criminal justice system crimes are gradated by degree of seriousness. **Felonies** such as premeditated murder or aggravated assault, are the most serious crimes. Felonies are further subclassified into Class A, B, C (etc.) felonies depending on the state. For example, in New York, murder is a Class A Felony, and assault in the second degree is a Class D Felony. Each level of felony is associated with a given penalty guidance. **Misdemeanors** are crimes that are less serious than felonies. An example of a misdemeanor is involuntary manslaughter, where one kills someone by accident rather than doing it with forethought. Misdemeanors are also broken into sub-classifications. Finally, there are **infractions**—crimes that are considered less serious than a misdemeanor. One can plead "no contest" to an infraction and the infraction will not appear on one's Department of Justice record. That is not the case with felonies and misdemeanors. Thus, the more drug use is treated as an infraction, not as a misdemeanor or felony, the fewer the people in prison. Below is a table summarizing the three types of crimes.

Decreasing Crime by Eliminating Laws against Victimless Crime.   Drug use falls into a class of crimes often called victimless crimes. Prostitution and gambling also fall into this category. Whereas most people agree that violent crimes such as premeditated murder should be a crime, there is far less agreement whether something like selling or smoking pot should be a crime. Nationally, it is a crime; but in some states it is not, and in the court of public opinion it both is and isn't depending on who you are talking to. Drinking in public is another behavior upon which people disagree about whether it should be a crime.

Table 8.1

Classification of Crimes

CLASSIFICATION	APPROXIMATE PENALTY
Felony	fines, probation, up to 1 year in county jail, or possibly state prison, for more than 1 year, parole
Misdemeanor	fines, probation, maximum 1 year in county jail
Infraction	fines only, no probation, no jail time

Were the United States to take a more lenient view of such activities, or even a more tolerant approach to the enforcement of the laws prohibiting such activities, "crime" in the United States would be significantly reduced. Let me give an example. There is a lot of underage drinking on residential college campuses, but the laws against it are seldom enforced, so it doesn't show up as a crime. College students are given a pass, whereas non-college students are often not.

A wide range of social scientists on both sides of the political spectrum believe that the war on drugs is a war that the United States cannot win, and that while the United States should do whatever it can to discourage drug use, trying to prevent drug use by criminalization and strict enforcement of drug use laws causes more harm than good. For example, in 2011, in a major global study of drug policy—signed by a former president of Brazil, former U.S. Secretary of State George Shultz, and former U.S. Fed Chairman Paul Volcker—came to the conclusion that the war on drugs has totally failed and that the trillion dollars spent on it have served little purpose. It recommended a new policy of decriminalization and discouragement as a way of undercutting the power of organized crime and reducing the number of prisoners in the United States.

The classification of crimes can also play an important role in determining the amount of crime in various subsectors of society. For example in the 1980s and 1990s, crack possession (a type of cocaine that was prevalent in black communities) was enforced more strongly than was cocaine possession (more prevalent in white communities.) How differently were these "crimes" enforced? In a study which led to the Fair Sentencing Act of 2010, researchers found that people charged with the possession of one gram of crack received on average the same sentence as people charged with the possession of 100 grams of cocaine, even though crack and cocaine are almost identical molecularly. Even after the law change in 2010, there was still a significant difference. On average, those charged with possession of just one gram of crack are given the same sentence as those found in possession of 18 grams of cocaine.

There are many reasons for this difference between crack and cocaine sentences, and it was not just because crack was more prevalent in the black community. It was also because, on average, whites tended to have more access to good legal advice and representation because they were more likely to afford it. That captures another problem with the justice system. If you can afford a good lawyer, you can often manage to get your sentence reduced to a lower-level crime—or even dismissed.

Inmates (except female instructor in the middle) take cooking course at Halden Prison, Norway's second largest prison.

© OMAR TORRES/AFP/Getty

A prison in New Orleans.

© Alex Masi/Corbis

Rich and middle-class people can afford a good lawyer; poor minorities often cannot.

Even if society does not totally decriminalize drug use, it can reduce the number of people imprisoned by reducing the classification of drug use and sales. Were society to keep all the same crimes that they currently have, but reduce the general level of classifications of most crime, society could reduce the number of people in jail and prison even while maintaining pressure against the norm violations. For example, many victimless crimes, such as drug use and prostitution, could be treated as infractions.

Society might even consider creating a fourth level of crime that is below an infraction—let's call it a more (remember it is pronounced mor-ray) violation. What are "more violations" could be decided on by legislatures, just as laws are currently.[1] These laws would be put on the books not as crimes, but as *more violations*. Giving legislatures the duty to define mores could let them serve a useful purpose without creating criminals. They are deciding on *guides for reasonable behavior.*

A "more violation" would not be classified as a crime; instead it would be classified as a deviant behavior, and there would be no enforceable-by-force prohibition of the action. Violators would not face any fine or jail time, but they might face a public rebuke and shame. (Such "shame" punishments currently take place. For example, some "criminals" have been sentenced to wear "I am an idiot" signs. You can find a number of such imaginative punishments that judges have given online.)

Broken Windows

Police face the continual problem of how strictly laws should be enforced. People break laws all the time, and if the laws are tightly enforced, you waste effort on crimes that people care less about, leaving crimes that people care more about to go unsolved. So police often let small crimes—jay walking, loitering, drinking in public places—go by, and concentrate on big crimes—armed robbery, assault, murder. But one line of thinking holds that if you stop small crimes, you develop a commitment to upholding the law and thereby deter large crimes as well. This is called the "broken windows theory" of policing.

It makes some sense, and when New York implemented it in the 1980s, it led to a decrease in crime. But it also has negative side effects, especially if it is not applied equally to all. Minorities were often subject to broken windows policing, and arrested for small crimes, which undermined their belief in the fairness of the system. The broken windows approach would almost always be accompanied by a "stop and frisk" policy, in an attempt to prevent serious crimes from happening. This also was often applied much more to minorities, and it has been at the center of a number of racial profiling scandals.

---

[1] The term "mores" comes from Latin and is the plural of "mos," so an argument can be made that what I call more should be called mos. I don't call it mos because mos doesn't sound right, and doesn't have the right ring to it. Languages, like societies, are living evolving systems and are continually adding and deleting words as they evolve.

Problem 2: Is Justice Applied Equally to All in the United States?

Let's now turn to a second reason for the United States's poor showing in international comparisons of justice systems—implementation both in policing and in court. While the theoretical structure of U.S. law sounds great, the implementation of that law is far from great. The first problem is in policing. While police do a good job in enforcing the law compared to most other countries, they do not do such a good job when it comes to minorities, especially young black men. One reason why is that police in minority areas often do not reflect the ethnic background of the area. This makes it hard for minorities and police to relate and understand each other to the degree that is necessary for mentoring to work.

A second problem is in the courts and legal system. To use the U.S. legal system you need a lawyer, and with the high cost of lawyers in the United States, lower-income individuals simply do not have the ability to get a fair treatment from the U.S. legal system. Whereas a well-off person can hire an expensive lawyer who can negotiate an offense down, or get a client off on a legal technicality, poor people cannot.

It is not only the high cost of lawyers that prevents low-income individuals from getting a fair treatment from the justice system. The situation is made worse by the practice of charging defendants for part of the cost of prosecution, either in the form of a fine or in the form of a required payment for the use of the court system. If a fine or required reimbursement of court expenses is at a level an individual cannot pay—and in many jurisdictions that is the case—the result is that, while a person's crime may have been minor, the person ends up in jail or prison, not for the crime but for not paying the fine associated with it. An extreme example is of a man arrested for stealing a $2 can of soda. He served twelve months in jail for failure to pay the fine he was given.

Oftentimes a poor person feels in an almost impossible position when arrested, and he or she may plead guilty to a crime he or she did not commit. How can that happen? When a person is arrested or in court, there are usually significant negotiations about how a crime will be classified—the same crime can be classified as a felony, misdemeanor, or infraction. Felonies have long-term consequences that carry through one's entire life. A convicted felon cannot vote or own a firearm, and can often find it very difficult to find a job. Oftentimes, prosecutors will offer plea deals to lower-level charges if a person pleads guilty. If a person doesn't have good legal representation, often pleading guilty to a lesser-category crime is the best option, because, even if he or she is innocent, there is a high probability he or she will be convicted.

Faced with such situations, for many of the poor, the justice system seems more like a "shakedown" system than a justice system. Once you are caught in it, it requires you to pay and pay to keep from getting brought deeper and deeper into the system. Most social science researchers believe that significant reform is needed in how poor people are treated by the courts so that individuals of any income level do not have the perception that they are being "shaken down."

Recent scholarship has suggested that the shortcomings of our courts and legal system are especially pronounced in the way the U.S. justice system treats racial minorities. In her 2010 book *The New Jim Crow*, author and legal scholar Michelle Alexander argues that, just like the systems of slavery and Jim Crow segregation that came before it, mass incarceration has created a racial caste system that disenfranchises black communities. Her thesis stems from the evidence that the war on drugs has disproportionately disadvantaged black people, owing to higher rates of enforcement in black communities and disparate sentencing policies. The result has been that one-third of black men can expect to go to prison in their lifetimes, despite white people being just as likely or even more likely to commit drug crimes. These black men then become second-class citizens unable to vote, serve on juries, or support themselves and their families, which perpetuates the cycle of poverty and discrimination that feeds back into even more mass incarceration.

*T*he Author's Bias[2]

As I have emphasized throughout the book, social scientists are supposed to be neutral in their presentations, and in most of the book, I try hard to maintain that neutrality. But in the text, you likely detected a bias in the discussion of the U.S approach to crime. If you did, you're right. I am sufficiently disgusted with the United States approach to crime that I have found it impossible to maintain the scientific objectivity I strive for. So I might as well admit it. I can't be objective in discussing how the United States deals with crime. The reason is that, while I certainly cannot place myself in the shoes of a young black teenager, I can partially do so, and from that perspective, I simply cannot justify the U.S. approach.

I grew up moderately poor, but had a loving stable family, so I was lucky. Nonetheless, I was a rebellious ADHD-type child, one who could not sit still. Nor could I put up with actions of people in power that I considered inappropriate. My school, my parents, and the justice system were lenient in their treatment of me; they provided guidance much more than punishment. I turned out okay, probably in large part because I was white. I suspect that, had I been black, I would not have been treated so leniently, and I might well have followed a different path—ending up in jail, rather than being a respected professor and author of your textbook.

Based on that experience, I have come to believe that there is little inherent difference among individuals, and one small different reaction can lead to enormous differences in one's life path. Because of my experiences, I am strongly biased toward the argument for judicial leniency and the guidance approach to the justice system, especially when dealing with young people.

I fully recognize that there are also arguments on the other side. The expectation of leniency can become built into behavior, which can cause antisocial behavior to increase. In social policy, when it is almost impossible to choose between two arguments based on the empirical evidence, one must choose based on one's gut. And my gut tells me that in most cases, "enlightened guidance,"—a combination of empathy, shaming, judicious counseling, and using strict criminal punishment only as a last resort—is the best way to deal with the general problem of deviance.

Problem 3: Deciding the Purpose of the Justice and Criminal System

Now let us turn to our third reason why many social scientists have problems with the U.S. justice system. It is focusing on the wrong goal. Let's distinguish two views. One is that the purpose of the justice system should be to punish criminals and get them off the street. The second is that the purpose of the justice system should be to provide guidance for people who have made a mistake; the goal, for most social scientists, is to return people to the street to be productive citizens as soon as they have gotten that guidance. The two views lead to quite different methods of enforcement and views of what should happen if a person ends up in jail or prison.

The "punishment" view sees the role of police as catching criminals and putting them behind bars so that they cannot commit more crime. The more people in prison, the more people are being prevented from committing crime, and the better the police are doing their job. If one holds this view, prison should be as unpleasant as possible—otherwise it wouldn't be punishment. Put enough of the criminals behind bars and crime is reduced. Moreover, the fear of imprisonment for crime reduces crime. According to this view, crime fell in the early 2000s because many of the criminals had been put in jail, and others were prevented from committing crime by the fear of punishment.

The "guidance" view has a different take on the role of the justice system. It sees prison as a last resort in rehabilitating a person. Prison time is not a time for punishment but a time for learning. It should be structured so that a person is socialized and prepared to go back into society as fast as possible. In certain cases, rehabilitation may be impossible, but in most cases it is possible. In the "law enforcement as guidance" view, most of the people in prison should

---

[2] Although the book has two authors, the lead author died a number of years ago. We keep him as a co-author because the book has become known as Hunt and Colander, and his sensibility still guides the book. This section is a departure from the standard social science detachment, so, while I believe that my co-author would have agreed with the sentiment it expresses, I cannot be sure. I, Dave Colander, use "I" in this box to emphasize that it is a personal sentiment expressed here, not a general social science sentiment.

not be thought of as sociopaths or natural-born criminals. Rather they should be thought of as people who made a bad decision, did not get appropriately socialized, or somehow got caught on the wrong side of the system that specifies what a crime is.

This guidance view sees the U.S. prison system, as it is currently run, as too often creating criminals. Once a person gets caught up in the criminal justice system, it is difficult to escape. Prison often hardens people and teaches them to be criminals. People getting out of prison or jail generally have no skills and no way of earning income. People with records have a difficult time finding jobs, and anyone classified as a felon has an almost impossible time finding a job. Given the inability to get work, someone coming out of prison is left with almost no alternative to crime. The entire process becomes a downward spiral and results in the feeling of being shaken down. That reinforces any antisocial behavior and creates hardened criminals, who actually do have to be put in prison to protect society.

This guidance view sees the difference between a criminal and a leader in society as often very small. This is especially true when one is dealing with young people who are still in the process of being socialized. Strict enforcement of a law too early can turn potential leaders—individuals who are naturally rebellious and who rebel against what they consider unfair treatment—into criminals.

Some social scientists call the U.S. approach to criminal justice the "school-to-prison pipeline" approach in which early arrests for relatively minor infractions destroy a child's long-term prospects and create a criminal out of someone who could have been a productive citizen. As former Attorney General Eric Holder put it, excessively strict enforcement of minor infractions of rules can have "negative effects on the long-term well-being of our young people, increasing their likelihood of future contact with the juvenile and criminal justice systems."

The difference between these punishment and guidance views of the role of the justice system can be seen in the introduction of this chapter that compared the treatment of two prisoners. Norway follows the "guidance" view and the United States follows the punishment view. The differential results reflect that difference. In fact, the United States has followed the punishment approach to a much greater extent than just about any other developed society. It imprisons many more people per capita than does any other developed country, and yet the United States has the highest crime rates of any developed country.

The Empirical Evidence is Insufficient to Guide Policy.   The empirical evidence does not tell us which of these two views is appropriate. The causation and correlation of different explanations is so complex that statistical analysis cannot provide definitive answers. But we must admit that the authors of this text fall strongly in the "guidance view of justice" camp. The reason is the interaction of the three problems listed above: Were the people in prison a representative sample of all society, so that everyone's friends and children were facing similar punishment, then the punishment view might possibly be justifiable if that punishment serves the general good and does not affect subgroups of society differently. That isn't the case in the United States. Very few rich and upper-middle-class people end up in prison; prison is disproportionately the fate of the poor and of blacks, especially young black men. That unequal application of justice suggests that the justice system is not equally applied to society.

Police Bias, Driving while Black, and the Downward Spiral.   The empathy and judicious counseling necessary for the guidance view of dealing with crime to work best occurs long before a person enters the criminal justice system—it takes place with mentoring by family and friends. That mentoring has broken down in many poor households. Fathers are often not to be seen, and other members of the family are working multiple jobs and coping with the stresses of poverty, which means that teachers and other adults in authority such as police have to assume that mentoring role. If more people in authority can relate to the youth they are mentoring, they can provide much better counseling. This presents another problem of our criminal justice system—many of the policemen are white, and even if they try hard (and the large majority of them do), because of differences in background, they are not especially good at providing role models or empathy for black male teenagers.

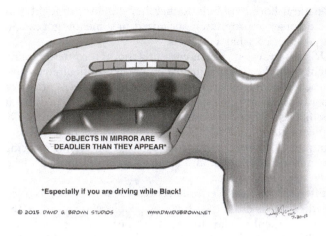

OBJECTS IN MIRROR ARE
DEADLIER THAN THEY APPEAR*

*Especially if you are driving while Black!

© 2015 DAVID G. BROWN STUDIOS   WWW.DAVIDGBROWN.NET

© David G. Brown

The Racial Reality of Policing.   In 2015, a number of killings of young black men by police provoked a set of demonstrations and outrage. A "Black Lives Matter" movement started, and rioting occurred in a number of cities. Some of the issues involved in forming an opinion on these events were nicely captured in an essay entitled "The Racial Reality of Policing" by former New York City police detective and author Edward Conlon. In it he describes a training exercise used by the NYC police department. The instructor had two white and two black police officers come up to the front of the class. He had one black officer face the wall with his hands up, and two white police officers pretend to point guns at him. He would than ask the class what was happening, and all would agree that it was an arrest. Then he would have one white officer face the wall with his hands up, and two black police officers pretend to point guns at him. He would then again ask the class what was happening. The class generally didn't answer because they knew the point of the exercise—what both black and white police thought was happening in this case was a mugging.

Rates of Impunity: It Could Be Worse

As bad as the criminal justice system is in the United States, it is also important to recognize that it could be far worse. The basic structure of the U.S. justice system is solid, and there is a rule of law that governs behavior and applies to government as well as the people. The problems with the U.S. system are around the edges and in its application, not at its core. In other countries, where the rule of law does not work, the situation is much worse. The entire system is seen as corrupt and unfair, not only for a subgroup, but for the large majority of people in the society.

One example is Guatemala, where, until recently, corruption was so deep and went so high into the government that no one believed that the justice system represented anything even approaching fairness. In response, Guatemala turned part of its judicial system over to a UN-sponsored agency, the International Commission Against Impunity in Guatemala or CICIG. This agency was given the right to investigate all types of crime. The results included charging the president, vice president, the head of the central bank, judges, and the head of congress with corruption. The UN commission claimed to have increased the rate of conviction for crimes committed by government officials from 5 percent to over 70 percent.

Conlon went on to argue that such perceptions are the reality, and that police should be excused for treating young black men as potentially dangerous. The reality is a higher percentage of them are dangerous, so these perceptions are themselves based in reality. Moreover, those perceptions are held by other blacks as well as by police. The reality is that a black man is much more likely to be killed by another black man than he is by the police. In 2011, almost 7,000 black men were murdered, mostly by other black men, and 129 were killed by police.

So, according to Conlon, the problem is not so much with the police as it is with the breakdown of mentoring of young black people. Aspects of black gang culture glorify gun violence, and promote norms that defy and challenge society's norms. This leaves the majority of black people who live in areas in which there is significant violence with a difficult choice—do they support the police or not? All too often they don't, and without that local support, officers cannot adequately police an area. It becomes a lawless area run by gangs, and both police and law-abiding individuals are hurt.

The distrust with which minority areas treat the police means that the necessary working relationship between the police and many groups in society is not there. That leads to a high **rate of impunity**—the ratio of committing a crime to being punished for that crime—for many crimes in low-income areas. The reality is that large percentages of murders in low-income areas go unsolved, and many who are arrested manage to avoid conviction because victims and witnesses from the area are unwilling to come forward, either because of fear of retaliation or mistrust of the police and the judicial system. The system becomes self-reinforcing, with police becoming seen as the opponents, instead of the supporters, of society's norms.

The point in raising these issues is to emphasize to you that there is no easy answer to this problem, and that all too often people fail to be willing to step back and see both sides of the issue—to play the objective impartial spectator who works hard to put himself or herself in someone else's shoes. While just about everyone agrees that one part of the answer is to have much more sensitive police, a much larger percentage of whom come from the geographic area and social group that they are policing, it is not something that can be easily achieved even when police are trying hard to do it.

Conclusion

This has only been a brief introduction to issues of deviance and crime, but we hope that we have conveyed to you the importance of the topic and the different ways of dealing with crime. The issue is not a conservative or liberal issue, and people on both the right and the left favor changing the system. This was demonstrated in 2015, when the Koch brothers, leading funders of the right wing of the Republican party, and former President Obama both agreed that the criminal justice system was broken and needed to be changed. They began exploring ways in which they could work together to bring about change. They all believed that the high level of incarceration in the United States, especially of young black males, is unacceptable. To highlight the issue, President Obama visited a federal prison and praised the efforts of the Koch brothers in bringing about change in federal sentencing laws and in how people convicted of a crime are treated once released.

What makes it possible for both of these groups to work together is that they are following the "walk in the other person's shoes" approach to thinking about problems. The Koch brothers' interest in criminal justice came about when they became, they believed unfairly, the target of criminal charges. Those charges were dropped as inappropriate, but the fact that they could be targeted made them aware that others, who did not have access to expensive lawyers, were also being targeted, and they decided to try to stop that.

Similarly, President Obama could relate to the felons. He stated: "These are young people who made mistakes that aren't that different from the mistakes I made and the mistakes that a lot of you guys made. That's what strikes me—there but for the grace of God . . . "

Social scientists don't have the answer to how to correct the criminal justice problem in the United States, but we do have the approach that is most likely to lead to an answer: Apply the "Walk in the other person's shoes" approach to thinking about the problem and honestly search for reforms that can be accepted by all sides.

 Study and **Review**

Key Points

- Norms are relative, differ among subgroups of society, and include a norm that encourages a certain degree of deviance.
- Deviant behavior is not a crime unless there is a law against that behavior.
- The rule of law is meant to place restrictions to how governments deal with deviant behavior.

- Five sociological explanations of crime are differential association theory, control theory, labeling theory, strain theory, and illegitimate opportunity theory.
- The economic explanations of deviance emphasize costs and benefits to an individual.

- Crimes can be classified as felonies, misdemeanors, and infractions, with felonies being the most serious.
- Three reasons for poor showings of the U.S. justice system include its attempt to do too much, unequal implementation, and lack of clarity over whether the purpose is punishment or guidance.

- To many poor people and black people, the justice system seems to be more of a shakedown system than a justice system.
- For policing to be effective, the police must work with the population, not against it.

Some Important Terms

control theory (151)
crime (152)
deviance (142)
differential association
    theory (149)
felonies (154)
functionalist perspective (149)

illegitimate opportunity
    structures (152)
infractions (154)
labeling theory (151)
misdemeanors (154)
mores (143)
norms (142)

personality disorder (148)
Prohibition (153)
rate of impunity (160)
rule of law (145)
strain theory (151)
symbolic interactionist
    perspective (149)

Questions for Review and Discussion

General Questions

1. What are norms and how do they differ from mores?
2. Why do sociologists emphasize that it is society's reaction to an act, not the act itself, that makes an action deviant?
3. Why may an act be a crime in one society but not in another?
4. Explain how criminal behavior could be behavior conforming to a group norm.
5. What is the difference between a civil law and a common law tradition?
6. What is the rule of law and why is it important?
7. Does social science tell you whether spanking a child to punish him or her is wrong?
8. Does the common law or civil law tradition give more emphasis to past judgments?
9. According to the strain theory, is crime necessary for a successful industrial society?
10. In what way is the labeling theory similar to the illegitimate opportunity theory of criminal behavior?
11. List three interrelated problems with the U.S. system of justice.
12. How would you distinguish a felony from a misdemeanor?
13. What are two different views of the purpose of the justice system?
14. What is meant by the Broken Windows theory of policing?

15. Is a young black man more likely to be killed by a white policeman or another black man? What implications does that have for police policy?
16. What are the causes of the high rates of impunity for crime in low-income black communities?
17. How would having more police coming from the geographic areas they are policing help in achieving a fairer system of justice?

Internet Questions

1. Visit the site https://www.thoughtco.com/folk ways-mores-taboos-and-laws-3026267. What is the difference between norms and mores?
2. Does Ice T's "Gangsta Rap Made Me Do It" video (https://www.youtube.com/watch?v=HzeZhCt5 PVA) serve a useful social purpose? If so, what is that purpose?
3. What is an example of a Class I felony (http://www.courtregistry.org/criminal_court_records/felonies/felony_class/)?
4. What is an alternative to imprisonment suggested by the Office of National Drug Control Policy (https://obamawhitehouse.archives.gov/ondcp/alternatives-to-incarceration)?
5. Go the Jon Stewart's interview of Edward Conlon on YouTube (https://www.youtube.com/watch?v=I3bR_Cbngzc). At what age does Conlon say that cops stop being cool in minority areas?

For Further Study

Books to Explore

Alexander, Michelle, *The New Jim Crow: Mass Incarceration in the Age of Colorblindness*, New York: The New Press, 2010.

Butler, Paul, *Chokehold: Policing Black Men*, New York: The New Press, 2017.

Clear, Todd, and Natasha Frost, *The Punishment Imperative: The Rise and Failure of Mass Incarceration in America*, New York: New York University Press, 2013.

Conlon, Edward, *Blue Blood*, New York: Penguin Publishers, 2004.

Dobbert, Duane L., and Mackey, Thomas X., *Deviance; Theories on Behaviors that Defy Social Norms*, New York: Praeger, 2015.

Downes, David, and Paul Rock, *Understanding Deviance: A Guide to the Sociology of Crime and Rule Breaking*, Oxford: Oxford University Press, 2011.

Drucker, Ernest, *A Plague of Prisons: The Epidemiology of Mass Incarceration in America*, New York: The New Press, 2013.

Forman, James, *Locking Up Our Own: Crime and Punishment in Black America*, New York: Farrar, Straus and Giroux, 2017.

Fortner, Michael, *Black Silent Majority: The Rockefeller Drug Laws and the Politics of Punishment*, Cambridge, MA: Harvard University Press, 2015.

Looman, Mary, and John Carl. *A County Called Prison: Mass Incarceration and the Making of a New Nation*, Oxford: Oxford University Press, 2015.

Pegues, Jeff, *Black and Blue: Inside the Divide Between the Police and Black America*, New York: Prometheus Books, 2017.

Plantinga, Adam, *400 Things Cops Know: Street-Smart Lessons for a Veteran Patrolman*, Fresno, CA: Quill Driver Books, 2014.

Rios, Victor, *Punished: Policing the Lives of Black and Latino Boys*, New York: New York University Press, 2011.

Schenwar, Maya, *Locked Down, Locked Out: Why Prisons Don't Work and How We Can Do Better*, Oakland, CA: Berrett-Koehler Publishers, 2014.

Spence, Gerry, *Police State: How America's Cops Get Away with Murder*, New York: St. Martin's Press, 2015.

Internet Sites to Explore

"http://www.civilrights.org/" The Leadership Conference.

"http://www.nij.gov/Pages/welcome.aspx" National Institute of Justice.

"https://www.thoughtco.com/sociological-explanations-of-deviant-behavior-3026269" Sociological Explanations Of Deviant Behavior.

"http://www.sociologyguide.com/basic-concepts/Social-Norms.php" Sociology Guide.

"http://www.justice.gov/" U.S. Department of Justice.

The Family

After reading this chapter, you should be able to:

- List four variations in family patterns and discuss where such variations can be found
- List three functions of the family and explain how variations in family patterns serve those functions
- Discuss the state and problems of the U.S. family today
- Discuss the effects of technology on the family and what effect future changes in technology are likely to have on the family

It is characteristic of man that he alone has any sense of good and evil, or just and unjust, and the like, and the association of living things who have this sense makes a family and a state.

—Aristotle

Of all the institutions that shape our personalities and help us adjust to changing environments, the **family**—a group of persons closely related by marriage, blood, or some other bond who deal as a unit with the outside world—is the most important. It is within the family that we are initially socialized. If our family unit is not working, we are likely to have personal and social problems. In the United States, families are recognized by civil and religious authorities. Families typically are formed by **marriage**—a social institution marking a commitment between individuals to live as a family which is recognized by civil and/or religious authorities.

Variations in the Family Pattern

Many variations of marriage and families are possible. Until recently most people in the United States tended to think of the family in terms of a mother, father, and one or more dependent children, often with the father working and the mother staying at home. That kind of family is now in the minority in the United States; in fact, fewer than 10 percent of our households meet this description. Today U.S. households are much more diverse. Single-parent families, families with no children, and single-person families are much more common and accepted. Similarly, many of our other ideas about marriage and the family are not universally held. For example, marriage used to be thought of as a union between a man and a woman. That is no longer the case with the legalization of same-sex marriage in the United States.

In thinking about the changing views of marriage, it is useful to consider the history of marriage as an institution underlying the family. Looking at that history, we see that marriage has both a religious and a secular component. Marriage's civil history goes back further; and, from early on, governments have adopted changing rules about what constitutes marriage (for example, whether polygamy is allowed) and the rights that individuals have in marriage. These rules become built into society's legal code (for example, until recently, when women married in Western society, they had to transfer all their property to their husband), and those legal codes form the civil or secular foundation of marriage. Marriage's religious history differs among different religions. In the West, the history of marriage goes back to the Middle Ages, when the Catholic Church sanctioned marriage as a sacrament between a man, a woman, and God. Other religions took different views, and some religions saw marriage as simply a government issue. The dual civil-religious aspect of marriage complicates debates about marriage and leads to the possibility of individuals being married in the eyes of a religion, but not in the eyes of the law, and vice versa. Polygamy in the United States is an example of marriages accepted by some religions but not by U.S. laws. Same-sex marriage is an example of marriages accepted by U.S. law, but not by some religious groups.

The change in views of marriage has led to changes in the nature of the family. Is family defined by tradition, by the state, or by religious organizations. The reality is that it is defined by all three, which means that formal marriage status has become less important in classifying families. There is much more openness about the disconnect between marriage and family. Whereas, even twenty years ago, families would keep quiet about their children who were living with a partner, but not married, or of a daughter having a child but not being married, today, it is much more accepted, and discussed openly as an acceptable social option. Still, there are both legal and social limitations on marriage and allowable family structures, and in the next section we describe some of the options.

Number of Mates

In the Western world, monogamy is the traditional and, in most places, the only legal form of matrimonial relationship. **Monogamy** is a form of marriage in which there is one husband and one wife. This is by far the most widespread form of marriage all over the world, even where other forms are allowed or encouraged. Given the increasing frequency of divorce in the United States, some researchers have suggested that we should develop a new name—serial monogamy—to describe our standard formal relationship, which is marriage between one husband and one wife followed by a dissolution of that marriage and a subsequent marriage between that same husband or wife and another partner.

Polygamy is the term used for plural marriage, but this is divided into two types: **polygyny,** meaning one husband and two or more wives, and **polyandry,** meaning one wife

*M*arriage Around the World

In this book we concentrate on the role and state of marriage in the United States. Other countries are subject to the same general forces as is the United States but can be at a different place in the evolution, or can have reacted to those forces differently. For example, in the United States 40 percent of children are born to unwed mothers; in France it is 60 percent. In Colombia it is 84 percent but in Japan it is only 2 percent. Alternatively, in the United States the average age of marriage for a woman is 30. In Bangladesh it is 19.

In all countries, the richer someone is the more likely they are to be married. This is especially true for males.

For example, in China about 4 percent of male university graduates aged 35 to 39 have never been married. For those who haven't been to university the percentage is much higher, and in 2020 it is predicted that 30 million more men than women will not have been to university, meaning that many men without a university education will not be able to find a wife.

One probable reason for the high number of unmarried non-college educated men in China is China's one-child policy which led to many more men than women as female babies were aborted. With that shortage of women, women get their choice of mates, and they opt for those with the best prospects.

Indian parents often arrange marriages for their children.

and two or more husbands. A polygamous family may be thought of as two or more nuclear families bound together because all the children have one parent in common. Some writers also recognize a form of plural marriage called group marriage, or cenogamy. **Cenogamy** is a form of union in which several men are married to several women, but such relationships are uncommon. **Same-sex marriage** is a union between adults of the same gender.

Where polygyny is sanctioned, it is generally practiced both for its prestige value and for its economic advantages. Among the Tupis of South America, for instance, as well as in sections of Africa, wealth and distinction are measured in terms of how many wives a man has. Often the wives not only perform domestic services but also work in the fields, and thus contribute to the support of the entire family group. Sometimes, as in the Trobriand Islands of Micronesia, the income of a chief depends on the annual endowments received from the families of his wives. The first wife usually has the responsibility of administering the affairs of the household, but she is not necessarily the favorite wife. In many cases, each wife keeps a separate household, and the husband rotates his attention among them.

Polyandry is comparatively rare. It is found mainly in some parts of Tibet and among some aboriginal tribes of India, where a woman may marry two or more brothers. There are also cases of polyandry among a certain few indigenous people of Canada, in the Marquesas Islands, and among the Bahima in Africa, but it is the least common of the main forms of marriage.

Selection of Mates

The rules governing the choice of mates are as diverse as the societies in which they have developed. The rules differ not only from one society to another but also among subgroups, such as social classes, within a society. They usually include various limitations on the persons who are eligible to marry any given individual.

Let us first consider some of the rules governing eligibility. For instance, in India a person of one caste finds it difficult to marry an individual from another, and, until recently, in a country such as South Africa a person of one race was not permitted to marry someone from another race. In some societies, one may never marry a blood relative, no matter how distant, and in others one may marry only within the kinship group.[1] The governing factors on the one hand are the fear of incest, or sexual activity among people who are close kin, and the desire for alliances. At the other extreme is the fear of marrying anyone too unlike the social group to which one belongs (in the case of certain small groups, this necessarily means marrying a relative). In the majority of modern societies, both forces operate, and therefore most people find their search for acceptable marriage mates limited to persons not closely related but within the same general social group.

Rules govern the actual choice of a marriage partner. Some societies have **arranged marriages**—marriages that are arranged by one or more persons other than the marriage partners—because it is believed that a marriage is as much the concern of the families as of the individuals involved. The arguments in favor of such marriages include alliances of wealth, property, or political power, or the belief that young people are too immature, inexperienced, and impulsive to consider properly all the factors necessary for an enduring and successful marriage.

Many Asian families in the United States still arrange marriages for their children, many of whom are highly educated. In some societies, wives are obtained by kidnapping or by capture, perhaps in a raid on a neighboring tribe. Sometimes the kidnapping is genuine, and sometimes it is a ritual that carries out a previous understanding.

The other principal type of selection we call personal-choice mating. **Personal-choice mating** implies the custom of personal freedom in mating, with relatively little interference from others. This is the type of marriage we are familiar with in mainstream society. However, this freedom of choice is not restricted to our own country, nor indeed to our own time, although we again emphasize that mating activities are almost always carried on within the framework of the prevailing local laws and mores.

The techniques involved in personal-choice mating differ from one society to another, as do the moral and legal sanctions governing them. For example, among the polar Eskimos in earlier days, there was not only complete freedom of choice by mutual agreement in the making of a permanent marriage, but before marriage there was also a sanctioned period of group living, during which experimental mating took place among the youth of the community. Children resulting from this arrangement were not considered illegitimate but belonged to the mother and the man who eventually became her husband. One of the criteria often used by the man in choosing a wife was her demonstrated ability to bear children, just as one of the criteria for the woman in choosing her husband was his demonstrated ability to provide for her and her children.

Family Control

No one type of family control has ever been universal, but three main patterns have prevailed: patriarchy, matriarchy, and the egalitarian family. A **patriarchy** is a form of social organization in which the father is the supreme authority. A **matriarchy** is a form of social organization in which the mother is the supreme authority. An **egalitarian family** is one with shared control, with neither the father nor the mother as superior.

In a patriarchal culture, not only is the father the head of the family, but society also considers that the children belong to him and that he has authority over their lives, even, in some cases, the right to give or sell them in marriage. The patriarchal family was found among the early civilizations around the Mediterranean and has been carried down through Christian civilizations to modern times. Our colonial fathers maintained the patriarchal system, and there are still many families in the United States, as well as in other parts of the world, in which the father is the recognized authority in the family, although with some modifications.

Societies in which family control actually rests with the mother are exceptional. In most so-called matriarchal cultures, as among the Zuni Indians in the southwestern part of the

---

[1] Marriage within the kinship or other social group is known as *endogamy*. *Exogamy* refers to marriage outside the group.

United States, the mother usually does not have direct control, as one might suppose. More often, the mother's brother wields authority and controls the children. But the family takes the mother's name and usually lives with the mother's parents or other relatives. The husband may move in with them, but he is apt to spend more time with his own mother or his sisters' families, helping to control their children. Because he has no control status with his own children, he is more of a playmate and friend to them.

Family control in the United States has gradually shifted toward the partnership, or egalitarian, form. As women have increasingly gained equal or greater education and more equal economic and political rights and privileges, the control of the family has more and more come to be shared by both marriage partners or primarily controlled by the woman.

Single-Parent Families

The above discussion about family control was about families in which there are two parents at home. That traditional family is no longer the norm, especially at the lower end of the income

What's Wrong with Men?

Psychologist Jonathan Peterson, whose work we discussed in a previous chapter, thinks he knows what's wrong with men. They haven't been trained to be "men." By that he means that the today's society has created a culture of victimization, and instilled in men a belief that life will be easy, and that they deserve things from others and from government. He argues that men should stop whining and not blame others, and that they should reject immediate gratification. Children, boys especially, should be strictly disciplined, and if they are they will once again find their role in the family.

Most academic observers see his work as "vague exhortatory banality" whose recipe for men is nonrelational and unemotional; it leaves out love. But he has become an Internet sensation, and his emphasis on strength of will and call to toughness seem to relate to many, and his YouTube videos have gone viral, as have videos pointing out the problems with his arguments. The best way to introduce yourself to them is to take a look at one of the videos, and then to take a look at a video pointing out the problems with his arguments. See for example The Tragic Story of the Man-Child (https://www.youtube.com/watch?v=JjfClL6nogo) and What's Wrong with Jordan Peterson (https://www.youtube.com/watch?v=Gy5j-Sm4Ur8).

Interview with Jordan B. Peterson in Amsterdam, on October 31, 2018. Photo by Romy Arroyo Fernandez/Nurphoto via Getty Images.

spectrum. There the traditional family has been replaced by single-parent households in which the mother is the family and the father is seldom around. Currently about 67 percent of black households, 42 percent of Hispanic and 25 percent of white families are single-parent families. Generally the single parent is the mother; she both works, and cares for the children. Sometimes the father or a boyfriend live with her, but they are often not seen as an integral part of the family. Men are seen as needed to conceive children, but otherwise tangential. In fact, many women report that the father or boyfriend is more like another child.

There are many reasons for the breakdown of the traditional family; part of it has to do with the lack of the traditional manual jobs that less educated men took; part has to do with culture, and part has to do with government policy such as our way of dealing with crime. Whatever the reason, it places enormous pressure on the mother, who finds herself as both primary caregiver and breadwinner. These single-parent women get some help from their extended families and friends, but the amount of work they do is substantial. Sometimes, in addition to being the breadwinner and caretaker, they attend college to improve their earning capacity, giving them the equivalent of three full-time jobs.

Reckoning of Descent

In the Western world, we use the bilateral method of reckoning descent, counting our ancestors on both our father's and our mother's side because our biological inheritance comes from both. However, this is not the universal practice. Some societies use the unilateral method, in which an individual is deemed to belong to either the father's or the mother's family, and ancestors are reckoned only in the male line of descent or in the female line. A **patrilinear system** determines descent through the male line; a **matrilinear system** determines descent through the female line. Not using a bilateral method may not seem logical to us, but it does simplify matters for those who use it. Imagine being asked to name your ancestors going back twenty generations. The African chief who reckons his ancestry by patrilinear descent would know the twenty names required. In our society, we would have to remember 1,048,576 names. Few carry their family tree back that far, but many families keep a family tree like the one in Figure 9.1.

Western societies generally are patriarchal and use a bilateral method of reckoning descent. These customs do not seem to fulfill significantly any of the functions of the family other than

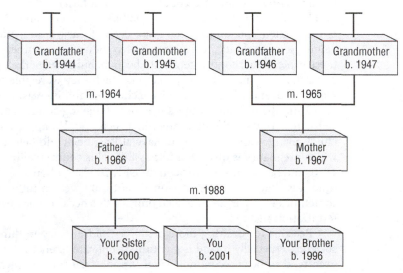

Figure 9.1

How to draw a family tree.

the need for the psychological adjustment of the male. Society does need to fulfill the child-rearing function, and it is true that women bear and nurse children and have evolved both genetically and socially so that, on average, a woman is better able to deal with children than a man is, at least until the child reaches the age of about three. Maternal instincts exist. But this patriarchal reality only suggests that the male will most likely maintain the uninterrupted income-earning activities, not that the male will have control of the family.

What maintains the patriarchal system is, in large part, social and genetic inertia. Male dominance is built into the social and genetic structure of society. The fact that it is built in does not mean that it cannot, or will not, be changed. It simply means that it will only be changed through conscious effort and moral commitment to equality.

Names and naming systems are important symbols. In the United States, although we generally acknowledge our descent bilaterally, the name we carry usually is that of our father or husband, emphasizing the patrilinear line of ancestry; however, in recent times, more married women have been keeping their birth names.

*F*unctions of the Family in Society

Despite such diversity of family structure, there are important underlying reasons for the survival of this institution through all the changes that have taken place over centuries. These reasons can be found in the functions of the family. The family has many functions:

- It must reproduce the species, otherwise the species will end.
- It must see to it that the young are reasonably well adjusted, so that they don't cause trouble for society and that they grow up to be productive in the biological and physical sense.
- It must provide sufficient satisfaction for parents to keep their children well adjusted so they don't make trouble for society.

Society relies on families to fulfill these functions, and when they do not succeed, other social institutions must adapt.

Let's consider an example: the biological function of families, or the need to reproduce. Until recently, few married couples were voluntarily childless, but in the last twenty years the number of families having no children has been increasing. During this time, many women, both married and unmarried, delayed childbearing and pursued professional education, gaining a foothold in their careers. Often they married other professionals. The incomes of these professional couples tended to be high, but so were their expenses and their ambitions. They chose to put off having children, which they were able to do because of, among other reasons, advances in contraceptive techniques and increasing sanction of these techniques.

A number of those couples who put off having children are experiencing what might be called the 37-year-old syndrome, in which couples approaching the end of the woman's childbearing years are opting to have at least one child before the woman reaches an age at which pregnancy is unwise or impossible. This countervailing trend became apparent in the 1980s and has continued through the early 2000s. A phenomenon surfacing at about the same time was that of unmarried women not only welcoming but actively seeking pregnancy, sometimes with partners selected only for this occasion or through any of a number of other fertilization methods.

Reasons for desiring more or fewer children vary in different societies. In agricultural societies, especially if land is plentiful, people are likely to desire large families because children tend to be an economic asset. In industrial societies, where children are more costly, families tend to have fewer of them. If the trend toward childless couples continues, society will have to find some other way to reproduce itself. For the United States, this may well mean an increase in immigration.

Matching Family Patterns with Family Functions

What family structure best meets these functions? That's hard to say because it depends on individuals' psychological development and the technology and exigencies of the society. Let's consider the variations of family groups in reference to modern Western society.

Number and Stability of Mates

As stated earlier, our society has a monogamous model of the family, in which a family group includes a male and a female, as its "ideal type." Why?

One of the reasons is that this family grouping works well for reproduction. Given current technology, that is the way society reproduces itself. If reproductive technology required three (or only one) for reproduction, there would be pressure for a different number of mates.

Another reason is that children take enormous amounts of time. A one-parent family has a difficult time meeting either the child's or the parent's psychological needs. As a matter of fact, a two-parent family has a difficult time meeting the child's and the parents' psychological needs, especially if both parents are working. This places two types of pressure on social institutions. One pressure is for an extension of the family, either by including a third mate or by extending the family and including grandparents, aunts, or uncles as part of the primary family unit. The second pressure is for society to develop institutions such as day care to remove part of the childrearing burden from the family.

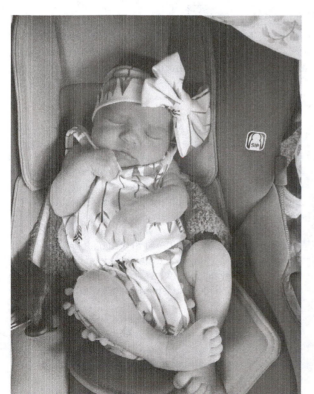

The little darlings (sometimes).

A third important reason the family group consists of a monogamous male and female is for the psychological adjustment of the individuals. According to some social scientists, "three's a crowd" is more than just a pat phrase. Individuals have psychological needs to be accepted and loved, making mates of some type necessary, and the need for security argues for a single mate. Some individuals might prefer more than one mate for themselves, but few would prefer that their mate have more than one mate. The development of strong friendships outside of marriage often results in strong feelings of jealousy. Those feelings are in part genetic; most species have developed instincts that encourage the propagation of the individual's genes, and humankind is no exception.

Recent work in evolutionary psychology emphasizes this psychological aspect. Some experts claim that those traits leading to procreation will be fostered in individuals and that there is a relationship between physiology and human characteristics. Thus, while there is a strong tendency toward one-to-one mating, there is also a strong tendency in both the male and the female to stray and have other mates.

Finally, a fourth reason is that from society's point of view the monogamous relationship provides a mate for most people because males and females are born in nearly equal numbers.

As pointed out earlier, even for relationships that are monogamous, there is a frequency of turnover of mates—called **serial monogamy**—and a certain amount of

A traditional family.

infidelity within marriages. Thus, while our system is monogamous, it is not so in a strict sense.

Selection of Mates

Western societies generally allow individuals to select their own mates. Such a selection process is by no means universal; families in Eastern societies often choose mates for the children. The problem with family selection is the possible incompatibility of mates and a failure to fulfill the psychological function of marriage, although, as some of our Eastern

Living and Loving

A key role of the family is procreation. A society needs children, but not too many. Maintaining the proper balance of numbers of children is a difficult social problem. Take Singapore, for example, a small, rich country in Asia. Singapore's population control incentives were very successful and reduced the birthrate from a 4.7 percent annual increase in 1965 to a 1.5 percent annual increase in the late 1980s. Then the government began worrying that the country would have too few young people to support the elderly, so it switched tactics and strongly encouraged marriage.

The government established a number of programs to encourage the 30 percent of college-educated women who were unmarried to get married. The programs included dating services, "love classes," and advice to men about how to act on a date. One of the program booklets lists "some nutty ideas" for dates, such as "playing Scrabble on the beach armed with a dictionary and a thesaurus." We leave it to you to decide whether this advice is transferable to the United States. Perhaps we could modify it some: Why not ask your date if he or she wants to go to the beach and discuss the questions at the end of this chapter? How about . . . ?

The measures didn't work so well in Singapore either. After they were introduced, the birthrate continued to fall. In the early 2000s, Singapore established financial incentives for having children. A second child earns couples about $3,000, and a third child is worth about $6,000.

Even countries that do not provide direct financial incentives for having children offer implicit subsidies. In the United States, taxpayers get a child tax credit, and in other countries parents get paid leaves and free child care, policies that are designed to make children less costly.

*I*s an Arranged Marriage in Your or Your Child's Future?

Dating is a pain, love is nonexistent, and romance is for the birds. According to Ramdas Menon, a sociologist at Texas A&M University, more and more Americans, especially those with Asian, African, and Middle Eastern backgrounds, are taking this view and leaving the problem of whom to marry up to their parents. They want their parents to arrange marriages for them, often to people they never meet until the parents of the prospective bride and prospective groom have settled things among themselves. Does this make sense? Maybe it does. It takes pressure off the mates. The custom also preserves culture, brings individuals from similar backgrounds together, often unites and strengthens economic ties, and keeps premarital expectations low.

friends point out, given the number of divorces and unhappy marriages in the West, self-selection does not seem to do such a good job of meeting the psychological functions.

The advantage of family selection is that it is more likely to fulfill economic and social stability goals. When hormones play an important role in mate selection, economic and social considerations often are forgotten.

Of course, as we saw in Chapter 4, some degree of social instability can be helpful for a society to allow cultural diffusion. One of the reasons Western societies have adapted better than Eastern societies to the changing technologies may be that self-selection of mates creates social instability that allows and generates change.

Other Western Family Characteristics and Functions of the Family

We could go on listing Western family characteristics and discussing their function, but there isn't space, and besides, it is an activity best left to you. Think of other characteristics, such as the age at marriage. Estimate what the average age is (later in the chapter we give you the information), and then try to explain what functions are served by getting married at that age. Why not earlier, say at age 13 or so, as soon as people are sufficiently developed sexually to have children?

Another interesting question in relation to the functions of the family is what is likely to happen to the family as the age structure of society changes. Consider Figure 9.2, which shows the increase in the elderly as a percentage of the total population. What is likely to happen to the family as this occurs? How will the family unit deal with the changes incurred by such a population shift?

A final question concerns the impact of the large increase in single-parent families, especially at lower income levels where it is now predominant, on the stability of society. What is the cause of that increase? Will it perpetuate, and increase, inequality in the system? And, if so, what should and can be done about it? Here is the reality—traditional marriage is still the norm at higher income levels. Both parents work, and, while they have troubles, they have the income to deal with those troubles. At low income levels traditional marriage is the exception. The mother is both caregiver and breadwinner with a job that pays a low wage. She faces a triple disadvantage—low pay, little childrearing support, and little financial support from the father of the child—which means that her children will likely have a hard time competing with those of a well-off married family with two high paying jobs and two people to share the childrearing.

In the next section, we look at the U.S. family today. As you read, consider the functions of the family and how well the characteristics fulfill those functions.

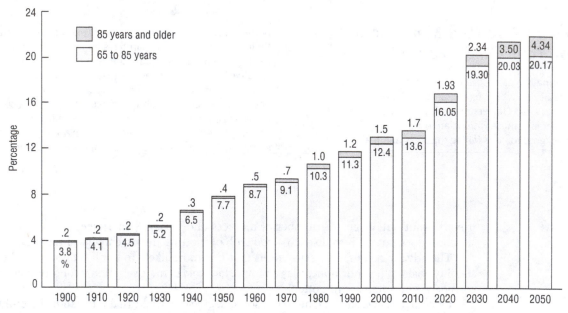

Figure 9.2

The aging of the United States. By the year 2050, it is expected that about 25% of Americans will be over the age of 65. (Source: U.S. Bureau of the Census)

The Family in the United States Today

One of the causes of the revolutionary changes in twentieth-century life in the United States was our massive transition from an agricultural, rural nation to one that is mainly commercial-industrial and urban. With the mass movement of people to cities throughout the late nineteenth and early twentieth centuries, housing costs increased and both family and home size shrank. People no longer worked mainly at home, although initially most women stayed home to care for the family. However, technological advances in labor-saving household appliances and family planning freed women for leisure and market-oriented activities. Children's help around the house was no longer required as much as it was on the farm; the number of children per family declined, and the city's recreational offerings often drew parents and children in different directions.

Modern transport—the car in particular, which came into widespread use in the 1920s—served to make us an on-the-go nation; home became a place to sleep or to get away from. The car itself and the two-car family helped in large measure to build the post–World War II commuter suburb. Postwar affluence, fed by commercial wealth, advertising, and the credit economy, helped lure us away from the "waste not, want not" Puritan ethic of the nineteenth century, when debt meant disgrace. Smaller families and the dramatic increase in the number of families in which both parents work—often earning two high incomes—have led to a return from the suburbs to city life, as many seek the distractions and satisfactions of the fast track.

With women playing more vital roles away from home, their dependence on males for survival has lessened. Moreover, many other forces have driven women toward more self-sufficiency and a search for satisfaction both in marriage and outside of it. Today, both males and females demand more of marriage and of each other, which adds to the stresses of modern life. The fully liberated man (of whom there are still only a few) shares major decisions, roles, and work with his wife, but many women find that they continue to be allotted the major share

As more and more women have entered the labor force, fathers have had to become nurture providers, not always with the most finesse.

of the domestic duties, even while working full-time. In other households, the patriarchal male finds great difficulty in accepting the wife's autonomy, but at higher income levels where both the mother and father have jobs a great many do, nevertheless, make the adjustment. At lower level incomes, men not only earn lower pay, but they have a much harder time finding a job. This places even more responsibility on the mother. She must be full-time mother and full-time breadwinner. The positive aspect of this is that she is de facto autonomous; she makes the decisions. The bad aspect of this is that the demands on her are almost unmeetable. The father or current boyfriend, who is sometimes around for companionship and childcare, may attempt to play the role of patriarch, but in reality he generally cannot since he is not bringing in an income and pulling his load. The mother often sees him as just another child she has to deal with. Getting married to him would only increase her responsibilities, not reduce them.

Even with shared responsibilities, the two-earner family cannot provide full-time care for children. This situation has placed more responsibility on the schools, many of which provide not only lunches but also breakfasts and may stay open beyond the normal school day to provide someplace for the child to remain until the parents' workday is over. Fortunate families have found good day-care centers, but these are not equitably distributed and tend to be expensive. Moreover, most good centers have waiting lists. Many children come home after school to empty houses or apartments and fend for themselves, sometimes even supervising younger brothers or sisters, until a parent arrives.

The sexual revolution of the 1960s and the enhanced sense of independence experienced by both men and women loosened many moral restraints. The mobility and easy anonymity of modern cities have made it possible for husbands and wives to widen their circle of friends. Often this freedom has caused them to become less content with one lifelong mate. Initially it led to a phenomenon described as serial marriage, in which people have several husbands or wives over the course of their lives, although not more than one at a time. Because each partner may bring to the new marriage one or more children and may be sharing the custody of those children with other former mates, family relationships can become complicated and challenging to emotional and material resources. More recently, serial marriage has evolved into serial relationships, where two individuals never get married, thereby making it easier to move on when the relationship ends.

How to Be a Good Wife

One way to get an idea of the change that has occurred in the nature of the family is to look at old textbooks. For example, a 1960 home economics textbook included a section entitled "How to Be a Good Wife." It included suggestions such as the following:

- Have dinner ready for him when he comes home from work; let him know you have been thinking about him and his needs.

- Touch up your makeup and be refreshed when he arrives.

- Prepare the children; wash their hands and faces. They are little treasures and he would like to see them play the part.

- Clean up the house before he arrives. Make him feel that he has reached a haven of rest and order.

- At the time of his arrival, eliminate all noise. Greet him with a warm smile.

- Let him be the first to talk.

- Never complain. Try to understand his world of strain and pressure and his need to be home and relax.

When one of the authors showed the list to his wife, she smiled and reminded him to have dinner ready for her and the kids when she got home from work.

Percent of households by type

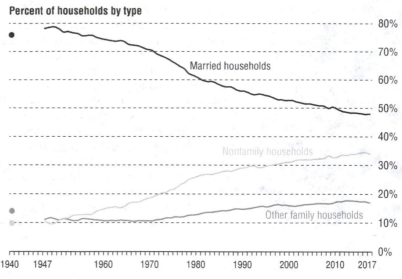

Figure 9.3

Percent of households by type. (*Source: U.S. Census Bureau, Decennial Census, 1940, and Current Population Survey, Annual Social and Economic Supplements, 1968 to 2017*).

Despite these changing roles, the traditional family remains a goal for most people in the United States, and we suspect that most of you would like to see marriage and a family somewhere in your future if you do not already have one.

Figure 9.3 gives you an overview of some U.S. family characteristics and how they have changed in the last thirty years. Notice that only about half of all U.S. households consist of married couples. There also tends to be significantly more unmarried female-headed households than there are male-headed households. One reason for the greater number of female-headed households is the fact that women live longer than men. Another is the breakdown of the traditional family, especially at the lower end of the income scale.

As we discussed above, today women both maintain and support many families. One reason for this is the lack of jobs for less educated males. Because of changes in technology, jobs requiring strength but not a lot of thinking have been replaced by machines. This has led men without education to have few job prospects. Those who cannot find jobs become dependent on others for their income. This changes the decision process for women thinking about marrying them. Rather than seeing them as a source of financial support for the family, more and more they are seeing them as simply another financial burden; they see themselves as better off without being married to them, even if they are the father of their children. They are just another mouth to feed. At upper-income levels, highly educated men have earning prospects that are still good, and at these higher income levels, the traditional family is more common. Women figure that even if men don't help all that much around the house, they at least provide some income, and are sometimes even good companions.

To provide you with a better sense of the changes that are occurring, in the next part of the chapter we consider the issue of matchmaking and "dating" in the United States. Because much of the material presented

Dating in the 1940s.

about dating is familiar to you, we approach it in a slightly different way—as if it were written by an anthropologist about people from another culture. This allows you to take a more objective look at issues in which you are active.

Matchmaking and Dating

Because U.S. custom allows self-selection of mates, people who eventually marry must first meet. Some of the ways people meet are through Internet matching services, school, work, religious institutions, sports, social meeting places such a bars, and networks of friends. Social networks such as Facebook allow people to stay in touch with others outside their immediate geographic area, and online dating and social mingling sites provide all types of opportunities for individuals to meet new people with similar interests for various reasons, from a casual hookup or fling to a serious attempt to meet a long-term partner.

After two people meet, they need to get to know one another. This process in the past was called dating, but that term is used far less today. Nonetheless, we will still use the term for lack of a better one. Dating can be either formal or informal. Dating is a time when people get acquainted with each other. It also gives them an opportunity to evaluate themselves in an interpersonal situation outside the family and serves as a form of recreation. In the 1950s, dating was often formal, with the boy picking up the girl and escorting her to a social event. Although the boy was no longer required to ask her parents' permission to take the girl out (as he would have been in the 1800s), he was obliged to see the parents and exchange some conversation when he came to the girl's house to pick her up. At these—often awkward—meetings, the parents would "size up the lad" and inform him that they expected their daughter home by a certain hour (say, midnight, if it were a weekend evening).

Today, arranging a date is generally much more informal. Often one person, male or female, will text the other and suggest they get together and possibly do something, often as part of a larger group. Individuals may pair off from that group, sometimes just for a one-time hookup, at other times to establish a longer-term relationship. Ideally, both individuals in the relationship know the reason for pairing off, and what the nature of the relationship is, such as: whether it is ok that the other person pairs off with someone else. When both individuals have a different sense of how much freedom the relationship allows them in terms of seeing, talking to, and being with other individuals, trouble often results. A vocabulary often develops to describe how individuals feel about relationships. For example, at my college some students who want a one-to-one relationship are described as "velcro."

Most relationships are not necessarily expected to end in marriage. Usually an individual has relationships with a variety of people before finding one that seems right. In fact, there are likely to be several right ones, or no right one. An eighth-grade girl explains: "Next year we'll be in high school, and then I'll ditch him to date a sophomore. No freshman girl ever dates a freshman!" Older individuals are likely to be less concerned about age or year in school and more concerned with emotional, economic, and social compatibility.

On-line dating.

© CartoonStock.com

Once one moves beyond high school and college, people tend to give relatively more thought in dating to whether the person is "marriageable material." Is this someone I can build a life with, have children with, and grow old with? Will they make my life better, or just add more burdens? Women face the hardest decisions since women generally end up with the primary responsibility for childrearing. To the degree that men can walk away from a relationship and child, they can take less interest in finding marriageable material, and more in finding someone to have a good time with now, and someone who makes them feel good about themselves.

Sex and Singles

An important reason for the movement away from the traditional family is the change in sexual mores and codes, and the degree to which they put responsibilities on men who father a child. There are enormous differences in the mores and sexual codes, even within the same

*T*inder: Stay Woke

What would you rather have from me?

A. A nice date, dinner and a movie

B. Meaningful intelligent conversation

C. Multiple orgasms

Is there a D? All of the above

Wow; that was skillfully played Sir

The above was an interchange on Tinder, a location-based "Social search" (https://en.wikipedia.org/wiki/Social_search) "Mobile app" (https://en.wikipedia.org/wiki/Mobile_app), or in more vernacular terms a dating and hookup app. It puts your profile out in cyberspace and allows you to connect with people in your geographical area and to chat by swiping right if you want to chat and swiping left if not. It can lead to a raunchy casual hookup or an evening at the opera, and it is part of the cultural revolution that is going on in relationships. There are many additional dating apps, and some estimates are that 20 percent of marriages began with an online meeting.

Of course lots of one-night hookups also began with an online meeting, and cultural rules have evolved that govern people's interaction. One interesting rule concerns last names. It seems that it is inappropriate to ask for last names on a first, or even an early date. Providing a last name is a bit like what having the person meet the family used to be.

Tinder is a social search mobile app that allows users to like or dislike other users, and further allows users to chat if both parties swiped to the right.

town; the sexual revolution that started in the 1970s spread in a complicated pattern. Depending on the individual's upbringing, sexual relations can begin at any stage of the relationship. Prohibitions against sexual relations are decreasing among college students, and "hooking up," in which one has sex with someone else supposedly without any emotional commitment, has increased. Today, students often talk about "friends with benefits" rather than about their "girlfriend" or "boyfriend."

In large cities and in suburban communities, sexual relations often begin as early as age 12, which could be an argument for starting marriage much earlier. In families in which religion or other organized moral standards prevail, however, the slogan "good girls don't" still carries some weight, and in such families, girls wait until the serious stage of a relationship, or later, before having intercourse. It should be noted that a dual standard still exists; for males, there is a less strict guideline than "good boys don't."

Over 40 percent of U.S. births are now to unmarried women, and for black women the proportion is even higher. Over 70 percent of all black children are born to unmarried mothers. In the black community as a whole, over 50 percent of all one-parent families are headed by mothers who have never been married.

Through the 1980s, the issue of teenage pregnancy was seen as a predominantly black issue, but beginning in the 1990s, with an increasing proportion of white teenage pregnancies, the issue now extends beyond racial lines. In the early 2000s, teenage birthrates declined across all racial and ethnic lines, although rates for African American and Hispanic teens continue to be higher than those for other groups, with about 20 percent of African American births being to teenage mothers compared to 10 percent for whites. The birthrate is about 26 per 1,000 teenage women, which, although a significant decrease over the past decade, is nonetheless still the highest rate of all industrialized nations. (Both increased use of contraception and increased abstinence are credited for the decline.)

Another issue that confronts singles—indeed, anyone, married or single, who is not in a monogamous relationship—is sexually transmitted disease. In addition to centuries-old venereal diseases such as gonorrhea and syphilis, there are now herpes, chlamydia, genital warts, HIV, and AIDS.

Even intense relationships often do not lead to marriage. Individuals often have a number of serious relationships before they finally marry. It is also now common for couples to live together for periods of anywhere from a month to many years before making a decision to marry, and some decide never to marry. Living together is much more common than it was in the past, and more and more parents are accepting that their children will live together with someone rather than get married immediately. In the 1960s, only about 10 percent of couples in the United States moved in together before marriage, but in the early 2000s, that percentage is closer to 50 percent.

In deciding whether (and whom) to marry, romantic love plays a role, but increasingly individuals are considering, in addition to love, other issues, especially in relationships in which both members are planning a career. Whose career will come first? What happens if they are assigned jobs in different locations? If one supports the other in order to further his or her education, what obligations are incurred? To meet these complex issues a number of couples are entering into formal marriage contracts (prenuptial agreements) that spell out the obligations and expectations of both so that the love relationship is not shattered.

After a period of decision, most individuals marry. Marriage is a more or less permanent contract between a man and a woman under which they are expected to live together and to provide a home for their children. The contract has legal, and in many cases religious, sanctions.

Entering into this contract creates many new responsibilities involving not only the couple but also the families from which they came and various other social groups. The partners immediately assume new statuses: the husband/wife status, the in-law status, and the family status. Even if the parties have previously lived together, marriage involves a major change.

Such an important shift of roles, even though desirable and pleasurable, involves a good deal of adjustment. This has not been made easier by the swift pace of social change in the United States. In a static society, the role expected of each spouse is well understood, but in a dynamic society such as ours it is easy to be uncertain about just what is expected. This confusion may be increased in cross-marriages between faiths, nationalities, or races. Even if hazards are eliminated, our common heritage of diversity is constantly changing the social pattern for everyone. Hence, adaptability has become an important personality characteristic in marital adjustment.

Children

As we stated earlier, for an increasing number of families, marriage and having children are not necessarily linked. This has contributed to creating what is sometimes called an underclass that has little chance of escaping the poverty it grew up with. This underclass has to deal with a different set of pressures than the middle class.

People in the underclass often get a poor education and little encouragement to take advantage of the educational opportunities open to them. They find themselves in social environments that offer little hope for long-term advancement and build that into their worldview and actions. Their immediate concerns are often for their safety and getting enough to eat, concerns generally far from the minds of middle-class (and even lower-middle-class) individuals.

Middle-class culture, although it has more or less condoned living together, tends to put pressure on middle-class individuals to get married if they have children or want to have children. Thus, most middle-class couples choose marriage. Marriage establishes the economic responsibilities for both mother and father, and even if the parents split up, both retain legal responsibility for the children. Thus, the spouse who does not have legal custody is responsible for child support and possibly alimony. Later, when we consider divorce, we deal with these issues in more detail.

The decision to have a child is not an easy one. Children involve major responsibilities and hard work. Often it means giving up one spouse's potential income or, if both parents work, worrying about child care, education, and privacy. Moreover, parenting is no longer eighteen years and out. Many adult children are coming home to live with their parents (see Figure 9.4).

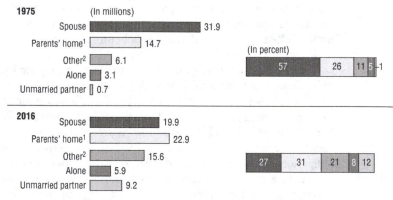

[1] College students who are living in dormitories are counted as living in the parents' home.
[2] "Other" includes people who are living with relatives besides a spouse, such as siblings or grandparents, and nonrelatives such as roommates.

Figure 9.4

Living arrangements of adults 18–34: 1975 and 2016. More young adults lived with parents than lived with a spouse in 2016. (Source: U.S. Census Bureau, 1975 and 2016 Current Population Survey Annual Social and Economic Supplement)

In spite of the responsibility and hard work children bring to a couple, most people feel that the rewards are compensatory. The number of children that couples are willing to have, however, is smaller than two or three generations ago, and following a temporary rise in the 1940s and 1950s, the average has been dropping.

Senior Citizens

As children grow up and leave home for college, for a job, or to establish their own households, the family dwindles in size to the original two.

For the middle-class ideal traditional family, a number of years then follow, perhaps as many as fifteen or twenty, before retirement—years in which there is time for more active participation in social and civic affairs or, for spouses who have not worked outside the home before, for employment. Companionship is now the strong bond between the couple. Shared experiences throughout the childrearing years cement this bond, but a new and satisfactory pattern of life without the children at home must be developed if the couple is to remain happy. Generally, couples are able to make the adjustment. In fact, research studies have shown that a couple's happiness declines with the birth of a child and tends to renew when the children leave. Thus, for the parents no less than for the children, maturing of the children represents a period of weaning or emancipation. When the children return on visits, their relationship is on an adult, companionable basis, and if there are grandchildren, they can provide the grandparents with a new interest in life.

The family ideal is not always reached. In the less-than-ideal family, the couple can't stand each other but stay together because they don't have enough money to live apart, or one leaves or has already left the other in order to take up with someone else or just to live alone. Whether they stay together when they want to be apart or one leaves and sets up another household, often there is a haunting loneliness for one or both members of the couple. Another less-than-ideal family type is the one in which the parents aren't speaking to the children because they have had to take second jobs to pay the kids' college loans, which the kids have defaulted on. There are countless variations of the less-than-ideal family. For the less-than-ideal family, retirement can mean being kicked out of a current job and shunted into a low-paying one that is necessary to make ends meet. As the Russian novelist Leo Tolstoy wrote in the opening sentence of his novel *Anna Karenina,* "Happy families are all alike; every unhappy family is unhappy in its own way."

When the time finally comes for the couple to retire from their regular jobs, many couples, if in good health, still have years of activity ahead. Successful adjustment to retirement also depends on personal temperament. Some individuals welcome the release from routine and responsibility—they are flexible enough to have little trouble in finding interesting ways to spend their time—while others feel lost when deprived of their previous work. Health and money are also important factors.

Family Disorganization and Divorce

The preceding section described the development over time of a married couple who remain married. More and more, this is a less typical chronology. Figure 9.5 gives the marriage rate and the divorce rate since 1900. The marriage rate has generally fallen and in 2017 was about 6.9; in other words, 6.9 people out of every 1,000 got married in a given year. The divorce rate increased in the 1970s but has been decreasing since the 1980s.

We must, however, remember several qualifications when considering the divorce rate. For instance, if in a given year there is one divorce for every two marriages, it does not mean that half the marriages in that year ended in divorce; rather, in that year some people got married and others, who had been married for anywhere from one day to fifty years or more, got divorced.

Statisticians have various methods for determining the number of marriages that end in divorce. One study of a group of married couples over time indicated that nearly 40 percent of

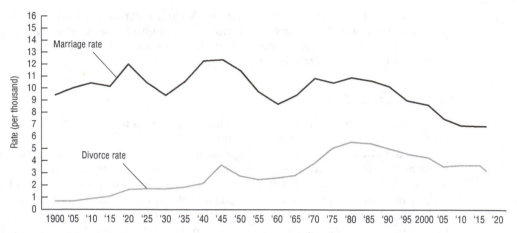

Figure 9.5

Marriages and divorces, 1900 to 2017. (Source: U.S. Bureau of the Census, Statistical Abstract of the United States, and monthly Vital Statistics Report)

first marriages end in divorce, about 80 percent of those people enter a second marriage, and almost 45 percent of the second marriages also end in divorce. Though we now have approximately one divorce for every two marriages, only about one in four households is a single-person household because many divorced people marry again.

Why Do People Get Divorced?   There are almost as many reasons why people get divorced as there are divorces. Most can be combined into some type of incompatibility: One or both of the partners are not getting what they want out of the marriage. Sometimes a third party is involved whom one of the partners finds more attractive than his or her mate, but often the marriage would have been in trouble even if there had been no third party.

When we think about the institution of marriage, the number of divorces is not surprising. Most friendships don't last a lifetime, so why should a marriage? Those marriages that don't have serious problems often are with partners who share a common set of values and who not only love each other but also respect each other's capabilities and integrity. Not many partners fit these characteristics, so there aren't many rock-solid marriages.

People often marry in the hope, belief, or expectation that their partner will change. A maxim of marriage counselors is that people don't change, or if they do change, you can expect it to be in the opposite direction from what the other partner wants. In word processing, most personal computers use WYSIWYG (pronounced wizzywig)—what you see is what you get—presentations. Most courtships involve WYSIBTWYG (pronounced who knows how)—what you see is better than what you get—presentations.

Some Caution about Divorce Statistics.   Divorce statistics often are used as a measure of family disorganization, and the present high divorce rate is cited as proof that the U.S. family is in serious trouble. However, higher divorce rates today than in the past are not entirely the result of more family unhappiness. In earlier generations, many couples avoided divorce even though their married life was unhappy. They avoided it because it meant social ostracism or, in the case of women, poverty, because there were few opportunities for them to earn a good living. As the possibilities for divorced people increased and it became easier to get divorces, more unhappy couples have chosen this route. Moreover, with fewer people getting married, there are fewer divorces.

Legal Grounds for Divorce.   There are many legal grounds for divorce, and they vary with the laws of each state. Among these are incompatibility, adultery, desertion, cruelty, nonsupport, bigamy, felony conviction, and fraudulent contract. Although the legal grounds for divorce are of some interest and significance, often they have little to do with the real reason behind a couple's desire to end a marriage. Often a husband and wife who wish to divorce cooperate to bring about real or apparent fulfillment of the necessary legal conditions.

Beginning in the 1970s, many states introduced **no-fault divorces,** in which irreconcilable differences serve as sufficient grounds for divorce. Under these laws, a marriage partner need not be declared guilty or at fault as was previously required, making the process of divorce much easier. In the 1990s, the movement shifted back in some circles. Louisiana introduced voluntary **covenant marriages,** in which divorce as an option is harder for people to get. In the early 2000s, legal covenant marriages were available in Arkansas, Arizona, and Louisiana. In most states, you do not have to be a state resident to get married in the state, or to "upgrade" an existing marriage into a covenant marriage. So, when someone proposes marriage, he or she may now have to specify whether it is a covenant marriage proposal or a regular marriage proposal.

Breaking Up Is Hard to Do. Even if one is not in a covenant marriage, divorce often presents serious difficulties, especially when a couple has joint property and children. The parties must decide who gets what. Some of the problems are demonstrated by the following four examples.

1. A wife has put her husband through school and has not furthered her own education. One year after he becomes a lawyer, they decide to get divorced. They have no property or children.
2. The same as (1), only it is the husband who put the wife through school.
3. A couple decides to break up after six years of marriage. They have two children, a house, a dog, and innumerable items of personal property. Both have careers but the wife's is more successful, and her income is twice that of her husband's.
4. The same as (3), only this time the husband's parents have given them the house.

In these examples, as in real life, there are no easy answers to what responsibilities two divorcing people have to each other, and couples often end up in court. Generally, however, both parties are encouraged to come to a reasonable pretrial settlement.

Singles

The number of individuals choosing not to marry and the large number of divorces have created the class called singles. These people live alone or as a parent in a single-parent family. As a group, singles have increased substantially in the past twenty years. This group includes divorced people but also an increasing number of people who have never been married. As you can see in Table 9.1, more and more people are postponing marriage. As the number of singles has grown, so too has the number of activities designed for them. Health clubs for singles, singles clubs, singles bars, and video dating services have proliferated.

Not only has there been a significant increase in the number of singles, but there has also been an important increase in the number of single-parent households. Whereas in 1960 there were approximately 2 million single-parent families, in the early 2000s that number had grown to more than 12 million, or about 34 percent of all families with children under age 18. Most of these are female-headed households. In theory, ex-husbands or fathers are required to help support their children, but in practice many shirk this responsibility.

Living Together

In the 1970s, statisticians documented a dramatic increase in the number of unmarried people living together. This trend has continued, and in 2017, the number of unmarried couples

Table 9.1

Singles Who Have Never Been Married

	1970	1980	1990	2000	2010	2017
Men						
25 to 29 years	19.1%	33.1%	45.2%	49.1%	65%	68.5%
30 to 34 years	9.4%	15.9%	27.0%	29.5%	39%	42.8%
Women						
25 to 29 years	10.5%	20.9%	31.1%	34.5%	53%	56.0%
30 to 34 years	6.2%	9.5%	16.4%	20.6%	36%	39.7%

Source: U.S. Bureau of the Census, *Current Population Reports.*

living together was about 9 million, up 29 percent from a decade earlier. Some of the reasons people live together without getting married are unwillingness to commit themselves to long-term relationships of any kind, desire to avoid legal complications when breakups they believe to be inevitable occur, experimentation, and the existence of an undissolved marriage of one or both partners. The practice, although traditionally frowned on, has gained acceptance, and many parents refer as casually to their children's living-together arrangements as they do to marriages.

The Future of the Family

The changing role of the family has left society with hard questions. Who will guide future generations? Who will be tomorrow's parents? What can prevent today's family crisis from becoming tomorrow's national disaster? Can adults please themselves as much as they hope to while producing equally happy, well-adjusted offspring who will be the solid citizen mothers and fathers we would wish for the next generation? Can both wife and husband find the satisfaction they seek at home, at work, and in their leisure hours, combining the goals of personal freedom and success associated with "single-blessedness" with the emotional security and commitments of wedlock?

Many individuals and groups have suggested what they believe to be effective ways to reinvigorate the family. Some of their ideas include outlawing abortion, banning busing, allowing school prayer, and prohibiting sex education in the schools. Without taking a stand on any of these issues, we doubt that they will contribute to the stability of families, although they may well be desirable for other reasons. Society changes and so too do the institutions in it. With new technologies, the optimal economic division of labor changes, and as it changes, so too do the functions of families.

Serious challenges to the family's survival are realities. With more women brought up to

" We *must* be great parents... our children all hate us. "

© CartoonStock.com

Same-Sex Marriage and Discrimination

The recent push for legalization of same-sex marriage in the United States is an interesting example of how cultural norms evolve and interact with legal structures. One of the major arguments put forward for same-sex marriage is that not to allow same-sex marriage discriminates against individuals according to sexual preference. This is true, but it is also irrelevant, because laws by their very nature discriminate. A law must draw arbitrary lines somewhere, and the debate about legalizing same-sex marriage concerns where to draw an arbitrary line, not necessarily any deep-seated discrimination or homophobia.

For example, the United States has laws against polygamy in all forms, and those laws are just as discriminatory as laws against same-sex marriage. In fact, the United States actively prosecutes polygamists, and that prosecution is supported by a large majority of the population. Were there to be no discrimination based on sexual preference, all types of marriages, including cenogamy, would have to be legalized.

The point is not that same-sex marriage should or should not have been given legal standing. The point is simply that laws inevitably include arbitrary lines that discriminate. Whether a law should be changed does not depend on whether the law discriminates, but on whether we, as a society, want that type of discrimination inherent in the law.

regard higher education and careers as their birthright, marriage will be only one of several paths they can choose. Many couples, deterred by high divorce rates, are deliberately opting not to marry or, if they do wed, not to have children, in view of the staggering costs of parenthood. When they do have children, those children often are left much more on their own than in the past. Consequently, rather than deriving their values from the family, these children acquire most of their values from films, television, music, magazines, the Internet, and peers.

It seems likely that changes to adapt the family to the new realities—such as flexible working hours, more shared jobs, infant care, and familial leave for both sexes—will help achieve the goal of holding the family together. The family may take new forms as social trends demand; it may bend with the winds of change. But the diagnosis of the family unit's imminent death seems premature.

 Study and **Review**

Key Points

- Four variations in family patterns are determined by the number of mates, selection of mates, family control, and reckoning of descent.
- Three functions of the family are the biological function, the psychological function, and the economic function.
- Family patterns evolve to meet these functions.
- The U.S. family today is quite different from its counterpart of seventy years ago.
- The diagnosis of the family unit's imminent death is premature.

Some Important Terms

arranged marriage (167)
cenogamy (166)
covenant marriage (183)
egalitarian family (167)
family (164)
marriage (164)

matriarchy (167)
matrilinear system (169)
monogamy (165)
no-fault divorce (183)
patriarchy (167)
patrilinear system (169)

personal-choice mating (167)
polyandry (165)
polygamy (165)
polygyny (165)
same-sex marriage (166)
serial monogamy (172)

Questions for Review and Discussion

General Questions

1. Why is the family often regarded as the most important of all social units?
2. State some important considerations in choosing a mate.
3. What are some methods of family control?
4. Why is it easier to trace your descent under a unilateral system than a bilateral system?
5. In today's circumstances, is the institution of the family really necessary for the propagation of the species? Defend your answer.
6. Monogamy is the most widespread form of marriage. Give some reasons for this.
7. What changes have the economic functions of the family undergone? Are they less important than formerly? Why or why not?
8. What changes has the physical-care function of the family undergone in the last few generations? Is it still important?
9. Describe the custom of dating as practiced in the United States, and explain the purpose it serves.
10. Describe some types of families other than the husband-wife-children household.
11. Does marrying for love eliminate consideration of compatibility and economic and social factors?
12. Can you think of some major adjustments that a newly married couple must make in their way of life? What further adjustments would be required by the arrival of children?
13. What are some of the problems a married couple must meet after the children have left home?
14. What are some of the factors that have contributed to high divorce rates?
15. What is no-fault divorce?
16. What implications does the increase in single-parent homes have for society?
17. How can family disorganization be reduced? By better marriage laws? By making divorce more difficult? Or by other methods?
18. Is the family likely to retain its present importance as a social institution? Why or why not? Could a satisfactory substitute be devised?

Internet Questions

1. Go to the site https://electronics.howstuffworks.com/family-tech/tech-effects-on-family/5-ways-technology-has-negatively-affected-families.htm. What are the top five ways that technology has affected families today?
2. Go to the website https://billofrightsinstitute.org/educate/educator-resources/lessons-plans/landmark-supreme-court-cases-elessons/loving-v-virginia-1967/. What does *miscegenation* mean? When did the Supreme Court decide *Loving v. Virginia*?
3. Go to https://www.youtube.com/watch?v=NJ5QuSoVJlU and watch the video on genealogy and DNA. How can DNA be used by genealogists or people interested in their own ancestry? Can DNA be used to identify specific ancestors like Alexander the Great or Genghis Khan?
4. Go to http://gaymarriage.procon.org/view.resource.php?resourceID=006193. What was the vote on the Obergefell v. Hodges case? Which justices supported which position?
5. From http://www.pewsocialtrends.org/2015/12/17/1-the-american-family-today/, what percentage of children lived with a single parent in 2014? (For reference only: answer 26 percent.)

For Further Study

Ansari, Aziz, and Eric Klinenberg, *Modern Romance*, New York: Penguin, 2015.

Ball, Carlos A., *Same-Sex Marriage and Children: A Tale of History, Social Science and Law*, Oxford: Oxford University Press, 2015.

Conley, Dalton, *The Pecking Order: Which Siblings Succeed and Why*, New York: Pantheon, 2004.

Coontz, Stephanie, *The Social Origins of Private Life: A History of American Families, 1600–1900*, New York: Verso, 2016.

de Marneffe, Daphne, *Maternal Desire: On Children, Love, and the Inner Life*, London: Little Brown, 2004.

Gottman, John M., and Nan Silver, *The Seven Principles for Making Marriage Work*, New York: Harmony Books, 2015.

Harper, Sarah, *Aging Societies: Myths, Challenges and Opportunities*, London: Hodder Arnold, 2006.

McClain, Linda C., *The Place of Families: Fostering Capacity, Equality, and Responsibility*, Cambridge, MA: Harvard University Press, 2006.

Moynihan, Daniel Patrick, *Family and Nation*, New York: Harcourt Brace Jovanovich, 1986.

Perel, Esther, *Mating in Captivity: Reconciling the Erotic and the Domestic*, New York: HarperCollins, 2006.

Ryan, Christopher, and Cacilda Jetha, *Sex at Dawn: How We Mate, Why We Stray, and What It Means for Modern Relationships*, New York: Harper Collins, 2010.

Stanley, Rosalind Caldwell, *Family Life: Revolutionizing the Way Families Live and Love*, CreateSpace Independent Publishing Platform, 2015.

Ugwueze, Uche Lynn-Teresa, *Reimagining the African American Family Through African Cultural Values and Structures*, Bloomington, IN: AuthorHouse, 2014.

Vance, J.D., *Hillbilly Elegy: A Memoir of a Family and Culture in Crisis*, New York: HarperCollins, 2016.

Internet Sites to Explore

"http://www.divorcereform.org/cov.html" Covenant Marriage Links.

"http://www.divorcenet.com" Divorcenet – Divorce Resources.

"http://www.cyndislist.com/" Genealogy Sites.

"http://www.ncfr.org" National Council on Family Relations.

"http://www.familyandparenting.org/" National Family and Parenting Institute.

Religion

chapter 10

After reading this chapter, you should be able to:

- Explain why religion has existed in all societies
- List the five great religions of today and summarize their beliefs
- State the problem that fundamentalist religious views pose for the state
- Discuss the role of religion in society

The more I study science,
the more I believe in God.

—Albert Einstein

From A.D. 1095 to 1272, Europeans went to war to recapture territory which had traditionally been controlled by Christians from the Muslims. The Crusades, as those wars were called, changed the nature of society. As evidenced in today's problems of worldwide terrorism and fighting in the Middle East, religion is still leading to wars and still changing the nature of society. The importance of religion to society cannot be overemphasized.

If we think of religion as including all beliefs in supernatural powers, conceived of as controlling people's lives, and including various types of spirits and gods, then religion probably had its beginnings in some of the earliest human societies. The findings of archaeologists and anthropologists suggest that from time immemorial humans have sought explanations of their existence and of natural phenomena that went beyond the range of what they could learn from the ordinary experiences of life or from observation of the natural world.

An aspect of life that from very early on troubled people was the inevitability of death, and religion often promised them a life beyond death. Also, as cultures and civilizations developed, people longed to find purposes and satisfactions in life that would transcend the needs and desires of everyday living and thus give human existence greater dignity and meaning. Religion helps satisfy this longing because of the concepts common to all of its forms: the incorporation of a code of ethics; the use of myths or stories; the organization of intellectual doctrine; the display and comfort of ritual; the fostering of community and regard for others; and the hope of some intense, personal experience such as the answering of prayer.

That religious beliefs, institutions, and rituals have been a major element in the cultural patterns of most societies cannot be doubted. Even in modern industrial societies many of our oldest values and traditions are rooted in religion. In our own country, evidence of religious influence is rich. It includes the millions of people who attend religious services; the thousands of houses of worship; the celebration of holidays (holy days) such as those associated with

Christmas, Easter, Passover, Yom Kippur, and Ramadan; and those ceremonies that are both private and official, such as weddings and funerals, and rites such as baptisms and bar mitzvahs.

In this chapter, our purpose is not to show the truth or falsehood of the doctrines of any particular faith. Rather, it is:

- To describe the nature of religion and the general character of certain major religions of the past and present.
- To give some attention to the role that religion has played in the development of human societies, not only to integrate and stabilize them but also, at times, to create conflicts.
- To consider the present-day influence of social change on religion and, conversely, the influence of religion on social change.

The Nature of Religion

Today, when we say that a person is religious, we usually mean he or she believes in the existence of a supreme being and that this belief determines moral precepts and behavior to an important degree. Religious people believe that some things are of great value, or sacred, and they are likely to belong to a religious organization such as a church or synagogue; at the least, they attend religious services, even if on a sporadic or occasional schedule, where they commune with others whose beliefs are similar.

Religions vary greatly. Most include a belief in God or gods, some concept of an afterlife, and some theory of salvation, either by earning the right of entry into heaven or the privilege of reincarnation in a higher form of life or a higher social status. But some religions seem to have no God in any sense in which we ordinarily use that term. One of these is original Buddhism, which, unlike some later forms of this faith, is a religion without a deity, without a personal concept of God, and without any theory of salvation except the bliss of escaping perpetual rounds of reincarnation and suffering by achieving **nirvana,** a state in which all desire and even all consciousness is lost.

Religions can have both spiritual and civil elements. **Civil religion,** a term that was first used by Rousseau, refers to religious beliefs that lead people to want to live by the laws of the land. It is a means of motivating people, out of fear of the divine power over them, to "subject themselves willingly to the governmental laws." This is in contrast to spiritual religion, which is only concerned with heavenly things and cares little what happens in this world. Neither civil nor spiritual religions are a threat to the state. However, when the two elements of religion combine, and the spiritual aspect of religion becomes interested in the happenings of the world and unwilling to accept the laws of the land, the state and religion can come into conflict. Fundamentalist elements of religions, such as fundamentalist Christianity and fundamentalist Islam, often combine the two and hence come into conflict with the state. No longer does the individual subject himself or herself willingly to government laws; instead he or she is often in direct conflict with those laws. Sometimes this conflict becomes violent. We can see this in both fundamentalist Christian attacks on abortion centers and fundamentalist Islamic attacks on Western targets.

It is not easy to give a formal definition of religion that is wholly satisfactory, but the one suggested by Hans-Joachim Schoeps in the *Religions of Mankind* is useful and is the one we will use. According to him, "**religion** may be defined, in its

All religions are based on faith.

The inscription expresses the views of many different religions.   *The Great Sphinx and the Pyramid of Khafra.*

broadest sense, as the relationship between man and the superhuman power he believes in and feels himself to be dependent upon." Such a relationship is expressed in various ways, including feelings of trust or fear, legends, myths, prayer, rituals, and the application of religious precepts to the conduct of life.

What religions the earliest human beings practiced is a matter for speculation, but there are some tribal groups today, such as African bushmen, whose way of life is, or has been until very recently, so removed from modern technology that it is tempting to liken their beliefs to prehistoric ones. A graphic example can be seen in the classic film *The Gods Must Be Crazy*. In the first fifteen minutes of this film, Kalahari bushmen are seen living a life that we feel must have been unchanged for thousands of years. Suddenly, a Coke bottle is tossed out of a plane passing overhead and lands among them. The bushmen view the bottle as a gift from the gods, but it causes changes, including tests of faith, which themselves celebrate the imagination of the primal human spirit. Ultimately, the bushmen decide they want to get rid of this "new technology" in order to preserve their way of life.

The Great Religions of Today

Today there are innumerable religions and sects, including the religions of people who still live in tribal groups. But if we are to list the great religions of the world, each of which is still a vital force in the lives of many millions of human beings, we should include at least five, namely, Hinduism, Buddhism, Judaism, Christianity, and Islam. In the world, about 70 percent of the population identifies itself with some organized religious group, although many people are only loosely affiliated. In the United States, Protestant or Catholic Christians are the largest groups, as you can see in Figure 10.1a. The Christian religion is also the largest in the world, as you can see in Figure 10.1b. Unlike in the United States, however, the largest percentage of Christians in the world is Roman Catholic rather than Protestant. Muslims and Hindus are the next two largest religious groups in the world. Were we to look at world religious affiliation over time, we would see that since 1950 the largest change has been the decreased importance of Buddhism. In large part, this decrease is due to the decline in religion in China after the communists took control in the 1950s.

The percentages in Figure 10.1 are of different affiliations. Many people are affiliated with a religion but do not attend services. If we include people who, while affiliated with a religion,

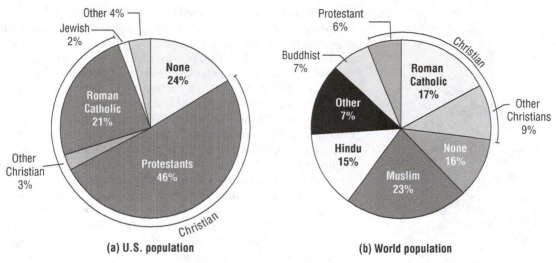

Figure 10.1

(a) Religious identification of U.S. population; (b) Religious identification of world population. (Source: Pew Research Center)

do not attend services more than once a year, the total number of people in the United States classified in the "none" category would rise to more than 50 percent, which is a substantial rise over past decades.

Whether Confucianism and Taoism in China and Shintoism in Japan should be included in the great religions of today is questionable. Since the current regime, the status and future of China's ancient religions are uncertain. Furthermore, Confucianism often is said to be more a philosophy than a religion. Shintoism is the ancient religion of Japan but has had strong competition from Buddhism. In 1868 reformed Shintoism was made the official religion of Japan, but after World War II religious freedom was declared. However, some calculate that millions of Japanese still retain their faith in Shintoism. It is a mixture of nature, ancestor, and emperor worship and is closely associated with Japanese nationalism, although the concept of the emperor's divinity was officially abolished in 1945.

Hinduism

Hinduism is the religion and social system of the Hindus, the majority of whom live in India. Since ancient times, it has had a strong hold in India, and even today it dominates the lives of the majority of its people. A minority of Indians have been converted to foreign faiths such as Christianity or Islam, or to religions such as Buddhism, Jainism, or Sikhism, all three of which developed out of Hinduism itself.

Unlike many religions, Hinduism has no founder, no distinct set of creeds, and, although it has many clear-cut paths to salvation, no unique path. It holds that the soul inhabits successive bodies in its journey through the universe, and thus all life, including insect and plant life, has a soul. All beings, even the gods, must die and be reborn in an endless cycle. Some believe that this cycle can be escaped through asceticism, in which personality is lost and the believer becomes one with the Absolute. Although Hinduism claims to be monotheistic, its High God has many forms, of which the two best known are Vishnu the creator and preserver and Shiva the destroyer. There are thousands of lesser gods. No one attempts to remember all of them, but each has its place in folk affection; the believer will tell you, "They are all the same god."

Shiva, a Hindu god.

In Hinduism all life is sacred because all life has a soul. The sacrifice of living creatures, a characteristic of some Hindu ceremonies, is explained by precisely this: Because life is sacred, its sacrifice to the gods is vitally meaningful. Today, however, partly because of the economic value of animals, sacrifices are almost always represented by flowers and food. (The gods eat the spiritual portion of the food; the material portion is consumed by the givers.) Many animals are sacred: The cow is revered because she represents Mother Earth. She is never to be injured or killed. (Sick and starving cows roam the countryside and crowded city streets; they have been known to attend the movies in Calcutta.) Other sacred creations are monkeys, snakes, the banyan tree, the herb known as basil, all mountains and rivers, and rocks of unusual shape.

Hindus are divided into four castes: (1) scholars and priests (Brahmans, a word meaning "source of life," or "expansive force"); (2) administrators of the state; (3) commercial and agricultural entrepreneurs; and (4) workers who perform the tasks the three higher classes shun—for example, sweeping floors, cleaning bathrooms, and repairing shoes. This **caste system,** in which individuals are differentiated in the jobs they can have, is hereditary, and although it has been officially outlawed for decades, it has proved almost impossible to eradicate, and to transfer to a higher caste is very difficult.

There are hundreds of kinds of Hindus, of which the Sikhs form one of the most important in the modern world. *Sikh* is derived from a Hindi word meaning "disciple," and **Sikhs** are disciples of a group of gurus whose tenets are most easily expressed by naming principles to which they are opposed: the caste system, the priestly hierarchy and ritual, and idolatry. Sikhs are skilled farmers and shrewd businesspeople, and they are considered among the world's finest soldiers. They subscribe to such Hindu beliefs as birth and rebirth and the transmigration of the soul. In India, intense religious hatred exists between Sikhs and followers of the dominant Hinduism, and this enmity is fortified by political and regional rivalries. In 1984, after the Indian Prime Minister Indira Gandhi had ordered a military attack on the sacred Sikh temple of Amritsar (which resulted in many Sikh deaths and great damage to the edifice), she was assassinated on the grounds of her official residence; Sikhs are widely believed to have been responsible. Since then there has been ongoing tension in the Punjab region of India, where the majority of Sikhs reside.

An outward sign of Hinduism is its concentration on counting and classifying, creating categories into which to fit individual manifestations. This usually is explained as a method of imposing order on a complicated world, but it can also be seen as a means of imposing disorder, or of proving, by the endlessness of the effort, that the world cannot be categorized. This characteristic enables Hinduism to incorporate diverse and even contradictory principles if Hindus find them good.

Buddhism

Although Buddhism, for the reasons outlined in this section, is now rare in India, it remains important in the Eastern world. It teaches that by right thinking and self-denial its followers can achieve nirvana. It developed out of early Hinduism, and one of its chief objectives is to free people from the endless cycle of reincarnations that is part of Hindu doctrine. Buddhism was founded more than 500 years before Christ by a young Nepalese prince, Shakyamuni Gautama, who later became known as Buddha ("the enlightened one"). He is also sometimes called Siddhartha, "the perfected" or "completed one." After observing the troubles of his father's subjects, the prince became convinced that all life results in suffering and that the

Buddha, revered in the Far East.

only escape is to overcome desire for life and its pleasures. Therefore, he left his parents and his princely existence and became a wandering ascetic monk in order to seek a cure for suffering.

He succeeded in entering a trance in which he remembered his former incarnations and perceived himself as having already passed through so many stages that he was ready to have himself born to his current circumstances in order to preach to others. Gautama had thus reached Enlightenment and could be called Buddha. He emerged from this state of contemplation, or nirvana, although tempted by evil forces to remain dallying there, and went to Banaras, on the Ganges River in India, to explain how others could attain nirvana— namely, by realizing that life is suffering, suffering springs from a burning thirst for material and spiritual riches, suffering ceases when the thirst is renounced, and we cease to thirst by passing through eight stages: right views, right aspiration, right speech, right conduct, right livelihood, right effort, right mindfulness, and right contemplation.

All of these concepts can be, and have been, divided into their own subcategories, but the heart of Buddha's teaching is gentleness, compassion, rationality, and moderation. Everyone can become a Buddha, although very few actually do so. More numerous than Buddhas are *bodhisattvas,* people who have given up or delayed entering nirvana in order that they may stay to help others. The Buddha's preaching did not involve appeals to a higher being, because his experience of widespread suffering rendered him incapable of believing in a beneficent creator. It did involve contemplation and relinquishing; in an advanced state, one realizes "There is nothing."

The Buddha's birthplace (Kapilavastu), the place of his Enlightenment (Bodh Gaya), the place where he gave his first sermon (the deer park in Sarnath), and the place where he died (near Kapilavastu)—all in India or Nepal—are today the main destinations for Buddhist pilgrimages. Nevertheless, Buddhism is not one of the major religions of India today, having declined for many reasons, but principally because Islam overtook it both philosophically and materially, and in the eleventh century A.D. Muslims destroyed the Buddhist monasteries and dispersed the monks.

Over the centuries, as Buddhism gained converts and spread to other countries, it underwent many changes, some of which greatly increased its popular appeal. Also, a variety of sects developed. It spread to Tibet, China, Korea, Japan, Southeast Asia, and Sri Lanka, taking on markedly different forms in different areas. In the south of Asia, in countries such as Sri Lanka, Myanmar, and Thailand, Buddhism is firmly established and is said to have retained more of its original character than in other regions.

Although Buddhism is primarily an Asian religion, in the 1970s small Buddhist sects sprang up in the United States. Many of these sects disbanded in the late 1980s, but a few remain. The Buddhist monastic community was founded by the Buddha himself, and its organization and character are said to be the one element in Buddhism that has changed relatively little over the centuries. Even to this day, Buddhist monks shave their heads and wear the traditional yellow robes. You are likely to see some sect members in the streets of a big city dressed in this traditional garb. Zen Buddhism, transcendental meditation, and yoga, all Buddhist practices that do not require more than several hours of practice a day, have also spread.

Judaism

We now turn to the three major **monotheistic religions** (religions with one god)—Judaism, Christianity, and Islam—which all share a common history. We begin with Judaism, which, although it has played an important role in world history, has a relatively small number of adherents. In 2018, the entire Jewish population of the world was probably only about 14 million, compared with about 2.3 billion Christians and 1.6 billion Muslims.

Judaism developed out of the religion of the ancient Hebrew tribe. According to the Bible story, a great leader of this tribe, Abraham, put his trust in a single God to guide him and his people in their migrations. During their wanderings, the Hebrews, or Israelites, as they came to be called (after Jacob, or Israel, the grandson of Abraham), moved into the fertile Nile delta to escape famine. There they were eventually enslaved by the Egyptians.

During the period of their slavery, probably sometime between 1450 B.C. and 1400 B.C., there arose a great leader, Moses. He led the Israelites to freedom, as God had directed him, and came to be commonly regarded as the real founder of Judaism. After the escape of the Israelites from Egypt, Moses ascended Mount Sinai, where God appeared to him and through him made a sacred covenant with what were by then the twelve tribes of Israel. That covenant required that the Israelites acknowledge "the God of Israel" as ruler of the world and creator of heaven and earth. In return, God recognized the people of Israel as his chosen followers. Moses had been instructed by God to call him *Yahweh,* or as it is sometimes translated, Jehovah. When Moses came down from the mountain, he brought with him two stone tablets on which were inscribed Yahweh's Ten Commandments. These were later amplified into the many commandments and prohibitions set forth in the **Torah**—the Pentateuch, or the Five Books of Moses—which is part of both Jewish scriptures and the Christian Old Testament.

Judaism has several unique characteristics. First, though it makes claims to universality, it was and still is primarily the religion of a group of people who can, with qualifications, regard themselves as descendants of the ancient Israelites. Jews believe that they were chosen by God, but they do not believe that being chosen by God makes them special. They do not understand why they were chosen, and they regard it as a burden as much as a blessing. In fact, in the Book of Exodus, God suggests to Moses that perhaps he should begin again with a less fractious tribe. According to Jewish theologians, God chose the Jews simply because he had to begin somewhere. They do not see it as an honor or as a sign that they are superior, attitudes that are attributed to them by some non-Jews.

Second, Judaism has preserved much of its essential character for more than 3,000 years. It has done this in spite of the fact that for more than 1,900 years, ever since their last major rebellion against Rome was crushed by the Emperor Hadrian in A.D. 135, Jews have been a widely scattered and often persecuted minority among alien peoples. Finally, and most important, Judaism was the first great religion to develop a clear and unequivocal concept of a single God as the creator and ruler of the universe.

Although some Jews believe in the resurrection of the dead and that people must account beyond the grave for their good and evil deeds, unlike some other religions Judaism is a world-affirming, not a world-denying, faith, and it requires that Jews enjoy this life and use their abilities for the service of humankind. It looks for the coming of the **Messiah**—the expected deliverer of the Jews—and for a messianic age in which the kingdom of eternal peace will prevail and all evil impulses will be removed from the human heart. But it rejects the Christian belief that the Messiah has already come with his message of salvation.

From the Middle Ages to early modern times, the rights of Jews in Europe were greatly restricted, and they were forced to live in special sections of the cities called ghettos. The French Revolution and Napoleon did much to free Jews from the ghettos. But later there was a backlash, and it was not until after the social upheavals of 1848 that in most countries Jews received full rights of citizenship on a more or less permanent basis. This, however, did not end their troubles, for the very success that many of them soon enjoyed in their professions stirred up new waves of **anti-Semitism,** or feelings of hatred and dislike toward Jews.

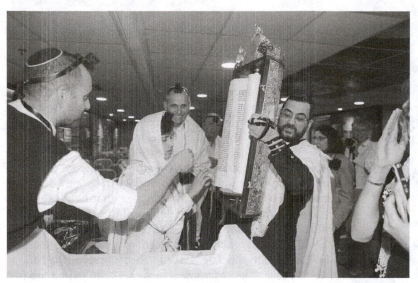

Boy reads from Torah during Bar Mitzvah celebration.

© Dan Porges/Getty

The freeing of the Jews in the nineteenth century from their former restrictions brought about great changes in Judaism. Gradually Jews, not only in Europe but also in the United States, became divided into three major groups: the Orthodox, who resist change in beliefs and ritual; the Reform, who reject much of Jewish traditionalism and believe that Judaism should be regarded as a changing and developing religion; and the Conservatives, who cannot accept the orthodoxy but who object to an extreme break with traditions and therefore seek a middle way.

Jews sometimes are called a race, but anthropologists remind us that this term is inaccurate. Originally, they belonged to that branch of the Caucasoid race that inhabited the Arabian peninsula and spread into the fertile crescent to the north of it. They once formed a nationality, the ancient Hebrew nation. But later they were dispersed over almost the entire world, and over the centuries they interbred to some extent with the non-Jews of the countries in which they lived. Also, they converted several non-Jewish peoples to Judaism. The word *Jew* comes from Judaism, which is their religion. After World War II, some of them migrated to the ancient homeland and created the new nation of Israel.

To determine the number of Jews in the United States with any great accuracy is impossible. This is partly because many persons of Jewish ethnic background maintain no affiliation with any temple or other Jewish organization, partly because there has been an appreciable amount of intermarriage between Jews and non-Jews, and partly because Jews disagree on who is a Jew. Tradition says anyone born to a Jewish mother is a Jew. However, in the 1980s the Reform rabbinate, representing about a quarter of U.S. Jews, extended recognition to those whose only Jewish parent is the father.

There is an increasing emphasis on individual choice in Judaism, including rising numbers of conversions. Some Jews see these processes as endangering their traditional view of themselves as chosen by God, but others welcome these trends. At present, it is estimated that there are about 6 million people in this country who can be classified as Jews. More than one-third of all U.S. Jews live in metropolitan New York, and considerable numbers are concentrated in other large cities such as Los Angeles, Philadelphia, Chicago, and Miami.

Jews are sometimes considered primarily a religious group, but in a poll taken by *Newsweek,* only 43 percent of U.S. Jews said they considered themselves religious. According to political scientist Daniel Elazar of Temple University, only 20 percent of the Jewish population worships regularly. Of the others, 40 percent maintain nominal affiliation with a temple but usually attend services only on their high holy days of Rosh Hashanah and Yom Kippur.

On the average, U.S. Jews have markedly higher incomes than the rest of our population, though over half a million fall below the family poverty level as set by agencies of the federal government. Jews also, on average, have higher levels of education than other groups and, in proportion to their numbers, are much better represented in business and the professions.

Prejudice against the Jews, or anti-Semitism, has existed for centuries and has been strong in certain countries. Sometimes it has been tied to religion; sometimes it has been rationalized by dislike on the part of the majority of the population for certain cultural or "racial" characteristics, largely imaginary, attributed to the Jews as a group. In some parts of eastern Europe,

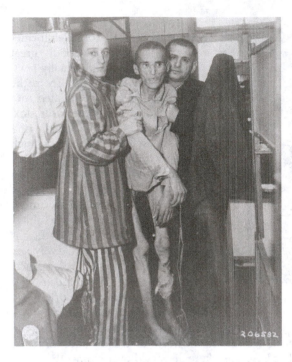

An inmate at a Nazi concentration camp.

anti-Semitism has at times gone to such extremes that thousands of Jews were killed, as in the **pogroms,** or organized massacres, that occurred in czarist Russia. But it was in Nazi Germany that anti-Semitism reached its height, and the Holocaust, in which 6 million Jews were killed, has affected Jews and everyone else in a variety of ways.

Partially because of feelings of guilt for allowing the Holocaust to occur, the Western nations supported the establishment of the state of Israel after World War II. Israel was established from lands over 50 percent of which were owned by Palestinian Arabs. After the 1948 war for control of this land, a huge number of Palestinian Arabs were displaced and moved to refugee camps in neighboring Arab states where they and their descendants still live. This area of the Middle East became a prime source of international friction.

In 1994, after almost fifty years of conflict, the Jews and the Palestinians officially agreed to become reconciled and to live in peace. That agreement was meant to culminate in a permanent peace treaty between the Palestinians and the Israelis, but disputes about borders prevented any permanent agreement, and today the two sides remain engaged in fighting and serious disputes.

Christianity

Christianity, the principal religion of the Western world, developed from Judaism, and the greater part of the Christian Bible (the Old Testament) still consists of Jewish sacred writings. The ancient Jews believed that at his chosen time God would confound their enemies and set up a new Jewish kingdom under a Messiah (deliverer) descended from King David. Later, some came to believe that the Messiah would come down from heaven at the end of the world, at the time of the resurrection of the dead, and would carry out the last judgment.

Jesus of Nazareth, the founder of Christianity, was born in Bethlehem, about A.D. 1. This date in itself is an example of the power of religion. In Western cultures, events that took place before the birth of Christ are dated "B.C.," meaning "Before Christ." For instance, in Chapter 3, we said that humans first appeared in China about 20,000 B.C. The term "A.D." stands for the Latin words *anno domini,* which literally translated mean "in the year of our Lord." This term is used to begin numbering all over again, with A.D. 1 as the year of Christ's birth. The year A.D. 2000 means the two thousandth year after Christ's birth.[1]

At some point in Jesus' life, he became convinced that he was the Messiah, or Christ, and the divine son of God. Often he is called Jesus Christ, which simply means Jesus, the Messiah. Soon after he started his ministry, at about the age of thirty, he gathered around him the **Apostles,** the twelve close associates who were to be his chief aides and who were to carry on his ministry after his death.

Our knowledge of Jesus' teachings comes to us indirectly. He did not write them down but depended on his disciples to preach from memory what he had taught. Our chief sources are, first, the Gospels of the New Testament and, second, the Epistles. But these were prepared long

---

[1] Twentieth-century scholarship indicates that Christ actually was born about 4 B.C. There will be no attempt to renumber dates, as that task would be impossible, and the Western world's dating system will continue to use A.D. 1 as a reference point. An alternative, secular, way of designating A.D. and B.C. is C.E. (Common Era) and B.C.E. (Before the Common Era).

Pope in front of a large crowd.

© imageBROKER/Alamy Stock Photo

after Jesus' death. The four Gospels are thought by historians to have been written between A.D. 65 and about A.D. 100. Presumably, they were based on documents in which some of his followers had recorded his sayings as they remembered them. But how accurately his sayings and the events of his life were recorded, or how much was changed or added by successive copiers or revisers of the Gospels, historical scholarship cannot tell us with any certainty.

Jesus never doubted the reality of God or of his own special relationship to God. But he knew he had not been sent, as some of his hearers hoped, to deliver the Jews from Rome by reestablishing the earthly kingdom of David. Rather, he had been sent by his Father to show all of humanity, Jews and Gentiles alike, the way to heavenly salvation. Like many Jews of his day, he believed that the long-foretold messianic kingdom of God would come rather soon, but for him it was a kingdom in heaven, which was only for those who would believe in him, who would truly repent of their sins, and who would surrender to the will of God before it was too late.

Jesus taught that the most important things are to believe in God, do His will, and believe in Jesus as the son of God. God is utterly good: supremely righteous and just, but also forgiving and merciful. Therefore, people should trust him completely and regularly seek spiritual aid through prayer. Jesus also taught that God demands we love one another, friend and foe alike, and this has been one of the most difficult teachings for devout Christians to interpret and to apply as a practical guide in daily conduct. In addition, Jesus taught his disciples to obey the Ten Commandments, which God transmitted to Moses on Mount Sinai, and to follow the golden rule. The latter states, "Do unto others as you would have them do unto you."

Jesus' success in drawing crowds in Galilee soon attracted the attention of the leaders of the two principal Jewish sects, or parties, in Jerusalem—the Sadducees and the Pharisees. They had their own differences, but both became enemies of Jesus because his teaching and his actions did not always follow the dictates of either Judaic law or tradition. After he had been preaching for three or four years, Jesus decided to go to Jerusalem at the time of the Passover, when Jews from a wide area would be assembled for the great annual festival. This gave the enemies of Jesus an opportunity to stir up ill feeling against him among the people. Finally they seized him, made accusations against him, and denounced him to the Roman governor, Pilate, on the grounds that he claimed to be king of the Jews. Pilate doubted Jesus' guilt, but when the crowd demanded death, the governor acquiesced and ordered Jesus' crucifixion at Golgotha.

Three events reported in the Gospels and the Epistles are of crucial significance for Christianity: (1) the Last Supper of Jesus with his disciples on the evening before the crucifixion, (2) his crucifixion, and (3) his resurrection on the third day after his death. Even before coming to Jerusalem, Jesus had foretold his death and resurrection to the twelve apostles. A key belief of the Christian religion is that Jesus died to redeem the sins of humankind and thus opened for them the way to salvation. In the sacrament of Communion, or the Eucharist, which was first celebrated by Jesus with the twelve disciples at the Last Supper, devout communicants believe that they enter into a special relationship with Christ. The wine they drink and the bread they eat symbolize, or in Catholic doctrine actually become, the blood and body of Christ. The communicant is thus strengthened in his or her attempts to achieve salvation by the redemptive power that Christ achieved through his death and resurrection.

Gaudi's Barcelona Cathedral.

© Stanley Chen Xi/Getty

The Early Christians. The spread of Christianity after Jesus' death was relatively rapid, but the early Christian groups, or churches, were only loosely linked. By the end of the first century, however, administrative organization had begun to develop in Rome and elsewhere, and bishops began to assume authority not only to appoint priests to oversee local churches but also to settle disputes over doctrine. Gradually the primacy of the bishop of Rome became recognized throughout the empire, and by the end of the third century, he had taken the title of pope.

The Middle Ages and After. Before the final collapse of the Roman Empire in the West in A.D. 476, the Church of Rome had become strong enough to prevent the complete breakdown of order and civilization that might otherwise have resulted from the successive invasions of the empire by Germanic tribes. During the Middle Ages, the church dominated the religious and intellectual life of Europe and to a great extent its politics and economics. Meanwhile, the eastern Roman Empire with its capital at Constantinople (now known as Istanbul) still survived, and the Eastern Church, later known as the Orthodox Church, became increasingly independent of Rome. The final break, or schism, between the two parts of the church occurred in 1054 and remains to this day.

The next great defection from the Church of Rome did not occur for several hundred years. In the fifteenth century, or perhaps even earlier, many Christians felt that the church was undergoing moral decay. The Renaissance, which brought a renewal of interest in art, literature, and the works of classical antiquity, undoubtedly contributed to a general unrest. Reformers began to urge that religion revert to its sources. The result was the **Reformation,** the Protestant revolt against traditional Catholicism, which began in 1517 when Martin Luther posted his call for reform on the door of the church in Wittenberg, Germany. Other important leaders of the Reformation included Ulrich Zwingli and John Calvin in Switzerland and John Knox in Scotland.

The Reformation led to a considerable period of religious and political turmoil, including religious wars and repression of dissident groups in various countries, and though it did not win over the majority of Catholics to Protestantism, it did result in substantial defections from the Roman Catholic Church. But the Protestants who succeeded in gaining freedom from control by Rome did not succeed in joining to form a major independent church body. Instead, they divided into a considerable number of sects, or denominations. Several of these, including the Puritans and Quakers, played an important role in the settlement of the British colonies in America.

European migration to the Americas and to areas such as South Africa, Australia, and New Zealand carried Christianity with it. In some areas, such as the United States and Canada except Quebec, Protestant settlers from northwestern Europe were in the majority. In other areas, as in practically all of Latin America, settlers came largely from overwhelmingly Catholic countries such as Spain, Portugal, and Italy. Christianity was also carried to other parts of the world by the strong missionary movement that developed in the nineteenth century, but in most non-Christian countries missionaries succeeded in converting only a small fraction of the people.

Modern Christianity in the United States. The United States is primarily a Christian state, but there are many different groups of Christians; a Unitarian or an Episcopalian differs significantly from an evangelical Christian in terms of worldview and beliefs. For the most part, U.S. Christianity functions smoothly with the state, but conflict between religion and state can arise when the moral views of certain Christian fundamentalist groups on issues such as abortion differ from the moral views as expressed in the laws of the state. When such differences exist, individuals are forced to choose between the two. The state integrates best with religion when each stays in its own sphere. That view is captured in Jesus' edict that his followers were to "Render unto Caesar that which is Caesar's and unto God that which is God's."

Islam

Islam, like Judaism and Christianity, is a religion based on divine revelation, and its messenger, Muhammad, like Moses, made no claims to divinity for himself. He believed only that he had been chosen by God, or Allah, to receive from the angel Gabriel revelations of Allah's will. These revelations, which became frequent, he repeated in full to those who would listen, and shortly after his death they were assembled by his friend Abû Bakr to form the **Qu'ran,** the holy scriptures of the Muslims. Abû Bakr became the first successor, or caliph, to carry on Muhammad's work. The Qur'an begins as follows:

> In the name of Allah, the Beneficent, the Merciful.
> All praise is due to Allah, the Lord of the Worlds.
> The Beneficent, the Merciful.
> Master of the Day of Judgment.
> Thee do we serve and Thee do we beseech for help.
> Keep us on the right path.
> The path of those upon whom Thou hast bestowed favors. Not [the path] of those upon whom Thy wrath is brought down, nor of those who go astray.

The Qur'an is accessible on the Web in formats that are easily searchable for specific topics, and, given the importance of Islam to modern world affairs, browsing through it is definitely a worthwhile activity.

Muhammad was born about A.D. 570 at Mecca, in the western part of what is now Saudi Arabia. According to tradition, he was orphaned and became a ward first of his grandfather and then of an uncle, both of whom were prominent members of the Koreish tribe. Later he was a merchant, and at about the age of 25 he became the business advisor to a rich widow, fifteen years his senior, whom he eventually married. Meanwhile, he had come into contact with the Arabian religion of his time, which was a mixture of animism and polytheism. Muhammad had also learned something about Judaism and Christianity from his acquaintances in Mecca who were followers of both religions. His contacts with Jews and Christians may have contributed to his dissatisfaction with the beliefs and practices of his fellow Arab tribesmen.

Though Muhammad himself initiated the religion of Islam, he was greatly influenced by Christianity

Temple Mount (Jewish name) or Haram esh-Sharif (Muslim name).

© Claudiad/iStock

and Judaism. He considered that he was completing and perfecting the work of Moses, Jesus, and other heavenly messengers whom he recognized as his forerunners. But Muhammad denied the Christian doctrine of the Trinity and the divinity of Christ. According to the Qur'an, God is one and God is eternal. He neither begets nor is begotten.

In Arabic, *Islam* means "submission," and Muslims are submitters to the will of God. The devout Muslim's goal is fairly simple: It is to perform one's duties as outlined in the Qur'an and as exemplified by the acts of Muhammad in his lifetime. For devout Muslims, the Qur'an is infallible.

The so-called Five Pillars of Islam state the indispensable religious duties of a believer:

1. Acceptance and frequent repetition of the creed, "There is no God but Allah and Muhammad is his messenger."
2. The performance five times a day of prescribed rituals of prayer and devotion.
3. The giving of alms to the needy.
4. The fast during Ramadan, the month when the angel Gabriel appeared to Muhammad.
5. The pilgrimage to the Kaaba stone at Mecca once in a lifetime by those who can afford it.

From the seventh century A.D. to the eighteenth century, Islam spread as far west as Spain and as far east as the Philippines. It was able to do this through its access to trade routes from its original home in Arabia and through military conquest. Islam's influence ebbed and flowed, but by the end of World War I in 1918 it had reached a low. By the second half of the twentieth century, however, with political independence and national consciousness, Islam was enjoying a resurgence and again extending its influence. Today its principal distribution is in the Arabian peninsula, North and West Africa, the Middle East, Turkey, Afghanistan and the Indian subcontinent, parts of the former USSR, and Indonesia. In both the United States and Europe, the number of Muslims is growing, and some authorities predict that there will be more Muslims than Jews in the United States in coming decades.

One of the reasons for the growing number of Muslims in the United States and Europe was the conflicts in Syria, Libya and Afghanistan, which displaced millions of people, and led Europe to classify them as political refugees. This classification made them eligible to emigrate, whereas had they been classified as economic refugees—refugees who are moving for economic reasons, they would not have been eligible. In 2015 Germany took in over 1 million migrants, most of whom were Muslims, leading to a backlash among voters in Germany who argued that it was too many in a short space of time.

The Denominations of Islam. After Muhammad's death, Islam split into two factions: the **Shiites** (the sectarians, followers of Ali, cousin to the Prophet), who believed that Ali was the legitimate successor to Muhammad, and the **Sunnis** (the traditionalists), who believed that Abû Bakr, the oldest companion of Muhammad, was the legitimate successor. Today Sunnis constitute about 85 percent of all Muslims and Shiites constitute about 15 percent. There are also smaller sects of Islam, including the Sufis and the Wahhabis, and though they are small in number, they can play important roles in the interaction between the Islamic world and the Western world.

The difference between Sunnis and Shiites concerns who should be seen as the legitimate religious authority in society. Shiites follow a system of Imamah. They believe that the existing Imam is the true leader of Muslims, and that all true Muslims must submit to his rule. Imams are appointed by existing Imams, which means there is a line of succession that always assumes a

The Qur'an is the Holy Book of Islam.

living Imam as ruler. Because Imams carry enormous power among believers to tell people what to do, Imamah can, and often does, come into conflict with governments, which also claim the right to tell people what to do. An example is Iran, which has a Shiite majority. Iran has both a religious authority—the Imam—and a democratically elected government, and there is often confusion about which authority is in charge.

Sunnis do not follow a system of Imamah. This means that Sunnis generally are more content with having a secular ruler as long as that secular ruler does not interfere with the spiritual dimension of religion. In Iraq there are both Sunnis and Shiites, with the Shiites in the majority. However, Iraq had never been a democracy, and until 2004 the Sunnis were in charge. It was in part to keep the Shiite majority out of power that the United States had earlier supported Saddam Hussein in his war with Iran.

After invading Iraq in 2003, the United States struggled with setting up a democratic government, which the United States stated was one of the goals of the invasion, in a country with a Shiite majority whose beliefs often put religious rule by an Imam above secular democratic rule. The type of problem the Shiite sect presents today was the kind of problem that led Rousseau early on in his discussion of democracy to despair of the relationship between religion and government, and to call on government to set up a civil religion that avoided the conflict.

Islamic Fundamentalism.   In recent years, there has been much discussion of what is sometimes called Islamic fundamentalism and its connection to terrorism and **jihad.** In Arabic, *jihad* means "striving," but it is commonly used by the Western press to denote a sacred war against the Western world. As with all fundamentalist religious groups, there is much dispute about what is meant by fundamentalist Islam and whether some groups should be considered as fundamentalist Muslims. According to the dictionary, *fundamentalism* consists of "strict maintenance of ancient or fundamental doctrines." The problem is that there is generally ambiguity about what those doctrines are, and the issue comes down to who is interpreting them. For some fundamentalists, such as Al-Qaeda and ISIS (the Islamic State of Iraq and Syria) the empowerment of Islam, which they see as God's plan for humankind, is a sacred end, and it can be achieved only through the establishment of an Islamic state. They interpret these doctrines as requiring Muslims to fight against the Western world and to reestablish an Islamic state, regardless of the costs to society and humanity. This interpretation of Islam had led to justification of terrorist attacks and wars in Islamic countries to replace existing governments with fundamentalist Islamic governments.

Other Muslims interpret them quite differently; many simply want to be left alone to follow their spiritual beliefs, leaving secular matters to government. Their concern is with religion, not government. For them, religious fundamentalism is simply strict adherence to the Five Pillars. The difference between the two views of fundamentalism has sometimes been called the difference between revivalists, who want to be spiritually devout, and fanatics and extremists, who exploit this devotion for political ends.

Ayatollah Khomeini, who led the Islamic revolution in Iran, combined fundamentalism with the Shiite belief in the role of the Imam and argued that because Islamic government is a government of law, and because a knowledge of law is necessary for anyone to rule, the person who should rule is the person whose knowledge of the law surpasses all others. Under this interpretation, it is appropriate to revolt against existing secular governments and replace them with rule by Islamic clerics, such as himself. This perspective fit Shiite views much better than it fit Sunni views, which posited a separation between religion and secular government. Khomeini also claimed that the West was on a crusade to eliminate Islam from the world and that Western ways were evil. In so doing he portrayed the United States in particular as the great Satan, claiming that good Muslims would reject U.S. technology and way of life.

More recent Islamic scholars such as Hasan alt-Turai and Sayyid Muhammad Husayn Fadlallah have argued that the problem is not that the West is on a crusade to eliminate Islam, but instead that the West has dispossessed Muslims. Unlike Khomeini, these scholars argue that Islam could selectively borrow technology and institutions from the West. These debates are still going on in Islamic society, and the outcome will play an important role in the peace of the world.

The Role of Religion in Society

There can be little doubt that in most primitive societies and the earliest civilizations, religious beliefs and practices were a strong integrative factor. Because of these beliefs and practices, people knew how they must behave individually and as a group to avoid the ill will of the gods and to win their favor. They knew certain things were sacred and that if the group was to avoid famine or other misfortunes, no one must be allowed to treat the gods with disrespect. Religious beliefs were tied to rules of behavior and usually gave strong support to custom and tradition.

In the early history of civilization, almost every "nation" had its own gods, and sometimes, as in ancient Egypt, the king himself was regarded as divine. Even in twentieth-century Japan, until 1945 Shinto doctrine held that the emperor was a descendant of the sun goddess. As a result, the people were drawn together not only by their common beliefs but also by their participation in common rituals of prayer, praise, and sacrifice.

Not infrequently, however, in the more highly developed civilizations of the world, differences in religious beliefs have been a source of social conflict, especially when groups with different religious beliefs have lived within the same national borders. To get an idea of the potential problem, look, for example, at Northern Ireland, where Protestants and Catholics clash, and at India, where Hindus clash with Muslims.

Religion as a Source of Moral Values and Social Change

Religion, then, can be a socially disruptive force, but it seems clear that over the years its major influence has been to integrate and stabilize nations and cultures. In the Western world, where Christianity in its various forms is by a wide margin the predominant faith, our ethical and moral values have, over the centuries, been modified and given greater vitality by the teachings of the Christian religion.

Religion's integrative force derives from the fact that it gives divine authority to ethical and moral principles. Without people's adherence to such principles, it would be difficult to maintain an orderly society with free elections and a wide range of personal freedoms, to produce goods with enough efficiency to hope to eliminate poverty, and in general to maintain the level of civilization we have already achieved.

Through its influence on individuals, religion also has an impact on economic and political institutions. The great German sociologist Max Weber (1864–1920) developed this thesis in his book *The Protestant Ethic and the Spirit of Capitalism.* According to his theory, the new Protestant sects that developed out of the Reformation, especially those that were influenced by the doctrines of Calvin, made a major contribution to the economic prosperity of Britain and western Europe and to the development of modern industrial capitalism. They did so because they believed in the **Protestant ethic,** the theory that God expects good Christians to work hard, to save, to invest their savings, and to show business initiative. The Protestant ethic also played a major role in the development of the American ideals of rugged individualism, private enterprise, and financial success.

Putting a high value on work and on the kinds of behavior necessary for material progress was never a Puritan or Protestant monopoly. It is a characteristic found everywhere among people who are determined to improve their condition, and it can be found in all societies and cultures.

Because religion is a source of moral values, it can also be a source of social change. For example, churches led the way in the civil rights battle, just as they had earlier in the antislavery movement. Churches have also been active in the push for more general economic and social equality, and for adding issues of morality to the political dialogue.

Impact of Religion on Education, the Arts, and Literature

The influence of religion on education, the arts, music, and literature is pervasive. During the Middle Ages, the church and especially the monasteries preserved ancient literature and kept learning alive. In the United States, from colonial times until well into the nineteenth century, most of our colleges and universities were started and controlled by religious organizations. Many of them are still church-controlled, and some religious bodies operate extensive systems of secondary and primary schools. Many of the great works of art of ancient Greece and the European Renaissance are representations of personalities or events with religious significance. In the field of religious music, we find such outstanding composers as Bach and Handel, and in literature we have great poems such as Dante's *Inferno* and Milton's *Paradise Lost.*

Buddhism and Hinduism have inspired temples, paintings, and sculpture of great sophistication, mystery, ferocity, and beauty. Particularly in India, these represent unparalleled fecundity and vitality. In some countries such as Indonesia and China, the entire history and development of the religions are carved over acres of temple structures or wrested from vast rock-cut caves and cliffs, constituting some of the greatest artistic and historical monuments in the history of human ingenuity. In Japan, hundreds of great gardens have been created to the quiet glory of Buddhism and Shintoism. An Islamic prohibition of representations of the human figure means that the classics of Islamic art are exhibited in architecture, calligraphy, and intricate floral and geometric patterns. Sanskrit, which means "perfect language," was developed in India to preserve religious traditions. In fulfilling this function, Sanskrit also became a great literary language and one of the Indo-European languages from which have derived most of the major languages spoken today in Europe, Iran, parts of Asia, and the Americas.

In China, the poetry of the eighth-century figure Wang Wei is one of the reasons the Tang dynasty is called the golden age. It has some Buddhist undertones, but only sixty years later the poetry of Han Shan became overtly Zen Buddhist. In India the *Ramayana* and the *Mahabharata* embody nearly all of the religious stories and myths on which the country is nurtured. In Japan we might mention the Shingon Buddhist novel of the eleventh century *Tale of Genji.*

Interfaith Efforts for Peace

Despite the many differences, significant similarities exist among religions. Religious leaders have attempted to build on these similarities by creating organizations of multiple religious denominations committed to creating better understanding among the world's population. In her book, *The Mighty and the Almighty,* former Secretary of State Madeline Albright argues that because many of the major conflicts in the world have religious roots, interfaith religious efforts are central to solving them.

The Potential Conflict between Religion and Government

The previous two sections discussed the positive elements of religion for society. But religion also plays what some consider negative roles. Specifically, it can undermine the state and lead people to fight others, all in the name of religion. The Crusades were an example of Christianity leading to war against Muslims, and recent jihad terrorist attacks are an example of Islam leading to attacks against Western countries.

Christianity and democratic government have made their peace with each other, with religion playing the spiritual role that Rousseau saw for it as a type of civil religion. The pope's decrees do not undermine Western governments, and a Catholic in government is seen as following his or her own judgment rather than the pope's decrees on issues such as gay rights or abortion. The same is true of many other religions.

This is not the case, however, with Islam, and Islamic fundamentalism poses the threat of religion to secular government that Rousseau foresaw. How those theological decisions play out will make a significant difference to the future of both the Middle East and the world.

 Study and **Review**

Key Points

- Humans have always been troubled by the inevitability of death and the meaning of life; their interest in these issues has led them to religion.
- The five great religions of today are Hinduism Buddhism, Judaism, Christianity, and Islam.
- In current society, religion is a source of moral values, and it significantly influences all aspects of life.

- Modern religions face serious questions. Disputes arise both within religions and among religions.
- Religion has played a central role in society for thousands of years and is likely to do so for thousands of years in the future.
- Religion presents a potential problem for secular government if religion extends its influence beyond the spiritual realm.

Some Important Terms

anti-Semitism (194)
Apostles (196)
caste system (192)
civil religion (189)
jihad (201)
Messiah (194)

monotheistic religions (194)
nirvana (189)
pogroms (196)
Protestant ethic (202)
Qur'an (199)
Reformation (198)

religion (189)
Shiites (200)
Sikhs (192)
Sunnis (200)
Torah (194)

Questions for Review and Discussion

General Questions

1. Why has religion had a strong appeal to human beings from earliest times?
2. To Westerners, Hinduism seems a strange faith. Why?
3. How did Prince Shakyamuni Gautama found Buddhism?
4. What are the unique characteristics of Judaism?
5. Why is our knowledge of Jesus' teachings indirect?
6. List as many as you can of the more important teachings of Jesus.
7. How did Islam begin? What was the origin of the Qur'an?
8. What are the Five Pillars of Islam?
9. What potential problems does fundamentalist Islam pose?

10. Explain how Islam spread from Arabia to other parts of the world from the seventh century to the eighteenth century.
11. State some of the similarities of Islam to Judaism or Christianity; also state some of the more important differences.
12. Why are religious beliefs likely to strengthen the moral and ethical principles of a society? How are they likely to create dissension and war?
13. On balance, has religion been an integrative or divisive factor in today's society? Defend your answer.
14. Why did Rousseau believe that governments needed to create a civil religion?

Internet Questions

1. Go to http://www.dalailama.com. What is a Dalai Lama? Who is the current Dalai Lama?
2. Using information found at https://www.deadseascrolls.org.il/learn-about-the-scrolls/introduction, explain what the Dead Sea Scrolls are. Why do you think this discovery is important?
3. Who were the Knights Templar, according to http://www.knightstemplar.org/? What was their original purpose?
4. Go to http://www.pbs.org/mormons/etc/genealogy.html. Why are Mormons so interested in genealogy?
5. Go to https://www.pbslearningmedia.org/resource/sj14-soc-religmap/world-religions-map/#.Wr0KMIhuZyw and launch the World Religions Map. In which countries is indigenous faith more popular than other faiths?

*F*or Further Study

Books to Explore

Albright, Madeline, *The Mighty and the Almighty*, New York: HarperCollins, 2006.

Bass, Diana, *Christianity after Religion*, New York: HarperOne, 2012.

Carter, Jimmy, *Faith: A Journey for All*, New York: Simon and Schuster, 2018.

Douthat, Ross, *Bad Religion: How We Became a Nation of Heretics*, New York: Free Press, 2012.

Eagleman, David, *Sum: Forty Tales for the Afterlife*, New York: Pantheon, 2009.

Evans, Michael D., *The American Prophecies: Ancient Scriptures Reveal Our Nation's Future*, Nashville, TN: Warner Faith, 2004.

Flood, Gavin, *The Truth Within: A History of Inwardness in Christianity, Hinduism, and Buddhism*, Oxford: Oxford University Press, 2015.

Jones, Gareth (editor), *The Religions Book*, New York: DK Publishers, 2013.

Kidwai, Abdur Raheem, *The Qu'ran's Essential Teachings*, Markfield: The Islamic Foundation, 2015.

Mailer, Norman, and John Buffalo Mailer, *The Big Empty: Dialogues on Politics, Sex, God, Boxing, Morality, Myth, Poker and Bad Conscience in America*, New York: Nation Books, 2006.

Mishra, Pankaj, *An End to Suffering: The Buddha in the World*, New York: Farrar, Straus, & Giroux, 2004.

Prothero, Stephen, *God Is Not One: The Eight Rival Religions That Run the World*, New York: HarperOne, 2011.

Radford, David, *Religious Identity and Social Change; Explaining Christian Conversion in a Muslim World*, Abingdon: Routledge, 2015.

Stewart, Matthew, *The Courtier and the Heretic: The Fate of God in the Modern World*, New Haven, CT: Yale University Press, 2006.

Warren, Tish Harrison, *The Liturgy of the Ordinary*, Downers Grove, IL: Intervarsity Press, 2016.

Internet Sites to Explore

"http://www.academicinfo.net/religindex.html" Academic Info Religion Gateway.

"https://uri.org/kids/world-religions/jewish-beliefs" United Religions Initiative.

"http://www.thearda.com/" Association of Religion Data Archives.

"http://www.buddhanet.net/" Buddhist Education and Information Network.

"http://www.christianitytoday.com" Christianity Today.

"http://www.islamonline.net" Islam Online.

"http://www.jewfaq.org" Judaism 101.

Education

After reading this chapter, you should be able to:

- Explain how schools serve as agents of social control
- Give a brief history of the development of U.S. education
- Discuss the main problem facing our school system
- Summarize the evolution of the college curriculum
- Explain why the methods of funding education contribute to unequal education

A human being is not, in any proper sense, a human being till he is educated.

—Horace Mann

Everything you do involves, or should involve, learning or education. Education is a never-ending process that begins with the socialization of the child and continues through all of adult life. In common usage, however, the term *education* has a more limited meaning. **Education** refers especially to efforts, usually by the more mature members of a society, to teach each new generation the beliefs, the way of life, the values, and some portion of the knowledge and skills of the group; it also refers to efforts to learn on the part of those who are the objects of teaching.

In modern society, there is so much to learn that any one person can acquire, at most, only a very small part of the total knowledge. Therefore, individuals must specialize in particular fields. Furthermore, in many fields, such as medicine and engineering, the knowledge and skills required have multiplied until they not only take years to learn but also require highly specialized educational arrangements in colleges, universities, and research institutions. Thus, as our modern industrial society increases in complexity, it becomes more and more dependent on formal education—that is, on a system of schooling—both for transmitting and for developing its cultural heritage. In the United States, we have created a school system that provides more opportunities for more people than any the world has ever known. In 2018, U.S. citizens and government spent over $1.5 trillion on education.

There is enormous concern about what we are getting for that money. Are we simply **credentializing** individuals, which means using school diplomas as a way to limit entry into jobs but not to train people appropriately? Why do U.S. students rate so poorly when compared internationally? Should we be providing "schooling"—the teaching of knowledge and skill—or should we be providing broader educational and social skills—the teaching of critical thinking and multicultural topics? And, finally, how can we get more for less?

Schools as Agencies of Social Control

In her book, *Miss Manners' Guide to Rearing Perfect Children,* Judith Martin writes that "every child is born ignorant ... and is civilized by two things, example and nagging." In many ways, example and nagging are education, and it is education that civilizes us. Put more formally, it is through education that society transmits to individuals the knowledge dealing with the ways of life of the group. Education is a prime agency of social control, and decisions made about how to educate play crucial roles in deciding the direction society will take.

The Dual Thrust of U.S. Education

In the United States, such socialization is deeply embedded in the schooling process, but it is modified by attempts to foster individuality and to maintain individual and **academic freedom**—the freedom of students and teachers to pursue, discuss, and teach knowledge without hindrance or censorship. In other countries, education concentrates more on instilling discipline; individuality is frowned on (see the box on "'Real' Education in Pakistan"). For example, in Japan and in other Eastern countries students face strict disciplinary codes and, according to international tests, they learn more.

The **dual thrust of U.S. education**—both the development of individuality and the socialization of students—leads to a tension in our attitude toward education. The tension shows itself in many ways. For example, some educational philosophies emphasize teamwork and cooperative learning, whereas others emphasize competition and individualism. The tension between these two approaches inevitably leads to debates: How much freedom should students be given? Should government determine what is taught, or should teachers and parents decide at the local level? Should private schools be subsidized with government money? And if they are, should they be subject to government control? Private schools have pushed for government financial support without control; public education advocates have resisted such moves.

"It's one thing for the National Commission to comment on the quality of teaching in our schools. It's another thing entirely for you to stand up and call Mr. Costello a yo-yo."

Education and U.S. Democracy

The dual thrust in education exists because the education system not only educates people but also prepares them to fit into society. It makes the many disparate parts of our population fit together. For that reason, education serves as a fundamental building block of U.S. democracy. It does so in the following four ways:

1. *By teaching the masses of our citizens to be literate,* public education makes it possible for them to communicate with one another more effectively beyond the local community and to learn something of politics and public policy by reading newspapers, magazines, and books. This enables people to vote more intelligently and to choose leaders more wisely.

2. *The public schools teach children to get along with people of different backgrounds.* In many areas, the students who attend these schools come from

The Thinker, *by Auguste Rodin.*

widely varied social, economic, national, and racial backgrounds. Also, extensive efforts have been made to integrate children who have special learning, physical, or emotional problems into the mainstream classrooms. Though going to school together will not necessarily make all children love one another, it does tend to create better understanding and to give all groups a keener sense of their common U.S. heritage.

3. *Our system of public support for education reduces inequalities of opportunity at all educational levels.* The masses of our people, even at the lower income levels, are now receiving an education up through high school. Large numbers are going on to college or technical and professional schools, in part because they can attend publicly supported schools with low tuition and in part because there are many government loan and grant opportunities.

4. *Our public school system has enabled us as a nation to make much more effective use of our human resources.* In the public schools, we discover many students who have unusual ability, including those who come from unfavorable social backgrounds. The talents of most such students would never be brought to light if it were not for free public schools. Once discovered, these students often can be encouraged and helped to develop their capacities to the maximum. Thus, not only do they themselves lead fuller lives, but as scholars, scientists, or leaders in other fields, they also make a contribution to the welfare of the nation.

Our public school system is by no means a perfect instrument, either for achieving complete equality of educational opportunity or for enabling us to make maximum use of our human resources, but it has helped us to take great strides toward both of these objectives.

*T*he Development of U.S. Education

American interest in education goes back to earliest colonial times. Within about fifty years after the first settlement at Plymouth, Massachusetts, in 1620, all the New England colonies except Rhode Island had passed legislation making it mandatory for parents and the masters of apprentices to ensure that their charges learned both a trade and the elements of reading, writing, and religion. Before long, laws were passed making it compulsory for towns to establish elementary schools. These early schools received some public support, but they also charged tuition.

In spite of early beginnings in New England, the idea that all citizens of a democracy should be taught at least reading, writing, and arithmetic was slow to take hold. The founders of our republic were not thoroughly democratic in all senses of the word. Although the Declaration of Independence pronounced that all men are created equal, most of our early leaders had limited faith in the ability of the common citizen either to vote wisely or to profit from education. Everywhere, the right to vote was restricted to the few by property and other qualifications, and, except perhaps in New England, only a small minority of the people even learned to read and write.[1]

This situation did not change radically until well into the nineteenth century, when a new spirit of democracy began to be felt. It permeated the entire country but was especially strong in the recently settled regions west of the Alleghenies and along the rapidly advancing western frontier.

---

[1] Women were not allowed to vote in national elections until 1920.

"*R*eal" Education in Pakistan

Education in Pakistan reflects the country's hierarchically structured society. It has different tiers of schools for different classes of students. The top-tier schools attended by the children of the elite are demanding and strict. They provide an education that, in terms of knowledge learned, is comparable to or better than most U.S. schools. The middle- and bottom-tier public schools are just strict, and are generally far less satisfactory. Often teachers don't even show up every day. The education described here is that provided by a top-tier school.

In Pakistan, the concept of individual freedom is subordinated to the demands of self-discipline and obedience to elders. When your father (men are given more respect than women) says to do something, you do it, or you get beaten. (Physical punishment is quite acceptable in Pakistan.)

When you enter school, normally at the age of four, you have already been thoroughly indoctrinated by your parents to give the teacher that same respect and unquestioning obedience. The school day is rigidly organized; it has none of the free-form organizational structure that permeates U.S. schools. School begins with a general assembly in which all students line up in rectangular formations to recite the Qur'an and sing the national anthem. If you refuse to sing, you're beaten—but nobody refuses.

The dress code is strictly enforced, and improperly attired children are either punished by their teachers or sent back home with a note telling the parents to turn up the next day with their child. Students up to the thirteenth grade (the final year of high school) are required to stand up when a teacher enters the classroom, greet him—the teachers are mostly men, especially in the senior classes—and sit down only when allowed to do so by the teacher. Throughout the lecture, all students are expected to sit in an upright position and preserve utter silence. Troublemakers (i.e., noisy kids) are caned (i.e., beaten). Students are not to question what the teacher says; the teacher's word is supposed to be almost as sacrosanct as the Qur'an.

After the eighth grade, students normally split up into two streams, the science group and the arts group. The students have little choice in this matter; their grades and parental pressure are the two most important determining factors. Generally, the brighter students are channeled into science and the second-raters are channeled into the arts.

Most Americans wouldn't like this system; they would see it as demeaning to the students and inconsistent with U.S. cultural mores. But in Pakistan, it works. It instills in students a work ethic and discipline that serves them well at the university level, both at home and abroad, and most Pakistani university students are glad they went through it, rather than through what they would describe as the namby-pamby U.S. educational system. The poor in Pakistan have the worst of both worlds and there is a strong movement there to either reform public schools or to privatize elementary and secondary education.

This new surge of democratic sentiment brought about the election of Andrew Jackson to the presidency in 1828. Jackson was a product of the frontier, and he represented the new democracy of the expanding West. In the period from Jackson's election to the Civil War, public elementary education became firmly established. In the 1830s, Alexis de Tocqueville, a French author, visited the United States and expressed astonishment at the ever-growing belief in and commitment to public education. In Europe, education was still restricted to members of the wealthy class and the clergy.

By 1860, tax-supported elementary schools had opened in many states. During these years, some publicly supported high schools were also established, but for the most part secondary education continued to be provided by the private academies that had succeeded the early colonial Latin grammar schools. These academies increased rapidly in number, but not until sometime after the Civil War did the idea of publicly supported high schools begin to gain wide acceptance.

Since 1865, there has been a phenomenal expansion of education in this country. In 1870, five years after the end of the Civil War, the number of children attending elementary schools was less than 7 million, and enrollment in public high schools was only 80,000. Some children were also attending private grade schools and academies. In 2018 total enrollment in elementary schools, public and private, was about 40 million, and enrollment in high schools was about 17 million. In 1870, less than half the children 5 to 17 years old were attending

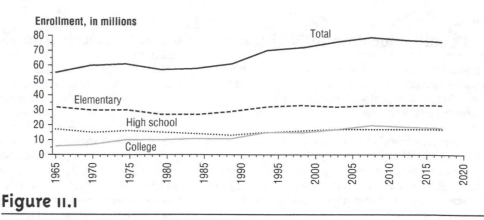

Figure 11.1

School enrollment by level of instruction, 1965 to 2017. (*Source: The U.S. Bureau of the Census. In parens add the note: (Total includes kindergarden and pre-school enrollment.*)

school, and the average number of days attended by each child was only fifty. Today, almost 100 percent of children from the ages of 5 to 17 attend school at least some days every school year, and on average children attend school for about 167 days a year.

The most striking expansion of education in the twentieth century was in the colleges and universities. In 1920, fewer than 600,000 students were enrolled in all of our institutions of higher learning. By 2014, the number of students in colleges and universities had increased to about 21 million. In 2015, college enrollment dropped as questions arose about the value of a college education and whether it was worthwhile for students to take out loans to finance their education.

The overall trends since 1965 are shown in Figure 11.1. Until 1970, school enrollment rose at all levels. Then, in the 1970s, school enrollment began to decline. This trend was in large part caused by the completion of schooling of the children of the World War II baby boom. Enrollment in elementary schools started to rise again in the late 1980s due to the secondary baby boom (baby boomers' children). As the children of this secondary boom grew older, the enrollment in later grades also rose. Through all these trends, until recently, college education and other post secondary certification programs has risen as higher percentages of students went on to college and as older individuals decided they needed more education to find or keep their job.

Democratic Structure of the U.S. School System

The school structure of the United States is quite different from what is traditional in most countries. Before World War I, nearly all European countries had a dual school system, and, in spite of some changes since, European schools still retain much of this dual character. A **dual school system** separates, at an early age, the children who expect to go on to a college or a university from those who do not, and provides a different type of education for each group. In Mexico, all children are given an exam at about the age of twelve, after completing six years of primary education. Students who do well are sent to special "secondary" or university pre-paratory schools; others are sent to vocational, agricultural, or technical schools after completing their elementary education. This holds true in most European countries, too, although the age and grade level at which children are segregated varies from country to country. In Germany, the age at which the examination is usually taken is ten; in Great Britain, it is twelve.

In the United States, we developed in the late nineteenth century a so-called unitary system. In a **unitary school system,** most children (unless they have dropped out along the way) attend the same type of school and follow a course of study that eventually leads to graduation from

*E*ducation in Some Other Countries

In this chapter we focus on the U.S. educational system. Our system is not the only way to educate. Let's take a brief look at how educational systems work in some other countries.

Germany

Schools are divided into three categories: grammar, technical, and vocational. The system grooms the gifted students and tests the abilities of those who will become skilled workers. Equal emphasis and status are accorded the sciences and the arts. Adolescents are treated like adults, and students see how success in education is connected to earning a living. Its technical/vocational training has attracted interest from other countries, as it has provided a skilled workforce to work in manufacturing that countries such as the U.S. have not been able to duplicate

Denmark

The general structure is similar to that of Germany. In Denmark, however, if parents are dissatisfied with their public school, they can get together to set up their own school, and the government will pay 90 percent of the cost. At the university level, where students used to be able to take as long as they wanted to get a degree, there are now detailed schedules to discourage students from wasting time.

France

Scientific and technical schools enjoy a high status. Adolescents understand the tradition of spending most of their time working for a rigorous general examination. Vocational training has been weak, but recently the government has mandated employers to spend 1 percent of their sales receipts for training workers. Simultaneously, the government has encouraged vocational schools to expand, setting forth clear, ambitious goals.

Britain

Britain has a national curriculum, tested by national exams. Parents can send their children to the best available school, and the government finances schools on the basis of how many students they are able to attract. Exam results are published and schools are ranked comparatively, so parents can make informed decisions about which school to choose. Schools are encouraged to escape from supervisory bureaucracies and run themselves independently. As in some other European countries, vocational schools need improvement, but Britain is working on this task.

Japan

Japan has what some call "a cult of education." Students attend for long hours. Even after regular school hours, many attend evening, holiday, and weekend "cramming" schools to get extra education. Schools are run economically. Most of the school buildings are shabby and ill-equipped by Western standards. Students are required to help with some tasks, such as serving in the cafeteria. These tasks are believed to improve character, and they help keep school costs low. Competition is intense because students know their adult careers depend on how well they do in school. Also, the importance of education is demonstrated by the parental pressure exerted on children to excel. Parents endure financial and other sacrifices to pay for extra schooling. In recent years, the Japanese Ministry of Education has tried to discourage overly long hours, as they have been embarrassed by the statistics on teenage suicide and nervous breakdowns attributed to overwork at school.

high school after twelve years. They are then ready, supposedly, to go on to a college or university. The door to further education is, so far as possible, kept open all along the line.

Of course, not all courses prepare students to enter a college or university. Even so, our school system is fairly successful in keeping open the doors to further educational advancement because the student who has not taken a college preparatory course can often qualify for some type of college training by merely making up a few required admission courses. Also, many colleges are flexible in their entrance requirements for students who give evidence, by test scores or otherwise, that they have the ability to do good work in college.

Formalization of the School System

An institution as important as education quickly acquires a formal structure, and by 1880 the structure of schools in the United States had evolved into the 8-4-4 system—a graded eight-year elementary school, a four-year high school, and a four-year college. As inevitably as a formal structure developed, so did the criticism and evolution of that structure. Increasing criticism of the 8-4-4 system after World War I led initially to the establishment of junior high schools in many communities. These schools took over the seventh and eighth years of schooling from the grade schools and the first year from the senior high schools. The junior high school made it possible to begin secondary education earlier and facilitated the introduction of new types of courses. In the 1970s, the evolution continued, and elementary school was reduced to five years, junior high was changed to three years of middle school, and high school was extended to four years, making the 5-3-4-4 system common for most communities in recent years.

Education prior to the grade school years also changed. For example, in most U.S. communities a year of kindergarten was added at the bottom of the scale, preceding the first grade. Later still, private nursery schools became common for very young children, and in more recent years, programs have been introduced for young children from disadvantaged backgrounds. For example, **Head Start** is a federal program that seeks to enhance the social and intellectual development of students as young as 3 years old.

Evolution has also occurred at the college level. A good example is the community college movement, which developed slowly at first. In the early 1920s, only a few such schools existed throughout the country. The first public community colleges were usually established by school districts as a kind of extension of high school. Often, they were begun in high school buildings and their classes were taught by high school teachers, preferably those with some graduate school training. Just as some educators had argued earlier that the first two years of college should be moved down to the secondary level, some now regarded the community college as an extension of secondary education. In fact, however, most of the early community colleges followed rather closely the curricula of the first two years of the four-year colleges and universities, and they were chiefly concerned with preparing their students to enter such institutions in their junior year. By the end of the 1930s, the number of community colleges had substantially increased, and because most of them were established in areas where college education had not earlier been available, they gave many young people a better opportunity for getting at least some college training.

After World War II, in response to the increased demand for higher education, the number of two-year colleges, both private and public, rose rapidly. In the early 2000s there were about 1,650 in the United States, with a total enrollment of 7.7 to 10.5 million, depending on what one includes within the measure. About 60 percent of all community college students are part-time. Community college enrollments account for 45 percent of all black students and 55 percent of all Hispanic students.

Gradually, as community colleges multiplied and more and more students crowded into them, their function changed to parallel more closely the initial concept of such colleges as an extension of high school. Now **community colleges** are colleges designed to meet the diverse needs of students who could benefit from some extension of their high school education. Community colleges are no longer regarded primarily as institutions preparing students to

Community colleges play an important role in U.S. education.

© *PHOTO.ZOOMMER.RU/Alamy Stock Photo*

*T*he Decline of Standards

A big-city school system requires a student in the seventh grade to be able to read as well as a fifth grader,

who, by the way, must be able to read as well as a fourth grader,

who, in turn, must be able to read as well as a third grader.

What would be wrong with demanding that a seventh grader be required to read like a *seventh* grader?

How would you like to be operated on by a brain surgeon who graduated from a school that allowed its students to be a year and a half behind in their skills?

United Technologies advertisement.

enter four-year colleges in the final two years. They still do this, but their design has been expanded to meet the needs of the community in which they are located. Especially for students who want to save money, community colleges, dollar for dollar, are a wonderful bargain. Recent proposals to reduce community college tuition to zero will make it even more of a bargain. Various types of vocational training have been introduced, some of them technical. Courses are offered to train auto mechanics, hair salon operators, salespeople, medical and dental assistants, laboratory technicians, and various other types of workers. The community college has become an institution that seeks to provide training that not only will produce better citizens but that also will meet the needs of our economy for a greater number of trained workers and the needs of young people for jobs that will yield both satisfaction and a reasonable level of income.

Exactly what that training should be is subject to debate. Some advocate traditional academic studies and others favor a vocational focus. Vocationalists argue that courses should provide skills needed in business. Traditionalists argue that there is a danger of students becoming narrow job specialists without common interests. They feel that job-specific skills can be learned on the job and that colleges should be designed to teach people to think and understand the world around them. The debate is likely to continue.

In recent years, private, for-profit universities have developed, which often offer many online courses that better fit working students' schedules. For-profit colleges account for about 10 percent of all college students. These for-profit schools have recruited heavily from groups of students within communities that often have not gone to college, and have assisted students in applying for government-guaranteed student loans for 90 percent of their revenue. Many of the students they have recruited have not completed their courses or, if they have done so, have found it difficult to repay their loans because their college degrees have not led to their getting jobs that pay enough to do so. Significantly less than half of the students at many for-profit colleges are repaying their loans. These problems have led government to rethink its student loan policy and to put pressure on colleges to see that the recruited students are capable of doing the work and are not being promised more than the colleges can deliver. In response to abuses, it has cut off loans to students at a number of for-profit schools forcing some to shut down and others to shrink.

*E*xamining the School System

The preceding history of the school system should give you a good sense of the U.S. educational system and how it developed. It is a compulsory system through age eighteen, usually the last year of high school, and it is a broad-based college system. It is also an expensive system that costs hundreds of billions of dollars. Given the significant role of education in modern society, it should not be surprising that there is a constant examination of the school system: how it delivers its services, how it is paid for, what it teaches, and what results it produces. These continuing efforts to understand and improve the system will inevitably introduce changes.

Technological Change and Teaching

As with other institutions, technology changes both the method of teaching and what needs to be taught. With the development of computers, for example, the process of writing is changing. Computer programs are now available that correct grammatical, spelling, and stylistic mistakes. Books have moved online, and with full online bibliographies available through computers, many library skills are no longer necessary; we simply need to know how to use the relevant search program. It is predicted that some time in this century computer programs will expertly translate onto paper the words and ideas that a person speaks into them, making obsolete much of what is now taught in grammar and composition classes. Such changes would parallel those already accomplished in math by calculators, which have made nearly obsolete the necessity to do arithmetic mentally or on paper.

What the long-range future holds is limited only by our imagination. Perhaps with advances in the analysis of the brain, by 2040 teachers and schools may be obsolete, and students may simply hook up their brains to various data banks that directly translate knowledge from computer memory to student memory. Luckily for teachers, that time is not yet here.

Private Schools and Home Schooling

Private schools have always been a part of the U.S. educational system, and their total enrollment includes about 10 percent of all schoolchildren. Schools defined as private or independent include religious schools, private nonsectarian schools, and home schools. In the early 2000s, there were about 30,000 independent schools. Of the 55 million school-age children in the country, more than 6 million attended independent schools and about 1.8 million were home-schooled, together representing about 14 percent of total school enrollment.

A large number of private schools have religious affiliations. Instruction in some of the religious schools is based on systematized programs, such as the one published by Accelerated Christian Education, Inc., of Lewisville, Texas. The pool of students in religious schools is estimated to be more than 1 million, and about half of these use the Accelerated Christian Education method of silent, individual study using workbooks and programed studies. There are several thousand different workbooks compiled to be "distinctively Christian," and each student goes through as many as sixty-five different workbooks in a school year.

These systems are inexpensive and easy to set up. They use church space and incur no additional expenses for heat, utilities, and most equipment. While they include biased presentations of science, where science and faith interact, they do reasonably well in providing students with basic reading, math, and writing skills.

Despite the significant amount of such activity and the fact that the choice of independent schools is growing rapidly, the total number of students in and from these schools is still statistically small. There is speculation that such schooling may lead to isolation, narrow interests, poor socialization, and alienation from the mainstream. These conclusions have not been subjected to testing by non-partisan researchers. Public school researchers find problems; private school researchers find success. When research results reflect the beginning views of the researchers, they provide little in the way of objective evidence. Hopefully, in the future, there will be more independent analysis.

An alternative to private schools is home schooling, in which parents teach their own children at home. As concern about public schools has increased, so, too, has home schooling, but it remains uncommon.

Charter Schools, Privatization, and the Problem of School Finance

Good schooling costs money, and it is not surprising that the taxpayers who pay for it often try to pay less. Historically, education in the United States has been paid for largely by local property taxes—taxes on land, houses, and businesses in the school district. Because many

Good teachers are a key to success in school.

property owners do not have children in school, some of them object to increases in property taxes. This leads to periodic community dissension and failure of the voters to pass school budgets. A second effect that local financing of schools has is significant differences in tax burdens among school districts. School districts with large amounts of valuable taxable property find that they can support schools with a much lower tax rate per property owner than can districts with little valuable taxable property. The result is significant differences in availability of funds for schools.

The inequity in this funding method has come under attack in the courts, and a number of states face legal mandates to change school finance methods by instituting some method of equalizing tax burdens and available resources. In Michigan, for example, the school property tax was eliminated and replaced with a sales tax. Other states are making similar changes.

Attempts to change these financing methods have led to more dissension and to calls for privatizing education so that it is no longer supplied by government, but is instead supplied by private, for-profit businesses. Under the typical privatization plan, students are given a voucher worth, say, $5,000, which they can use to attend whichever school they want. Advocates push for such privatization programs using the phrase "school choice," because students would have a choice of schools. Opponents of such schemes argue that the private schools would "skim the cream," taking the easy-to-educate students and leaving the difficult and expensive-to-educate students in public school. They also argue that it would significantly change the socialization function of the public schools and, hence, change the nature of U.S. society. With President Donald Trump's election in 2016, the federal government started to push schools to privatize. He appointed a strong supporter of privatization, Betsy DeVos, as Secretary of Education and she has advocated and encouraged school choice and competition.

One initiative that has passed in many states is **charter schools**—decentralized schools based on a charter between an individual or group (usually teachers, parents, and others in a community) and its sponsor (usually the local or state school board). Charter schools are designed as an alternative to private and public schools. Although largely controlled by parents and teachers, their financing usually is provided by the state in which they are located. About 10 percent of charter schools are run by for-profit businesses. The structures of charter schools are designed to minimize bureaucracy and promote innovative approaches to learning by empowering teachers and parents to create the curriculum. Accountability is achieved by performance tests that determine whether the charter is renewed. Over the next few years, these schools will be watched closely so that the quality and breadth of the programs that emerge can be measured.

One of the most comprehensive reforms was instituted by Florida where they (1) started grading their schools based on student proficiency and progress in reading, math, and science; (2) eliminated social promotion—the practice of letting students move to the next grade even though they have not mastered the skills needed to advance; (3) introduced merit pay; (4) allowed parents much greater choice; and (5) set up new methods of teacher certification to allow alternative ways for someone to become a teacher. While these reforms showed some positive results, the reforms also introduced problems, and researchers' assessments of the program almost invariably reflect their prior views.

Textbooks

After systematic testing had been developed as a research tool beginning in the 1920s, educational testers reached the conclusion that the elementary curriculum was too hard, and they targeted the textbook. Since then, textbooks for elementary schools have tended to become less and less rigorous. Long words and complex grammatical constructions are frowned on, as are connective words. According to Harriet Bernstein, textbook expert of the Council of Chief State School Officers, the word *because* does not appear in most U.S. schoolbooks before the eighth grade. Some believe these simple books continue to be used because overworked, undertrained teachers need something easy to teach from.

The situation is complicated by the claims of various ethnic, religious, political, and other pressure groups. For instance, nutritionists who believe that refined sugar is a health hazard have succeeded in some states in having removed from children's textbooks most references to cake and candy. The results can sometimes be unintended; in one case, these omissions resulted in stories about a child having a birthday—with no birthday cake.

Textbooks developed for high schools and colleges have some of the same characteristics. Open several and stand back so that you cannot read the print: You will find that they all tend to look alike. Popular strategies include frequent subheads, charts and pictures, boxed material appearing in the middle of a page to relieve the blocks of print, and chapter summaries that enable the student to get the gist of the chapter without reading the main text. Publishers demand these devices because that is what sells, and textbook writers comply.

In our view (yes, it is true that textbook authors have views), textbooks coddle students too much. We make learning too easy, so students don't have to think. Nevertheless, we coddle (a word that probably shouldn't be used because it is too unusual), although less than other textbook writers do, because teachers and publishers say that a truly thought-provoking (and therefore painful) textbook would not get published and would not get read.

School Dropouts

When education becomes too painful, students drop out. According to data compiled by the U.S. Bureau of the Census, as many as 50 percent of high school students in some major cities drop out before graduating. The dropout rate has fallen somewhat over the past decades, from about 14 percent nationwide in the 1970s to about 6 percent in 2018. It remains higher for Hispanics at about 9.2 percent and blacks at about 6.5 percent than it is for whites at 4.5 percent. (This 6 percent dropout rate for blacks may look good, but this is partly because so many black male teenagers have ended up in jail and are not counted as being eligible for school or as dropping out.) The number of students actually dropping out of regular school is higher, but many return to school and earn a GED (General Educational Development) degree or its equivalent.

In the early 2000s, about 63 percent of dropouts obtained a GED within eight years of dropping out. In 2014 the number of students getting GEDs fell precipitously when the GED exams were reworked and made much more difficult. In response a number of states created alternatives to the GED.

A number of programs have been established to deal with dropouts. In New York City, for example, dropouts from high school are contacted by phone in an attempt to persuade them to return to school. Other areas have tried flexible school scheduling, work-study plans, and identification and counseling programs. In a cash-for-class project, one California school paid students to attend school.

Dropping out is a problem not only for the individual student but also for the entire community. Education has an inverse relationship to crime and, in the long run, the higher the average level of education, the lower the crime rate. Dropping out of high school also affects one's ability to get a job; the unemployment rate among dropouts is roughly twice as high as the unemployment rate for high school graduates.

Multiculturalism, Collaborative Learning, and Institutional Fairness

People learn in different ways, and various groups respond differently to alternative learning environments. Much of our current learning environment is what Peggy McIntosh, an education specialist at the Center for Research on Women at Wellesley College, calls "winner-killer competitive," which she argues is not conducive to some minority cultures' and women's backgrounds. The current system, she argues, is biased toward white males and does not provide a **collaborative learning environment,** in which students learn to work together, helping each other excel rather than competing with others to beat them down.

The ways in which discrimination occurs can be subtle, although sometimes, when pointed out, they are not so subtle after all. For example, Gary Mitchell, a New Jersey attorney, sent his child to a progressive school and was struck by the awards given out in the child's kindergarten class. The awards given to students of one gender were for best thinker, most eager learner, most imaginative, most enthusiastic, most scientific, best friend, best personality, hardest worker, and best sense of humor. The other gender's awards were for all-around sweetheart, sweetest personality, cutest personality, best sharer, best artist, biggest heart, best manners, best helper, and most creative. We leave it to you to figure out which gender got which list of awards.

McIntosh's theories are highly controversial, but aspects of them are making their way into mainstream educational practices in what is called the **multiculturalism movement,** the movement to make social institutions unbiased with respect to all ethnic and cultural groups.

Another example of this multicultural movement is Uri Treisman's work with black college math majors. Treisman is a mathematics professor at the University of Texas at Austin who has studied in depth the reasons why black students made up a disproportionately small number of college math majors, whereas Asian students made up a disproportionately large number. Together with a number of social scientists, he conducted research to find out why. He found that the cause had nothing to do with ability. The groups he was looking at (students at the University of California at Berkeley) had equal ability in math in their high schools and on standardized tests. The difference was more in the institutional structure of the program. He found that Asian students tended to work on problems together in informal social groups, so studying math became part of their social interaction. On the other hand, he found that black students' social activities did not include any such interaction, as they were drawn to black cultural centers that did not include other math majors. Thus, they did not experience the type of collaborative learning that the Asian students did. He set about to change that and successfully instituted collaborative learning exercises that, together with other institutional reforms, significantly increased the percentage of black math majors at the University of Texas.

Learning environment can significantly affect educational outcomes in other ways as well. Harvard social science professor Roland Fryer has found that, adjusted for income, black children preform equally well as white children through kindergarten, but by third grade they fall behind. He tested the hypothesis that cultural pressures deterred black students from studying. The culture viewed "studying" as "acting white." He found strong support for that hypothesis and suggested a variety of policy suggestions to offset that cultural pressure.

How Good Are U.S. Schools?

Probably the most important questions we can ask about our educational system are: Does it deliver and are students receiving a good education? The answers are not a unanimous yes. Many argue that our schools are not succeeding; they cost too much and achieve too little. Students are graduating without knowing the fundamentals of reading, writing, spelling, and arithmetic. A number of empirical measures suggest that this is the case. For example, in international comparisons of student achievement in the fourth grade, U.S. students were in the middle of an international comparison of twenty-six nations. By the eighth grade, they had fallen to the bottom third; and by graduation, they had fallen to the bottom.

Despite increases in the amount of money put into education, the situation does not seem to be improving. Scores on the Scholastic Aptitude Test (SAT) and the American College Testing (ACT) exams, which are used to measure whether students are ready to enter college,

Are Boys Discriminated against in School?

Discrimination takes many forms, and as one type of discrimination is corrected, others are created. Take the discrimination against girls in education alluded to in the text. In the 1970s and 1980s, this topic was much discussed, and a large majority of the population felt that the educational structure discriminated against girls. That view led to the passage of the Gender Equity in Education Act in 1994, which specifically banned discrimination against girls in school. Fifteen years later, it was not girls who social scientists felt were being discriminated against; it was boys. The signs of discrimination are many. Girls, on average, get higher grades than boys; girls are more likely to be in advanced placement and honors courses; and girls attend college in higher percentages than boys.

The suggested reasons are varied. Some include:

- Teachers tend to choose "feeling" books that appeal to girls rather than "action" books that appeal to boys, so boys don't learn to read.
- Math is being taught with words, with which girls excel, rather than with numerical algorithms, with which boys excel.
- Competition, which boys thrive on, is portrayed as bad, and "cooperative learning," a learning style that girls do better with, is portrayed as good.

Also varied are the suggested solutions. Some want to make boys more like girls, so that they relate to feelings rather than to action. Others want to make school more conducive to masculine ways of learning. Still others say we should simply get rid of the Gender Equity Act, which was too much, too late; it went into effect when women had already achieved equity.

Whatever the answer, we can expect to hear more about the issue in the future.

© PeopleImages.com/Getty

suggest that only between 25 percent and 43 percent of students are prepared. Average SAT scores have been falling in recent years in all parts of the exam. From 2011 to 2016, Average Critical Reading scores fell from 497 to 494; average Mathematics scores fell from 514 to 508, and average Writing scores fell from 489 to 482. So students are even less prepared for college than they were. In 2016 the SAT exams were redesigned so the results are no longer comparable over time. The tests now include only math and reading, and the average scores on these new exams are higher—533 for reading and 527 for math in 2017—but that increase is due to the different normalization process used, not to any improvement in students' reading or mathematics ability.

Educators justify the shortcomings in our schools in a variety of ways. They argue that many modern-day students do not want to learn and have little ability to master traditional academic subjects. Teachers are then under pressure to lower standards. It seems unreasonable to give failing grades to, say, 50 percent of a class, no matter how poor it is; naturally, many principals and parents would blame the teacher. In addition, teenagers with little schooling now have difficulty getting jobs. If they leave school, they may just wander the streets and get into trouble. So, in many schools, most marginal students are promoted regardless of their lack of achievement.

The tendency to pass students from grade to grade on the basis of little or no achievement is strengthened in some schools by the policy of social promotion. This means promoting students along with their classmates regardless of whether they reach a minimum standard of achievement in their studies. The theory is that it is better for social reasons to keep them with their own age group, whether they learn anything or not, and at all costs to avoid stigmatizing them as failures. However, promotion on this basis does not help matters much. Students who

Can You Read This?

About 9 percent of adult Americans whose native language is English can't read English. That's what the U.S. Bureau of the Census says. If we're talking about people whose native language is not English, then the Census Bureau says 48 percent can't read English. Put these two groups together and they add up to more than 27 million people.

Here are a few of the test questions that many people couldn't answer:

1. Pick another word for *sickness:* The patient has the right to ask for information about his sickness. benefits/payments/expenses/illness
2. Pick the best fill-in for the blank: Don't allow your medical information card to —— by any other person. be used/have destroy/go lose/get expired

3. Choose the answer that means the same as the phrase with a line under it:
   We cannot see you today. <u>When can you return?</u>

   When was the last time you came?
   Who should you call when you come?
   On what date can you come again?
   Are those the papers you can return?

Of course, no test is perfect. For instance, all the preceding questions seem to imply that the person taking the test is sick. Some authorities have challenged the Census Bureau study by criticizing the test. But as one of the critics said, "What does it matter if there are 10 million or 20 million? We're not even taking care of a small fraction of them. There are too many."

have not learned elementary mathematics in the lower grades become completely frustrated or indifferent if they must attend math classes in the upper grades. Thus, so-called education consists only of going through the motions of attending classes. Not only do these students become a problem to the teachers and hinder the other students from learning, but they also often feel their own inadequacy more keenly than if they had been held back. Whether under these conditions students gain anything by remaining with their own age group or by staying in school at all is open to question. If this problem is to be solved, we probably must address it early in a child's life.

The Search for Excellence

In response to many criticisms of the U.S. educational system, measures to stem what critics call a tide of mediocrity have been instituted. The reforms have been mostly on the state and local level and have increased salary scales, lengthened the school day, improved teacher certification standards, given teachers more responsibility, and put in place frequent standardized testing in a variety of grades and subjects so that students' performance will be monitored in a measurable way.

Education is primarily run and paid for on the state and local levels, but increasingly the U.S. federal government has been becoming involved. Periodically, it passes laws and initiatives designed to achieve excellence in education by setting standards and introducing performance measures. For example, in 2001, Congress passed the No Child Left Behind Act, a sweeping reform that redefined the federal government's role in K–12 education. It was based on four principles: stronger accountability, increased local control, expanded parental options, and emphasis on proven teaching methods. The most expensive and controversial aspect of this program was its emphasis on standardized testing. One side saw high-stakes tests as defining accountability, the other as stifling broader learning and forcing teachers to teach to a test, not to teach for understanding. The debate about this program is ongoing, with no definitive results about its effectiveness.

Changes in the College Curriculum

Until the middle of the nineteenth century, higher education consisted chiefly of learning the ancient languages, mathematics, philosophy, and theology. Some attention was also given to modern foreign languages and the social sciences, but these held a place of less importance. After the Civil War, however, the curriculum began to show the effects of new developments in science, technology, and other fields of knowledge. As enrollments increased and the interests of students became more and more diverse, scientific, technical, and vocational training were increasingly introduced at the college level. Subjects and courses of study multiplied until it became impossible for any student to take more than a very small portion of the total offerings.

The Development of the Elective System. To meet this problem, the elective system was adopted. This permitted students, with some restrictions, to determine their own courses of study. But the results were not always satisfactory, for often students chose a hodgepodge of unrelated subjects, and at the same time they frequently missed entirely any acquaintance with some of the basic fields of human knowledge.

The shortcomings of the elective system led to two developments. First, colleges began to require students to major in one field of knowledge by taking a substantial proportion of their work in this field. At the same time, they began to require students to spread some of their courses in such a way that they became acquainted with at least several of the basic fields of knowledge. The expression *liberal education* came to be associated especially with the attempt to give students breadth of understanding.

This attempt led to the rapid spread in the 1930s of survey courses covering broad fields of knowledge such as physical science, biological science, social science, and the humanities. Sometimes all students were required in their freshman and sophomore years to take a core curriculum consisting of several of these survey courses. After World War II, courses of this type continued to spread; this book originally was written for such a survey or basic course in the social sciences.

To this period belong terms such as **general education,** college programs intended to broaden students' intellectual horizons. Sometimes the term is used merely as a substitute for the older term *liberal education.* Both expressions refer to a type of training designed to go beyond narrowly practical or vocational objectives. But although liberal education emphasizes the desirability of learning something about a variety of subjects, general education puts more stress on the importance of not missing completely any of the major fields of human knowledge.

Following the Fads. In the late 1960s and throughout the 1970s, colleges and universities restructured their curricula to be relevant. Students in the 1960s were interested in the social issues of their times. As the 1970s progressed, students became less interested in social issues and more interested in money and how to get it. As a result, institutions of higher learning experienced a demand for courses related to business and professions such as law, medicine, engineering, and banking. Since 1985, the majority of college students have been majoring in business or business-related subjects.

Since the 1950s, college enrollments have quintupled, which has contributed to the relaxing of standards, the dropping of course requirements, and the introduction of courses

*S*ocial Science: No Fad

Social science has been around a long time; it is no fad course. It is one of the courses that provides students with an education in their culture and civilization. Various incarnations of this particular book have been a staple of social science courses since the 1930s when nine Chicago professors put their notes together and created a selection of readings for their students.

It has since been revised many times to keep it current. It has been "Hunt and Colander" since the early 1980s.

As the social sciences have split into their various components, it's been harder and harder to find professors with training and inclination to teach the course, but because it provides a necessary and broad overview of social science thinking, it is precisely the type of course that reformers are advocating.

such as family food management and automobile ownership. Today, about half of the students who enter college as first-year students fail to get degrees.

Almost as soon as colleges began to allow flexible requirements and courses of study, and instituted courses and even whole departments in response to trendy demands, they started thinking about making the curriculum more rigorous. By the late 1970s, some colleges and universities were experiencing the equivalent of the back-to-basics movement in elementary and secondary school practice. This took the form of eliminating superficial survey courses, returning to requirements of Greek and Latin, asking students to take more math, and trying to ensure that students had at least some knowledge of fields that are considered part of a broad liberal education but that many students would not study unless they were required to.

Nevertheless, in 1984, a report entitled *Excellence in Education* by the National Endowment for the Humanities (NEH) argued that colleges had not made good on "promises to make you better off culturally and morally," and that "colleges have been ripping off students." It attributed this to poor management and ill-conceived curricula, and suggested that the money invested in a college education would serve a more useful purpose if the parents would instead give that sum to a child to buy a small business. Despite attempts to change it, many observers believe that this situation has not significantly improved.

Is the U.S. Educational System Equal?

Although the U.S. educational system provides greater opportunities for the masses than any other country, it still perpetuates inequalities that are difficult to justify. The most striking of these is found in comparing the situation of blacks with whites, as we already discussed in earlier chapters.

Figure 11.2, which shows the percentage of black adults compared to the total number of adults who have completed four years of high school, demonstrates some of the strides we have made since 1950, but also shows our need to make further gains.

As discussed, a second inequality in education is based on wealth and income. Because most localities finance their education with property taxes, variations of taxable wealth in different regions and localities cause significant variations in educational opportunities. In many poor areas, residents find it impossible to provide adequate school facilities for their children. In the 1970s, a Supreme Court case determined that the use of the local property tax, to support education perpetuated inequality, and states were directed to explore alternative financing methods. Thus, over the past decades, we have seen some states shift from local property taxation as their only school financing tax, to statewide property taxation or state income or sales taxes as additional sources of funding for schools. We can expect further change in the future.

Even if all localities received equal support for education, inequality would still exist. There is a close correlation between the amount of schooling received by children and the income status of their families. The higher the family income, the greater the likelihood that a child will finish high school or go to college.

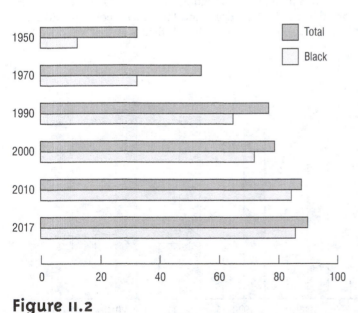

Figure 11.2

Percentage of adults who have completed four years of high school or more, 1950 to 2017. (*Source: U.S. Bureau of the Census, Pew Research Center*)

How Much Education Should the Average Citizen Receive?

How far should the formal education of the average citizen be carried? Grade school? High school? Junior college? This basic question must be answered as our school system changes and develops, but there is no simple response. For every person, there is certainly a limit to the time that can be spent in acquiring a formal education. Where this limit is depends on the temperament, abilities, interests, and purposes of the individual; on the kinds of education available to the person; and on the costs that must be met by the student, the parents, and the community.

Today, few people would question that a grade school education is worth the cost for almost everyone. Also, there is general agreement in this country that a high school education is desirable and worth the cost for the majority of young people, though perhaps for many of them we are not providing the most helpful kind of curriculum. The situation with respect to higher education is somewhat different, and we may well question whether it is desirable for the great majority of young people to complete four years of college. Many people believe we should set admission standards that would limit enrollments in four-year colleges and universities. But there seems to be increasing support for the point of view that eventually most young people should have at least the equivalent of a two-year community college degree. As you can see in Figure 11.3, the percentage of our population receiving a high school and college education has increased substantially since 1960.

With community colleges becoming more responsive to current educational needs of our society, high school graduates today can more easily find the kind of further education that suits their abilities and needs. For those who have no liking for it, the indefinite extension of formal academic education holds no magic. But it is increasingly difficult for adolescents without training to find jobs. This largely explains the increasing emphasis on providing more vocational schools and more vocational courses in community colleges. However, this may also reflect both the recent conservative trend that has swept the country and a return to concern with developing skills that make the U.S. competitive in the world economy.

But what of individuals who are not interested in further schooling and who in some cases may have little ability to benefit from a high level of vocational training? There is still a great deal of relatively unskilled work that needs to be done and for which people would pay if willing workers could be found at reasonable wages. One difficulty is that we have been

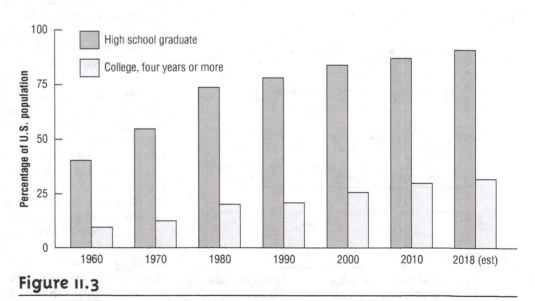

Figure 11.3

Educational attainment (persons age 25 years and over). (*Source: U.S. Bureau of the Census*)

downgrading the dignity of commonplace work, of jobs that are extremely useful and necessary, but only provide moderate pay and offer no glamorous future. In doing this, we have robbed many young people with limited ability of the chance to learn how to work and, by gaining confidence and experience, to find a useful and independent place in life.

Interaction of Economics, Politics, and Social Institutions

Most subjects in social science must be isolated for purposes of study, but in reality they are not isolated. So it is with the educational system. Our educational system includes cultural values and thereby plays an important role in shaping other social, economic, and political institutions, but simultaneously it is shaped by them. The current state of education is a case in point. All agree that school systems could and should do a better job. The question is: how? Some argue that the answer is to spend more—for instance, to improve teachers' pay and to provide schools with the latest technological equipment. Others argue that the ideal answer is for schools to become more efficient—for teachers to work harder, for students to study harder, and for administrators to decide that schools do not need so much administration and to eliminate their own jobs. But don't hold your breath waiting. Individuals in educational institutions are likely to opt for the easy path. Students aren't going to be motivated to study harder unless provided with incentives to do so. It's the same with teachers. And there is almost no way administrators are going to eliminate their own jobs.

The interaction of economics, politics, and social institutions can be illustrated in the setting of teacher standards. The concepts of setting standards, certifying competence, and mandating the teaching of certain basic subjects are admirable, but all are liable to abuse. Teachers are divided in their view on certification. Teachers who have been teaching for years feel it is unfair for their competency suddenly to be questioned and tested. New teachers feel that their own recent education qualifies them in the latest methods and believe that if the older teachers had nothing to fear, they would not protest competency tests. Both groups can unite in their scorn of agencies that set educational standards when the staffs of the agencies have no professional educational training. Yet taxpayers do not want to leave certification in the hands of the very people who are to be certified.

The point of this example is twofold: First, there are no easy answers to difficult questions, and second, what we do in one area of society is likely to have significant effects in other areas. Only by considering all those effects and recognizing the pitfalls in implementing the easy solutions can we hope to develop wise social policy.

 Study and **Review**

Key Points

- The U.S. educational system has a dual thrust: It attempts to develop students' individuality and to socialize students.
- Educational institutions in the United States are a product of their history.
- The main problem facing our educational system is how to provide excellent, equal education

- efficiently, inexpensively, and in a manner that appropriately socializes the students.
- The college curriculum has evolved from a rigid system that taught specific subjects to an elective system with significant freedom and varied courses.
- An important reason why our educational system is not equal is the methods used to fund it.

Some Important Terms

academic freedom (207)

charter school (215)

collaborative learning environment (217)

community college (212)

credentializing (206)

dual school system (210)

dual thrust of U.S. education (207)

education (206)

general education (220)

Head Start (212)

multiculturalism movement (217)

unitary school system (210)

Questions for Review and Discussion

General Questions

1. Explain the difference between education and socialization.
2. How does free public education contribute to the development of U.S. democracy?
3. Discuss the development of U.S. education since colonial times.
4. What factors have contributed to increasing enrollments at the primary and secondary levels?
5. How does the structure of the educational system in the United States differ from that of Europe?
6. Discuss the history of community colleges.
7. Discuss the changes that have taken place in school curricula over the past hundred years.
8. What differences in educational opportunities exist?
9. How can multiculturalism and collaborative learning improve the effectiveness of schools?
10. Discuss some types of schools that are alternatives to public schools.
11. What conclusions can be drawn concerning the progress made in U.S. education over the past hundred years? What still remains to be done?

12. Give an example of a political issue influencing an educational issue.

Internet Questions

1. According to http://www.ericdigests.org/1995-1/multicultural.htm, what are the three basic types of multicultural education programs and what is the focus of each?
2. Go to http://www.amshq.org/. What is the Montessori approach to education?
3. Go to http://www.pewresearch.org/fact-tank/2016/07/28/5-facts-about-latinos-and-education/. What has happened to Hispanic and black dropout rates in recent years? (for reference only: ans: They have fallen.)
4. Go to https://www.youtube.com/watch?v=8dAujuqCo7s and watch the video or just listen to the song. What current education policy is being criticized? Name three criticisms of this policy.
5. Go to https://www.edreform.com/2012/03/15/just-the-faqs-charter-schools. According to the Center for Educational Reform, what are charter schools?

For Further Study

Books to Explore

Bloom, Allan D., *The Closing of the American Mind: How Higher Education Has Failed Democracy and the Impoverished Souls of Today's Students*, New York: Simon & Schuster, 1987.

Caplan, Bryan, *The Case Against Education: Why the Educational System is a Waste of Time and Money*, Princeton, NJ: Princeton University Press, 2018.

Carr, Sam, *Motivation, Educational Policy and Achievement: A Critical Perspective*, Abingdon: Routledge, 2015.

Dwyer, James G., *Vouchers within Reason: A Child-Centered Approach to Education Reform*, Ithaca, NY: Cornell University Press, 2002.

Labaree, David F., *A Perfect Mess: The Unlikely Ascendancy of American Higher Education*, Chicago, IL: University of Chicago Press, 2017.

Ravitch, Diane, *The Death and Life of the Great American School System: How Testing and Choice Are Undermining Education*, New York: Basic Books, 2011.

Sander, Richard, and Stuart, Taylor Jr, *Mismatch: How Affirmative Action Hurts Students It's Intended to Help, and Why Universities Won't Admit It*, New York: Basic Books, 2012.

Schooling for Tomorrow: Think Scenarios, Rethink Education, Centre for Educational Research and Innovation, Paris: Organisation for Economic Co-operation and Development, 2006.

Stern, Sol, *Breaking Free: Public School Lessons and the Imperative of School Choice*, New York: Encounter Books, 2004.

Westover, Tara, *Educated*, New York: Random House, 2018.

Wolff, Edward N., *Does Education Really Help? Skill, Work, and Inequality*, New York: Oxford University Press, 2006.

Internet Sites to Explore

"http://www.aacc.nche.edu" American Association of Community Colleges.

"http://www.eric.ed.gov" Educational Resources Information Center.

"http://www.nheri.org/" Home Education Research Institute.

"http://www.ihep.org/" Institute for Higher Education Policy.

"http://www.nces.ed.gov" National Center for Education Statistics.

"http://www.ed.gov" United States Department of Education.

"http://www.usdla.org" United States Distance Learning Association.

Social and Economic Stratification

chapter 12

After reading this chapter, you should be able to:

- List three types of social stratification
- Discuss the role of social mobility in making some social stratification acceptable to society
- List three sources of income inequality
- State what the poverty threshold is in the United States
- Discuss six issues that any practical program for meeting the problems of economic inequality must take into account
- Explain what is meant by the U.S. class system and how it relates to class consciousness

> *. . . all the animals are equal here, but some are more equal than others.*
>
> —George Orwell

The people of every society can be divided into groups—sometimes along clear-cut lines, sometimes only roughly. **Stratification** is the grouping of people according to differences in income, occupation, power, privilege, manner of living, region where they live, age, gender, or race; you can probably think of other categories. Stratification, in the sense of differentiation, is not necessarily bad. People differ and that difference adds diversity to life. But when there is a **hierarchy**—when one group considers itself better, or maintains privileged access to society's resources—questions of social equity are raised. Many systems of social and economic stratification do create a hierarchy of superior, intermediate, and inferior groups; that hierarchical stratification is our primary concern in this chapter.

Social stratification appears to be unavoidable. Some activities and some kinds of work are more important to a society than others. Some can be carried on only by people of outstanding ability with special training or experience. Political offices must be filled, economic activities must be organized, medical services must be provided, and military forces must be commanded. Those who play important roles in such activities acquire power and prestige. Usually they also acquire larger than average incomes and various special privileges. In addition, because these individuals tend to associate principally with one another, they develop common attitudes and modes of living. Sometimes they entrench themselves in their positions by means of legal and religious sanctions, but even without these safeguards, they can often pass their superior status along to their children.

When firmly established, social stratification contributes to social stability. It means general acceptance of the fact that certain groups perform certain functions, as do their children after them. Competitiveness is reduced because people know their place in society and the paths they are expected to follow. When social stratification is less rigid and there are more opportunities for an individual to change status, dissatisfaction and conflict may be more evident, even though the situation is objectively fairer in the sense that there is more social mobility. Thus, a lessening of stratification often is accompanied by social unrest because that reduction focuses attention on the unfairness of the system.

Types of Social Stratification

There are three principal types of social stratification: estates, castes, and social classes. We are chiefly interested in the last type because social classes represent the major form of stratification found in modern industrial societies. However, some knowledge of estate and caste systems will contribute to our understanding of the nature of social classes.

Estates

When used in a discussion of stratification, the term **estate** refers not to land but to groups such as the nobility, the clergy, merchants, artisans, and peasants. The estate stratification system developed in Europe under feudalism. The estate to which a person belonged and its place in the social hierarchy were determined chiefly by custom, occupation, rights and obligations with respect to land, and other legal sanctions.

In an estate system, the position of an individual in society is nearly always inherited from parents; the lines between groups are clearly drawn, and almost everyone knows just where he or she belongs. They may even be required to dress in a particular way to indicate their station in relation to others. The opportunity for mobility is small, but it is entirely possible within the framework of law and custom. In feudal times, a noble could free a serf from bondage to the land in return for a special service, or a king could bestow a title of nobility (the Queen of the United Kingdom still bestows titles today). Military service and the priesthood are also possible avenues of upward mobility in an estate system.

The medieval estate system, with its relatively rigid social categories, was better suited to a static than to a dynamic society. It gradually disintegrated under the impact of changes such as the decline of feudalism, the Industrial Revolution, and the rise of democratic ideology, with its strong emphasis on freedom and equality.

Poor, low-caste Indian farmers.

Castes

Caste is a rigid class distinction based on birth, wealth, or some other distinguishing characteristic. Within a discussion of stratification, the caste system is usually associated with India, where until recently it had prevailed for about 3,000 years. Since caste-based discrimination was banned in the 1950s and additional laws were passed against it in the 1970s and 1980s, the legal underpinnings of the caste system have been removed in India, but the cultural legacy remains and caste still plays an important role in Indian life.

Under the caste system, an individual acquires a social position at birth. The great vitality of the caste system seems to arise from the fact that, besides being firmly established by custom, it is an integral part of the Hindu religion. It is based on the ideas of dharma, karma, and transmigration. **Dharma** is the law that sustains the system. **Karma** refers to the actions a person takes in fulfilling the duties associated with membership in a caste. The doctrine of **transmigration** holds that if a person fulfills duties sufficiently well in this life, that person will in a future life be reincarnated into a higher caste.

A symbol of apartheid in South Africa.

A caste system is even more rigid than an estate system because in theory there is no way of moving to a higher status except through death and reincarnation. In practice, a very limited amount of upward shifting occurs. Recently, the Indian government attempted to increase the upward shifting by creating a quota system, which holds places open in universities for members of the lower castes. This move has been controversial as the higher-level castes argue that such a quota system is unfair to them.

Social stratification systems having some of the characteristics of the one in India have been found in other societies. In the United States, blacks, especially in the South, have been called a caste by some writers. To support this designation, they point out that blacks belong by birth to a socially underprivileged group and that, at least in the past, it was very difficult for them to enter groups predominantly occupied by whites. For example, until 2000, it was technically illegal in some states for blacks and whites to intermarry. Alabama, in 2000, was the last state to repeal its law. (The law had not been enforced since the 1960s.)

Despite these similarities, most observers believe the position of U.S. blacks differed considerably from that of the members of a low Hindu caste. In the first place, even before recent reforms, blacks were subject to no rigid occupational limitations, and some achieved high positions in government, business, and the professions. Even more important, their inferior social position was not based on religious sanctions; rather, it was and is contrary to most Americans' religious teachings and democratic ideals of freedom and equal opportunity for all human beings.

A closer analogy to the caste system than the U.S. situation is the **apartheid system**—a separation of the races—that existed in some African countries. In an apartheid system blacks could not hold the same jobs or live in the same places as whites, and their interrelations with whites were severely limited. Apartheid was condemned by most other countries; in the early 1960s, it was overthrown altogether in the southern African country of Zimbabwe. In the 1990s it was abolished in South Africa.

Social Classes

Although most modern industrial societies do not have formal stratification systems, they do have a type of social stratification called a social class system. Unlike estates and castes, these social classes are not supported by any legal or religious sanctions. They are not clear-cut, definitely delimited groups into which every person in the community can be placed. The fact that social classes are not perfectly clear-cut entities is proven by the inability of social scientists to come to any general agreement on just how many of them should be recognized as existing. In a democratic industrial society, social status is a continuum, with individuals and families scattered along it from top to bottom. If we divide people on this social scale into two, three, or more social classes, we must do so arbitrarily.

Social scientists also have difficulty deciding just what criteria should be used in determining social status. Some would place an individual (or family) in a given class entirely on the basis of economic considerations. Those who take this point of view usually put their chief emphasis on income. Others, probably the majority, would determine the status of an individual by general social standing—that is, by whether the community, on the basis of various

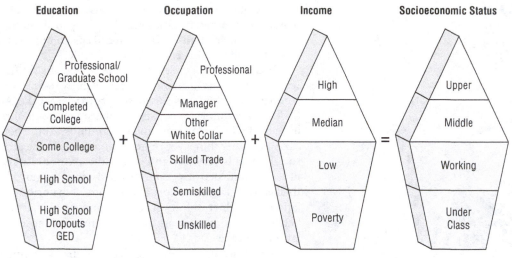

| Education | Occupation | Income | Socioeconomic Status |

Figure 12.1

Socioeconomic hierarchies.

criteria, places the individual high or low on the social scale. Income would be only one factor. Some of the common stratification hierarchies are shown in Figure 12.1. The combination of hierarchies—education, occupation, and income—forms an individual's socioeconomic status.[1]

Notice that the hierarchies shown in Figure 12.1 are drawn as pentagons with a sharp point at the top and a somewhat wider base. This shape represents a change from the way earlier editions of the book presented this material. Back in the 1930s when this book was first published, the shape was a pyramid—narrow at the top and wide at the bottom. This reflected the way social scientists had talked about income inequality for hundreds of years because the social stratification of European societies of the seventeenth and eighteenth centuries, with most people at the bottom and very few at the top, could be reasonably well represented by a pyramid.

In the 1950s and 1960s, that began to change; the lower classes decreased in relative size as more people moved into the middle class. The pyramid no longer was appropriate to represent the situation. To capture that change, we shifted to a diamond shape, suggesting that the majority of people fell in the middle class, with smaller upper and lower classes. We made the change to the diamond shape in the expectation that the lower class would continue to shrink as the members moved up the social ladder. Those expectations were wrong; the lower classes have stopped shrinking as upward social mobility has slowed and as immigration has increased in the United States. Hence, the need to expand the bottom of the hierarchies led to the pentagon shape.

Social Class Defined. A **social class** consists of those people in a community who are somewhat similar in their economic status, their attitudes and beliefs, their educational attainments, their ways of living, the regard in which others hold them, and their power or lack of power to influence community affairs. According to this definition, social class is, to some degree, a subculture. People whose social statuses are similar are not only likely to live in the

---

[1] There are many ways to classify the population. One imaginative survey undertook to see if "You are what you eat" is a defensible statement. The survey, done a number of years ago, covering some 13,000 households, identified five strata: (1) meat and potatoes households (30 percent); (2) child-oriented households: hot dogs, peanut butter, and soft drinks (25 percent); (3) seriously concerned over diet (15 percent); (4) natural-food enthusiasts (15 percent); and (5) sophisticates: quiche, raspberry tofu, and instant gourmet dinner (15 percent). Since then, groups one and two have decreased and groups three and four have increased.

Class structure in the United States. Shoe shines are almost invariably given by minorities. Some argue that this is because society fails to offer better opportunities.

same neighborhoods, associate largely with one another, and marry one another, but they are also likely to show similarities of speech, manners, and moral standards as compared with people who are higher or lower on the social scale.

Because social classes, like other types of stratification, represent superiority/inferiority relationships, some writers have compared the class structure of society to a layer cake. At the top of the cake is a thin layer consisting of a small group of people who have the highest economic and social status. At the bottom of the cake is another thin layer representing those whose economic and social status is very low and whom the community regards as of little account. Between these two extremes, at various levels, lie thicker layers, which represent the great majority of the population. The chief objection to this analogy is that the divisions between social classes are not as definite as those between the layers of a cake.

Social classes are not organized groups like families or communities. Rather, they are useful concepts. They are also social realities, but only in the sense that the people of any complex society can be divided roughly into a few large groups in such a way that those in each group have about the same general social standing and other similarities. Because the lines of division among classes are both vague and arbitrary, many individuals are difficult to place. The more class layers, the greater the difficulty of distinguishing between them and determining just where individuals fit.

In order to classify individuals into socioeconomic classes, it is generally necessary to average a variety of characteristics. This is normally done by a weighting system; points are allocated for various characteristics, these points are added up, and individuals within certain ranges of points are assigned to certain categories. For example, people with advanced education may get many points, but high income also confers many points, so somebody with high income and low education and somebody with low income and advanced education may fall into the same socioeconomic group after the weighting process. Using the weighting system allows us to organize people into upper class, upper-middle class, middle class, lower-middle class, and lower class. Some of the characteristics looked at are occupation, sources of income, type of housing, and the area within which the subject lives. Figure 12.2 presents typical class divisions and characteristics.

Most people do have some idea of the social class to which they belong, though they may not give it the same name that a sociologist would. For example, a family may think of themselves as ordinary people; a sociologist might classify them as belonging to the lower-middle class. Members of a social class recognize that they have more in common with others at a similar social level than they do with those above or below them. Also, as we have noted, they are likely to live in those areas and do those kinds of work that bring them into especially close association with people like themselves.

The Family Basis of Social Class.　The primary unit of stratification is the family, for except in rare cases all members of a family are regarded as belonging to the same stratum, or layer. The same social status is shared by all members of the immediate family group. As a rule, the most important factors in determining social class are the occupation, wealth, and income of the breadwinners in the family.

Occupations such as law and medicine, high government positions, and the management of large business enterprises yield considerable prestige because they require more than average ability and training; other occupations, such as keeping small stores or working at

Class levels	Approximate percentage of population	Likely occupation	Likely education	Approximate annual income (some overlap between classes)	Residential neighborhood	Newspaper reading
I. Elite	5	Independently wealthy Lawyers Doctors CEOs, CFOs, COOs	Seventeen or more years of school, elite college, and beyond	Over 400,000 Some extremely high Much inherited wealth	Very elite neighbor-hood Expensive houses Gated communities	Wall Street Journal New York Times
II. Upper-middle class	20	Small businesspeople Teachers Lawyers Professors Managers of small firms	Around sixteen years High-ranked college	Between 100,000 and 500,000 Most earned income by salary	Good neigh-borhoods Moderately expensive homes	Wall Street Journal New York Times
III. Middle class	35	Administrative Clerical Chain store managers Technicians Salespeople	High school and lower-ranked college	Between 30,000 and 125,000 Salary Some wages	Private homes, medium-sized Some tract homes	USA Today
IV. Lower-middle class	25	Low-skilled labor Part time employees in close to minimum-wage jobs	Ten to twelve years GED	20,000 to 40,000 Hourly wages	Apartments Small tract homes Trailers	USA Today National Enquirer
V. Lower class	15	Unskilled labor Unemployed	Eight to twelve years	Under 20,000 Poverty and welfare	Blighted areas Poor apartments	None

Figure 12.2

Social classes. *Sociologists do not completely agree about how many classes there are in the United States because classes overlap considerably and there are not sharp breaks between them. It is generally possible, however, to identify five or six basic social classes. (Source: Authors' modification of U.S. Bureau of the Census, "Money Income and Poverty Status of Families and Persons in the United States")*

skilled trades, are regarded as respectable; but some occupations, especially those that require unskilled manual labor, are looked down on by many members of the community. In general, the regard in which an occupation is held is closely correlated with the income it yields, although there are exceptions to this rule. A federal judge, for example, may have more prestige but less income than the owner of a catering service.

Membership in social classes tends to be transmitted in the same family line from generation to generation because children are likely to acquire much the same attitudes and modes of living as their parents, to receive similar educational advantages, to enter similar occupations, and to inherit whatever wealth their parents may possess.

In 2012, Charles Murray wrote a provocative book, *Coming Apart: The State of White America, 1960–2010,* in which he argues that the upper class has become insulated from the rest of white society. Its members attend elite universities, intermarry, and live in separate areas, which he calls SuperZips, where neighborhoods are whiter and more Asian than others. So not only is there a cultural separation based on race, but there is also a cultural separation based on habits and income. Murray argues that the elite have become out of touch with the rest of U.S. society. For example, they do not watch Oprah or Judge Judy; they drink wine and craft beers (in appropriate moderation); and they do not smoke. They eat out a lot, not at Denny's, the American Legion, or Sonic, but at upscale ritzy restaurants with fancy wine lists. They tend to have stable marriages; they work hard, are good parents, and have children within marriage; and often they are affiliated with a number of social groups. As one moves lower on the class ladder, one moves farther away from these characteristics. Many men don't work; children do not have a stable family life; religion is being lost; and the social nature of the community is ending.

The problem, according to Murray, is that the elite tend to make decisions on the basis of their atypical lives, as if everyone were like them. This is important because the elite hold a disproportionate amount of power over decisions that society makes. Murray argues that attempts to fix the situation through government only make it worse, and that what is needed is a "civic great awakening" that will reintegrate the elite with the other classes and help spread the elite values, which Murray sees as useful values for a society, to other classes. Whether or not Murray's "solution" is the right one, a number of commentators have found that his diagnosis that the United States is becoming more separated fits their perceptions, and that this issue needs to enter the public debate.

Social Mobility

Any class system is somewhat inconsistent with the democratic ideal of equal opportunities for life, liberty, and the pursuit of happiness. Certainly, lower-class children do not have the same opportunities as those in the upper classes. In the United States, we try to avoid thinking in terms of "low class" and "high class," but there is no escaping the fact that some people are economically and socially better off than some other people.

What made this situation acceptable to most Americans was that the United States had an **open class system**—a system in which class lines were not definite, and for many people the possibilities of moving up were excellent. The important element was not the size of the various groups or the disparity, but the ability of individuals to move among the groups. The degree of **social mobility**—the comparative ease with which a person in a society can improve (or worsen) his or her social and economic status—was considered quite large in the United States, so people at the bottom could imagine their kids moving to the top. Until recently, most observers viewed the United States as having significant social mobility. This view of a socially mobile U.S. society was captured by a nineteenth-century U.S. novelist who gave his name, Horatio Alger, to stories of ordinary Americans who improved their social and economic status through commitment, dedication, hard work, education, thrift, moral rectitude, and, very often, help from family, friends, teachers, employers, and scholarships and government programs.[2] Downward mobility is also a possibility, and although there is not much proof, many believe that the spoiled children of the idle rich will eventually land in the gutter.

Fifty years ago, social scientists found that significant upward mobility existed. In a 1960s study, Gerhard Lenski found that 33 percent of all males in the period from 1945 to 1965 were upwardly mobile. Downward mobility at that time was clearly present but its incidence was not well documented. However, in the 1970s, the U.S. expectation of upward mobility began to erode. A study by Featherman and Hauser in 1978 found that one-fourth of all persons age 21 to 53 had slid to an occupational level below their first jobs. A study by Greg J. Duncan and colleagues compared mobility between the 1968–1979 and 1980–1987

---

[2] Horatio Alger was born in 1834. He wrote hundreds of stories with titles such as *Ragged Dick* or *Luck and Pluck* in which his young heroes went "from rags to riches." Alger worked hard, saved up a fortune, and gave his money away. He died poor in 1899.

periods and found that the incidence of upward mobility for those in the lower class declined, while upward mobility for those at the upper income levels rose, leading to a shrinking middle class.

In the early 2000s, social scientist Brent Bratsberg and his colleagues found further erosion, and discovered that Europe had more social mobility than did the United States. Specifically, they ranked countries on a scale of 0 to 1, with 0 meaning perfect mobility (a child's income bears no relation to parental income) and 1 meaning no mobility (a child's income is identical to parental income). They found that for sons, Sweden scored a .2; Britain scored a .36 and the United States scored a .54, suggesting that the United States had only about half as much social mobility as did Sweden and Britain. The situation was worse at the bottom; children born to families in the bottom fifth of the U.S. income distribution were the least likely to move up. Further, this situation was exacerbated by the large increase in income and wealth inequality in the United States, where the rich have been getting much richer and the poor have been essentially treading water. Their incomes have hardly increased, or have even fallen. Thus, when social scientist Bhashkar Mazumder studied the issue in 2014, he found that social mobility was limited in the United States and that it was difficult for children to rise up. The situation was particularly difficult for blacks; of those born to low-income families only 29 percent would rise to middle class or higher.

These changes in social mobility have the potential to undermine the political and social stability of the United States because much of that stability is based on a belief that, although there are large inequalities in the United States, such inequalities are acceptable, since they reflect effort on the part of the rich. There remains a belief in the United States that, with hard work, people with low incomes can move up. That belief is eroding, and many attributed the large support that the self-declared socialist presidential candidate, Bernie Sanders, received in the 2016 primaries to the sense that social mobility was decreasing.

Who Are the Upwardly Mobile?

Although overall upward mobility has decreased, it is still possible to move up if a person has certain traits. Studies of people who have achieved upward mobility have identified certain related traits: race, gender, being an only (or first) child, and a belief in deferred gratification, which is when a person is willing to trade off an immediate pleasure for a future goal. The first and second of these are so important that we treat them in a separate chapter under the subject of discrimination. The third is probably related to income (it has been found that rich people are more likely to have only one child) and is not within an individual's control. The last trait, however—deferred gratification—can be and is probably the most important, as demonstrated in what is sometimes called the Marshmallow study.

In 1972, a psychologist ran an experiment in which he gave 4-year-olds a marshmallow and told them that he would give them two if they would wait for twenty minutes before eating it. Some waited, and some did not. He then followed their progress through life and found that those who waited were psychologically better adjusted, more dependable, and did significantly better in school than those who did not wait. The implication: The ability to delay gratification is an important factor in determing success.

How much a belief in deferred gratification can be fostered is debatable. Your beliefs are, in large part, transmitted from your parents through continually supportive feedback, and by the time you reach college age, these beliefs are probably set.

Thus, for most of you, whether you are to be upwardly mobile may have already been determined and is partially built into your personality. Of course, luck (such as being in the right place at the right time for a job) plays an important role, and many people who have the traits associated with being upwardly mobile may find themselves disappointed. For example, if you had a crisis the night before you took the college boards, you might have done poorly on them, which might have played a role in whether you won a scholarship. Bad luck is not pleasant, but it is a fact of life and should not be considered unusual. No one ever said life is fair.

Up, Down, and Out

If you pay $25,000, can you get your name in the *Social Register?* If you drop your subscription, can you get your name out of the *Social Register?* Should you let people know you are in the *Social Register?* Do you use the *Social Register* as a phone book? Do you know anyone who knows what the *Social Register* is? To some people, these are important questions but the number is shrinking.

Exactly how one gets into the *Social Register* is unclear. The book tries to limit the number of names to around 33,000. Some people get into it without trying; some people have always been there and can't get out; some people are in it by virtue of their office (U.S. presidents, for instance). Marrying up won't get you in and might get your spouse deleted. If you get in and want to be sure to stay in, don't get divorced, start an acting career, or go to jail.

Discussions of mobility often overlook one simple fact: Room at the top is always limited. When we talk about social mobility, we are apt to think of opportunities to move upward on the social scale, but we must remember that as some people, or their children, move up, others, or their children, are likely to move down.

What are the conditions that contribute to social mobility? Probably most important of all is social change. In a changing society, the old order is always being disturbed, and new ways of achieving wealth or position keep appearing. For the past 200 years, industrialization, with its ever newer methods of production and types of business organization, has provided opportunities to climb the economic and social ladder.

What's changing now for people is globalization. From a global perspective, U.S. workers, even poor ones, are on the high end of the income distribution ladder. People want to immigrate to the United States even if it means accepting a "low-wage" job because that low-wage U.S. job is a "high-wage" job for them. With U.S. companies increasingly willing to (or forced to, because of global competition) shift production to low-wage countries throughout the world, and with low-wage countries increasingly developing their own companies that compete with U.S. companies, the avenues for U.S. citizens at the bottom of the income/social scale to move up are decreasing. Thus, we can expect that social mobility will be of increasing concern over the coming years.

Education and Social Mobility

One of the best ways to advance from one class to another is through education (see Table 12.1). Education allows individuals access to job possibilities that otherwise would not be open to them, and in doing so it raises their income.

Table 12.1

Starting Salary Offers to New College Graduates in 2017, by Selected Fields of Study

CATEGORY	2017 AVERAGE SALARY
Engineering	$66,097
Computer Science	$65,540
Math & Sciences	$59,368
Business	$54,803
Agriculture & Natural Resources	$54,364
Healthcare	$50,839
Communications	$51,925
Social Sciences	$53,459
Humanities	$48,733

Source: NACE Salary Survey.

One method that *doesn't* lead to class advancement is to increase income without attention to other issues. Social scientist Susan Mayer developed a statistical model that predicted what would happen to a child's prospects for success in life if the annual income of the child's family were doubled. She found that if the increased income were the only factor in the life of a child in that family, the child's chances of becoming a successful adult would hardly improve at all. Intelligence, determination, good health, and a willingness to cooperate were far better predictors of advancement.

Class Consciousness in the United States

Most Americans are not highly **class conscious,** that is, overly concerned about their status in society and the standing of other people in relation to them. Ambition usually takes the form of a desire for a more satisfying job, more income, or more personal prestige. Any resulting change in social status usually is secondary or wholly incidental. Relatively few Americans have a strong desire to move into a higher social class except insofar as this may help them to achieve other objectives.

Why are Americans so comparatively free of class consciousness? Partly, the reasons are historical. We never did have a hereditary nobility, and throughout our early history rapid growth and expansion resulted in considerable social mobility. It is more than a coincidence that, although a number of our presidents have come from wealthy or aristocratic families, some have had very humble origins.

One factor that has tended to keep class consciousness at a low level is the general rise in standards of living that has occurred. Even though people were not changing their position in the social scale, they felt they were making progress when their incomes rose and when they could improve their way of life.

Another factor that has tended to reduce class consciousness and discontent is **horizontal mobility,** the opportunities that exist for moving from one job to another, and often to a better-liked job. Horizontal mobility is important because, while U.S. citizens are not especially class-conscious, they are group-conscious and their desire to be in the "in group" is strong. This desire begins early in life as cliques form in schools, and students are classified as nerds, druggies, preps, and jocks, for instance. Advertising takes advantage of our group consciousness, portraying goods as providing group cachet to the buyer. Celebrity endorsements are common in advertising, under the assumption that if some movie or sports star uses the product, if you also use it, you will fit in with the group to which they belong. Take a look at the shoes or clothes you are wearing. Did you buy them because they were the least expensive but still comfortable clothes you could find? Or did you buy them because they made you feel "in"? This horizontal mobility gives people the feeling of making progress, even though the change has little effect on income or social status.

With globalization, the factors militating against class consciousness have been somewhat reduced. Wages for lower-income individuals are not rising, and horizontal mobility is getting harder. To date, these changes have not led to an increase in class consciousness, but they may well do so in the future.

Class Consciousness, Marx, and Weber

In his criticism of capitalist society, Karl Marx, the nineteenth-century father of communism and one of the founders of the field of sociology, divided the populations of industrial societies into two classes—**capitalists,** or owners of the means of production, and the **proletariat,** or workers, who were exploited by the capitalists. The proletariat's labor was used to further the capitalists' own profits, without consideration of the workers' needs. Marx felt that the increasing exploitation of workers would lead to an increasing class consciousness among the proletariat.

Homeless person on the streets.

Riches in the United States.

Marx believed that under capitalistic exploitation the condition of the workers would become worse and worse. Eventually workers would rise up in revolt, seize the means of production, and establish a socialist state under the "dictatorship of the proletariat." Actually, the standard of living of the working people in most industrial countries, quite contrary to Marx's prediction, tended to rise.

Marx's division of the classes is not the only division. Max Weber, an outspoken critic of Marx's views, argued that property is not the sole basis of class. Instead class is determined by the three *p*'s—property, prestige, and power. Weber's more general concept of class is accepted by numerous sociologists, but their views of how to quantify prestige and power often differ substantially. We shall use Weber's concept.

*E*conomic and Social Inequality

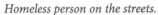

We focus on an individual's monetary income because that is what we collect figures on. True inequality depends on much more. For example, say you have a choice of poor health and an income of $100,000 per year or good health and $25,000 per year. Which would you choose? Probably the latter, for people's true income includes all aspects of their position. Because we cannot measure true income, most studies focus on monetary income and individuals' standard of living.

Even if we focus on monetary income, we still have difficulty in determining how much of a problem income inequality is. For example, how much poverty do we have in the United States today? That depends on how the word is defined. In terms of what poverty means in India or China, or even in terms of what it meant in this country or Europe a hundred years ago, we have very little poverty. Almost no one in the United States today actually dies of starvation, but tens, and sometimes hundreds, of thousands do in Africa.

It is true that homeless persons sleep on the streets or in all kinds of makeshift shelters such as large packing cartons in the cities of the United States, but this is most often because of other kinds of social problems (a spirit of independence carried to psychotic extremes, for instance, or policies of releasing marginally competent people from mental facilities). It is not because there are no programs or funds available to shelter this population.

On the other hand, large numbers of people depend on public assistance to live, and many who do not receive such payments have incomes so small that they must live in depressing or

Union and labor activists in New York City demonstrating for a $15 minimum wage.

© a katz/Shutterstock.com

unsafe surroundings, wear shabby clothes, and buy cheap food. They cannot afford to spend money for travel, entertainment, or education, and if they are out of work or if an emergency such as serious illness arises, their only recourse is public aid or charity.

In 1996, Congress passed a welfare reform law designed to drastically reduce the number of people on long-term public assistance and to help them improve their economic status through measures such as education, job training, child care facilities, and medical assistance. Two results of this law have been to put millions of low-income people in jobs and to reduce public assistance rolls significantly. However, some of the people who found jobs did not make enough money to support themselves and their families, and there is still a large population of low-income people. Although its effects are continuing to be monitored, most observers see that public assistance reform was a success in reducing the number of people on welfare and in channeling them into more productive activities. But that success was dependent on the law being fine-tuned to eliminate some of its harshest effects.

Causes of Income Inequality

Differences in income arise directly from three sources: variations in earnings from personal services, differences in the amounts of property owned, and variations in transfer payments from government. Differences in the earnings of individuals are the most important. These differences are based partly on occupation and partly on the personal qualities of those engaged in each occupation. The most basic of the factors that determine income variations between occupational groups is demand and supply.

In general, occupations that are not easy to enter because they require special aptitudes and long training are highly paid because the supply of workers is small relative to the demand. On the other hand, occupations classified as common labor, which anyone can enter with relatively little ability or training, tend to be poorly paid. But within each occupational group, there are often great differences in individual earning power, especially at the higher professional and managerial levels.

Tables 12.2a to 2.2d show the distribution of income by percentage of families; by occupation; by representative states; and by race, gender, and household status. As you can see, income is distributed unequally in the general population and also by the place where one lives, by race, by gender, and by occupation.

Jobless Recovery and Globalization

Over the past thirty years, the U.S. economy has been significantly affected by globalization and large trade deficits. Globalization has been hardest on the least-skilled workers, who have seen their jobs evaporate as companies have moved production abroad to places where labor costs are much lower. But globalization has been the most kind to upper-level management and highly skilled workers, who have benefited from the low cost of imported goods, and also have seen the demand for their services and their compensation grow. The result has been a large increase in measured inequality in the United States; the rich have gotten richer and the poor have gotten poorer. During this time period, the top 1 percent has doubled their share of income compared to thirty years ago. A study by the government's Congressional Budget

Table 12.2a

Measures of Relative Incomes: Upper Limit of the Bottom Four Quintiles, 2017

Bottom 20%	$24,500
Bottom 40%	$47,500
Bottom 60%	$76,000
Bottom 80%	$118,000

Table 12.2b

Median Annual Income by Sector, 2017

Education, Training, and Library	$52,104
Health Care Practitioners and Technical Occupations	$58,448
Protective Services	$44,304
Personal Care and Service	$27,040

Table 12.2c

Median Household Income by Region, 2017

Northwest	$66,998
Midwest	$57,778
South	$55,135
West	$66,485

Table 12.2d

Household Median Family Money Income by Race, Gender, and Household Status, 2017

White	$65,845
Black	$40,232
Hispanic	$49,793
Single Male Householder	$35,700
Single Female Householder	$27,339

Source: U.S. Bureau of the Census. *American Community Survey.* Extrapolations by author.

Office found that from 1979 to 2007, average inflation-adjusted, after-tax income grew by 275 percent for the top 1 percent, but for the bottom 20 percent, it rose by only 18 percent. While the recession starting in 2008 slowed the relative gains of the top income earners, it has not stopped it and as the economy has grown in recent years, most of the gains have gone to top income earners.

Measuring Poverty

In order to measure poverty in a country, we must define the term. It isn't easy to do so. In the United States, the Social Security Administration and the Bureau of the Census attempt to do this by determining the **poverty threshold,** that is, the minimum amount of income needed to maintain a living standard above the poverty level. Obviously, the poverty threshold will be lower for an individual than for a family, and it will differ for families of different size. It will also change with fluctuations in the cost of living.

To be above the poverty level, an individual or family must have enough income to obtain food, clothing, and shelter that will maintain health, plus some margin for other necessary expenditures. Just what minimum income is essential at any given time and place cannot be determined with any great precision, and hence any specific poverty threshold is to some degree arbitrary. However, after a careful and objective weighing of the facts, the determined cutoff can have enough meaning to be useful. Each year, the Bureau of the Census publishes poverty thresholds for single ("unrelated") individuals and for families of various sizes. The level at which the poverty level is set is important because that level determines which families receive government assistance.

According to census estimates, the total number of Americans who lived in poverty in 2017 was about 39.7 million, or 12.3 percent. For a family of four (excluding Alaska and Hawaii), this represented an annual income of $25,100 in 2018. For a single person, it is about $12,140. As you can see in Figure 12.3, the percentage of people in poverty

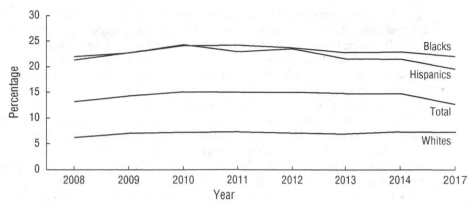

Figure 12.3

Percentage of poverty by race. (*Source: U.S. Bureau of the Census*)

depends on race and ethnicity. Blacks and Hispanics are more than twice as likely as whites to be poor.

These measures of the number of Americans who live in poverty should be accepted with some reservations. Undoubtedly, many of those included had incomes that were only temporarily extremely low, or had savings with which to supplement current income, or owned homes and lived in communities where they could get along reasonably well on a small income, or were young people getting help from parents. However, after all such allowances are made, it is clear that a substantial amount of poverty exists in this country.

Increasing Social and Economic Inequality

It would seem that a country as rich as the United States should be able to eliminate poverty, if what we mean by that is simply providing everyone with enough income for physical comfort and security.[3] To do so, the United States has instituted a variety of programs, including public assistance, unemployment insurance, Medicare, Social Security, and Supplemental Security Income (SSI). In many ways, these programs have succeeded, but they have also introduced new problems.

Being poor in the United States is quite different from being poor in a developing country; it is consistent with having air conditioners and cable TV. That said, it should also be noted that most people view their positions in society relatively, not absolutely. And relatively, over the past twenty-five years, inequality has been increasing substantially. Median family income has risen by about 20 percent over those twenty-five years, but the median income of the top 1 percent has increased by 200 percent over that same period. Moreover, the median income of most families has risen over that period only because women have entered the workforce in increasing numbers. The wage (adjusted for inflation) that a worker makes has actually fallen. The result is that U.S. income is much more unequal than it was in the 1970s. In terms of wealth, the situation is even more unequal. The top 1 percent of the population controls 50 percent of the nation's wealth. The bottom 50 percent controls less than 2.5 percent.

---

[3] If we define poverty in relative terms, as many sociologists do, then to some degree the problem will always be with us. No matter how much incomes rise, if we assume the continuance of substantial inequalities, people with relatively low incomes will continue to be deprived of various things that the rest can enjoy.

The reasons for these changes are both structural and policy-related. Structurally, global competition has hit low-income, nonspecialized workers hardest. They were presented with a difficult choice: Lower your wage or your job will be **outsourced**—transferred to a low-wage worker outside the United States, or transferred to a low-wage recent immigrant willing to do the same work for much lower pay. High-wage workers with specialized skills are also now beginning to feel the pressure of global competitiveness, as new technologies have allowed more and more of their jobs to be outsourced.

These structural forces pushing for inequality have been compounded by policy changes—the progressivity of the U.S. income tax has been significantly reduced, the inheritance tax has been reduced, and the capital gains tax—a tax on the increase in value of assets that falls mainly on the rich—has been reduced. Advocates for these policy changes claim that they kept the U.S. economy expanding, and that the focus of attention should not be on inequality, but on the overall health of the U.S. economy. Critics see the policy changes as giveaways to the rich—taking from the poor to give to the rich.

Policies to Reduce Inequality

The view that economic inequality should be reduced is widely shared. While there is nothing inherently correct about this view, it is prominently held, which raises the question of how to do it. High progressive taxes are one way, but they tend to hurt entrepreneurial incentives. Moreover, they are hard to enforce and they tend to create numerous evasion and avoidance schemes that misdirect resources and cause economic inefficiency. As government tries to prevent this evasion and avoidance, the taxes often become bureaucratic and legal nightmares. These serious problems with highly progressive taxes have led to the **supply-side argument** that in some cases lowering tax rates actually can raise tax revenues. That said, most economists believe it is technically possible to have an effective, more progressive tax system in the United States than we currently have, although the political process of implementing the system usually so distorts it from the ideal that the end result is often problematic. The bottom line: What can be achieved with a progressive tax system, given the political climate in the U.S., is limited.

Another way for government to redistribute income involves government programs to help the poor, but these too tend to have serious negative incentive effects—for example, they usually have a cutoff, so if you work or earn above a certain amount, you are no longer eligible. That cutoff discourages work—to stay eligible for the program, people don't work. It was such negative incentive effects that led to the welfare reforms in the 1990s, which limited public assistance eligibility to a five-year window and placed a work requirement on those collecting public assistance benefits.

Both these government approaches attempt to redistribute income after it has been distributed by the market. But because the government sets the laws that govern the economy, it can equalize income in other ways. Specifically, it can directly affect the way in which income is distributed through legislation. For example, patents, copyrights, and intellectual property rights tend to create income inequality. Shortening the length for which these are given out would lead to less inequality, although it would also reduce the incentive to innovate. All economists agree that an appropriate trade-off must be found between equity and incentives to innovate, but many economists believe that the current trade-off leans far too heavily toward those with intellectual property rights protected by government patents and copyrights.

In developing countries, economist Hernando de Soto found that the lack of capitalizable property rights (property rights that can be used as collateral for loans) was a major reason why the poor stayed poor, and that a key element to reducing inequality would be for government to reduce the number of restrictions on the poor's activities. He also argued that governments should simultaneously formalize the titles to property of the poor.

Some Conclusions about the U.S. Class System

In spite of the statement in the Declaration of Independence that "all men are created equal," everyone knows that in many ways people are not equal. They are not born with equal potentialities for learning and achieving, nor are they born into equally favorable social environments. Nevertheless, equality before the law and equality of opportunity are strongly cherished democratic ideals. Over the years, we have been striving in the United States to come closer to these ideals, and since the Declaration of Independence was written, we have made considerable progress toward them. Recent structural changes in the U.S. economy have led some to be concerned about whether the country is providing equality of opportunity, and this issue will likely be much in debate in the next decade.

 Study and **Review**

Key Points

- Three types of social stratification are estates, castes, and social classes.
- The existence of social mobility allows people to move from one class to another and makes the social and economic stratification more acceptable to society.
- Three sources of income inequality are variations in earnings from personal services, differences in the amounts of property owned, and variations in transfer payments from government.
- The poverty threshold in the United States is the level of income needed to maintain a living

standard above the poverty level. In 2018, the poverty level was set at $25,100 for the average family of four.
- Any practical program for meeting the problems of economic inequality must take into account the poorest people, the need for health care, justice, children's rights, and the need for savings and incentives.
- The U.S. economic class system is not strongly developed, in part due to historical factors and in part due to the market economy, the government, and the underlying U.S. ideology that sees class consciousness as a negative trait.

Some Important Terms

apartheid system (228)
capitalists (235)
caste (227)
class-conscious (235)
dharma (227)
estate (227)

hierarchy (226)
horizontal mobility (235)
karma (227)
open class system (232)
outsourced (240)
poverty threshold (238)

proletariat (235)
social class (229)
social mobility (232)
stratification (226)
supply-side argument (240)
transmigration (227)

Questions for Review and Discussion

General Questions

1. Name the three principal types of social stratification and briefly describe the nature of each.
2. How has the position of blacks in our society resembled, and how has it differed from, the position of a low Hindu caste?
3. Societies can be stratified in a variety of ways. What is the major form of stratification in modern industrial societies?

4. Why has the kind of class conflict Karl Marx predicted never developed anywhere?
5. Why are Americans not highly class-conscious?
6. What difficulties are encountered when we attempt to divide the people of an industrial society into clear-cut social classes?
7. Why is social class a family matter rather than an individual matter?

8. What are some of the principal factors that may contribute to class mobility?

9. Why is upward social mobility necessarily limited in any society?

10. What factors have been operating in the United States in recent years to reduce class distinctions? Can you name any factors that, in your opinion, have had the opposite effect?

11. Characterize the U.S. class system from the standpoint of (a) the sharpness of class distinctions, (b) the degree of class consciousness, and (c) the amount of social mobility.

12. Is U.S. society becoming more stratified? Defend your point of view.

Internet Questions

1. Using http://www.hinduwebsite.com/hinduism/h_caste.asp, explain how the Vaisyas differ from the Chandalas. (ans: for reference only: The Vaisyas are the merchant and peasant class; the Chandalas are the lowest of the Shudras caste and were treated as untouchables.)

2. Looking at the U.S. Department of Health and Human Services' poverty guidelines, http://aspe.hhs.gov/poverty/index.shtml, what is the most recent poverty threshold for a family of six? In Alaska?

3. Go to https://www.usgs.gov/about/organization/science-support/human-capital/upward-mobility-program-0, the site of the U.S. Geological Survey, Upward Mobility Program. What is the purpose of this program?

4. Go to http://www.salary.com/ and use the Salary Wizard. In your area, what is the income range for the middle 50 percent of teacher's aides? What is the range for associate professors of economics?

5. Using https://www.census.gov/newsroom/press-releases/2018/cb18-41-population-projections.html, in what year is the U.S. population expected to exceed 400,000,000? (ans: for reference only: 2058)

For Further Study

Books to Explore

Clark, Gregory, *The Son Also Rises: Surnames and the History of Social Mobility (The Princeton Economic History of the Western World)*, Princeton, NJ: Princeton University Press, 2015.

Drennan, Matthew P., *Income Inequality: Why It Matters and Why Most Economists Didn't Notice*, New Haven, CT: Yale University Press, 2015.

Ehrenreich, Barbara, *Nickel and Dimed: On (Not) Getting By in America*, New York: Holt, 2004.

Harford, Tim, *The Undercover Economist: Exposing Why the Rich Are Rich, the Poor Are Poor and Why You Can Never Buy a Decent Used Car*, New York: Little Brown, 2005.

Hughes, Chris, *Fair Shot: Rethinking Inequality and How we Earn*, New York: St Martin's Press, 2018.

Isenberg, Nancy, *White Trash: The 400-Year Untold History of Class in America*, New York: Viking, 2016.

Keller, Bill, and *The New York Times*, *Class Matters*, New York: Macmillan, 2005.

Lindsey, Brink, and Steven Teles, *The Captured Economy: How the Powerful Enrich Themselves, Slow Down Growth, and Increase Inequality*, New York: Oxford University Press, 2017.

McCarty, Nolan, Keith T. Poole, and Howard Rosenthal, *Polarized America: The Dance of Ideology and Unequal Riches*, Cambridge, MA: MIT Press, 2006.

Murray, Charles, *Coming Apart: The State of White America, 1960–2010*, New York: Crowne Forum, 2012.

Putnam, Robert, *Our Kids: the American Dream in Crisis*, Simon and Schuster, 2015.

Reeves, Richard (editor), *Does Character Matter?* Washington, DC: Brookings Institution, 2015.

Wilson, William Julius, *More than Just Race: Being Black and Poor in the Inner City*, New York: Norton, 2009.

Internet Sites to Explore

"http://www.bls.gov" Bureau of Labor Statistics.

"http://www.naceweb.org" National Association of Colleges and Employers.

"http://www.nccp.org" National Center for Children in Poverty.

"https://www.bls.gov/ooh" Occupational Outlook Handbook.

"https://www.census.gov/" U.S. Bureau of the Census.

"http://www.hhs.gov/" U.S. Department of Health and Human Services.

Stratification, Minorities, and Discrimination

After reading this chapter, you should be able to:

- List four reasons for ethnic and racial prejudice
- Distinguish between minority and dominant groups
- Discuss the race problem in the United States today
- Explain the problem of illegal Mexican immigration
- Discuss briefly the problems of religious minorities
- Discuss briefly the problems of sexual minorities
- Give arguments for and against age discrimination

Wrong never lies in unequal rights, it lies in the pretension of equal rights.

—Friedrich Nietzsche

In Chapter 12, social stratification was considered primarily along economic and social lines. Societies are also stratified along racial, ethnic, and cultural lines. Questions of discrimination based on a person's race, religion, ethnicity, age, gender, physical disabilities, or sexual preferences, and issues of busing, job quotas, and right to jobs—these issues are not of the past, but rather remain relevant to our daily lives.

Many of you may feel that you are well aware of these issues, either because you have lived them or because they have been extensively discussed at home or in school. This chapter is necessary, nonetheless, both to provide you with a sense of the history and dimension of the issue and to give you a standard by which to judge your own views. The issues of equality and discrimination are as pertinent today as they were seventy years ago, when social scientists first considered these issues.

Race and Ethnicity

Although all human beings belong to the same species, *Homo sapiens*, they exhibit many physical and cultural variations, including differences in height, weight, skin color, and the shape of the head and face. Any group of people, if isolated from others over a long period of time, will develop differentiating physical characteristics. Thus, it is possible to distinguish groups of people by these characteristics and to call those groups races.

While it is possible to distinguish groups of people by characteristics, it is also problematic. There are few natural dividing lines, and those dividing lines are arbitrary. In addition, a range of gradations within any group one makes can be found. One classification

243

Due to mixing of races, "race" as a classification system is losing significance.

© Goodluz/Shutterstock

system has divided most people into three groups based on physical variations—Caucasoids, Mongoloids, and Negroids. The problem with this classification is twofold. First, it reflects social constructions loosely based on biological differences. However, the biological differences between so-called races often are far fewer than the biological differences between individuals of the same "race." What do we mean by social construction? Consider hair color: There are redheads, brunettes, and blondes; yet because our social system doesn't distinguish among them, hair color does not delineate race. But skin color does, not because blacks and whites are inherently different, but because our social system differentiates them.

Second, over time, migration has led to a mixing of the races, and ranges of gradation within races can be found. Thus race as a classification system is losing significance. The U.S. Bureau of the Census dealt with this classification problem when it prepared its census forms by listing a large number of ethnicities, such as black, white, Hispanic, of Hispanic origin, Pacific Islander, and many others, including "Other," leaving people to classify themselves in any way they pleased. Golf star Tiger Woods, who is of Thai and African American descent, tried to devise a unique term for his heritage, Cablinasian (a combination of the words *Caucasian, black, Indian,* and *Asian*), and this may mark a trend. The Census Bureau is continually changing its race classification system, as society's view of how we should distinguish groups changes. In response to feedback from people of mixed race who found it difficult to select only one race when prompted, the Census Bureau has allowed people to select "one or more" options for their race since 2010. Some even argue that the government should be prevented from collecting information on race because having that information leads the government to be less race-neutral in its policies than many believe it should be. Why should the government care how many people consider themselves black or Hispanic? We are all Americans.

A concept closely related to race is ethnicity, which is a more defensible way of classifying groups of people. It is important to distinguish between race and ethnicity. The reason for doing so is the following: Whereas race is a biological classification system, ethnicity is a cultural classification. An **ethnic group** is a group of people who identify with each other on the basis of common ancestry and cultural heritage.

In popular usage, ethnic differences often are confused with racial differences. Ethnic differences between groups in matters such as nationality, language, and religion are important, but they do not constitute differences in race. It would be incorrect, for example, to speak of the French race or the German race. France and Germany are adjacent countries, and the people who live on one side of the border are physically little different from those who live on the other side. It is also misleading to call Jewish people a race. They have no physical characteristics by which they can be dependably distinguished from non-Jews in our population. Primarily, what holds them together as a group is religion, history, and social tradition—that is, ethnicities.

Racial and ethnic differences fall into distinct categories and are largely independent of each other. The frequently made assumption that race determines culture has little scientific or factual basis. Where different racial groups have lived in close association for some time, as in Hawaii, they are likely to have much the same culture; on the other hand, members of the same race living in different parts of the world often exhibit cultural patterns that are radically different. To see the truth of this last statement, we need only compare the culture of black Americans with that of blacks living in the Congo basin of Africa.

Questions of Ethnic and Racial Superiority

Some people believe that one race or one ethnic group is innately superior to others in intelligence and creativity, and that this superiority largely explains the high degree of civilization certain groups have been able to achieve. This may seem superficially plausible because many of the recorded scientific and social advances (or at least the ones familiar to whites of European descent) in the last several hundred years have been made by the European-descended ethnic groups.

Such a view would be extremely shortsighted. Over the centuries, the particular groups who have taken the lead in the advances of civilization have changed. First, it was the Sumerians and the Egyptians; later, the people of India and China, the Jews, the Phoenicians, and the Persians; still later, the Greeks and Romans; then, for a while, the Arabs; and finally, the peoples of northern and western Europe. But we need go back only 2,000 years or less to find Roman writers who looked on the then primitive Britons and Germans as not only crude and uncivilized but also stupid. In other parts of the world, well-organized societies developed but they either disintegrated or were destroyed by invaders, disease, or natural disasters. These include the Maya and Inca civilizations in the Americas and various kingdoms in black Africa south of the Sahara.

There is no convincing scientific evidence to support the contention that some races biologically inherit a greater capacity for development than others. Which society leads the world development of civilization is the result of a combination of other factors such as favorable climate and soil, migrations that stimulated change by bringing together peoples with different cultural backgrounds, and fortuitous discoveries and inventions. Such advances tend to lead to further advances, a gradual accumulation of technical skills, an increase in food output, a slow growth of population, and the development of towns and cities. Every group of people has its bright and dull individuals, its great intellects and its idiots.

It is possible that, on average, there are some inherited mental and psychological differences between ethnic groups, just as there are physical differences. Statistics collected by Richard Herrnstein and Charles Murray in a controversial book entitled *The Bell Curve: Intelligence and Class Structure in American Life* suggest that in the United States, on average, Americans of Asian descent score a few points higher than whites on IQ tests, and black Americans score about 15 points lower than whites. These statistics, and the usefulness of IQ tests in measuring mental abilities, have been challenged on a variety of levels. But even if the statistics are correct and IQ tests actually measure mental ability, it is not clear whether the difference in scores is inherent in ethnic groups or is socially determined. Moreover, averages say nothing about individuals, so most social scientists say that no policy inference can be drawn from such statistics.

Even if some inborn mental and psychological differences exist, they do not necessarily mean superiority or inferiority any more than do differences in skin color, hair texture, or head shape. In any case, such differences are minor compared with the great differences that exist among individuals in every ethnic group.

Some social scientists argue that the concept of race is so socially determined that such discussions do not belong in social science. The problem is that discussions of race are often emotionally charged and emotion is anathema to good science. We agree. The reasons not to discuss race include:

- The term *race* is a social, not an important physical, construction.
- Biological differences within a race tend to far exceed biological differences among races.
- The race concept has a history of being inappropriately used.

These reasons lead most social scientists to focus on other ways of classifying people. We discuss the issue of race here not because we believe races are distinguishable in any meaningful biological way, but simply because race is much discussed in our society and we believe it is necessary to address issues of societal concern. Regardless of whether the concept of race is a meaningful concept in a democracy, the important thing is to treat all people as human beings, to judge people on their individual merits, and to provide every opportunity for people to develop and use whatever capabilities they possess.

Ethnic and Racial Prejudice and Discrimination

Ethnic relations vary greatly in different societies and in different social situations. In some cases, relatively little friction exists among members of different ethnic groups. **Prejudice**— an

*E*thnic Cleansing

Ethnic divisions affect every country, and in many ways they are worse abroad than they are in the United States. Let's consider two cases where they have been particularly bad: Bosnia and the countries of central Africa.

Bosnia

In Bosnia, significant hatred exists among the many different factions that make up the population of the country. The most numerous are Bosnians, Serbs, and Croatians. Bosnians, who are primarily Muslims, make up about half of the population; Serbs, who are mainly Eastern Orthodox Christians, make up about one-third of the population; and Croats, who are primarily Roman Catholic, make up about one-sixth of the population. This diversity in the area has existed for more than a thousand years and has been the cause of continuing tension. When Yugoslavia collapsed in 1991, widespread and devastating political, economic, and religious fighting broke out.

The various factions embarked on programs of "ethnic cleansing." As one side or another was temporarily victorious, the temporarily defeated were killed, tortured, or driven from their homes, causing most of the rest of the world to worry about the stability of the country and the fate of its people. Efforts by many

Skulls and bones from a mass grave.

countries, including several European powers and the United States, resulted in an international conference held in Dayton, Ohio, in 1995 that ended the worst of the incidents. However, the hatred aroused and intensified by the ethnic cleansing has persisted.

Central Africa

In the early 1990s, the world became aware of a fierce tribal war in the central African country of Rwanda, where two principal tribes, the Hutu and the Tutsi, tried to exterminate each other. In 1994, a group of militant Hutus massacred more than one million ethnic Tutsis (and moderate Hutus). Hundreds of thousands more managed to escape into the neighboring country of Burundi. Burundi could not support such a huge number of refugees, and worldwide assistance was only partially effective. In Burundi, the Hutu were in the majority but the Tutsi controlled the military, and so the warfare continued. This led to hundreds of thousands of refugees escaping to the neighboring countries of Zaire and Uganda.

The influx of refugees into Zaire upset the ethnic and political balance there between Hutus and Tutsis, and hundreds of thousands of members of both tribes were killed. In 1997, a radical change of government took place, and even the country's name was changed (from Zaire to the Democratic Republic of Congo). While international organizations tried to find solutions, in 1997 the situation in Zaire became so intolerable for the Rwandan refugees that those who had survived the warfare made their way back to Rwanda.

Because large numbers of members of these tribes live in all of the countries of central Africa, the Hutu-Tutsi conflict is not confined to any one of these countries. The Congo is mineral-rich and the competition for the land and its resources exacerbates the rivalries in this politically unstable area. Political alliances shift often. In 2002, the first Tutsi president of Rwanda signed a peace accord with the Congo, which agreed to a disarming of Hutu militiamen. The conflict is far from resolved and will continue to warrant international concern into the indefinite future.

adverse judgment or opinion formed beforehand or without knowledge or examination of the facts—exists, but ethnic barriers are not sufficient to prevent considerable social contact and frequent intermarriages. This seems to be the situation today in Hawaii, where the principal ethnic classifications are Caucasian and Asian/Pacific Islander. Though the various ethnic groups have not yet lost their sense of identity, residentially, economically, and educationally, they are nearly integrated. But there are other places in the world where prejudice and **discrimination**—actions, behavior, or treatment based on prejudice—are intense and where racial segregation is the accepted pattern.

What is the explanation for these great variations? Many people feel that prejudice is inevitable, that it is an inherited aversion. But the belief that human beings inherit attitudes has long been discredited by psychologists, and racial prejudice cannot be accounted for by any such simple explanation. Moreover, attitude and prejudice need not necessarily lead to discriminatory actions.

Writers have suggested various reasons for ethnic and racial prejudice. Prominent among these are the following four:

1. Influence of tradition
2. Psychological need of individuals to belong to a particular, identifiable group
3. Building up of the ego by cultivating a feeling of superiority
4. Usefulness of prejudice as an economic and political weapon.

Each of these could be expanded enormously, but we will leave that to sociology courses. Here, we simply want you to consider your own attitudes, to ask yourself whether they reflect prejudice, and, if so, to consider the reasons behind that prejudice. After you've done that, take the next step and ask yourself whether your prejudices show up in discriminatory actions. If they do, evaluate whether you find those actions justified.

The Melting Pot

Because of its heterogeneous population and the tendency of immigrant groups ultimately to become assimilated, the United States often has been called a melting pot. Although the white colonial population was predominantly British, other nationalities were also represented. During the nineteenth century, this country received 30 million immigrants, and in the early twentieth century millions more arrived. A few came from almost every section of the world, but the great majority were Caucasians from Europe. In the last thirty years, immigration from Asian and Latin American countries to the United States has been high and will likely continue to be high through the early 2000s.

Groups whose basic patterns of life were not too unlike those of the early British settlers became assimilated in a relatively short time; others were assimilated more slowly. But from the beginning there were non-Caucasian groups whose assimilation seemed impossible because they differed not only culturally but also racially from the majority of the American people. Today there are still unassimilated groups. The best known of these are blacks, but they also include Hispanics, who are largely Caucasian but who have come to this country rather recently; Asians, whose physical characteristics set them apart from white Causasians and

On July 10, 2015, the Confederate flag was removed from the Capitol grounds in Columbia, South Carolina after 54 years.

© John Bazemore/AP/Corbis

Black Lives Matter: Racial Hatred in the US

In August, 2014, a police officer shot and killed a young black man in Ferguson, Missouri, whom he had tried to detain, and who the officer said resisted arrest. This killing resulted in protests and riots in Ferguson and other U.S. cities. Protesters complained that police are prejudiced against blacks and don't respect black lives.

In June, 2015, a young white man walked into a Charleston church Bible study. He was welcomed by the church members, and he sat through the discussion. Then he pulled out an automatic gun and began shooting, killing nine of the people in the group. Why did he do it? Because they were black.

These, and other similar incidents, have placed the issue of racial prejudice in the U.S. front and center in policy debates, with impassioned views on both sides.

What does social science have to say about these incidents? Lots of things, but the issue we will focus on here is that the two incidents are different.

The Ferguson Killing

The Ferguson killing, while it may have been unjustified and symptomatic of the police's problematic treatment of blacks, was not, in and of itself, an example of blatant prejudice. The young man who was killed had just robbed a store and had resisted arrest. An argument can be made that the police officer was just doing his job—policing the community. Policing is a difficult job and police officers are allowed by law significant benefit of the doubt. They have to make split-second decisions.

Whether the killing was the result of underlying prejudice is debatable. The officer was white, and the young man was black, and individuals of all races have inherent tendencies to think of young black men as scary, and hence to react differently to black people than they would to whites. In some ways this is natural, since, on a probability basis, young black men are more likely to be threatening than an older black man, a white person, or a young black woman. To pretend that people don't react that way is to pretend that prejudice that exists does not exist.

The debate about such probability-based prejudice is a highly nuanced debate in which there are social scientists on both sides of the issues. There are reasonable arguments on various sides and reasonable differences of opinion about what might be done about it to best deal with it. Social scientists have strongly advocated having more police come from the neighborhoods they police. So what social science says here is that, in drawing conclusions about this incident, one needs to put oneself in the shoes of both people, and to work out how to reform organizations to deal with the inevitable problems that come up.

The Charleston Killing

The Charleston killing is quite different. This killing had no nuance. Here, all social scientists agree—the perpetrator was unjustified and wrong. The perpetrator should be punished, and society should look for ways to eliminate the set of racist beliefs that led him to kill. Ironically, this Charleston killing, which was far more unambiguously an example of racial hatred than the Ferguson killing, did not lead to rioting. The relatives of the victims urged forgiveness and encouraged all people to avoid hate and retaliation. What the perpetrator had hoped would lead to race war instead led to a coming together of all people marching against such racist beliefs. It also led to the Confederate flag, which was seen by many as a symbol of racial hatred, being removed from the South Carolina statehouse, and being placed in a historical museum. Furthermore, it sparked a larger movement to remove Confederate monuments from public spaces in the south. When a statue of Confederate general Robert E. Lee was removed from the grounds of the Virginia statehouse in August 2017, white supremacists protested the action, which they saw as a challenge to their heritage.

who sometimes find themselves the subjects of economic and educational discrimination; and individuals of Middle Eastern descent, whose connections with Islam have subjected them to discrimination as the United States struggles to balance its fight against terrorism with individual liberties.

Minorities

If various groups were different but essentially equal, prejudice and discrimination probably would not be a central concern of social scientists. But as was the case with social and economic stratification, racial and ethnic groups are not viewed equally: **Minority groups** are groups of people singled out for unequal negative treatment and who regard themselves as objects of collective discrimination, and **dominant groups** are groups of people singled out for positive treatment. The term *dominant group* is used rather than *majority* because the dominant group may be a minority, as was the case with white people of European descent in South Africa.

In the remainder of this chapter, we introduce you to the important minority groups in the United States.

Native Americans

The Native Americans were the first settlers of what is now the United States. Although the date is uncertain, most anthropologists believe they came from Asia about 30,000 years ago. After Europeans began to colonize North America, a combination of deadly diseases that ravaged the continent and colonial expansion ensured that Europeans soon outnumbered and eventually conquered the Native American population. Today, they are a relatively small minority, and for a long time they were the most isolated of all minority groups and perhaps the most deprived in education. Recently, Native Americans have taken the initiative in efforts to increase ties with the dominant U.S. culture, to improve their educational and employment opportunities, and in some cases to restore lands taken in the eighteenth and early nineteenth centuries by procedures that Native Americans have attacked in the courts.

The policies of the dominant white population toward Native Americans have undergone changes in the past century from (1) enforced isolation and segregation, to (2) forced integration into U.S. society, with almost disastrous results for Native Americans culturally, economically, and physically, to (3) a policy of much more gradual assimilation. The present government policy toward them is based on the Indian Reorganization Act of 1934, which was designed to encourage Native American tribes to revive their traditions and to manage their own political and economic affairs. Although many Native Americans choose to live on land designated as Native American homeland, they can live where they like; they are U.S. citizens and can vote; they pay certain taxes, and they receive Social Security benefits; they may own private property; and they are free to seek employment anywhere they wish. But they sometimes encounter prejudice and have difficulty in adjusting to the dominant U.S. culture outside of areas designated as Native American lands. Also, some of them are disadvantaged by poor health, a lack of education and skills, and a language barrier. Each of the tribes has its own language or dialect, which usually is very difficult for a person who is not a member of the particular tribe to learn. According to the federal Bureau of Indian Affairs, there were originally about 300 different languages spoken by Native Americans in what is now the United States, and possibly as many as 200 still survive. If in addition the tribe is isolated, the process of assimilation is extremely slow.

Blacks (Americans)[1]

Blacks constitute approximately 45 million people, or about 13.5 percent of the U.S. population. Black Americans are for the most part descendants of slaves brought over to the United States in the seventeenth, eighteenth, and early nineteenth centuries. According to one estimate, at least 14 to 15 million black slaves landed in the Americas (North and South, with a majority sent to sugar plantations in the Caribbean; only 5 percent of slaves were on ships bound for the United States) from 1600 to the latter part of the nineteenth century.

---

[1] Debate continues about whether "African American," "Afro-American," or "people of color" should be substituted for "black." The issue is complicated by the fact that not all black people identify as African Americans (such as in the case of immigrants from the Caribbean).

The African Origins of U.S. Blacks.   The main source of slaves in the seventeenth and eighteenth centuries was the Gulf of Guinea in Africa. This area was more densely populated than most of Africa, and as merchants had already established trade with the outside world in ivory and gold, it was easy to provide slaves as well. The trade routes of the Guinea people were evidence of a relatively advanced culture. Although they were a nonliterate people, the inhabitants of this area were among the leaders of black Africa in agriculture, metalwork, pottery, and sculpture.

Slave trading has a long history. Muslim Berbers and Arabs exported black slaves from Africa as far back as the early 900s. In the fifteenth century, Spain and Portugal imported slaves from Africa, whom they bought from other Africans. The first ship of slaves did not arrive in the territory of what is now the United States until 1619, carrying blacks to Virginia for labor in the British colonies. Plantation owners needed a large force of controllable workers, and black slaves were the answer to this need.

Although importation of slaves to the United States became illegal in 1808, the need for a workforce did not subside, and thousands of slaves were smuggled in despite the laws. These practices continued until the Civil War, when, in 1863, Abraham Lincoln signed the Emancipation Proclamation. Abolitionists were a strong force in the North, but aside from humanitarian concerns, political leaders also saw emancipation as a way to further cripple the South during the war.

The Emancipation Proclamation and the Thirteenth Amendment to the U.S. Constitution changed the legal status of slaves but not their social status. The systematic legal segregation of blacks was promoted by what were called Jim Crow laws,[2] and the voting rights of blacks were effectively blocked in the southern states. White supremacy propaganda became intense and was often accompanied by violence.

Continuing Discrimination against Blacks.   The problems of blacks in the United States today differ from those of any other minority group in this country. To begin with, blacks in the United States are so far removed from their African homeland that much of their cultural heritage is difficult to identify today. Though their cultural patterns may differ somewhat from those of other Americans, they essentially are American by culture, as reflected in their language, customs, education, and religion. But the position of the black minority still is influenced unfavorably by the fact that it is the only minority in this country whose ancestors once served a long period of slavery to whites. No other minority groups have experienced the social and psychological upheavals caused by slavery, followed by sudden emancipation and then by a long period of discrimination and segregation, some of it enforced by law. In addition, blacks tend to differ from whites in skin color, hair, and features more than other

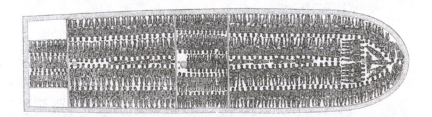

An illustration shows the cramped quarters on a slave ship.

---

[2] The name Jim Crow is thought to have come from a character in a popular minstrel song written by Thomas D. Rice in 1832. It is the name used to describe the system that perpetuated the subordination of blacks in the American South after the abolition of slavery.

*I*vory and Ebony or Evory and Ibony?

Over the years, there has been a considerable amount of mixing of black-skinned and white-skinned people, just as there has been mixing of people with many other different physical attributes. Much of this mixing occurred under slavery when slave owners fathered children by black mothers. The great abolitionist leader Frederick Douglass was the son of a white father and a slave mother. Just how much white ancestry U.S. blacks have cannot be determined with certainty, but some geneticists have attempted to make an estimate.

Most of the ancestors of U.S. blacks came from certain areas in West Africa. By comparing the percentages of the West African natives who carry a certain gene (the

rhesus-factor allele R⁰) with the percentage of U.S. blacks and U.S. whites who carry it, geneticists estimate that, on the average, the ancestry of U.S. blacks is probably about 30 percent white. Other researchers have estimated that about 75 percent of all U.S. blacks have at least one white ancestor.

Similarly, it is estimated that about 25 percent of whites have at least one black ancestor. As intermarriage continues, these percentages will increase, making black- and white-skinned physical characteristics less noticeable. Perhaps, someday we will arrive at a society in which skin color will not comprise an ethnic grouping and will instead be just another physical characteristic on a par with hair color, eye color, and height, and in which it will be just as strange to think of a person as "black" as it is to think of a person as "green-eyed."

minority ethnic groups, and this has contributed to the strong personal prejudice that sometimes exists between whites and blacks.

Although the status of blacks has advanced in many ways in recent decades, they still suffer from prejudice and discrimination and from disadvantages that are the legacy of past discrimination.

Legal Discrimination and Segregation.   We have already described briefly the rise of legal segregation in the South. The constitutionality of the state laws on which it was based was long a matter of dispute because the Fourteenth Amendment to the Constitution of the United States, adopted in 1868, provides that no state may deny any person equal protection under the laws. The question was whether segregation constituted denial of equal protection. Those who attempted to challenge these laws in the courts had no important success until 1954, when the U.S. Supreme Court, in the case of *Brown v. Board of Education,* outlawed segregation in public schools.

The *Brown* decision reversed a decision made by the Court in 1896, when, in the case of *Plessy v. Ferguson,* it had issued a decision approving segregation of blacks and whites by state legislation. The decision in *Plessy* was based on the so-called **separate-but-equal doctrine,** that is, the theory that providing separate educational, recreational, and other public facilities for blacks was not denying equal protection under the laws if these facilities were equal to those for whites. In practice, this equality proved to be a myth.

The *Brown* decision outlawing school segregation opened the way for challenging other segregation laws, and within a decade or so it became clear that they were all unconstitutional. However, the deconstruction of systems of segregation, especially in the case of schools, has proved to be a slow and difficult

Martin Luther King Jr. at the 1963 civil rights march in Washington.

process. Some confusion has resulted from disagreement about whether court decisions and civil rights acts passed by Congress merely annul laws and public policies that require or encourage attendance at segregated schools, or whether they also place an obligation on communities and school boards to take positive measures to eliminate **de facto segregation**—segregation that occurs because of social and cultural, not legal, reasons. **De jure segregation** is segregation based on actual segregation laws.

Since 1954, many major pieces of civil rights legislation have been passed. For example, the Civil Rights Acts of the 1950s and 1960s enforced the voting rights of blacks and prohibited discrimination on the basis of "race" (as was then the terminology), sex, or national origin in public accommodations, federally assisted programs, and housing.

Causes of Blacks' Frustration.   Despite all of this legislation, for many blacks there has been little progress, and the frustration level has at times led to riots and civil disturbances. Their frustration is grounded in both social and economic conditions. Though the economic condition of blacks has, on the average, improved greatly, it has by no means caught up with that of whites. In the early 2000s, blacks earned a median income that was less than 60 percent of that earned by whites.

The reasons for this lower income are complicated and varied. They include discrimination, family structure, age structure, occupation, and education. Blacks make up a higher proportion of the labor force for low-skilled jobs than is proportional to the general population, and a lower percentage of managerial jobs. Additionally, their unemployment rates are higher. Table 13.1a shows that black unemployment rates have consistently remained at higher levels than those of the other major groups (whites and Hispanics). The unemployment rate is especially high among young black males, as can be seen in Table 13.1b.

Much of the problem can be attributed to past and present discrimination against blacks. Discrimination has robbed some blacks of the incentive to acquire the necessary education and training to fill jobs that require not only willingness to work but also more than average skill, training, and education. They believe they will not be given such jobs even if they are qualified to fill them. As a result, to them it makes no sense to acquire marketable skills. To make matters worse, a large proportion of blacks live in neighborhoods where crime is rampant and housing substandard.

The economic and social disadvantages that black people face in the United States today cannot be discussed without touching on the topic of mass incarceration. The fact that one in

Table 13.1a

Unemployment among Races, 1975–2018

YEAR	ALL ETHNIC GROUPS (%)	WHITE (%)	BLACK (%)	HISPANIC (%)
1975	8.5	7.8	14.8	Not available
1980	7.1	6.3	14.3	10.1
1985	7.3	6.5	14.0	10.6
1990	5.5	5.1	12.0	8.7
1995	5.6	4.9	10.4	9.3
2000	4.0	3.9	8.5	7.0
2005	5.1	4.4	10.0	7.1
2010	9.6	8.7	16.0	12.5
2015	5.2	4.5	9.5	6.5
2018	3.8	3.4	6.1	4.5

Source: U.S. Bureau of Labor and Statistics, *Employment and Earnings*.

Table 13.1b

Male Unemployment by Age Group, 2018 (third quarter)

AGE GROUP	WHITE (%)	BLACK (%)
16–19	12.1	25.3
20–24	6.2	11.3
25–34	2.9	6.2
35–44	2.1	5.2
45–54	2.1	4.4
55–64	2.4	4.0
65 and over	3.4	5.5

Source: U.S. Bureau of Labor and Statistics, CPS.

three black men will go to prison in their lifetime compounds many of the problems already affecting that community, such as unemployment and family instability. This system, and other systems of discrimination, have hampered the development of the black community.

Progress toward Equality.   Notwithstanding these problems, the average economic condition of blacks has improved. Many blacks have moved into career-level and skilled jobs. The major credit for the job advancement of blacks should probably go to those individuals among them who have had the ambition and the willingness to acquire education and training. But they have been helped by organized efforts to give blacks far greater opportunities than were available to them in the past. These efforts are made by government agencies, colleges and universities, corporations, and various other private groups, including some organized by blacks themselves. They range from trying to train the hard-core unemployed for specific jobs to providing qualified blacks with scholarships or fellowships for advanced study.

In the past, a significant factor in restricting the economic progress of blacks has been discrimination by labor unions, many of which refused to accept them as members. Some still strongly resist admission of blacks, but the number of unions that discriminate is declining. Construction trade unions in large cities have been especially slow in accepting black apprentices except in token numbers, but under pressure they are adopting more liberal policies.

In the past, black business people or professionals were generally limited to their own community as the market for their services. Today the situation is changing. Many corporations are actively seeking qualified blacks to fill professional or administrative positions. This is not always easy, because there are still relatively few blacks with good college training and even fewer with degrees from graduate or professional schools, and the competition to hire them is sometimes intense. But progress is being made, and black enrollment in college and professional schools has risen significantly in the past decades.

From 1960 to 2015, the percentage of blacks completing four years of college rose from about 3.5 percent to over 20 percent; the percentage of blacks completing high school rose from 23 percent to over 90 percent. In addition, as black political power has grown and the demands for equality have mounted, more and more professional and administrative jobs have been opened to blacks in public institutions such as hospitals, schools, and state and local government agencies.

Part of the reason for this increase was **affirmative action programs,** programs designed to favor minority groups as a way to prevent and compensate for the effects of racial discrimination. Such programs came under attack beginning in the late 1990s and early 2000s. For example, in California and Texas, affirmative action programs were overturned by the courts and replaced by need-based and race-neutral programs. As a result, the number of blacks in higher education decreased. This decline has led to the development of programs that seek diversity in other ways, such as admitting a certain percentage of the top students from public high schools. Though this has boosted minority enrollments, many college officials remain opposed to ending affirmative action.

Affirmative action continues to be a hot topic in the United States. Much of the debate concerns precisely what is meant by affirmative action and how it translates into policies. Does it justify numerical quotas, and, if so, what is the nature of those quotas? Does it require that race be the major factor in decision making, or does it simply allow race to be considered as one of the factors in decisions? And if it allows a consideration of race, how much weight can be given to race? Does it require or allow that specific preferences be given to minority groups (and if so, how strong can those preferences be), or must all groups be treated equally?

As an example of the issues that can arise, let's consider the college admission program at the University of Texas. That program was changed after its affirmative action program, which gave specific preferences to blacks, was one of the programs that the courts struck down. (Its program giving specific preferences to football players or to legacies—children of alumni—in admissions was not struck down.) In response, the University of Texas decided to allow automatic admission to the top 10 percent of all Texas high school students. Because many of the inner-city high schools in Texas are predominantly black and, on average, score low on standardized tests, whereas suburban high schools are predominantly white and, on average, score high on standardized tests, this new program gave blacks an advantage compared to their chances of admission if only test scores had been considered. Was this new program allowable under an affirmative action plan that used a "top 10 percent" standard, or did it represent a strategy to avoid the accusation that the schools were still giving preference to blacks? Even if it were allowable, is it desirable? (There were stories about some whites transferring into inner-city schools so that they would get admitted to the University of Texas.) The bigger question is: What is reasonable discretion in admissions (discretion similar to the allowable attempt of colleges to have a geographic diversity in their student body) and what is unreasonable discretion when it comes to race? Many such issues will have to be dealt with in the near future.

Another example involved the University of Michigan, where applicants were selected on the basis of points. Applicants were given 20 points for being black and 20 points for attending a predominantly minority high school, out of a total of 150 points. (SAT scores accounted for only 12 points.) Was this too much of a preference, and, if so, what would not be too much? When thinking about an answer to this, consider also that legacies, who are generally white and well-off, were given 1 to 4 points for their alumni relationships. Was that too much, and, if so, what would not be too much? The U.S. Supreme Court, which has the ultimate power to make these decisions in the United States, decided that, at an undergraduate level, the points for black students were too much like affirmative action. However, it held that colleges could take race into account in their admission decisions, thereby legalizing affirmative action. Future decisions may, however, be different. The reason it is difficult to predict what the Court will decide is because the Court's composition changes over time, as judges retire and are replaced by others with different judicial philosophies. The death of Justice Scalia in 2016 is an example. He was a conservative justice, and President Obama nominated a moderate justice to replace him. Republicans refused to take up his nomination, hoping that in the 2016 election, a Republican president would be elected, who would nominate another conservative justice to replace him. Their strategy paid off, and in 2017 a new conservative justice picked by President Donald Trump, Neil Gorsuch, was sworn in to the Supreme Court.

Eliminating the Vestiges of Discrimination. When we consider the extent to which discrimination against blacks prevailed throughout this country from early colonial times to World War II, the progress toward equal treatment since that war has been substantial, even though it has fallen far short of the hopes and expectations of many. Segregation in the armed forces, formerly the unchallenged rule in all branches of the service, was completely abandoned as a policy by the mid-1950s. Discrimination against blacks in hotels, motels, restaurants, and other public places has been virtually eliminated, partly because of changes in public attitudes and partly because of laws forbidding it. To be sure, not all the subtler forms of discrimination have disappeared, but at least they are on the defensive.

Another area in which discrimination against blacks has been reduced is in the right to buy property. Formerly, the purchaser of a house might be required to sign a restrictive covenant in which he or she agreed not to rent or sell to members of specified racial or cultural groups. This covenant sometimes made it impossible for blacks to buy or rent housing except in overcrowded black neighborhoods that were often slums. But in 1948, the Supreme Court ruled that restrictive covenants are contrary to public policy and may not be enforced by the courts. In 1968, Congress passed a Fair Housing Act prohibiting racial discrimination in the sale or rental of about 80 percent of all housing, and in the same year the Supreme Court interpreted an 1866 federal law as banning racial discrimination in the sale or rental of any housing. Although these actions have not completely eliminated discrimination in the sale of housing, they have made it difficult, especially for real estate firms.

One place where social scientists have found significant discrimination against blacks is in entry-level jobs and low-skilled positions. Researchers had young high school graduates with similar job histories apply for the same jobs. Thirty-four percent of the white applicants were called back; 14 percent of the blacks were called back. In another experiment, social scientists had fictitious individuals apply for jobs online. Some had white-sounding names, such as Greg Kelly, and some had more African American names, such as Jamal Jackson. They found that the white-sounding names received many more callbacks and that the white-sounding name was worth approximately eight years of experience, meaning that a person with a black-sounding name had to have eight years' more experience to have the same callback rate as an otherwise similar white. The discrimination was even greater when both black and white applicants had criminal records; in the first experiment, a black person with a criminal record had only a 5 percent chance of getting a callback, whereas a white person with a criminal record had a 17 percent chance of getting a callback. Since almost one in five of all black men have served some time, this presents a serious problem for integrating them back into the community.

Black-White Social Relations.   In his classic book, *An American Dilemma,* economist Gunnar Myrdal observed that the area of strongest white prejudice against blacks had to do with intermarriage and other intimate social contacts. This seems still to be true. The great majority of whites believe that blacks should have equality of opportunity in employment, housing, education, health facilities, and legal rights, but many of them are still uneasy about intermarriage (just as many blacks are) and often are awkward in developing close social contacts.

Among some groups, especially in the younger generation, there is a trend toward breaking down the obstacles to social contacts between the races, including those barriers to interracial marriages. After World War II, more than half of our states had laws prohibiting marriage between a white person and anyone defined legally as a "Negro," but in 1967 the Supreme Court ruled that no state may ban interracial marriages. Still, today only about 9 percent of all marriages are interracial. This is up from 3.2 percent in 1980. That statistic overstates the change in attitude about black/white marriages; less than one fifth of those interracial marriages are between blacks and whites, and the avoidance of black-white interracial marriage, from both whites and blacks, is still strong.

Children tend to have little inherent prejudice.

© Christopher Futcher/iStock

Discrimination occurs not only between blacks and whites but also among blacks, with darker-skinned blacks called derogatory names and treated differently by lighter-skinned blacks. Moreover, the discrimination that does occur by whites seems to be more pronounced the darker the skin the black person has. In a study of brothers from the same family who differed by skin color, it was found that the lighter-skinned brothers tended to have higher incomes and experience less discrimination.

In 2008, the United States made a major step forward in race relations with the election of a light-skinned black president with a very African name—Barack Obama. That election was, to many, an indication that the United States had come a long way in solving the race problem. But, as can be seen in the continuing racial tension, it has a long way to go.

Ultimately, we will know that the race problem has been solved if bringing home a black fiancée to a white family, or bringing home a white fiancée to a black family, raises no more eyebrows than bringing a blonde fiancée home to a brunette's family, or a brunette fiancée home to a blonde's family.

The Future of Black Americans.   In the early 1960s, some twenty years after he had completed *An American Dilemma,* Gunnar Myrdal was asked if he foresaw any solution to our race problems. He replied, "Well, you can find solutions to technical problems; but in social problems, particularly those that are so intrinsically difficult and mixed up as the [black] problem, there is no solution in an absolute sense."

In his study, Myrdal called the race problem in the United States a white problem because the whites are the great majority and hold the bulk of wealth and power. He saw progress by blacks to be dependent on white cooperation; on a lifting of the bars of discrimination. But it is clear that even if all whites (and blacks) could quickly and completely rid themselves of ethnic prejudice, it would still take time for blacks as a group to overcome completely all the effects of generations of slavery followed by decades of extreme discrimination.

Some have even argued that blacks are owed reparations for the injustices of the past, and that such reparations are necessary to achieve equality. They have collected information about companies' and universities' pasts and have shown that a number of them profited from the slave trade and oppression of blacks. They argue that companies and universities need to repay those profits to the descendants of those slaves. Others argue that reparations are precisely the wrong way to achieve equality, since reparations are unlikely to achieve significant results from a practical point of view. To hold people today accountable for wrongs of their ancestors is a highly tenuous proposition. Trying to do so will move the debate away from the more important issue of how to provide better opportunities for blacks now and in the future. Regardless of what is decided about reparations, no group can give equality to another group except in the sense of treating its members fairly and sympathetically and helping to provide them with opportunities. No disadvantaged people of any race will achieve equality with the average citizen merely by being given jobs for which they are not qualified or by being admitted to colleges whose academic standards they cannot meet. They can, however, be offered opportunities for job training and, if they have the will and ability, chances to make up for academic deficiencies.

The debate over what to do about inequality has manifested itself in the debate about affirmative action programs. Advocates of affirmative action programs argue that such programs are necessary to offset past discrimination. Critics charge that such programs are unfair both to the minorities and to whites. They say that affirmative action programs place blacks in situations for which they are unqualified and that preference for blacks discriminates against needy whites.

As we stated earlier, in response to criticism some states such as Texas and California have started substituting "need" for "race" and "gender" as the determining factor for preferential treatment. For instance, in 1996 California passed a law designed "to abolish affirmative action." According to this law, "The state shall not discriminate against, or grant preferential treatment to, any individual or group on the basis of race, sex, color, ethnicity, or national origin in the operation of public employment, public education, or public contracting." This statement of forced neutrality abolished previous legislation that had favored preferential treatment for minorities and women, in addition to other types of affirmative action. Other states are considering similar legislation.

Eliminating affirmative action on the basis of skin color will not necessarily mean an end to giving preference to blacks; it will simply be preference not solely based on skin color, so a white child and a black child of upper-middle-class families will be treated equally. However, because many blacks are poor and come from backgrounds without a strong focus on education, they, along with whites from similar backgrounds, can be given preference in admissions and hiring because, to achieve what they have, they had to overcome greater obstacles than a person from a rich, pro-education background.

It is doubtful whether ethnic prejudice and discrimination can be completely eliminated as long as blacks constitute a distinct ethnic group in our society. Discrimination is inherent to some degree in most social relationships all over the world. It occurs in the contacts between individuals, between individuals and groups, and between groups of many types, including families. But, in the view of the textbook authors, to deny to an entire ethnic or cultural

DWB and Racial Profiling

A black man is much more likely to be pulled over when driving a car than is a white man. In fact, it has occurred so often that it has acquired a name—driving while black (DWB). The issues are complicated and have no easy answer. Our society has decided that profiling by police is wrong, and some of the most egregious racial profiling, in which police didn't even need a presumption that the person being stopped might have done something wrong, has ended. But, even with these policies being prohibited, a young black male will be stopped by police much more often than a young white male, especially if the young black man is "looking suspicious"—for example, wearing a hoodie. Society develops stereotypes and people react to stereotypes, not to individuals. That's the point Hillary Clinton was trying to make when she said, "if we're honest, for a lot of well-meaning, open-minded white people, the sight of a young black man in a hoodie still evokes a twinge of fear." To that she might have added that it isn't only whites who find some young black men scary; it is also blacks and Americans of other races. The question is: How does society deal with that fear?

The social science answer to this problem is not a direct answer, but a set of indirect suggestions. The first is that we should be open about our views, and not hide them. Lack of communication can lead to serious misunderstandings. It is hard to be a police officer, just as it is hard to be a young teenager. Discussions that encourage people to reflect on their natural proclivity to make quick, often inappropriate judgments about others on the basis of the physical characteristics can make them more aware that they do it, and reduce their tendency to do it.

The second is that there should be as much informal social interaction of police with the people they are policing as possible. Informal social interaction provides both the police and the public with a knowledge of the culture and the problems the other group faces. One city started having police issue "good deed" tickets to young people, in which, when a police officer observes a young person doing a good deed, he or she issues a "ticket" that the young person can redeem for a small present.

The third is that, wherever possible, police should come from the same cultures of the geographic area that they police. If the person you are stopping reminds you of your son or your neighbor, you may still stop and question the person, but you will likely treat them a little bit differently.

Finally, both sides should be respectful of the other. Young blacks should recognize that the police's job is to enforce the law, and that, in doing that job, sometimes they have to stop and question people. Police should recognize that they are often disproportionately checking young black males, and that doing so is unpleasant and degrading for the person. They should treat them with deferential respect and not enjoy the power being a police officer gives them. One social scientist suggested that whenever a police officer stops someone in search of a suspect, and it turns out not to be the suspect, that he or she not only should give the person an apology for inconveniencing them, but that he or she should also give them a coupon for a free milkshake at a local restaurant to partially compensate the person stopped for the inconvenience. Perhaps young black men could also be provided with coupons that they could give to police who treat them with appropriate respect.

Hispanics are the fastest-growing minority in the United States.

group equal civil rights and equal educational, political, and economic opportunities is a type of discrimination that a society should not tolerate.

Hispanics

The largest minority group in the United States is **Hispanics,** or individuals of Spanish-speaking origin. From 1988 to 2000, the Hispanic population in the United States more than doubled, and from 2000 to 2012 it grew even faster. In 2019 about 61 million U.S. citizens (more than 18 percent of the population) identified themselves as having historical links to Spain. Of the total number, about 67 percent gave Mexico as their family's place of origin, about 9 percent gave Puerto Rico, about 4 percent gave El Salvador, and the remainder gave other Latin American countries. The majority of Hispanics, over 65 percent, are second-generation and now tend to have higher birthrates, so their role in the United States will likely become more important in the future. Immigration, both legal and illegal, has been an important part of Hispanic population growth, and in 2016 there were about 11.3 million undocumented immigrants in the United States, about 70 percent of whom were Hispanic.

Mexican Americans make up the largest of all Hispanic minority groups and they are one of our most rapidly growing groups. Because of their high birthrate, a large proportion of them are young. Four out of five Mexican Americans live in the Southwest. The great majority are concentrated in Texas and California, but substantial numbers are also found in Arizona, New Mexico, and Colorado. Many immigrants from Mexico are migrant workers who depend upon moving seasonally from place to place to find work. The U.S. economy's high demand for workers in states such as Iowa, Kansas, and Georgia has meant that in the 1990s and early 2000s many Mexican Americans moved to those states. In fact, many farms throughout the United States have come to rely on undocumented Mexican immigrants because of the Mexicans' willingness to work for lower wages and do harder jobs than U.S. workers. Although some are of Spanish descent, most are of mixed Spanish and indigenous ancestry. They tend to live in segregated residential areas, to retain their own customs, and to continue to speak Spanish. They often lack the level of education of their neighbors of other races, and their parents often do not speak English fluently (although children who were born here do). In states where there has been a large influx of immigrants in recent years, they sometimes are discriminated against not only by the long-established population but also by Mexicans who have been in the country longer than the newest arrivals. All these factors work together to slow their economic and social progress.

Though many Mexican Americans still live in the Southwest and are employed in agriculture, and a relatively small number of them are still migrants, the great majority—close to 85 percent—live in urban areas, where they sometimes form small colonies. In cities, Mexican Americans work in many job areas, but as yet relatively few are found in high-ranking occupations. As a group, their incomes are much lower than those of white Americans of European descent. But like the descendants of earlier immigrant groups, some are finding their way up the social and economic ladder, and today about 34 percent of them hold white-collar jobs.

Asian Descent

In 2019 about 20 million people of Asian descent lived in the United States. They have spread throughout the country, but most live in large cities. Despite prejudice against them, many of them have done well both financially and socially.

Ethnic Chinese.   Immigrants from China first came to this country in large numbers when gold was discovered in California. In the single year of 1852, some 20,000 were admitted. They worked as cooks and launderers and as laborers in the mines. When the gold rush was over, many of them were employed in building the western portion of the transcontinental railroad. They also spread out into occupations such as agriculture and fishing. But to the white settlers, they were strange and unwelcome. As their numbers grew, antagonism increased and they endured many types of discrimination. There were even riots in which they were chased through the streets and beaten or lynched. Part of this antagonism resulted from competition for jobs. Chinese workers were willing to live on very little and, if forced to do so, would work for extremely low wages. Finally, in 1882 Congress passed the Chinese Exclusion Act, which virtually suspended all Chinese immigration until it was repealed in 1943.

In 1965, a revision of immigration laws ended discrimination against the Chinese and the immigrants from all other countries by abolishing quotas based on national origin. Due in part to U.S. response to the upheavals in Southeast Asia that began at least as early as 1970, immigration laws have undergone several subsequent liberalizations, especially for highly trained individuals. Immigration law is complex, but at the present time we can say that it has permitted a significant increase in the number of Chinese and Southeast Asian immigrants to the United States.

Japanese Ethnic Descent.   After Congress passed the Chinese Exclusion Act, the Japanese began arriving on the West Coast in increasing numbers. Most of them settled in California, and before long they, like the Chinese before them, began to encounter prejudice and discrimination. As with the Chinese, the feeling against them was partly based on conflicting economic interests. Many Japanese became truck gardeners (growers of fresh vegetables), and because whole families were willing to work hard and live on very little, the native California truck gardeners complained that they could not meet Japanese competition. Also, it was argued that the strong loyalty of the Japanese to their homeland made assimilation impossible.

During World War II, anti-Japanese sentiment came to a head. The U.S. government forcibly moved 117,000 people of Japanese birth or ancestry away from the West Coast to relocation centers further inland. This move was explained as a security measure, but it is now generally recognized as an inexcusable injustice, for removal was not based on disloyalty but only on national origin, and it meant gross discrimination against thousands of loyal U.S. citizens. Furthermore, these citizens were deprived of their civil liberties, having been forcibly taken from their homes and detained in camps that differed little from military barracks. In 1945, the evacuation order was rescinded, but many Japanese did not return to the West Coast, preferring to live in areas where prejudice against them was less marked.

In recent years, prejudice against the Japanese has greatly diminished. In 1988, the U.S. government finally apologized to the surviving Japanese Americans who had been interned and agreed to pay each of them $20,000.

Other Asian Ethnic Groups.   Over the years, there have been varying numbers of other Asian immigrants. In the 1970s, hundreds of thousands of Vietnamese immigrants were allowed into the United States to escape political oppression in their native country. More recently, many highly trained Indians, Pakistanis, and other Southeast Asians have been allowed in because of a shortage of workers in high-tech fields. In a number of high-tech companies, foreign-born workers outnumber U.S.-born workers.

A U.S. Gulag?

On February 11, 1942, U.S. authorities began rounding up Japanese Americans and shipping them to internment camps simply because of their Japanese heritage. Fear that these Americans would support Japan in that country's war with the United States was the ostensible cause, but anger at the Japanese attack on Pearl Harbor in Hawaii on December 7, 1941, and ethnic prejudice were major unstated reasons. Although these internment camps were far more humane than the Soviet Gulag, in which prisoners were inhumanely treated and in which millions died, the fact that the U.S. government created these camps at all is considered a travesty by many. Just as angry people often strike out in vengeance without thinking, angry societies sometimes strike out in revenge and ignorance.

Asian American immigration has been highly self-selective. It has primarily consisted of highly educated individuals who have found it relatively easy to succeed in the United States. Often they have taken low-level jobs that only had loosely regulated working conditions, and they have worked hard to advance. For example, many Indians worked in motels and then, having learned the business and saved enough money, bought the motels and thus provided jobs for new Indian immigrants. Today, many local motels are owned by people of Indian descent. The same is true of doughnut shops and some other occupations; for example, most doughnut shops in California are owned by Indians.

The success of Asian Americans has led to the stereotype of them as a "model minority." Thus, even though they are a minority, they attend top schools in greater numbers and often achieve better results than other groups, including whites. Thus, to maintain diversity, some colleges, especially those located in areas with a large Asian population, discriminate against Asian Americans by making it more difficult for them to get accepted into those colleges. This leads to complaints of unfairness; not all Asian Americans are rich, educated, and successful.

Arab Americans and Americans of Middle Eastern Descent

The last minority we will discuss is Arab Americans, of whom there are more than 3.5 million, over 90 percent of whom live in urban areas. As a group, Arab Americans have done relatively well, and their average incomes are 22 percent higher than the U.S. national average. Traditional multicultural efforts often overlook this ethnic group, though they face stereotyping and prejudice. The first wave of immigration of Arabs from the Middle East took place between 1875 and 1920. Most of these early Arab immigrants were from Lebanon and Syria; most were Christians seeking economic opportunities. Immigration then slowed as the United States began imposing restrictions. The second wave began in the 1940s because of the Arab-Israeli conflict and regional civil wars; this group came from a much more diverse area, and many practiced Islam. But like the earlier group, most were more financially secure when they came.

The 2000s were particularly difficult for Arab Americans. Because the 9/11 terrorists were of Middle Eastern descent, many Arab Americans have been subject to discrimination and prejudice, even though almost all of them strongly condemn the terrorists and consider themselves Americans. Although they may feel that U.S. policy in the Middle East is tilted in Israel's favor, that is a feeling shared with many other Americans, and with many individuals throughout the world, and is in no way unpatriotic. New Arab American immigrants are especially singled out. The U.S. government has implemented a mandatory registration for nonimmigrant aliens from the Arab and Muslim world. They are also profiled and subject to special surveillance by law enforcement. Thus, the "crackdown" on terrorism created discrimination toward Arab Americans in travel, housing, and educational and work opportunities. Whether that discrimination was a necessary side effect of the government's need to provide security, or was an unacceptable form of discrimination, is currently debated.

Immigration and Minorities

In the early 1900s, when immigration into the United States reached its peak, some 1 million persons were arriving every year, the great majority from Europe. Nationalities tended to group together. For a while, they became isolated islands of culture, continuing among themselves to speak their own language and to perpetuate their own traditions. At first, most immigrants took unskilled jobs and occupied the lowest place in the class structure, consequently pushing into the upper classes a larger proportion of older immigrant residents than might otherwise have been occupying the lowest place themselves. These older residents had the advantage of being more integrated into and comfortable in American society earlier, as a result of which they not only knew the language and customs, but also in many cases had accumulated property.

Undocumented immigrants sometimes die during their attempts to sneak into the United States.

In some ways, the situation of European immigrants was like that of a minority ethnic group. The difference lay in the fact that although most second- and third-generation individuals from ethnic groups were still set apart and considered unassimilable no matter how Americanized they became, those from the Caucasian nationality groups had little trouble, in a generation or two, in identifying as a part of American society.

Restrictions on Immigration.   Until 1890, most immigrants to the United States were from northwestern Europe. Then immigration from southern and eastern Europe began to grow, and Mexican immigration also increased. Many "old" Americans, and even some of the earlier immigrants, were strongly prejudiced against southern and eastern Europeans. Demands for restrictive legislation led to laws limiting immigration.

In 1921, the first **Immigration Quota Act,** designed to reduce immigration to specified annual quotas for each national group, was passed. The quota for each country was 3 percent of the number of people living in the United States in 1910 who were of that national origin. The effect of this legislation was a sharp reduction in immigration from the countries of central, eastern, and southern Europe. Later, the quotas were reduced, and in 1924 the maximum total number of immigrants to be admitted annually was cut to 150,000. The quota laws did not apply to countries in the Western hemisphere.

During the years following World War II, Congress passed various immigration acts to admit considerable numbers of immigrants over and above the quotas. Most of these were Europeans displaced from their homes by World War II or by the 1956 Hungarian rebellion against communist rule. Later, as we have already mentioned, Cuban and Asian refugees were admitted under special legislation.

But in 1965, under pressure from people who considered our immigration laws discriminatory, Congress passed an act that provided for the complete abandonment of national quotas by mid-1968. Under this act, admittance is based not on national origin but on the U.S. need for the training or skills of a would-be immigrant. Various special immigration laws applying to groups such as Cubans, Southeast Asians, Irish, and political refugees have been passed since 1965. In addition, many classes of immigrants are exempt from any numerical limitations—such as immediate relatives of U.S. citizens. The change in the composition of immigration can be seen in Figure 13.1.

In 1989, the United States again changed the quotas, cutting the number of Asians allowed and increasing the number of people from the former Soviet Socialist Republics. These actions created a political stir. In 1990, Congress overhauled the immigration laws, raising the quota of immigrants by nearly 50 percent and allowing entry for a larger percentage of immigrants who were not related to U.S. citizens. It also created 30,000 slots for wealthy foreigners of any origin who would guarantee that they would invest at least $1 million in the United States. This led to charges that the United States was selling U.S. citizenship.

In 1997, the Illegal Immigrant Reform and Immigrant Responsibility Act went into effect. It substantially deliberalizes the conditions under which a U.S. citizen or legal resident can sponsor a would-be immigrant and makes permanent residency much harder to achieve than under the older laws. It also increases the requirements for various formal certificates, such as birth and marriage, that an immigrant has to meet. This legislation makes it harder for immigrants to comply with the formalities of the law, and directs employers to investigate before giving a job to an immigrant. Currently, the Trump administration is lobbying congress to move away from

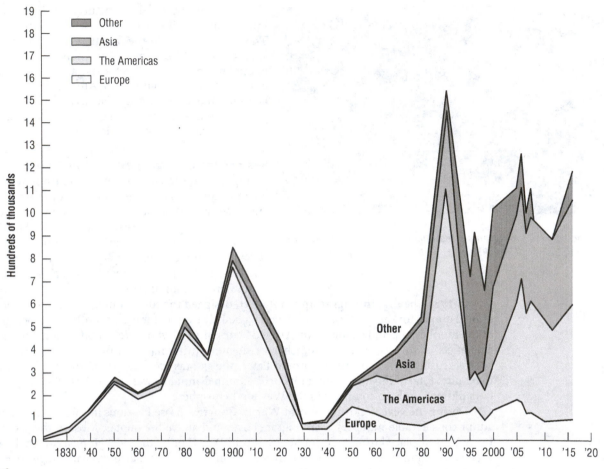

Figure 13.1

Legal immigrants by continent, 1820 to 2016. The large jump in 1990 is due to the legalization of many Mexican immigrants (later years on the time axis are extended for easier viewing of recent changes). (Source: U.S. Bureau of the Census, Statistical Abstract of the United States; Yearbook of Immigration Statistics)

the current immigration system, in which a majority of legal immigrants entering the United States every year are family members of immigrants who have already established themselves here. President Trump calls this process, whereby legal immigrants can apply to bring their immediate family members to the United States after they themselves have received citizenship, "chain migration," and argues that it is not bringing the "best" immigrants to the United States. Instead, he hopes to create a merit-based immigration system, in which a majority of immigrants would be people deemed to be of high value to our society, such as doctors, engineers, and technology developers.

The effectiveness of our immigration laws, especially when we consider that some seem to conflict with others, has been questioned. First, their application and enforcement have not been consistent: Leverage can and has been exerted for individuals or small groups. Second, the crucial task of controlling illegal entry along our long northern and southern borders and the approaches by sea (not to mention exotic tactics, such as parachuting) is a formidable one for the available authorities. Even legal admissions are difficult to enforce because there is insufficient monitoring of students and other visitors to see that they comply with the restrictions of their visas or do not outstay their permissions.

Dealing with Unauthorized Immigrants. As of 2016 there were about 11.3 million undocumented aliens who live in the United States, a number somewhat lower than its peak in 2007. The decline is due to the recession of 2008–2012 and laws that have limited the hiring of undocumented workers. About 40 percent of undocumented immigrants have entered the country legally but outstayed their visas; the others primarily are unauthorized Mexicans. This 11.3 million does not include those immigrants folded into the population when in 1986 the United States passed legislation imposing more restrictions on new illegal immigration while at the same time making provisions for legitimizing the status of some of the 2.7 million aliens already illegally living and working in the United States at that time. This law legalized a large group of formerly undocumented aliens, but also made employers subject to penalties for employing illegal aliens. The resulting large one-time jump in the number of naturalized citizens from Mexico is evident in Figure 13.1.

The 1986 law had limited success. After the passage of the law, illegal Mexican immigration initially held constant. However, then it started increasing, and it increased until the 2007 recession, as the demand for low-wage workers in the United States was high. President Trump's election and policies brought immigration to the forefront of politics. President Obama had issued an Executive Order, called the Deferred Action for Childhood Arrivals (DACA) Order that directed officials not to enforce immigration laws for children brought here illegally and had been here for a long time, and to offer them temporary work permits and protection from deportation. Trump ended the program in September 2017 and told Congress that they would have to pass legislation to extend DACA. This led to political and legal fights, which will likely continue for years. In the meantime DACA immigrants are allowed to work and stay, but they face significant uncertainty.

Religious Minorities

A number of religious groups in this country espouse beliefs that lead them to follow ways of life somewhat different from the general pattern of U.S. culture. These include sects such as the Amish, the Seventh-Day Adventists, and the Jehovah's Witnesses. But their total number is small. At one time, Mormons could have been included, but after they officially abandoned polygamy, they became, in their relation to U.S. culture, not very different from any other Christian sect.

Jews, however, form an important minority group whose influence on our society is greater than their numbers alone would seem to indicate. We have already considered the nature of Judaism in Chapter 9, but we will take up here a brief discussion of anti-Semitism. Prejudice or severe discrimination against Jews, called anti-Semitism, has existed for centuries and has been very strong in certain countries at certain periods. Sometimes it has been tied to religion; sometimes it has been rationalized by dislike on the part of the majority of the population for certain cultural or "racial" characteristics, largely imaginary, attributed to Jews as a group. In some parts of eastern Europe, anti-Semitism has at times been taken to such extremes that thousands of Jews were killed, as in the pogroms, or organized massacres, that occurred in czarist Russia. But it was in Nazi Germany that anti-Semitism reached its height, for Jews constituted 6 million of the more than 10 million people who were murdered in Adolf Hitler's concentration camps.

Anti-Semitism continues to exist, although in the United States it has slowly diminished, perhaps in part because it was overshadowed by the greater problem of black-white relations. But in recent years, some Jews have felt that the level of prejudice was rising. Two factors may have contributed to this. First, when the new nation of Israel was established and conflict with the Arabs began, the majority of Jews were drawn together by a sense of pride, and many gave their full support to Israel. Often non-Jews do not share their sentiments. Second, as blacks have increased their demands for equality, some of them have tended to identify the Jewish merchant in the black ghetto as the symbol of white oppression.

Leading up to the 2016 election, the growth of the conservative movement calling itself the "alt-right" led to a resurgence of anti-Semitic rhetoric in the United States. Energized by the success of Donald Trump's presidential campaign, the people of the alt-right movement began making their anti-Semitic views known on a larger scale, resulting in white supremacist rallies and even the vandalism of Jewish graveyards in the days after Trump won the election in November 2016.

In spite of such developments there is no clear evidence that in the country as a whole anti-Semitism is increasing. The long-term trend appears to be in the other direction. Intermarriage seems to be more and more common, although, according to polls taken in recent years, Jewish opposition to it has fluctuated. The majority of people claiming Judaism as their religion are ethnically Jewish, but Judaism has come more and more to denote a cultural classification as opposed to a racial one. Thus, as the ethnic composition of Jewish people may become less and less concentrated, this does not necessarily mean that Jewishness itself will become diluted as well. On the contrary, because Jewish cultural identity is not dependent upon Jewish ethnic identity, it is unlikely that Jews will lose their identity as a separate cultural group any time soon, despite trends such as intermarriage.

Another religious minority that has been experiencing discrimination is the Muslim population. Although we discussed discrimination against some Muslims earlier, it is important to remember that not all Arabs are Muslims and not all Muslims are Arabs. The Muslim population, estimated to be about 3.5 million, is diverse, with only about 12.5 percent ethnically Arab. A large percentage of Muslims are also blacks; they make up over 40 percent of all U.S. Muslims. The next largest percentage is South Asians at about 25 percent. Muslims can be found in every state, with the largest numbers in California and New York. Since 2001, many U.S. citizens have associated Islam (the religion of Muslims) with terrorism, even though only a minuscule percentage of Muslims are terrorists. But all too often in recent times Muslims are judged guilty by association.

An example of an issue that the United States is currently grappling with regarding discrimination against Muslims is President Trump's travel ban. Initially implemented in the first days of his presidency in early 2017, Trump's travel ban aimed to reduce the threat that terrorism posed to the United States by prohibiting entry to individuals coming from countries deemed to be sources of terrorism. The first ban was almost immediately blocked in federal court, because a judge deemed it to discriminate against Muslims since all the countries under the travel ban were majority Muslim. Trump then modified the travel ban so that it included some non-Muslim countries, and the revised travel ban met court approval.

Although discrimination on the basis of religion exists in the United States, relative to many other countries, the United States has a fairly good record. In China, a Christian is subject to persecution by the state. Even more severe persecution occurs in some Islamic countries. In Iran, for example, a person who converts from Islam to another religion may be subject to the death penalty.

Women

In today's society, the roles of men and women differ: Women are in some ways subordinated to men. Thus, although women make up a majority of the U.S. population, given this subordinate position, they still are often referred to as a minority. Whether this subordinate position is acceptable is up to each one of us to decide, but in making that decision, we must be aware of the facts.

One fact is that our society has decided that discrimination is not legally allowed on the basis of sex, age, ethnicity, or national origin. Despite the law, there is still discrimination against women. This discrimination takes many forms. Sometimes it is disguised as protection: Women are not allowed to do

Pornography treating women as objects.

things because they are perceived as *the weaker sex;* the prohibition against women serving in combat in almost all of the armed forces was an example that only recently ended. Other times, the discrimination is built into the way men treat women—as objects rather than as human beings; most pornography is a good example. Still other times the discrimination is in women's access to jobs: The perception that firms have of women's abilities often differs from the reality. The list goes on. We cannot provide a comprehensive list of the various practices of discrimination, partly because our space is limited and partly because the perception of discrimination varies from individual to individual.

To deal with this complex, subtle discrimination, many people supported a constitutional amendment, the **Equal Rights Amendment (ERA),** which stated simply: "Equality of rights under the laws shall not be denied or abridged . . . on account of sex." It needed ratification by three-fourths of the states, which it did not receive. Supporters point out that the state legislatures that defeated this amendment, and all state legislatures, were overwhelmingly staffed by males. (This should not overshadow the fact that women played a key role in the defeat of the ERA, with many conservative female voices helping to convince those state legislators that it was not in women's best interests for the amendment to be ratified.)

History of the Women's Movement. We can trace the women's movement, sometimes called feminism, a belief in the equality of the sexes, at least as far back as the early nineteenth century. In the late 1800s and early 1900s, the suffragist movement continued its work. Women whose primary aim in the women's movement was to win the right to vote were called suffragettes. The women won this campaign in 1920. During World Wars I and II, women were called on to assume many of the tasks that had been assigned to men until the men were called into military service, such as working in factories, and many women enjoyed their new role. They found it difficult and, indeed, absurd to give up the freedoms they had won just because the wars ended and the men came home. But, as can be seen in the movie *Rosie the Riveter,* the government exerted strong pressure on women to resume their so-called proper role at home and to give up their jobs to men.

The principal permanent achievement marking women's contributions in World War I is the passage of the Nineteenth Amendment to the U.S. Constitution (1920), which gave them the right to vote. During World War II, women's performance in the civilian economy and their actual service in the armed forces gave them confidence to assert claims for greater equality. They played vital roles in the Persian Gulf War, after which Congress passed a law authorizing women pilots to take part in combat. In the latest Iraq war, women served honorably in combat roles, and women were captured and held as prisoners of war. Still, the army is far from sex-neutral. Even disregarding outright discrimination, approximately one in five women in the armed forces have been sexually assaulted and 80 percent have been sexually harassed. Additionally, all men are required to sign up with the Selective Service System and thus may be drafted should the need arise. Women are not required to sign up and under present law cannot be drafted.

Over the past decades women have made significant gains in many areas. There are now more women in better-paying jobs: more women in colleges and graduate schools, in government offices, in corporate boardrooms, in the highest-ranking positions of financial institutions, and in professions such as medicine, the law, and engineering. Yet when we examine the record more closely, in many areas these gains seem to have had little overall effect on equality. For example, only 20 to 25 percent of state legislators are female. In 2018, only 87 out of the 435 members of the House of Representatives were women, and there were only 23 female senators. Thus, primarily men are both the lawmakers and the law enforcers.

The average earnings of a woman are still less than the average for a man, even when equal work is performed. At managerial levels, women usually rise only to middle-management jobs, and they tend to stay there. Many women tend to be segregated into "pink-collar jobs" such as teaching, nursing, and library work, which pay less than white-collar jobs. The fact that women are often pushed toward jobs that are inherently lower-paid is one of the explanations

Table 13.2

Earnings for Men and Women by Occupation, 2017

MEDIAN EARNINGS FOR VARIOUS FULL-TIME WORKERS BY
OCCUPATION IN 2017 (WEEKLY, IN DOLLARS)

OCCUPATION	MALE	FEMALE
Managerial, professional, and related	1,442	1,052
Office and administrative support	735	691
Service	608	501
Farming, fishing, and forestry	585	474
Installation, maintenance, and repair	883	736
Production	769	564

Source: Bureau of Labor Statistics.

for the portion of the wage gap that is not due to women blatantly being paid less to do the same work as men. Other reasons why women's income tends to be lower is that they, on average, do not work as many hours as men due to maternity leave and keeping a household, and that they simply are not chosen for better positions because they are perceived to be less capable and/or less committed to the job than male candidates. A 2017 study of Danish women found that almost all the lower pay Danish women received was highly correlated with women's choice to withdraw from the workplace after they had children, and that Danish women without children had pay equal to men. To see how women's earnings compare with those of men, see Table 13.2.

In addition, as women have comparatively recently entered occupations such as construction work, firefighting, and police forces, they tend to be the last hired and the first fired. None of these acts is necessarily discriminating on the individual or firm level. For example, many companies have established a seniority system that governs their hiring and firing. Thus, they are required by the system to fire the last one hired, of which women constitute a larger percentage. With respect to pink-collar jobs, the schools, hospitals, museums, and libraries that offer these positions say they merely hire from the pool of those who apply and that they are not directing women to take the jobs.

Much of the gender discrimination occurs too early and is too subtle and built into the system to attribute to specific individuals. If you take a poll in your class, you would likely find that the men have higher career aspirations than the women. Why?

It might be that in childhood the boys were pressured harder; it was made clear to them that they would be ultimately responsible for their own lives. When a girl had difficulty completing a project, she might have been treated leniently. Or it might have been a career counselor who guided girls in a different direction from boys. A woman who was, say, a brilliant mathematician and a straight-A student might have been counseled into education courses rather than to professional schools of business, finance, or international relations. Frustrated with teaching, she might leave that occupation to marry and have children. The fact that she made that decision does not mean she is unhappy or that her life is any less fulfilling (it may be more), but it does show the process by which women are channeled into certain careers.

Reasons for Women Entering the Workforce.   Former Congresswoman Patricia Schroeder pinpointed one of the most important reasons for women to enter the workforce when she argued that the primary reason they do so in such unprecedented numbers is that they have to maintain their families. Many family women work because they must work. For others, although families have become smaller, wants have become larger. Therefore, for some women,

*O*ne Woman's Struggle

Stratification is a key obstacle in millions of personal stories. What breaks down stratification is individual fortitude and initiative. Here's one of those stories.

Burnita S. Matthews, who was born in 1894, was the first woman ever appointed as a judge to a U.S. federal court. She had to wait until she was 64 years old to get that judgeship.

Her father sent her brother to law school and Burnita to a music conservatory. On her own, she went to law school at night, graduating in 1919. She then applied to the U.S. Veterans Administration for a lawyer's job; the Veterans Administration told her they would never hire a woman. She sent her membership dues to the Bar Association; they returned her check. She opened her own law office anyway.

In 1949, President Harry S. Truman appointed her to the judgeship. All the other judges in her court were men, of course. One of them made a public announcement: "Mrs. Matthews would be a good judge, but there is one thing wrong—she's a woman." The other judges agreed among themselves to give her the most boring work the court had. She did the work and stuck to her job. In fact, she never officially retired. She heard her last district court case in 1983, when she was 88 years old.

As the years went on after her appointment, things got better for women. Matthews eventually got important cases on which to work. For instance, she ruled that black Muslims had a right to attend religious services of their choice, even though they were in jail. She ruled that people who receive disability benefits from Social Security cannot have the money suddenly cut off just because the government decides they are not disabled anymore. The people are entitled to a hearing and a chance to show that the government is wrong, and they are allowed to keep their checks unless the government can justify stopping the money.

A federal judge always has younger lawyers working for them as clerks. Matthews always employed women lawyers. She said, "I always chose women because often when a lawyer does well, the authorities say that some man did the work. I wanted everyone to know that when one of my lawyers did well, the work was done by a woman."

Burnita Matthews died in 1988, her life a symbol of overcoming barriers of stratification.

---

work is not an actual necessity but rather a social need: It is a way the family can meet its desires. However, for black and other minority females, work has been a necessity for much longer than for white females.

Women in the workforce as a percentage of total women of working age rose from 32 percent in 1972 to over 60 percent in the early 2000s. Then it started decreasing slightly, and in 2018 that percentage was about 59 percent. According to the 2000 census, 64.5 percent of two-parent families with children under age 18 had both parents working. (This percentage had risen from 33 percent in 1976.)

It is sometimes argued that for many women the decision to work is not as important as that for men because they work only to provide "extras," often listed as a second car, a vacation home, restaurant meals—items that can be seen as frivolous or self-indulgent. If this is so, then women can be paid less because their earnings are not essential and their attachment to the labor force is intermittent. Others claim that this argument is wrong for two reasons. First, not all women are one-half of a couple. Their need for income is as great as, or greater than, a man's. But, more important, the argument is wrong because it is both immoral and illegal to pay one individual less than another individual for the same work.

The breakdown of the family has had its most telling impact on women. The outlook for women and their children who do not have the child's father living with them is not bright—many absent fathers make no child support payments, or do so at a level substantially lower than the amounts ordered by the court. In the last thirty years, laws have been passed to improve the situation. For example, in 1984 Congress allowed attachment of wages in certain cases, and in 1991 a federal law authorizing wage

More and more women are doing "male" jobs.

attachment for all absent parents who did not live up to their child support obligations was passed. Subsequent adjustments to federal law have mandated additional measures such as that employers must report newly hired employees to a national data bank to find out whether any of them owe child support payments. But it is still difficult for most single parents (generally women) to collect.

The situation for divorced women is also precarious. It has been said that for a woman the surest road to poverty is divorce. Numerous women who should receive alimony payments often do not, as many men who are supposed to make these payments default (some, in all fairness, cannot meet these financial demands). The tendency to give child custody to women still prevails, because women are perceived as being naturally better caretakers, although recently judges have more often been awarding custody either jointly or solely to the father. Because most women earn less than men, the financial burden of a divorced woman with children can be overwhelming.

We have been saying that women work for the same reasons men do: to make a living and provide for their families. But there are other reasons, which women share with men, for their desire to work: self-fulfillment and personal satisfaction. Apart from the basic satisfaction of seeing their work rewarded with money—the symbol of reward in our society, whatever opinion we may have of that symbol—women want to accept the challenges of competition and the acquisition and manipulation of new skills, to associate with peers, and to make contributions to the success of projects and enterprises.

Many men feel threatened or inconvenienced by the changes at home and at work caused by new attitudes and conditions. Men who were raised by traditional patriarchal fathers are sometimes baffled and confused by what has amounted to a kind of social revolution.

Yet the women's movement has affected men in several positive ways. Large numbers of men, either married or divorced, have become stay-at-home dads, taking on household and child care tasks and finding a new joy in being closer to their children. Although many women still end up with a larger share of the housework and the care of the children, men for the most part are beginning to appreciate the burdens and drudgery that women have long handled alone. Significant numbers of men have found themselves liberated from ancient stereotypes that barred them from kitchens and nurseries at home and nursing and clerical work in the workplace. Some men have begun to realize that to equalize duties is also to free males from the superman image of sole provider and family mainstay, reducing their tension and liberating them from toxic masculinity.

Not all men are willing or able to take on the duties of child care. Good (and affordable) day care is hard to

Braver, Kinder World

With the rise of social media, media icons such as George Clooney and Lady Gaga have enormous cultural and social influence, which they can use in various ways. George Clooney has chosen to highlight the suffering in Darfur, Sudan; and Lady Gaga has chosen to encourage a multi-cultural pluralism with her Born This Way Foundation to inspire youth. The foundation's emphasis is on bravery, acceptance, and love.

THE THREE PILLARS OF THE BORN THIS WAY FOUNDATION

SAFETY — CREATING A SAFE PLACE TO CELEBRATE INDIVIDUALITY

When provided with a safe environment, young people are able to explore themselves. So we'll provide you support through an online community that engages users in ways that celebrate their individuality.

+

SKILLS — TEACHING ADVOCACY, PROMOTING CIVIC ENGAGEMENT, AND ENCOURAGING SELF-EXPRESSION

It's not enough to simply tell you about the importance of making a change. We're going to provide you with the skills, tools, and resources you need to feel empowered and lead.

+

OPPORTUNITY — PROVIDING WAYS TO IMPLEMENT SOLUTIONS AND IMPACT LOCAL COMMUNITIES

Our organization is only as strong as supporters like you. That's why we'll be providing opportunities for you to bring the work we are doing to your local communities. You will be able to lead the charge in impacting your surroundings.

=

BY HAVING HANDS ON THESE THREE PILLARS, YOU WILL HELP BORN THIS WAY FOUNDATION CREATE:

A BRAVER, KINDER WORLD

BORN THIS WAY FOUNDATION
· EMPOWERING YOUTH · INSPIRING BRAVERY ·

BTWFOUNDATION.ORG

come by, and although some firms have established on-site day-care facilities, these companies represent a tiny minority. One solution has been the classic method of changing the problem instead of finding the answer: namely, to reduce the number of children. Especially among professional women earning high incomes and enjoying the exhilaration of the competitive business or professional world, childbearing has been postponed or even specifically declared to be completely outside their plans because of such inconveniences as childcare.

This tendency has been countered in recent years by a number of women finding that the desire to have at least one child is strong, resulting in an upsurge in the number of children born to mothers between the ages of 35 and 45. Such a development brings us full circle: Trying to work at a full-time job while simultaneously caring for a house and family, even if the family work is shared, is demanding, requiring almost a superwoman to achieve it. Women are increasingly questioning whether they want it all. They can do it, but do they want to do it?

Despite the problems, the issue of women's rights will not disappear—their proportion of the total workforce and their need to work and earn a decent wage cannot be denied. Many men remain unconvinced that helping women surmount the obstacles still in their path will probably be good for men. It is, however, quite possible that both sexes can gain from a more equitable policy toward women and that both men and women can find, through their less traditional roles, a new sense of trust, mutual respect, and cooperation.

Discrimination Based on Sexual Orientation.   People are also discriminated against based on sexual orientation. Members of the lesbian, gay, bisexual, and transgender community argue that they experience enormous discrimination, both in the way people think about them and in finding work. For example, until recently the U.S. armed forces had a rule that all homosexuals must resign from the army. An instance in which people with same-sex sexual preferences have tried to overcome discrimination by going to court is the case of the Boy Scouts of America. The Boy Scouts refused to let a scoutmaster continue in that work when they found out he was gay. He sued on his own behalf and on behalf of other gays, but he lost in every court to which he appealed, including the U.S. Supreme Court, which in 2000 decided that as a private organization the Boy Scouts had a right to exclude persons based on their sexual orientation. In 2013, however, the Boy Scouts reviewed their policy and decided to allow gay men to participate in the organization.

To try to counteract that discrimination, gay people have been pushing for explicit gay rights laws and hate-crime bills. Some of the proposed gay rights laws specifically prohibit discrimination on the basis of sexual orientation, and the proposed hate-crime bills make crimes that reflect underlying prejudice subject to stronger than normal penalties. More recently, a number of states passed laws legalizing same-sex marriage, and the U.S. Supreme Court found the federal Defense of Marriage Act, which defined marriage as a union between a man and a woman, unconstitutional. With that battle won, the civil rights focus changed to laws affecting transgendered individuals.

Senior Citizens

Another characteristic that plays an important role in our society is age. Age stratification must be considered on a slightly different basis from the other characteristics we have been discussing. Whereas we are born either male or female, the characteristics of aging are universal for both sexes. Aging is inevitable, and Ponce de León's fountain of youth remains a legend.

Some stratification according to age is inevitable. As children, we are unable to care for ourselves and are thus separated from older age groups who productively contribute to society. As we grow old, our physical abilities decline and we are not able to do all that we once could, again creating a group separate from others. There is, however, no clear demarcation line as we move from youth to middle age to being elderly. **Chronological age,** or age measured in years, often does not reflect a person's mental age or capacity to work and contribute to society.

Senior Citizens' Role in Society. In primitive societies, few individuals live to an old age because of poor health care systems and their difficult lifestyle in general. The few who do live to old age are venerated as sources of information and wisdom. In modern industrial societies, because of advanced technology, life expectancy has almost doubled since 1900, and the number of elderly are increasing quickly. Because in these societies, great value is placed on physical achievement, grace, and agility, the normal physical slowdown that characterizes aging has been accompanied by decreased status for the elderly. Sometimes the output of senior workers has not been thought to be worth their wages. Even though it is against federal law for employers to discriminate against older workers, businesses often have been successful in finding ways around the law to get rid of these workers. Most of the elderly live productive and active lives, but when they can no longer do so, they have retreated to retirement communities if they can afford them, or, if they need a lot of care, they have had to enter nursing homes, some of which have been described as "waiting rooms for death."

As medical technology has advanced, the perception of what it is to be an older person, and what an older person can do, has changed. In the early 2000s, a significant number of older people were reaching their mid-eighties or older in good health. The proliferation of knowledge about DNA and gene function has fostered so much research that previously unheard-of increases in life expectancy have been predicted, although today the work is highly theoretical. Practical results, if any, are probably decades in the future. But it is not outside the realm of possibility that in the coming decades life expectancy could increase by 20 or 30 percent should the "aging gene" be found and science discover how to modify it.

The Growth in the Proportion of Senior Citizens. As you can see in Figure 13.2, the proportion of the elderly population has been growing. In 1900, less than 4 percent of the total population was 65 years of age or older. In 2019, they numbered about 47 million, about 15 percent of the total population. Projections are that their number will rise to about 70 million by the year 2030, or about 20 percent of the projected population. The growth is more substantial for those over 85. In 1985, there were more than 2 million people over age 85; in 2000, there were more than 4 million, and it is projected that by 2050, there will be about 21 million, or about 5 percent of the projected population.

This growth of the elderly population is beginning to present significant economic and social problems. For instance, the amount of Social Security benefits, including medical insurance payments, for the elderly has placed a strain on the Social Security system, and as the proportion of mostly nonworking elderly grows in relation to the number of younger, working contributors, fewer and fewer workers will be supporting more and more elderly. This causes anxiety about the solvency of the fund and resentment on the part of younger workers.

In the early 2000s, over 35 percent of the federal budget was spent on the elderly, and federal spending on the elderly is projected to rise significantly in the future. This is despite the fact that the over-65 group is financially better off than younger groups, partly because of relatively generous Social Security benefits and partly because of various tax advantages. Many younger workers believe they will find the Social Security fund empty when it is their turn to seek benefits as elderly persons; in the meantime, they are making high Social Security tax

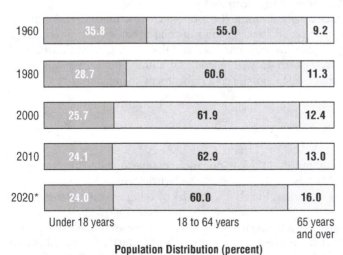

Figure 13.2

Resident population: age distribution. (*Source: U.S. Bureau of the Census,* Statistical Abstract of the United States) (* estimated)

payments—in many cases higher than their income tax liability—and some are bitter about this mix. They ask why they should pay for all of these giveaways.

The problem of care for the elderly is increasing, along with the difficulty of providing older people with opportunities for a meaningful life. These problems have been worsened by changing family structures. With the decline of extended families, children often do not include their parents in social activities. Additionally, declining birth rates mean that there are fewer workers to pay into the social security account and a smaller family to support the elderly. These changing family structures are likely to continue for many years, and, as they do, the problems of finding a role for grandparents and great-grandparents in the family are likely to increase. To argue that a role for grandparents in the family is desirable does not mean that grandparents should be considered an appendage of their children's family. On the whole, the elderly prefer to live independently; yet at the same time contact with family and friends remains a vital part of their lives.

Age Discrimination. In reaction to the problems facing older people, the gerontological set has turned to political and social activism, demanding their rights as individuals and as workers. They have formed groups, such as the American Association of Retired Persons (AARP), which play an active role in the political arena. These groups helped to win passage of the Age Discrimination in Employment Act of 1967, which prohibits discrimination against persons between the ages of 40 and 65. Moreover, in the amendments to that Act 1978, the mandatory retirement age was raised from 65 to 70, and in 1986 it was eliminated for most occupations. The elderly are an effective political force; when the AARP, which has more than 38 million members, speaks, lawmakers tend to listen. The effect of these groups is compounded by the fact that elderly people vote at much higher rates than young people, so their interests are on the whole much better represented in government. Because the numbers of older Americans are expected to continue to grow at such an impressive rate, their influence can only increase over the next few decades.

The issues involved in age discrimination are not simple ones. For example, a 60-year-old person differs from a 25-year-old person; each relates to people in a different way. If a store believes customers prefer to have younger salespeople, should it be against the law if it "discriminates" on the basis of age? Under current laws, it is. Alternatively, some firms used the 65 or 70 retirement age to ease out employees who were unable to keep up, without having to state explicitly the reason for their release. Under the Age Discrimination in Employment Act, they cannot blame the change on a general rule and thus save face for both. Training older persons as new employees presents another problem. Many jobs require years of training, and in order to recoup an investment in a worker, a firm counts on that employee working for the firm for a sufficiently long period of time.

The argument can, of course, be reversed. Some firms have fired workers right before retirement in order to save pension payments. Others have merely fired older workers in order to have a better image, using "training" or "customers' perception" as an excuse. Age group conflicts are beginning to appear as the percentage of wage earners goes down and the number of pension recipients increases. The dilemma in many firms is in deciding whether to keep on older workers, who have had much more experience, or to hire in their place a younger workforce with more energy and newer ideas. In fact, in the early 2000s, as worker shortages developed, some firms began to welcome workers at and above retirement age because of their reliability and their work ethic. In the future, we are certain to hear more about the issue of age and employment, whether discussing a young workforce or an older work-force, because, as discussed here and earlier in the chapter, it is indicative of an ongoing change in the structure of our society.

Physical Disabilities Discrimination

Yet another type of discrimination that has been the subject of public policy is discrimination against people with disabilities. In 1990 the United States passed the Americans with Disabilities Act (ADA), which prohibits employment discrimination on the basis of workers' disabilities. The law, which was amended in 2008, prohibits companies with fifteen or more employees from discriminating on the basis of physical or mental disabilities, or past or current medical conditions, and from creating or maintaining worksites that include substantial physical barriers to the movement of people with physical disabilities. Such discrimination is sometimes called "ableism"—discrimination against people on the basis of their abilities—which makes it comparable with racism or sexism—discrimination against people on the basis of race or gender.

The "ableism" terminology also captures some of the problems with this law, since, in most people's views, how able a person is to do a job should be a key element in whether that person gets the job. What the law attempts to do is to prevent firms from discriminating in hiring based on physical disabilities that do not affect job performance, not physical abilities that are central to job performance. Making that distinction, however, is often difficult, and thus what is and is not perceived as allowable discrimination has been the subject of numerous court cases. These cases provide what are called "case law" guides to making the distinction.

Conclusion

At this point we end our discussion of stratification and the issues it raises, but not because we have exhausted the topics—we have only touched on many of them. We end it because of the pressure of space and the variety of other topics to be covered. Most of these other topics—social institutions, economics, and politics—deal with some of the same issues from a different perspective, and each perspective provides yet another insight into the problems of society and the workings of social scientists' minds.

Our discussion of stratification was designed to encourage you to draw your own conclusions. Obviously, merely in the way the chapters are written, certain biases became clear, although we worked hard to keep the analyses as objective as possible.

We can, however, conclude that stratification and discrimination do exist. Of that there is little doubt. It also seems fair to say that the issues are far more complicated than the advocates of either side generally present, and we must be careful not to focus too strongly on one side's argument. We raise the methodology issue at this point because most of us are involved in some type of discriminatory action—either discriminating or being discriminated against (and often at the same time in different contexts). It is at precisely such instances that our objectivity leaves us and we find the fairness or unfairness of the situation clear and beyond question. At this point, rational discourse breaks down. Whenever you seem to have such a strong belief, count to ten and try to "walk a mile in the other person's shoes."

 Study and **Review**

Key Points

- Four reasons for ethnic prejudice are the influence of tradition, psychological needs, ego, and economic advantages.
- A minority group is a group of people singled out for unequal, negative treatment, whereas a dominant group is singled out for positive treatment.

- Although the United States has made progress in dealing with the problem of prejudice against various ethnic groups, it still has a long way to go.
- Undocumented Mexican immigration continues to be a problem despite several recent laws meant to deal with it.

- Anti-Semitism has been reduced, but it remains a potential problem.
- Anti-Islamic discrimination is on the rise in the United States.

- Women have made strides toward equality but still have a way to go before they achieve full equality.
- Senior citizens are likely to be a major political force in the twenty-first century.

Some Important Terms

affirmative action programs (253)
chronological age (269)
de facto segregation (252)
de jure segregation (252)
discrimination (247)

dominant groups (249)
Equal Rights Amendment (ERA) (265)
ethnic group (244)
Hispanics (258)

Immigration Quota Act (261)
minority groups (249)
prejudice (246)
separate-but-equal doctrine (251)

Questions for Review and Discussion

General Questions

1. Why are racial and ethnic differences largely independent of each other?
2. Has it been proved that some ethnic groups are superior to others in their capacity for mental development? Has it been proved that all ethnic groups are alike in their inborn capacities for mental and emotional development? Explain.
3. How would you explain the existence and the extent of ethnic prejudice in the world?
4. What is the relationship of prejudice to discrimination?
5. Why is the position of the black minority different from that of any other minority group in the United States?
6. What effect did the Supreme Court cases of *Plessy v. Ferguson* and *Brown v. Board of Education* have on legal segregation?
7. What are the obstacles to the elimination of de facto school segregation?
8. How does the economic position of blacks compare with that of whites? List the major factors that have brought economic gains to blacks.
9. What advances have been made in protecting the civil and political rights of black Americans? Which do you think have been most significant? Discuss what still needs to be accomplished.
10. Are blacks continuing to improve their social, political, and economic position? Defend your point of view.
11. What does Gunnar Myrdal mean when he says that no social problem as complex as the U.S. race problem is ever solved in an "absolute" sense?

12. Why are friendly relations between ethnic groups important to both the dominant and the minority groups?
13. Discuss the history of Asian migration to the United States.
14. How do you account for the existence of anti-Semitism in both Europe and the United States?
15. Is discrimination against Muslims acceptable because of national security needs?
16. What might be some of the reasons the average earnings for a woman are lower than the average earnings for a man? Does this necessarily imply discrimination by individuals or firms?
17. What determined your career aspirations? Do those aspirations reflect institutional discrimination?
18. How is the growth in the proportion of people over age 65 in the population likely to affect our society?
19. What differentiates age discrimination from other types of discrimination?
20. If a store prefers to hire younger salespeople, should it be allowed to do so? Why or why not?

Internet Questions

1. What is the National LGBT Bar Association (https://lgbtbar.org)?
2. Go to http://www.eeoc.gov/, the website of the U.S. Equal Employment Opportunity Commission. What is their latest news announcement?
3. Go to http://www.newsweek.com/minorities-women-highly-satisfied-military-work-90615 and read the article. What group is the most satisfied in the military? How does this compare to civilian

occupations? What is the likely reason for these results?

4. The Arab American Institute (http://www.aaiusa.org/) identifies some famous Americans of Arab descent. List the names familiar to you, perhaps through sports or entertainment.

5. Based on http://www.hrw.org/news, what does the Human Rights Watch organization list as one of the current issues involving the United States and human rights?

*F*or Further Study

Books to Explore

Alexander, Michelle, and Cornel West, *The New Jim Crow: Mass Incarceration in the Age of Colorblindness*, New York: The New Press, 2012.

Bonilla-Silva, Eduardo, *Racism Without Racists: Color-Blind Racism and the Persistence of Racial Inequality in the United States*, Lanham, MD: Rowman and Littlefield, 2006.

Ephron, Nora, *I Feel Bad about My Neck: And Other Thoughts on Being a Woman*, New York: Knopf, 2006.

Gates, Henry Louis, Jr., *America Behind the Color Line*, New York: Warner Books, 2004.

Kendi, Ibram and Cornel West, *Stamped from the Beginning*, New York: Nation Books, 2016.

Lareau, Annette, *Unequal Childhoods: Class, Race, and Family Life*, 2nd ed. with update a decade later, Berkeley, CA: University of California Press, 2011.

Lentin, Alana, and Gavan Titley, *The Crises of Multiculturalism: Racism in a Neoliberal Age*, London: Zed Books, 2011.

Litman, Malia A., *Evolution of the Feminine Mystique: Searching for Happily Ever After*, Malia A. Litman, 2015.

Myrdal, Gunnar, *An American Dilemma*, 2 vols., New York: Pantheon, 1975.

Obama, Barack, *Dreams from My Father: A Story of Race and Inheritance*, New York: Crown, 2004.

Rothstein, Richard, *The Color of Law: A Forgotten History of How Our Government Segregated America*, New York: Norton Publishers, 2017.

Sanberg, Sheryl, *Lean in: Women, Work, and the Will to Lead*, New York: Knopf, 2013.

Slaughter, Anne-Marie, *Unfinished Business: Women Men Work Family*, New York: Random House, 2015.

Smoak, Gregory, *Ghost Dancers and Identity: Prophetic Religion and American Indian Ethnogenesis*, Berkeley, CA: University of California Press, 2006.

Tatum, Beverly Daniel, *"Why Are All the Black Kids Sitting Together in the Cafeteria?" and Other Conversations About Race*, rev. ed., New York: Basic Books, 2003.

Thurston, Baratunde, *How to Be Black*, New York: HarperCollins, 2012.

Williams, Lena, *It's the Little Things: The Everyday Interactions That Get under the Skin of Blacks and Whites*, New York: Harcourt, 2000.

Zangwill, Isreal, *The Melting Pot*, CreateSpace, 2015.

Internet Sites to Explore

"http://www.aarp.org" American Association for Retired Persons.

"http://www.adl.org/" Anti-Defamation League.

"http://www.hrw.org" Human Rights Watch.

"http://www.naacp.org" National Association for the Advancement of Colored People.

"http://www.now.org" National Organization for Women.

The Functions and Forms of Government

chapter 14.

After reading this chapter, you should be able to:

- List five primary functions of government
- Identify three contrasting views of government
- Explain the liberal, conservative, radical, reactionary, and anarchist philosophies of government
- Distinguish a democracy from an autocracy
- List some distinguishing characteristics of a democracy
- Explain the democratic concept of the individual
- List the common justifications for an autocracy
- List four characteristics of an autocracy

> *Government after all is a very simple thing.*
>
> **—Warren G. Harding**

> *There never was a more pathetic misapprehension of responsibility than Harding's touching statement.*
>
> **—Felix Frankfurter**

Are governments necessary? To answer this question, all we have to do is look around the world to see what happens when an effective government does not exist: to Libya, where the lack of an effective government led to anarchy, looting, and devastation; and to Somalia, where, up until recently, because no effective government existed, competing factions fought for control, spreading devastation throughout the countryside—looting, raping, and murdering almost indiscriminately. The list could go on, but these two examples make the point: Effective government is necessary.

Government is the set of institutions by which a society is ruled. People often disagree violently about the role that government should play in society, which accounts for many of the political conflicts within a nation. Much of the controversy over the proper role of government in society arises from different conceptions of society and government, and any discussion of political and governmental concepts requires some common agreement on the meaning of these terms.

In the first part of this chapter, we look at the various functions of government. Then in the second part we consider the various forms of government and how they operate. Finally, in the third section we examine various views of government.

As with all social institutions, there is a presumption that if an institution exists, it serves some function. Government is no exception. The **functionalist approach** to government argues that what exists must exist as it is and not be tampered with because it serves a necessary function. That is too rigid a position for most social scientists but that does not mean that the functionalist approach is not important. In this book we have emphasized change and how change modifies the role that institutions play in society. Thus, we may find that institutions that once played a functional role may now play a quite different role, maybe functional, maybe dysfunctional. To decide that, we have to consider carefully the functions government serves in our society.

The Primary Functions of Government

In every society of any size, some form of organized government develops due to the need for an agency capable of exercising overall social control. The role of government can be better understood if we examine the specific functions governments perform or claim to perform.

Maintaining Internal Order and External Security

Though the functions of government are many and varied, its basic job is to protect its citizens from internal and external enemies. The highest value in every political society is self-preservation, and the government is the one agency equipped to protect a nation. It alone possesses the power to enforce obedience to the rules of life that the society has established, and it alone has at its disposal all the military might that the nation can provide to repel aggression.

Government, as the guardian of internal social order, employs police, prisons, and courts in its attempts to protect persons, property, rights, and whatever society designates as worthy of preservation. None of our other social institutions could exist without the "domestic tranquility"—the peace and safety—that government provides. Wherever law and order break down, the government is unable to perform its other functions; the people become fearful, and all aspects of society begin to disintegrate. **Anarchy** is a society without government or law.

Anarchy generally is so injurious to society that, after a period of social confusion, people sometimes welcome as a blessing a dictator who can restore peace and order. Recognition of this fact led Thomas Hobbes, the seventeenth-century English philosopher, to conclude that government results from a contract among free men desirous of preserving life and of increasing its contentment—"that is to say, of getting themselves out from that miserable condition of war" that necessarily results from the absence of effective government.

Most advanced modern nations have eliminated internal warfare and reduced internal violence to such a low level that nearly all the conflicts that arise among their citizens are settled in an orderly and peaceful manner. When countries have not succeeded in doing this, bloodshed, destruction, and agony tear them apart, as we have seen clearly in places such as Syria, Yemen, Rwanda, Sudan, the Republic of the Congo, and others on a sad list.

Ensuring Justice

The belief in justice appears to be universal, and every modern government professes devotion to it. **Justice** is the maintenance or administration of what is considered fair—by law or by judicial proceedings. It is a concept that involves the relationships of individuals (and groups) both to society and to one another. Though justice means different things to different people and no one definition has been agreed on that describes its content, nearly every society considers it to mean "to everyone their due."

Not all governments strive for justice, although most generally profess to do so. All governments based on popular support aspire to convince the people that they are being treated justly. In fact, justices of the peace, sheriffs, judges, and courts exist in some form almost everywhere, and their main function is to administer justice.

People have confidence in their governments to the extent that they deal out rewards and punishment in accordance with the popular conception of justice. People willingly submit their private disputes for public settlement when they have faith that justice will be done. For example, a person whose home has been burglarized is generally willing to have the burglar prosecuted in a court of law, rather than attempting to secure personal revenge, as long as that person is convinced the courts will deal fairly with the matter. When government fails to perform this function adequately, or loses the ability to enforce its decisions, lawlessness begins to spread, and revolution may even result.

Yemen: A Failed State

There are numerous examples of failed states and the problems faced by countries with no effective government. In this edition I have chosen Yemen as my example. Yemen is an Arab country (https://en.wikipedia.org/wiki/Arabs) in Western Asia (https://en.wikipedia.org/wiki/Western_Asia) at the southern end of the Arabian Peninsula (https://en.wikipedia.org/wiki/Arabian_Peninsula). It is the poorest country in the Middle East and was established as a country in 1990 with the combination of North and South Yemen. From its inception, it never had an effective government; instead, it had various sheikhs claiming power with the strongest of them becoming the president. Essentially it was a power-sharing agreement among the elite rather than a government with rules and laws. Yemen was often described as a *kleptocracy*—a country in which the leaders use the state to expand their wealth rather than to govern.

As bad and ineffective as this government was, it at least held the country together and prevented war. The situation became worse in 2011 when the power-sharing agreement broke down and the country entered into civil war, with Saudi Arabia supporting one side and Iran supporting the other. Aid coming into the country was blockaded and much of the aid that did come in was pilfered by one side or the other. Saudi Arabia started a bombing campaign in support of its side, devastating a number of cities. The result was famine and lack of clean drinking water causing the world's worst outbreak of cholera. In 2016, the UN named Yemen as the country most in need of humanitarian aid. Political philosopher Thomas Hobbes wrote that "life is solitary, poor, nasty, brutish and short" without government. Yemen is proving his point.

Destruction due to war in Yemen.

Safeguarding Individual Freedoms

Without some kind of government there can be no organized, stable society, and without a stable society there can be little real freedom for individuals. All governments profess to try to safeguard certain freedoms by maintaining law and order. But like the case of ensuring justice, not all governments actually do so. Democratic governments go further than nondemocratic governments; they have come to accept the defense of individual freedoms as a primary function. For example, the Constitution of the United States declares that a fundamental purpose of the union is to "secure the Blessings of Liberty to ourselves and our Posterity."

But in past times, when modern democracies were in the early stages of their development, government was often considered the enemy of freedom. Faith in government as the defender of individual freedoms has developed slowly over the years, until now in modern democracies there is a trend to look toward government for protection. Our federal government, for example, has taken action against monopolies, corrupt political practices, and discrimination against ethnic minorities and women.

There are, to be sure, two sides to this picture. Sometimes government regulations unjustly or needlessly restrict personal freedom, and there is always the danger that government may fall under the influence of special interests and fail to reflect the will of the majority.

There is also likely to be debate about how much individual freedom should be infringed on to protect society. For example, after the 9/11 attacks, the U.S. Congress passed the **Patriot Act,** which gave the government the right to detain people it felt might be terrorists or others who might support them. The act greatly broadened the circumstances under which surveillance was permitted, especially with online activities. It required financial institutions to provide information on client transactions and bookstores and libraries to provide information about what books individuals checked out or bought.

Some felt this law went too far; others felt it didn't go far enough. These debates are healthy. The reality is that individual freedoms can be safe only when large numbers of individuals, and also organized groups, are dedicated to their defense. The preservation of these freedoms necessitates an active and responsible vigilance on the part of the people who enjoy them. Individual freedoms are responsibilities as well as rights, and as such, they must be defended to ensure their continued strength and legitimacy.

Regulating Business's and Individuals' Actions

In the growth of modern societies, many institutions and groups have developed to perform various functions. Some of these institutions and groups provide important social services, but often they pursue selfish interests that are contrary to the welfare of society. In such cases government plays the important role of regulating people's activities so they are coordinated. Finding the appropriate amount of regulation and freedom is difficult, and democracies tend to go through cycles of increasing and decreasing regulation. For example, in the 1980s and 1990s financial institutions were deregulated as the regulation was slowing down growth and hurting the economy. Then in 2007, a financial crisis, followed by the election of President Barack Obama, led to a period of reregulation as government attempted to prevent such crises in the future and institute more government control over business. With President Trump's election in 2016 the United States has again started to reduce the number of regulations in the economy.

Promoting the General Welfare

Government as the agency for overall social control cannot escape the task of promoting the general welfare in a variety of ways that go beyond the functions we have discussed. The general welfare activities of government have multiplied many times in recent decades, but governments have always to some degree undertaken measures to promote the material well-being of their citizens. Even the governments of antiquity carried on some welfare activities. At times they gave aid to farmers, subsidized private enterprises, and controlled prices. The Bible relates how Joseph in Egypt supervised an extensive government program of buying and storing surplus grain to provide food in times of famine. The modern state has extended and intensified this ancient function of government.

Government provides the institutional structure within which economic and social interaction can take place. It regulates the economy; levies taxes; and prohibits, protects, and provides services to benefit individuals, groups, and the whole of society. Whether we think about it or not, every person every day is affected by the demands of government and by the benefits it provides. Whenever citizens leave home in a car, they drive on streets and roads provided by government; they can enjoy parks set aside by government; they can send their children to government-supported schools; they travel abroad with government-issued passports, and in case of trouble can go to the consular or diplomatic agents of their government for aid; they can receive help from the government when they are unemployed or disabled; and if accused of breaking a law, they can be heard in a court established by government. These are only a few of the ways in which individuals are affected, controlled, or benefited by government, all for the purpose of promoting the general welfare. Welfare activities of government include health services, education, Social Security, and various other benefits.

Governments furnish these benefits to meet public demands and to increase their own strength. Even dictatorships find it in their interest to provide workers with vacations and pensions on retirement. People, even if deprived of their liberties, are less likely to revolt against a government that appears to show consideration for their welfare. In democracies, where the political system makes public policy more directly responsive to public opinion, government has greatly broadened its welfare activities in response to the wishes of an enlarged electorate.

For centuries, students of politics have believed that if the masses were given the right to vote, they would demand a redistribution of wealth and privileges. In modern democracies, wealth and income have been redistributed by such means as progressive income taxes, inheritance taxes, Social Security benefits, public assistance payments, and public housing projects. This redistribution has happened to varying degrees. For example, in the 1960s, the income tax was highly progressive, inheritance taxes were high, and there were numerous government programs to help the poor. In the 1980s and 1990s that tendency toward redistribution was reduced. For example, the degree of progressiveness of the income tax was lowered. Many of these changes were supported by the lower-middle class, even though it did not help them economically. This support can be explained by a belief, held by many in the United States, that more effort should go into increasing total outputs—raising everyone's income—and less into redistribution of income. Under President Obama there were moves towards more redistribution with new government programs such as health care expansion, but with President Trump's election, the pendulum swung back to a focus on growth and increasing total output.

Debates about the Nature of Government

The preceding brief discussion summarized the various functions of government and debates about those functions. As you can see, although a government serves definite functions, there are spirited debates about these activities. In the evolution of the state over the centuries, the nature of government functions has in many ways remained the same. However, as other social institutions, such as the family and social mores, have evolved in response to technological change, the ways that governments carry out these functions have changed and so have the forms of government. Differences in culture have led different states down different paths and, therefore, to differing forms of government. We now turn to these issues.

Political Theory and Government

Government is by far the most powerful of all social institutions. It controls resources of extreme physical coercion, and it has taken over countless functions and responsibilities that once resided in the family, religion, and business enterprises, such as education and various social services. For example, in earlier times children took care of elderly parents; today, the government often does this through social programs such as Medicare. Although government today is in a position to regulate and control all other social institutions, it is in turn controlled by them. People's beliefs and attitudes and the ways they behave in the family, religion, and business enterprises determine the kind of government they develop, and often the expansion of government functions results from the failure of other institutions to meet social needs.

Politics is the means by which individuals affect government. Because of the importance of government and politics, an immense area of study, called political theory, has developed to study governments and politics. **Political theory** is that area of inquiry dealing with the nature of government and politics. Political theory has its origins in the writings of Aristotle, but our current systems of government are founded more on the writings of political theorists John Locke or Thomas Hobbes. Their alternative views of the relationships between the individual and the state form the basis of many modern **political ideologies,** deeply held beliefs in an idea—held so deeply and with such conviction that a person is willing to die for those beliefs. For example, **democracy**—the rule of the people—is the ideology of the United States, and it is rooted in the writings of John Locke. An alternative ideology, **fascism**—the belief in the rule of an elite whose members have special abilities—is the basis for what some people have argued is a preferable form of government as compared to democracy.

When two political ideologies meet, there often is conflict. For example, World War II was in some ways a conflict between fascism and democracy. Ideologies are closely related to various views of the nature of government. If we believe that there is no role in society for government, we will likely have a significantly different ideological position than someone who believes that government has a positive role.

Three Views of the Nature of Government

To organize our thinking about these issues, it is helpful to differentiate the following three views of the nature of government: (1) government as a necessary evil; (2) government as a positive good; and (3) government as an unnecessary evil.

Government as a Necessary Evil. Government follows us all through life, telling us what we can and cannot do. If we want to drive a car, we must first pass a government examination and buy a government license; then government forbids us to park in convenient places and fines us for exceeding the speed limit. It forces us to stay in school when we want to go to work. (We are told that we are too young to work.) It has the right to take us out of school and compel us to enter military service. We can only become a lawyer or a doctor by securing a license from the government. If we earn any money, government claims a share in taxes. If we are fortunate enough during our lifetime to accumulate enough wealth to leave to our children, government may impose an inheritance tax. Such activities as these make government the object of complaint and abuse and cause many people to feel that, at best, government is a necessary evil.

The very essence of government is to prohibit, to restrain, to regulate, to compel, and to coerce. For example, government possesses the authority to pass laws and the power to enforce them. Parents, therapists, and employers may cajole and condemn, but only government can legally imprison. It regulates the affairs of family and economic enterprise in accordance with its conception of public security, morality, and welfare. Of all institutions of social control, government is the most inclusive and the most powerful. Here, indeed, is a power so great that no one can safely ignore it.

Government as a Positive Good. Another picture of government can also be painted. Many years ago, Supreme Court Justice Oliver Wendell Holmes was asked by a young law clerk, "Don't you hate to pay taxes?" Justice Holmes is reported to have answered, "No, young man, I like to pay taxes. With taxes I buy civilization."

Some years later, when taxes were much higher, Supreme Court Justice William O. Douglas made another classic statement about government. He wrote:

> Government is the most advanced art of human relations. It dispenses the various services that the complexities of civilization require or make desirable. It is designed to keep in balance the various competing forces present in any society and to satisfy the dominant, contemporary demands upon it. As a result it serves a high purpose; it is the cohesive quality in civilization.

People such as those we have quoted think of government as a positive good. They realize there is some truth in Thomas Paine's contention that government is necessary "to supply the defect of moral virtue," to force us to do right when our moral weakness would lead us to injure one another. For these people, government is more than a "punisher"; it is a promoter of the common good. It is the proper social instrument for positive action to bring the essentials of the good life to all the people.

Government as an Unnecessary Evil.   Writers of communist doctrine offered another picture of government. **Communism** is a theory of social organization based on the holding of all property in common, actual ownership being ascribed to the community or state. Marx, Lenin, and Stalin, for example, portrayed government as an instrument of oppression, "special machinery for the suppression of one class by another." All capitalist governments, so the argument runs, are tools of the rich used to enforce the exploitation of the poor. Capitalist democracy allows the people "once every few years, to decide which particular representatives of the oppressing class should be in parliament to represent and oppress them." In communist theory, the **bourgeoisie** is the class that, in contrast to the proletariat or wage-earning class, is primarily concerned with property values.

In this way of thinking, machinery for suppression will be necessary only until the internal and external enemies of communism are converted or destroyed. In general, communist theory pictures government, or at least the coercive powers of government, as an unnecessary evil, to be abolished as soon as possible.

In this respect, communist theory resembles that of the anarchists. Communists have always considered government to be an unnecessary evil and have advocated the eventual abolition of all political authority and all instruments of coercion. It should be noted, however, that although Karl Marx, the early communist theoretician, wrote that there should be an end to the "coercive powers of government" and a "withering away" of the state, the former USSR and other communist nations found it difficult to follow their own ideology. Communist governments in the Soviet Union and a number of eastern European countries ended not because they withered away, but because they were removed by the very people whose interests, in theory, they were serving. Today there are almost no purely communist governments. In China the Communist Party still rules, but it has reduced its pervasive role in the economy, even as it strengthens its control over politics.

How Powerful Should Government Be?   Another way to classify people's views of government is by how strong a role they see government playing. Figure 14.1 represents various classifications of people's views, starting with those who see the least role for government and ending with those who see the strongest.

Individuals who believe in the least role for government, such as anarchists and libertarians, argue that government necessarily limits individual freedom in an unacceptable way. **Anarchists** are people who believe that the institutions of society, such as private property and the state, exploit and corrupt humans. If these authoritarian structures were removed, people would be free to realize their intrinsic goodness and establish the communal lifestyle instinctive to all human beings. **Libertarians** are people who advocate greater freedom for individuals. They dislike arbitrary authority and argue for active freedom and the free expression of the individual personality. Libertarians, such as the philosopher Robert Nozick, see a role for a minimal state. They disagree with the anarchists, arguing that we need the state to provide defense against other states, but that much of what modern states do is harmful.

Next in our classification system come reactionaries. **Reactionaries** believe that more than a minimal government is necessary, but that the role government currently plays in society is much too large. They prefer turning back the clock and organizing under the smaller role they believe the government played in earlier times.

Anarchist, libertarian, and reactionary views are not widely held in the United States. Most individuals accept the need for government in a form similar to that which we now have. They differ primarily in degree and in the role they see government playing. The most commonly used terms, with their generally accepted descriptions, are the following: **Conservatives** favor a smaller role for government than currently exists; **moderates** favor about

Figure 14.1

Views of the role of government: some exaggerated characterizations.

the same role for government as exists; and **liberals** favor a broader role for government than exists. These views of government are the predominant ones in the United States.

By considering the three different views of the role of government, you can see that the distinction between liberals and conservatives is not as clear-cut as the listing in the previous paragraph implies. In actuality, liberals tend to see government as a necessary evil and thus they favor limiting government's role of infringing on individual rights, emphasizing concepts such as freedom of speech and freedom to worship as one wishes. When liberalism was founded, its focus was on limiting the role of government—the position we now call conservatism. But over time, liberalism became associated with government establishing a framework within which individuals' freedoms have real meaning, and thereby it became associated with increasing the size of government, even though liberalism maintained its view of government as a necessary evil.

When conservatism was founded, its focus was on a strong government because conservatives saw the government as a keeper of the public morals and, hence, as a potential public good. Therefore, conservatives felt that it was proper for government to legislate morality and to tell people what was right and what was wrong. With the rise in the 1980s of the Christian Coalition political groups in the United States, we can see some of these conservative positions being taken up again. The conservative viewpoint in the United States is also associated with policies such as lower taxes; elimination or reduction of regulation, both of public and private activities; highly structured elementary and secondary education, with frequent tests to be sure students are learning the basics; and an emphasis on the family values of stable marriage and careful rearing of children by the parents.

To illustrate, it is the conservatives who generally support the government's right to legislate whether certain sexual activities such as sodomy are legal. Liberals generally oppose the government's right to control an individual's intimate life. In this example, liberals support less, not more, government. New Right conservatives generally support the government's right to control individual sexual practices, because these conservatives see the government as a positive good—as the keeper of the society's moral code. Therefore, on such issues conservatives favor a stronger government role whereas liberals favor a weaker government role. Over such issues the commonly accepted distinctions break down.

*R*epublicans, Democrats, and Political Ideologies

In the text, we develop a number of classifications of views of government, distinguishing conservatives, liberals, and moderates. Most of the political discussion in the news does not relate specifically to these groups, but instead to two political parties—Republican and Democrat. Democrats are often classified as liberals and Republicans as conservatives, but those classifications are misleading. The parties actually are coalitions of groups developed to win elections, not to espouse a particular political ideology, unless doing so will help them win elections. Thus, there is no close relationship between the two parties and the classifications, the meanings of which are themselves changing. Because of the difficulty of equating a political party with a particular ideology, more and more people in the United States are classifying themselves as political independents who will support whichever candidate espouses positions most consistent with their overall views at a particular time.

This tendency of moderates to pull away from the party affiliations has let small groups of political activists increasingly control the agendas of the two parties—social conservatives in the case of the Republicans and social liberals in the case of the Democrats. These groups often combine with private interest groups, which have no specific political ideology other than to design laws to channel more money to themselves, to control the parties. This leads candidates on both sides to pander to the social activists and private interest groups during primary elections in which candidates are chosen. Then, once they win the primary, candidates portray themselves as more moderate in the general election as they try to put together a winning coalition.

The 2016 election was an unusual one. The Republican nominee Donald Trump, was elected by the Republican rank and file in primaries; he was not supported by the Republican elite, since he held policy positions that were quite different from theirs. The Democratic nominee, Hillary Clinton, was supported by the Democratic elite, but many of the rank and file Democrats favored her primary opponent, Bernie Sanders. This limited her ability to swing to the middle, without alienating them.

The result was that she lost the election, Donald Trump became president, and the Republicans controlled both houses of Congress and the White House. But that did not really put the Republicans in charge since Trump was a quite different type of a Republican than most. He had few ideological convictions, and had been a Democrat previously. His demeanor was quite unRepublican, and many of the elite in the Republican Party had vehemently opposed Trump, finding him psychologically unsuited to be president. As opposed to bringing the Republicans together, Trump's election divided it further, demonstrating how difficult it is to shoehorn either party into an ideological box.

Not all groups fit this classification. For example, you may often hear the term *radical*. **Radicals** believe that the existing government must be changed from what it is to something else. They do not necessarily favor a larger or smaller role for government—just a change from the existing situation. Progressives also advocate for change and reform of government, but are considered less "radical" than radicals. Theodore Roosevelt was one of the United States' most prominent progressives, and when he ran as a Progressive Party candidate in 1912, he won the largest share of votes for a third-party candidate in U.S. history.

Elements of Truth in Each of the Views

All of these views of the role that government plays in society contain elements of truth. Differences of opinion arise in part from differences in governments and in part from the different functions that every government performs. Governments have been oppressive and have exploited the masses; they have at times been almost exclusively concerned with restraining the unruly elements in human society. But they have also been used by society to promote by positive means the common good. A rational evaluation of government must be based on many considerations, and there will inevitably be debate about the role that government plays in our lives.

Forms of Government

Of the many ways to divide governments, none is perfect. The first distinctions we draw are democratic, nondemocratic, and partially democratic countries.

Both the word and the concept of *democracy* come from the Greeks: *demos* means "people" and *kratos* means "rule." Thus, democracy means rule of the people. Democracies are governments based on a popular vote; elections decide who will be in power.

The map on the next page shows one way in which the countries of the world could be divided in the early 2000s. About 35 percent were democracies, 25 percent were partial democracies, and 40 percent were autocracies. (The lines between the various characterizations are sometimes vague.) In later chapters, we discuss each in more detail. Here we simply present a basic overview.

Democracies

Democracy is a word that means different things to different people. To the ancient Greek philosopher Plato, it meant mob rule, or anarchy. To some people today, it means capitalism; to others, it means socialism. Before the nineteenth century, few people in the world considered democracy desirable. But today, comparatively few people will admit opposition to democracy. Now almost every important nation, including the republics of the former Soviet Union, claim to be democratic. In pre-1990 Soviet terminology, communism, in which individuals' rights to undertake actions within the economy were limited, was the only true form of democracy. Soviet and some U.S. scholars argued that in capitalist countries control is actually in the hands of a small group of people—sometimes called the power elite (the wealthy and the political establishment)—and that the so-called democratic states of the West are in reality states serving the interests of the power elite.

These arguments may have been correct, but they were discredited by the reality of most of these communist states. In these states, the communist parties were not the protectors of the workers; often they were the exploiters. With their inefficient economic systems, to live well they had to exploit a lot, creating enormous animosity among the people. That's why most people in the Western democracies believed that the communist states were dictatorships. Some people in the West even went so far as to maintain that democracy and any form of extensive governmental interference in the economy, such as they had in the Soviet Union, are in the long run incompatible—that we can have one or the other, but not both. That's debatable, but what happened in the communist countries has been an enormously positive advertisement for democracy. As Winston Churchill aptly noted, "It has been said that democracy is the worst form of government except all the others that have been tried."

Characteristics of a Democracy. Obviously, democracy cannot be defined in any precise way that satisfies everyone. However, we can clarify some of the concepts and opinions involved. For instance, we can distinguish between democracy as a form of government and democracy as a theory of economic and social relationships. We can describe the characteristics that the West includes under the term *democracy* and, having done this, we can distinguish between profession and practice and between democratic ideals and democratic realities.

In thinking about a democracy, the first thing that usually comes to mind is the concept of popular sovereignty. **Popular sovereignty** is the right of individuals to select their leaders by voting for them. A state that does not have popular sovereignty cannot be a democracy. We use the complicated term *popular sovereignty* rather than *voting* because the mere act of voting does not guarantee that the people decide who will be their leaders. In deciding whether a government is really democratic, we must consider whether popular sovereignty prevails, or

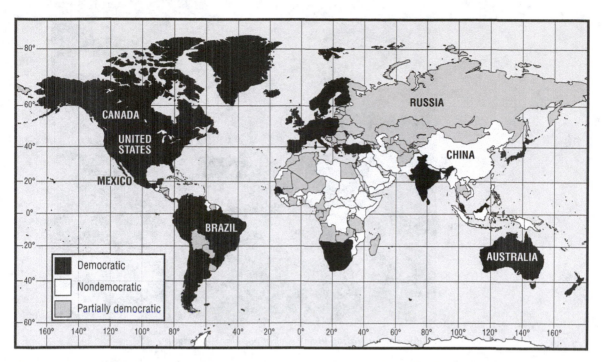

Democratic, partially democratic, and nondemocratic governments of the world. *There is some ambiguity about how democratic a number of countries are, and this list reflects judgments of the authors over the last decade. Countries can change quickly if there is a coup. Almost all countries call themselves democratic. For example, North Korea calls itself the Democratic People's Republic.*

whether the voting is simply a matter of form. Universal adult suffrage is not sufficient to make a political system democratic if the voters have no real choice among candidates.

The essential requisite for political democracy is that the people (not a king, an elite, or a class) are ultimately sovereign. Not only are the people the source of all political power, but they also are the masters of any government they establish to serve their interests. The "consent of the governed" means more than passive acquiescence; it means the power to control. In order for the people to control the government, there must be (1) freedom of speech, (2) effective legislative organs to represent the people, and (3) free elections in which the people may change the government by legal and hence peaceful methods.

Most modern democrats in the West consider freedom or liberty to be an essential element of democracy. But popular sovereignty means, in effect, majority rule, and there is always some tension or conflict between majority rule and the ideal of individual liberty. There is no way of completely resolving this conflict, but if the ruling majority is reasonably tolerant, it attempts to limit personal freedom only in situations in which such freedom would seriously interfere with the freedom and rights of others.

Key words that indicate important aspects of the democratic method are *free discussion, accommodation, compromise, moderation, tolerance,* and *reconciliation.* If these aspects exist to a sufficient degree, the definition of democracy as majority rule is perhaps acceptable. But democracy really means more than majority rule, for in the absence of these methods of resolving conflict, a majority can be just as tyrannical as any absolute monarch or modern dictator. It means that the majority will respect and guarantee the rights of the minorities, and that it will allow the minorities the right to try to become the majority. Democracy means that the end, no matter how noble, cannot justify the means. It holds that no goal, however desirable, is worth the price of sacrificing democratic methods.

People demonstrating their belief in popular sovereignty.

Democratic Concept of the Individual.   Every philosophical, social, and political system is based on certain assumptions about the nature of human beings, and no political system can be understood without a knowledge of the assumptions it makes about humans and their relationship to society and government. Democratic assumptions are worlds apart from those made by dictatorships. Not all democratic assumptions can be scientifically demonstrated, but they are part of the democratic faith and the democratic ideal. In the absence of these assumptions, democracy could not operate successfully, for no other system of government puts so much faith in the average person or depends so much on the average person for its success. Democracy demands that the common people exercise sovereign authority over themselves, maintain freedom, and employ the judgment needed to secure the blessings of good government.

Rationality and the Democratic Way of Life.   Democratic theory assumes that people are capable of developing a culture in which individuals will have learned to listen to discussion and argument, and in which they will try to discover the truth by a rational weighing of the evidence. It assumes that a human society is possible in which the people will realize that they cannot get all they want from government, and that it is therefore in everyone's interest to make compromises. In a successful democracy, every important group must be willing to make such concessions to the interests of others as are necessary

Equality.   Democratic theory holds that all humans should be regarded as equal, not in ability or in achievement, but in legal status and in their right to seek the good life. It does not insist that people are equal in beauty, brawn, and brains; in money and morals; or in power and prestige, but it does assert that all are equal before the law. It may even be said that the basic assumption underlying democratic government is that all—or at least most—citizens potentially are capable of reaching wise political decisions. It follows, therefore, that all should be given equal opportunities to participate in the political process: to vote, to hold office, to have opinions, and to strive to make their opinions prevail. No individual group is regarded as having a monopoly on political wisdom. Equality implies that public laws apply equally to all and that they will be impartially administered.

The democratic ideal of equality has developed considerably in the United States since the Declaration of Independence was written and has played an important role in eliminating slavery, in expanding educational opportunities, and in stimulating efforts to eliminate extreme poverty. Its work is still unfinished and necessarily always will be, but the widespread sharing of respect and power that democracy implies depends on a broad distribution of economic goods and the means of intellectual enlightenment. Further movements toward equality of opportunity will bring us closer to full realization of the ideal of popular control of government and should improve the quality of political decisions.

Primacy of the Individual.   Democratic philosophy and democratic government put primary emphasis on the dignity and worth of the individual. Government and society are considered to exist for the individual. The best organization of society—the best form of government—is regarded as the one that enhances the dignity of the individual and provides for the fullest and richest development of personality. The individual is considered to be the primary unit, one whose interests should be served by all social institutions. Individuals are not to be considered as means; they are the ends for which all else exists.

The primary values of liberal democracy are freedom and respect for the individual personality, and these values provide the basis for resolving the apparent contradictions between other democratic values. For example, freedom and equality are permitted and promoted insofar as they create the best environment for the development of individual personality. Freedom that disrupts social order is prohibited because order in society is necessary for the fullest exercise of the kind of freedom that promotes the development of wholesome personality. Individual or group freedoms that seriously limit the freedoms of either the majority or minorities are curtailed because the goal is as much freedom as possible for all, in order that all may lead full and satisfying lives. Complete social equality is not enforced, because such enforcement would destroy the individual freedom required for personality development. The line between freedom and order is a difficult one to draw, and inevitably there will be differences of opinion.

Where Democracy Works Best.   Democracy is a Western ideology, and, in the West, we often think that it is the solution to all political problems. Unfortunately, it is not. For democracy to work, one needs the right environment. The right environment includes a tradition of respect for individual rights, a commitment to solving problems peacefully, a relatively homogeneous population (in which subgroups of the population are not antagonistic to one another), a commitment to minority rights, a commitment to democracy over other obligations such as religion, a generally acceptable distribution of income and wealth, an educated population, a free press, and a commitment to law. In many countries of the world, this environment does not exist, making the establishment of a well-functioning democracy difficult if not totally impossible. Attempts to impose democracy, rather than to let it develop endogenously, tend not only to fail, but to lead to the destruction of government, making the situation worse, not better.

Alternative Forms of Democracy.   The fundamental requirements of democracy are not to be confused with any precise type of governmental organization. Students of government agree that political democracy exists in many forms. It may be direct (as in a New England town meeting, which every citizen can attend) or representative (as it must be in all units with large populations). It may be presidential (as in the United States) or parliamentary (as in Britain, Canada, and Italy). It may be unitary (as in Britain and France) or federal (as in the United States). It may exist where there is either a written or an unwritten constitution, but there must be in some sense a constitution or fundamental law that the government respects. It may exist in a republic (as in the United States and France) or in a constitutional monarchy (as in Sweden and Britain).

Autocracy

In the preceding discussion, you saw that the term *democracy* was far more complicated than you might have thought. The same is true of the term **autocracy,** a government in which a single person or a small group of people has or claims unlimited power. Like democracies, autocracies come in many varieties. Antiquity had rulers in the clan, tribe, city-state, and empire. The names of some of the great Roman dictators are well known: Julius Caesar, Augustus Caesar, and Marcus Aurelius. The short-lived and limited democracy of the Greek city-states was replaced by autocracies under men such as Pisistratus, the Athenian tyrant.

The absolute monarchies that emerged from the disintegration of feudalism in the Middle Ages constituted the type of authoritarian rule commonly found before the emergence in the twentieth century of fascism and communism. Like many twentieth-century autocracies, these earlier absolute monarchies were marked by arbitrary rule, which at times tended to become irresponsible. Nevertheless, many of their rulers provided "popular" or "benevolent" government. Unlike most contemporary autocracies, the absolute monarchies were fairly stable because usually one hereditary ruler followed another without introducing any basic changes in society. In modern societies, we generally do not have absolute monarchies. Instead, we usually have limited monarchies in which the monarch plays a ceremonial role but has little to say in the governing of the country. Despite the trend away from monarchies, especially absolute monarchies, more than twenty-five national monarchs still remain, holding varying degrees of governing power. British Queen Elizabeth II can claim more than fifteen countries as her kingdoms, although her real power is effectively none. On the other side of the spectrum, Swaziland, Brunei, Oman, Qatar, and Saudi Arabia are still ruled by almost absolute monarchs.

In the twentieth century, various types of autocracies developed in accordance with different conditions in different countries. The two basic types of autocracies that remain are the authoritarian and the totalitarian.

An **authoritarian autocracy** is one in which the society is ruled by a dictator or clique that forbids all activities that threaten its position. Although this group ruthlessly guards its power, it generally is indifferent to activities that do not threaten its rule. It wants to rule because it likes ruling or because it likes the benefits of ruling, such as the enormous potential income. The societies of the eighteenth-century Empress Catherine the Great of Russia and, in the twentieth century, Francisco Franco of Spain are examples of past authoritarian autocracies,

*L*etting a Guilty Person Go Free

The primacy of the individual can be seen in various aspects of life in the United States. One example is Miranda rights, which were established by a decision of the U.S. Supreme Court in 1966 (*Miranda v. Arizona*). In that case, Ernesto Miranda had been convicted of kidnapping and rape after appearing in a police lineup, being questioned, and signing a statement of guilt. The Supreme Court held that the courts cannot use statements obtained by the police while a suspect is in custody unless the suspect has been warned of the protection against self-incrimination provided by the First and Fifth Amendments to the Constitution. The Court laid out the points that must be covered. You may have heard them on television crime stories.

The Miranda Warning: *You have the right to remain silent. Anything you say can be used against you in a court of law. You have the right to the presence of an attorney. If you cannot afford an attorney, one will be appointed for you prior to the questioning if you so desire.*

If these individual rights are not read to the suspect, or are not understood by the suspect, the individual's statement cannot be used as evidence against him or her. Other examples of our concerns for the rights of the individual include limitations on how evidence is obtained. For instance, illegal wiretapping and unwarranted search may also be grounds for letting a person who may be guilty go free.

and the military juntas in some countries of Africa are examples of current authoritarian autocracies.

A **totalitarian autocracy** is one that wants to control all aspects of an individual's life. A totalitarian ruler is different from an authoritarian ruler who does not care who teaches in a school as long as he or she takes no political stand and does not threaten the ruler's power. Put simply, "an authoritarian wants obedience; the totalitarian wants worship." The concept of totalitarianism was not formally introduced until the twentieth century. The reason is that overwhelming dominance of the political authority emanating from a totalitarian nation was not possible until twentieth-century technology succeeded in significantly increasing the scope of the state's control.

Most totalitarian autocracies are based on an ideology. With this ideology, they can justify their actions in terms of the goal of a better world. Nazism and Marxism are two examples of ideologies underlying totalitarian rule.

An authoritarian autocracy is not necessarily better or worse than a totalitarian autocracy. For example, authoritarian autocrats often plunder their countries' wealth, living in splendor while the people they rule may starve. Because totalitarian autocracies are generally based on ideology, totalitarian leaders are often far less interested in wealth for themselves and are more interested in seeing that individuals in their society share their own ideology. Thus, in a totalitarian autocracy people can be better off financially but have fewer personal freedoms.

Justifications Given for an Autocracy. Because most of the countries that we classify as autocracies claim to be democracies, to gain a better sense of an autocracy we must consider their arguments about why they do not allow free elections. Here we find ongoing debate about what is meant by *free*. For instance, some communists argue that when workers depend on businesses for jobs they are not free to express their own will—that their will is just an expression of the capitalists' and power elite's will. They argue that the control of a government by the Communist Party is a temporary expedient necessary to prevent the existing vested interests (the bourgeoisie) from thwarting the state's movement to a higher, freer stage. The theory is that only by accepting some limitation on freedom in the present can citizens under communism achieve true freedom in the future. Given the upheavals that ended communist rule in most former communist countries, this justification did not satisfy many of those who lived under communism.

In similar fashion, the autocracies of many underdeveloped countries claim that they are merely caretakers, that if, they were not in charge, some other group far less benevolent and far less committed to democracy would take over and eliminate any possibility of the country ever becoming a democracy. They argue that because the environment of their country is not suitable for democracy, they must preserve order so that the environment can be made safe for democracy. They argue that they are not antidemocratic; on the contrary, they are protective of democracy. An example of a relatively beneficent caretaker autocracy is the African country of Uganda, where the president, Yoweri Museveni, led Uganda back from chaos and created the stability needed for economic growth while at the same time maintaining a relatively uncorrupt government. He tried to be inclusive in his government, but nonetheless has not allowed significant political

Egypt has struggled to achieve democracy.

© Cartoon Stock

opposition, arguing that with the ethnic hatreds that are so pervasive in Uganda, the country is not yet ready for Western-style democracy. This lesser-of-two-evils justification for autocracy goes back to the political philosophy of Thomas Hobbes, who justified monarchy in this fashion.

Each of these arguments has some validity. Democracy has its weaknesses. Modern democracies were developed to reflect Western cultural values and social institutions, and, as mentioned above, these may not flourish when transplanted. The will of the people is not well defined and the concept can be manipulated. Moreover, democracies operate within certain legal frameworks that restrict individual liberties in certain areas. As recently as the 1950s here in the United States, during what is called the McCarthy era,[1] a congressional body, the House Un-American Activities Committee, summoned people suspected of being communists or of being "fellow travelers" (having friends who are communists). As a result of their testimony, or refusal to testify, some lost their jobs or could not find work in their professions, and some were even arrested and jailed. More recently, as part of the war on terrorism, individuals of Islamic beliefs or origin are being singled out as possible terrorist supporters. They can lose their jobs, even be arrested or jailed for having contact with suspected terrorists. Some believe that this treatment is a reasonable price to pay to root out terrorism. Others believe it has trampled on the rights of individuals that are supposed to be sacrosanct.

Similarly, developing countries often have problems making democracy work. In a country with two (or more) separate and opposing cultures, democracy is almost doomed to failure. Examples include Nigeria, with its many tribes and deep divisions between the Christians and Muslims; Iraq, with the Kurds, Shiites, and Sunnis; Afghanistan, with its many tribes; and the Democratic Republic of Congo, with its many ethnic divisions.

Western countries have been frustrated with recent efforts to promote liberal democracy in Asia, Africa, and Latin America. However, the leaders in the West need to realize and accept that it is difficult to impose the typical Western model of democracy on non-Western societies, which possess distinct (and often contrary) cultural and sociopolitical characteristics. Therefore, classifying a country as an autocracy does not necessarily mean it is bad; it means it is not responsive to the will of the people in the same way as Western democracies.

"Frankly, it's no better or worse than any other form of government."

Autocracy and Power. As we stated earlier, an autocracy is a government that exists independently of, or beyond, the will of its citizens. It may or may not act contrary to the wishes of those it governs. It is important to note that, in an autocracy, the people have limited means of calling the government to account. Its right to rule does not depend on majority support but, rather, derives from power that for authoritarian autocracies can be an end in itself. However, even in an autocracy, a leader who has lost the support of the people may find it difficult to stay in power.

A dramatic overthrow of an autocratic dictator occurred in Romania in 1989. Nicolae Ceaușescu had ruthlessly governed Romania during the Cold War and was

---

[1] This era takes its name from a U.S. senator of the time, Joseph McCarthy, who conducted an infamous campaign against communists in government and in influential positions throughout U.S. society.

responsible for numerous human rights violations. When the tide of the pro-democracy movement engulfed eastern Europe in the late 1980s, Romania was the stage for a massive revolt against the incumbent dictatorship. On December 16, 1989, Ceaușescu declared a state of emergency after hundreds of protestors died during demonstrations in the city of Timisoara. The wave of protest spread rapidly throughout Romania and people openly marched into the capital, Bucharest, demanding Ceaușescu's dismissal. Army units joined the rebellion and on December 22, 1989, a group calling itself the National Salvation Front announced that it had overthrown the government. A bloody conflict followed between security forces still loyal to the dictator and the new government. The National Salvation Front gained control and Ceaușescu and his wife were captured. After a speedy trial, they were found guilty of genocide and were executed on December 25, 1989. On the same day, Ion Iliescu, the leader of the rebellion, was sworn in as the new president of Romania. In 1991, a new constitution set up a system by which the president and the legislature are elected by popular vote.

Whereas for authoritarian autocracies power is an end in itself (and possibly a tool for personal enrichment), and they need claim no other justification, for totalitarian autocracies the power is nearly always a means to a higher ideological end. There generally is some belief that the ruling elite possesses the "best brains," the "best blood," the "highest political insight," and the "capacity to rule."[2] Autocrats do not expect people to know what is good for them; they tell the people what is best and hope the people will believe it. If the people do not believe it, the autocrats can try to do what is good for them anyway. Of course, they can also listen to the people and carry out popular wishes, either because they believe that is the right thing to do or because they fear an uprising or a coup. Thus, we can have autocracies that are responsive to the general will. They remain autocracies because the decision to be responsive rests with the ruler, not the people.

Characteristics of an Autocracy. The central characteristic of the totalitarian autocracies that came into power after World War I was their policy of controlling the total life of individuals and private groups. They employed whatever devices they could to make possible the effective control by the state of all social activity. The sphere of private freedom, which democracy attempts to maximize, is narrowly restricted by totalitarianism. Totalitarian government attempts to regulate all of life for state ends. Capital and labor, press and religion, family and fraternal organizations, work and play, individuals and society—all are subject to strict controls designed to promote the general welfare and to enhance the power and prestige of the state.

Loyalty to the Party and the State. Totalitarian autocracies demand complete loyalty and obedience to the party and the state. Fascist theory glorified and exalted the state. Some forms of communism exalt the social revolution and require of the individual complete dedication to the objectives of the Communist Party. But under both systems, the political party has direct control of the government and determines what government policy will be. Totalitarian communist states, for example, are the instrument for carrying out the policies of the Communist Party. Both fascism and totalitarian communism demand that individuals, where there is any conflict, subordinate their own interests to those of the party or the state.[3]

---

[2] For example, the classic totalitarian autocrat Adolf Hitler wrote: "A philosophy of life which, by rejecting the democratic concept of the mass-man, endeavors to give this earth to the best nation, the highest type of human beings, must in turn, logically, obey the same aristocratic principle within that nation and must secure leadership and greatest influence for the best brains. It rests on the basis of personality, not on that of majority." Translated from *Mein Kampf,* Munich, 1938, p. 493 (earlier editions in 1925 and 1927).

[3] Benito Mussolini, the fascist leader of Italy between the two world wars, wrote: "For Fascism the State is an absolute before which individuals and groups are relative.... When one says Liberalism, one says the individual; when one says Fascism, one says the State.... The Liberal State does not direct the interplay and the material and spiritual development of the groups, but limits itself to registering the results; the Fascist state has a consciousness of its own, a will of its own." "The Doctrine of Fascism," quoted in William Ebenstein, *Great Political Thinkers: Plato to the Present,* New York: Holt, 1951, pp. 597, 598.

In recent times, there were signals of a possible resurgence of fascism in Europe, with the relative success of extremist parties in France, Germany, Italy, and Russia. These movements exist, but at least in recent years they have generally remained without effective power.

Rule by Leaders.   Democracy emphasizes constitutionalism and rule by law; an autocracy is often characterized less by the rule of law and more by the rule of leaders. Until 1215, England was a complete autocracy and no rule of law limited the ruler's power. In that year England adopted the **Magna Carta,** or "great charter," which forced King John to agree that free men had rights and liberties that could not be trampled on. After King John accepted the Magna Carta, his rights were limited, and England took a step from autocracy to democracy. As we have stated, autocracies differ from one another, and so do countries. However, where the power of the autocracy is strong and the ruler or ruling party unresponsive to the wishes of the citizens, the autocrat can change the political rules arbitrarily to meet the purposes of the moment; no law or established procedure is permitted to interfere with the continued existence and absolute rule of the power holders. Under such circumstances, life, liberty, and property are insecure, for a person may be found guilty on false charges without any genuine trial.

One-Party Monopoly   Autocracy desires a monopoly of control; it generally tolerates no organized opposition, but it sometimes makes use of a political party. The one highly disciplined party that exists may have begun as a traditional political group struggling for parliamentary control. Once in power, however, it loses its private character and becomes the official control agency of the state. The purposes it serves are very different from those served by parties in a democracy. It offers the people no alternatives and it gives them no opportunity to participate in the formulation of public policy. Its purpose is to serve the organizational needs of the autocratic leaders and their followers. It provides for close contact between the rulers and the people, for the dissemination of the party line, and for the control and regimentation of the people in the interest of the rulers. It may, as in China, possess a legal monopoly on the power to nominate candidates. Regardless of its legal position, the state party carries out the will of the autocratic leaders and prevents the people from forming an effective legal opposition party to challenge the present rulers. Thus, the party becomes in practice synonymous with the state; its personnel, policies, and programs become those of the state.

Hitler's Germany embodied fascist theory.

A Controlled Press.   If a leader is to maintain control without resorting to elections, she or he often finds it necessary to control the press and the other media to ensure popular support for the regime. **Propaganda** is the product of the state controlling the press and structuring the flow of information to the people in order to make the state look good. Totalitarian autocracies often employ an elaborate propaganda machine designed to secure mass support through intellectual conformity. The people are denied the privilege of hearing any other side of an issue. For these reasons, autocracies often have strong public support, but without a free press and freedom of expression for individuals it is difficult to say whether that support

Figure 14.2

Continuum of autocracies.

would exist if people were offered a wider range of choices.

Communism, Fascism, and Autocracy. When thinking of autocracy, we often think of communism and fascism because the terms *communism* and *fascist Nazism* have sometimes been used synonymously with *totalitarian autocracy*. This is somewhat misleading because communism and fascism are not really types of government. Rather, they are different systems of social, economic, and political theory that have produced totalitarian governments of a similar character. The differences between them are largely matters of detail and ideology, but as we stated at the beginning of the chapter, ideological differences are important.

Under communism the totalitarianism is meant to be temporary, and rule by the Communist Party is said to be a transition toward a higher stage of society in which "the State will wither away" because true equality and freedom have been achieved and totalitarian rule no longer has any function. Fascism, originally developed as an ideology to combat communism, does not see itself as a mere stage; it sees itself as a complete system capable of withstanding all assaults. (Adolf Hitler, the German founder of fascist Nazism, proclaimed that the Third Reich, which he established, would last a thousand years— it lasted less than twenty.)

The development of fascism in reaction to communism shows the problem that ideologies present to society. The goals of communism (to each according to his needs; from each according to his abilities) sound noble, but when that ideology conflicts with a democratic ideology, one or the other must give. In the 1930s, communist ideologists argued that the democratic ideology must give. Once one group in a democracy no longer accepts the democratic ideology, it becomes more and more difficult for other groups to accept the limitations democratic ideology places on them. For example, if you're playing cards and the person you're playing with cheats, at some point you are likely either to cheat too or to quit playing. In the 1920s and 1930s, fascists argued that because communists were not playing by the rules, fascists didn't have to play by the rules either. In Germany that argument carried the day, and Germany became a fascist state to "protect itself from the communists." The ultimate result was World War II.

Often fascism and communism are seen as opposite ends of the spectrum—communism on the left and fascism on the right. It is better to think of a circle, as depicted in Figure 14.2. At the top of the circle are autocracies without any ideological commitment. Traveling all the way around the left side of the circle to the bottom would bring us to communism, and tracing around the right side would end in fascism. Thus, almost at the bottom, but not quite touching, are communists and fascists.

Governments Are Far from Simple

Having come to the end of this first chapter on political systems, we are in a better position to see why a former Supreme Court justice, Felix Frankfurter, attacked President Warren Harding's view that government, after all, is a very simple thing. Government is far from simple. Understanding the role of government is not like understanding mathematics or logic. There is an art to government, and although the goals of government may remain constant, the means of achieving those goals may vary with the temper of the times.

We could go on about the nature of governments, but you'll learn far more by considering examples.

 Study and **Review**

Key Points

- Five primary functions of government are maintaining internal order and external security, ensuring justice, safeguarding individual freedoms, regulating individuals' actions, and promoting the general welfare.
- Three contrasting views of government are government as a necessary evil, government as a positive good, and government as an unnecessary evil.
- The liberal, conservative, reactionary, and anarchist philosophies of government differ in their view of how strong government should be.
- The two primary forms of government are democracy and autocracy.

- Three distinguishing characteristics of a democracy are freedom of speech, effective representation of the people, and free elections.
- The democratic concept of the individual is that he or she is rational, equal to all others, and primary.
- Common justifications for an autocracy include the repressiveness of markets, the need for a temporary caretaker, and the lack of the requirements for a democracy.
- Four characteristics of an autocracy are loyalty to the party and state, rule by leaders, one-party monopoly, and a controlled press.

Some Important Terms

anarchists (281)
anarchy (276)
authoritarian autocracy (288)
autocracy (288)
bourgeoisie (281)
communism (281)
conservatives (281)
democracy (280)
fascism (280)

functionalist approach (275)
government (275)
justice (276)
liberals (282)
libertarians (281)
Magna Carta (292)
moderates (281)
Patriot Act (278)
political ideologies (280)

political theory (279)
politics (279)
popular sovereignty (284)
propaganda (292)
radicals (283)
reactionaries (281)
totalitarian autocracy (289)

Questions for Review and Discussion

General Question

1. What are some of the functions of government that make it such a powerful institution?
2. Distinguish between anarchists and libertarians.
3. What three different attitudes toward government are predominant in the United States?
4. What are some of the reasons people disagree over the role government ought to play?
5. What does equality mean to you?

6. How do you think a government can administer the ideal of individual freedom without infringing on the freedom of other individuals?
7. Some forms of government advocate individual liberty; some others advocate individual control. Name one or two ideologies on each side and describe what you think each would mean for a citizen under such a government.
8. What are some of the differences between an authoritarian autocracy and a totalitarian

autocracy? Name a state governed under each of these systems, and give reasons for your choices.

9. In what ways can communism be said to advocate liberty? In what ways can democracy be said to lead to repression?

10. What kind of government provides open elections but with only one candidate on the ballot? What kind might give voters a choice of candidates but have soldiers stationed at the polling place?

Internet Questions

1. Go to the Frontiers of Freedom website http://www.ff.org/. What is their mission statement?

2. Go to https://www.aclu.org/about-aclu. Would the American Civil Liberties Union defend entities such as the Ku Klux Klan? Are they correct in doing so?

3. Looking at the Homeland Security threat and protection information at http://www.dhs.gov/, what was the content of the most recent National Terrorism Advisor bulletin or alert?

4. Who was Idi Amin? Go to https://www.youtube.com/watch?v=DCSpABIwY8s and watch the video.

5. Take the "World's Smallest Political Quiz" on the Libertarian Party website, http://www.theadvocates.org/quizp/index.html. How do you score?

For Further Study

Books to Explore

Acemoglu, Daron, and James Robinson, *Why Nations Fail: The Origins of Power, Prosperity, and Poverty*, New York: Crown Business, 2012.

Aristotle, *Politics*, trans. H. Rackham, Cambridge, MA: Harvard University Press, 1944.

Diamond, Jared, *Guns, Germs and Steel: The Fates of Human Societies*, New York: Norton, 2006.

Friedman, Thomas L., *Longitudes and Attitudes: Exploring the World after September 11th*, New York: Farrar, Straus, & Giroux, 2002.

Hayek, Friedrich A., *The Constitution of Liberty*, Chicago, IL: University of Chicago Press, 1960.

Hitler, Adolf, *Mein Kampf* (1927), Boston, MA: Houghton Mifflin, 1962.

Hobbes, Thomas, *Leviathan* (1651), Baltimore, MD: Penguin, 1982.

Levitsky, Steven, and Daniel Siblatt, *How Democracies Die*, New York: Crown Publishing, 2018.

Locke, John, *Of Civil Government, Second Essay (1690)*, Chicago, IL: Henry Regnery, 1960.

Marx, Karl, and Friedrich Engels, *The Communist Manifesto (1848)*, ed. Samuel H. Beer, New York: Appleton-Century-Crofts, 1955.

9/11 Commission Report: Final Report of the National Commission on Terrorist Attacks upon the United States, Philip Zelikow, Commission Executive Director, New York: Norton, 2004.

Roberts, Cokie, *Founding Mothers: The Women Who Raised Our Nation*, New York: Morrow, 2004.

Snyder, Timothy, *On Tyranny: Twenty Lessons from the Twentieth Century*, New York: Tim Dugan Books, 2017.

Tocqueville, Alexis de, *Democracy in America (1835)*, Garden City, NY: Doubleday, 1969.

Internet Sites to Explore

"http://www.theadvocates.org" Advocates for Self Government.

"http://www.aclu.org" American Civil Liberties Union.

"https://en.wikipedia.org/wiki/Democracy" Democracy.

"http://www.dhs.gov/index.shtm" Department of Homeland Security.

"http://www.politics1.com/parties.htm" Directory of U.S. Political Parties.

Governments of the World

After reading this chapter, you should be able to:

- Give a history and describe the key features of the French government
- Give a history and describe the key features of the Chinese government
- Give a history and describe the key features of the Nigerian government
- Give a history and describe the key features of the Russian government
- Give a history and describe the key features of the Saudi Arabian government

If the gods should hand down to mortals, as mortals now are, a perfect system, it would be all banged up and skewed twist-ways inside of ten years.

—Don Marquis

The ideas behind governments are one thing—how the ideas work in practice is another. In this chapter we try to give some concreteness to the ideas of the previous chapter by providing a brief description of five governments: France, China, Nigeria, Russia, and Saudi Arabia. Our goal in doing so is not to make you an expert on these governments, but to show you how the historical context within which each country developed has shaped its specific form of government, and to demonstrate how much variance there is among both autocracies and democracies.

French Government

France, the country where democracy was reborn, is a good country with which to begin our consideration of governments besides our own. The current system of French government developed in reaction to the absolute monarchy that had become nonresponsive to the changing social conditions of the eighteenth century—specifically, the emerging middle class. **Bastille Day** is the equivalent of our Fourth of July and commemorates the storming of the Bastille prison in Paris. The French celebrate it every year on July 14.

The storming of the Bastille in 1789 marked an uprising of the people—the **French Revolution,** the revolt in France against the monarchy and aristocracy, lasting from 1789 to 1799—and led to a decade of chaos and terror, with the revolutionaries tearing down the political structure and other social institutions of the country but not replacing them. This chaos ended when dictator Napoleon Bonaparte took control. Although Napoleon reversed the process of democratization and returned France to an autocracy, after his reign there was a

Emmanuel Macron, the president of France.

© Alamy

gradual evolution away from autocracy and toward a liberal parliamentary system that characterizes the French government today. In 1871, after France was defeated in a short war with Germany, the Franco-Prussian War, all vestiges of autocracy were ended, and the democratic French republic was established.

Although the republics of France have always had a written constitution, the French constitution has never been as firmly established as the U.S. Constitution. In fact, there have been sixteen constitutions since the revolution of 1789. There is some continuity, however, and their present constitution refers to the Declaration of the Rights of Man (http://avalon.law.yale.edu/18th_century/rightsof.asp), part of the preamble to the original constitution written in 1789.

The lack of a stable constitution has made the French people regard laws differently than they are regarded in the United States, where for many people the law is the law; the law is right. For the French people, laws are simply technical rules under which they live. The difference is not so much in what actually happens in each country—in both some people break the law. In the United States, if you break the law (for example, by evading taxes), you probably feel guilty about it. In France, people often are proud of having broken what they regard as mere rules made by people who made different ones last week and will make still different ones next month.

The French Parliamentary System

France is now organized under what is called the Fifth Republic. Each of its republics has had a different constitution. Ever since the Third Republic, established in 1871, France has had a modified parliamentary system, modeled after the British parliamentary system. Perhaps the most distinctive aspect of French government and politics has been their instability. During the seventy years of the Third Republic (1871–1940), France had more than a hundred prime ministers, each one holding office less than eight months. This occurred because of the many political parties and the unwillingness of the members of the legislature to compromise. The Fourth Republic, established in 1946 after World War II, was even worse than the Third Republic. In response, on September 28, 1958, with the country on the brink of civil war, the Fifth Republic was instituted. In the Fifth Republic, it is much more difficult for the parliament to vote on a **censure motion,** a motion that, if successful, means the prime minister does not have the support of parliament and a new government must be formed via elections. A **vote of confidence** is a formal and constitutionally binding motion indicating that parliament still supports the current government and premier.

The legislative branch of French government is elected every five years and consists of two houses: the National Assembly, whose members are elected directly by all citizens over age 18, and the Senate, which is chosen by an electoral college and provides stronger representation for rural areas than does the other house. When there is disagreement between the two houses, the National Assembly takes precedence. Compared with the U.S. Congress, however, neither of these legislative bodies has significant power. Once having elected executive officers, the executive branch can in many cases both legislate and carry out the laws. The strength of the executive branch was a change made in the Fifth Republic and accepted because the previous governments had been so unstable.

The French Executive Branch

The executive branch of the French government has two leaders: a prime minister and a president. Unlike many parliamentary systems, in France both leaders wield considerable power.

The president is the head of state and the executive head of government. He or she is elected every five years by direct popular vote. The president appoints the prime minister, and together they choose the cabinet.

In 2017, an independent centrist, Emmanuel Macron, won the presidency. He was pro-EU and pro-business, but most of all he presented himself as someone outside of France's traditional political structure. He was not associated with any traditional French party, and he promised a change in the way politics was conducted in France. So in many ways the 2017 election symbolized the French people's growing dissatisfaction with the existing

France

Population: 67 million

Area: 211,209 square miles (547,030 square km)

Distribution: 80% urban; 20% rural

Capital city: Paris

National anthem: "La Marseillaise"

Government leaders: President Emmanuel Macron (since 2017), Prime Minister Edouard Philippe (since 2017)

Ethnic divisions: Celtic and Latin with Teutonic, Slavic, North African, Indochinese, and Basque minorities

Literacy rate: 99%

Religion: 63–66% Roman Catholic; 7–9% Muslim; 25% nonreligious; others include Protestant and Jewish

GDP: $2.8 trillion; per capita: $43,600 (purchasing power parity)

Currency unit: euro

Monetary conversion rate: 1 euro = $1.23 USD (Feb 2018)

Internet users: 57 million

Cell phones: 67 million

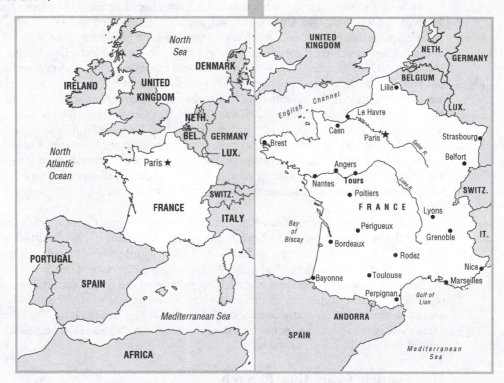

Map of France

*T*he Difference between a Parliamentary and a Presidential System

Democracy has many forms. To hold meetings where everyone in the country can come and be heard is impossible when countries have millions of people. Therefore, every democracy must establish systems of representation. The United States has a **presidential system**, where the head of government and head of state are the same person, but most democratic countries in the world use a parliamentary system. The difference is found in who elects head of government. In a presidential system, the people elect the leader, called the president, by direct election or indirectly through an electoral college. In a parliamentary system, people elect the members of the legislature and the legislators elect the head of government, or the executive, generally called a prime minister. Thus, in a presidential system, the legislature and the executive can be of opposing parties (as

happened recently in the United States when Barack Obama, a Democrat, was president but Congress was controlled by the Republicans). In a parliamentary system, the majority in the legislature and the executive are of the same party or collection of parties. If the prime minister loses the support of the parliament, the government is said to fall and the prime minister must call for a new election or resign.

Parliamentary systems also often have presidents, whether elected by the legislature or by popular vote. The job of a president in such a system usually is to be a head of state—that is, to attend receptions and play a largely ceremonial role. In Great Britain, the king or queen serves the function that a president serves in other parliamentary systems. France presents an exception to both the parliamentary and the presidential system. In France, the president is elected by popular vote, but then the president appoints the prime minister from the party or coalition of parties that rules the legislature, instead of the prime minister being chosen by the legislature.

government's political elite, as have elections throughout the world. It remains to be seen whether Macron can bring about the type of change that will satisfy the French people.

Chinese Government

Because of its growing importance in the world, both militarily and economically, China's government is crucial to discuss. It differs from other governments described in this chapter in that it is a communist autocracy, by which I mean that it is run by the Communist Party. To say that it is run by the Communist Party is not to say that China does not have a state government; it does. It is only to say that there is a parallel Communist Party structure that dominates and controls what the state does. This means that to understand the Chinese government, one must understand that Communist Party structure as well.

I start with a brief discussion of Chinese governmental history that contextualizes the cultural setting for the modern Chinese government. Then I look at the recent history of the Chinese state government. Finally, I look at the Communist Party structure, and conclude with a discussion of how the interaction works in practice.

Chinese Governmental History

China has a long and deep history that goes back far beyond most Western governmental histories; Chinese dynasties go back to 2070 B.C. These dynasties were essentially royal autocracies in which emperors ruled the kingdoms of China with varying degrees of control. Because China has always included a large area with many different ethnic groups, that rule was often limited the further one got away from the central ruling group in Beijing.

Chinese governmental history differs from Western governmental history in an important way. China has a history of territorial integrity going back millenia; European government split up and divided into smaller autonomous states, such as Germany or France, which Europe is now trying to put back together with the European Union. Since 2000 B.C., dynasties have claimed to rule the entirety of the territory of China. Some dynasties managed to defeat all their enemies and rule alone, while in some periods three or even four warring states, each of which claimed the entirety of China as their territory, existed at once. Dynasties changed when one group overthrew another, or conquered all the other separatist governments. The crucial point is that Han Chinese people have considered themselves part of a single Chinese nation for over 4,000 years.

The last of the dynasties was the Qing Dynasty, which ruled from 1644 to 1911, when Sun Yat-sen led a revolution that overthrew the Qing Dynasty and established the Republic of China. The republic was unstable, and was characterized by enormous internal fighting. When Sun Yat-sen died in 1925, there was a struggle for power between the nationalist party led by Chiang Kai-shek and the Communist Party led by Mao Zedong. In 1949, Mao's Communist Party won, and the Nationalist Party retreated to Taiwan, an island off the coast of China. It was at that time that China became a communist country, and modern Chinese governmental history begins.

Chinese State Structure

After taking power, the Communist Party of China established an interim constitution, which was formalized into a governing constitution in 1954. The constitution was adjusted a number of times since then. In 1982 the current constitution of the People's Republic of China was adopted. It remains the governing structure for China and it places the Chinese Communist Party above the state.

The government of China consists of a legislature, the National People's Congress (NPC), a president, a premier, and a state council. The NPC is the legislature, the president is head of state, the premier is head of government, and the state council is the operational division of the government.

The National People's Council has about 3,000 members who are elected to terms of five years. It meets for about two weeks every year. You may wonder how the legislature can handle governing China meeting only two weeks a year, and the answer is that it does not. In effect, the NPC is a largely ceremonial body whose job is to pass decisions made by the Communist Party of China. The president is elected by the NPC, but that election is ceremonial; in practice, the person selected as president is determined by the Communist Party. In 2018, the president of China was Xi Jinping.

The third branch of the Chinese government, the State Council, consists of about thirty-five to fifty members who are heads of various national and local government agencies. (The country is divided into twenty-two provinces, five autonomous regions, and four municipalities.) Thus, the State Council is a bit like the cabinet in the U.S. government. It is headed by the premier, who is nominated by the president.

Communist Party Control. While the governmental structure looks somewhat like a democratic governmental structure, it isn't. The Communist Party of China makes all the decisions and Communist Party members occupy almost all the positions of power within the government. This central role of the Communist Party

Xi Jinping, the president of China.

© Alamy

of China is enshrined in the Chinese Constitution, which states that the Communist Party is essentially the only political party allowed within China.

The Chinese Communist Party has about 100 million members and is organized under the principle of **democratic centralism**, which is a system that allows for discussion of policy matters within the party. But once the decision of the party has been made, all members of the party are expected to uphold and not actively disagree with the decision. It has been described as "freedom of discussion, unity of action."

The actual decision-making power of China lies with the Communist Party's Politburo, which is a group of about twenty-five members. They oversee the Communist Party and generally have simultaneous appointments in government. Thus, Xi Jinping is both president and head of the Politburo. The Politburo meets once a month. How they formally make decisions is not spelled out, since the "unity of action" guiding mandate of the party strongly discourages vocal dissent once a decision is made. That's why we classify China as an autocracy, rather than a democracy.

Just how much power the Communist Party has can be seen in its decision in 2004 to become a more market-oriented economy. At that time, China introduced private property and allowed private businesses, both of which had previously been prohibited. It did this by simply making some amendments to the constitution. These amendments recognized private property, and promoted the non-public sector of the economy, essentially legitimizing the market sector of the economy and changing the Chinese economy from a command and

China

Population: 1.38 billion

Area: 3,705,407 square miles (9,596,960 square km)

Distribution: 58% urban; 42% rural

Capital city: Beijing

National anthem: "Zhōnghuá Mínguó guógē" ("March of the Volunteers")

Government leader: President Xi Jinping (since 2013)

Ethnic divisions: 91.6% Han Chinese; 8.4% 55 other ethnic minorities

Literacy rate: 96.4%

Religion: 52.2% nonreligious; 29.1% Chinese folk; 18.2% Buddhist; 5.1% Christian; 1.8% Muslim; 0.8% other

GDP: $23.12 trillion; per capita: $16,600 (purchasing power parity)

Currency unit: Renminbi (Yuan)

Monetary conversion rate: 1 yuan = $0.16 (Feb 2018)

Internet users: 731 million

Cell phones: 1.36 billion

Map of China

control economy to a market economy. There was no internal public political discussion. Such a major change without internal public discussion would have been impossible in a Western-style democracy.

While the Chinese government has enormous power, especially at the national level, with such a large country, its control over local government and affairs is limited. China is so large and diverse, both geographically and in population, that many local government officials within the Communist Party do what they want. Their confiscation of land, often with minimal compensation, has led to many local demonstrations and riots and anger at the government. Such complaints have been stifled by the enormous growth that the Chinese economy has experienced in recent years. But with the recent slowdown in growth, many outside observers suggest that maintaining quiet may be more difficult. In response President Xi has cracked down on corruption within the Communist Party and the Chinese government, especially on those who might pose a threat to his rule.

Nigerian Government

The next country we consider, the African country called the Federal Republic of Nigeria, provides a good example of the governance problems faced by many of the former European colonies in Africa. To understand the problems and government of Nigeria, it is helpful to take a brief look at the nation's precolonial and colonial history. The roots of Nigeria lie in its tribal foundations, with each tribe representing a unique blend of language, religion, and culture. The main tribes occupied separate geographic areas in the region and were differentiated by region: Muslim tribes in the North and Christian tribes in the south. These religious differences were tied to major cultural differences as well, which made cooperation among tribes difficult.

Before British colonization, there were distinct tribal regions with many subregions. For administrative ease the British grouped together various regions—the three largest of which were Lagos, the Niger Coast, and the Northern Protectorate—into the area that came to be known as Nigeria. Today, Nigeria remains a country of more than 250 ethnic groups with varying languages and customs. Its official language is English, which was chosen to facilitate cultural and linguistic unity. Nigeria's other major languages are Hausa, Yoruba, and Igbo, among more than 500 others.

Since its early beginnings—through colonization to the emergence of its first democratic republic to now—the history of Nigeria has been marked by ethnic conflict, civil war, and military rule. Since gaining independence from the British in 1960, Nigeria has progressed through three separate republics and survived the aftermaths of their collapses. With intervention from Western powers, the most recent—the fourth republic—hopes to mark the starting point for a lasting stable government in this important African country.

British Influence

The British became interested in West Africa at the time of the slave trade. British-based companies such as the Royal Niger Company occupied the region. As the companies slowly gained influence, so did the British Empire. This growth eventually climaxed in the establishment of the Protectorate of Nigeria at the beginning of the twentieth century. Despite the revocation of the charters of several of the British companies, the influence of the British government in the region continued to grow. With colonization under way, an influx of Christian missionaries brought churches and schools to the predominantly Muslim region. Within the first few years of the new century, several protectorates had been established, growing outward from the original stronghold in Lagos on the southern coast.

Nigeria

Population (approximate): 190 million (2018)

Area: 356,668 square miles (923,768 square km)

Distribution: 49% urban; 51% rural

Capital city: Abuja

National anthem: "Arise O Compatriots, Nigeria's Call Obey"

Government leader: President Muhammadu Buhari (since 2015)

Ethnic divisions: 29% Hausa and Fulani; 21% Yoruba; 18% Igbo; 10% Ijaw; 4% Kanuri; 3.5% Ibibio; 2.5% Tiv

Literacy rate: 60%

Religion: 50% Muslim; 40% Christian; 10% indigenous beliefs

GDP: $1.12 trillion; per capita: $5,900 (purchasing power parity)

Currency unit: Naira

Monetary conversion rate: 1 naira = $.003 (Feb 2018)

Internet users: 84 million

Cell phones: 154 million

Map of Nigeria

Each protectorate came under the authority of a lieutenant-governor, whose job was to keep order and generate revenue for the British government. Slow steps toward unification of the separate regions were taken in 1906, with the incorporation of Lagos into the Southern Protectorate. Several ideas were proposed to unify the remaining regions, and by 1914 the British had established the unified modern foundations of Nigeria, with Sir Frederick Lugard serving as its first governor. He set up an advisory body known as the Nigerian Council, which featured representation from each former protectorate and limited input from the native Africans.

Meanwhile, the National Congress of British West Africa established itself as a growing force in the region. Though ongoing fights with the British government failed to establish this group as part of the legislative council, native Africans slowly gained more representation. In 1922, the British Empire ratified the first constitution of Nigeria. However, the constitution failed to give equal weight to all of the former protectorates, and it continued the strategy of indirect rule of the northern and predominantly Muslim areas by the Christian southern areas. Over the years, Britain made numerous efforts to unite the northern and southern regions of Nigeria. At the same time, changes to the constitution, combined with growing nationalism, led to a push toward national sovereignty.

The sixty years of British rule were marked by continual fights for independence. With each of these fights, Britain allowed greater local Nigerian self-government, and created

President Muhammadu Buhari of Nigeria.

© dpa picture alliance / Alamy Stock Photo

various constitutions that were meant to demonstrate the efficacy of self-rule. Ultimately, Nigeria was given its independence in 1960, and it established a republican parliamentary system of government.

Modern Nigeria's Government: The Fourth Republic

Though British rule was not especially successful, the constitutions that Britain created to govern Nigeria became important guides for the development of the modern state of Nigeria. First, the legacy of British rule led to the creation of a government with both a legislative and executive branch; second, it led to the establishment of a system of common law based on British common law; and third, it spurred the creation of political parties. In short, the constitutions embodying British ideas became integrated with domestic Nigerian traditions to create the modern structure of the Nigerian government.

In addition to the national government, Nigeria has various regional governments and is divided into thirty-six states and 774 local governments. This large number of local governments is an attempt to provide a degree of home rule to the many different tribes that make up Nigeria.

The fourth republic can be considered a transition republic, as control has shifted from the military rule of the third republic to civilian rule. Nigeria uses a presidential system in which the president serves as both head of state and head of the government.

Nigeria has a bicameral legislature. The Senate has 109 seats—three from each state plus one from the capital, Abuja—and its members are elected by popular vote to serve four-year terms. The House of Representatives has 360 seats; its members are also elected by popular vote for four-year terms. There are two main parties, the People's Democratic Party (PDP) and the All Progressives Congress (APC), a coalition of opposition parties created prior to the 2015 elections in order to more forcefully challenge the president at the time, Goodluck Jonathan. Starting in 2015, the APC has held a majority in both houses of the National Assembly.

Nigeria's legal system is composed of four distinct systems of law: English law, common law, customary law, and **sharia law**, which is a form of Islamic law that gets significant press in the West because its punishments are often considered harsh by Westerners. Sharia is practiced primarily within the northern states of Nigeria, but it is being slowly introduced elsewhere in the country. The judicial system has a Federal Court of Appeals appointed by the federal government, and a Supreme Court whose members are appointed by the president.

Difficulties Facing Nigeria

Just as Britain found it difficult to govern the diverse cultural areas that made up the country, so too has the elected Nigerian government. It has faced fighting among political parties, uncompromising religious division, and a lack of cohesiveness between the former protectorate regions. These problems set the stage for subsequent upheavals and constant transitioning through various governmental structures. A military coup in 1966 overthrew the first republic, which led to civil war and enormous turmoil. Eventually, in 1979, a second republic was created, this time as a presidential system, but in 1983 it too ended in a coup and military rule.

At about that time, Western countries became interested in Nigeria, in large part because it was becoming an important oil-producing country in the world. They played a role in the establishment of a third republic, which resumed elections and attempted to establish a two-party system.

Nigeria emerged as a somewhat stable democracy in 1999 with the creation of the fourth republic. While this republic has been marred by the same pattern of violence and civil unrest that undid the first three republics, it has survived even though it is characterized by many of the inefficiencies and problems that plagued previous republics.

More recently, there have been positive signs in the development of a Nigerian democracy. In 2010, Umaru Yar'Adua, the first civilian and university-educated leader of Nigeria, died and was replaced by his vice president, Goodluck Jonathan, who was reelected in 2011 in what outside observers saw as a relatively free election. He, in turn, was defeated in 2015 by a former military dictator, Muhammadu Buhari. Many feared that Jonathan's supporters would riot and not accept the result, but Jonathan urged his supporters to accept it. He stated: "Nobody's ambition is worth the blood of any Nigerian. . . . The unity, stability and progress of our dear country is more important than anything else." His acceptance of the election results made him a contender for the Ibrahim Prize. (See Box.)

Buhari's victory marked the first time a sitting president had conceded power to another leader, and is seen as a victory for democracy in Nigeria. But it will only succeed if Buhari is successful in dealing with the two major problems that led to Jonathan's defeat: governmental corruption and the insurgency and terrorist activities of an extreme and secretive Islamic sect named Boko Haram. As of 2018 he was struggling with both, as well as facing serious health concerns, which limited his ability to deal with problems even if he wanted to do so.

Government corruption is rampant throughout Nigeria, as government "oil money" seems to evaporate from government reports and suddenly appear in government officials' personal accounts. This has led the population not to trust the government. Boko Haram's success is partially due to that corruption—if people don't trust government, they don't support it, which creates the conditions for lawlessness. The inequality in the Nigerian economy is another reason for Boko Haram's success. It operates mainly in the Islamic north of Nigeria, which lags behind the richer south of Nigeria in almost all measures. Boko Haram takes advantage of people's economic grievances to radicalize them. This inequality, and the religious differences that exist between the north and the south, present serious problems for any Nigerian leader.

And the Winner of the Ibrahim Prize for Achievement in African Leadership is . . . Nobody

Most of you will have heard of the Nobel Prize, but you probably haven't heard of the world's richest prize—the Ibrahim Prize, which is a prize for excellence in African leadership. The winner gets $5 million plus an additional annual $200,000 pension for life. The prize was established in 2007 by the Sudanese billionaire Mo Ibrahim as an annual award, but for several years, the award was not given out because the award committee decided that it couldn't find a deserving winner from any of the more than fifty African countries. The winner needs to be a democratically elected former African head of state who has left office peacefully in the last three years and who has demonstrated exceptional leadership.

Goodluck Jonathan was not seen as an especially effective leader. There was rampant corruption under his rule, and his party worked hard to "influence" the election by buying votes and stuffing ballot boxes (as did the other parties running for election—such practices are common in Nigerian elections). But as the incumbent, Jonathan was in a stronger position to succeed in his efforts than the opposition. However, public opinion was so strong against him, because of corruption and failure to effectively fight against terrorists, that he lost by a substantial margin despite that advantage in rigging the election. Faced with those clear-cut election results, he accepted defeat. It was that gracious acceptance of his election loss that made him a strong candidate for the Ibrahim Prize, despite his leadership failings in office. He didn't win; instead, in 2017, the prize was awarded to Ellen Johnson Sirleaf, who had just stepped down as the president of Liberia and was the first female head of state in modern African history.

A couple of points are worth noting in this history. First, the geographic area that became Nigeria did not develop organically; it was imposed by the British to make colonial rule easier. The combination of diverse cultural regions is problematic because Nigerians often see themselves first as tribal members, then as Nigerian citizens. Second, Nigeria has oil wealth, which one would think is a blessing, but which, in many ways, is a curse. The problem is that the oil wealth creates a prize to fight for, making it difficult for Nigeria's non-oil-producing regions to accept a breakup in the country, because then they would get none of the wealth. At the same time, that oil wealth provides a strong reason for the oil-producing regions to support a breakup because then they would reap the financial benefits from the oil. Oil wealth also means that outside interests will fund the side that promises them some of that wealth. Consequently, the civil unrest that has marked recent Nigerian political history may continue for a long time.

A Final Comment

The history of the Nigerian government demonstrates the problems that multiculturalism presents for democracy. For a democracy to work, its people must share certain values, one of the most important of which is that people will not resort to armed conflict even when they feel they have been wronged. That value depends on a level of goodwill and belief that others will not take advantage of situations when they are in power. In part because of the diversity in Nigeria, that goodwill often does not exist, and Nigeria continues to struggle with the problems imposed on it by its colonial history.

Russian Government

To understand the current government in Russia, we need to consider its history. That history is one of a centralized Russian Empire ruled by tsars. The empire included not only what is now Russia, but also a number of surrounding countries and areas. World War I created severe economic difficulties for the Russian Empire and led to political confusion and civil war. In 1917, the **Bolsheviks,** members of the more radical majority of the Russian Social Democratic Party, under the leadership of Vladimir Lenin took over the Russian government and, after winning the civil war, established control over the country.

In 1922, Lenin designed a federal type of constitution that incorporated republics surrounding Russia, republics that had previously been part of the Russian Empire. The constitution marked the beginning of the Union of Soviet Socialist Republics (USSR). Although the constitution was revised in 1936 and again in 1977, this constitution was, in principle, the same as the one that Lenin wrote in 1922, until the fall of the USSR in 1991. The republics that made it up each became independent states, connected by history and a loose commonwealth. These former Soviet states are home to many Russian speakers, and Russia still sees many of them as within its sphere of influence.

A key element of the Soviet constitution and the government of the Soviet Union was the relationship between the government and the Communist Party. Article 6 of the Soviet constitution stated: "The Communist party of the Soviet Union is the leading and guiding force of the Soviet society and the nucleus of its political system and of all state and public organizations." The Communist Party's dominant control of the Soviet government meant that the government was largely a rubber stamp and administrative institution for carrying out policies made by the Communist Party.

There was a radical change in the Soviet political system in the late 1980s when Soviet leader Mikhail Gorbachev introduced a number of liberalizing reforms. These reforms reduced the power of the Communist Party and unleashed a wave of nationalistic and economic upheaval. Faced with this upheaval and reduction in power of the Communist

President Vladimir Putin of Russia.

© ITAR-TASS Photo Agency/ Alamy

Party, a number of communist leaders attempted a **coup d'état**—an extra-constitutional takeover of a country. That coup failed because the military and a majority of the people in the former Soviet Union resisted, and leaders such as Boris Yeltsin, the head of the Russian Republic, refused to accept the coup and began a struggle against it. The coup leaders were arrested and the Soviet Union ceased to exist. Russia, the largest and most dominant state in the Soviet Union, inherited much of the government and institutional structure of the former Soviet Union. Each of the republics that had formerly been part of the Soviet Union claimed its independence. In the 1990s a number of the republics joined together with Russia in what they called the Commonwealth of Independent States, but it was primarily a symbolic organization. Chaos reigned in the early 1990s in all the countries that made up the former Soviet Union, but by the mid 1990s Russia's new governmental structure took shape.

Specifically, Russia created a governmental system consisting of a president, a legislative branch, called the Congress of People's Deputies, and a judicial branch. The three branches of government shared roughly equal powers, causing many gridlocks in policy decisions in the early years. A new constitution in 1993 created a stronger president but also maintained a Federal Assembly composed of an upper Chamber of the Federation and a lower State Duma with checks on presidential power.

In 2000, Vladimir Putin was elected president. Throughout his years in office, he has been an extraordinarily popular president, in part because he brought stability back to Russia, and in part because he brought pride back to being Russian. In 2004, he was elected to a second term. Because of a two-term limitation on service as president, he could not run for election in 2008, but his handpicked successor, Dmitry Medvedev, won in a landslide after hardly campaigning. After the election, Medvedev appointed Putin as prime minister.

In 2012, Putin and Medvedev exchanged positions, and Putin ran for president once again for a six-year term. (It had been increased by two years since the 2008 election.) This was allowed by the Soviet constitution, since technically Putin was out of office when Medvedev was president. Medvedev ran for prime minister. Both won by large amounts, and while the actual voting seemed relatively fair, many believed that the underlying process was unfair, since strong opposition candidates were prevented from running in a variety of subtle ways. Because of this belief, major demonstrations occurred in Russia following the elections, with demonstrators claiming that the elections were rigged.

Neutral observers saw some voter fraud but not enough to change the results of the election. But they also agreed that the success of Putin and Medvedev was in part because some of their strongest opponents, who might actually have been candidates with a good chance of beating them, had been arrested for a variety of reasons or were otherwise prevented from running. Differences of opinion existed about the legitimacy of the reasons that prevented them from running. So while Putin currently remains in power and has significant popular support, an undercurrent of discontent exists.

This opposition movement reared its head in the run-up to the 2018 presidential elections, with opposition candidate Alexei Navalny spearheading a campaign promising to fight corruption and decrease tensions between Russia and the West. Two months prior to the

Russia

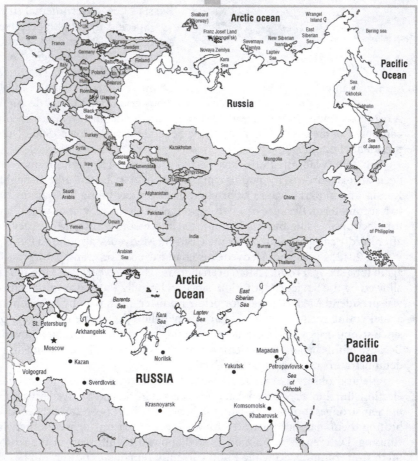

Population (approximate): 142 million

Area: 6,601,650 square miles (17,098,200 square km)

Distribution: 74% urban; 26% rural

Capital city: Moscow

National anthem: "Hymn of the Russian Federation" (formerly "The Patriotic Song" and "God Save the Tsar")

Government leaders: President Vladimir Putin (since 2012); Prime Minister Dmitry Medvedev (since 2012)

Former Soviet Union: Russia is the largest country of the former Soviet Union. The other countries were Armenia, Azerbaijan, Belarus, Estonia, Georgia, Kazakhstan, Kyrgyzstan, Latvia, Lithuania, Moldova, Tajikistan, Turkmenistan, Ukraine, and Uzbekistan.

Ethnic divisions: 80% Russian; 4% Tatar; 2% Ukrainian; 1% Bashkir; 1% Chuvash; 12% other

Literacy rate: 99.7%

Religion: 67% atheist; 15–20% Russian Orthodox; 10–15% Muslim; 2% other Christian

GDP: $4 trillion; per capita: $27,900 (purchasing power parity)

Currency unit: Ruble

Monetary conversion rate: 1 ruble = $.018 (Feb 2018)

Internet users: 90 million

Cell phones: 231 million

Map of Russia

election, Navalny was prevented from becoming an official candidate on the basis of charges brought against him for organizing unofficial protests and campaign rallies. In response, he called for a boycott of the general election, arguing that the vote was rigged by the fact that no viable challengers to Putin's reelection were allowed to have their names on the ballot. Despite all this, most Russians value stability, continuity, and a strong Russian state over the values that Navalny espoused, and Putin remains highly popular in Russia.

Putin and Medvedev are less popular in the West than in Russia, as they have tried to exert Russia's influence on the world political scene. Because of its authoritarian history, Russia is not seen by many in the West as a Western-type democracy, but since it does rely on elections to select its leaders, and the fact that its leaders have widespread popular support, many choose to call it an authoritarian democracy.

Saudi Arabian Government

Unlike the other four countries we have considered, all of which call themselves democracies, Saudi Arabia makes no such claim. It is a monarchy, and it provides us with an example of an authoritarian autocracy.

The Saudi Arabian government is relatively modern; the present kingdom was established in 1932. Before that time, what is now Saudi Arabia, like the other countries in the Arabian Peninsula, was a collection of tribes generally following Islamic religious traditions. Life in the individual tribes and among the various tribes was governed by those traditions and by the **Qur'an,** the primary Islamic religious body of writings. Until the twentieth century, no single long-term leader emerged from this collection of tribes.

That changed in the early 1900s, when Ibn Saud conquered most of the tribes in central Arabia and became the political and spiritual leader of the Bedouin tribes. He extended his authority during the first third of the twentieth century and created the Kingdom of Saudi Arabia in 1932.

The kingdom has no written constitution, relying instead on historical precedent, the Qur'an, and royal decrees as its guides. Until recently, there were no legislative bodies and no political parties. It is was in a very real sense an absolute monarchy. But even absolute monarchies have their limits. Although the Saudi state has no constitution and no laws that restrict the king's powers, the Qur'an and historical custom limit what the king does, and over time a quasi-constitutional system has developed. The ruler is chosen by members of the royal family from among its thousands of members, subject to the approval of a group of Muslim leaders (the *ulema*). The *ulema* can remove the ruler, and he is also dependent on support from tribal leaders and, more recently, from important businessmen. Notice that there is no question of female rule in Saudi Arabia, because Islam's view of women precludes them from taking any such role.

Running a government is too much for any one person, and in 1953 King Saud created a Council of Ministers to assist him, with a prime minister playing a significant role partially independent of the king. The prime minister appoints the council, along with other advisory councils which assist him

Crown Prince Mohammed bin Salman.

© Khalid Mohammed/AP

Saudi Arabia

Population (approximate): 28.6 million

Area: 830,000 square miles (2,150,000 square km)

Distribution: 83% urban; 17% rural

Capital city: Riyadh

National anthem: "Aash Al Maleek" ("Long Live Our Beloved King")

Government leader: King and Prime Minister Salman bin Abd al-Aziz Al Saud (since 2015)

Ethnic divisions: 90% Arab; 10% Afro-Asian

Literacy rate: 95%

Religion: 100% Muslim (90% Sunni, 10% Shia)

GDP: $1.8 trillion; per capita: $55,300 (purchasing power parity)

Currency unit: Riyal

Monetary conversion rate: 1 riyal = $0.27 (Feb 2018)

Internet users: 20.8 million

Cell phones: 47.9 million

Map of Saudi Arabia

in both legislative and executive matters. When King Saud died, he was replaced by one of his descendants, King Faisal, who, working with a council of ministers, chose a successor from the thousands of descendants to be crown prince, along with someone who became second in line to the throne. These two chosen successors were given important roles in government to provide training and to see how well they did.

Until recently the chosen leaders had always been older senior members of the Saud family. But in 2015, a relatively young Salman bin Abd al-Aziz Al Saud became king and he appointed a 59-year-old crown prince and a 30-year-old deputy crown prince, who upon his appointment as deputy crown prince became the Saudi defense minister. In November 2017, this young deputy crown prince, Mohammed bin Salman, became crown prince and first deputy prime minister. Soon thereafter he led a purge of more than forty members of the royal family and Saudi Arabian elite, arresting them on various corruption charges. Some people saw this as a consolidation of bin Salman's power, while others applauded the effort to hold elites accountable for their crimes. Such a drastic restructuring of the upper echelons of the Saudi Arabian government was

*T*he Arab Spring and Saudi Arabia

In 2011, there were uprisings against the rulers in many Arab countries, including many of Saudi Arabia's neighbors, such as Bahrain and Yemen. Saudi Arabia avoided an uprising in part because soon after the uprisings in other countries, it distributed $30 billion in additional funds to its population. The lack of jobs that other Arab countries face is less of a problem in Saudi Arabia, where its oil wealth allows it to provide economic support for its citizens. But it faces other serious problems—including dissension between the ruling Sunnis and the Shiites, who claim discrimination.

Another issue involves women's rights, which according to traditional Islamic values are limited for the good of the women. Since Saudi Arabia is a highly traditional society, these values limiting women's rights are embedded in the constitution. For example, all Saudi women must have a male guardian, without whom they cannot make most major decisions. Not all women object to these limitations. For example, in an interview reported in the *New York Times* in 2010, one woman stated:

> In Saudi culture, women have their integrity and a special life that is separate from men. As a Saudi woman, I demand to have a guardian. My work requires me to go to different regions of Saudi Arabia, and during my business trips I always bring my husband or my brother. They ask nothing in return—they only want to be with me. The image in the West is that we are dominated by men, but they always forget the aspect of love. People who aren't familiar with sharia often have the wrong idea. If you want stability and safety in your life, if you want a husband who takes care of you, you won't find it except in Islam.

Other more secular women find the limitations to be a violation of their basic rights. With such deep divisions in its cultural views, we can expect to see further unrest in Saudi Arabia in the future.

unprecedented, and it remains to be seen whether a new stability has been found or whether more changes will take place in the coming years. In 2018, a dissident journalist was murdered in the Saudi embassy in Turkey. Many believed the murder was done under the direction of the crown prince, leading to a loss of support by Western governments.

As is the case with many governments, especially those established in the twentieth century, the Saudi system of government is still evolving. It is exploring the use of a Consultative Council, which would play a more influential role in policymaking in the future. That council now has the right to draft and interpret laws, but most power still resides with the king.

People tolerate strong autocracies in which the people have little or no power for numerous reasons, including military force wielded by the government, historical precedent, fear of the chaos that a change would bring, or satisfaction with the existing state of affairs. In the Saudi case, despite the enormous income taken by the Saudi monarchy, the Saudi people are relatively satisfied. The reason is the huge amount of oil income received by the government that allows it to undertake numerous social projects for the people. For example, all Saudis are entitled to free medical care, and state employees often receive bonuses equivalent to thousands of U.S. dollars in the name of "offsetting the increasing cost of living." These projects are financed without significant taxation, even while providing lavish lifestyles for the Saudi royal family.

The stability of the Saudi Arabian autocracy depends very much on the price of oil. A high price allows the monarchy-led government to "buy its legitimacy." The country's oil revenues constitute more than 75 percent of its annual budget, and therefore its economic health goes up and down with oil prices. Low oil prices squeeze the government budget and lead to austerity measures that create agitation. Thus, the discovery of shale oil outside the kingdom, which led to a drastic fall in the price of oil worldwide, presented difficulties for the monarchy. If oil prices fall, there could well be considerable turmoil in the Saudi system of government in coming years.

The Saudi government finds itself in a difficult position. Internally, the ultra-religious Sunni Muslims advocate a return to more strict Islamic tradition, while externally it faces intense criticism from human rights groups and Western-oriented Saudis who call for increased democracy, less strict punishments for criminals than called for in sharia law and equal treatment for women under the law.

The structure of the Saudi government is changing. In 2005, municipal elections were held and were seen by some outside observers as a first step toward democracy in the kingdom. In 2011, the Saudis announced that women would be allowed to run for local elections and vote. Such Westernization of Saudi Arabia has infuriated a number of Saudis, such as rich businessman/terrorist Osama bin Laden, who masterminded the 9/11 attacks on the United States.

One of the things that makes it difficult for Saudi Arabia and other Islamic states to be friendly with the United States is the United States' strong support for Israel. That support has fueled anti-American sentiment in Saudi Arabia and throughout the Middle East. If Saudi Arabia does evolve into a democracy, which the United States has stated that it ostensibly wants, the result will likely be a government far less supportive of U.S. Middle East policy than the current government.

Some Lessons about Governments

This survey of governments of the world should give you a sense of the variety and diversity of governments—both democratic and autocratic. From it you can see that there are many types of democracy and autocracy and that it is difficult to compare one with the other.

A number of general points about governments can be made:

1. Governments reflect their history (for example, the Nigerian government reflects its British heritage, and the strong French government reflects its unstable history).
2. Governments are evolving. France, Nigeria, and Saudi Arabia do not have the same governmental structure they had fifty or sixty years ago, and the Soviet Union no longer exists. These countries are unlikely to have the same governmental structure fifty years from now as they have today. The rate of change depends on the historical tradition as current government practices become embodied in society and place limitations on change.
3. Autocracies are more likely to change than long-standing democracies. The reason is that the process of change is easier. When the former Soviet Union decided to change governmental form, it could do so relatively easily compared with the United States. Saudi Arabia would be able to do so even more rapidly.
4. Changes in autocracies occur from within as much as from without. The change in the former Soviet government is an example. Often the process of liberalization brings about opposition that otherwise would have been silent or suppressed.

More rules and insights are embodied in the examples, but we leave them for you to draw out.

Future Changes in Governments

What does the future hold for these and other governments? As usual, it is unclear. We are likely to see significant changes in the structure of Middle Eastern autocracies as the aftershocks of the Arab Spring continue to reverberate around the region, and as these countries struggle to adapt to an ever-changing world. How much change we see will likely depend on the economic situation. If the coming years hold prosperity, the present forms of most governments are likely to continue. If the economic and social conditions remain bad or worsen, however, more changes can be expected. And if there is a major nuclear war, who knows what will remain of government? Obviously, we hope such major changes will not occur because of war, but current troublesome social and economic conditions could dash those hopes.

Some of these social and economic conditions are high unemployment rates in many countries, including much of industrialized Europe; the proliferation of destructive weapons systems in areas of the world where social, political, economic, and religious quarrels are already disrupting ordinary life; repression and denial of opportunity to large populations in some countries; widespread financial hardship in some countries burdened with heavy debt they owe to more prosperous nations; refugee crises in Europe and Southeast Asia that threaten political and economic stability; and environmental pollution that threatens to change whole areas of the world. Fortunately not all of these conditions exist in any one country, and it is always possible that diplomacy and, ultimately, good sense exercised by governments will enable the compromises and adjustments necessary for peacekeeping to prevail.

 Study and **Review**

Key Points

- The French government is a parliamentary democracy with both a president and a prime minister.
- The Chinese government is an autocracy in which the Communist Party, through its policy of democratic centralism, retains significant control over the state.
- The Nigerian government is a republican democracy whose political instability in large part reflects its colonial heritage.

- The government of Russia is probably best described as an authoritarian democracy.
- The Saudi government is an autocracy based largely on Islamic principles.
- Some lessons about governments that can be drawn from these examples include the following: governments reflect their history, governments are changing, autocracies can change quickly, and autocracies often change from within.

Some Important Terms

Bastille Day (296)
Bolsheviks (306)
censure motion (297)
coup d'état (307)

democratic centralism (301)
French Revolution (296)
presidential system (299)
Qur'an (309)

sharia law (304)
vote of confidence (297)

Questions for Review and Discussion

General Questions

1. What is the relationship between the Declaration of the Rights of Man and the French constitution?
2. How can the French prime minister be removed from office?
3. What is an important way in which Chinese governmental history differs from European governmental history?
4. When did China become a communist-ruled state?
5. What is meant by democratic centralism?
6. What is meant by "freedom of discussion, unity of action"?

7. Why is it harder for Nigeria to maintain political stability than it is for many other countries?
8. What is the official language of Nigeria? Why was it chosen?
9. How does the discovery of oil in a country make it harder to govern that country?
10. How does the new Russian Federation differ from the former Soviet Republic?
11. President Putin enjoys widespread support in Russia and was elected in a vote that was seen as fair. Given this fact, why do many Western observers call Russia an authoritarian democracy?
12. Does the Saudi autocratic government have unlimited power?

13. Why do the Saudi people tolerate the Saudi autocracy?

14. State four lessons about government that can be derived from this chapter.

15. What do you believe would be the ideal system of government?

Internet Questions

1. Using http://www.gouvernement.fr/en/composition-of-the-government, list four of the sixteen minister posts under the French Prime Minister.

2. Go to http://www.nigeriaembassyusa.org/index.php?page=test-sub. In terms of population, how does Nigeria rank compared to other African countries? How does it rank in terms of physical size?

3. According to http://www.saudia-online.com/saudi_arabia.htm, what does the legislative branch of Saudi Arabia's government consist of?

4. Go to http://www.time.com/time/specials/2007/personoftheyear/ and watch *Time's* interview with Vladimir Putin. According to the reporter, why was Putin chosen as the 2007 *Time* Person of the Year? According to Putin, what is a country's sovereign right?

5. Using the CIA World Factbook, https://www.cia.gov/library/publications/the-world-factbook/, what are the administrative divisions of Mexico?

For Further Study

Books to Explore

Aarts, Paul, and Carolien Roelants, *Saudi Arabia: A Kingdom in Peril*, London: Hurst, 2015.

Fenby, Jonathan, *Penguin History of Modern China*, London: Allen Lane, 2009.

Gaffney, John, *Political Leadership in France: From Charles de Gaulle to Nicolas Sarkozy*, New York: Macmillan, 2012.

Gassen, Mash, *The Future is History: How Totalitarianism Reclaimed Russia*, New York: Riverhead Books, 2016.

Isikoff, Michael, and David Corn, *Russian Roulette: The Inside Story of Putin's War on America and the Election of Donald Trump*, New York: Twelve, 2018.

Lacey, Robert, *Inside the Kingdom: Kings, Clerics, Modernists, Terrorists, and the Struggle for Saudi Arabia*, New York: Viking, 2009.

Mcfaul, Michael, Nikolai Petrov, and Andrei Ryabov, *Between Dictatorship and Democracy: Russian Post-Communist Political Reform*, Washington, DC: Carnegie Endowment for International Peace, 2004.

Myers, Steven Lee, *The New Tsar: The Rise and Reign of Vladimir Putin*, London: Knopf, 2015.

Nwogu, Nneoma, *Shaping Truth, Reshaping Justice: Sectarian Politics and the Nigerian Truth Commission*, Lanham, MD: Lexington Books, 2007.

Sakwa, Richard, *The Crisis of Russian Democracy: The Dual State, Factionalism and the Medvedev Succession*, New York: Cambridge University Press, 2011.

Shambaugh, David, *China's Future*, Cambridge: Polity Press, 2016.

Internet Sites to Explore

"https://www.cia.gov/library/publications/the-world-factbook/" CIA World Factbook.

"http://www.gouvernement.fr/en/news" The French Government.

"http://www.gov.ru/index_en.html" The Government of the Russian Federation.

"https://www.ted.com/talks/martin_jacques_understanding_the_rise_of_china?language=en" Martin Jacques: Understanding the rise of China.

"http://statehouse.gov.ng/" The Nigerian Government.

"http://www.kantei.go.jp/foreign/index-e.html" Prime Minister of Japan and His Government.

"http://www.saudiembassy.net/" The Royal Embassy of Saudi Arabia.

Democratic Government in the United States

chapter 16

After reading this chapter, you should be able to:

- Give a brief account of the development of the U.S. government
- List the five key elements in the Declaration of Independence
- Outline the structure of the U.S. federal government
- Explain the distribution of powers as set out in the U.S. Constitution
- Describe the political process in the United States
- Summarize the role of the fourth estate, the political elite, the military-industrial complex, and PACs in the political process

An oppressive government is more to be feared than a tiger.

—Confucius

In the previous chapter, we briefly considered the governments of five countries. In this chapter, we look specifically at the U.S. government and how it works. As you will see, government, like other aspects of your life, is in an ongoing process of evolution. With the election of Donald Trump as president, that evolution was sped up significantly. Trump was different than other recent presidents. He ran against the establishment, not as part of it, and had no experience in politics. Instead he was a real estate mogul and reality TV star.

Many voters liked that. They felt that both parties had let them down, and did not relate to their concerns. Voters liked that Trump dumped on the establishment—that he promised to drain the swamp, and that he didn't convey a sense of book smarts or even political smarts, but rather business smarts—he knew how to make a deal, and to tell it like it was.

The election of Trump captures much of what is good and bad about U.S. democracy. First, his election didn't destroy democracy. Rather than a coup, there was a peaceful transfer of power. That would not have happened in some countries. Second, his election forced a rethinking of the positions of both the Republican and Democratic elite, and a reduction in the self-satisfaction that had previously prevailed.

The bad was that it reinforced, or at least exposed, the polar divisions that had developed. Democracy works by compromise and checks and balances on the power of not only of government, but also of the elite. Trump's election was part of the check on the political elite's power, and it suggested that they had lost sight of the broader public's views which blended a commitment to individualism and fairness in ways that neither party captured. We will discuss these issues later in the chapter, but before we do it is useful to review the historical development of our government.

Historical Development of U.S. Government

Because the United States started as a colonial possession of Great Britain, it is natural that our government reflects a British heritage. Initially, ties to Britain were strong, but when Britain tried to tighten control over colonial trade and to levy taxes on the colonists without obtaining the consent of the colonial legislatures, the colonies took action to end British rule and set up their own state.

The most important event in the formation of the U.S. government took place when the Second Continental Congress met in 1776, issued the Declaration of Independence, and resolved to draw up a plan for the United States of America. The Declaration of Independence states that:

- The people have the right to revolt against oppressive government.
- Legitimate government must be based on the consent of the governed.
- Both the ruler and the ruled are obligated to preserve a government that pursues legitimate purposes.
- All men are created equal.
- All men are endowed with certain inalienable rights, including life, liberty, and the pursuit of happiness.

These principles became the foundation of the U.S. form of government.

The Declaration of Independence formalized the war that had begun with the Battle of Bunker Hill in April 1775. It proclaimed the colonies "free and independent states." Having declared themselves independent, the states faced the problem of establishing a workable form of government. This was done in a Constitutional Convention held in Philadelphia in May 1787.

The Constitutional Convention succeeded because the delegates were willing to compromise. The decision to have a federal government was probably the biggest compromise. It satisfied both supporters of a **unitary government**—a government in which all the power is centralized in the national government, and the central government is absolutely supreme over all other government within such a nation—and supporters of a **federation,** a number of separate states, each of which retains control of its own internal affairs. The federal system of government had aspects of both. States retained control of some issues; the central government retained control over others.

Other important compromises included:

- The differential representation in the House (by population) and Senate (two per state).
- The establishment of an Electoral College to choose the president. The **Electoral College** is a body of electors chosen by the voters in each state to elect the president and the vice president. In the Electoral College, each state is allowed to have as many electors as it has representatives and senators in Congress, and each state can determine the method of choosing its electors.
- The direct election by all the people of a particular state of its House members and the selection by state legislatures of the two senators allowed each state.[1]

In addition to those just mentioned, compromises on many other issues were necessary because of the extensive conflict of interests and opinions. In essence, the Constitution can be characterized as a bundle of compromises.

The U.S. Constitution—the foundation of the U.S. government and legal system—was signed on September 17, 1787, and forwarded to Congress with the recommendation that it

---

[1] The election of senators by the people is one change that has taken place in the Constitution.

be submitted to state conventions for ratification and that it become effective on acceptance by nine states, which it was after much struggle.

Many of the states ratified the Constitution on the condition that amendments protecting private rights be adopted as soon as the new government was formed. The first ten amendments, adopted in 1791, accomplished this insofar as the national government was concerned. This **Bill of Rights**—a formal statement of the fundamental rights of the people of a nation—forbade the national government to invade basic private rights.

The Structure of U.S. Government

Because of the compromises in the Constitution, the United States has a federal government. It operates on three levels: national, state, and local. Over time, the relative strengths of these various levels have changed. Specifically, the national government has been strengthened in part by wars, in part by advances in communication and transportation, and in part by the increasing complexity and nationwide scope of social problems. Nevertheless, state and local governments are still of great importance both to the individual and to our entire society.

Each of the fifty states, with its independent constitution, its own supreme court, and its own governmental agencies, exercises jurisdiction over most personal relationships, such as those of husband and wife, parent and child, and employer and employee, and also over property and business matters, including contracts, deeds, wills, corporations, and partnerships. Each state regulates commerce within its borders; establishes and controls local government; protects health, safety, and public order; conducts elections; and provides education.

Local governments are subdivisions of the state, are incorporated by the state, and possess varying degrees of autonomy. They include the county, city, town, township, village, borough, and school district and also include special agencies such as park districts, sanitary districts, and planning and zoning boards. Local governments are close to the individual, who can hardly escape noticing the services they provide. The sidewalks, lights, schools, public health service, police and fire protection, parks, beaches, and libraries are largely provided by local governments.

Structure of the National Government

Because the national government has become most important, we describe it in some detail. The national government of the United States as established by the Constitution is divided into three branches: the executive branch, the legislative branch, and the judicial branch. Figure 16.1 is worth careful study; it provides an outline of the structure of our national government.

The **executive branch,** the branch of government charged with the execution of laws and the administration of public affairs, is headed by the president, who is in charge of enforcing or executing the laws. Under the president, to whom all members of the executive branch are directly responsible, are the vice president, who would become president if the president were unable to serve, and the **Cabinet,** the heads of the major administrative departments of government. These Cabinet members, called secretaries, are appointed by the president, subject to approval by the Senate. Within the executive department there are also a number of agencies and commissions such as the Environmental Protection Agency. The extent to which these are responsible to the president is determined by law. The executive branch of the government is primarily concerned with enforcing the laws and with carrying on daily the many activities in which a modern government must engage. However, the president also plays an important role in determining governmental policies.

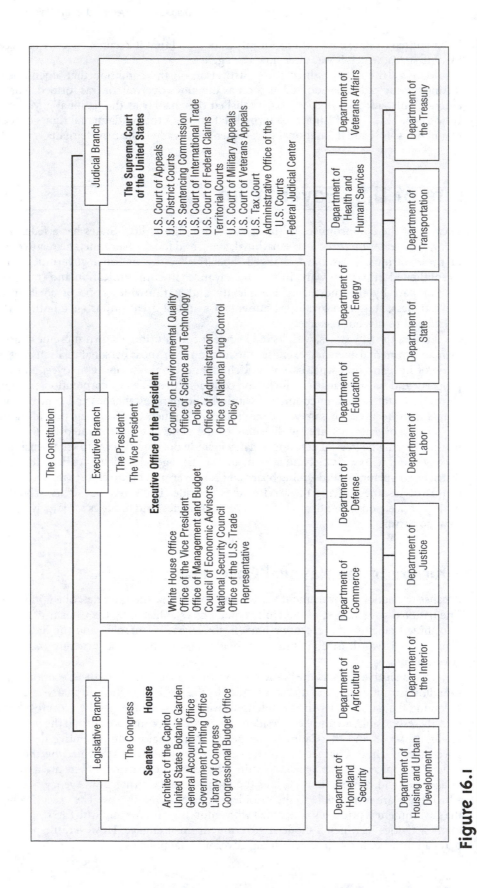

Figure 16.1

Diagram of the government of the United States as of 2018. The U.S. government is organized into three branches: the legislative, executive, and judicial. (Source: U.S. Bureau of the Census, Statistical Abstract of the United States)

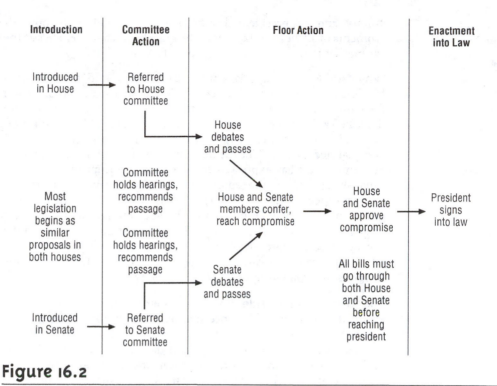

Figure 16.2

How a bill becomes law. *This diagram illustrates the most typical way in which proposed legislation is enacted into law. There are more complicated, as well as simpler, routes. Most bills fall by the wayside and never become law.*

The **legislative branch** is the branch of the government vested with the power to enact and legislate the law. It consists of the two houses of Congress: the House of Representatives and the Senate. The legislative branch is chiefly the policymaking agency of government. It determines government policies by passing laws, or statutes. (See Figure 16.2 and the box on page 324 for a better understanding of how a bill becomes a law.)

The **judicial branch** is the branch of government that interprets the laws as they apply to particular cases that may arise. It consists of the Supreme Court and of the various lower and special federal courts. Once the meaning of a law has been decided in its application to a case, a precedent is said to have been established, and similar cases are likely to be decided in the same way. The federal courts interpret not only the laws passed by Congress but also the Constitution itself. For legal purposes, the Constitution of the United States means whatever the Supreme Court says it means. If the Court should obviously and persistently misinterpret the Constitution, the primary redress would be for the House of Representatives to impeach the justices responsible. Then the Senate would try them and, if they were convicted, remove them from office.

We now turn to the broad issues, clarifying our national government.

The Nature of Our National Government

A short answer to the question "What kind of national government do we have?" would contain as few as four words: democratic, republican, federal, and presidential. Our national government is democratic rather than dictatorial or oligarchical; it is republican rather than monarchical; it is federal, in contrast to most of the governments of the world, which are unitary; and it is presidential rather than parliamentary. It should be noted that the governments of all the fifty states have the same basic characteristics as the national government except that they are unitary rather than federal.

Why Our Government Is Both a Democracy and a Republic. There is an old but fruitless argument as to whether the United States is a democracy or a republic. Actually, the nation has the essential characteristics of both of these forms, and therefore it may be described as both democratic and republican. A **republic** is a form of government in which the head of state, the president, does not inherit the office but is elected by those citizens who are qualified to vote. The United States is a republic according to this definition. Our Supreme Court has expressed the American concept of a republic as follows: "The distinguishing feature of the republican form of government is the right of the people to choose its own officers." This makes *republic* synonymous with *democracy,* which is the kind of government we have. Technically the United States has a **representative democracy,** a form of government in which the people make most governmental decisions not directly but through elected representatives, rather than a **pure democracy,** a political system under which all citizens vote directly on every piece of legislation. Pure democracy is possible only in very small communities.

The Meaning of Presidential Government. We have noted that the U.S. national government is presidential. In a **presidential form of government,** the chief executive (usually called the president) is elected for a definite period of years independent of the legislative or lawmaking body and has certain powers derived directly from the Constitution. In contrast, under the **parliamentary form of government,** the executive branch is a committee, or cabinet, that represents the majority party in the legislative body and holds office only as long as it can command a majority in that body.

Great Britain presents a good example of parliamentary government. There the cabinet and its chief, the prime minister, are responsible to Parliament, and they can hold office only as long as Parliament supports their policies. The Parliament may withdraw its support for the prime minister by approving or introducing a vote of no confidence against the government. This system makes for close coordination of the executive and legislative departments. Under the presidential system, as exemplified in the United States, it is possible for the president and the majority in Congress to represent different parties and therefore fail to cooperate. This has happened frequently in recent years.

The president has two major functions: to take the lead in formulating policies and proposing legislation to Congress, and the administrative task of keeping the vast and unwieldy government organization operating smoothly and efficiently to perform its various normal duties. The latter involves many important responsibilities, including acting as commander in chief of the nation's armed forces. Thus, when the United States went to war against Iraq, it was the then President George W. Bush who ultimately was responsible for making the decision to do so.

Distribution of Powers by the Constitution. A broad view of the national Constitution as originally devised and as it stands today reveals a wide distribution of political power. The Founding Fathers, though desiring a central government strong enough to govern, feared too great a concentration of power and therefore attempted to

President Trump.

© The Photo Access / Alamy Stock Photo

devise a means for preventing the abuse of power. Broadly speaking, power is distributed in accordance with four constitutional principles:

1. **Federalism**—power is divided between the national government and the separate states.
2. **Separation of powers**—legislative, judicial, and executive powers are divided among three separate branches of the national government, each with its own duties and limitations of power.
3. **Checks and balances**—the decisions of one branch must be ratified by different branches of government. This system is designed so that no one branch of government can become too powerful.
4. **Limited government**—power is divided between the people and the government. This fourth principle includes the democratic doctrines of popular sovereignty, the inviolability of personal rights, and constitutionalism.

Division of Powers between the Nation and the States. One of the great problems under federalism is how to divide powers between the central government and the states. In the United States, the national government theoretically possesses only the powers delegated to it, and all others belong to the states. Powers delegated to our federal government are of two kinds, enumerated and implied. The **enumerated powers** are expressly delegated by the Constitution and include the grant of legislative powers to Congress (Article I, Sections 1 and 8), executive powers to the president (Article II), and judicial powers to the Supreme Court and other federal courts (Article III). In general, the enumerated powers delegated to the national government deal with all international affairs and domestic affairs of a national, rather than merely state, concern. The **implied powers** can only be inferred from the Constitution and have no explicit provision. They have, however, provided the flexibility necessary for the national government to meet the new problems arising over the years from economic and social change. They have also, as some critics of expanding federal powers put it, enabled the central government to encroach on the rights and functions of the states. The implied powers are based on the so-called **elastic clause** (Article I, Section 8), which gives Congress the power "to make all laws which shall be necessary and proper for carrying into execution the foregoing powers, and all other powers vested by this Constitution in the government of the United States, or in any department or officer thereof."

The constitutional provisions for the division of powers also distinguish, though not very clearly, between exclusive and concurrent powers. **Exclusive powers** belong only to the national government or only to the states. **Concurrent powers** belong to both the national and state governments, such as the power to tax, borrow, and spend. Many government powers were not mentioned in the original Constitution, and the general understanding was that these belonged to the separate states. The Tenth Amendment made it plain that these reserved or residual powers "are reserved to the States respectively, or to the people."[2]

In the final analysis, however, it is clear that in spite of a careful attempt to separate powers, national supremacy has become a principle of the U.S. constitutional system. This principle grows out of the supreme-law-of-the-land clause, which states that the Constitution, laws of Congress in pursuance thereof, and treaties are the supreme law of the land, despite anything to the contrary in state constitutions and laws. In case of conflict, the states must make the necessary changes to conform to national law. Moreover, a branch of the national government, the Supreme Court, decides the issue when a conflict exists, so that in effect the national government judges its own case.

Separation of Powers of the Branches of Government. As an additional safeguard against tyranny, the Founding Fathers divided governmental powers on a functional basis in accordance with the principle of separation of powers. James Madison wrote:

---

[2] In some federal systems (Canada, for example), the reserved powers belong to the national government.

No political truth is certainly of greater intrinsic value, or is stamped with the authority of more enlightened patrons of liberty, than that … the accumulation of all powers, legislative, executive, and judiciary, in the same hands … may justly be pronounced the very definition of tyranny.

The overconcentration of power in the colonial royal governors and the exalted position of the legislatures in the state governments of the Revolutionary War era had both proved unsatisfactory. The founding fathers feared tyranny by a majority of the electorate as well as by a strong executive. Most of the fathers were conservatives who wanted, among other things, to safeguard property against the "ill-humor" of popular majorities. They decided to place legislative, executive, and judicial powers in three different branches, each independent of the others. Each of the three branches of government was designed to be not only independent of the others but also directly dependent on different sources for office. The president was to be chosen by the electors in the Electoral College for four years; senators by state legislatures for six years; representatives directly by the people for two years; and judges by the president and Senate for life. As a consequence, it would be difficult for even the majority of citizens to "seize" complete control of the government and "tyrannize" over the minority, even though these constitutional mechanisms might not frustrate the will of the majority forever.

Checks and Balances. Supplementing and modifying the principle of separation of powers is the principle of checks and balances. Because of this principle, there has never been in practice a complete separation of executive, legislative, and judicial powers. Broadly speaking, the separation of powers is part of the checks-and-balances system, for it fulfills Madison's dictum, "Ambition must be made to counteract ambition." Strictly speaking, however, checks and balances refer to restraints placed on each branch by requiring it to divide some of its powers with the others so that it cannot exercise independently the major functions allotted to it. Despite some popular opinion to the contrary, the authors of the Constitution never intended the three branches to be completely independent of each other. What they wanted to prevent was all legislative powers and all executive powers from falling into the same hands.

The Constitution clearly provides for interdependence between the three branches, which Madison also said was essential to free government.[3] Each branch of the government has some responsibility and power to influence the functions of the other two. Congress enacts laws, but they are subject to the president's veto, and that veto can be overridden by a two-thirds majority in each house. The Supreme Court can declare acts of Congress void, but

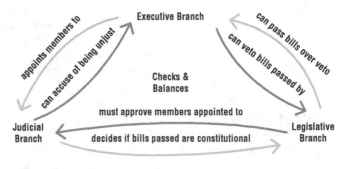

Check and Balances.

---

[3] He wrote that "unless these departments be so far connected and blended as to give to each a constitutional control over the others, the degree of separation which the maxim requires, as essential to free government, can never in practice be duly maintained."

Congress determines the appellate jurisdiction of the Court, and the president and the Senate appoint the judges. The president can make treaties, but only with the advice and consent of the Senate, and presidential appointments to government offices must receive Senate confirmation. The president and two-thirds of the Senate can make a treaty, but the House of Representatives must approve if any money is involved. The president administers the laws, but Congress must establish the departments and agencies and provide for their support. Many of the regulatory commissions (which are administrative agencies) created by Congress actually exercise executive, legislative, and judicial powers. Congress, by investigative committees and other means, attempts to secure the faithful administration of the laws. In a very real sense, all three branches participate in the making and the administration of public policy.

The extent of the power of the various branches is continually being tested. For example, the Constitution (in Article I, Section 8, paragraph 11) specifically gives Congress the right to declare war; yet presidents have often entered government forces into battle without having Congress declare war. When they do this, presidents say it is not really a war but a "police action." The Vietnam conflict is the most vivid example.

In response to the Vietnam "police action," Congress passed the War Powers Act, which was meant to define clearly when the president must consult Congress about a warlike action, but it has not worked out that way, as you can see by considering the invasion of Grenada, the actions of U.S. ships in the Persian Gulf off Iran in the war between Iraq and Iran, and the bombing of Kosovo in 1999, all of which were done without congressional approval. In the Persian Gulf War of 1991, President George H. W. Bush (the father of George W. Bush) maintained his right to commit forces to war unilaterally, as did President Clinton in Kosovo and President Obama in Libya. However, usually presidents do try to get congressional approval before entering into war (as President George W. Bush did in the 2003 Iraq War), even though they argue that they do not need it.

An Independent Judiciary and Judicial Review. U.S. tradition places great faith in an independent judiciary, one free of all pressure and all fear of political reprisal. Democratic theory has not demanded that the courts be directly subject to popular control. The U.S. Constitution provides for a Supreme Court relatively free of the executive and legislative branches, and once the judges are appointed, they can be removed only by impeachment and conviction by Congress. The function of the courts is to interpret the law and apply it in individual cases. For this task, independence is necessary in order to avoid decisions influenced by public sentiment or thoughts of job security and patronage.

The power to interpret the law is an enormous power. As you have seen throughout this book, concepts are often vague and somebody must give them specific meaning. Does "equal rights for all" require busing students to particular schools? Are segregated private clubs violating the rights of nonmembers? Do we have a constitutional right to doctor-assisted suicide? How much newly presented evidence, and what kind, is necessary to overturn a death sentence? Making these decisions and others like them is the main function of the courts.

As the Supreme Court has evolved, it has become a protector of the rights of the people (as it interprets those rights). Every law passed in the United States is subject to judicial review by the Supreme Court of the nation or the supreme court of the state in which it was enacted. Under **judicial review,** the Supreme Court passes judgment on the constitutionality of a legislative or executive act. If the Court decides a law is unconstitutional, it is no longer a law. This independent judicial review, the third in our system of checks and balances, is a unique U.S. contribution to government and it has served us well. The national Constitution does not expressly grant or deny the Supreme Court the power of judicial review, but the Court has exercised it since 1803, when Chief Justice John Marshall concluded in the case of *Marbury v. Madison* that the Court must do so to fulfill its expressed duty of exercising jurisdiction over all cases arising under the Constitution.

*F*unny Things Happen to an Idea on Its Way to a Law

So that you can get a sense of how the national government functions, let's briefly follow a fictional idea through the various stages from conception to law. Let's say the idea begins with a social science professor who figures out that if the government establishes a new reform of the public assistance system, everyone will be better off. At a cocktail party, she meets a legislative assistant for one of the congresspeople (all of whom have a number of assistants analyzing potential bills for them). The legislative assistant hears the idea, likes it, and decides to talk it over with some friends who work as assistants at the White House. If the White House staff like it, they may make it part of their proposals; if the White House doesn't like it, the congressperson or a senator may introduce it as a bill (a proposed law) on his or her own. If it is to get any further than that, other congresspeople or senators must be interested in it, and often, if they like it, several will become joint sponsors.

If possible, a similar bill will be introduced in the other legislative body. Then the bill will be sent to the appropriate committee, which will decide whether to consider the bill. The committee chair has significant flexibility in deciding which bills to consider. The bill might also be sent to subcommittees. By now, if the committee has chosen to, it will consider the bill for a formal vote and bring it up to the House or Senate with its recommendation (many bills die in committee). At this stage, it is important that the bill have other backers. For example, if the bill is part of the president's program, the president can probably generate significant pressure to bring the bill to the floor—that is, to introduce the bill to the full House and Senate. Let's say one of the legislative bodies passes the bill. Then it is sent to the other legislative body. At each stage, the bill is subject to debate and can be amended. Thus, even if the bill passes both houses, it will probably be different from the originally proposed bill.

If both houses of Congress pass the bill in some form—say, by a simple majority vote—it is sent to a resolution committee that irons out the differences between the two versions (the one passed by the House of Representatives and the one passed by the Senate). Once that's done, the bill is sent to the president, who can either sign it, at which point it becomes law, or veto it. If the president vetoes it, Congress can override that veto with a two-thirds majority. But that is a rather hard thing to come by, and usually the politicians will try to compromise on a bill so that the president will agree to it in the first place.

Now the professor's idea is a law. But it's still subject to judicial review—an examination by the Supreme Court to determine whether the law is in accordance with the Constitution when a case relevant to that law is brought before it. If the Supreme Court holds that it is unconstitutional, that idea is no longer law.

This is a fairly succinct description of how an idea becomes a law. In reality the process is more complicated, but this summary should give you some idea of what happens to a bill on its way to becoming a law.

Whether the Founding fathers intended it to be so is uncertain, but our system of government required that this function be performed by some agency, and the Court was the logical choice. Marshall's opinion may have been partially political, but it was logical and has proved expedient. His basic assumption, which democratic theory endorses, is that the Constitution is superior to ordinary law.

The necessity for judicial review arises from federalism, the separation of powers, and the inviolability of private rights. The Court decides whether the national government has encroached on the powers reserved to the states, whether the states have exceeded their constitutional powers, whether the president or Congress has encroached on the rightful sphere of the other, and whether the national or state governments have violated constitutionally guaranteed private rights. This, of course, provides no safeguards against encroachment by the Court on the allotted spheres of the other agencies, including the states.

The aspect of judicial review that has provoked the greatest opposition is the voiding of acts of Congress. To nullify acts of Congress is to frustrate the will of the people expressed by democratically elected representatives, or so the critics have argued. There is truth in this accusation, but most Americans prefer having the majority will occasionally frustrated to having a system of government in which the majority is free of constitutional restraints. If a measure really has powerful public support, the people can always resort to a constitutional amendment or new legislation, adjusted to meet the Court's objections.

The Supreme Court Justices as of late 2018. Standing from left: Associate Justice Neil Gorsuch, Associate Justice Sonia Sotomayor, Associate Justice Elena Kagan and Associate Justice Brett Kavanaugh. Seated from left to right, bottom row: Associate Justice Stephen Breyer, Associate Justice Clarence Thomas, Chief Justice John Roberts, Associate Justice Ruth Bader Ginsburg and Associate Justice Samuel Alito.

© Mandel Ngan/AFP/Getty Images

The Supreme Court is theoretically unpolitical, and its decisions are meant to reflect a neutral consideration of the issues. But such neutrality is impossible, and in recent years, it has been possible to predict many justices' decisions based on their ideological views. The Court has a conservative and liberal branch which balanced one another. In February 2016 a conservative justice, Justice Scalia, died, and President Obama nominated a moderate to replace him. That appointment would have swung the balance of the court toward the liberal ideology. Republicans refused to consider the nomination, in the hope that they would win the 2016 election. When they did win, President Trump appointed Neil Gorsuch, and because the Republicans had a majority of votes in the Senate, he was confirmed. Then in 2018, Justice Anthony Kennedy retired and President Trump nominated Brett Kavanaugh to replace him. After a highly partisan vote, he was confirmed. As these two appointments demonstrate, the process of appointing a Supreme Court Justice has been politicized on both sides, and the sense of a non-political justice system has been undermined.

Federal judges do not sit in an ivory tower rendering their decisions completely apart from public opinion. When the Court reverses a previous decision, this almost invariably reflects a basic change in public opinion. For example, in 1954, the Supreme Court rendered a long-awaited decision on the constitutionality of "separate-but-equal" public school facilities. It reversed a fifty-six-year-old decision and found segregation in public schools to be a denial of "equal protection of the laws." Similarly, in 2015, the Court legalized same-sex marriage. In both those cases the decisions reflected changing social mores in the country as a whole.

Limited Government.   Our national government under the Constitution has limited power. First, it shares power with the states. Second, at fairly frequent intervals, the voters, in free elections, may reject those in office or extend their tenure. Third, every citizen has certain inalienable rights recognized by our Constitution. These include freedom of speech, assembly, and religion, and they also include the right not to be tried, convicted, and punished for crimes without due process of law—that is, without being given the benefit of certain procedures and privileges that the law provides for an accused person in order to ensure a fair trial.

Two characteristics of U.S. government, both of which are closely related to the subject of judicial review, require special comment at this point. One is the recognition by our laws and Constitution that every citizen has certain inalienable rights. The second is the fact that, though our federal Constitution is difficult to amend, the meanings ascribed to many of its clauses change gradually, as new situations arise, through the process of reinterpretation by the courts. For this reason it has sometimes been called a living constitution.

Individuals' Inalienable Rights. The Preamble of our Constitution contains the declaration that one of the great purposes of government is "to secure the blessings of liberty to ourselves and our posterity." The U.S. concept of limited, constitutional government is based on the proposition that the people reserve to themselves certain areas of freedom that government may not invade, that people have inherent rights no political authority may either give or take away, "and among these are life, liberty, and the pursuit of happiness." Democratic government assumes that the majority will rule but also that the minority has the right to dissent. In the United States, as in any democracy, the majority rules legitimately only so long as it respects minority rights.

The Founding Fathers considered government to be largely an enemy of freedom rather than a friend. As stated earlier, the original Constitution and its Bill of Rights provided safeguards against the national government, and the Fourteenth Amendment extended most of these to the states.[4] We have learned through experience that government can be both the enemy and the friend of freedom. Most of us do not regret that our government was forbidden the right to invade a wide sphere of private rights, though we may no longer believe that government is a necessary evil. We know that liberty and security are inseparable and that without the security provided by stable, effective government, there would be few freedoms to enjoy. Thus, the trend for more than a hundred years has been toward popular dependence on government to promote basic human rights.

Rights versus Duties. Rights are never absolute. Furthermore, rights involve duties. The right to freedoms involves the duty of respecting the freedoms of others, whether these concern their choices of religion, political party, economic philosophy, or place of residence. Our freedoms are guaranteed only so long as we exercise them responsibly and refrain from using them as a cloak for obscenity, slander and libel, murder, public nuisances, incitement to riot and insurrection, and other unlawful acts. It is always the duty of the courts to draw a line between the legitimate and the illegitimate exercise of freedom, between controls essential for the welfare and safety of society and controls that unnecessarily invade the area of protected personal freedoms. No duty of government is more important or more difficult than this one.

There is no simple way of drawing a hard-and-fast line between the inalienable rights and freedoms of the individual and the controls required to protect the rights and freedoms of others. Many people, including a number of respected lawyers and judges, feel that in recent years the Supreme Court, in its efforts to guard the civil rights of individuals, has shown more concern for the rights of those accused of crime than for the rights of their alleged victims. Other critics, equally respected, defend the Court's decisions on the ground that protection of accused persons who may be innocent requires strict adherence to correct legal procedures. Since 1985, however, the Supreme Court has begun to crack down on criminals by giving the police more rights. The 9/11 terrorist attacks on the United States led to the passage of the Patriot Act, which gives the government significant power to detain individuals suspected of terrorist motives. Under this law, it is possible to keep these detainees for an indefinite period

---

[4] All responsible U.S. citizens would do well to acquaint themselves with the Bill of Rights and its significance for their welfare. These rights include (1) substantive rights, such as freedom of religion, of the person, of speech and the press, and of peaceable assembly; and (2) procedural rights, such as due process of law, just compensation for property taken for public use, specific warrant for arrest or search, writ of habeas corpus, speedy and fair trial by jury, and freedom from excessive bail, unusual punishment, bills of attainder, double jeopardy, compulsory self-incrimination, and ex post facto laws.

without charging them with a specific crime or allowing them to speak with a lawyer. The reviews on the Patriot Act are mixed. Some see it as undermining the basic rights of individuals; others see it as a necessary deterrent to terrorism.

Figure 16.3 shows the basic rights that, under our U.S. system of government, are designed to protect an accused person against an unfair trial. One great protection is the right to trial by jury. In criminal cases, conviction requires a unanimous decision. (Some states do not require unanimity for deciding civil cases.)

Growth of the Living Constitution. U.S. government is constitutional government, and we Americans are proud of our written Constitution. In Great Britain, democratic government and the fundamental principles on which it is based developed slowly, so that no need was felt for a formal written document expressing these principles. But in the United States, a new nation had to be suddenly created out of thirteen independent colonies or states, and the only solution for this problem was to draw up in writing a formal agreement describing the structure and powers of the new government and also expressing the principles on which it was based. Because of our long and successful experience with this written Constitution, we have perhaps come to feel that fundamental political principles cannot be trusted to provide a framework for government unless they have been formally agreed on and duly recorded.

A written constitution is, however, rigid in that it cannot be easily amended. The amendment procedure stated in Article V of the U.S. Constitution provides for two methods of proposing and two methods of ratifying amendments. They may be proposed by two-thirds of both houses of Congress (the only method ever used to date) or by a constitutional convention called on the petition of two-thirds of the states. A number of states have called for such a constitutional convention, although most observers do not believe as many as two-thirds of the

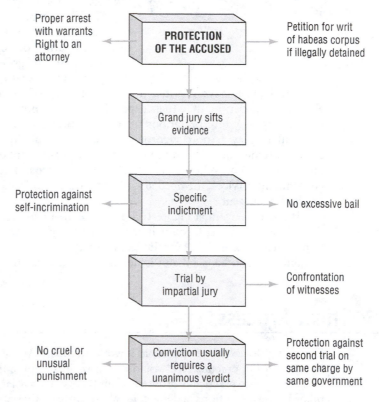

Figure 16.3

*Civil liberties: **an American heritage.***

The Constitution.

© Pgiam/iStock

states would agree to petition Congress to call such a convention. Once proposed, amendments may be ratified by legislatures in three-fourths of the states (the method used all but once) or by conventions in three-fourths of the states (the method used to ratify the Twenty-first Amendment). The procedure was set up to ensure that the integrity of the document will not be violated by frequent revisions prompted by transient shifts in public and governmental opinion.

In spite of the difficulty in amending it, the Constitution has been a flexible instrument. It has changed, not so much through amendment as through reinterpretation by the courts, to meet new practices and new situations that those who drew up the Constitution could not have foreseen. It has thus become a living constitution in the sense that it has been able to adjust in many ways to the changing beliefs and needs of the people. For example, through custom the undemocratic elements of the Electoral College were largely eliminated. Originally, the people elected leading citizens to the college and these then selected the president. But the practice soon evolved for candidates to the Electoral College to pledge themselves to a presidential candidate in advance, so that for all practical purposes when a citizen voted for an elector, the vote was for a certain presidential candidate.

The rise of national political parties has helped bring about unity to our national government in spite of the separation of powers provided for in the Constitution. Also, the growth of nationalism, the need for giving the executive great powers in times of crisis, and other influences have resulted in the emergence of the president as a strong unifying element in government. Much expansion of government functions has also been made possible by new interpretations of the Constitution. When the people wanted the government to play a more vigorous role in the regulation of business activity, they and their Supreme Court found the necessary authority implied in the enumerated powers of the Constitution. When new social problems arose and the people demanded more government services, the needed authority was again found to exist, by implication, in the original document.

If you look again at Figure 16.1 and note the major agencies of the executive branch of the federal government, you will have some idea of the vast expansion in government functions that has taken place over the years. Whether that expansion should continue or whether it should be reduced is a major issue that must be faced in the coming years.

The Political Process

Earlier, we described democracy as it works in theory. We also touched on some examples of its workings in practice. We would be remiss in stopping there because, as with just about everything else, practice is different from theory. In our large country, decisions cannot be made by the institutions of democracy alone. Instead, they are made by a political process that includes numerous influences, some of which have no lofty goals—only the goal of establishing and using a power base. Others play a more beneficent role, but it is a role that was not foreseen by the early proponents of democracy. Political pressure groups and elites that have direct influence on governmental decisions are prime examples of practices deviating from theory.

Individuals influence government in our democracy through the political process. This political process includes numerous factors that determine policy formation, including public opinion, political pressure groups, the military-industrial complex, political parties, nominations and elections, and, finally, legislation. We can't give a complete discussion of each of these, but we can mention the most important.

Political Parties

Although political parties in the modern sense did not begin to develop until the middle or later part of the eighteenth century, today they are universal in democracies. George Washington advised the new American nation to avoid dividing into parties, and they are not mentioned in the U.S. Constitution. But as democratic government developed, political parties came into existence because they fulfilled two important functions: interest aggregation and policymaking. They are not the result of theory but of practical experience, and they are necessities in representative democracies.

Compromising Conflicting Interests.   Probably the most important role of political parties is in compromising conflicting interests. In a dynamic society, many conflicting interest groups compete for control of the government and for favorable legislation. The majority of these sincerely believe that their programs represent justice, progress, and the general welfare, but they cannot all have their way. No government can provide at the same time for prohibition of and the right to manufacture, sell, and consume marijuana; for outlawing strikes and the freedom to strike; for the complete separation of church and state and publicly supported church schools. If all the conflicting groups that arise from differences in race, nationality, social class, creed, economic interest, and geographic location refused to accept any compromises, a unified national policy would be impossible. In the United States and other countries with two-party systems, most of the necessary compromises are brought about within each political party.

The political party, especially in the two-party system, acts as a mediator and cushion between, on the one hand, the individuals and groups that belong to it and, on the other hand, the government. Individuals and interest groups can bring pressure to bear on the party to adopt policies they favor. The organized party then seeks to reach compromise agreements and to convert them into legislation.

The Two-Party System.   Although the number of parties is not determined in the Constitution, the United States has generally operated on a well-functioning, two-party (Republicans and Democrats) system. Most observers believe that this provides a more workable system than the alternative multiparty system. However, because of the necessary compromise on issues, a two-party system often does not exhibit sharp and clear-cut differences in program or principle, and often differences that appear to exist before an election tend to disappear once a party gets into power. The need of each of the two major parties to appeal to a large segment of the population contributes to the development of relatively moderate philosophic orientations. Moreover, in their attempt to attract people from all interest groups, the two parties tend to promise far more than they can possibly deliver. Voters who want to influence some particular policy (such as extension of civil liberties, more public housing, gradual elimination of farm price supports, or a planned reduction of foreign aid) often feel frustrated because they cannot make their voices heard in the party. Periodically, there have been attempts to establish a third party. For example, in 2016, when Donald Trump won the Republican nomination for President, much to the consternation of the Republican elite, there was a movement by some in the Republican

Supporters of Trump at a political rally.

© Alamy

Party to support an alternative third party candidate. But such a movement would likely have broken up the Republican Party and guaranteed that the Republicans would lose in the general election, so it was not followed up.

The argument in favor of two parties is that in a nation as large and diverse as the United States, unity is essential, and each of our major parties performs the valuable function of bringing together under one umbrella a number of groups whose interests vary considerably. If a portion of the population is not happy with the policy alternatives presented by the two major parties, however, it is at liberty to create an alternative party. This potential for the development of an alternative party helps keep the two major parties responsive to the needs and demands of the people. Trump's election did however present new problems for the Republicans, many of whom had strongly opposed Trump during the campaign, and as of 2018 there were serious fractures within the Republican Party. Similarly, there were fractures in the Democratic Party: one, a progressive wing that wants a more socialist society; the other a more centrist wing, which is less radical in its goals.

An important trend in party affiliation that has been increasingly evident is the decline in the number of people who identify themselves with one or the other major party. Today, more than 40 percent of voters in the United States describe themselves as independents. Some of the reasons for this are that (1) people do not need to rely as much on favors extended to them by their party as they did seventy-five or one hundred years ago, when formal support systems were less common; (2) they wish to split their votes among candidates of different parties; (3) they are disillusioned with the party system or with some kinds of government activities; and (4) they have so many social and professional interests that they no longer see a political party as a kind of club. Relaxation of party ties does not mean, however, that people have given up the privilege of voting, and of voting within the choices offered by the two-party system.

Elections

Democratic government implies the wide extension of the **franchise**—the right to vote. Citizens of modern dictatorships also enjoy this privilege, though for them it is a privilege stripped of power. The right to elect government officials and to vote on public policies has been achieved by centuries of effort. We have already noted how suffrage was restricted in early America by property and religious qualifications. Because of such requirements, in 1790 only about 15 percent of adult white males, and no women, could vote.

Over time, the United States has done away with property, religious, racial, and gender qualifications. The gradual trend throughout the world has been to extend the franchise and make it universal for all responsible citizens. In the United States, black males won the right to vote in national elections in 1870, when the ballot was awarded them by the Fifteenth Amendment to the Constitution. It was not until 1920, when the Nineteenth Amendment to the Constitution was ratified, that women won the right to vote in U.S. national elections, although some individual states had granted them local rights much earlier. The most recent such movement in the United States was to reduce the voting age from twenty-one to eighteen, which was accomplished by the ratification of the Twenty-Sixth Amendment to the Constitution in 1971.

Selecting a Candidate: The Problem of Primaries

Democracy requires that the president be elected, but some process must exist to select the two parties' candidates. That process involves the parties' national conventions, and the rules by which the national conventions select candidates. Today, those conventions rely heavily on state presidential primaries which select delegates tied to a candidate, at lease for the first vote. This means that the race for the White House begins long before the actual election, as candidates run in presidential primaries. Prior to the 1970s, primary elections were held but those primaries were non-binding, which meant that they were often simply ignored. That changed in the 1970s as primaries (and other mechanisms for selecting candidates, such as caucuses) were given more importance. Today the nomination is won or lost in the primary elections.

The rising importance of primaries has had two negative side effects. First, since running in state primaries is extremely expensive, it has made it much more expensive to run for office, giving those with the wherewithal to finance the elections more power, precisely the opposite of the initial goal of the primary system. Second, it has tended to polarize the political process. By that we mean that while the increased importance of primaries has given more power to the people, it has also given more power to the extremes of the party, since they are much more likely to vote in the primaries. The result is that in running for office, candidates reflect the views of the party base. Highly conservative Republicans and highly progressive Democrats are more likely to win the nomination than they were before. Candidates who are willing to compromise, a willingness that is necessary in a democracy, find it harder to win the nomination. Some moderate compromisers do get through, but they often find it necessary to "sell" themselves initially as true believers to win the primary. Then, having won the primary, they revert to a more middle of the road position to attract the independents in the actual election. This promotes a sense that these candidates have no true beliefs, and are beholden to financial interests. It also reduces their ability to compromise, leading to ineffectual government.

As we discussed earlier, one of the important compromises of the original Constitutional Convention was the establishment of the Electoral College. The people elect members of the Electoral College, which then elects the president. In a number of elections, such as the election of President Trump, the popular vote and the Electoral College vote differed. While Trump won the electoral college vote, he lost the popular vote. This led to calls for the elimination of the Electoral College, but we are unlikely to see any such change because constitutional change comes very slowly, and small states, which would lose power, are likely to block any such effort.

Obstacles to Effective Popular Control.   The right to vote is not equivalent to the power to control the government. The electorates in democracies throughout the world have had their ballot power weakened in many ways, including the following:

- Overburdening voters with a long ballot
- Permitting voters to participate only in indirect elections
- Forcing voters to declare their choices publicly
- Providing inadequate voting facilities
- Allowing nominations to be controlled by the privileged few
- Limiting categories of those who can hold office
- Conducting corrupt elections
- Use of psychological methods to guide people to vote in certain ways
- Placing on the ballot only candidates sponsored by the official government party

Some of these limitations have existed and still exist in the United States and other democracies. In the early 1990s, some electorates, such as those of Colorado and California, limited their own power by voting to limit the number of terms their elected representatives could

Protesting voting rights.

© Alamy

serve. They did this because they disliked the idea that the representatives, once elected, tended to get reelected indefinitely. However, the voters were also preventing themselves from constantly reelecting individuals if they liked them well enough. The debate over whether term limits should be repealed or whether more electorates should adopt them is likely to be discussed well into the future.

The Nonvoter. In the United States, perhaps 60 percent of the civilian population of voting age exercise their franchise in presidential elections; in the off-year congressional elections, only about 40 percent participate; and in local elections, a mere 15 percent is not uncommon. In Britain and the other democracies, the percentage is considerably higher (it is over 75 percent in Britain). Why do Americans fail to vote? The many reasons include the long ballot, the belief that politics are irrelevant to contemporary concerns, lack of interest, or feelings that one vote cannot matter.

Probably the most important reason is indifference produced by lack of political education and experience. People simply feel no compulsion to participate in the electoral process. Many of them come from homes with a long tradition of nonparticipation in political affairs. Such people are often considered selfish and unpatriotic, but in many cases ignorance of issues and candidates is the main reason for not voting. Only increased education can improve the percentages of voters.

Another reason people don't vote is the belief that their vote cannot make a difference. Generally, they are right—one vote does not swing an election, but in the 2000 elections numerous votes were extremely close, and a few votes either way could have changed the result in various House and Senate races. In the U.S. presidential race, the election came down to who would get Florida's twenty-five electoral college votes. After initial recounts of the votes, only about 900 out of 6 million votes separated the candidates, and there was much legal wrangling about which votes could be counted. The number of partially punched ballots in those counties that had punch card ballots far exceeded the 900-vote difference, so the presidential election hinged on decisions made about these ballots. Ultimately, George W. Bush was declared the winner, but only after a Supreme Court decision. Had a few more Gore supporters voted, or even had they been more careful when they voted, Al Gore might have won. So individual votes can matter.

Referendums, Recall Elections, and Direct Democracy. In the United States, most elections are indirect—we elect a governor and a legislature and they then determine the laws. Decisions can, however, be more directly related to the voting public if a referendum is held and the people decide directly what the law will be. These referendums avoid the governmental structure and allow direct voter input into a law.

The direct approach is used most in California, which allows voter initiatives on a large number of issues, and these voter initiatives often play an important role in the laws that are passed. For example, property taxes are limited due to a referendum, and in 2003 the then governor, Gray Davis, was recalled and former actor Arnold Schwarzenegger was elected.

Gerrymandering and the U.S. House of Lords

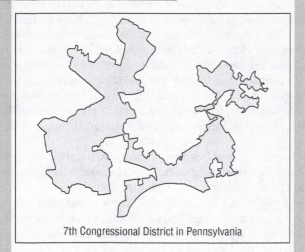

7th Congressional District in Pennsylvania

Gerrymandering.

U.S. democracy doesn't work perfectly. Incumbents use their powers—PAC (Political Action Committee) money, free use of the postal service, perks of office, the large support budgets they are given to pay for staff—to vest themselves in office. These powers are sufficiently great that in the last forty years, 80 percent of all members of the House of Representatives who have run for reelection have indeed been reelected. In 1988, 99 percent were reelected, leading the *Wall Street Journal* to call this body "The House of Lords."

One of the ways incumbents win reelection is to have the districts from which they are elected gerrymandered, or drawn up in such a way that it is difficult for them to lose. For example, consider the pre-2018 strange shape of the 7th District of Pennsylvania. Why did it have that shape? Answer: Because demographic characteristics make the odd-shaped district a safe district for the incumbent; a "reformed" district might not be safe. Its shape (which acquired the name Goofy Kicking Donald Duck) changed when the Pennsylvania Supreme Court ruled that degree of extreme gerrymandering illegal and directed Pennsylvania to redraw its districts.

Shaw v. Reno (1993) illustrated some of the problems that plague democracy in the United States. In that case, white voters claimed that a long, skinny North Carolina district was unconstitutional because it was drawn to include blacks and exclude whites. The Supreme Court sent the case back to the lower court for a review of the issues: the meaning of the constitutional "right" to vote and the propriety of racially motivated state legislation designed to benefit members of historically disadvantaged racial minority groups. The lower court then said that the district was constitutional because it helped remedy past discrimination and that its odd shape alone was not enough to void the legislation. The white voters appealed the decision by going back to the Supreme Court in 1995, this time in a case called *Shaw v. Hunt.*

When the Supreme Court decided *Shaw v. Hunt* in 1996, it said that the legislation was indeed unconstitutional because North Carolina had not overcome the presumption that the use of race as the "predominant factor" in drawing district lines is unconstitutional. In response, North Carolina wrote a new version of the statute, and the case again worked its way up to the Supreme Court. This time, the Court said that to think that states must absolutely eliminate the use of race in drawing up their electoral districts was to misinterpret the 1996 decision. Instead, the Court said, a state might have other reasons, besides focusing on black voters, for drawing a district that happened to have large numbers of black voters, and that anyone challenging such a law must be prepared to prove that the state's main motive was to isolate or favor black voters. Boiled down, the Court meant: "Case not proved." North Carolina was left to ponder yet again the reasons for the shape of the district. In 2001, the case was ultimately decided, and the Supreme Court ruled that race could be used in redistricting, as long as it was not the predominant factor.

Debates about redistricting are continuing, with the party in power in state government using the power of redistricting to set districts most favorable to them. Cases are sporadically reaching the Supreme Court which attempts to split hairs on what is allowable and what is not. Numerous cases are working their way up the legal ladder. See https://www.brennancenter.org/blog/state-redistricting-litigation.

The California experience demonstrates both the benefits and the problems with direct democracy. To pass an issue by referendum requires large spending on advertising and organization, and this means that some special interest is usually behind those referendums that pass. So, whether these referendums lead to better government or are simply another means through which special interests can achieve their desires is much in debate.

The Fourth Estate

Most politicians now acknowledge that what is often called the **fourth estate**—the journalistic profession or its members, including the print and broadcast media—is equal in importance to the president, Congress, and the judicial system. *Public opinion* is a general term that everyone talks about, but no one is quite sure what it is or what determines it. Nonetheless, it is extremely important, and political leaders keep a close watch on the mood of the public by listening to feedback from their local representatives and through opinion polls. Politicians try to shape public opinion by giving speeches, selectively granting interviews, and allowing information leaks. As they do this, they must listen to the press and television because these institutions control the information that flows to the general population. The ease of publicizing one's individual opinions by means of the Internet can also affect public opinion, but unlike print or television the Internet is not a good medium for political control because it does not organize concentrated action.

Inherent in our Constitution is the guarantee of freedom of the press, but the press is not free from influence by private pressure groups and businesses. The media is important because it plays such a central role in influencing public opinion. For example, consider our earlier discussion of the process by which a bill becomes a law. If the social scientist who had the idea has good contacts with the media and can get it to cover stories on how wonderful the idea is, she will probably be much more effective in getting her idea considered by the political process. Similarly, if the media does not like the idea, the idea will probably disappear quickly.

Despite the time, energy, and skill they devote to obtaining favorable media coverage, politicians are often not pleased with the results. For example, Presidents Nixon, Carter, and Clinton felt hounded by the press. Both Nixon and Carter believed it to have played an important role in their political defeats. On the other hand, President Reagan, whose career until well into middle age was based in radio announcing and film and television acting, was called "the Teflon president" because press criticism would not stick to him. His personality and experience served him well in politics, where he was also called "the great communicator" because he could get his points across to the American people so effectively. President Obama has demonstrated a similar ability to communicate through the press.

Perhaps no President has seen himself as hounded by the press as much as President Trump; he continually rails against the biased press and their presentation of what he often calls "fake news." Unlike previous presidents, Trump communicates directly with the public with continual tweets giving his immediate, unvarnished, reaction to events of the day. This is possible because the Fourth Estate is no longer just the print and television press—it is the media, which includes many more outlets than existed before. Individuals can select curated news feeds to fit their world-view, and get their news without it being filtered by the mainstream press.

Trump sees the majority of reporters as tied in with the power elite; they accept their accounts of events, and look for any way they can to undermine Trump's accounts of events. He sees most colleges, universities, government agencies, and reporters as reflecting a one-sided view that is not open to other views. Whatever the truth, Trump has shown himself to be able to set the discussion agenda in ways that few other presidents have. A mainstream press discussion of Trump's methods of squelching the press can be found at http://robertreich.org/post/153748549760.

The Political Elite

A basic assumption in the United States is that all individuals are created equal, but it would be a mistake to assume that practice follows that ideal. In practice, there is an elite in the

United States whose feelings, aspirations, and influence carry more weight than those of other groups, either because they can use money or power to influence events or because they have direct access to those in power. If they don't like what is going on, they contact a high-ranking U.S. official to let him or her know their concerns.

Who are the political and economic elite in the United States? Any list would have to include the president, U.S. senators and representatives, governors, state senators, state representatives, and high executives in government, which, using U.S. civil service rankings, would be Grade Service Level 15 and above. To these we would need to add approximately 15,000 to 20,000 executives who hold most of the power afforded by their positions as heads of business and nonprofit enterprises; the executives of the top financial organizations, law firms, universities, and religious bodies; judges; and independent professionals such as writers, doctors, and scientists. Roughly estimated, we would arrive at about 100,000 people who would have to be considered the political elite of our society.

Does the political elite rule our country and thwart democracy? That's debatable. For example, consider the 2016 election, when the initial presumptive nominees—the choices of the party elites—were Jeb Bush, son and brother of former presidents, and Hillary Clinton, wife of a former president. Despite the fact that the elites in the respective parties favored them, the primary voters did not. Bernie Sanders, a self-declared socialist, gave Hillary Clinton a strong challenge, before she finally won the Democratic nomination.

Jeb Bush never excited Republican primary voters and he dropped out of the race as Donald Trump, a candidate that many of the Republican elite refused to support both because of his behavior on the campaign trail—attacking other candidates personally and making crude comments during debates (such as an innuendo about the size of his genitalia)—and because of his lack of knowledge of policy issues. Many Republican primary voters liked Trump precisely because he didn't have those elite airs about him—he related to real people in a way that other Republican candidates didn't. Sanders' and Trump's performance in the primaries is a demonstration of the limits of power of the elite, and also an indication of how they have lost touch with the average person in the US. Trump's election is an even stronger indication of this. It reflects the fact that the United States has lost the overall societal cohesion that pulls a nation together. Whether Trump's election will bring about a rethinking and recommitment to compromise, or whether it will further pull it apart remains to be seen.

The Military-Industrial Complex and Pressure Groups

In a living democracy, the division among the various groups is often not as clear-cut as it seems. A good example of this is what is often called the **military-industrial complex,** the nexus between the armed forces, the Pentagon, and defense industries. The term was originated in 1961 by President Dwight D. Eisenhower, who had just ended his term of office. In his farewell radio and television address, he said:

> This conjunction of an immense military establishment and a large arms industry is new in the American experience. The total influence—economic, political, even spiritual—is felt in every city, every statehouse, every office of the federal government. We recognize the imperative need for this development. Yet we must not fail to comprehend its grave implications. Our toil, resources, and livelihood are all involved; so is the very structure of our society.
>
> In the councils of government, we must guard against the acquisition of unwarranted influence, whether sought or unsought, by the military-industrial complex. The potential for the disastrous rise of misplaced power exists and will persist.
>
> We must never let the weight of this combination endanger our liberties or democratic processes. We should take nothing for granted. Only an alert and knowledgeable citizenry can

I HAVE 1,800 NUCLEAR MISSILES, 283 BATTLESHIPS, 9,400 PLANES... I SPEND MORE ON MY MILITARY THAN THE NEXT 12 NATIONS COMBINED AND DESPITE SPENDING MORE EVERY YEAR I STILL FEEL INSECURE!

IT'S SIMPLE. YOU HAVE A MILITARY-INDUSTRIAL COMPLEX

© Matt Wuerker/Politic Universal Uclick

compel the proper meshing of the huge industrial and military machinery of defense with our peaceful methods and goals, so that security and liberty may prosper together.

Eisenhower's warning is no less relevant today than it was in 1961. The simple reality is that there is money to be made in defense (in 2019, defense spending totaled about $900 billion), and when there is, firms and individuals will try to make money by expanding their particular areas, using whatever political means they can to ensure political support. Thus, it is possible to have weapons systems that serve little purpose other than to make profits for defense firms, jobs for their workers, and votes for congresspeople. This means that once the building of such a weapons system is begun, it is extremely hard to stop.

Of course, it is not only industry and the military that combine to create pressure groups for continuation of their programs. Advocates of other kinds of programs also form pressure groups. But the potential damage from weapons systems is so great that the military-industrial complex deserves special mention.

Another way in which groups interact is by means of **pressure groups** that have organized to influence the political process. Pressure groups play an important role in trying to shape public opinion. In addition to exerting indirect influence, they often try to influence legislators directly. Thus, pressure groups fill a gap in a two-party system, enabling people with common interests to petition government for redress of grievances and to make their will known on many specific issues. Through the use of lobbyists, they keep national and state legislators and executives informed about what the people they represent really want from government. They also present a threat to well-functioning democracies in that certain special interests may become so powerful that, unless the public is alert, they frustrate the will of the majority and thus obstruct government by and for the many.

Fortunately, one powerful interest group (such as organized labor) is often balanced by another powerful interest group (such as business). However, certain interest groups that lack effective organization, such as hired farm labor and consumers, tend to suffer from pressure-group government. But to say that consumers are likely to suffer from the activities of pressure groups is only one way of saying that the public interest is likely to suffer, for everybody is a consumer.

Political Action Committees.   The problems presented by special-interest pressure groups have surfaced in a new way with the advent of political action committees (PACs). **PACs** essentially are campaign committees established by individuals to raise money for particular political purposes. They sprang up as a result of the revised 1974 federal election laws that limited the amount of money individuals were allowed to contribute to a candidate. Under the law, an individual contributor could give only $1,000 to a candidate's primary and general election campaigns, whereas a PAC could give $5,000 to each.

In 2002, the Congress passed the Bipartisan Campaign Reform Act (BCRA). This law eliminated all soft money donations to the national parties; however, it doubled the allowable hard money contribution. The act also addressed issue ads, placing a limit on advertisements paid for with **soft money**—money contributed to political parties rather than to individuals. The act requires that any ad that supports a specific candidate aired within thirty days before a primary election and sixty days before a general election must be paid for with hard money. However, parties are free to spend whatever they want before that cutoff. In 2010, the effectiveness of this act was reduced when the U.S. Supreme Court ruled that it was in violation of corporations' and unions' first amendment rights to free speech, and that their spending to support a candidate's election cannot be limited. This led to the creation of what are called SuperPACs, and their spending has played an important role in recent elections.

Other recent advancements in campaign finance reform include the passage of "Clean Money" bills in several U.S. cities. A Clean Money election proposes to publicly finance candidates who can show enough public support through signatures and small donations. These candidates must agree to additional stipulations that limit outside donations and use of personal money to finance the election campaign.

A voluntary funding system is in place for presidential elections in which taxpayers are allowed to check a box on their tax returns that allows a small amount of their tax payments to support presidential campaigns. In return for public money, candidates are required to adhere to spending limits. In the 2008 election, Barack Obama, who, as a primary candidate, had promised to abide by the limits and accept the federal money, decided not to accept the money when it became clear that he could raise far more through private donations. His challenger, John McCain, accepted the federal campaign money and the spending limits that went along with it. Obama won the election decisively, and the additional money he had may well have played a part in his election.

Some writers maintain that the most effective defense against special-interest groups is the organization of still other groups to check and balance those that now exist. The weakness of this theory is that if great numbers of people cannot organize effectively to protect themselves, the general interests of the public—which may constitute the most vital interests of every group—often are neglected.

*E*valuation of the Democratic Political Process

The political process in the United States is complex, confusing, and challenging. To win election to a major office takes time, work, money, and patience; from an idea to the enactment of a law often is a long journey. To reach such goals, mountains of obstacles must be scaled and arid deserts of electoral inertia must be crossed. Compromises are necessary, and concessions must be made by many conflicting interest groups, each of which has a somewhat different destination in mind. Ignorance and other human limitations must be taken into account all along the route. Fraud and favoritism are constant dangers. But democracy offers ordinary people the challenge of the opportunity to rule themselves.

In the United States, the democratic way of life has become so firmly embedded in our culture and has brought us so many personal and social advantages that few of us can really conceive of living under any other social system. No other system can give us such a high degree of personal liberty or protect our individual rights so well. If at times we complain about the faults of democracy and its failure to achieve perfection, we are only being human. When we consider the alternatives, most of us believe that our U.S. brand of democracy is providing us with benefits that can be matched in few other countries, and we believe that if we meet our responsibilities, democracy will provide these benefits in greater measure in the future. Most Americans believe that, on balance, our government is and will continue to be a government of the people, by the people, and for the people.

Study and **Review**

Key Points

- The United States revolted from Britain in 1776 and became a new nation in 1787.
- The Declaration of Independence declared that the right to revolt is reserved by the people, consent to be governed is necessary, governmental action is limited, and all people are created equal and are endowed with certain inalienable rights.
- The national government of the United States as established by the Constitution is divided into three branches: the executive, the legislative, and the judicial.
- The Constitution provides for federalism, separation of powers, checks and balances, and limited government.
- The political process in the United States is a mess that works.
- The fourth estate, the political elite, the military-industrial complex, and PACs all play an important role in the political process.

Some Important Terms

Bill of Rights (317)
Cabinet (317)
checks and balances (321)
concurrent powers (321)
elastic clause (321)
Electoral College (316)
enumerated powers (321)
exclusive powers (321)
executive branch (317)
federalism (321)
federation (316)

fourth estate (334)
franchise (330)
implied powers (321)
judicial branch (319)
judicial review (323)
legislative branch (319)
limited government (321)
military-industrial complex (335)
PACs (336)
parliamentary form of government (320)

presidential form of government (320)
pressure groups (336)
pure democracy (320)
representative democracy (320)
republic (320)
separation of powers (321)
soft money (337)
unitary government (316)

Questions for Review and Discussion

General Questions

1. Is the United States a democratic society? Explain your answer.
2. In what way does President Trump's victory in the 2016 election capture what is good and bad about U.S. democracy?
3. What important decisions were made by the Constitutional Convention?
4. What major compromises were made at the Philadelphia convention?
5. Compare federal government with unitary government.
6. What are the three levels of government in the United States, and how are they related to one another?
7. What are the three branches of our national government, and what is the function of each?
8. What are the four basic characteristics of the U.S. system of government?
9. Compare presidential government with parliamentary government.
10. In what ways does the Constitution distribute power?
11. How does the principle of checks and balances modify that of separation of powers?
12. What is the meaning and significance of judicial review?
13. How is the "living constitution" related to the written one, and how does it keep pace with changing conditions and new problems?
14. What role do political parties play in a democratic system?
15. What are the primary reasons people do not vote?
16. What is the "fourth estate"? How does it influence our government?

17. What is the military-industrial complex? How does it influence our government?
18. What role do PACs play in shaping legislation? Is it a positive or negative role?

Internet Questions

1. Go to http://www.270towin.com. Which states have more than twenty electoral votes? Which states have fewer votes now than in 1988?

2. Who are your present senators and in what year were they first elected? Check https://www.govtrack. us/.
3. Use http://www.supremecourthistory.org/ to find out who are the current justices on the Supreme Court today.
4. What is the Preamble to the United States Constitution? See http://www.usconstitution.net/const.html.
5. Using http://www.whitehouse.gov/, who is in the president's advisory cabinet?

*F*or Further Study

Books to Explore

Clinton, Hillary Rodham, *What Happened*, New York: Simon and Schuster, 2017.

Conrad, Jessamyn, and Naomi Wolf, *What You Should Know About Politics . . . But Don't: A Nonpartisan Guide to the Issues That Matter*, New York: Arcade Publishing, 2016.

Graber, Doris, *Mass Media and American Politics*, Washington, DC: CQ Press, 2009.

Hacker, Jacob, and Paul Pierson, *Winner-Take-All Politics: How Washington Made the Rich Richer—and Turned Its Back on the Middle Class*, New York: Simon and Schuster, 2010.

McCullough, David, *The American Spirit: Who We Are and What We Stand For*, New York: Simon and Schuster, 2017.

McDougall, Walter A., *Freedom Just Around the Corner: A New American History, 1585–1838* (vol. 1 of proposed 3 vols.), New York: HarperCollins, 2004.

Mounk, Yascha, *The People vs. Democracy*, Cambridge, MA: Harvard University Press, 2018.

Obama, Barack, *The Audacity of Hope: Thoughts on Reclaiming the American Dream*, New York: Crown, 2006.

Scott, Tim and Trey, Gowdy, *Unified: How Our Unlikely Friendship Gives Us Hope for a Divided Country*, Carol Stream, IL: Tyndale House Publishers, 2018.

Taylor, Paul, *On Obama: (Thinking in Action)*, Abingdon: Routledge, 2015.

United States Government Organization Manual, Office of the Federal Register, National Archives and Records Service, Washington, DC: Government Printing Office, issued annually.

Wood, Gordon S., *Revolutionary Characters: What Made the Founders Different*, New York: Penguin, 2006.

Internet Sites to Explore

"http://www.reformparty.org" Reform Party.
"http://www.usa.gov/" USA.gov.
"http://www.usconstitution.net" The U.S. Constitution.
"http://www.house.gov" The U.S. House of Representatives.
"http://www.senate.gov" The U.S. Senate.
"http://www.supremecourtus.gov" The U.S. Supreme Court.
"http://www.whitehouse.gov" The White House.

The Organization of Economic Activities

After reading this chapter, you should be able to:

- Define the economic problem
- Discuss the evolution of our economy from feudalism to mercantilism, to a market economy, and to a pragmatic market economy
- Summarize the historical development of socialist thought
- Distinguish between a planned and an unplanned economy
- Explain the terms *supply* and *demand,* and use them to explain how a market economy works
- Explain why all modern economies are pragmatic market economies

The ideas of economists and political philosophers, both when they are right and when they are wrong, are more powerful than is commonly understood. Indeed, the world is ruled by little else.

—John Maynard Keynes

Traditionally, economics was that branch of social science concerned with the ways in which people provided themselves with material goods and services. More recently, economics has broadened its scope and sees itself as the science of choice. It considers how people and societies allocate resources among alternative ends to achieve their wants. Thus, we will define **economics** as the study of the social organization through which people satisfy their wants. In the process of satisfying these wants, economic institutions develop that govern individuals' economic interactions in the same way that social institutions govern individuals' social interactions. These economic institutions include government organizations, business firms, unions, and the laws that facilitate the production, distribution, and consumption of goods. To understand how an economy operates, we must be well acquainted with these institutions. In this chapter, we consider how economies are organized. Before we do that, because economists tend to play a more active role as policy advisers than do other social scientists, let's briefly consider how economists approach problems.

Economists bring a unique analytical approach to looking at social problems, an approach that emphasizes *rational choice* and *costs and benefits*. They take as a starting point that everything has to be paid for by someone and argue that society should take explicit account of costs and benefits so that it can make rational decisions. Economists picture a world populated by individuals doing precisely that—they search out benefits, and they weigh those benefits relative to the costs. If the benefits exceed the costs, they do it; if not, they don't do it. Economists define rationality in relation to this cost–benefit approach: Rational individuals are individuals who weigh the benefits and costs of decisions and make decisions that have the largest benefits at the lowest costs. Economists extend that reasoning when they analyze social problems, arguing that government and society need to establish rules and institutions that require decision makers to take the costs of laws and regulations into account as well as the benefits.

*T*he Nature of an Economy

In modern industrial societies, economic relationships are complex. Almost nothing can be produced and made available to the final buyer without the help of a variety of economic institutions and the conscious or unconscious cooperation of great numbers of workers. This is true of almost every commodity, whether it be a shirt, a computer, a ballpoint pen, or frozen yogurt. Our ability to satisfy our daily economic wants depends on the existence of many highly systematized social arrangements. Without these organizations, our economic efforts would be largely futile, and most of us, especially in the cities, would soon starve to death.

Taken together, all the complex social arrangements by which we satisfy economic wants constitute an economic system, or an economy. An **economy** may be defined as the social organization by means of which the people of a given society produce and distribute economic goods.

Functions of an Economy

An economy must perform at least four basic functions, and ideally it should perform them in such a way as to confer maximum benefits on the community. It must determine:

1. The kinds of goods to be produced
2. The amount of each good to be produced
3. The resources that are to be allocated to a good's output
4. The ultimate division of the goods among those who are to enjoy them

In addition, an economy should provide a favorable environment for economic progress.

Economics and the Social Sciences

Before we consider these issues, we need to consider how economic issues fit in with other issues in social science.

Some economists argue that economic issues are at the center of all social science issues. We disagree. Although economic issues are important, we would not argue that they are the central elements of our lives. Often economic goods are wanted for only social and cultural reasons (if you have enough money to buy that sports car, that cute girl or guy will go out with you; otherwise, she or he won't give you the time of day). Ultimately, it is not money or economic goods that we desire—it is happiness (satisfaction or contentment with one's life), and recent research on happiness has found that after society has reached an annual income threshold (of about $15,000 per capita), additional income does not seem to make a society happier.

Although economic wants are not the *most* important, they are important. If you're hungry or lack adequate clothing or shelter, you're probably not happy; and if all your friends have new cars, you probably aren't happy unless you have a new car, too. Thus, it is important to study economic needs and wants, and how societies fulfill them.

Economic Wants and Economic Goods

Economic wants are desires for things that can be obtained by labor or through exchange and on which, in a modern society, a money value can be placed. Not all wants are economic. People want love and affection, respect, health, happiness, and many other things that cannot be measured in money. These things may be affected by the economic circumstances of the individual, but they are not primarily economic. A certain amount of money and the things that money can buy are necessary to sustain life and to make it worth living, but beyond that, the relationship between money and happiness is not so clear.

Economic goods are the things that money can buy and that are the objects of our economic wants. If we possess such goods, we can obtain money or other valuable things in exchange for them. If we wish to acquire them, we can do so by offering enough money to pay the price demanded. In some cases we can produce them for ourselves if we are willing to invest the necessary labor. **Wealth** is what we call the material economic goods—the kind we can see, feel, and accumulate. All economic goods take the form of either wealth or services.

Economic goods have monetary value because they are desirable and because they are scarce. By scarce, we mean that if the goods were free, the amount that individuals want would exceed the supply, the amount available. Because the whole supply is owned or controlled by people, if we want more of such goods than we already have, we must either produce them for ourselves or offer something valuable in exchange to induce others to part with them.

Economic goods are not necessarily material. They may consist of services such as those of a housekeeper or a doctor, and, more and more, services are becoming the most important economic goods in the United States. Anything that offers benefits in exchange for a definite sum of money is an economic good. Economic goods in the form of services can be obtained from things as well as from people. If people want to enjoy the benefit of a house, they usually have a choice: They may buy the services of one in return for a monthly payment called rent, or they may buy one outright, thereby obtaining all the benefits the house is capable of yielding until it wears out or falls down. But when we wish to enjoy the benefits of a housekeeper or a doctor, we can't buy this choice; we have to rent it, because slavery is illegal.

The Economic Aspects of Culture

We have already emphasized many of the economic aspects of culture in earlier chapters. People's problems in adjusting to their physical environment are largely economic. The solutions require producing the kinds of goods that the environment demands; for example, in a cold climate, warm clothing, fuel, and well-insulated housing are necessary goods. Our attempts to improve our economic situation motivate technological progress.

Economic factors also play an important role in shaping the mores and the institutions of every society. Many of our most firmly held beliefs of what is right and wrong have to do with property and property rights, as illustrated by our strong condemnation of theft, robbery, cheating, and embezzlement. Most of our social institutions, even those that are not usually regarded as primarily economic, have economic aspects of major importance. The family is an excellent example. When two people marry, they not only signify their intention of living together and establishing a family, but they also undertake important economic obligations to care for each other and, if they have them, their children.

The Standard Economic Problem

Producing economic goods to satisfy human wants requires resources. **Factors of production** are all the human and nonhuman resources that go into the production of material goods. These resources are of three principal types: first, **labor,** or the efforts of human beings; second, **natural resources,** such as the land, raw materials, and so on, that are the basis of all the material products that humans make; and, third, **capital,** or productive equipment, which includes tools, machines, factory buildings, and all the things that human beings have made to help them produce more easily and efficiently the kinds of goods they ultimately require to satisfy personal wants. Goods in the form of capital do not *directly* satisfy human wants. Their importance is that they ultimately enable us to produce a much greater quantity and variety of consumer goods than would otherwise be possible, and often goods of a more desirable kind or quality.

All productive resources—labor, natural resources, and capital—are limited in quantity, whereas in modern societies human wants seem practically unlimited. Our own society may be affluent in comparison with others, and a very small minority of its members may have few wants of consequence that remain unsatisfied, but the vast majority find it difficult to stretch their incomes enough to provide all the things they desire. The **great economic problem** facing every modern society is how to make scarce resources satisfy as fully as possible the ever-expanding wants of its members. But, as we have noted in earlier chapters, we cannot continue indefinitely to satisfy greater and greater economic wants for an ever-increasing population without encountering shortages of resources and more and more environmental pollution. In the 1970s, the trend in thinking was that economic growth was undesirable and that "small is beautiful." By the 1980s and continuing into the twenty-first century, most people were seeking ways to have increasingly higher levels of economic growth without diminishing efforts to control pollution and conserve and extend resources. This led to serious concerns that the energy consumption associated with economic activity was causing climate change, which was bringing about some major physical changes in our world.

Economizing—making the best possible use of the resources that we employ at any time, regardless of what we think of growth—is one of the most important functions of an economic system. Determining the best mechanism for economizing, or allocating resources, is the fundamental task of economic policy.

The Other Economic Problem

The above discussion is the way economists have traditionally discussed the economic problem. But there has always been a second theme in economic writing and thinking that has emphasized a second type of problem. As we discussed above, the goal of life is not to get as much stuff as you can, but to live a fulfilling and satisfying life, so that when one gets old, one can look back on one's life and say that was a life well lived. What happens when society has developed technology to do the producing of all the goods that people want? What happens when the standard economic problem has been solved? What will people do with their lives?

For many people, a life well lived currently involves work. It is satisfying to achieve some end through work—tending a garden, writing a book, diagnosing a disease, teaching a class, even keeping the streets clean. There is inherent pleasure in being good at what we do, and in feeling needed. Take work away and people will have to find other ways of satisfying their need to be needed. Additionally, work plays a central role in deciding how much of society's stuff one gets. Those who work harder get more. Take away work and you take away that way of dividing up society's output.

Solving the standard economic problem has been making solving this other economic problem more difficult for us for centuries. Most humans in the 1600s didn't have to worry about finding a purpose or discovering a meaningful life. Getting enough to eat, a place to sleep, and caring for one's family was meaningful.

Technology has eaten away at those aspects of life that were obviously meaningful. The Agricultural and Industrial Revolutions took away many of the physical challenges that provided meaning. You don't have to be strong and especially physically fit to drive a tractor, or to operate a backhoe. So the nature of work shifted from meaningful physical labor to meaningful mental labor. Physical activities became part of play—sports or exercising for the fun of it. People joined gyms, hired physical trainers, and created activities that were ends in themselves—10ks, marathons, ironman competitions—to give them physical fulfillment.

Today we are in the midst of an Information Revolution that is doing to mental work what machines did to physical work. Computers can now calculate and compute much better than humans, thereby eliminating the rote aspects of mental work. They are also becoming more and more able to "think" (process information about abstract issues and draw conclusions about the implication of that information) better than even the brightest humans can. The inroads being made by information technology into all types of thinking is, for a human, mindboggling. With what is called **deep learning** (information processing based on finding patterns in data that is not based on new human programming of algorithms, but on algorithms that program new algorithms), thinking, as we humans normally think of it, will become as obsolete as plowing a garden by hand. Want a book on social science? Simply tell the tenth-generation replacement for Siri and Alexa to do it and out it comes. So much for me being useful.

When these Information Revolution changes are combined with the ongoing Industrial Revolution changes, there is almost nothing that we need humans for anymore, other than to sweep up and clean up loose ends after the machines and algorithms have done all the fun work. The economic problem will be solved. But society still has a problem; the other economic problem will be worsened. What will give us life satisfaction? It is this other economic problem that social scientists will likely be working on over the next century.

The Evolution of Economic Systems

Throughout the Middle Ages, markets grew as trade among diverse areas expanded. Governments were not well developed in those times, and for the market to exist it was necessary to work out agreements with leaders of the various towns. As the Western political system evolved, first controlled by local lords or nobility and then by monarchs, all individuals who wanted to undertake economic activities were required to get permission from the noble or the royal head of state. Those who did not have permission were not allowed to undertake such economic activities.

From Feudalism to Mercantilism

As we discussed in Chapter 3, early on the economic system of the Western world was **feudalism,** in which tradition ruled and most people were peasants tied to the land and their feudal lord. A few individuals escaped this pattern; these included the workers who built the great medieval cathedrals of Europe (and who gave the term *Freemason* to our vocabulary) and traders who traveled in caravans they set up as temporary markets in or near feudal estates. These traveling workers and traders played a pivotal role in spreading culture and ideas from one estate to another and in establishing the political geography that evolved into our modern states. For example, many of the temporary markets became permanent and formed the centers around which towns and cities grew. Traders brought ideas as well as goods, providing peasants with a view of the wider world. As trade progressed, people began living in towns and producing goods full-time for the market.

As people moved into the city, the economic system evolved into the **mercantilist system,** in which manufacturing or processing was favored above agriculture, and governments determined who could do what. The important aspect of the mercantilist system was that permission to engage in economic activity had to be obtained from local authorities, and as increasing trade fostered the development of the nation-state, traders soon found they had to obtain permission from the evolving governments.

Open-air trading continues today, as this scene of a person selling fish in New York City's Chinatown demonstrates.

From Mercantilism to a Pragmatic Market Economy

Beginning in the eighteenth century, the Industrial Revolution brought about a change from artisan production to machine production, which required a large number of individuals to work at specific manufacturing tasks in a common place (instead of scattered around in small enterprises). The Industrial Revolution was characterized by specialization of individuals in their work tasks. It unleashed an engine for material growth through growth in technology that transformed not only the economy and economic institutions, but also the social institutions of society.

The Industrial Revolution placed an economic strain on the mercantilist system, which had incorporated so many limitations on individual enterprise that many who might have been very good at some economic activity were simply not allowed to undertake that activity; this created tension and opposition to the existing social structure. By the mid-eighteenth century, opposition to the limitations of the mercantilist system had grown important. In 1776, moral philosopher Adam Smith wrote *The Wealth of Nations,* in which he expressed the underlying economic ideas that became central to the development of modern Western economic institutions.

Smith argued that for the government to prevent individuals who were good at something from doing it was not beneficial to society. Individuals, he held, should be free to do what they want, and he argued that such freedom would not lead to chaos. Instead, the market's **invisible hand**—the rise and fall of prices that guide individuals' actions in a market—would guide individuals' choices, so that each individual pursuing his or her own self-interest would simultaneously help society and create the greatest wealth for the greatest number of people in that society. For example, Smith argued that bakers will supply bread to people when they can make a profit, and this bread will satisfy people's hunger. If the baker charges too high a price, as long as there is competition, others will enter and drive the price down to its cost of production. Alternatively, say there is too little bread. The price of bread will rise, and as it does, as long as individuals are free to become bakers, more people will become bakers, more bread will

be produced, and there will no longer be too little bread. Then the price of bread will fall. People's needs are met by the market not because people are nice or concerned about others' welfare, but because people are selfish and pursue profit. The market, through changes in prices, guides individuals' choices like an invisible hand, so that what helps them personally also helps society.

Laissez-faire is a policy that allows the market to operate with a minimum of government regulation. The policy of laissez-faire was quite different from the mercantilist economic system in which the government played an important role in determining who could and could not produce certain goods. The debate that began between mercantilism and laissez-faire has continued. On a global scale, it is tied to the debate between planned and unplanned economies. Within the United States, we see it surfacing currently in the debates about how much government involvement in, and regulation of, the market should exist. Laissez-faire advocates argue that the government should stay out of economic activities except to provide the framework within which individuals can themselves carry out those activities.

Historically, opponents of the market have argued that the market causes people enormous pain, and that government has to enter in to alleviate that pain. During the Industrial Revolution, wages were low, living conditions were poor, and often people were thrown out of work and left starving on the street. Whereas individuals under feudalism had a society with built-in supports to fall back on, they had none

Adam Smith.

under capitalism. Many industrialists liked it that way: The fear of starvation kept wages low and profits high.

The opponents of the market offered two alternatives. One was that the government should intervene in the market to alleviate the worst problems and to see that the market interactions achieved a degree of fairness, They argued for keeping the market, but keeping it under control with laws and regulations. The second was much more radical. It called for an overthrow of the market economy and the establishment of socialism or communism.

The Push for Socialism.   The complaints about laissez-faire capitalism increased through the early 1800s, and by the mid-1800s, when laissez-faire capitalism was at its peak, there were many groups devoted to exploring and instituting alternatives. Those interested in socialist alternatives turned to the writings of utopian socialists such as Charles Fourier and Robert Owen, who favored establishing new communities where all members would contribute to the output of the community and use whatever community resources they needed. There, the decision of the community rather than the decision of the market would be the determinant of the allocation and distribution of goods. Utopian socialists believed that the market system was flawed, but they did not see a need for revolution against the system, nor did they see the development of an inevitable class struggle between workers and the owners of the means of production.

More radical reformers did see such needs and developments. These radical social reformers, such as Karl Marx and Friedrich Engels, saw the market system as inherently flawed. They argued that as the capitalists, or the owners of the means of production, exploited the workers, the workers would unite and establish a new form of economic organization called *communism,* under which each person would work according to his or her ability and each would consume according to his or her needs. Thus, communism would evolve into somewhat the same type of economic system as that envisioned by the utopian socialists, but the path by which society would reach its destination was different. Under socialism, the path would be peaceful, with everyone joining in for the good of society; under communism, the path would be one of revolution against the existing social structure.

Socialism and Communism.   The terms *socialism* and *communism* are not easy to define; they developed slowly over time, and the nature of the concepts themselves has changed and is continuing to change. From the 1930s until about the late 1980s, both were associated with what we now call **Soviet-style socialism**—an economic system in which the government, rather than the market, makes decisions about the allocation and distribution of goods. Communism was a type of Soviet-style socialism in which the Communist Party played a key role in the economy. In the 1990s, as the former Soviet-style socialist countries underwent tremendous upheavals, some socialists were suggesting different definitions under which socialism was compatible with the use of markets to distribute goods. Most people, however, still used the definition that associates socialism with government decisions about the allocation and distribution of goods. But a change in that definition should not be surprising; the nature of socialism has continually changed.

In the mid-1800s, for example, the French writer and reformer Louis Blanc, one of the originators of socialism, argued that all individuals had an inherent right to a decent job. Capitalism failed to achieve that goal and, therefore, violated individuals' rights. Initially, the right to a job was a central tenet of socialism.

Having a right to a job means that somehow jobs must become available, and quickly the principle expanded to include not only the right but also the means by which government would supply jobs to all—through government ownership of the means of production. As this happened, government ownership of the means of production became a key element in the definition of socialism. The focus on jobs also switched to a focus on equality of income, and the advocacy of equality of income became another key element of socialist thought. Thus, programs designed to equalize income in a country are often called socialistic.

Given this evolution, there is no unambiguous description of socialism. Because we need some definition, however, we define **socialism** in the traditional way, as an economic system under which society as a whole takes the primary responsibility for producing and distributing economic goods. Using this broad definition, Soviet-style socialism is a particular type of socialism. Although there is no inherent political system associated with socialism, the focus on society as a whole as the producer and distributor of economic goods quickly linked the theory of socialism to a comprehensive plan of government and hence autocracy, but the relationship is subject to debate.

In practice, socialism has taken on a variety of forms, and elements of socialist thought have influenced the evolution of capitalist societies. For example, the establishment of social security systems was originally a socialist goal, as were many of the social welfare programs that we now regard as part of our capitalist economic system.

We formally define **communism** as a type of autocratic or state socialism in which the Communist Party (a small group of people not subject to elections) determines society's goals. But communism also includes specific political elements and thus must be differentiated from socialism. Communism includes a set of beliefs following from communist writers such as Karl Marx and Vladimir Lenin. As we stated earlier, Marx's criticisms of capitalism were more widely focused than those of the socialist writers; he saw capitalism as being doomed by the laws of history. He argued that history progressed in stages and that each stage had two opposing elements—thesis and antithesis. Each stage played a role in history, but once the role was played, society would progress to the next stage.

In capitalism, Marx saw one of the opposing forces as the bourgeoisie—the capitalists who brought about growth by exploiting the workers. This exploitation, he argued, played an important role in causing the economy to grow, but once that growth had brought society enough income, he believed that the workers would unite to overthrow the capitalists who were no longer needed. Then the workers would constitute a communist form of economic organization, with the following creed: From each according to his ability, to each according to his need.

Marx had little to say about how a communist economy would operate. In practice, it involved the same key points as socialism—a stated belief in the equality of income and a centralized system of distribution and production. Marx also argued that under communism the state would wither away, which might be interpreted to mean not the complete disappearance of an administrative mechanism but the complete disappearance of any need for controlling people by force. Presumably, after the state had withered away, production would be carried on by cooperative groups of workers in complete harmony and without any need for coercion. But in no country that we called communist has the state withered away.

The following list summarizes five reasons why Soviet-style socialism was abandoned:

1. Soviet-style economies were not delivering goods.
2. Communist Party members were using their position to obtain desired goods and favorable treatment.
3. Socialist economies were significantly lagging behind capitalist economies.
4. New technological developments made it more difficult for the government to repress information and ideas that were contrary to the interest of the ruling parties.
5. Long-standing ethnic and cultural differences undermined the ability of the societies to form a national consensus.

In response to these problems, socialism and communism underwent enormous changes. Most Soviet-style socialist countries dumped Soviet-style socialism completely; others, such

Karl Marx.

as China, attempted to integrate the market into their socialist institutions, freeing up certain areas of the economy while keeping others under government control. Still others talked about following some as yet undefined third way—an alternative path that was neither socialist nor capitalist.

Planned and Unplanned Economies

In the past, economies were differentiated by whether they were unplanned market economies or planned socialistic economies. **Unplanned economies** were economies that relied primarily on the market to control economic decisions. Because they relied on private capital markets to raise money for building production facilities such as factories, and because any profits or losses from production accrued to the owners of those facilities, these societies were also sometimes called *private enterprise* or *capitalist economies*. In an unplanned or market economy, individuals have significant freedom to own and operate productive enterprises, to produce economic goods, and to develop specialized institutions, such as banks and insurance companies, to fulfill their needs. The U.S. and Western European economies were given as examples.

Planned economies were economies that relied on government-controlled production and distribution systems. In a planned economy, the money for building the production facilities came from government, and any profits or losses from production accrued to government. In a totally planned economy, some central governmental authority has the power to plan, own, and operate directly all productive activities. The former Soviet Union and China were given as examples.

How Planned Economies Are Supposed to Work

To understand the difference between planned and unplanned economies, let's consider how they are meant to work in theory.

Let's start by considering how bread is produced in a planned economy. Wheat is raised on government-owned farms. The central planners decide on a set of production goals for a five-year period and determine what they will need in the way of equipment, seed, money, and other efforts to meet those goals. Once those decisions are made, the farms and central planners are responsible for meeting the goals. The farms do not calculate profit or loss (although the central planners may consider such issues), nor is there any necessary relationship between the costs of production and the price of the wheat. Production goals are set in terms of quantities, not economic value.

After the wheat is produced, the flour is sent to a bakery, which has also negotiated with central planners about its own five-year plan. Wheat is one of the "inputs" for which the bakery planned. Thus, the bakery's goal might have been to produce 5 million loaves of bread with 4,500 tons of wheat. Having baked the bread, the bakery sends it to a government-owned retail store, which sells it to the consumer at whatever price the government tells the retailer to charge. In the Soviet planned economy in the 1980s, the price set for bread was far lower than the price of a loaf of bread in the United States because the Soviet government wanted to make this essential food widely available.

There is one other element, or input, in the production process that we should mention, and that is labor. Each of the government production facilities needs a certain number of workers. Once the planning commission has determined the labor requirements of the firm, the government assigns individuals to various jobs in that facility. Thus, in the pre-1990 Soviet economy, when a Soviet citizen graduated from school, she or he was assigned to a job. However, students in the top 2 percent of their class were allowed to choose their jobs. The government also set the wages that workers received.

Why Central Planning Did Not Meet Its Goals

The goals of socialist or communist economies are admirable. In the ideal society envisioned by communist theorists, citizens would be completely free of coercion by the state and would be happy enough to accept all their social responsibilities. Social classes would disappear. Everyone would work, the entire product of the economy would go to labor, and all workers would have equal rights to share it. They would share, however, not equally but according to need. If money were used as a medium of exchange, presumably wages would be paid to workers according to their needs. In any case, certain basic essential goods would be provided free to all citizens.

To some degree, communist countries achieved their goals. Basic necessities were relatively much cheaper in the former Soviet Union and China than they were in market economies; however, luxuries were much more expensive. For example, in 1986 an average two-room apartment in the former Soviet Union cost approximately $24 per month, and all workers were guaranteed a one-month holiday. Similarly, medical care and education were free. In China, the communist government made the provision of health care a top priority. It instituted a "barefoot doctor" program that sent doctors out to teach paramedics the basics of sanitation, hygiene, preventive medicine, and birth control. It similarly embarked on an educational program for all its people.

Despite these impressive showings, both the Chinese and the Soviet systems often fell short. The $24-a-month apartments often required a ten-year wait, and consumer goods were generally rationed or impossible to get except on the black market, where they were enormously expensive. The medical care was inept. There were serious shortages of goods of all kinds. Productivity—the amount of output per worker—lagged and economic growth slowed. New technologies were not developed because no one had an incentive to develop them.

Another goal they did not meet was equity and fairness. The shortages did not fall on all people equally. Through special commissaries, government leaders and Communist Party members easily got the goods that were in short supply, while other people had to wait in long lines. By the 1980s, the general view of most social scientists and of many citizens in communist countries was that the planned economy was not delivering the goods. The people were becoming dissatisfied.

In response, China introduced major modifications in its economic system, allowing the development of private markets while the Communist Party maintained overall political control. The former Soviet Union and a number of the countries of Eastern Europe took much more drastic measures. They essentially abandoned the socialist planned economy.

Planned economies were characterized by significant food shortages, causing people to line up to buy scarce goods.

How Market Economies Are Supposed to Work

As you can see, planned economies have many problems. But so too do market economies. We can see some of the problems of the market economy in the United States by considering the recent plight of unskilled workers who, in the recent recession, have lost their jobs. In the planned economy, all workers would have a job and access to earning income. In the United States, people are left on their own to find a job. In the planned economy, all graduates have jobs. The complaints about market economies that led people to search for alternatives did not come from nowhere. As we stated previously, the complaints were rooted in suffering the market caused that people were unwilling to accept. To better understand how market economies are supposed to work, let's briefly consider economists' theory of a market economy.

A **market economy** is an economic system that relies on the initiative of private citizens for the production of economic goods. In the market economy, no production quotas are assigned. Farmers, bakers, and retail stores individually decide how much they want to produce on the basis of expected prices and costs of inputs. If they make a mistake, they— not the government—are responsible for the loss, and if they make a profit, they—not the government—receive that profit. Workers are not assigned to jobs; they seek their own. Those who organize and control production must have incentives, and in a market economy the chief incentive is the possibility of making profits. Subject to the law of the land, anyone who chooses to is free to undertake the establishment of almost any kind of business enterprise. Businesspeople can choose both the products to be produced and the methods to be employed in their production; they can buy materials, labor, and managerial services; they can sell their products wherever people will buy them and at any price that customers are willing to pay. The chief problem in getting started is likely to be finding sufficient capital. If the new business is small, the owner's capital plus personal credit or borrowing power may be sufficient. But if the business is larger, the owner must interest other people and induce them to contribute capital as partners or, if a corporation is formed, as stockholders.

Institutional Foundations of a Market Economy. There is no such thing as a pure or absolute free market economy in which the government plays no part at all—because freedom itself is always relative. When we sometimes describe the U.S. market economy as a free enterprise system, we do not mean that anybody can establish just any kind of business without meeting obstacles. We mean that in most cases it is quite feasible for people who can obtain capital, and who have the necessary personal qualities, to organize and operate new business enterprises, and that they have a wide range of freedom in making the decisions involved. But in some industries, certain obstacles are difficult to overcome. In the automobile industry, for example, the capital required to establish a new company is huge, and the risk of failure is great, and in the public utility industries, local monopolies are sometimes supported by law because this is believed to be in the public interest. Free enterprise, however, means more than the right to start a business. Fully as important is the right of those who already own business enterprises to operate and control them—to determine policies—subject only to laws and restrictions deemed necessary and reasonable by government.

The government must provide the legal and economic framework and the general rules within which private enterprises operate. Although government participation in economic affairs may be great or small, no government follows a complete policy of laissez-faire with respect to the economic activities of private individuals.

Figure 17.1 provides an example of the interrelationships within a market economy. In it we see that producers (firms) and consumers relate through the market. Workers earn income from firms and, in turn, spend their income on goods that the firms produce. What the workers don't spend they save in financial institutions that, in their turn, lend money to firms. The government enters the picture in three ways. It establishes the laws and regulations that govern the interaction of individuals and producers; it collects taxes and provides services for firms and consumers; and it redistributes income.

© Gustavo Frazao/Shutterstock

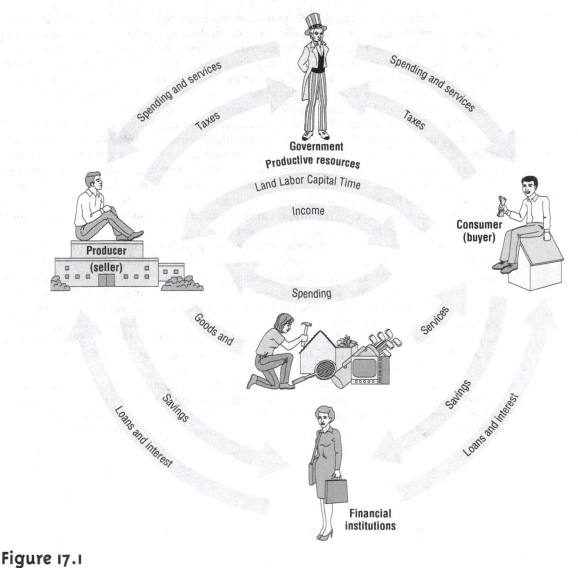

Figure 17.1

Model of a market economy.

Supply and Demand

In a free enterprise system, markets and prices play a dominant role in organizing and controlling economic activities. Any commodity that cannot be sold in the market at a profitable price will not be produced, at least not for long, whereas any commodity that can be sold at a profit is probably going to be produced by someone sooner or later.

When prices are not regulated and when markets are highly competitive, price changes keep adjusting production to consumption and consumption to production. For simplicity, let us assume that by a competitive market we mean one in which there are many small independent sellers of the same product and many independent buyers. Under these conditions, if people wish to increase their purchases of a commodity, the resulting increase in demand will cause the price to rise and production to be stimulated. Simultaneously, the rise in price will restrict the increase of market demand.

If people decide to decrease their purchases, the price will fall and this will discourage production, but the lower price will tend to limit the decline in sales and consumption. As long as more of the commodity is still being produced and offered for sale than people are willing to buy, the price will continue to drop. In competitive markets, the price always tends to rise or fall until the amount of a commodity that is being produced and offered for sale is equal, at the market price, to the amount that consumers are willing to buy. This determines the **equilibrium price,** or the price at which demand exactly equals supply.

Figure 17.2 is far too simple to take into account all the conditions in a real market, but it does illustrate the tendency under competition for the price of a commodity to rise or fall until **demand,** the amount of a product that people are willing to buy at a given price and time, equals **supply,** the amount that others are willing to sell. The vertical *y*-axis measures the price of potatoes per bushel; the horizontal *x*-axis measures the number of bushels. The **demand curve,** *DD,* shows the amount of a good buyers would be willing to purchase at different prices in the market on a certain day. The **supply curve,** *SS,* shows the amount of a good sellers would be willing to offer at different prices on the same day.

The point of intersection, *P,* shows that under the assumptions made in constructing these curves, the market price would tend to be $6. The price could not, for example, stay at $7, for then buyers would take only 300 bushels, whereas sellers would offer 600 bushels. Because there are many competing sellers, some would soon reduce their prices as they saw sales lagging. Likewise, the price could not stay at $5, for in that case buyers would want 700 bushels, but sellers would offer only 300. As soon as buyers sensed that there were not enough potatoes to go around, some would raise their offers. Only at the equilibrium price of $6 would the forces of supply and demand be in balance, for at that price, buyers would be willing to purchase 500 bushels, just the amount that sellers would offer.

To see the way markets work, it is useful to consider two important historical events: an oil "crisis" and the computer revolution. Numerous times in the last seventy years, there has been a sudden dramatic decrease in the supply of oil. In each case, the market's reaction has been a rise in the price of oil. The resulting price rise hurt consumers, and it made them change their

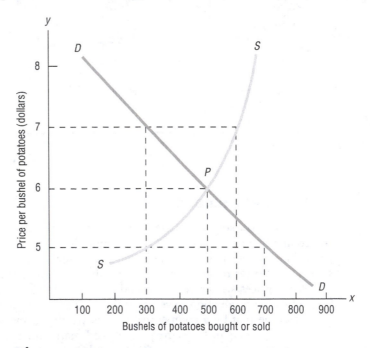

Figure 17.2

Determination of equilibrium price.

consumption habits. For instance, smaller, more energy-efficient cars were developed. The result was a decrease in the quantity of oil demanded, induced by the higher price. The higher price acted like a stick, leading people to decrease the quantity of oil they used. Simultaneously, the higher price acted like a carrot, encouraging oil-producing firms to produce more and explore for more oil. As they produced more, the price of oil fell.

Now let's consider the computer revolution, which represents a more pleasant side of the market for consumers. Major technological breakthroughs in the development of computers increased supply, quality, and capacity. In response, prices of computers fell, and individuals, firms, and schools developed new ways to use computers, increasing the quantity demanded. This revolution is continuing and will be an important phenomenon well into the twenty-first century. An increase in supply causes prices to fall, giving individuals more for less. Thus, not only does the market act as a stick as individuals are forced to change their ways because of higher prices, but it also acts as a carrot, causing individuals to find new uses for goods and services whose prices have fallen.

*M*odern Economies Are Pragmatic Market Economies

The preceding discussion should make it clear that the distinction between planned and unplanned economies has broken down. First, those countries that had a planned economy in the strict sense of the word abandoned it. The Soviet Union dissolved, and its component countries adopted markets. Similarly, China abandoned large portions of central planning and adopted markets as well. So, planned economies in the traditional sense are no longer of central importance. Second, the United States and Western European countries adopted significantly more planning and government involvement in the economy than anything envisioned by the theory of a market economy. In the U.S. economy today, government is involved in all levels of economic activity—either directly or indirectly. Consider the 2008 financial crisis. When large U.S. banks and automobile companies were on the verge of going under, the government stepped in and bailed them out. It poured trillions of dollars into the economy to support these companies.

Our point is that, today, the distinctions among countries are much more nuanced than planned or unplanned. All modern economies, whatever their history, have evolved into **pragmatic market economies**—*economies that use markets as a central way of allocating resources, but which also regulate and control those markets and change market outcomes to varying degrees.* Along with the downplaying of the differences in the planned and unplanned nature of economies has gone a downplaying of the differences between capitalist economies and socialist economies. Modern economies are blends of both and are guided more by what works than by a strong ideological commitment to either. Today's economies reflect pragmatism more than the other "isms." Pragmatism, not ideology or economic theory, has become the primary driving force in determining how modern economies operate and the degree of government involvement.

What really differentiates modern economies is their institutional and historical settings, which affect how government interacts with markets. For example, in China, most people expect that the government will step in and change the results of markets if it does not favor those results. In the United States, that expectation is far less.

In China and Russia, property rights and the rule of law are far less established than they are in the United States, which means that the Chinese and Russian governments can more easily step in and change a market outcome they do not like than can the U.S. government. People's property rights are determined by the government, and a change in government can change these property rights. In the United States, greater reliance on what is called the "rule of law," which stands above whatever government is in power, places restrictions on what government can do. Specifically, the rule of law limits any government's ability to change property rights. This limitation allows businesses to plan ahead more easily than they otherwise could.

Although we have also seen many examples of government intervention in the United States, the law under which businesses are run is largely independent of who constitutes the government in power and therefore can be relied upon to be relatively stable. That is far less so in China and Russia. Because the rule of law is less established, the law and property rights can be more easily changed by the specific government in power, if it chooses to do so. So, one's ownership of property is seen as at the will of government. This makes longer-term planning more difficult and gives government a more important role in the economy than in the United States. So, even though both China and Russia are now market economies, they are different market economies than the United States. In China and Russia, there is an implicit government control on economic activities that is stronger than in the United States. The difference is, however, nuanced, not the stark difference that was sometimes conveyed in the past.

Conclusion

Fifty years ago, there were enormous debates about whether planned or unplanned, market or nonmarket, socialist or capitalist economies were better. Some said that the collapse of many Soviet-style socialist planned economies showed that the market is definitely preferable to other ways of organizing economies and used that event as an argument for laissez-faire and against regulation. That argument is wrong. While the market certainly has its advantages, the history of the U.S. economy reflects the serious problems markets can create, and what has survived is not a pure market economy, but a pragmatic market economy with enormous government involvement. The United States has government-sponsored unemployment insurance, government-regulated retirement programs (Social Security), government-owned schools, and an enormous number of government regulations that limit our actions in the market. We have a pragmatic market economy rather than a pure market economy.

Today's economies in the world are almost all pragmatic market economies where government and the market interact in nuanced ways to solve problems that present themselves. There are problems with markets and there are problems with government regulation and government planning, and societies make pragmatic decisions about how to handle these, at times relying more on markets, at other times relying more on government.

In short, there is no perfect economic system. Organizing the economic affairs of millions of people is a difficult process and will be continually marked by problems. As new problems are faced, it is likely that economies will continually evolve, perhaps into types we have not yet classified. Economic systems, like culture and human beings, adapt to changes and evolve as new ways of coordinating behavior are tried and as those new ways create new problems.

 Study and **Review**

Key Points

- The great economic problem that every modern society faces is to make the scarce resources available satisfy as fully as possible the ever-expanding wants of its members.
- Our economy has evolved from feudalism to mercantilism to a market economy and finally to a pragmatic market economy.

- Socialist thought developed in reaction to the problems caused by a nonregulated market economy.
- Unplanned economies rely on markets to control economic decisions; planned economies rely on government.
- All modern economies have market economies that involve different amounts of government

involvement and planning. Pragmatism has become the primary driving force in determining the nature of the economy.

- Soviet-style socialism was abandoned because its economies were not delivering the goods. Many of the goods were distributed unfairly, economic growth lagged behind that of capitalist countries,

technology in communications promoted dissent, and ethnic and cultural differences undermined national unity.

- Markets create carrots and sticks when supply differs from demand, leading the invisible hand to get people to do what is in society's interest.

Some Important Terms

capital (342)
communism (347)
deep learning (343)
demand (352)
demand curve (344)
economic goods (342)
economics (340)
economic wants (341)
economizing (343)
economy (341)

equilibrium price (352)
factors of production (342)
feudalism (344)
great economic problem (343)
invisible hand (345)
labor (342)
laissez-faire (345)
market economy (350)
mercantilist system (344)
natural resources (342)

planned economies (348)
pragmatic market economy (354)
socialism (346)
Soviet-style socialism (346)
supply (352)
supply curve (352)
unplanned economies (348)
wealth (342)

Questions for Review and Discussion

General Questions

1. Economics studies the social organization through which people satisfy their wants for scarce goods, including services. Give some examples of economic wants.

2. What four important functions must every economy perform?

3. What are economic goods? What are economic needs? What are economic wants?

4. What three factors of production are necessary to produce economic goods?

5. What is the great economic problem facing every society?

6. What does the author mean by "the other economic problem"?

7. How did the Industrial Revolution contribute to economic growth?

8. In 1776, Adam Smith published the book *The Wealth of Nations*. How did he believe a nation could become wealthy?

9. In a planned or socialist economy, who is responsible for building the factories and distributing the goods?

10. In an unplanned or market economy, who raises the money and builds the factories? Who gets the profits or suffers the losses?

11. If the government controls the means of production, what is produced, and how the goods are distributed, what are the advantages? What are the disadvantages?

12. In a planned economy, if weather and plant disease caused an agricultural disaster, would farms go out of production? Why or why not?

13. What are some of the reasons why consumer goods are scarce and of poor quality in a socialist economy?

14. If the price of Coca-Cola went up to $5 a can, what would you expect to happen to the quantity of Coca-Cola demanded?

15. Do you believe that everyone has a right to a job? If so, whose responsibility is it to provide that many jobs?

16. Give an example of how a socialist idea has been adopted in a market economy.

17. Give an example of how a capitalist idea has been adopted in a socialist economy.

18. In market economies, such as the United States and Sweden, taxes are quite high. How does this blur the distinction between the terms *capitalist* and *socialist*?

19. Why is the distinction between a planned and an unplanned economy less relevant today?

Internet Questions

1. Read about the experiences of laborers in early coalmines at http://www.saburchill.com/history/chapters/IR/039.html. How do working conditions then compare to those now? Are these working conditions an unavoidable result of laissez-faire capitalism?
2. Using information found at http://www.auburn.edu/~johnspm/gloss/index.html, what is the definition of a black market?
3. Go to http://www.spicker.uk/social-policy/wstate.htm and read about the welfare state. What lesson can be learned from Sweden's experience?
4. Using https://www.forbes.com/sites/dougbandow/2013/01/21/when-you-ban-the-sale-of-ivory-you-ban-elephants/#7a04975d4b03, explain the argument that banning ivory trade will result in more elephants being killed?
5. Go to http://www.economist.com/displaystory.cfm?story_id=13743310. What does the article mean by the visible hand, and how does it relate to a pragmatic market economy?

For Further Study

Books to Explore

Bornstein, David, *How to Change the World: Social Entrepreneurs and the Power of New Ideas*, updated ed., New York: Oxford University Press, 2007.

Friedman, Milton, *Capitalism and Freedom*, Chicago, IL: University of Chicago Press, 1962.

Galbraith, John Kenneth, *Economics and the Public Purpose*, Boston, MA: Houghton Mifflin, 1973.

Gladwell, Malcolm, *Outliers: The Story of Success*, New York: Little Brown, 2008.

Hodgkinson, Tom, *Business for Bohemians*, New York: Overlook Press, 2018.

Haskel, Jonathan and Stian Westlake, *Capitalism without Capital*, Princeton, NJ: Princeton University Press, 2018.

Hayek, Friedrich, *The Road to Serfdom*, Chicago: University of Chicago Press, 1944.

Klein, Naomi, *This Changes Everything: Capitalism vs. the Climate*, New York: Simon & Schuster, 2014.

Prestowitz, Clyde, *Three Billion New Capitalists: The Great Shift of Wealth and Power to the East*, New York: Basic Books, 2006.

Sandberg, Sheryl, *Lean In: Women, Work and the Will to Lead*, New York: Alfred Knopf, 2013.

Schumpeter, Joseph A., *Capitalism, Socialism and Democracy*, New York: Harper & Row, 1962.

Stiglitz, Joseph, Amartya Sen, and Jean-Paul Fitoussi, *Mismeasuring Our Lives: Why GDP Doesn't Add Up*, New York: The New Press, 2010.

Stockman, David A., *The Great Deformation: The Corruption of Capitalism in America*, New York: Public Affairs, 2015.

Taleb, Nassim Nicholas, *Skin in the Game: Hidden Asymmetries in Daily Life*, New York: Random House, 2018.

Thiel, Peter, *Zero to One*, New York: Crown Publishers, 2014.

Walter, David Moberg, *The Wal-Mart Effect: How the World's Most Powerful Company Really Works—and How It's Transforming the American Economy*, New York: Penguin, 2006.

Weber, Max, *The Protestant Ethic and the Spirit of Capitalism* (1904), New York: Scribner, 1958.

Internet Sites to Explore

"http://www.capitalism.org" Capitalism.org.

"http://www.economist.com" The Economist.

"http://www.communism.org" Informal Communist Discussion.

"http://www.mpiew-jena.mpg.de/english/" Max Planck Institute of Economics.

"http://www.oecd.org/" Organization for Economic Cooperation and Development.

The Economy, Government, and Economic Challenges Facing the United States

chapter 18

If you don't know what you are doing, for God's sake, do it gently.

—William Brainard

After reading this chapter, you should be able to:

- Distinguish government's indirect and direct roles in the economy
- Summarize the costs and benefits of regulation, and explain why regulation should be seen as a continuous process
- Discuss two contentious roles of government
- Give examples of two ways the government influences the distribution of income
- Define monetary policy and fiscal policy
- Give a short summary of economists' view of the fiscal crisis, globalization, and global warming
- Define globalization, and explain the importance of the law of one price

As we discussed in the last chapter, our economic system is best thought of as a pragmatic market economy. That means we are continually searching for the right mix of government and market control to meet society's desires. In this chapter, we explore that mix and the challenges facing the U.S. economy in the coming decades.

In talking about the government's role in the economy, it is useful to distinguish government's indirect role—its role in specifying what individuals and businesses can and cannot do through laws and regulation—from its direct role—its role in the economy as an institution that spends and taxes. Let's begin with government's indirect role.

Government's Indirect Role in the Economy

The government's indirect role in the economy is to provide a legal and institutional setting for the workings of the market by establishing and enforcing laws that regulate actions of individuals and businesses. Such laws have significant influence on who gets what, how people spend their money, and how people conduct economic activities.

Let's first consider government's influence on who gets what. Say the government passes a law that people can freely share downloadable songs and movies, or even that they can provide a site that allows other people to share songs and movies. Such a law will transfer income away from the producers of songs and movies to consumers of songs and movies.

The Enormous Increase in Regulations.

© Reuters/Kevin Lamarque

Alternatively, if the government establishes laws that prevent someone from practicing law or from teaching without a license—even if other people want to hire them despite their lack of a license—that law will transfer income to licensed lawyers and teachers and away from consumers. The list of ways in which the government indirectly determines the distribution of income with such laws of regulation is long and can be extended almost infinitely. In other words, what someone earns reflects not only his or her efforts but also the rules the government establishes that govern how the income is earned.

The government's influence on how we conduct economic activities is just as pervasive. For example, if you want to drive a car, most states require you to have car insurance. You must wait until you are a certain age to begin to work, and when you do work, you must keep certain records and file tax returns. Firms must abide by certain nondiscriminatory practices when hiring, provide proof of insurance, and ensure their products meet certain standards. It is because of government's large indirect role that we called our economic system a pragmatic market economy rather than a free market economy as it is sometimes called. A free market economy would be anarchy. The U.S. economy is far from anarchy; it is a highly regulated market economy where the regulations reflect pragmatic considerations and attempts to correct problems caused by markets and problems caused by government. Both are problematic, and all societies continually search for the right combination.

The Problem of Regulating the Economy

All individuals agree that some regulation is needed. The questions are: How much? And what type? One type of regulation that has come under specific attack is **unfunded mandates,** or regulations by the federal government that impose significant costs on individuals and states but do not provide the funds to pay those costs. One example of an unfunded mandate is the law passed by the federal government to make all public buildings in the United States accessible to all individuals, including people with physical and mental disabilities. Passing the law was easy and seemed right to many Americans. But the law imposed serious costs on many businesses, and the law did not provide those businesses with a way to pay for them. Governments pass many such laws and regulations every year that impose large costs on individuals and firms in the economy—costs that someone, either the firm or their customers, must pay.

The debate over regulation is ongoing. Supporters of a particular regulation generally argue that the regulation serves an important purpose of protecting individuals and of ensuring that economic activities are carried out in a way that the legal system considers fair. Opponents of a particular regulation generally argue that the costs of the regulation are too high, citing examples such as the following, which appeared in the *Wall Street Journal.* An upstate New York nursing home had been cited by state officials as "a shining example" of what such an establishment ought to be. However, not long afterward, the owner of this home closed it down with the following explanation: "It was just impossible. There were eighteen state and federal agencies putting forms, questions, and statistical requests across my desk. Medical reports . . . census figures . . . Social Security . . . unemployment insurance . . . workers' compensation . . . withholding taxes . . . daily time sheets . . . work plans . . . It was just one thing after another." According to the owner, she sometimes spent eighteen hours a day just handling the government paperwork required for only twenty patients and fourteen employees. Such large-scale regulations have brought about a reaction on the part of some people supporting the doctrine of **laissez-faire,** the theory that government should interfere with business as little as possible.

The problem for strong advocates of laissez-faire is that while there are many examples of large-scale and intrusive regulation, there are also many examples of regulations that have helped society, and there are parts of society that most observers would consider under-regulated—areas of the economy where the lack of regulation has caused significant problems for the economy. Let's consider a couple of them. The first involves pollution. In the past, firms and people have been able to pollute without facing any limitations on their actions. That pollution has often made streams unusable, the air unbreathable, and has destroyed beautiful areas and public lands. In economists' parlance, such problems are caused by **externalities**— the effects of a firm's actions or decisions that negatively affect others but that the firm does not consider when undertaking the action. When there are externalities, the situation is made worse for the majority of people by the action that caused the externality. Economists agree that even in a primarily market-based economy, regulation is needed to see that those creating negative externalities stop doing so at least to the degree that others would be willing to pay them not to undertake those activities.

Another example of an area where lack of regulation has caused problems involves financial firms that borrowed enormous amounts of money to buy highly speculative mortgage-backed securities (bonds backed by risky mortgages in the first decade of the twenty-first century.) When the value of those bonds fell in 2007, the firms could not pay back the loans, and they would have collapsed without government intervention. Many felt that these financial institutions deserved to collapse. Unfortunately, their collapse would have brought down the entire U.S., and probably world, economy along with it, which would have made the situation worse for everyone. They were considered "too big to fail," which means that the U.S. government felt it necessary to step in and bail out the firms, and it did so in 2009. The problem here is the fact that if a firm is too big to fail, it is too big *not* to be regulated; and following the bailout, the U.S. government explored ways to increase the regulation of financial firms in an attempt to avoid another financial crisis in the future. It passed a law, called the Dodd-Frank Act, for this purpose; however, the rules were about 900 pages long and were nearly impossible for anyone not specializing in the law to understand.

There are huge differences of opinion about how much and what kind of regulation is desirable. It is clear that many government regulations have served the public interest, but it seems equally clear that some intended to do so have not. What makes finding the right mix of regulation so difficult is that the problem of regulation cannot be solved once and for all and then forgotten. Technology and social situations are continually changing, which means that regulations appropriate in the past may no longer be appropriate. People also figure out ways to get around regulations, so that the regulations become less effective over time. Thus, regulation must be seen as a continual process, which requires regulators to stay ahead of the firms and the individuals regulated. Successfully doing so requires enormous expertise and commitment— expertise that is expensive and often beyond the budget of governments.

Whose Desires Does the Government Reflect?

If government always reflected "society's will," there would be far less debate about regulation and government's role. But it doesn't. "Society's will" is an artificial construct; there is no society that has a will of its own that can be specified separately from the collective will of the individuals within the society. Whose desires will be reflected by government as society's desires is subject to enormous political infighting; it reflects the political power of various groups: Those with political power get their desires met, while those without political power do not.

Often, from many outside observers' perspectives, government laws and regulations are not designed to help the general public, but instead are designed to help special interests. Consider the issues of patents and copyrights. All agree that some patent and copyright protection is useful because it creates incentives for the development of new technologies and products, but many argue that the length of time that patents and copyrights last is far longer than necessary to encourage such developments and that the length of patents and copyrights in the United States could be shortened significantly, thereby benefiting the general public with minimal negative effects on incentives.

Why don't governments shorten these times? Critics claim that the reason is that it would reduce the patent and copyright owners' income—and those owners lobby Congress hard to prevent that from happening. An example of this is the Copyright Term Extension Act of 1998, often called the "Mickey Mouse Protection Act" because the Disney Corporation was a big

© Wiley Miller and CartoonStock.com

beneficiary of the law. Disney's copyright on Mickey Mouse was about to expire after 75 years. That would have let anyone produce Mickey Mouse goods without paying Disney. Disney lobbied Congress hard, and Congress extended the copyright for decades longer, essentially transferring billions of dollars from consumers to Disney. Many similar examples exist.

So while most people agree that, in principle, regulations *can* improve the workings of an economy, there is far less agreement on whether, in the real world, regulations *do* improve the workings of the economy or whether regulation simply provides an alternative method through which special interests can improve their position.

Fluctuating Attitudes toward Regulation

Attitudes in the United States toward regulation have fluctuated. In the 1960s and early 1970s, regulation was seen as a necessary limit to private powers. About the mid-1970s and well into the 1980s, the pendulum of public opinion shifted, and many believed that the U.S. economy was suffering from overregulation. This led to a belief that deregulation, or the removal of those excessive regulations, would improve the workings of the economy. Then, in the 2000s, the pendulum swung again as first accounting scandals, and then the financial crisis of 2008–2009, rocked the economy and brought it to the verge of collapse because of financial risk-taking by large banks and insurance companies. In response, public opinion shifted to favor more, or at least better, regulation.

In recent years, however, voters began to support the idea that government regulations were hindering the growth of small businesses and U.S. industry once more. These sentiments were inflamed by the rhetoric of the 2016 presidential election, and strong support from voters favoring deregulation is one of the factors that carried Donald Trump to victory.

Government's Direct Role in the Economy

Besides its indirect role of making laws and regulations for the economy, government also plays a direct role in the economy. By that we mean that it is an active participant in the economy and that it collects and spends trillions of dollars a year. The reason government has a direct role in the economy is because some things are better done collectively than individually, and government is the natural institution in our society to carry out collective action. Let's consider one example of something best done collectively: defense. If each of us provided for our own defense for attack from another country, our country would likely be taken over by another country—each individual in our country could not afford to provide even one plane or one battleship. These collective consumption goods, sometimes called **public goods,** are more efficiently supplied by government than by individuals.

Where the Government Spends Its Money

Each year, the federal government spends about $4 trillion to finance its activities, and state and local governments spend more than $3.4 trillion to finance their activities. Figure 18.1a shows the division of federal government expenditures; and Figure 18.1b shows the division of state government expenditures.

As you can see, the federal government spends the largest percentage on social welfare programs. By contrast, after administration, state governments spend most of their money on education and public welfare. In addition to federal and state governmental activities, there are also local governmental activities. Local governments spend most of their budgets on education and roads.

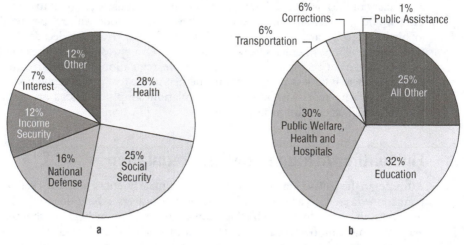

Figure 18.1

(a) Approximate federal outlays by use, 2018 (b) Approximate state outlays by use, 2018. (Source: U.S. Department of Commerce, CBO, U.S. Department of Treasury)

Where Government Gets Its Money

If government is to supply a good, it has to pay for it. The three main options for paying are voluntary contributions, taxes, and borrowing. The most prominent of these is taxes. To have a government is to have taxes. Why not pay for those goods through voluntary contributions? The reason is that people have a natural tendency to avoid contributing toward public goods, even when they are receiving the benefits. Therefore, all governments have the power to tax—to force people to pay for the goods that government supplies. Borrowing is also used by government, but borrowing does not eliminate the need for government to pay for the goods or for taxes; it simply puts it off until later. Moreover, borrowing means that the government not only has to pay the money back; it also has to pay interest on the loan.

Each year, the U.S. federal, state, and local governments together collect about $5 trillion in taxes. Figures 18.2a and 18.2b show the divisions of tax revenues for the federal and state governments. As you can see, the federal government's primary sources of revenue are individual income taxes, Social Security taxes, and corporate income taxes. State and local governments' primary sources of revenue are a combination of three sources—income taxes, property taxes and sales taxes. Local governments get most of their income from property taxes.

What the two charts in Figure 18.2 miss is the fact that on both the federal and state levels, government spending often significantly exceeds tax revenue. When that happens, the spending has to be financed by borrowing, not taxes. Currently, the U.S. national debt is more than $20 trillion, or approximately $170,000 per taxpayer. It is projected to increase to $30 trillion by 2026. Most of this debt is "public debt," meaning that it is held in the form of Treasury securities by outside investors, including companies and foreign governments. The two largest foreign holders of U.S. public debt are the governments of Japan and China.

Alternative Methods of Supply in a Pragmatic Market Economy

Once a government exists, the political process can decide which goods the government should provide, which goods should be supplied privately through the market, and what other roles the government should have. Many different arrangements are possible. Consider primary and secondary education. It could be supplied privately with individuals paying for the

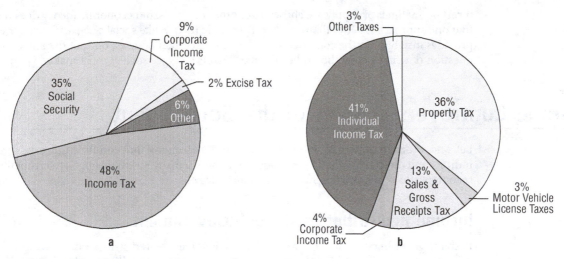

Figure 18.2

(a) Federal revenue by source, 2018. (b) Approximate State and local tax revenue by source, 2018. (Source: U.S. Department of Commerce, U.S. Department of Treasury, OMB, U.S. Bureau of the Census)

education they want, in the same way that people pay for their cars. But this is not the way most societies provide education. Most societies provide education for all students by paying for it with money collected in taxes. Why? Because they feel education benefits the society as a whole as well as the individuals getting the education. In the United States, tax-paid public education ends with the completion of high school, although most states have colleges and universities that receive part of their budgets from tax money.

Currently, there is a debate about whether public schools are doing an adequate job of providing a quality education and whether their costs—more than $12,000 per student per year—are excessive. Some reformers advocate a hybrid system—public funding but private provision—through vouchers given to parents, allowing families to choose which school to send their children to and to pay for at least part of the school cost with the government vouchers.

Education is not the only good that can be paid for and supplied either by government, individuals, or private firms. For instance, health care and prescription drugs are goods that could be paid for and supplied privately but are actually paid for in part by the government, although in the United States, supply remains private.

In 2010, the United States passed a mandatory health insurance law, the Patient Protection and Affordable Care Act (the ACA), that required all individuals to have health insurance, and provided for subsidies for lower-income individuals to pay for that insurance. These mandates were challenged as being unconstitutional by twenty-six states, but in 2012, the Supreme Court declared the ACA constitutional. Implementation began in 2014, but that implementation has been problematic. The fight over health insurance, and how to provide it in a cost-effective manner, reflects the wide divide between those who favor a larger direct role for government and those who favor a larger role for individual responsibility.

Since the beginning of his presidency in 2016, Donald Trump has worked toward repealing the Obama-era health care reforms. Since the Republicans did not have the votes to repeal the law, Trump focused on modifying the program by making administrative rulings that changed the plan. Since the Democrats did not have the votes to fully implement the plan without numerous administrative rulings, Trump was able to do this. For example, he eliminated the mandate that all people had to buy specific types of insurance.

The direct role of government in the economy will always be an important issue of debate in a pragmatic market economy. Economics gives guidance about problems that will likely develop if certain methods of supply are chosen over other methods, but economic theory does not say that one approach is better than another. Economic theory, like social science theory generally, provides insights into the consequences of adopting certain policies, but not the answer to the question of which policy should be adopted. That is a choice society must make.

Some Controversial Roles of the Government

Let's now turn to some roles of government in the economy that combine the government's indirect and direct roles. First, we will look at income redistribution through government; and, second, we look at government's macroeconomic role.

Income Redistribution through Government

Perhaps government's most controversial role involves the redistribution of income. Redistribution of income is achieved both through the government's direct and indirect roles. We have spoken of the indirect role's effect on distribution above. By allowing long-term patents and copyrights, the government creates inequality by redistributing income from large numbers of consumers of books and music to a small group of people who own those copyrights and patents. Another example of such indirect redistribution involves the allocation of the broadcast spectrum, which the government has given to a small number of corporations, providing billions of dollars in wealth for them and higher costs for the public. A third example concerns the recent proposed allocation of CO_2 rights for the cap-and-trade policy by which the government is attempting to help fight global warming by reducing CO_2 emissions. Ignoring the advice of almost all economists, the government has proposed to give the majority of these rights to existing polluters rather than auctioning them off. The existing polluters will then be free to "sell" those rights if they cut their pollution. By allocating the rights in that manner, the government is creating a transfer of hundreds of billions of dollars to these companies and to the people who buy their outputs—and away from the government that would have received the income from auctioning off these rights.

A final example involves the licensing of professions such as lawyers, medicine, and real estate. Those licenses force suppliers of these services to go through an often expensive schooling before they are allowed to practice that profession. In doing so, the government limits certain activities to those who have gotten the credential. That limitation raises the price of the service considerably from what it would be if entry had been less restrictive. Consider a couple of examples—a person (even a medical doctor) is not allowed to charge for administering a rabies shot to a dog, even though he or she might know how to do so from his or her training. Similarly, a person who has specialized in writing wills is not allowed to charge for writing a will for a friend. Doing either would be practicing a profession without a license, which is against the law. There are, of course, benefits of people having qualifications, but often the training doesn't really make someone qualified; it simply serves as a hurdle that people must meet to enter a profession. Government could let people know who has qualifications with a certification program, rather than a licensing program. Then people could decide if they wanted to hire a "certified" lawyer or an uncertified lawyer. Through such a program, it would be possible to have much more freedom of entry into professions than there currently is, while still giving people the option of hiring a certified professional. Alternatively, government could provide narrower sublicenses in which a non-lawyer could be licensed to do particular types of activities, such as writing a simple will, but not other types of activities, such as defending a client in court.

Government also directly influences the distribution of income through its use of its taxing power and its spending functions. Generally, this involves imposing relatively higher taxes on people who have high incomes and using that tax money to provide additional

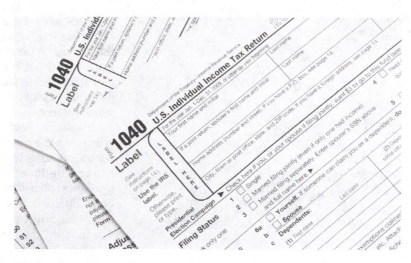

The income tax is a major source of government's income.

© Oxford/iStock

income to people whose income would otherwise be much lower. There are three ways this is done in the United States:

1. We have a **progressive income tax system**—people who earn high incomes are taxed at a higher rate so that the government can use tax money to provide programs for lower-income people. Although our income tax is progressive, it is far less progressive than it has been in the past. During World War II and for a short while thereafter, the top federal tax rate on high-income individuals was over 90 percent. Today, top federal tax rates on earned income such as wages are about 40 percent.
2. We have low-income tax credits. Low-income people are given a tax credit, so instead of paying taxes, they receive a direct payment from the government.
3. We have entitlement programs that favor the poor. The majority of income support our government provides is through entitlement programs such as Social Security, Medicare, and Medicaid, which are designed to favor the poor somewhat. For example, the federal government subsidizes health insurance premiums for many low-income people.

Each of these programs is complicated, and we could write a book about each one just trying to explain their intricacies; we won't do that here. We focus our discussion on one example, the Social Security program, the largest government expenditure program.

The U.S. Social Security System.   The first comprehensive government-administered social insurance system was enacted by imperial Germany in 1889, sponsored by the famous German chancellor Otto von Bismarck, who apparently conceived of it as a plan for allaying social unrest. Over the next three decades, similar plans were adopted by most other major industrial nations. It was not until the Great Depression of the 1930s that the United States passed the Social Security Act of 1935, a broad program of social insurance. Under pressure from President Franklin D. Roosevelt, Congress enacted the **Federal Insurance Contributions Act (FICA),** a plan providing a broad program of social insurance funded by a tax levied half on employers and half on employees. The plan was a compromise between liberals who wanted a much larger guarantee of government income support and conservatives who opposed any such plan.

Social Security Is Not Insurance.   Because of the debate surrounding it, Social Security was described to the public as a type of contributory insurance plan, even though it really did not meet that definition. A true insurance plan would collect money, invest it, and out of the

© Oxford/iStock

proceeds pay people who found themselves in the circumstances against which they were insuring themselves. As it developed, the Social Security system paid out the money almost as soon as it took it in. Thus, it was not funded like an insurance plan but was a system in which there was only a small reserve; benefits were paid from current contributions. Such a procedure does not necessarily mean the system is unsound. As long as new contributions at least equal expenditures, the system can continue forever. However, by calling it an insurance plan when it was actually something quite different, the government laid the foundation for future problems.

Initially, the problems were not evident: The plan was a modest one, contributions were very small, and monthly benefit levels were very low. In those initial years, it was not planned as a retirement system but, rather, as a cushion against destitution in old age and as a supplement to whatever other plans workers made for retirement income. Through the 1980s, the law was amended many times, almost always to increase the amount of an individual's benefit and sometimes to increase the number of people who could become eligible. As legislated expenditures of the program have increased, the tax has greatly increased as well. Beginning in the 1980s, fear about the stability of the system led to some cutbacks such as computing current benefits at slightly lower amounts and, for the future, setting the retirement age higher.

Social Security Benefits and Taxes.　How much do people pay for Social Security? In 2018, individuals paid a tax of 6.2 percent on their wages up to $128,400 and an additional tax, dedicated to health benefits, of 1.45 percent on their total wages. Businesses that hired them paid an equal amount, which is in addition to the income tax that individuals pay, so combined they pay over 15 percent in Social Security taxes.

How much do people get back for what they put in? That depends on how long they worked, how much they earned when they worked, and when they started claiming benefits, along with a variety of other factors. To give you a rough idea of how much someone would get, say a worker earned $50,000 a year when he or she retired, and worked consistently most of his or her life. That worker would receive about $1,650 a month if he or she retired at 62, but if he or she delayed retirement until 70, would receive closer to $2,900 a month.

The Future of the Social Security System.　Because Social Security is a pay-as-you-go system, not an insurance system, how solvent it is depends on how many people are paying into it and how many are drawing out of it. When the program began, many paid in and few took out. In 1950, for every one person drawing benefits, 16.5 people were paying in. Recently, that ratio has changed to about one person drawing out for every three people paying in, necessitating a much higher tax rate applied to a much higher base (in 1937, the tax was just 1 percent and applied only to the first $3,000 of income). But the real crunch will come between 2020 and 2030, when a large majority of the baby boomers retire. At that time, the ratio of people paying in to people drawing out will move closer to two to one. When that happens, the Social Security system will have to borrow money, the tax rate will have to rise considerably, or benefits will have to be cut.

The Social Security Trust Fund, which has been built up by raising the FICA tax above what is necessary to fund the current benefits, provides some cushion against the future imbalance between the number of people paying in compared to the number of people drawing out. But the United States cannot escape the fact that in the near future, the Social Security system will be supporting many more retirees than it does now, and have fewer contributors per retiree.

Government's Macroeconomic Role

Another important, but controversial, form of government involvement in the economy reflects its **macroeconomic role**—its role in protecting and increasing society's welfare by reducing economic fluctuations in the economy and providing a stable financial environment. To understand government's macroeconomic role, it is useful to contrast it with government's **microeconomic role**—a role that involves protecting and increasing society's welfare based on the consideration of individuals' welfare. Both roles consider society, but microeconomics builds up from the individual to create systemic effects, while macroeconomics starts with the whole system and then works down to the individual. The reason it is called macroeconomics is that it focuses its concerns on the aggregate (macro) society—whereas microeconomics focuses its concerns on the individual. Both categories consider the welfare of society, but they approach it differently. What this means is that the difference between the two is more one of approach than of focus.

Thus, for economists, government's microeconomic role is concerned with individual problems such as health care or old-age pensions. Government's macroeconomic role is concerned with the economy as a whole—seeing to it that the overall economy remains stable, does not fall into a depression, or experience runaway inflation.

Stabilizing the Economy.   Over the past hundred years, there has been significant fluctuation in unemployment, inflation, and output. These fluctuations in aggregate output are called **business cycles.** A typical business cycle is shown in Figure 18.3; it has a boom period and a recession period.

Up until the 1930s, most economists thought such business cycles were inevitable. Society should put up with them just as one endures minor aches and pains in one's body. So there was felt to be little macroeconomic role for government in stabilizing the economy. Fluctuations and unemployment were seen as inevitable parts of life. Economists believed that government should be concerned with preventing inflation, and figuring out how to control its tendency to spend without taxing to pay for that spending. To do that, most economists of the time supported government running balanced budgets—except in periods of wartime—and in limiting increases in the money supply.

That view of the role of government changed in the 1930s when the economy fell into a deep depression. A **depression** is a period of drastic decline in an economy, characterized by decreasing business activity, falling prices, and unemployment. Most Americans, judged by today's standards of income and consumption, were relatively poor in the middle and late 1920s, but we must be cautious in judging the past by the present, for in comparison with anything they had known before, people were enjoying a period of unprecedented prosperity. True, some groups, including farmers, did not share in this prosperity, but most Americans had achieved higher incomes than ever before. Furthermore, a great speculative rise in the prices of real estate and stocks had helped to create a general feeling of optimism.

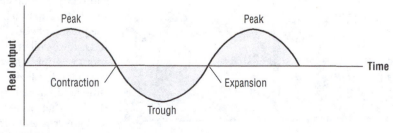

Figure 18.3

Idealized business cycle.

This feeling was soon dissipated by some rude shocks. In October 1929, there was a spectacular break in the stock market, and this was only the first of a series of developments that, by 1932, brought the country to the greatest depths of depression in its entire history. From 1929 to 1932, industrial production and national income dropped by about half, and unemployment rose from about 3 million to between 12 and 15 million, or about a quarter of the nation's labor force. These developments brought losses, discouragement, and great hardship to millions of people.

In response to that depression, in the 1930s the government instituted many of its income security programs. It also took a much greater role in maintaining the level of employment in the economy and in stabilizing the economy. This change was closely tied to what has become known as the **Keynesian view**—the view that government can and should play a stabilizing role in the economy. It is named after John Maynard Keynes, the English economist whose work played a big role in bringing about the change. The widespread adoption of the Keynesian view of the economy created the field of macroeconomics as distinct from that of microeconomics.

Monetary and Fiscal Policy.   Government's macroeconomic role is performed by both the executive branch of government, which has responsibility for fiscal policy, and the Central Bank of the United States (the Federal Reserve Bank, or Fed)—a type of banker's bank that has responsibility for monetary policy. Let's discuss each in turn.

Fiscal policy is a policy of using the government budget surplus or deficit to influence the level of spending and income in the economy. The economist's standard rule of thumb for fiscal policy is that if total spending in the economy is too low, the government should run a budget deficit; this deficit adds spending to the total flow of income and has a multiplied effect on the total level of spending. If total spending is too high, the government should run a budget surplus; this surplus subtracts spending from the total flow of income and has a multiplied downward effect on the total level of spending.

This rule of thumb allows that some government budget deficits can be useful in stimulating the economy out of a recession. Therefore, if the U.S. economy falls into a recession, we are likely to hear calls for increases in government spending or decreases in taxes in order to stimulate the economy. That is precisely what we heard in 2008 when the U.S. economy seemed to be in freefall. In response, the government ran a massive deficit and in doing so avoided a depression. But it also created an enormous problem—how to wean the U.S. economy from the deficit spending and the bailouts, and in 2018, the United States was still struggling with this problem.

A second macroeconomic tool to control a country's economy is monetary policy. **Monetary policy** is a policy in which the Central Bank varies the level of money and credit in the economy to affect the level of income. The **Federal Reserve Bank (Fed)** is a semiautonomous agency that is only indirectly responsible to Congress and the president. It is run by a Board of Governors appointed by the president and serves as a bank to banks. It issues IOUs (also called notes) that serve as the basis of our money supply. (If you look on a dollar bill, you will see that it is a Federal Reserve note.) Whereas at one time gold backed the dollar, presently only trust in the fact that others will accept this dollar backs it. The government provides no backing for the dollar except its ability to tax. What gives money its value is that the Fed is committed to issuing only a limited quantity of its notes, or IOUs.

The Federal Reserve Bank.

© usschools/iStock

Credit and the financial sector are the equivalent to an economy's heart. They are essential to the economy because a failure of the financial sector means its heart stops beating; if that happens, firms and individuals cannot borrow or pay their bills, and they have to cut production. These cuts in production can push the economy into a downward spiral that ends in a depression.

The discussion of the technical operation of monetary policy is best left to economics courses. What you should know now is that monetary policy does not affect the level of income directly; rather, it affects the interest rate by making it easier or harder for individuals and firms to borrow. When the Fed increases the money supply, it is called expansionary monetary policy. Expansionary monetary policy makes credit easier to get and lowers interest rates; as interest rates fall, investment increases, which in turn has a multiplied effect (upward) on the level of income. When the Fed decreases the money supply, it is called contractionary monetary policy. Contractionary monetary policy makes credit harder to get and raises interest rates. As interest rates rise, investment decreases, which in turn has a multiplied effect (downward) on the level of income.

The Federal Reserve has become a key player in determining government macroeconomic policy despite the fact that the Fed is semi-autonomous. Its chairperson (Jerome Powell as of 2018) is often seen as the second most powerful person in determining U.S. economic policy, right after the president.

Since 2008, the Fed has been keeping the U.S. interest rate low, by significantly increasing the money supply and available credit in the economy, in order to stimulate the U.S. economy. The initial reason for doing so was the 2008 financial crisis, which threatened to lead the U.S. economy into a depression. The stimulative monetary policy saved the U.S. economy from a depression, but it also built into the economy an expectation of low interest rates, and the Fed continued the low interest rate policy through 2016. Some economists have argued that these low interest rates are encouraging people, businesses, and government to borrow more than they will be able to pay back, which will cause serious debt problems for the U.S. economy in the future. In 2017, the Fed started increasing the interest rate again, which is a trend anticipated to continue for the coming year, since the economy has been expanding.

*E*conomic Challenges Facing the United States in the Future

There is much more to be said about the government's macroeconomic role, but discussion of such issues is best left to economics classes. Here we simply want to introduce you to the institutions, terms, and ideas of economists. We will do this by considering economists' views on some challenges facing the United States—the debt challenge, the **globalization** challenge, the income inequality challenge, and the climate change challenge.

The Debt Challenge

The accompanying box captures a key element of economists' thinking about the debt problem. Economists call it the **"no free lunch" principle** (everything has a cost and must ultimately be paid for). Economists see this principle as universal for individuals, governments, and businesses. One of the central policy propositions that economics has come to is that successful societies are those that have figured out ways to build this principle into the decision-making process of all decisions makers, so that it occurs almost without thinking. That's an important reason why economists tend to support markets: Markets let people make voluntary trades that improve their lot. So when people trade in the market, they believe that the benefits they get from the trade exceed the cost, which means that they are made better off by the trade, even when the trade takes into account that something must be given up. So in a

There Ain't No Such Thing as a Free Lunch

It is sometimes said that economics is simply the application of some tautologies (statements that are true by definition) to a consideration of social issues. One of those tautologies is captured by the following apocryphal story about a tyrannical king who decided that he wanted all economic knowledge summed up in a ten-volume work, so that he could read it and better rule his country. He assembled the best economists in the nation and told them to complete the task in four years. They set to work, and at the end of four years they had all ten volumes completed.

Unfortunately, the king had become busy with affairs of state in the interim, and he no longer had time to read ten volumes. So he told the economists to reduce it all to one volume within the next year. They dutifully set to work doing so. But at the end of one year, the king became much busier and felt he no longer had time to even read a book. Moreover, he had become a tyrant, so he ordered the economists to reduce the information in the book to one sentence within the next week. He told them he would put them to death if they did not complete the task.

After lamenting their fate for a couple of hours, they decided the task was hopeless and that they might as well order one last meal before they were put to death. They called in their order for a thick-crust, super-veggie pizza. When the delivery man who came with their pizza asked for his money, the economists realized that they didn't have any. The king had taken away their checkbooks and credit cards. When they told the delivery man that, he took the pizza back and walked away, saying, "You guys are economists; you should know that there ain't no such thing as a free lunch." Upon hearing this, the hungry economists looked at each other with a grin, saying in unison, "We're saved; that's it—that's economic knowledge summed up in one sentence." They ran and told the king, who thanked them, and sent them back to their respective universities, where they began teaching social science.

TANSTAAFL! It is a fact of life that you don't get something just for nothing. That's all!

© CartoonStock.com

market transaction, people are made better off even as the "no free lunch" principle is maintained. Trade allows people to get cheaper, not free, lunches.

While the "no free lunch" proposition is a tautology for the entire system, it is not always true for component parts of the system such as individuals, governments, or businesses. One part of a system can eat a lunch and leave the paying to other parts. Government, people, and businesses have a strong incentive to do precisely that, and much of economists' advice about the economic challenges facing the United States involves instituting measures that build the "no free lunch" principle into society's decisions.

Debt allows people to temporarily get around the "no free lunch" proposition. To the degree people are willing to accept debt—a promise to pay in the future—in return for something now, an individual who makes that promise can get something for nothing but the promise. If, when the borrower is asked to make good on that promise, he, she, or it doesn't have the wherewithal to do so, then there are problems. The reality is that if the person or government really can't pay, it does no good to try to force them to pay. That's the policy problem created by debt, and it is one that societies continually face.

Once one is in a position where individuals who have the debt cannot repay it, then some part of the debt will have to be forgiven. Once that position has been reached, economists don't have a good answer for what to do. One group of economists argues that we should just let the borrowers go bankrupt, even if it will cause enormous hardship and suffering not only for the debtor, but for all society. This position is often called "austerity," but supporters prefer to call it a policy of responsibility. The problem with bailing out a debtor is that it will encourage more debtors to get in such a position in the future. People will see the possibility of free lunches, and the market will not work right. Another group of economists argue that if people really can't repay the loan, you have no alternative but to bail them out, and that you should simply do your best to prevent the need to bail out debtors from happening again in the future.

We spend time on this principle since you will likely see defaults on debt in the news in the coming years. A major reason for that is student debt; many loans are now being made to students that will be impossible to repay, since the students' income from jobs that they will be able to get will be nowhere near high enough to repay what they have borrowed. So you can expect a student debt crisis in the future.

Another debt crisis on the horizon involves pensions—specifically the way pension plans by firms, local governments, and state governments have been structured. Many of these pension plans have promised payments in the future that far exceed the companies' and local and state government's ability to pay. The only solution in all these cases will be default—and enormous suffering and economic dislocation—or bailout by the federal government with the federal government assuming the loss as best it can. These coming debt crises will put significant strains on the stability of our social system.

To summarize economists' view of the debt problem: Debt allows individuals and governments to do things that they otherwise could not do. If debtors have the earning capability to pay that debt back, or at least to continue to pay the interest on the debt, then debt allows an expansion of the economy and serves a useful purpose. But there is strong pressure for borrowing to take place that exceeds the capacity of the borrower to repay. When that happens, the debt will eventually lead to a crisis for which economists have no good answer.

The Globalization Challenge

In the beginning of the twentieth century, the United States became the world's dominant economic power; throughout the twentieth century, it had higher wages, and much more industrial power than any other country in the world. That is now in the process of change, as industrial power is shifting from the United States to newly developed countries. Although the name globalization is fairly new, the phenomenon is not. It is a process that has been ebbing and flowing for centuries. For example, in the colonialization period of the 1600s and 1700s, colonial "possessions" were integrated into the economies that controlled them, and there was much trade between the home country and its colonies. In 1914, World War I ended the era of colonial globalization. Global trade did not begin to recover until the end of World War II. Since then, it has re-expanded greatly, but it is important to understand that globalization is not new to our generation, and that the world's economies have been in a continual process of integration, segregation, and reintegration for centuries.

During the twentieth century, it became taken as given by many Americans that U.S. per capita income would be higher than world per capita income. In the period immediately after

"THAT'S NOT IN ADDITION TO YOUR PENSION,
THAT IS YOUR PENSION."

World War II, U.S. power grew and U.S. wages rose far above those of other countries; U.S. technology also was far above others, and U.S. economic might was unchallenged. The globalization crisis involves coming to grips with the realization that U.S. economic dominance is not inherent and that very likely, in the coming decades, its dominance will decline. The reason why U.S. dominance will decline is because indefinite dominance by one country was not a stable situation to begin with. It violated what economists call the **law of one price,** which states that if a free flow of resources and technology exists, equally productive factors will tend to earn equal amounts, and tradable goods will tend to have the same price.

According to the law of one price, eventually—assuming they are equally productive—a Chinese, Indian, or African engineer will earn the same as a U.S. engineer. This law holds because, if it is not the case, firms will relocate production to areas with lower-cost workers. This process of equalizing wages of equally productive workers is called factor price equalization. It has been occurring since the end of World War II—first with the growth of the European, Japanese, and Korean economies, and more recently with the growth of India's and China's economies relative to the United States.

An important condition to note is that the law of one price is dependent on a free flow of resources and technology, and in many sectors of the economy that does not hold. For example, an American cannot get a haircut from someone in China or India, so haircuts are not tradable. This means that a Chinese haircutter can receive less than a U.S. haircutter without the U.S. haircutter worrying about losing his or her job. Similarly, if U.S. firms have access to better technology than Chinese and Indian firms, which was the case for much of the twentieth century, U.S. firms can earn higher profits and pay higher wages than Chinese and Indian firms.

In the late twentieth century and the beginning of the twenty-first century, those qualifiers —which made it possible for U.S. incomes of many U.S. workers to significantly exceed those of workers in other countries—have been fading away. One reason is because technology has opened up new areas where trade can take place that did not exist before. This expansion of trade has occurred in both goods and services. Trade has expanded in terms of goods because of enormous technological changes in shipping and transportation. Modern containers allow much lower-cost shipping of bulky items than was previously possible. Today, the oceans are filled with gigantic containerized ships that are unloaded at ports and sent on their way by computerized systems that have significantly lowered the cost of shipping.

Computers, the Internet, and modern communications technology have also allowed instant contact with firms all over the world, which reduces much of the advantage of producing for U.S. consumers in the United States. Simultaneously, countries previously hostile to markets have introduced markets into their economies and thus have become trading partners and competitors, creating billions of additional potential workers competing for a job. This has added enormous competition to the manufacturing sector in the United States and has changed its very nature, from one where most manufactured goods consumed by U.S. consumers were produced in the United States, to one where most U.S. manufactured goods consumed by U.S. customers are produced abroad. Today, U.S. manufacturing specializes in certain niche and high-tech consumption goods and in research and development. China is now the factory for the world much more than is the United States.

It is not only in goods that this movement has taken place. It is also in services, and the loss of service jobs to other countries goes under the name **outsourcing**—the shifting of jobs from the United States to lower-wage developing countries. Thus, while U.S. haircutters do not face competition from abroad, people working in service support positions do. For example, call centers now are typically found in India and other English-speaking developing countries. So when you call for technical support on your computer or with a question about your bill, the telephone call will likely be handled by someone in India.

Similarly, accounting and bookkeeping for firms is more and more done in India. The areas of competition are expanding. Say you need some tutoring. Now you can go online and hire an Indian tutor to help you with your homework. We can expect much more such competition in the future.

To maintain its dominance in a globalized economy, and the higher wages that go with that dominance, the United States will have to maintain a technological edge over other countries. Doing so will likely become increasingly difficult as India and China move up the technological ladder—just as Japan, Korea, and the European countries did earlier. This does not mean that U.S. income must fall from where it is now; it only means that the largest growth in income and output will likely be in countries such as China and India, and that the United States and Europe will experience relatively slower growth.

What do economists have to offer to meet the globalization crisis? If you are looking for an easy fix, the answer is "not much." They see globalization as an inevitable process, not a crisis. They argue that the best a country can do is to learn to live with it. It must concentrate on producing as efficiently as possible and must learn to no longer see itself as special. In an economy, you are only special to the degree that you can produce goods people want at a lower cost than others. President Trump has offered what he suggests is an easier America First approach. Instead of freer trade, he will implement tariffs as he did in 2018 on washing machines and solar panels. Most economists opposed that approach.

Why shouldn't the United States impose tariffs to project our jobs? As we will discuss in Chapter 20, economists argue that imposing tariffs would lead to other countries imposing tariffs, which would reduce demand for U.S. goods, and which could enter the world economy into a trade war. With the globalization process, the market is doing precisely what it is designed to do—channeling production to the lowest-cost area so that goods are produced as efficiently as possible. It is this globalization of goods and services that has allowed the United States to develop the high standard of living it enjoys today. So, economists' solution to the globalization challenge is that the United States should learn to live with it and compete as hard as it can to maintain its standard of living.

The Income Inequality Challenge

Now let's turn to a third challenge facing the U.S. economy—the income inequality challenge. Market economies are built on social contracts—an implicit understanding that individuals in society will be given freedom to act and people will not complain about income inequality too much as long as the large majority of individuals in society can be provided with chances for advancement—that if one works hard, and does what society expects from them, then one can have a fulfilling life. One can expect that one's prospects will exceed those of one's parents. From the 1930s to the 1970s, that was the case in the U.S. Income inequality fell, the difference between the rich and poor declined, while simultaneously the overall economy was growing.

The rising standard of living and the declining inequality were consistent with the general belief of most people in the United States that large inequalities in income cause problems for a functioning democracy. In the 1980s, the inequality stopped declining and instead began increasing. Unskilled workers at the low end of the income spectrum were the most affected. From the 1980s until today, they have seen their wages stagnate, so that when adjusted for inflation, their wages have not risen at all. Individuals on the high end of the income spectrum have seen their income shoot up, so that they have been earning double or triple what they were earning, even after adjusting for inflation.

The reasons for this increase in inequality are varied. They are political—the progressivity of the income tax was reduced during this time period; sociological—the mores changed, and

Occupy London protests against income inequality.

© Lucian Milasan/Alamy Stock Photo

it became acceptable for top managers in firms to give themselves large increases in pay even when most workers in the firm were seeing their pay fall; and technological—new technologies developed which allowed low- and medium-skilled jobs to be replaced with **winner-take-all** industries, in which the top firm makes billions but other competitors do not make a profit. New technologies also allow machines and computers to replace low-skilled and repeatable jobs. This has gone on for decades.

What is now different is that what is meant by "low-skilled" is changing. It used to mean jobs like digging a hole, or manning a machine. Now with the expansion of artificial intelligence, "low-skilled" includes driving; standard diagnostic work, the primary work that most doctors do; teaching standard material, the primary work that teachers and professors do; and choosing among investment alternatives, a primary job of many middle managers in finance. When what doctors, professors, and managers do is considered "low-skilled," society is in for some enormous changes, and the basic way in which society distributes income will likely need to be rethought.

Globalization has also played an important role in the income inequality challenge. Workers who faced global competition, including many lower-skilled workers in the manufacturing sector, have seen their incomes pushed down to low global levels, and workers in sectors who face less global competition, such as government workers, teachers, and lawyers, have seen their wages rise. As discussed above, that process is now changing, and what were considered solid middle-class professional jobs will be experiencing downward pressure on their incomes in the coming years.

Economists do not have a good answer on how to deal with this income distribution challenge, in part because they have not focused their analysis on income distribution and in part because the issues are more political than they are economic. So income inequality will likely continue to be a topic of discussion in the coming years.

The Climate Change Challenge

Let's conclude with a consideration of a fourth challenge—one that not only the United States, but the entire world, is facing—climate change. Climate change is occurring because too much economic production is using carbon-based fuels, which increase the levels of CO_2 in the atmosphere. In the words of economists, the use of carbon-based fuels is creating an externality, which, as we stated above, is the result of a decision that is not taken into account by the decision maker. Thus, while the private decision maker balances the costs and benefits facing him or her, those private costs do not match the social costs that the action imposes on society. This is occurring so much in the consumption of carbon-based fuels that it is changing the world's atmosphere by increasing CO_2 levels and thereby increasing the average world temperature. The result is a rising sea level and significant weather changes for many areas. Low-lying areas face flooding if, as predicted, the sea rises by one to five feet over the next century.

Economists' answer to the problem of climate change is to see that the costs of the decision to use carbon-based fuel are taken into account by the decision maker. This can be done either by placing a tax on carbon-based fuel so that people face the true social cost, or by creating a cap-and-trade system—essentially creating property rights in pollution.

Given the fiscal problems the U.S. government faces—and the need for additional revenue—the tax-based approach is the one most economists favor, but imposing taxes is difficult politically, and the United States has chosen to do little in the way of the substantial changes that will be necessary to make a difference. But, slowly, it is beginning to create cap-and-trade markets in pollution. As it set them up, it had to answer the question: Who would get the property rights? Most economists favored government receiving the property rights to pollution because it would have meant hundreds of billions of dollars in revenue that the government needs. All polluters would then have to pay for the pollution, and the United States would have revenue to reduce its deficit.

Initially, the U.S. government followed economists' suggestion, but it soon backed away from that and gave most of the rights to existing polluters. Thus, existing polluters would not have to pay; instead, they could sell pollution rights to new firms, gaining income for reducing pollution. This decision on property rights made the implementation of the cap-and-trade system politically feasible but, from economists' standpoint, highly problematic since it essentially entrenched existing companies, and made creating new firms more costly. In a cap-and-trade system, with existing firms having the property rights, new companies starting in the United States will have to buy pollution permits from existing firms who reduce their CO_2 output; this places them at a competitive disadvantage to existing companies, and thereby slows the introduction of new technologies that the new companies generally introduce.

Economists also point out that the solution to climate change must occur at the global level because, otherwise, firms will simply move to where restrictions are weakest. There will be a flight to the lowest level of regulation. Thus, without a strict international agreement that all countries of the world abide by, it is almost inconceivable that a climate change solution will be achieved. So, the economists' perspective on climate change is that society should expect a warmer world because effective solutions are beyond our current international institutional structure, and voluntary measures do not work when dealing with problems that involve costly solutions.

As we discussed in Chapter 5, an attempt to facilitate international cooperation to curb climate change took place in Paris in December 2015. A vast majority of the world's countries sent representatives to Paris with the goal of creating parameters for CO2 emissions that could help slow the pace of global warming. At this convention, the signatory countries agreed to take action to cap global temperature increase at 1.5 degrees Celsius above pre-industrial levels. A 2017 study concluded that if the goals of the Paris climate agreement were met, median sea level rise in the next century could be kept to 1.7 feet.

The United States agreed to more reduction than did countries such as China and India, and when President Trump took office he argued that the Accord was unfair. He decided that the United States would withdraw from the **Paris Climate Accord**. A number of U.S. states and companies, however, said they would continue to meet the agreement's requirements on their own, even if the country as a whole would not.

Conclusion

Much more could be discussed on all of these issues, but we don't have time. However, despite the cursory structure, this chapter and the preceding chapter should give you a sense of economists' approach and their thinking about the economic challenges facing the U.S. economy. Such thinking involves an explicit consideration of both the costs and benefits of government policy and actions. The goal is to minimize costs while maximizing the benefits that laws and policies achieve. Imposing those policies is not easy, and is often politically difficult, which is why economics alone does not provide answers to problems. It simply provides a framework. The answers to the actual problem have to be found in the realm of politics as much as in the realm of economics.

 Study and **Review**

Key Points

- Government plays both an indirect role in the economy—setting the rules and regulating the economy—and a direct role—spending and taxing to pay for its spending.
- Regulation has both benefits and costs. It helps limit people from activities that might hurt others, but in doing so restricts people's actions and often stops them from activities that would be beneficial to others.
- Regulation is a continuous process because technologies change and people learn how to get around existing regulations.

- Two contentious roles of the government are its income redistribution role and its macroeconomic role.
- An important federal government expenditure is the Social Security program, and financing the program may present problems in the future.
- The government influences the level of activity in the economy with fiscal policy—using the government budget surplus or deficit to control the level of spending in the economy—and by monetary policy—allowing the Federal Reserve Bank to control the level of money and credit in the economy.

- The United States faces a number of economic challenges in the coming years, including the debt challenge, the globalization challenge, the income inequality challenge, and the climate change challenge.
- One of economists' key principles is the "no free lunch" principle.
- Globalization is the natural process of economic integration and is driven by the law of one price.
- Economists believe that to deal effectively with climate change, the costs of activities that contribute to climate change will have to be raised considerably.

Some Important Terms

business cycles (367)
depression (367)
externalities (359)
Federal Insurance Contributions Act (FICA) (365)
Federal Reserve Bank (Fed) (368)
fiscal policy (368)

globalization (369)
Keynesian view (368)
laissez-faire (359)
law of one price (372)
macroeconomic role (367)
microeconomic role (367)
monetary policy (368)

"no free lunch" principle (369)
outsourcing (373)
Paris Climate Accord (376)
progressive income tax system (365)
public goods (361)
unfunded mandates (358)

Questions for Review and Discussion

General Questions

1. About how much does the federal government spend each year to finance its activities? As a result, does it run a deficit or a surplus?
2. What has the U.S. government done so far in response to the issue of global warming, and why does this issue require an international solution?
3. While spending more money on manufacturing goods is looked upon favorably, why do people feel uneasy about additional spending on health care and education?
4. On what major category do state governments spend the most money per year?
5. What is fiscal policy, and what entity conducts it?
6. What is monetary policy, and what entity conducts it?
7. What problems is the government likely to face in paying Social Security benefits in the future?
8. What is the Keynesian view?
9. Should the federal government allow an unlicensed lawyer to practice law? Why or why not?

10. What problem will most likely arise when tariffs are imposed?
11. What two measures did the U.S. government take to stop the 2008–2009 financial crisis? What effect will they have in the long run?
12. Will outsourcing ultimately lead to a shift of all U.S. manufacturing to lower-wage countries?
13. Give two examples of how government laws can indirectly influence the distribution of income.
14. What are the implications of the "no free lunch" principle for debt?
15. What is the law of one price, and what does it mean for the wages of U.S. workers?
16. How is the information revolution changing the politics of income distribution?
17. How does a winner-take-all industry increase income inequality?
18. What do the authors mean when they say that solutions to global warming are beyond our current international institutional structure?

Internet Questions

1. Go to http://www.taxadmin.org/, the website of the Federation of Tax Administrators. Does your state have an income tax? Using the latest figures, what is the lowest and highest income tax rate for your state? Is it a progressive tax system? Explain.
2. Go to https://www.cbo.gov/publication/51580, the site of the Congressional Budget Office. What percentage of the GDP was spent on social security in 2016? How will that percentage change by 2046?
3. Go to https://www.treasurydirect.gov/govt/rates/pd/avg/avg.htm, the site of the Bureau of the Public Debt. What is the current amount of the national debt? What is the interest rate for the latest month? For the same month in the previous year?
4. Using a quick calculator, http://www.ssa.gov/planners/calculators.htm, estimate your Social Security benefits with the information you have now. Do you think Social Security payments are worth the expense?
5. According to the Federal Reserve, http://www.federalreserve.gov/faqs.htm, what are its responsibilities?

*F*or Further Study

Books to Explore

Baker, Dean, *Rigged: How Globalization and Rules of the Game were Structured to Make the Rich Richer*, Washington, DC: Center for Economic and Policy Research, 2016.

Baumol, William J., Robert E. Litan, and Carl. J. Schramm, *Good Capitalism, Bad Capitalism, and the Economics of Growth and Prosperity*, New Haven, CT: Yale University Press: 2007.

Brynjolfsson, Erik, and Andrew McAffe, *The Second Machine Age*, New York: Norton, 2014.

Cogan, John, *The High Costs of Good Intentions*, Stanford, CA: Stanford University Press, 2017.

Ehrenreich, Barbara, *Nickel and Dimed: On (Not) Getting By in America*, New York: Holt Publishing, 2001.

Friedman, Milton, *Capitalism and Freedom*, Chicago, IL: University of Chicago Press, 1982.

Hacker, Jacob S., and Paul, Pierson, *Winner-Take-All Politics: How Washington Made the Rich Richer-and Turned Its Back on the Middle Class*, New York: Simon & Schuster, 2010.

Heilbroner, Robert, L., *The Worldly Philosophers: The Lives, Times and Ideas of the Great Economic Thinkers*, London: Allen Lane, 1969.

Judis, John B., *The Populist Explosion: How the Great Recession Transformed American and European Politics*, New York: Columbia Global Reports, 2016.

Klein, Naomi, *This Changes Everything: Capitalism vs. the Climate*, New York: Simon & Schuster, 2014.

McKibben, Bill, *Deep Economy: The Wealth of Economies and the Durable Future*, New York: Henry Holt & Co, 2007.

Reich, Robert, *Saving Capitalism for the Many Not the Few*, New York: Knopf, 2015.

Reid, T. R., *A Fine Mess: A Global Quest for a Simpler, Fairer, and More Efficient Tax System*, New York: Penguin, 2017.

Rogers, Melissa Ziegler, *The Politics of Place and the Limits of Redistribution*, New York: Routledge, 2015.

Temin, Peter, *The Vanishing Middle Class: Prejudice and Power in a Dual Economy*, Cambridge, MA; London, England: MIT Press, 2017.

Internet Sites to Explore

"http://www.federalreserve.gov" Federal Reserve.
"https://www.irs.gov/" Internal Revenue Service.
"http://www.medicare.gov" Medicare.
"http://www.whitehouse.gov/omb" Office of Budget Management.
"http://www.ssa.gov" Social Security Administration.
"http://www.treasury.gov" U.S. Treasury.

International Political Relations

After reading this chapter, you should be able to:

- Explain the role of the state in international relations
- Define power and explain why nothing is more basic to an understanding of international relations
- Define foreign policy and discuss five issues that policymakers must heed when forming foreign policy
- List the three ideologies that have been prevalent since World War II
- Summarize the role of the U.S. Congress and president in conducting foreign policy

We are trying to make a society instead of a set of barbarians out of the governments of the world.

—Woodrow Wilson

In early 2018 President Donald Trump tweeted:

> North Korean Leader Kim Jong Un just stated that the "Nuclear Button is on his desk at all times." Will someone from his depleted and food starved regime please inform him that I too have a Nuclear Button, but it is a much bigger & more powerful one than his, and my Button works.

That's not the way most academics believe foreign policy should be conducted, but President Trump seldom acts in a way approved of by academics. But he does get people's attention. In this chapter we discuss international political relations in the age of Trump.

What we find is that technology is changing the way foreign policy works, and the implications for stability and order of the world politic. The first thing we notice is that technology is shrinking the world. Earlier, it involved transportation technology. As transportation technology has improved, the world has shrunk. Whereas only a hundred years ago our community meant our town, today it means the entire world. More recently, it has involved communications technology—the way in which individuals and countries interact. Today, a tweet can go round the world in seconds, tying countries together in ways that they have never been tied before.

The State in International Relations

The goal of international politics is to understand this world community and to figure out ways for us all to live together, and avoid war. A central unit of analysis for this consideration is the state. The term *state* has a number of different meanings. In this country, it is most commonly used to refer to any one of the fifty members of our national union. But as the word is used in discussing international relations, and as we are using it in this chapter, a **state** is a body politic organized for civil rule and government. It is an independent political unit that can carry on negotiations or make agreements with other such units. In this sense, the United States qualifies as a state, but political entities such as Alabama, California, and Michigan do not.

Consider the map of the world on pages 380–381, on which you can count a total of about 190 states. Not all of these states are completely sovereign or independent, nor are they fully comparable. There are extreme variations among them in both physical characteristics and in cultural matters such as religion, education, ethnic background, industry, standards of living, and government.

For instance, in area they range from Russia, with an area of 6.6 million square miles, down to Monaco, with less than 1 square mile, and tiny Vatican City, with a mere 106 acres of

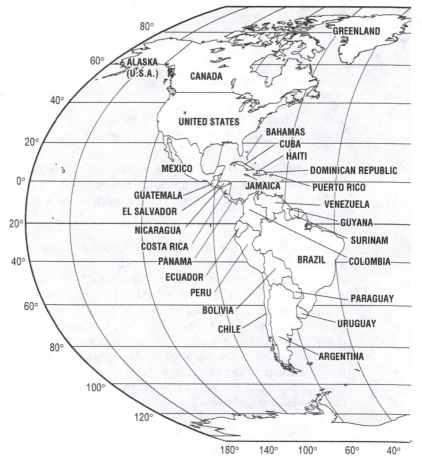

Nations of the world. *A few of the smaller countries have been left out. See how many of them you can name.*

land; only eight states possess more than a million square miles of territory. In population the largest states are China (about 1.4 billion people) and India (over 1.3 billion); the smallest are Tuvalu (12,000) and Vatican City (under 1,000). Some states are overwhelmingly Roman Catholic in faith (such as Spain and France); some are almost entirely Protestant (Denmark and Sweden); others are both Catholic and Protestant (Germany); some accommodate a wide variety of faiths (the United States). There are also states in which other religions prevail, including Islam, Buddhism, Judaism, and Hinduism. Income per capita ranges all the way from more than $100,000 per year in Liechtenstein and Qatar to estimates of less than $500 per year in some African countries.

*T*he Nation-State

In this chapter, we use the terms *state* and *nation* more or less as synonyms. Strictly, however, they carry different meanings, and in the precise language of international law and diplomacy, only "state" is employed; this is true, for instance, in the Charter of the United Nations, in the Statute of the International Court of Justice, and in treaties generally. The characteristics of a state, according to the Charter of the Organization of American States (1948) are (1) a permanent population, (2) a clearly defined territory, (3) a government, and (4) sovereignty that requires a capacity for international relations. The term **nation** was originally applied to groups of people with the same ethnic background, such as the Germans or the French, each of

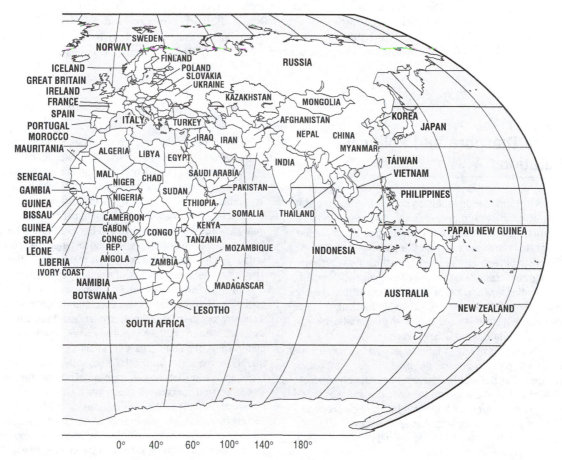

whom could point to a common language and a common cultural heritage. When a group of people share a cultural heritage with an area where they do not live, that group is called a **diaspora**. (See Box.)

The explanation of the modern popular practice of using state and nation as synonyms lies in the fact that for some centuries now, the **nation-state**—a state that has tended to include substantially the same people as the ethnic nation—has been one of the most prominent forms of state in existence. The French state, for instance, is for the most part made up of a French-speaking people with a common historical and cultural background. There are some nation-states, however—including Switzerland, India, Russia, Iraq, Spain, Turkey, and Canada—that do not have a common language or cultural background. These differences in language and in cultural and ethnic background can cause problems, as we have seen in recent years in Belgium, Sri Lanka, India, the emerging African states, the republics of the former Soviet Union, Nepal, and Kosovo.

As we saw in Chapter 3, the structure of the modern nation-state was built on the ruins of feudalism in Western Europe. In the conflicts among feudal lords, a certain lord within an area would emerge as victor, and eventually large areas where the people spoke similar dialects were brought together under a ruler who called himself king.

England was one of the first nation-states, and by the latter part of the twelfth century, the authority of King Henry II extended over almost all of the country, as well as over parts of what is now France. Most of France was unified a little later; by the middle of the fifteenth century, English authority had been forced off the continent. By the end of the reign of the French king Louis XI (1461–1483), France could claim to be a new nation-state. Other nation-states gradually emerged, so that in time the map of Europe showed a substantial group—England, France, Spain, Denmark, Hungary, Russia, Poland, Norway, and Sweden. The Peace of Westphalia (1648) put its stamp of approval on the new system by recognizing that the political authority of the pope and of the old Holy Roman Empire was dead.

*T*he Diaspora and Political Relations

When a group of individuals do not live in the same state with which they culturally identify, they are called a diaspora. Diasporas are naturally created when people emigrate from one state to another, allowing the nation of people to differ from the state. Over time, however, when immigrants assimilate into their new country, they cease to be a diaspora and become individuals whose heritage is from some other area. For example, the United States' identity as a state started with immigrants who, over time, assimilated into U.S. citizens.

This process of assimilation was slow but steady, and with each passing generation, it advances. For most groups, after three of four generations, the children of children of immigrants see themselves simply as Americans. They might have historical ties to their previous state or group of people, but they do not primarily associate with them. A few groups did not assimilate as much for a variety of reasons. Jews are an example.

When that assimilation does not occur, it creates an ongoing dispora. A Jewish dispora has existed for centuries and is spread around the world. Most groups assimilate, so diasporas are generally composed of people who have immigrated within the past fifty years or so.

In recent years there has been significant global immigration, such as from Africa to Europe; or from Latin America to the United States, making for large diasporas of various groups. These diasporas have many implications. They affect the foreign policy of a country by creating cultural and political ties between the new and old countries. They also can loosen the cultural glue that holds a country together since the diaspora doesn't primarily associate with the culture of the new state. When the cultural glue of a state is loosened too much, it can cause trouble for the state. One of the reasons the Soviet Union broke apart was that it was composed of different ethnic groups who did not culturally associate themselves with the dominant Slavic Russian culture. Starting in 2015, millions of people emigrated from Syria, creating a large diaspora of Syrians in Europe. How well they assimilate will be an important issue for Europe in the coming years.

The Establishment and Disappearance of Nation-States

Since 1648, many new nation-states have sprung into being, and from time to time old ones have died out. For example, during the nineteenth century, Turkish authority was expelled from most of Europe, and new states took its place on the Balkan Peninsula: Greece, Bulgaria, Serbia, Romania, Albania, and Montenegro (later included in Yugoslavia). By the mid-1990s, several of these nation-states were again in political turmoil. Yugoslavia and Czechoslovakia broke apart into a number of ethnically different states, some through war and some through negotiation.

Change occurred in the Western hemisphere in the 1800s. For example, approximately twenty new states were formed from the old holdings of Spain and Portugal in the New World. About the middle of the nineteenth century, China and Japan, ancient countries of the Far East, opened their doors to Western trade. They, too, were admitted into the community of nation-states, in 1842 and 1854, respectively.

World War I tore down the old multinational state of Austria-Hungary and built up several new states: Poland, Czechoslovakia, Austria, Hungary, Latvia, Lithuania, and Estonia. It also added to the territory of already existing states such as Romania. World War II snuffed out Latvia, Lithuania, and Estonia, but it led directly to the establishment of Israel and the divisions of Korea and Germany into new political units. With the collapse of the Soviet Union, Latvia, Lithuania, and Estonia reasserted their independence, and East and West Germany were reunited. After World War II, a surge of nationalism took place in the colonial areas of Africa, and in the 1960s a number of African and Asian states emerged from the British and French empires. These countries combined different ethnic groups and experienced turmoil at the turn of the century, not all of which has subsided. Their structure may yet change. Significant areas of turmoil in recent years include the Congo, Somalia, Zimbabwe, and Nigeria.

*T*he Rise of the European Union

As you can see, states are constantly evolving. Another aspect of this evolution involves the building up of states through combinations of previously existing states. An example is the ongoing development of the European Union (EU). The beginnings of the EU go back to 1951 when Belgium, West Germany, Luxembourg, France, Italy, and the Netherlands set up the European Coal and Steel Community. In 1952, this same group of countries expanded the organization into the European Economic Community (EEC), and the countries began to remove trade barriers between them, forming a common market. In 1962, a European Parliament was created, and with it the beginnings of a political union, but the union was still primarily economic. In 1979, direct elections for members of the European Parliament were held, and in 1992 the Treaty of Maastricht was signed. This changed the EEC to the EU, which was not only an economic union but also a political union. In the EU the countries were still independent, but there were forms of cooperation in defense, justice, and home affairs. Work toward common regulations and policies began, and EU laws started to replace, override, and sometimes conflict with laws within the countries. You can see the effect of these changes when you travel among most European countries—you no

The European Union as of 2018.

longer have to go through a border check. That European open border policy is called the **Schengen Agreement.**

In 1992, the EU made another move toward greater cooperation when twelve countries adopted a common currency—the euro. Now, when you go to Germany, for example, you no longer use German marks as your currency; you use the euro. As these changes occurred, membership expanded. Denmark, Ireland, and the United Kingdom joined the EU in 1973, followed by Greece, Spain, Portugal, Austria, Finland, and Sweden in the years up until 1995. In 2004, ten new members joined, and since 2007, three more countries—Bulgaria, Romania, and Croatia—joined.

All these changes, however, leave the EU a long way from being considered a state, and attempts at consolidation have floundered. For example, a number of countries, such as Denmark and Britain, chose not to adopt the euro. Another example is the 2003 Treaty of Nice, which laid down new rules governing the way the EU would work; it was to be a stepping-stone to a new EU constitution. But voters in France and the Netherlands, two of the original members, did not ratify the treaty. In response, the European Parliament instituted many of the provisions of the proposed constitution in a treaty called the Treaty of Lisbon, which did not require voter approval. The Treaty of Lisbon was signed in 2007 and went into force in 2009.

Another example is the Schengen open border policy mentioned above. In 2015 it was threatened when large numbers of Syrian and other refugees immigrated to Europe and claimed asylum, and some European countries tried to keep them out of their country by closing their borders. The Schengen Agreement allowing free travel among EU countries came under pressure, and some countries, such as Hungary, began building barriers on their borders, preventing free access into Hungary from its EU neighbors.

Two other examples of the limitations of the EU as a state occurred in recent years. The first is the Eurozone crisis that occurred when Greece could not pay its debts and the European Central Bank had to help bail Greece out. As a precondition for the bailout and to manage default of its debt, Greece had to accept an austerity budget that required cutting workers' pay by 20 percent and increasing taxes significantly. This provoked substantial political problems in Greece. If Greece were the only problem, it might be manageable, but Italy, Portugal, and Spain also had fiscal problems that are somewhat similar to Greece's. The second is a June 2016 referendum in which the United Kingdom voted to leave the EU. (Britain's exit from the EU is referred to as Brexit.) That decision to leave created a major crisis for the European Union, and over the coming years there will be difficult negotiations on how to extract the United Kingdom from the EU and on how to discourage other countries from following the United Kingdom's lead.

Sovereignty of States

All states are legally sovereign, which means they are not legally subordinate to any other state. In practice, however, their sovereignty is limited by economic and political realities. For example, some Latin American countries rely on aid from the International Monetary Fund and the United States. Therefore, they generally consider carefully the probable reaction of the United States and the Western "alliance" in determining their international position.

Similarly, after the 9/11 attacks on the United States and former President George W. Bush's war on terrorism policy of preemption—in which the United States claimed the right to attack a country believed to be harboring, aiding, or abetting terrorists—countries such as Pakistan and Syria needed to carefully consider the United States' views before undertaking any policy. With the strongest military power in the world threatening you, it is hard to consider yourself fully sovereign and independent.

Power in the World Community

Nothing is more basic to an understanding of international relations than an appreciation of the role of **power**—the capacity to compel another party to commit an action contrary to its explicitly stated will. Countries have national goals, and to achieve those goals they need power. Current expressions such as "power politics," "the great powers," the "small powers," and the "balance of power" all attest to the importance of that role. Power has many dimensions: military, economic, moral, geographic, and political, and in the next sections we discuss some of them.

The Nature and Sources of National Power

In the final analysis, the power of a state consists of the means it possesses for promoting its vital interests by influencing or controlling the behavior of other states. Although military force is the most obvious type of power, it is not the only one. The principal forms of pressure available to states in their dealings with each other are military power, power over opinion at home and abroad, economic power, and geographic power. Possession of any of these attributes tends to augment the power of an individual nation and thus increase its ability to realize its political, social, economic, and military goals.

Of all the sources of power, military power is the most important. The parallel to individual relationships is clear: If you can beat up everyone on the block, you are free to do pretty much what you want. There are, of course, limits if you want to maintain friendly, rather than fearful, relations with others, but a nation with clear military superiority can generally control its destiny. It is seldom the case, however, that one country emerges as indisputably superior militarily. Instead, competing spheres of military power develop, leading to a standoff.

In historical terms, the beginning of the twenty-first century was unusual in terms of military power. The United States was a **hegemon,** a country with almost indisputable military superiority. That military might gave it enormous power, and its desires became much more important than those of other sovereign countries. It had the power to say, "If you don't like it, tough—we're going to do what we want." Thus, when the United States wanted to use military force because it believed (incorrectly) that Iraq had **weapons of mass destruction** (biological, chemical, and nuclear weapons capable of significant damage) and it wanted to rid Iraq of those weapons, it did so, even though a majority of the world's countries felt that military force was not yet called for.

There was no overwhelming cry for the United States to apply its mandate equally—Israel had significant weapons of mass destruction, but when Arab countries tried to raise that issue, they were ignored by the United States. In fact, the very definition of weapons of mass destruction was itself a reflection of the U.S. point of view. Cruise missiles and Big Brother bombs, which the United States used against Iraq, were not classified as weapons of mass destruction, but chemical and biological agents, which the United States accused Iraq of developing, were.

The United States (and some other countries that joined the U.S.) attacked Iraq and found no evidence of these weapons. After doing so, the United States was not condemned by the United Nations (UN) for an inappropriate preemptive war. Instead, the UN Security Council officially recognized the United States and Great Britain as legitimate occupying powers. Such is the power of a military hegemonic state.

Military power depends on far more than weapons. Military power is also limited by social and cultural conventions. In its war with Iraq, the United States could have used nuclear weapons to achieve its objective much more quickly, but it was prevented from doing so by cultural, social, and political pressures. Thus, military power depends on the will to use that military power and the will to accept the losses that the use of military action entails.

A country's will to use military power depends, in part, on its ability and willingness to accept criticism of its actions. By showing that the United States was willing to use its military might on grounds that it determined, and that it would not accept outside limitations on its power, including UN limitations, the United States changed the international political landscape. Thereafter, all countries were a bit more careful in their interactions with the United States. Thus, the war initially extended the power of the United States. But the United States' "go it alone" attitude also undermined much of the world's view about the United States' commitment to fairness. The failure of the United States to bring about peace in Iraq and the loss of popular support for the war by the U.S. population undermined U.S. power.

Some of the hostility toward the United States subsided with the election of President Barack Obama in 2008. His use of military power reflected the lessons from the Iraq War. Under his presidency few countries believed that the United States would act as independently and unilaterally as it did in Iraq. The U.S. role in deposing Muammar Gaddafi as the leader of

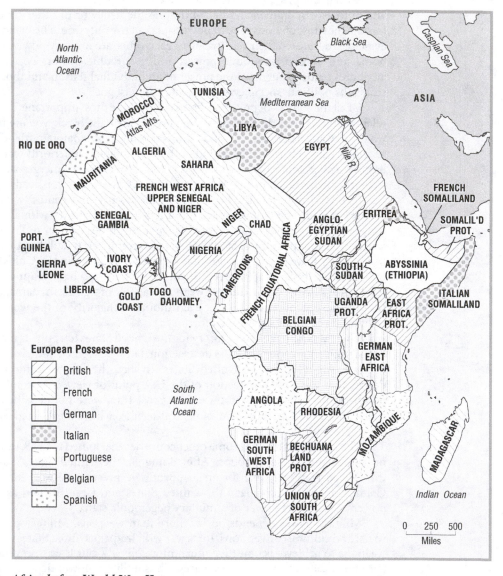

Africa before World War II.

Libya is an example of U.S. involvement in a post-Iraq world. While the U.S. supported Gaddafi's overthrow, it did not commit troops to fight in Libya but instead "led from behind," offering backup air support and diplomatic encouragement to other countries, such as France, that took the lead in support of Libyan rebels.

In 2016, the United States elected Donald Trump as president, who implemented a policy he called America First. Under this policy the United States would not lead from behind, nor would it lead from the front. Instead, it would follow its own policy that Trump believed was in the interests of the United States, with little to no concern for other countries. For example, he withdrew from the Iran nuclear deal even though all other countries wanted to continue with it, and he disparaged NATO, suggesting he might also withdraw the United States from that organization. If other countries wanted to follow suit, that would be fine, but they would have to recognize that the United States would be driving the decision-making, rather than making

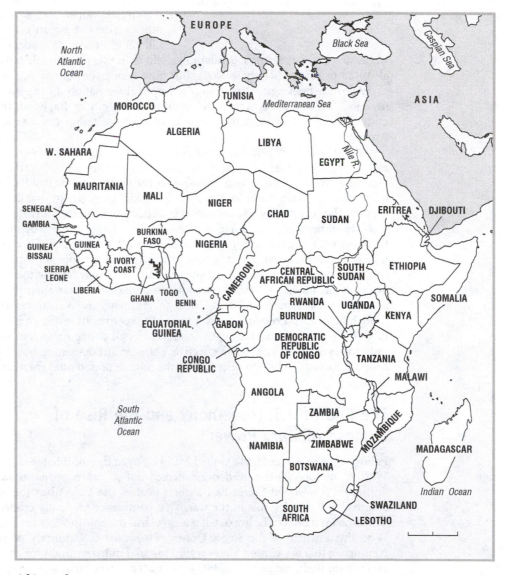

Africa today.

U.S. military might is often used as a threat by the United States to achieve its goals.

the decision collectively with its allies. In practice, the United States' position under Trump is not so starkly unilateralist, but it is far more so than under Bush or Obama.

The importance of social and cultural factors means that the structure of government plays a role in determining the military power of a country. In Western liberal democracies, in which the press and individuals enjoy extensive freedoms, public opinion plays a significant role in determining governmental policy. Public opinion plays less of a role in the policies of autocratic governments. Such governments can partially shape public opinion through tight control of the media. If, in spite of such control, dissent develops, they can use secret police or other repressive organizations to ferret out and kill or imprison its leaders and, in some cases, whole groups of dissenters. Saddam Hussein used this power ruthlessly in Iraq, and Bashar al-Assad used it ruthlessly in Syria. Just how strong the control of the press was in Iraq is shown by the briefings of the Iraqi Ministry of Information during the final days of the U.S. invasion. As U.S. tanks were driving through the city of Baghdad, the minister of information was briefing reporters on how Iraq was winning the war and driving back the Americans.

We should point out that while democracies have less control over public opinion, they can still influence it, and during times of war they directly control the flow of news that reaches reporters. In the 2003 Iraq War, members of the press were "embedded" within military units, giving them a much closer look at the war. Critics pointed out that embedding was a way of shaping the reporter's view, because it is difficult to criticize individuals who are protecting you. The difference in control of the press in an autocracy and in a democracy is one of degree. In an autocracy, the control over the press is often direct; in a democracy, it is generally indirect, with the government relying on creating an appropriate "spin" on the reporting.

Although the government of an autocratic state may be able to shape public opinion at home, it has no direct control over foreign opinion. In their attempts to influence opinion abroad, both autocratic and democratic governments are likely to resort to propaganda, and though there are no very dependable ways of measuring its results, it is safe to assume that the large-scale propaganda campaigns conducted by all strong nations would not be undertaken unless they were thought to be effective, either in strengthening home morale and winning support abroad or else in undermining the morale of potential enemies.

The End of U.S. Hegemony and the Rise of Chinese Military Power

Following World War II, the United States enjoyed the confidence and respect of most other Western nations. This confidence reflected not so much propaganda and military might (although the United States had a good deal of the latter) but the appreciation of most countries for the U.S. role in the war. That confidence gradually eroded through the 1980s. This erosion reflected the impact of issues such as our role in Vietnam and dissension at home. With the downfall of the Soviet Union, respect for U.S. military power returned, but the confidence that the United States would use that military might for the benefit of the world, and not for itself, did not. The 2003 Iraq War reinforced that reduced confidence. Today the United States is seen by many as just another country pursuing its own interests.

In recent years, China has been growing economically and expanding militarily. As it does so, it is exerting its military influence in the Far East, creating a counter power to the United States. An example of the type of problem that may develop involves control of the South China Sea. China claims much of the sea as its territory. Other countries, such as Japan and the Philippines, with whom the United States identifies and has defense treaties, do as well. In earlier years, when China did not have a strong military presence, it was unwilling to exert its claims forcefully, and there was a standoff that allowed the conflicting claims to exist. As China has become stronger militarily, it has been more willing to exert its claims, and to disregard the other countries' claims. To strengthen its claims, it has been taking small uninhabited atolls and building military bases and landing strips as a way of demonstrating its control of the South China Sea. These activities are viewed with alarm by the neighboring countries, and they are pressuring the United States to do something about it. In response, the United States sent naval ships to the area to demonstrate its right to open access to those waters. China sees such actions by the United States as an unacceptable intrusion into its affairs.

Other Sources of Power

The usefulness of economic power in international relations has often been demonstrated. During the struggle against Napoleon Bonaparte in the early 1800s, Great Britain's economic power enabled it not only to expand its own military forces but also to provide money and supplies for its allies. More than a century later, it enabled the United States to do likewise in both world wars; after World War II, it enabled the United States to make an important contribution to rebuilding the economies and the military forces of the countries of Western Europe that had been overrun by the Nazis and that later felt threatened by the expanded military power of the former Soviet Union.

Though the sources of a nation's power are varied, some of them are more basic than others. For a state to generate great national strength, it helps to be large, both in area and in population. Size is an advantage enjoyed by both Russia and the United States, and that size helps explain their importance. On the other hand, Japan is geographically small, but it is a major economic power. Industrial might is another vital source of power, for in its factories a country must produce the equipment for modern warfare, including tanks, ships, planes, missiles, and nuclear bombs. The high industrial output of the United States is a great asset in the power game, and Japan's industrial output is what its strength is based on.

Another major source of economic power is dependable access to adequate supplies of raw materials, because without these no nation can develop and maintain a large and efficient industrial complex. Yet another condition that is still a factor in national power is geographic location. This can, among other things, affect both access to raw materials and the degree to which a nation is vulnerable to a military attack. Geographic location is one element of U.S. strength. We are separated by oceans from any other major power, and though these can be crossed in a few minutes by nuclear missiles, there are, as we have pointed out, strong deterrents to the use of such weapons. Meanwhile, the oceans still protect us against attack by great armies using conventional weapons.

However, given size, a well-developed industry, and dependable access to adequate raw materials, probably the most important source of a nation's power is the characteristics of its people. Among the people there should be a substantial number of able scientists, artists, educators, businesspeople, military leaders, politicians, and many highly skilled workers of all types. In a democracy, perhaps the characteristic of a people that, if they have it, contributes most to the power of the nation in dealing with others is a strong sense of patriotism and loyalty that makes them willing to support their government in any policy they consider reasonable. But in dealing with foreign countries, the governments of democracies can face difficult problems at home. Negotiations cannot be carried on by all the people; they must be conducted by those who represent them in government.

Why Do So Few Americans Have Access to Al Jazeera?

Al Jazeera.

© Philip Lange/Shutterstock

Western countries have numerous news sources that provide news from a Western slant. While there are differences—Fox News provides a more conservative view than CNN, which provides a more liberal view than the BBC, which provides a more European liberal view—the overall view is definitely Western. These news sources broadcast around the world, and people in all countries have access to these news sources. There are other views, and a good source for those other views was the Al Jazeera English-language news network. Because one of the pillars of United States democracy is free access to all viewpoints, it would seem that the United States would support widespread access to Al Jazeera, but few in the United States watched it and it was not readily available to most U.S. citizens. Al Jazeera America ended its attempt to establish itself as a cable channel in the United States in 2016.

Many Arabs see political and social pressures as the reason why Al Jazeera had a difficult time establishing itself in the United States. Former Secretary of Defense Donald Rumsfeld called its broadcasts of the Iraq War "vicious, inaccurate, and inexcusable." Many in the United States agreed. The difficulty for the United States in maintaining that position and informally or formally restricting access to the Al Jazeera network was that the United States is also committed to free speech. To many observers, Al Jazeera, while providing a significantly different slant on the news, does not deviate from the truth significantly more than other networks. Thus, Europeans have wide access to the Al Jazeera network, and many Arabs see it as much more objective than either their state television networks or Western networks.

Because the Internet is open and does not rely on a cable company to provide it, Al Jazeera is available in the United States online.

This creates no great problem if those who represent the country are following policies with which the vast majority of the people agree. Frequently, however, there are large dissenting minorities, or there may even be an almost equal division of public opinion on the wisdom of government policies. When such differences of opinion concern issues about which people have strong emotions, the power of a government to formulate clear foreign policies and to make satisfactory agreements with other countries is likely to be impaired.

Maintaining Security

In a world community of sovereign nation-states, there are several ways in which a state could conceivably attempt to achieve security from attack without war and at the same time gain some of its other international objectives. If it is a large state, such as the United States, with adequate resources and industrial development, it might attempt to make a **unilateral**—independent or one-sided—buildup of its military power to such a degree that no other state or probable combination of states would dare to challenge it. In the contemporary world, this would be a difficult achievement for any nation. First, it would mean diverting to military uses vast amounts of resources needed to improve the living conditions of its people and needed to meet various other social problems. Second, other nations, fearful for their safety and their power to control their own affairs, might form alliances to protect their interests. Thus, after the start of the 2003 Iraq War—a war that a majority of U.S. allies strongly opposed—a number of European nations began reconsidering their alliance with the United States and began exploring the creation of a separate European defense organization that would operate independently of the United States.

Another conceivable approach to the problem of security, one that a group of cooperating states could attempt to implement, would be to organize all the states of the world into a system of world government. To have much chance of success, such a system or organization would have to include most of the states of the world, especially the more powerful ones. It would have to be a kind of federation or superstate, with courts for settling disputes between nations and with a military establishment capable of forcing a recalcitrant nation to accept court decisions. The chances of establishing such a system in the foreseeable future are small because most power is in the hands of several very large countries, many of whose interests appear to be in opposition.

Furthermore, few nations seem willing to give up much of their sovereignty or their right to adopt any foreign policies they please. The United Nations, which we discuss in Chapter 22, may be regarded as a first step toward a system of world government, but actually it has very little power to protect its members or to prevent war. It does, however, perform many useful international services.

The most common way of preventing or at least indefinitely delaying a disastrous war between the world's most powerful nations is to develop and, if possible, maintain a stable balance of power. The term **balance of power** means an equilibrium or division of power that for the time being no nation is willing to disturb. The power of one nation prevents the other nation from using its power. During the century that followed the Congress of Vienna (1815), a fairly effective power balance was maintained, for though that era did witness some adjustments of power and even several sizable wars, until World War I no state attempted to radically challenge the existing balance. After World War I, the United States became a major power, and its power significantly increased during and right after World War II. After World War II, the balance of power was between the Western bloc (the United States, Western Europe, Japan, and their allies) and the Eastern bloc (the Soviet Union, Eastern Europe, and their allies). This balance was structurally indicated by their membership in formal alliance organizations.

In the 1990s, that balance of power became unbalanced. The United States was the world's strongest military power, much stronger than any other country. Given that reality, there was talk of a **new world order**—an international order in which the United States would follow the dictum of right rather than might in its conduct of external and internal affairs—replacing the balance of power.

As social scientists discussed the emergence of a new world order, a political theory emerged to fit the changing order. It is called the **theory of complex interdependence,** in which the largest nation's powers are limited by a variety of interdependencies. This new theory is in contrast to the **realist theory,** in which a balance of power with two competing nations was necessary to maintain the peace. As the world gradually moved toward a unipolar system, with the United States as the primary superpower, without an equally strong offsetting balancing force, the theory of complex interdependence gained acceptance.

The emerging international realities brought into question the purpose of some international organizations. One example was the **North Atlantic Treaty Organization (NATO),** the organization responsible for the collective defense and protection of the West. In 2018, NATO had twenty-nine member states. Members of NATO include Belgium, Britain, Canada, Czech Republic, Denmark, France, Germany, Greece, Hungary, Iceland, Italy, Luxembourg, the Netherlands, Norway, Poland, Portugal, Spain, Turkey, and the United States. Montenegro joined in 2017.

With the breakup of the Soviet Union, in the 1990s NATO lost much of its former purpose. But, like many organizations that have lost their purpose, NATO continued in existence, searching for a new purpose. Because of the 2003 war in Iraq, a war that many NATO countries opposed, NATO scaled back its mission and began refashioning itself as an

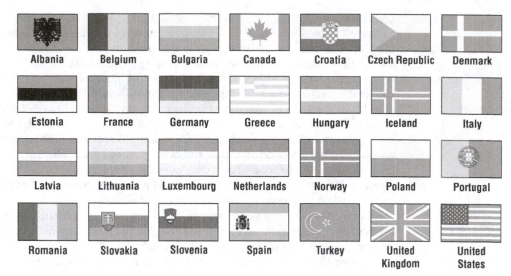

Figure 19.1

Flags of NATO member states before Montenegro joined.

"all-purpose military and political toolbox that can be tapped at short notice by ad hoc clusters of NATO countries." This change means that NATO can commit its NATO forces to peacekeeping activities even if all NATO countries do not agree.

As NATO searched for a new role, it expanded, adding some states that it had previously been established to counterbalance, such as Poland, Hungary, and the Czech Republic in 1997. Other states were also asking for membership, and NATO even worked out a cooperative agreement with Russia.

The Berlin Plus Agreement in 2002 also saw the European Union further enhance its military capabilities; it gave the EU access to NATO resources should the latter decline to intervene in a crisis. The expansion of the EU's military role posed questions about NATO's future. However, when Russia supported Ukrainian rebels and, in many reports, was taking an active role in supporting them, NATO members found more consensus. In 2014 NATO unilaterally ended its cooperation with Russia, and moved NATO troops to countries bordering the Ukraine, moving NATO closer to its original intent—as a balance for Russian power and aggression.

The theory of complex interdependencies lost some favor as China has emerged as an offsetting superpower, and the balance of power view regained currency. The question political scientists asked was what interdependencies were limiting the United States' use of power.

When there is a balance of power each country limits its actions for fear of upsetting that balance. In the new world order it is foreseen that each country will limit its actions according to "what is right." How is "what is right" determined? It is determined by the major power who, for the new world order to work, must interpret "what is right" in a way that seems right to most people regardless of what is in the countries' individual interests. Making the new world order work is a tall order, an issue that we discuss further in Chapter 22.

Foreign Policies

Relationships between states that affect the national security or general welfare of each are the core of international relations. The **foreign policies** of a nation are the courses of action a nation uses to achieve its international objectives. As a rule, the nation's primary purposes are to increase its own security and its own general economic welfare. Sometimes, however, a foreign policy may further the interests of some politically powerful pressure group rather than those of the nation as a whole. When this is so, those who support it usually attempt to convince the majority that it benefits the entire nation.

Generally speaking, the foreign policies of a state are designed to serve the national interests as these are conceived by the public or by those in direct control. Security and prosperity are always major objectives; other objectives may include the spread of an ideology and the expansion of national power and prestige. Unfortunately, there is no simple formula guaranteeing that the right foreign policy decisions will always be made. Debate is, therefore, inevitable.

An example of the problems of foreign policy involves the recent agreement with Iran, the United States and other Western nations. In negotiations about removing economic sanctions on Iran in return for Iran submitting to limitations on its nuclear activities, the United States arrived at an agreement with Iran that was strongly opposed by two of its strongest allies—Saudi Arabia and Israel. They were worried that the lifting of sanctions would make Iran a stronger player in the Middle East and that Iran would not stop its nuclear program. The United States argued that bringing Iran into the global economy would strengthen liberal reforms in Iran and make it less likely develop nuclear bombs, thereby giving it even more power regionally. Both sides believed that unreported side agreements were being made, and that their so-called allies were working against their interests. The intrigue of soap operas pales in comparison with the intrigue of foreign policy. The Iran deal became even more intriguing with the election of President Trump; he unilaterally pulled the United States from the agreement and reimposed sanctions on Iran, precisely what Israel and Saudi Arabia wanted him to do. How this all plays out remains to be seen.

Geography and Foreign Policy

Conspicuous among the facts and forces that act as determinants of foreign policy is, as we have pointed out, the geographic position of a nation. For the promotion of the country's security and prosperity, policymakers must give heed to matters such as the following:

- the defensibility of the state's boundaries
- the effects of distance on its powers of offense and defense by means of long-range missiles
- the availability of ports for useful trade and for naval bases
- the attitudes of neighboring states and their size and power
- the state's own size and natural resources

If a state is satisfied with its geographic lot in life, it can direct its efforts toward protecting what it has; if it is dissatisfied, it will, if possible, maneuver its policies toward the elimination of its alleged handicaps, asserting itself dynamically, perhaps even aggressively, in order to get from others what it believes it needs.

The term **geopolitics** refers to the relation between geography and security that foreign policymakers attempt to take into account. According to Nicholas Spykman, geopolitics is "the planning of the security policy of a country in terms of its geographic factors." No nation pursued the subject as seriously as did Germany in the 1930s. Under the Nazis, Germany embraced the theories of earlier geopoliticians, and it worked out a "scientific" policy of expansion calculated to secure Germany's position as a master power for an indefinite future, all at the expense of "decadent" neighbors.

Without constructing a complicated theory of geopolitics comparable to that of the Nazis, most states nevertheless have exhibited their geographic aspirations in their foreign policies. Russia for centuries has sought good warm-water ports; it has wanted control over the

Dardanelles, and it has tried to get buffer territory on its western frontier to make up for its lack of defensible boundaries there. Its activities in Iran and Afghanistan in the 1970s and 1980s reflected that desire. Its annexation of Crimea from Ukraine is another example.

Such geopolitical concerns have contributed to many wars. For example, France long felt that its geographic position required it to seek a frontier on the Rhine River in order to undermine the strength of its dangerous neighbor, Germany, which had several times invaded France's territory. In the Far East, Japan attempted before World War II to add to the security of its position by absorbing Korea, Manchuria, Taiwan, and many islands of the Pacific and by controlling China. Iraq's 1990 invasion of Kuwait was in part an attempt by Iraq to gain control of two of Kuwait's islands, which would give it better control of the shipping lanes out of the Iraqi port of Basra, and the 2003 Iraq War was seen by some observers as an attempt by the United States to gain a strong military presence in the Middle East so that it could protect its oil interests and provide better protection for Israel.

Values, Ideologies, and Foreign Policy

A term that one often hears when discussing foreign policy is **ideology**—a deeply held vision of what the correct form of government should be. Since World War I, the three ideologies that have been prevalent are the fascist ideology, the democratic capitalist ideology, and the communist ideology.

Fascist Ideology.   The **fascist ideology** holds that a natural leader will arise in a country to tell the people what they want. It gives enormous power to a small group of leaders, which means that it tends to overlook the rights of individuals and minority groups. Under fascist ideology, the leader will make the people, the nation, and their culture great. With the defeat of Hitler in Germany and Mussolini in Italy in World War II, fascism has declined as an ideology, but you can still see support for fascist ideology in the small Nazi Party in the United States and in some countries where significant social turmoil exists.

Democratic Capitalist Ideology.   The dominant ideology today throughout the world is the democratic capitalist ideology. It is an ideology that sees the people as making society's decisions through democratic elections of their government. The will of the people is dominant, and subject to the preservation of certain inalienable individual rights such as the right to hold property and the right to free speech. The working of the elections and the inalienable rights are spelled out in either a formal or informal constitution that is the core of the laws of the country. In democratic capitalist ideology, all leaders are subservient to the law. Thus, democratic capitalism is supposed to involve a combination of the rule of law and the rule of people.

Communist Ideology.   Communist ideology is an ideology that sees people as making society's decisions through a set of leaders who have the best interests of the people at heart. Thus, it places a small group of leaders above the political will of the people and above the law. It gives less weight to inalienable rights, private property, and the law than does democratic capitalist ideology.

The meaning of communist ideology is changing. When Karl Marx wrote *Das Kapital* and *The Communist Manifesto,* he spent almost no time discussing how a communist society would be implemented or would operate. It was only through the experience of the Soviet Union under its communist government after World War I and in the writings of the Soviet leader and practical theorist Vladimir Lenin that the nature of what we now call communist countries became clear.

Because, according to Marx, communism involves the eventual withering away of the state, even so-called communist countries agreed that they were in a transition stage. For many people, it is not communism that went against these values; it is the transition stage. During the Stalin era, large numbers of Soviet people were liquidated. Stalinist justification for that policy—that the end justifies the means—was, and is, unacceptable to most outside observers. They felt that nothing justifies such wholesale killing.

The 1980s and 1990s saw an enormous change in communism. Many states, including the formerly communist Eastern European states such as East Germany and Poland and many of the republics of the former Soviet Union, have simply abandoned it, and in others, such as China, communism has evolved both economically and politically. This evolution, to some, suggests a victory of democratic capitalist ideology, and in many ways, it is. People in the former Soviet Union focused their demands for reforms on achieving markets and democratic elections. Clearly, the totalitarian nature of Soviet communism and the favoritism the Soviet Union showed to Communist Party members were highly problematic.

But other observers point out that the Communist Party itself should also have been opposed by true communists. The party was meant to protect the rights of the working class, not to become a class of people with special privileges that it became. These other observers argue that communism failed because it abandoned communist ideals.

Most social scientists accept the argument that communism abandoned its ideals. They differ, however, on the question of whether that abandonment was inherent in the structure of communism—no society can ever give that much power to any group—or whether the communists simply didn't try hard enough to preserve their ideals. Whatever the answer is to that question, the reality is that communism is not yet dead. For example, communist parties still control the governments of China, Vietnam, North Korea, and Cuba.

Ideologies and Foreign Policies.   By emphasizing certain aspects of decisions, ideologies can be made to seem more or less desirable. A supporter of a certain ideology will likely provide a different spin on the ideology than an opponent of that ideology. If that supporter has rhetorical abilities, he can likely convince others to support it as well. Thus, a supporter of communism is likely to emphasize cases when personal property rights have led to what most people would see as undesirable outcomes, while a supporter of democratic capitalism is likely to emphasize cases when the small group of leaders have brought about undesirable outcomes. That's why societies generally come to share a certain ideology, and its implications for what is an acceptable form of government and action by government. We must, however, be extraordinarily careful about letting our emotions affect our considerations of those issues so that we do not become **ideologues**—individuals who are so fixated on certain ideologies that they cannot reasonably consider opposition arguments; ideologues tend to insist on everyone looking at the world as they do.

As we stated previously, the dominant global ideology today is democratic capitalism. It is an ideology that most people in the United States, including the authors of this text, support. While there is much to be said for the democratic capitalist ideology, we must take care to see that we supporters do not become ideologues—to make sure that our support is based on reasoned argument and that we are open to both the weaknesses of democratic capitalism and the positive aspects of other ideologies. Doing so is especially important in deciding on foreign policy. For example, often when we hear of what occurs in other countries, our immediate reaction is one of abhorrence, and we wish our country would "do something." There have been numerous examples: the severe punishment for being gay in Uganda; the restrictions of political rights in China; the slaughter by the Myanmar military of the Rohingya Muslim minority; the killing of an opposition journalist in Saudi Arabia; the systematic killing of millions in Cambodia under the Khmer Rouge; the mass genocide and ethnic cleansing in Bosnia and Rwanda; and the terrible atrocities in the Darfur region of Sudan.

These actions go against our ideological beliefs about what is acceptable action by a state. The question each of us must answer is: Do these actions rise to the level of contradicting our values such that we would support the United States using its power to stop and prevent such activities occurring in another supposedly sovereign country? And if so, what powers should we use?

Unfortunately, there is no easy answer to these questions. Not all cultures have the same regard for human rights as we do, and democratic capitalist ideology also holds that we generally do not have the right to impose our personal values on others. In all cases, it is proper to use diplomatic channels and public channels to do what can be done to support human rights, but in doing so a country must apply the same criteria to friendly countries as to unfriendly countries, recognizing that countries have different social values. For instance, if a country has a mandatory military draft, that draft may violate the concept some have of human rights, but it would be wrong to assume that such opposition is a universally agreed-on human right.

More difficult choices than one about a military draft confront us when issues such as forced labor camps for large minorities within a population, involuntary abortion, infanticide, restrictions on the rights of women, and apartheid surface. There comes a point when the offenses against human rights become too great to sit back and accept. Again, this is based on our particular value judgments, which are not universally shared. Examples include the annihilation of the Jews in Germany in the 1930s and 1940s (to which the United States initially responded by restricting immigration visas for Jews) and Pol Pot's massacre of millions of his fellow citizens in Cambodia in the 1970s (which the United States ignored, at least officially). The U.S. changing position in regard to Iraq shows the difficult choices. When Iraq used chemical weapons against Iran and the Kurds in the 1980s, Iraq was a U.S. ally and the United States said nothing; in fact, it shipped Iraq more weapons. However, in 2003 the United States used Iraq's previous use of chemical weapons as one of the reasons it should liberate Iraq from Saddam Hussein.

The United States in the World Community

The separation-of-powers doctrine, modified by a system of checks and balances, was embodied in the U.S. Constitution of 1787 to prevent tyranny, and it applies to the field of foreign affairs as well as to domestic politics. Although the judiciary has no hand in policymaking and is confined in its work to the interpretation and application of treaties and statutes, the other two branches of the government—the president and Congress (especially the Senate)—are both equipped with far-reaching authority to determine foreign policy.

The President and Foreign Policy

The president derives great power in foreign affairs from the right to appoint diplomats (with the consent of the Senate) and to receive the diplomats of other countries, and has ultimate responsibility for the diplomatic messages our government transmits abroad and for the operations of the Department of State generally. Presidential control of diplomacy gives the president a strong initiative in foreign affairs, for diplomatic correspondence can be a vehicle of policy, as in 1899, when Secretary of State John Hay originated the Open Door policy in China by messages to selected governments. The president's prerogative in diplomacy confers, too, the right to deny or to extend recognition to a new government or state, for it is usually by establishing diplomatic relationships that recognition is accorded. President

Obama demonstrated that policy when he established formal relations with Cuba in 2014, reversing U.S. policy of half a century.

The president has the initiative in treaty making, too, but here these actions require the approval of two-thirds of the senators present when a vote is taken. This arrangement, indeed, is a good example of the system of checks and balances that pervades all of government in the United States. Much criticism has been aimed at the Senate for its obstructive tactics in its consideration of treaties—notably the Treaty of Versailles (1919)—and several proposals have been submitted to amend the Constitution to substitute a majority of both houses of Congress in place of two-thirds of the Senate in treaty making, but such proposals have never had much support. Some of the problems that can develop from this dual responsibility can be seen in the Law of the Sea Treaty negotiated between 1974 and 1980 under UN auspices. This treaty was signed by President Jimmy Carter but was never approved by the Senate. When President Ronald Reagan was elected, he specifically disavowed the treaty, leaving the United States in an ambiguous position.

President George W. Bush took a strong position against U.S. involvement in international treaties, opposing multilateral cooperation, in which countries attempt to negotiate their differences through international treaties and organizations, and favoring unilateralism, in which each country goes it alone. President Obama worked much more closely with other countries, negotiating new international trade and climate partnerships, and working jointly with other countries toward consensus.

President Trump's victory marked a change in tone and policy. He pulled the United States out of the Paris Climate Accord, and the Trans-Pacific Partnership, which was a new trade pact with Japan and other Pacific basin countries. He called his policy the *America First* policy. Exactly how to interpret America First was unclear; often compromise is the best way to advance American interests and that means accepting less desirable aspects of an agreement so that one gains other aspects that are what one wanted. Without compromise there would be no agreement, which would be worse for everyone. The debate is inevitably over how hard one pushes in the negotiations. President Trump recognized this, and stated that he would compromise when he felt it was in America's interest. In many ways, his America First policy was primarily a negotiating ploy to allow him to drive a harder bargain than previous presidents had.

The president's authority in foreign affairs is augmented by some more general powers. As commander in chief of the armed forces, the president can dispatch the Army, Navy, Marines, or Air Force to any part of the world to carry out a policy and can conclude executive agreements by which bases abroad are placed at the disposal of the services. This gives the president enormous power, in effect, to enter into war without Senate approval. For example, during President John F. Kennedy's administration, the U.S. government supported the Bay of Pigs invasion of Cuba with no Senate approval. Similarly, in 1964 President Lyndon B. Johnson began the direct U.S. military role in Vietnam by ordering attacks on North Vietnamese military targets following attacks on U.S. warships in the Gulf of Tonkin.

In response to the latter incident, Congress passed a series of laws that placed stricter limits on presidential actions. Because the Constitution explicitly gives Congress the powers to declare war and control military and naval expenditures, it was argued that the president's discretionary powers as commander in chief had become too broad. These laws removed the president's power to "wage war, sell arms, conduct covert operations, or enter into executive agreements with foreign governments." According to these laws, a president can deploy troops to protect our interest only for a limited time without the consent of Congress.

U.S. Foreign Policies

Throughout much of the nineteenth century, the United States was deeply committed to a policy of isolation. **Isolationism,** a policy according to which the United States made no alliances abroad and kept as free as possible from the political embroilments of Europe,

The aftermath of a US drone strike in Yemen that killed three suspected Al-Qaeda militants.

© AFP/Getty

reigned supreme. Even after the Spanish-American War (1898), the nation remained aloof, though the acquisition of scattered dependencies such as Hawaii as a result of the war had widened U.S. interests a great deal. Isolationism broke down when the United States in 1917 became a belligerent in World War I, but it was revived in 1919–1920, when the Senate rejected membership in the new League of Nations. Although under attack in the 1920s and 1930s, isolationism continued to have strong support, as shown by U.S. neutrality legislation (1935 and later) and by the efforts from 1939 to 1941 to keep the United States from becoming involved in World War II.

But the Japanese attack on Pearl Harbor in 1941 changed all this and moved us from a period of isolationism to a period of internationalism. **Internationalism** refers to the belief that world peace can be realized by the friendly association of all nations. As a result, the United States quickly became enmeshed in world politics and has continued to be deeply involved ever since.

Since World War II, the United States has made or affirmed a number of alliances and maintained troops or military outposts in various parts of the world, especially in Europe and the Far East. The United States has committed large military forces to the fighting of four local undeclared wars: Korea, Vietnam, Iraq, and Afghanistan.

Much of our foreign policy in the postwar era has been dedicated to the protection of capitalism and "liberal" democracy. For example, our foreign policy immediately following World War II revolved around the Truman Doctrine of 1947. Essentially, the **Truman Doctrine** stated that if any country threatened by communist aggression was willing to resist that threat and asked for help, the United States would come to its aid. This was often referred to as a policy of containing communism and was part of what was called the **Cold War,** the tension between communist countries, such as the former Soviet Union, and the United States and its allies following World War II until the 1990s. During the Cold War, the United States believed that if it did not take the lead in resisting the aggressive moves of the Soviet Union and the other communist nations, there would probably be no effective opposition, and a **domino effect** would occur, with one country after another falling to the communists.

The basis of the peace in the Cold War was a **nuclear standoff**—a position of stalemate brought about by the recognition that, if attacked, the other party possesses sufficient ability to launch a devastating nuclear counterattack. In a nuclear standoff, because each country has the ability to destroy the other many times over, the concept of military superiority becomes difficult to define. This was especially apparent in the 1980s, when the United States and the former USSR negotiated a reduction of the arms buildup. Both sides claimed that the other had military superiority; which side actually did was unclear.

The containment approach to U.S. foreign policy lost favor following our involvement in Vietnam in the 1960s and early 1970s, and a period of **détente**—an easing or relaxation of strained relations and political tensions between countries—replaced the Cold War. Under détente, the U.S. involvement in world political affairs decreased, and the United States reduced its expenditures on defense as a percentage of total output. That changed in September 2001, when terrorists attacked the United States and the United States declared a war on terrorism.

An Outline of U.S. Foreign Policy*

1789–1897: Isolationism/unilateralism, with the following examples showing how we followed this policy:

> **1796**—Washington's Farewell Address: "Beware of entangling alliances" (balance-of-power entanglements in today's words).
>
> **1823**—Monroe Doctrine. U.S. promises not to interfere in European affairs and demands that Europe not interfere in Latin America.

1898–1918: Interventionism.

> **1898**—Spanish-American War: events leading to it and results of this interventionism.
>
> **1917**—U.S. intervention in World War I.

1919–1941: Return to isolationism/unilateralism as the nation sees the result of interventionism.

> **1919**—U.S. Senate rejects joining the League of Nations.
>
> **1930s**—Neutrality Acts of 1935, 1937, and 1939 as we see Europe heading toward war.
>
> **1941–1945**—No special change in policy necessary; United States simply responds to attack. Any nation follows a similar policy of defending itself.

*We are grateful to Prof. W. K. Callam for supplying an initial draft of this outline.

1945–1999: Internationalism. Actually starts with the Truman Doctrine (1947), even though we join the UN in 1945.

> **1949**—NATO.
>
> **1950**—Korean conflict (even though UN-sponsored).
>
> **1961–1973**—Involvement in Vietnam (really following tenets of the Truman Doctrine).
>
> **1969**—Nixon Doctrine (so called, although it should rightfully be called a corollary to the Truman Doctrine).
>
> **1990**—Foreign policy directed at working with, rather than against, Russia.
>
> **1991**—Persian Gulf War; beginning of new world order, or at least Western control.
>
> **1993**—United States tries to enforce its will with UN backing in a variety of states such as Haiti, Somalia, Bosnia, North Korea. The results are questionable.

2000—Alternative approaches

> **2001**—9/11 attacks on United States and beginning of war on terrorism.
>
> **2003**—Bush Doctrine of Preemption: President Bush declares the United States has the right to wage preemptive war against countries that allow terrorists on their soil.
>
> **2009–2016**—Barack Obama becomes president. He institutes a more multilateral foreign policy and away from preemption. Leading from the Rear.
>
> **2017**—President Trump declares his America First policy.

That war on terrorism pitted the United States not against a particular country, but against an ambiguous enemy who could be anywhere. A new Homeland Security Department was established in the United States, and military expenditures increased substantially. But exactly how this war on terrorism was to be fought remained open. Does the United States have the right to fight terrorism anywhere? Are preemptive wars truly justified? What limitations on individual rights are acceptable trade-offs for increased security? Does the United States have the right to eliminate governments it believes are harboring terrorists and developing weapons of mass destruction? What proof does it need to carry on such preemptive wars? And, finally, will fighting such a war do more harm than good, creating hatred for the United States that will lead to more terrorism?

In 2009, Barack Obama became president and signaled to the world that his administration would be less belligerent to other countries and would work with them to arrive at a multinational solution to problems. However, at the same time, he promised that the United States would be vigilant against terrorism and would carry on and even expand the war against the Taliban in Afghanistan. President Trump replaced President Obama in

2017 and took much stronger negotiating positions than did Obama. He named his policy the America First policy. He declared that the United States had military power and that it wasn't afraid to use it. It remains to be seen how this policy will play out in a changing world.

 Study and **Review**

Key Points

- The state is the institution empowered to conduct international relations for its citizens.
- Power is the capacity to compel another party to commit an action contrary to its explicitly stated will. Ultimately, power determines whether a foreign policy will be successful.
- Governments use foreign policy to achieve their international objectives, but they must take geography and other nations' strengths into consideration when they make policy.

- In the past century, the three most prevalent ideologies have been the communist ideology, the democratic capitalist ideology, and the fascist ideology.
- The president is responsible for foreign policy and is commander in chief of the armed forces, but only Congress can declare war.
- In the early 2000s, the United States adopted a policy of unilateralism and preemption, a policy that was modified somewhat under President Obama.
- President Trump introduces his America First policy.

Some Important Terms

balance of power (391)
Cold War (398)
détente (398)
domino effect (398)
diaspora (382)
fascist ideology (394)
foreign policies (392)
geopolitics (393)
hegemon (385)
ideologues (395)

ideology (394)
internationalism (398)
isolationism (397)
nation (381)
nation-state (382)
new world order (391)
North Atlantic Treaty
   Organization (NATO) (391)
nuclear standoff (398)
power (385)

realist theory (391)
Schengen Agreement (384)
state (380)
theory of complex
   interdependence (391)
Truman Doctrine (398)
unilateral (390)
weapons of mass destruction (385)

Questions for Review and Discussion

General Questions

1. In what sense do the nation-states of the world form a community?
2. List the more important differences between nations and states.
3. Historically, how did nation-states develop?
4. Would the European Union have been a state if the Treaty of Nice had been ratified? Why or why not?
5. The effectiveness of a nation's military power in supporting its foreign policies depends on what factors in addition to the size, training, and equipment of its armed forces?
6. Why are democratic governments more restricted in their actions by public opinion than are totalitarian governments?
7. What is a hegemon?
8. What factors make up a nation's economic power?
9. What are three possible approaches to the problem of achieving some degree of national security? Explain each.
10. Explain how the theory of complex interdependence is becoming a substitute for the balance of power in maintaining the peace in today's world.
11. How may foreign policies be influenced by (a) geography and (b) an ideology?

12. What powers does the president of the United States have in foreign affairs? What powers are held by Congress? Point out the advantages and disadvantages of this division of responsibility.

13. Do you believe that the president of the United States should have more power or less power to determine and carry out foreign policies? Defend your answer.

14. Was the 1991 Persian Gulf War justified? Was the 2003 Iraq War justified? Why or why not?

15. What is the U.S. policy of preemption, and is it justified?

16. How might Trump's American First policy be seen as a useful negotiating strategy? Is it a useful one?

Internet Questions

1. Pick a country to which you have never traveled. Using http://projectvisa.com/, find what type of travel visa you can get to enter the country and how to do so.

2. Go to http://www.archives.gov/exhibits/charters/charters.html. What does Article II, Section 2, clauses 1 and 2 of the United States Constitution state?

3. Watch the video at https://www.youtube.com/watch?v=okE3F7jiLI8. What is meant by the new geopolitics?

4. Using the website of the American Foreign Policy Council, http://www.afpc.org/, describe one of their latest news stories.

5. Using the NATO site, http://www.nato.int/, what is the Euro-Atlantic Partnership Council, and how many members are there?

*F*or Further Study

Books to Explore

Blum, William, *America's Deadliest Export: Democracy—The Truth about US Foreign Policy and Everything Else*, Chicago, IL: University of Chicago Press, 2015.

Chomsky, Noam, *Who Rules the World?* New York: Henry Holt and Company, 2016.

Hook, Steven, *U.S. Foreign Policy: The Paradox of World Power*, Washington, DC: CQ Press, 2010.

Kaplan, Robert, *The Return of Marco Polo's World: War, Strategy and American Interests in the Twenty-first Century*, New York: Random House, 2018.

Khalidi, Rashid, *The Cold War and American Dominance in the Middle East*, Boston, MA: Beacon Press, 2009.

Kynge, James, *China Shakes the World: A Titan's Rise and Troubled Future—and the Challenge for America*, Boston, MA: Mariner Books, 2007.

Laqueur, Walter, *After the Fall: The End of the European Dream and the Decline of a Continent*, New York: Thomas Dunne Books, 2012.

Maddow, Rachel, *Drift: The Unmooring of American Military Power*, New York: Crown Publishing, 2012.

Mearsheimer, John, and Stephen Walt, *The Israel Lobby and U.S. Foreign Policy*, New York: Farrar, Straus, & Giroux, 2008.

Rachman, Gideon, *Easternization: Asia's Rise and America's Decline*, New York: Other Press, 2015.

Smith, Rupert, *The Utility of Force: The Art of War in the Modern World*, New York: Penguin/Allen Lane, 2005.

Zakaria, Fareed, *The Post-American World: Release 2.0*, New York: Norton, 2011.

Internet Sites to Explore

"http://www.cfr.org/" Council on Foreign Relations.
"http://www.embassy.org" The Electronic Embassy.
"http://www.fpa.org" Foreign Policy Association.
"http://globalgeopolitics.net/" Global Geopolitics.
"http://www.state.gov/r/iip/" International Information Programs.
"http://www.nato.int" NATO.

International Economic Relations

chapter 20

After reading this chapter, you should be able to:

- Distinguish between a fixed and a flexible exchange rate
- Differentiate between the balance of payments and the balance of trade
- Compare the advantages and disadvantages of international trade
- State the arguments in favor of and against protective tariffs
- State whether the United States is a debtor or a creditor nation and explain what that means
- Discuss the advantages and disadvantages of limiting imports to protect U.S. jobs from the threat of globalization

One of the purest fallacies is that trade follows the flag. Trade follows the lowest price current. If a dealer in any colony wished to buy Union Jacks, he would order them from Britain's worst foe if he could save a sixpence.

—Andrew Carnegie

Can we be frank? Once we cut through many of the high-sounding moral positions nations (and individuals) take, often there is a crass materialistic or economic motive underlying those positions. Therefore, to understand international relations, we must understand international economics, which includes the study of international trade, determination of foreign exchange rates, and foreign investment.

In Chapter 3, we discussed the rise and importance of international trade in the development of society and the evolution of cultures. As nations developed, trade transferred culture and made merchants rich, which helped break up the feudal system and led to the modern nation-state. The modern role of international trade is no less important, but without the perspective of history we are less likely to see it.

In the 1930s, the United States followed an isolationist policy toward trade. Since that time, the importance of international trade for the United States has grown significantly, particularly over the last few decades, and now accounts for well over 10 percent of our total GDP. But even this percentage underestimates its importance. It fails to take into account the fact that once export industries become established, people employed in them furnish a part of the market for industries producing products for domestic consumption. Hence, if exports decline, production and employment, in accordance with the multiplier principle, also fall off in other industries.

That figure also does not take into account the importance of imports to us. A number of our imports are necessary or desirable commodities that we cannot produce ourselves, or cannot produce as much of as we would like, such as coffee, bananas, natural rubber, nickel, tin, and oil. The crisis and shortages in the U.S. economy as a result of the Arab oil embargo in the 1970s demonstrated the importance of international trade.

Over the years the United States has been a strong supporter of globalization, encouraging trade and entering into international agreements that encouraged trade. That changed in 2017 when President Donald Trump took office, and started to pull the United States out of trade agreements. In this chapter we provide economists' views of international trade.

What Makes International Trade Different?

One reason why International trade is different from domestic trade is because it involves the use of different currencies. When you buy something from China, the Chinese producer wants to be paid in yuan (the Chinese currency) and you want to pay with dollars. For that trade to take place, there must be an exchange of currencies—trading yuan for dollars. The market in which that takes place is called the Foreign Exchange Market.

Foreign Exchange Markets

Foreign exchange refers to the process of exchanging the money of one country for that of another and to the monies themselves. Thus, the Japanese yen is called foreign exchange in the United States. Goods are generally paid for in terms of money, but in international trade the buyer uses one kind of money and the seller another, so the price that one pays and the other receives depends in part on the rate at which their two currencies exchange. For example, in 1980, when the price of a British pound in terms of dollars was $2.20, a setting of chinaware selling for 10 pounds in London would have cost a U.S. tourist $22. In 1985, when the pound had depreciated to $1.20, the same setting of chinaware would have cost a U.S. tourist only $12. In fall 2018, a pound cost about $1.30, so the chinaware would cost that tourist about $13.

In studying foreign exchange, we are concerned first of all with exchange rates and how they are determined. It is desirable for exchange rates between two countries to be at a level that will encourage trade. They should also be reasonably stable. Erratic fluctuations in exchange rates are a handicap to trade because they increase the uncertainty and risk involved in transactions that require time for their completion.

Fixed and Flexible Exchange Rate Systems

For many years before World War I, the principal trading countries of the world maintained monetary systems based on **fixed exchange rates,** exchange rates in which the relative values of the various currencies are established by agreement. Under **flexible exchange rates,** in contrast, the government allows the market forces of supply and demand to fix the exchange rate of that country. A fixed exchange rate system was achieved during this time by using the **gold standard,** a system in which the prices of the various currencies are set in relation to the price of gold. During World War I, this standard broke down in most countries, and though it was revived for a time after the war, it suffered a second general breakdown with the coming of the Great Depression in the early 1930s.

When two or more countries are on the gold standard, only very small fluctuations can take place in the exchange rates between their currencies. Under the traditional gold standard, each country will exchange its paper money freely for a fixed amount of gold. When paper money and gold are freely interchangeable in each

Currencies are exchanged in foreign exchange markets.

© bostjan/iStock.

of two countries, the relative values of their currencies depend almost entirely on the relative amounts of gold they represent.

Let us suppose that the French franc once represented 4 grains of gold and the U.S. dollar 20 grains of gold.[1] Then a dollar would always exchange for approximately 5 francs. Slight variations in the exchange rate could still occur because of the cost of shipping gold. For example, though under the gold standard Americans could always exchange dollars in this country for a fixed amount of gold, in order to use this gold to obtain francs in Paris they would first have to pay the cost of shipping it to France.

The weakness of the gold standard was that, in order to maintain it, a government had to keep on hand enough gold to meet all demands for redeeming its currency. The advantage of this standard was that, as long as there was a determination to maintain it, it was an effective check on inflation. It forced a government to limit the expansion of bank deposits and the issue of paper money. Otherwise, demands for conversion of paper into gold would soon reach such a level that the government would be forced to stop redemption, thus automatically placing its money on a paper, or fiat, standard.

Paper Standards and the Gold Exchange Standard. A **paper standard** is a system under which the basic monetary unit of a country is represented by engraved pieces of paper. These have value only because they are limited in quantity and, in the country of issue, are legal tender and acceptable in trade.

After World War II, the Western world initially went on a modified gold standard, under which countries were allowed to adjust their exchange rate (devalue) slightly (by no more than 10 percent), but no major devaluations were allowed without approval from other countries. The approval came from the **International Monetary Fund (IMF),** an international organization set up just after World War II, both to aid in the adjustment and stabilization of exchange rates and to bring about the development of free exchange markets. The IMF could help its members meet temporary exchange difficulties by lending them limited amounts of gold or redeemable foreign currency.

Though the IMF has not entirely lived up to the hopes of its founders, it has helped stabilize foreign exchange markets and continues to do so today. It does so by providing loans for countries that are experiencing a loss of faith in their currency. For example, in 2011, when people became concerned about the stability of the euro, the IMF provided loans to the European Central Bank, which allowed it to buy euros and help reestablish faith in the euro.

From a Fixed System to Our Current System: The Dirty Float. The modified gold standard was more an illusion than an actual gold standard, and that illusion ended in 1971, when the foreign demand for gold was so great that the United States stopped convertibility, and our international exchange system moved from a fixed exchange rate system and a modified gold standard to a flexible exchange rates system. Under the new system, many of a country's reserves are no longer held in gold, but are instead held in reserve currencies, such as the dollar, and in special drawing rights, a type of paper gold. These special drawing rights can now be used, within limits, for meeting international obligations, and they can be lent by the IMF to countries whose other reserves are being rapidly reduced by an adverse balance of payments.

Other countries can no longer get gold for dollars from the United States, but they can exchange dollars for U.S. goods. As the supply and demand for U.S. goods fluctuates, the supply and demand for U.S. currency fluctuates also, changing its relative price. Thus, one month you might be able to buy a British pound for $1.60, and the next month it might cost

---

[1] Under the gold standard as it existed before World War I, U.S. gold coins actually contained 23.22 grains of pure gold per dollar, and French gold coins contained slightly less than one-fifth of this amount per franc. (A grain is equal to 1/7,000 of a pound.)

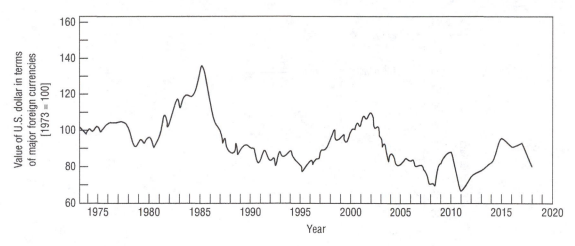

Figure 20.1

Fluctuations in the value of the dollar. (Source: Federal Reserve System)

$1.70. In that case, the value of the dollar has fallen, since the pound that previously cost $1.60 now costs $1.70. In a perfectly flexible exchange rate system, the balance of payments must always be in equilibrium. Put another way, the supply of currency must always equal the demand for that currency. This follows from the definition of balance of payments as the relation of total payments made abroad to total payments received from abroad, which we discussed above.

Actually, although the U.S. exchange rate system is generally a flexible rate system, it is not perfectly flexible. Every so often, the United States and other countries enter into the foreign exchange markets to attempt to raise or lower the value of the dollar. This makes our exchange rate system a **dirty float**—a partially flexible exchange rate system through which every so often the government enters into the foreign exchange market to affect the exchange rate. In some instances, a country attempts to significantly influence the value of its currency for a long period of time. China is a case in point. In recent times, in order to hold the value of its currency, the yuan, down, and thereby encourage exports, China bought large amounts of dollars and dollar-denominated assets, which increase the demand for dollars and thereby held the value of the dollar higher than it otherwise would be. The United States has objected to this Chinese policy, calling it currency manipulation, and the Chinese government has reduced the amount of dollars it buys.

Fluctuations in the value of the dollar can be seen in Figure 20.1. You can see that the value of the dollar has recently been on a roller-coaster ride. Although the value fluctuates, the general trend of the dollar value has been down. This trend is likely to continue until the U.S. trade deficit is eliminated.

*B*alance of Payments and Balance of Trade

Now that we've introduced you to foreign exchange markets, let's turn to the terminology of trade. In discussing international trade, two terms are used frequently: the *balance of trade* and the *balance of payments*. **Balance of trade** refers to the relation of our total exports to our total imports. It tells us the dollar difference between exports and imports. Figure 20.2 shows that the United States has had a balance of trade deficit since the 1970s. That deficit significantly increased in the early 2000s but then decreased somewhat with the recession of 2008. The

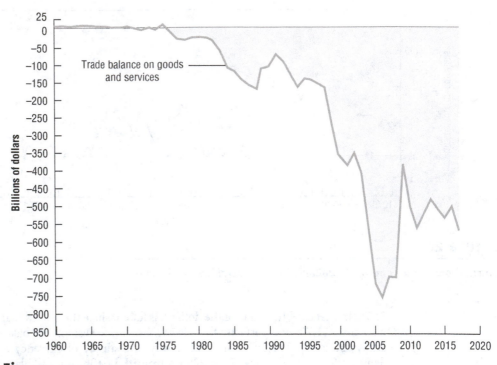

Figure 20.2

U.S. trade deficits: the United States has run deficits in its balance of trade for the last forty years. *(Source: Bureau of Economic Analysis)*

balance-of-trade deficits are cumulative; they represent the debt obligations of the United States going into the future. These debt obligations are growing, and today the United States is by far the largest debtor nation in the world. A significant amount of this debt is owed to China, which has been running balance-of-trade surpluses as the United States has been running balance-of-trade deficits.

Balance of payments refers to the relation of total payments made abroad to total payments received from abroad. It includes not only traded goods and services but also currency flows, such as loans and investments, among countries. Even though the balance of trade has been in deficit recently, the balance of payments has not, because the trade imbalance is being offset by large foreign capital inflows into the United States.

The difference between the balance of payments and the balance of trade can be seen by considering the U.S. position in 2007 when it ran a balance-of-trade deficit of over $500 billion. However, at that same time, foreigners were investing heavily in the United States, largely in the form of bonds. Therefore, because the balance of payments includes these financial flows, even though the balance of trade was in deficit, the balance of payments was not; it was balanced.

The fact that trade flow deficits are offset by capital flow surpluses does not mean we do not have to worry about the international trade deficit. When foreign money is invested in the United States, foreigners acquire U.S. assets and will be paid interest and profits from them in the future. They also can decide to no longer hold their assets in the United States, in which case the value of the dollar can fall substantially. A fall in the value of the dollar will make foreign goods more expensive in the United States and make U.S. goods cheaper abroad. Combined, these changes will eventually eliminate the U.S. trade deficit, but they also will mean that U.S. citizens will pay more for the goods they consume.

The Changing Nature of International Trade

In the 1960s, 1970s, and 1980s, international trade expanded in the developing countries, mainly in the area of manufacturing. One after another U.S. manufacturing plants moved abroad to take advantage of cheaper labor, and today the majority of goods you consume are manufactured abroad. The 1990s marked a new dimension in the expansion of international trade. Companies began dividing up their production processes into components and looking for ways to shift the various subcomponents of production abroad. Each aspect of production was separated—such as bookkeeping service, maintenance service, and advertising—and ways to achieve lower costs by outsourcing—contracting out for others to provide that activity for the firm rather than having someone in the firm do it—were explored.

Beginning in the 1990s, services began moving abroad. For example, accounting for some firms is done in India, where labor costs one-ninth what it does in the United States. Likewise with telephone service: When you actually reach a service representative, it might well be a person in India, Pakistan, or Bangladesh who has been trained to speak "American" and who receives a wage that is a fraction of what a U.S. citizen would get. Such movement overseas of subcomponents of production is likely to continue and even increase in the coming years.

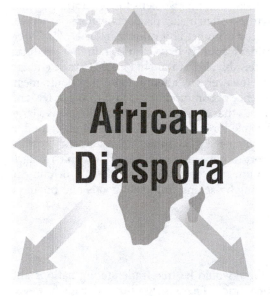

Many people, when they think of imports and exports, have in mind only the visible items of trade—material goods such as wheat, pianos, or machinery. But to think of foreign trade as consisting of these alone is misleading, because the so-called invisible items are just as important.

Invisible items of trade consist of services of all sorts for which the people of one country pay those of another. For example, in normal years, we pay British citizens and other foreigners large amounts in freight charges for carrying U.S. goods on their ships and planes. Tourists from the United States also pay British citizens, French citizens, Italians, and others large sums to buy hotel accommodations and transportation in their countries. Such items represent purchases abroad just as truly as do imports of coffee or shoes. Another important invisible item of trade is the interest Americans receive from foreign investments. This is payment for permitting foreigners to use our capital, something that is just as truly a service as their permitting us to use their hotel rooms. Capital remittances sent by non-U.S. workers living in the United States to their friends and families back home are another example of an invisible trade item. These flows sent by migrant communities (also called **diasporas** if the community members maintain close ties to their homelands) far exceed the total level of foreign aid in the world.

Advantages and Disadvantages of International Trade

Trade is the lifeblood of a modern economy, and the benefits of international trade are so great that it is inconceivable that a modern nation would adopt a policy of complete economic isolation. The full utilization of machinery, with its attendant specialization, requires mass production, and mass production calls for extensive trade in very wide markets. To limit the market of an industry to one country would often mean reduced efficiency and higher costs. Also, modern society requires a great variety of goods, both for consumption and as raw materials for its industries, including tea, coffee, cotton, rubber, petroleum, iron, manganese, aluminum, nickel, cobalt—a complete list would be long indeed. No country has or can produce all of these products. The missing ones can be obtained only through trade. When trade flows freely between countries, the world tends to become more prosperous. When trade languishes, production lags, unemployment increases, and the world's income shrinks.

Three Advantages of Trade

There are three primary advantages of international trade. The first is that it enables a country to obtain products that cannot be produced at home at all or that cannot be produced in adequate quantities and at acceptable costs. Sometimes the inability of a country to produce certain things is a matter of climate, such as the difficulty in growing tea and coffee in the United States. In other cases, it is a lack of certain natural resources. Italy, for example, has no good coal deposits, and Britain does not have enough good farmland to meet its demands for food.

The second advantage of international trade is that it often enables a country to get a better product than can be produced at home. This may be due to differences in climate and soil or to differences in natural resources. Sometimes, however, it is owing to the fact that the people of some foreign countries have, over a long period of time, acquired certain techniques that are not easily transferred. British factories for years produced finer woolens than most U.S. factories because they had specialized in fine woolens for generations.

A third advantage of international trade is that it often makes products available at a lower price than would be possible if they were produced at home. This raises standards of living by increasing consumer purchasing power. Consider a country like Great Britain that produces only about half of its needed food supply. Conceivably, Britain might be able to raise enough food within its own borders to feed its people. However, any attempt to do this would mean inadequate amounts of many foods and the absence of commodities such as oranges, tea, and coffee. It would also mean high prices for the foods that could be produced. Britain has a large population relative to the amount of land available for cultivation. To raise all of its food, it would have to cultivate its good land more intensively, in spite of the tendency toward diminishing returns; it would also have to resort to inferior land not really suitable for agriculture. Both methods are expensive and result in high prices. In the long run, Britain can provide its people with better standards of living by selling industrial goods and buying a substantial portion of its food supply abroad.

Disadvantages of Trade

If international trade had only advantages, there would be free trade among nations and little debate over what to do about international trade. There is significant debate, however, so obviously there must be some disadvantages to international trade. To see these disadvantages, let's consider some examples. Say, for instance, that China began building automobiles that would sell in the United States for $7,000. This would benefit the Chinese who make the automobiles and U.S. consumers of automobiles, but it would hurt one group of producers—U.S. automobile companies—and one group of workers—U.S. automobile workers—a lot. Other examples abound. Importing potatoes helps U.S. consumers but hurts Maine and Idaho potato producers; importing textiles from Bangladesh helps U.S. consumers but hurts textile firms here in the United States.

When we look at both groups together, we see that, in most people's eyes, the benefits of international trade almost always outweigh the costs, but the benefits are spread over a large group of people, whereas the costs are imposed on a few. Those few who are hurt express their opposition to international competition loudly, and so in the United States, as in most countries, there is often a tendency to encourage exports and discourage imports. The complainers argue something like the following: Imports rob U.S. producers of the profits and wages they might have received had these goods been produced at home.

International trade is expedited by standardized container shipping.

Why Economists Generally Support Free Trade

The notion that U.S. producers as a group are injured by foreign purchases is a fallacy. In the long run, the United States can sell goods to other countries only if it also buys goods from them. Though we may gain home markets for the products of some U.S. workers, we do this only at the expense of losing foreign markets for the products of other U.S. workers. For the country as a whole, these two things cancel each other out, and the long-term net result of restrictions on trade is that U.S. consumers pay higher prices or receive inferior goods.

Why You Can't Get the Advantages without the Disadvantages

Why is it that we can sell goods to other countries only if we also buy goods from them? Briefly, the reason is that, in the long run, foreign countries can pay for what they buy only with the goods they sell. Let us explain as simply as possible how imports pay for exports, and vice versa. For simplicity, we first assume that trade takes place only between Britain and the United States.

Suppose that at a certain time a British importer wishes to buy $1 million worth of U.S. machinery. The U.S. firms that have this machinery for sale are unlikely to want British money, or pounds sterling. Rather, they want dollars. Therefore, in order to buy the machinery, the British importer must find some way to change British money into dollars—that is, to find someone who has dollars and who is willing to sell them in exchange for pounds.

Who will have dollars and be willing to exchange them for pounds? For the most part, they can be found in two groups: (1) Americans who want pounds in order to buy goods or services from Britain, and (2) British exporters who have accepted checks or drafts in dollars for British goods that they have sold to Americans. In either case, the source of the dollars available to the British to buy American goods is the payments Americans have made, or plan to make, for British goods.

If for any reason U.S. imports of British goods should decline, the British would be forced to curtail their purchases of U.S. goods because they could no longer obtain sufficient dollars to buy in the previous volume.

The preceding explanation disregards certain complicating factors. Actually, as we discussed above, British importers do not go directly to British exporters to obtain U.S. money. The banks act as middlemen. If British exporters accept in payment dollar-value checks drawn on U.S. banks, they do so because they can take them to their own banks and there exchange them for pounds sterling and deposit them to their own accounts. Their banks can then deposit these checks in New York banks and sell dollar drafts to British importers who need them in order to pay for U.S. goods.

Another factor that our explanation disregards is that trade does not take place just between Britain and the United States. Other countries come into the picture. For example, British exporters might receive dollars for textiles sold in the United States, and British importers might in turn use these dollars to buy beef in Argentina. The dollars would then be available to Argentine importers to buy machinery in the United States. In this case, the dollars we spent for British textiles made it possible for Argentines to buy our machinery.

A final qualification is the time dimension. In the long run, any country's imports must equal its exports. In the short run, however, this statement must be qualified. Over considerable periods of time, one country may be able to buy substantially more from another country than it sells, or vice versa. This can happen for two reasons: (1) countries may have stocks of gold, reserve currencies, or financial assets that they are willing to send us in payment for their purchases, and (2) countries may be willing to sell goods on credit. This is the position that the United States has been in for the last three decades. People outside the United States have been willing to hold dollars and dollar-denominated assets, which has allowed U.S. imports to greatly exceed U.S. exports. However, this cannot continue indefinitely, and we can expect the situation to change in the coming years, probably with a major international currency crisis.

Restrictions on International Trade

We have seen that there are significant advantages to international trade, and in most cases nations would derive the greatest economic advantage from international trade if they allowed free trade. This, however, is not the usual practice; instead, numerous controls are applied. These controls include subsidies on exports, tariffs, quotas, exchange controls, and bilateral barter agreements. In the past, tariffs have been the principal device for regulating trade, but in recent years other methods of control, especially quotas, have assumed greatly increased importance.

The reason for these controls has to do with how economics relates to politics. As stated above, the benefits of trade are spread widely among consumers, who simply take the benefits for granted. The costs fall on a relatively small group and often affect them rather severely, causing firms that cannot compete to go out of business, which means that their workers lose their jobs. Often, even though the total costs are less than the total benefits, politicians will listen to, and make laws to protect, the few who are hurt. Therefore, there is continual pressure for trade restrictions. We now consider some of these.

Tariffs on Imports

A **tariff** is a tax, or duty, usually on an imported commodity. When tariff duties are levied as a fixed charge per barrel or yard, they are said to be *specific*. When they are levied as a percentage of the value of a commodity, they are said to be *ad valorem* (value-added). A tariff generally has one of two purposes: either to raise revenue or to protect the market of a domestic industry by keeping out the products of foreign competitors. To a degree, these two purposes are incompatible because a tariff that would keep the foreign product out entirely would raise no revenue at all. In practice, however, protective tariffs are seldom high enough to exclude imports completely and hence do raise some revenue. But if the chief purpose of a tariff is to raise revenue, it should not be high enough to discourage most imports. Further, instead of being levied on a commodity produced both at home and abroad, it should, if possible, be levied on one that cannot be produced at home. This eliminates the possibility that imports and revenues may fall off because buyers turn to home producers.

Although tariffs for revenue interfere with trade to some extent, that is not their purpose, and such interference is usually kept at a minimum. Their use is in no sense incompatible with a policy of free trade. Whether they represent a desirable kind of tax is another question, and we might point out that, unless they are levied chiefly on luxuries, they have the same drawback as a sales tax—namely, their burden falls more heavily on people of low income than on the well-to-do. The primary argument for tariffs is not that they generate revenue; rather it is a belief that it is in the public interest to keep people from buying goods abroad and to force them to buy at home. Most economists reject that argument and oppose the levying of protective tariffs and the setting up of other trade barriers designed to limit competition and maintain or raise prices. Studies of congressional hearings and debates indicate that protective tariffs are nearly always enacted as a result of political pressure from business and labor groups interested in the production of a certain product, and who expect to benefit from a reduction of foreign competition.

The Case against Protective Tariffs.

The basic argument against protective tariffs is that, by restricting international trade, they rob us of part of its benefits. A second argument against tariffs is that free admission of imports expands the foreign markets of home industries because it is payments for our imports that furnish foreigners with most of the funds with which to buy our exports.

A third argument against tariffs is that when one country institutes tariffs, it is likely that other countries will follow. The result will be a contracting spiral of trade, making all countries worse off. That is precisely what happened in the Great Depression from 1929 to 1933 (see Figure 20.3). As one country after another instituted tariffs to protect jobs at home—the United States instituted the infamous Smoot-Hawley tariff—trade declined, and the entire world fell into a serious economic depression.

The Arguments in Favor of Protective Tariffs.

The advocates of protective tariffs support their point of view with a number of plausible arguments: the home-market argument, the high-wages argument, the infant-industry argument, and the self-sufficiency argument.

Home-Market Argument.   One of the most effective of the claims made by the protectionists is the home-market argument. According to this reasoning, a tariff that keeps out foreign goods increases the market for U.S. goods and thereby increases home profits and employment. Undoubtedly, there is some truth in this contention if we consider only short periods of time, but, as we have already pointed out, the final result is that a home market is created for some goods at the expense of losing a foreign market for others. This loss of the foreign market comes all the faster

Figure 20.3

The contracting spiral of world trade, 1929 to 1933. Total imports of seventy-five countries (monthly values in terms of old U.S. gold dollars in millions). (Source: Original diagram by League of Nations)

because, when we raise our tariffs on their goods, other countries retaliate by raising their tariffs on our goods. Meanwhile, as we have seen, U.S. consumers pay higher prices or receive inferior products.

High-Wages Argument. A second claim that protectionists make is expressed by the high-wages argument. They assert that the tariff maintains the U.S. wage level and the U.S. standard of living by protecting our workers from having to compete with cheap foreign labor. This argument is also plausible, but a little analysis and observation robs it of much of its force. In the first place, if a tariff makes possible higher wages, it does so only by enabling producers to sell their products at a higher price. This may benefit one group of employers and workers, but it reduces the purchasing power and standard of living of all others who must buy the product. If this kind of price raising were applied to a great many products, the general reduction in standards of living might be serious.

Infant-Industry Argument. A third defense of the protective tariff is the infant-industry argument. Those who advance it often disclaim any wish to give permanent tariff protection to an industry not able to survive without it. But, they say, a small new industry in the United States cannot hope to produce at as low a cost as an old, established industry abroad. Let us give it protection until it can get established and grow. Eventually, it may become more efficient than its foreign competitors. If so, it can provide consumers with goods at reduced prices, and it will no longer need tariff protection.

The infant-industry argument has been advanced in the United States at one time or another in support of tariffs to protect various industries. In theory it is sound, but it is difficult to find any clear case in which it has been successfully applied—that is, where an industry has been established as a result of tariff protection and then has continued successfully without such protection.

Self-Sufficiency Argument. A final argument for protective tariffs is that they make a country more self-sufficient and thus less dependent on foreign countries for essential commodities in time of war. This argument is sound in theory, but the situations to which it can usefully be applied in practice are probably rather limited. Though our experience in World War II emphasized the importance of having dependable supplies of vital raw materials, to keep such products out of the country by tariffs would not always result in building up home production. Moreover, many products once deemed essential are less so today because of greatly improved substitutes. Familiar examples are wool, tin, and natural rubber.

When there is real danger of a shortage of strategic materials in time of war, the best solution is probably to build up stockpiles. The U.S. government has followed this policy with a number of minerals and with oil, but many students of the problem believe that much of this stockpiling has been unjustified and is a waste of the taxpayers' money.

Import Quotas

Another device for protecting home industries is the import quota. An **import quota** limits the quantity or the value of a commodity that can be brought into a country in a given period of time. For example, the government may decide to limit sugar imports to 2 million tons a year, and it may decide to assign definite parts of this quota to specified foreign countries.

Many advocates of freer trade consider quotas more objectionable than tariffs. For one thing, though quotas restrict trade, they bring no revenue to the government of the importing country as a tariff would. But for those who wish to restrict imports, quotas have certain advantages over tariffs. Often, they do not require special legislation but instead may be imposed or changed by administrative decrees. Moreover, a quota can be fixed to admit a definite amount of a commodity, whereas if a protective tariff is levied, there is no way of knowing just how much of it will enter.

Pro-trade organizations such as the WTO often face vigorous protests.

Removing Trade Restrictions

Most economists believe that if trade could flow freely and securely through the world, there would be a great expansion of its total volume and that in the long run all nations would be more prosperous. There would be less talk of have-not countries and less need for foreign aid because every country would have free access to the markets and raw materials of the world. The average price of consumer goods would be lower everywhere. Nothing would contribute more to the expansion of world trade than removal of the great mass of restrictions that have been placed on it by government action. But as we saw earlier, decreasing these restrictions will be a slow and tortuous process.

The General Agreement on Tariffs and Trade (GATT), established in 1947, was an agreement in which most Western nations agreed to a mutual effort to reduce trade barriers. In the mid-1990s, GATT was replaced by the **World Trade Organization (WTO),** an international organization designed to foster worldwide trade. More recently, much of the focus has been on regional trade organizations, which attempt to reduce trade barriers among a smaller group of countries. The North American Free Trade Agreement (NAFTA—subsequently renamed the United States-Mexico-Canada Agreement by President Trump), involving the United States, Canada, and Mexico, is an example, and until recently the United States was working on establishing a Transatlantic Trade and Investment Partnership with Europe, and a Trans-Pacific Partnership with countries in Asia. These agreements eliminate trade barriers among member countries and often establish common barriers against nonmember nations. Economists, who generally favor free trade, are of two minds about these associations. They favor associations because they reduce barriers among countries, but they fear that the associations make it harder to achieve a worldwide reduction in barriers. President Trump took a quite different view. He opposed both these smaller agreements among a group of countries and large trade agreements covering all countries. He pulled the United States out of the Trans-Pacific Partnership, and threatened to pull out of NAFTA, unless Canada and Mexico would agree to a better deal for the United States. This led to the NAFTA agreement being modified slightly and renamed. Following his anti-trade policies, he moved the United States away from its path of globalization—the integration of various world economies in terms of production, distribution, and finances.

Globalization

Globalization has occurred as countries have followed economists' policy suggestions to remove barriers to trade and integrate their economies. As part of globalization, both India and China have seen large increases in production, and billions of people have seen their standard of living improve. Although we are a long way from reaching a fully globalized world, in which international barriers would be of little importance to world trade, and global firms could move across national borders with ease, we have made significant strides in that direction.

Global firms have played a major role in expanding international trade, and in doing so, they have significantly changed the international economic environment. When workers in one country demand higher wages, a global firm is in a position simply to transfer production to another country where workers are willing to work for lower wages. For instance, IBM closed many of its production facilities in the United States and moved them to Asia where labor costs were significantly lower. Then, in 2004, it sold its entire personal computer business to a Chinese company, Lenovo. Many other companies have done the same, and manufacturing in the United States has languished over the past decades. In the early 2000s, it was not only manufacturing industries that were transferring jobs abroad, but it was also service industries. When you phone a company for technical assistance or to buy something, you are likely to speak to an operator in the Philippines or India.

Global corporations affect the trading environment in another way. Say, for instance, that the United States were to establish unilateral quotas for Japanese cars. By becoming a global company and establishing production or assembly plants in the United States, a Japanese company could avoid the quotas and sell as many cars in the United States as it wished. That is exactly what happened in the 1980s when a number of foreign-car producers established assembly plants in the United States. In the late 1990s and early 2000s, it was U.S.-based global firms that were establishing production facilities elsewhere. This upset some U.S. workers who felt they were losing their jobs and others who felt that the firms were being imperialistic and paying unacceptably low wages to their foreign workers. These beliefs led to demonstrations against globalization, and likely played a role in President Trump's victory in 2016, when he promised to make America great again and bring back blue collar manufacturing jobs that had been lost to globalization. To do that he stated that he would be much more open than previous presidents to protecting domestic jobs by establishing tariffs on imports, or limiting imports directly by quotas. As discussed above most economists oppose such policies, pointing out that job losses and other disadvantages of trade go along with the advantages of trade—the lower cost of goods. Were it not for trade and globalization, many of the goods we buy—the computers, shoes, shirts, telephones, and so on—would cost two, three, or four times as much, making us much poorer. On average, trade benefits both countries involved; otherwise they would not enter into the trade. President Trump and his advisors recognized that trade is a two-way street, and that it could benefit all countries. But whether it does, and how much it does, will depend on how good a deal the trade negotiators had negotiated. Trump's position was that the U.S. negotiators had not made good deals, and that he could make better ones.

The problem facing Trump is that once a deal is negotiated, it is difficult to backtrack and redo it. Attempting to do so creates ill will and can lead to a breakdown of trade relations that would make all sides worse off.

Globalization, Trade Imbalances, and Exchange Rates

Now that we've discussed both exchange rates and trade issues, we're ready to address the question of the future adjustment that the United States will experience due to globalization and the trade imbalances it has been running. Currently, countries are accepting dollars (U.S. promissory notes) for their goods and services. As discussed earlier, their willingness to do so has allowed the United States to run large trade deficits over the past few decades. At some point in the future, countries will stop accepting these U.S. dollars and promissory notes and instead want goods and services from the United States. When that happens, the value of the dollar is likely to fall substantially, especially in reference to the Chinese currency, the yuan, and the Indian currency, the rupee. At that point, Chinese- and Indian-produced goods will become more expensive in this country (making U.S. citizens less well off) and U.S. goods will become cheaper in India and China (making their citizens better off). As we buy fewer Chinese and Indian imports, and as they buy more U.S. exports, the U.S. trade deficit will end, but in the process the United States will no longer have the enormously higher standard of living over the rest of the world that it currently enjoys.

Conclusion

As you can see, there is much to be learned about international economic relations, and we have only touched the surface. The international economy is complicated and operates on faith and goodwill among nations. If countries each try to go their own way, instituting protective tariffs and other forms of protectionism, the entire world will likely suffer. Therefore, cooperation is as essential in the international economy as it is in the domestic economy.

What makes international economic issues all the more important is their close relationship to international political relations. Countries that trade together generally do not fight wars. Thus, international economic and political relations will probably determine the direction the world takes in moving toward peace or moving toward war.

 Study and **Review**

Key Points

- In a fixed exchange rate system, the relative values of currencies are set by agreement; in a flexible exchange rate system, the relative values of currencies are set by the market.
- Balance of trade refers to the relation of our total exports to our total imports. Balance of payments refers to the relation of total payments made abroad to total payments received from abroad.
- Trade enables a country to obtain better products more cheaply, but trade can hurt the domestic producers of those products.

- Protective tariffs restrict international trade and rob us of part of its benefits. This argument is countered by the home-market argument, the high-wages argument, the infant-industry argument, and the self-sufficiency argument.
- The United States is the largest debtor nation in the world; we owe trillions of dollars more to foreigners than foreigners owe to us.
- The large U.S. trade deficit will eventually lead to a fall in the value of the dollar, which will eliminate that trade imbalance.

Some Important Terms

balance of payments (406)
balance of trade (405)
diasporas (407)
dirty float (404)
fixed exchange rate (403)
flexible exchange rate (403)

foreign exchange (403)
globalization (413)
gold standard (403)
import quota (412)
International Monetary Fund (IMF) (404)

paper standard (404)
tariff (410)
World Trade Organization (WTO) (413)

Questions for Review and Discussion

General Questions

1. What is meant by the foreign exchange market?
2. Why were foreign exchange rates stable under the gold standard?
3. What is the purpose of the International Monetary Fund?
4. Why will the value of the U.S. dollar likely fall in the future, and what will that fall do to the relative standard of living in the United States and developing countries such as China and India?
5. What are the three main advantages of international trade? What are some disadvantages?
6. Exports depend on imports, and vice versa. Why is this true?
7. Is it more desirable for a country to build up its visible or its invisible trade? Explain.
8. Is a favorable balance of trade possible? Is it desirable? Explain.
9. Do most economists support President Trump's trade policy that uses tariffs to protect American jobs? Why or why not?
10. The use of quotas to limit imports has been spreading recently. Are import quotas less damaging to consumers than tariffs? Why or why not?
11. In what ways can a country meet an excess of foreign payments over foreign receipts? Can it meet such an excess indefinitely? Explain.

Internet Questions

1. Look up the exchange rate at http://www.economagic.com/fedstl.htm for U.S. dollars to the euro for the latest date and then for a year before. How did the rate change?
2. From U.S. census data at http://www.census.gov/foreign-trade/balance/index.html, pick a country and find the U.S. trade balance with that country now, in 2008, and in 2000.
3. Using http://dataweb.usitc.gov/tariff/database, the U.S. International Trade Commission's database, find out what the tariff is per liter of beer. Why are there two different tariff rates?
4. According to the World Bank website, http://www.worldbank.org/en/about, what are the World Bank's goals?
5. Go to http://newsweek.washingtonpost.com/postglobal/america/2007/07/inside_an_indian_call_center.html, read the article, and watch the video. In a typical day, how many sales does a sales representative make? Would you be willing to work for $10 per day?

For Further Study

Books to Explore

Bernstein, William, *A Splendid Exchange: How Trade Shaped the World*, New York: Atlantic Monthly Press, 2008.

Bhagwati, Jagdish, *In Defense of Globalization: With a New Afterword*, New York: Oxford University Press, 2007.

DeSoto, Hernando, *The Mystery of Capital: Why Capitalism Triumphs in the West and Fails Everywhere Else*, New York: Basic Books, 2000.

Friedman, Thomas, *The World Is Flat: A Brief History of the Twenty-First Century*, New York: Farrar, Straus, & Giroux, 2005.

Friedman, Thomas, and Michael Mandelbaum, *That Used to Be Us: How America Fell Behind in the World It Invented and How We Can Come Back*, New York: Farrar, Straus, & Giroux, 2011.

Pomeranz, Kenneth and Steven Topik, *The World that Trade Created: Society, Culture and the World Economy, 1400 to the Present*, New York: Routledge, 2015.

Rein, Shaun, *The End of Cheap China: Economic and Cultural Trends That Will Disrupt the World*, Hoboken, NJ: Wiley Publishers, 2012.

Rodrik, Dani, *Straight Talk on Trade: Ideas for a Sane World Economy*, Princeton, NJ: Princeton University Press, 2017.

Stiglitz, Joseph, *Globalization and Its Discontents Revisited: Anti-Globalization in the Era of Trump*, New York: W. W. Norton & Company, 2010.

Stiglitz, Joseph E., *Globalization and Its Discontents Revisited: Anti-Globalization in the Era of Trump*, New York: W. W. Norton & Company, 2017.

Van Overtveldt, Johan, *The End of the Euro: The Uneasy Future of the European Union*, Chicago, IL: Agate Publishing, 2011.

Walter, Carl, and Fraser Howie, *Red Capitalism: The Fragile Financial Foundation of China's Extraordinary Rise*, Hoboken, NJ: Wiley Publishers, 2012.

Internet Sites to Explore

"http://www.bea.gov/" Bureau of Economic Analysis.
"https://europa.eu/european-union/index_en" "http://www.census.gov/foreign-trade/index.html" Foreign Trade Statistics.

"http://www.imf.org" The International Monetary Fund.
"http://www.xe.com/ucc" Universal Exchange Rate Converter.
"http://www.usitc.gov" U.S. International Trade Commission.
"http://www.wto.org" The World Trade Organization.

*T*he Political Economies of Developing Countries

chapter 21

After reading this chapter, you should be able to:

- List six problems facing all developing countries
- Explain why each of those problems is so difficult to solve
- List three suggestions you might give to a potential leader of a developing country
- List and discuss the various policy options of developing countries
- Discuss developing countries' problems with specific reference to the cases of China, Venezuela, and Uganda

A poor country is poor because it is poor.

—Ragnar Nurske

A country becomes rich because it is already rich.

—P. Chaunu

There are 195 countries in the world; of these, about fifty-six might be considered developed. Others are called **developing countries**—countries still in various stages of economic and political development. Developing countries are called developing because they have far lower incomes than developed countries. As a group, they make up about 83 percent of the world's population but consume only about 30 percent of the world's output. Table 21.1 shows some other dimensions of the schism between developed and developing countries. As you can see, people in developing countries live shorter lives and earn less money.

Developing countries can be divided into a variety of groupings. The position of many Latin American countries, such as Mexico, Brazil, and Argentina, which have developed to some degree, is better than that of some others. Other developing countries, primarily those in the Pacific Rim, are in a second group that has managed to maintain rather rapid economic growth. These include South Korea, Taiwan, Singapore, and Hong Kong, which have had high growth rates (over 7 percent) during the last forty years. More recently China, India, and other neighboring countries have been experiencing fast growth. Because these countries have grown so much, they are sometimes considered to have left the developing country classification and entered the "newly industrialized country" classification. In the past decade, four countries that have been developing quickly have acquired the name **BRIC countries,** standing for Brazil, Russia, India, and China. They have called for the establishment of a multipolar world order in which they would have more say in world affairs.

Over the past decades the worst performers in terms of economic growth have been the countries of Africa, which, until recently, have not grown or have grown only slowly. Some have even seen their total output per capita decline. To differentiate these less developed countries in the early 2000s, the United Nations created a new category, **Least Developed**

Table 21.1

The Schism between Developed and Developing Countries in the Early 2000s

	HIGHER-INCOME DEVELOPED COUNTRIES	LOWER-INCOME DEVELOPING COUNTRIES
Population	1.12 billion	5.9 billion
Per capita GDP	$39,000	$3,500
Life expectancy	79 years	68 years
Literacy rate	99%	80%

Source: Estimates based on World Bank data.

Least Developed Countries

Afghanistan	Djibouti	Malawi	South Sudan
Angola	Eritrea	Mali	Sudan
Bangladesh	Ethiopia	Mauritania	Timor-Leste
Benin	Gambia	Mozambique	Togo
Burkina Faso	Guinea	Myanmar	Tuvalu
Burundi	Guinea-Bissau	Nepal	Uganda
Cambodia	Haiti	Niger	United Republic of
Central African	Kiribati	Rwanda	Tanzania
Republic	Lao People's	Sao Tome and	Vanuatu
Chad	Democratic Republic	Principe Senegal	Yemen
Comoros	Lesotho	Sierra Leone	Zambia
Democratic Republic	Liberia	Solomon Islands	
of the Congo	Madagascar	Somalia	

The above list includes countries with per capita GDP of under $1,025. Happily the number of countries in this category has declined in recent years. The forty-seven countries listed above fall into this category.

The different performance of these various groups is a result, in part, of their contrasting policies. Asian countries, such as China and India, have generally adopted policies to promote exports and have worked hard to maintain competitive exchange rates. Many of the African countries have not. Another difference concerns the government and political structure. Asian governments have been strong and stable; African governments have been weak and unstable; Latin American governments' stability has generally fallen between the two. Stable governments are a requirement of continued economic growth.

The economic growth of developing countries has varied. Figure 21.1 shows the growth rates of developing countries compared with those of industrialized countries. Since 1965, developing countries have grown at a faster rate than industrial countries, but the gap between the two in absolute terms has grown larger.

Developing countries were once called "backward," but, on belated recognition of the value judgment inherent in that term, we began to call them "underdeveloped," and, on belated recognition of the value judgment inherent in that term, we now call them "developing." Although developing is preferable to backward, even the current term embodies a value judgment and suggests that someday developing nations will turn into, or that they want to turn into, the western ideal of a "developed nation." That is not necessarily the case—it is possible that some countries may not want to "develop." One of the reasons is that the term *developing* refers primarily to economies, not cultures. So-called developing countries can

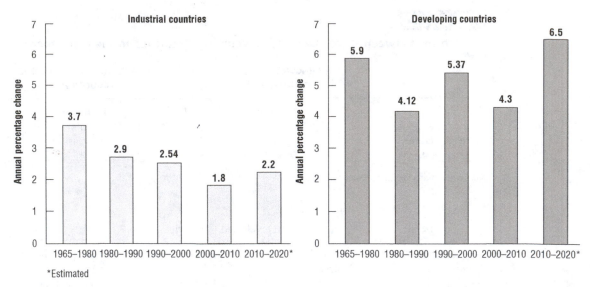

Figure 21.1

Economic growth rate among regions of the world. (*Source: International Monetary Fund, World Bank, and UN*)

have highly refined cultures that are inconsistent with modern economies. It would be ethnocentric of us to think that their cultures are any less refined than ours, or that they should want to become like us.

What is less developed, from the perspective of western countries, is their economies and their systems of government. Those developing countries that do not develop do not have the stable governments and social systems that hold a country together. In another world, that would not necessarily present a problem, but in today's world, without stable governments it is unlikely that they will be able to maintain their culture or their society as they currently exist. They will simply be overrun by the U.S. and other Western cultures. That is not good or bad; that's just the way it is. Thus, developing countries find themselves at a point of choice.

*P*roblems of Developing Countries

To summarize and review much of what we have previously written on politics, economics, and their interrelationship, in this chapter we consider some of the problems facing developing countries in choosing and maintaining social, economic, and political systems. Although these problems are not unique to developing countries—many of the same problems are faced by developed countries—their severity in developing countries makes them worth emphasizing.

In looking at their choices, we would like to consider the full range of possibilities open to developing countries. Given that there are 195 countries in the world, it would seem they have a wide range of existing societies from which to choose, but that is not the case. The various societies have not developed separately; they have been influenced by the other societies. Thus, we now have two main economic systems, capitalism and socialism, and two main systems of government, democracy and autocracy, although there are many variations of each. These systems do not necessarily span the range of possibilities, and probably many forms of society have not been tried. So we must keep an open mind about new possibilities.

The Political Consensus Problem

The central problem facing nonindustrial nations is what might be called the political consensus problem. **Political consensus** means sufficient political order and government efficacy so that the leaders of the state are able to rule. The political consensus problem is the following: Any state that is to operate as a nation-state must have a political consensus—a general understanding between the citizens and leaders of a country that their system of government is satisfactory. The ability to rule can be derived from military might, force of personality, or cultural and social mores, but it must exist if the country is to develop.

In the United States, we have information availability, an educated public, cultural unity, and a long tradition of democracy. That tradition limits individuals' actions and holds our society together. For example, when a political party loses an election, it does not declare the election null and void; it accepts the election results. Developing countries seldom have all of these qualities, and they often do not have any of them. In those countries, it is unlikely that the democratic model will serve them well in the present, although it may provide a goal for the future. Generally, the developing state evolves into, at best, a partial democracy, or an autocracy.

*P*olitical Instability in Africa

African countries have experienced the slowest growth among developing countries in recent decades, and a major reason for this is political instability. If a government does not offer effective control or protections for its citizens, its economy will not grow. Consider just some of the African political crises that existed in 2018.

Somalia Collapse of the military government in 1991 led to a civil war that killed thousands of citizens. Warlords continue to fight for power in a country of essential anarchy. In 2006 an Islamic leader declared a jihad on the Somali government, leading to civil war.

A new internationally recognized government was installed in 2012, but many parts of the country remained largely lawless.

Sudan Pro-government militias began ethnic cleansing campaigns, starting a humanitarian crisis in 2004 and continuing until today. South Sudan split off from Sudan in 2011, and there have been continual fights among various factions within South Sudan and between Sudan and South Sudan since that time.

Republic of Congo A series of wars between ethnic and military powerhouses has marked the country's history. All elections are contested and the country remains mired by ethnic disputes and civil strife. Attempts by the incumbent president to prolong his rule have led to protests and violence.

Rwanda In the early 1990s, economic collapse led to an outbreak of war that led to genocide and the killing of hundreds of thousands of citizens. Leaders of that genocide were recently convicted of crimes against humanity. It is currently ruled by one party, and fighting has been significantly reduced, but tensions remain.

Zimbabwe This formerly prosperous country has been marked by human rights abuses, political instability, and economic collapse. Hyperinflation made the currency useless, and it was abandoned and replaced with the U.S. dollar. In 2017, long-time leader Robert Mugabe was forced from office, but it remains to be seen whether the new leaders will be any less abusive than he was.

One of many victims of internal political strife being removed from the shores of Lake Victoria.

The wars in the Middle East have led to a large increase in refugees.

© AHMAD AL-RUBAYE/Getty

Both autocracy and democracy present problems for developing countries. Democracies often lead to continual changes of government, and the general population's will is not always what is best for a country. Autocracies often lead to arbitrary and capricious rule. The old saying that power corrupts is not without merit. However, when leaders are not strong, power bases often develop outside the state framework. These power bases have their own means of enforcement; they might require payment for protection and make their own rules. Drug dealers in Colombia are an example. In 1985, when the Colombian Supreme Court cracked down on drug dealers, the head of the Supreme Court in that nation was killed. Then one of the many terrorist groups in Colombia invaded the Hall of Justice, and in a shootout with the military, twelve more justices were killed. Mexico experienced a similar reaction when its then president, Felipe Calderón, attempted to crack down on drug dealers. In response, there were widespread killings of officials and the general public by the drug cartels. The Mexican government was not strong enough to prevent it, and continues to be undermined by regional de facto cartel rule and widespread corruption.

The difficulties of finding political consensus could also be seen in a number of Middle Eastern countries in 2012 when large portions of the general populations revolted against the ruling dictators. The result was not more democracy. Instead the result was turmoil since there was no consensus on who should rule, or even how to decide who should rule. In Syria and Libya, the struggle for control led to civil war among various factions, throwing the economies and societies into shambles. In Egypt, it led to the reimposition of authoritarian rule supported by the army. The bottom line: Democracy—the rule of the people—is a wonderful ideal, but in practice, "the people" have many different interpretations of what democracy means, and there is no one way to arrive at a single interpretation.

The Corruption Problem

Closely associated with the lack of an established government, one that has inherent legitimacy, is the problem of corruption. Corruption is a way of life in developing countries. For example, in Mexico City, when you park your car, a police officer might ask you for a protection payment. If you want to import an item, you often must bribe the appropriate authorities to obtain permission. No bribe, no importing. In the Philippines, former President Ferdinand Marcos amassed a fortune estimated at $5 billion to $10 billion, although his presidential salary was only

The World Bank

Various international institutions have been developed to assist developing countries. One of these is the World Bank. The **World Bank** is an international organization whose goal is to foster development by making loans and giving out economic advice. It receives funds primarily from developed countries, and makes loans primarily to developing countries. The World Bank was formed in 1944, and since that time it has provided low-interest loans to many developing countries. It has a staff of more than 10,000 (from http://www.worldbank.org/en/about/what-we-do).

The World Bank's initial loans focused on large projects such as dams and power plants. The World Bank received strong criticism in the early 1990s for the nature of its loans. Critics said that the loans were too heavily focused on large projects that hurt the environment. In 1994, when the bank celebrated its fiftieth anniversary, it responded to the criticisms by saying that it would change its lending practices. It reiterated its basic goal of promoting broad-based economic growth that benefits the poor, but it said that to achieve that goal it would increase its investment in human, as opposed to physical, resources.

Specifically, it would increase its support of educational, nutritional, and family planning programs. It also stated that it would concentrate on environmentally sound physical investments, and that it would help fund programs that build on and expand the role of women in development. Since that time, it has changed its lending practices, but it has continued to be the target of criticism because of its association with free trade and because protestors feel it is still not doing enough.

More recently there has been a debate in the World Bank about whether the focus should be on "small development"—highly targeting projects aimed at solving small problems, rather than "big development"— large projects aimed at transforming the system. The appointment of American Jim Yong Kim, who previously headed a small medical charity which developed new techniques for identifying small target groups that most need help, as head of the World Bank, suggests that in the future there will likely be more focus on small development than there has been in the past.

about $6,000 per year. Either he was an awfully shrewd investor, or he was heavily involved in skimming money from the Philippine economy and government.

The examples of the corruption problem are wide-ranging and are not tied to any particular country or party within that country. What we call corruption here may be simply accepted practice there. We see no easy answer, or likely even complicated answer, to the problem of corruption.

No system clearly offers a way around corruption. Only a deep-seated conviction built into the social mores offers some help; a conviction that regardless of the temptations, the leader will not take advantage of the situation to amass power and wealth. This is a bit like sitting you in a room of a hundred beautiful people of the opposite sex and telling you not to talk to any of them.

The Economic Problem

When income is below the starvation level, some form of economic development seems necessary. At that point, the question is not, "Should a country develop?" but, "How?" The answer is unclear. To develop, a country requires savings and investment, but when you don't have enough to eat, how can you save or invest? Therefore, at or below a certain level of income, societies find themselves in a vicious cycle from which there is no easy escape—and sometimes no escape at all. They must try, somehow, to pull themselves up by their own bootstraps to reach a point where they begin to grow.

To achieve takeoff into economic growth, a country needs to raise the level of investment to a certain minimum proportion of the national income. What is also essential, and what must develop along with any substantial increase of savings and investment, is an understanding on the part of the people of how a successful industrial society operates. The citizens must then be able and willing to develop the attitudes, the patterns of behavior, and the initiative required for vigorous economic growth. Simply pouring in capital is not enough.

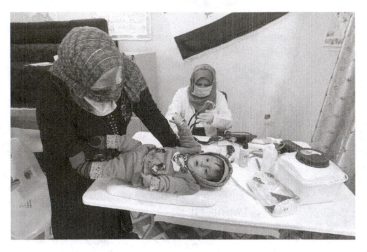

An Iraqi woman brings her baby to a clinic run by Doctors Without Borders.

© SABAH ARAR/Getty

Sometimes, because of lack of understanding, or to satisfy the pride of politicians, countries striving for economic growth spend their available capital on the wrong things. They may, for example, produce impressive government projects such as national airlines or power plants, when what would help most, initially, might be greater production of food. Economic growth will proceed faster if it is balanced and if a foundation is gradually laid for a broad expansion of output. Before too many new airlines are founded or power plants are built, increased provision should be made for certain types of education and training; basic transportation, communication, and banking facilities should be provided; and efforts should be made to raise standards of living in order to increase both the welfare and productivity of workers and also to make possible a significant amount of saving and investment.

As is always the case, social, political, and economic factors interact. For example, many companies simply will not invest in certain foreign countries because of the unstable governments there, and they are unwilling to pay the bribes necessary to carry on business in such countries. Here, we can see the clash of two different cultures. United States firms would be breaking U.S. law if they were to pay bribes to foreign government officials; yet without paying bribes, they could not operate in some countries.

Foreign Aid and Trade Barriers. When countries cannot pull themselves up by their own bootstraps by developing internal savings and investment, they have another option. They can seek foreign infusion of investment, which can come in the form of private foreign investment or governmental **foreign aid,** which consists of financial and practical assistance given by one country to another, especially by a technologically advanced country to a less developed one.

Over the last sixty years, in response to the developing world's need for assistance, the United States has given foreign aid at the rate of about one-half of 1 percent of our total output. The results of that aid have been mixed. Much of it has not been used for humanitarian purposes; rather, it has had political and military purposes.

The biggest recipient of U.S. foreign aid is Israel, and that aid has been provided based on blatantly political motives. Even aid that was given for humanitarian purposes has faced heavy scrutiny. Much of that aid was eaten up in bureaucracy and skimmed by foreign politicians; thus, it never reached its intended recipients. In response to these criticisms, more and more aid is flowing through nongovernmental organizations, or **NGOs**—privately established agencies that attempt to help countries and channel aid to those who need it.

Foreign aid and investment are only part of the answer. An equally or even more important part of the economic answer is removing developed countries' trade barriers. The reality is that developed countries are not very open to exports from developing countries. For example, the European Union (EU) provides enormous subsidies to its farmers, who then export subsidized farm products to countries that could have produced them, but which cannot compete with subsidized prices. In addition, the EU maintains tariffs against many farm imports. This combination of policies makes it difficult for developing countries to develop or expand their farm exports, countering much of the benefit of EU foreign aid. Combining all policies that help or hurt developing countries, the Centre for Global Development ranked twenty-seven rich countries in a "Commitment to Development Index." The United States came in twenty-third.

*H*ope and Development

Esther Duflo, an MIT economist, recently conducted an experiment about aid that suggests that the benefits of aid go far beyond the direct resources provided if it gives the people hope for a better future. She analyzed a program that gave small productive assets, such as a goat or chicken, as well as weekly training sessions on how to tend the animals, to poor people in West Bengal, India. She found that long after the program ended, people were earning 20 percent more—far more than could be explained by the productive assets. The reason: They had hope of getting out of extreme poverty, which led them to work harder (hours worked increased by 28 percent). By making them optimistic about their future, the program changed their actions and helped get them out of the poverty trap they were in.

Duflo found that people without hope have a pathological conservatism, which leads them to forgo potentially large benefits for fear of losing the little they have. By breaking through the poverty trap, small amounts of aid can have large positive effects.

The Historical Legacy of Colonialism.   When Western governments' budgets are tight, the amount of foreign aid they give often comes under attack. Opponents of aid argue that the developed countries owe nothing to the developing countries. Supporters of aid, on the other hand, point to history in providing justification not only for giving aid, but also for giving even more than we do. The historical argument goes as follows: Western countries colonized the developing countries, creating artificial political entities that brought together incompatible ethnic groups and extracted what they could from those countries. These developing countries were not allowed to develop in their own way. In following these policies, the West created many of the problems that developing countries face today. Given this history and the West's role in creating many of developing country's current problems that developing countries face, supporters of foreign aid argue that the West has a moral obligation to assist them.

The Debt Problem

The reliance on private investment, including loans from U.S. and other banks, has created a new problem for many developing countries: the debt problem. Private investment and loans must be serviced, which means that interest must be paid.

In the 1980s, the problem of the **international debt**—the amount of outstanding loans among different nations—grew in importance. The large borrowings of the developing countries throughout the 1970s, together with high interest rates, made it almost impossible for a number of developing countries to meet their debt obligations.

In the 1990s, that debt problem was greatly reduced by **debt restructuring**—allowing repayment of debt over extended periods of time—and a fall in the world interest rate. In 2001, the International Monetary Fund (IMF) granted debt relief for twenty-two countries, continuing the trend of debt restructuring.

In 2005, the Group of Eight, a consortium of eight "developed" countries that met to discuss solutions to problems of mutual interest, agreed to cancel more than $40 billion in debt owed by the poorest countries, in part due to pressure from U2's lead singer, Bono. The debt forgiveness allowed nations to use the money they saved to provide health care, education, and other social improvements. However, in order to qualify for the program, the countries had to comply with good governing practices and transparency. Despite this restructuring, particular developing countries still have large debt balances, and paying off that debt remains a problem.

The Population Problem

Even if they begin to grow, developing countries will not necessarily escape the vicious cycle of poverty because they face another large problem. Put simply, as long as population continues to grow at current rates, these countries are going to have enormous, perhaps insurmountable, difficulties in increasing their **per capita output**—the total output divided by the country's population. The poverty cycle that Thomas Malthus[1] wrote about is very real to many developing countries. Although with sufficient technological development there is virtually no limit to the amount of production one can get from land, one must overcome the initial investment hurdle that will provide one with the means to make that technological progress.

The Brain Drain Problem

As bad as the preceding problems are, they do not leave developing countries without hope. The emergence of nation-states and their development show that the transition to developed states is possible. But before we say, "We grew, why don't you?" we should consider that the nation-states of Western society enjoyed significant advantages over currently developing countries.

In the 1700s, when Western economies developed, travel was limited and individuals tended to stay home and to consider their life in relation to their society. Bright dynamic individuals modified their society, but because their lives were contained within their society, their modifications were generally small and consistent with that society's culture. That is often not the way it happens in developing countries today. Developing countries have a **brain drain,** a process in which the individuals who could make a country develop leave that country.

Having attended school in Great Britain and Germany, one of the authors came to know a number of the brightest and best students of a variety of developing countries. They were sent away to school because they were so outstanding. They often did well, but in doing so they became immersed in the developed culture.

When such students finish their studies, they often are presented with a choice between two totally different economies and cultures. One offers enormous amounts of material goods, intellectual challenge for which their training has prepared them, and excitement. The other offers traditional values from which their foreign education has taught them to escape, material shortages, and enormous intellectual challenges for which they have no preparation. Faced with these choices, many decide to remain in the developed country or to join an international agency that pays as well as a good job in the United States. The result is the brain drain.

Consider the brain drain problem from the perspective of an outside observer. Doctors trained in India, where doctors are in short supply, are constantly immigrating to the United States, where there are many more doctors per capita; the same is true with engineers and computer experts. The United States benefits enormously from this immigration, and immigrants constitute nearly one-fifth of all doctors and PhDs. The UN estimates that India loses $2 billion a year just from computer expert emigration to the United States. In addition, many of the brightest students are going abroad for higher education, causing a foreign exchange outflow of $11 billion annually. Removing the best and the brightest from a society makes it that much harder for the society to develop.

It is not all a loss for developing countries. Emigrants send hundreds of billions of dollars to their home countries and provide links that allow and encourage global companies to expand into the emigrants' home countries. They also create a pool of talent that can return to the country once the country develops sufficiently to need the emigrants' training. This is happening with both Indian and Chinese immigrants to the United States. More of them are returning to their home countries to take advantage of business opportunities there. That integration of economies leads to faster development for their home countries.

Mission Impossible: Advice to a Potential Leader

What, then, should a developing country do? Neither we nor any other social scientist knows precisely what to do. Advice has run the gamut of possibilities. The results have been so bad

---

[1] See Chapter 5 for a discussion of Thomas Malthus and his theories.

that we are going to deviate from standard textbook policy: We do not tell you what the experts think should be done. Instead, we are asking you what you think should be done. So, we hereby appoint you as social advisor to Hopelandia. (If you have foreign students in your class, you might find that the exercise is not so far-fetched. Many of them are the future leaders of their countries.)

Your task, should you choose to accept it, is to prepare a development plan and determine what set of policies a developing country should follow to solve the problems mentioned earlier. To make the assignment easier, we begin by providing you with some general advice that we would give a potential leader, a set of policy options to help formulate your thinking about the problems, and some initial background information on three developing countries.

Keep an Open Mind. The first piece of advice to an advisor to a developing country is: Don't rule out options arbitrarily, and do use all available knowledge of the interrelationships of various aspects of social science. Don't try to emulate any specific developed country. Do what is right for your country, because what works for one country might not work for another. For example, in Uganda, there are enormous tribal differences, and individuals' allegiance is to their tribe rather than to the larger society or to their country. Voting almost invariably means voting for whichever candidate is from one's tribe. Within such a situation, democracy is unstable. For democracy to have a reasonable chance of succeeding, the allegiance must be to the entire country, not to an individual subsection of that country.

Recognize the Difficulties. The second piece of advice is: Set goals and priorities with full recognition of the difficulties that the development plan will encounter. Should a country grow economically, or should it instead set different goals, such as maintaining its tradition and furthering its religion? In the Middle East, many Shiite Muslims tend to be more fundamentalist in their beliefs; they fear that economic growth means the infusion of Western values into their society and a worsening, not an improvement, of the society. Therefore, the goals they choose have little to do with economics other than as a means to the end of preserving their religion and their way of life. In other countries such as South Korea, economic growth is weighted more heavily, and although maintaining tradition always plays some role, when faced with the inevitable trade-off, these countries will make choices based on economic development.

Maintain Your Idealism. A final and most important piece of advice is: Maintain your idealism. Unless you love your country and are willing to use whatever power you have for the good of the country as well as you understand that good, and not for your own gain or that of your friends, then forget about being a leader and give your support to an individual who will.

Options of Developing Countries

Developing countries have a variety of ways to approach their almost impossible problems. Let's briefly consider their options.

Political Options

Political options include democracy, autocracy, and various shades in between the two. Somehow the system chosen must be one that combines the various ethnic and regional groupings into a complete whole and makes them feel that they belong together, rather than that they are blood rivals who must continuously fight with each other. The policies you suggest to meet this necessity will determine the type of policies you can advocate in regard to the economic problem.

Economic Options

The range of economic options goes from (1) variants of unfettered capitalism, in which the government enters into the economy as little as possible; to (2) socialism, in which individuals can operate in certain areas, but the government plays a much stronger role in guiding the choice of each individual decision; to (3) some new kind of economic organization that you think of. The choices are interrelated.

Foreign Policy Options

Countries do not develop in a vacuum. Other countries play a role, at times stabilizing a regime, at other times destabilizing a regime, depending on whether the individuals guiding these regimes are following the other country's goals, and on whether the particular major power can live with the operation of the regime to which it has lent support. Therefore, you have to choose a foreign policy.

During the Cold War, developing countries could play the former Soviet Union against the United States. With the breakup of the Soviet Union, this strategy ended. The United States and its allies were about all there was left to flirt with. That's why in the early 2000s most development plans were democratic, market-oriented plans. However, the significant economic growth in China, and China's increasing international presence, is once again presenting developing countries with a variation of the "flirting" option.

Population Options

You need to ask yourself some questions about population. First, do you have a population problem? Facing this issue is one of the most difficult tasks confronting human beings, whether on a personal level, a national level, an international level, or—now that space colonization is not just a wild, science-fiction dream—a cosmic level. Second, if you have an overpopulation problem (and in the countries we are talking about here, let us hint that you may likely have overpopulation problems), do you then go in and direct people not to have children, or at least limit the number to one or two? How would you do this? Third, having made the decision which way to go, and how to go that way, what consequences can you foresee will have to be dealt with when the results of your policy begin to show up in the census figures?

The Brain Drain Option

Should you encourage your top students to go abroad? If you do, how can you be sure they'll come home again to use their new skills in the country that sent them to be educated? Suppose you decide the other way, that is, to keep your most promising youth at home. In that case, how will you foster new ideas, youthful enthusiasm, and the importation of valuable ideas and methods that have already been developed in other countries? (You don't want to reinvent the wheel.)

Who Will Be the Next Leader?

What qualities do you want and what qualities does your country need in a leader? Should there be a committee or coalition of some kind, rather than a single leader? In either case, how will leadership qualities be developed? How will leadership qualities be recognized? What will the leader, or leaders, do once in power? How should the leadership be controlled, if it should be controlled? How can you search for and pick out the leaders in your country? Perhaps that search won't be fruitful, or not as fruitful as you expect. Should you look for imported talent? Where should you look for it, if this is your choice? Ask the same questions about the imported talent that you asked about possible homegrown leaders.

You could, of course, ask many other questions, but these few should start you on the way.

Case Studies

To really get a sense of the problems facing developing countries and their options, we need to look at specific experiences of real-world countries. Thus, we conclude this chapter with three case studies.

China

The first country we look at, China, is a success story in terms of economic growth, despite some recent problems. Starting in the late 1990s the Chinese economy grew at a rate of more than 10 percent for well over a decade. In 2018, it was still growing at about 6 percent. By almost any standard, that rate of growth for that long is phenomenal. Its growth has pulled hundreds of millions of people out of poverty, and has made its economy the second largest in the world. China may still be a developing country, but it is one with enormous clout and power. It did this with what some call a Chinese market socialism system. It allowed its economy to be essentially a market economy, but it did not allow political freedom.

One of the reasons for its clout and power is that it is the largest and most populous developing country in the world. It has approximately as large an area as the United States. Its main language is Mandarin Chinese, although there are eight separate dialects. Ostensibly, it is a federal republic with twenty-three provinces, five autonomous regions, and Hong Kong. It describes itself as a socialist state, with the Communist Party of China dictating the state ideology. (The box on page 431 gives an overview of the statistics relevant to China.)

Up until the late 1980s China was a planned socialist economy in which the government controlled most of the economic activity. After the tumult of decades of reforms that brought famine and political upheaval, in the late 1980s the government introduced markets and market incentives to try to encourage individual production. The Chinese economy moved away from central planning, although in what it considers key goods, government production still rules. It now sees itself as a type of socialist market economy. The freeing of the market in many sectors led to China becoming the world's fastest-growing economy at the turn of the century, creating a substantial middle class and many "newly rich" people.

The introduction of markets has not been without problems; the income growth has been highly skewed, and the large majority of Chinese remain poor, while a few, including many with close ties to the government, have become incredibly rich. This is especially true for children and descendants of the leaders of China, often called the princelings. The sense that the system is corrupt is a major concern for the Communist Party that leads China, and it recently created a strong anti-corruption program. What happens in China is of major concern to all countries in the world, since China has become a vital player in the international system, and is set to join the United States as a genuine international super-power in the coming decade.

Background of China.   China is surrounded by a variety of natural barriers: the sea to the east, and mountains and desert to the southwest and north. There are three naturally deli-neated regions: the west, an area of high plateaus and desert; the north, an area of fertile plains; and the south, mostly hills and valleys. The two main rivers, the Yangtze and the Yellow, are both of extreme economic importance. Ninety percent of the population of China are of Han ethnicity, and 95 percent are Chinese-speaking, although there are several dialects and a variety of other languages.

Though now officially atheist, most Chinese people practice variants of Buddhism, Taoism, or Chinese folk religion. Even before that, Confucianism, based on patriarchal dominance, had established extraordinarily strong family and social ties based on male supremacy. As one result of the communist takeover in the 1940s and the establishment of

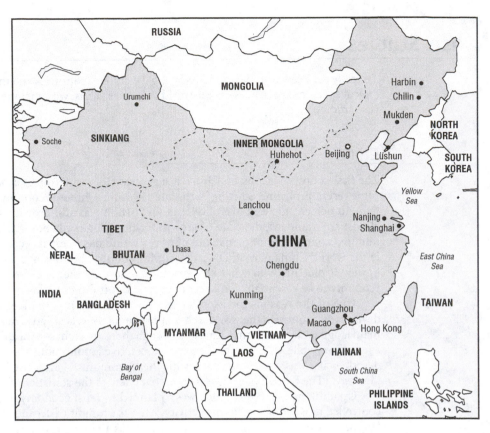

Map of China.

communes, many of these ties were significantly reduced. As that occurred, the status of women in Chinese society improved greatly.

The key to recent Chinese economic history is the communist takeover of the government in 1945 and its attempt to introduce socialism into the Chinese system and culture. Then, starting in 1978, a change in leadership gradually introduced market-oriented reforms and decentralized economic decision making.

China's Population Problem. In the 1970s and 1980s population growth was a key concern for China, and the government introduced a variety of rather strong policies to limit that growth. It started with an edict pronouncing as a norm the two-child family; that edict was soon changed to a one-child limit, and the system was backed by a variety of economic rewards for those who complied and penalties for those who did not. Families having more than one child lost rights and income, and were counseled by most of the leaders of their community that they were not doing the right thing.

The rule was draconian but it led to a significant decrease in the birthrate, and by 1982, the majority of newly formed families in the cities were having only one child. This was not the case, however, in the countryside, where the desire to have several children and, above all, to have boys, meant that families ignored the limit or, in some cases, killed newborn female babies, so that their one child could be a boy. Recognizing the difficulty of policing these vast rural areas, in the late 1980s the authorities relaxed their one-child policy for those areas.

In 2015 China replaced its one-child policy with a two-child policy, in part because social mores had changed and people no longer wanted large numbers of children, in part because people disliked it, and in part because China became concerned about the need for more

China: Selected Statistics

Population: 1.4 billion
   Urban: 58%
   Rural: 42%

Population growth rate: 0.4%
   Age distribution
         Under 15: 17.2%
         15–64: 72%
         Over 64: 10.8%

Fertility rate: 1.6 per woman

Birth rate per year per 1,000 population: 12.3

Death rate per year per 1,000 population: 7.8

Infant mortality: 12 per 1,000

Life expectancy at birth
   Male: 73.6
   Female: 78

Religions
   Nonreligious: 52.2%
   Chinese folk: 21.9%
   Buddhist: 18.2%
   Christian: 5.1%
   Muslim: 1.8%
   Other: 0.8%

School life expectancy: 14 years

Literacy rate among those age 15 and older: 96.4%

GDP: $23.12 trillion (purchasing power parity)

GDP per capita: $16,600 (purchasing power parity)

Population below poverty line: 3.3%

Cell phone subscriptions: 99 per 100 inhabitants

Internet users: 53.2%

workers to support the aging population. In 2018, China's population was a bit more than 1.4 billion, and it has remained relatively stable since the early 2000s.

China's Political Problems.   Politically, China remains controlled by the Communist Party. The way to its present state has been a zigzag path. Mao Zedong's attempts to modernize China with the Great Leap Forward contributed to a famine that lasted three years, from 1959 to 1961, killing tens of millions of people. From 1966 until 1976, China was governed by a radical faction that engineered the **Cultural Revolution** and encouraged the youth to purge the economy and society of external influences that it felt had adverse consequences for China. Universities were torn apart and strong attempts were made to break down the vested ruling interests. It is estimated by some that millions of people were killed in this movement. In 1976, after the death of Mao Zedong, the group that brought the Cultural Revolution to China was thrown out of power, and moderates, headed by Deng Xiaoping, took over. They started developing economic incentives and economic modernization, moving from a state-controlled economy to a market economy.

After Deng retired in 1986, Zhao Ziyang and Li Peng shared China's leadership. They cautiously continued Deng's economic modernization policies, while maintaining communist control. Economic modernization led to demands for political liberalization as well, and in 1989 the world saw millions of students and ordinary citizens clashing with China's government. The uprising was repressed and the Communist Party strengthened its control over the country. After a series of leadership changes, and concerns about corruption, Xi Jinping became leader in 2012. Over the next few years he consolidated his power by removing critics and competitors (often on charges of corruption) and through adroit political moves including continued economic reform and suppression of political dissension. In 2017, Xi was reelected for another five-year term, and his thoughts were included in the Communist Party Constitution, something that had not been done with a leader since Mao Zedong. In 2018, China's National People's Congress removed term limits for the presidency, clearing the way for Xi to maintain his grip on power for the foreseeable future.

Over the past thirty years China has grown at a fast economic pace, which means that China has gone through incredible changes. Hundreds of millions of people moved off farms and into cities. Much of the initial growth was focused on China's eastern seaboard,

The old Shanghai, overshadowed by the new Shanghai.

especially in the urban areas and in the southern part of China, creating significant inequality among individuals and regions. More recently growth has occurred in inland cities. In the process of growth local governments often seized what had been communal land from rural farmers, frequently with little compensation, creating even more inequality, and creating a significant gap between a rich minority and the millions of poor workers and peasants. The result has been unrest in a number of rural areas.

Starting around 2013, the Chinese economic growth rate began slowing. Its previous economic growth model, which was based on exports and government investment, no longer worked, as wage increases in China allowed other developing countries to take business away from China, and the government investment was often wasted and mired by corruption. As growth slowed, millions of migrant workers lost their city jobs and were forced back to their rural jobs, where they saw a halving of their wages as they reverted to farming and other occupations.

This slowing of growth is of serious concern to the Communist Party, which rules China with an implicit agreement—it will maintain high growth and economic gains for individuals in return for a lack of political rights. To deal with the slowing growth, the Communist Party implemented a highly publicized crackdown on corruption, although many observers felt that it was primarily enforced against President Xi Jinping's political enemies, not his political allies.

As China has increased in economic strength, it has also increased its military power and presence in the world. It has created assistance programs for African and South American countries, and has invested heavily in those countries. It has claimed rights to islands in the waters between it and its neighbors in the South China Sea—islands that its neighbors also claim. It has also increased its **soft power**—the cultural influence it gains through support of academic studies about China.

Some observers fear that if the Chinese Communist Party experiences domestic trouble because slow growth undermines the implicit agreement with its people of economic growth in return for few political rights, then it might try to gain support by "playing the nationalistic card," which means that they gain support domestically because of conflict with other countries. In summary, China is emerging as a full-fledged superpower, but it remains to be seen how its "market socialism" ideology—involving concurrent political repression and economic liberalization—will play out over the long haul.

Venezuela

Venezuela is a country of about 31.3 million people on the northern coast of South America. It has enormous biodiversity within its borders since it includes parts of the Andes Mountains as well as parts of the Amazon rainforest basin. Like many South American countries it has a complicated political history with numerous autocracies since its independence from Spain in 1811 until 1958, after which a series of democratic governments ruled. These democratic governments were weak and often experienced political coups and impeachments for corruption. A distinguishing feature of the Venezuelan economy is that it has enormous oil reserves, which means that there is substantial oil revenue. Much of the political fighting in Venezuela is centered on who will control the decisions about oil and who will get the oil revenues that flow in.

One would think that more revenue makes a society better off, and to some degree it does. But, often, the fights about who will get that revenue become so intense that they undermine the country's political stability. Moreover, because the demand for that oil can prop up the value of a country's currency, it can make it hard for other industries to compete in the world market. It is very easy for oil-rich countries to become totally dependent on oil revenue. Then, when oil prices fall, the countries fall into a fiscal crisis. That certainly has been the case in Venezuela, and is one of the causes of the political instability there.

Venezuela is of special interest because, as of 2018, it was one of the few countries existing that sees itself as following a socialist economic model. It began in 1998, when there was a collapse of confidence in the government, and Hugo Chavez, a self-professed socialist, was elected. Chavez argued that much more of Venezuela's oil revenue should go to help the poor. To do that, Chavez embarked upon a plan to establish Venezuela as a twenty-first century socialist economy, by which he meant that it was distinguished from earlier socialist economies in that it was more decentralized and had a more participatory planning process. A new Constitutional Assembly was created that wrote a new constitution to make that possible. The government took control of oil production and began providing more money to the poor. Chavez also provided low-cost oil to Cuba and promoted socialist parties in other countries, in an attempt to bolster the international socialist movement and perhaps create more socialist governments around the world.

Initially, the plan went well. Oil prices were high and there was significant money to support a variety of social programs. When oil prices fell, and the government received less revenue, it tried to continue those programs by borrowing, and printing money. This resulted in inflation, which the government attempted to slow by establishing price controls. In 2013

Venezuela: Selected Statistics

Population: 31.3 million
  Urban: 89%
  Rural: 11%
Population growth rate: 1.24%
  Age distribution
    Under 15: 27%
    15–64: 59%
    Over 64: 7%
Fertility rate: 2.32 per woman
Birth rate per year per 1,000 population: 18.8
Death rate per year per 1,000 population: 5.3
Infant mortality: 12.2 per 1000

Life expectancy at birth
  Male: 73
  Female: 79.1
Religions
  Roman Catholic: 96%
  Protestant: 2%
  Other: 2%
School life expectancy: 14 years
Literacy rate among those aged 15 and
  older: 97.1%
GDP: $389.4 billion (purchasing power parity)
GDP per capita: $12,400 (purchasing power parity)
Population below poverty line: 19.7%
Cell phone subscriptions: 89 per 100 inhabitants
Internet users: 60%

Map of Venezuela.

Hugo Chavez contracted cancer and died in office. He was replaced by his vice president, Nicolas Maduro, who attempted to continue in Chavez's footsteps. He found this difficult both because he lacked the charisma of Chavez and because the oil prices fell further, putting even more strain on the Venezuelan economy. Loans from China stopped the Venezuelan economy from crashing.

The declining Venezuelan economic conditions led to significant political protests. In response President Maduro jailed opponents and protesters. He put price controls on many goods, which created black markets with prices five or six times those of the "price-controlled" goods that could be legally bought, if they were available. So, people bought black market goods because, while many necessities had low prices in regular stores, they were unavailable. The economic difficulties caused Maduro's approval ratings to plummet. In response, Maduro restructured the Venezuelan government, imprisoned opponents, and essentially turned the Venezuelan democracy into an autocracy with him in charge. As of 2018, it was unclear how long this experiment with a new socialism would last.

What to make of this history? One lesson is that that oil is not a panacea for development. It can cause problems if the country becomes overdependent on it. A second lesson is that it is really difficult for a government to achieve its social goals by taking control of the economy. The economy is highly complex, and strong attempts at government control through socialist planning have almost always led to shortages and economic troubles. But that does not mean that trying to achieve social equality is an undesirable goal; it simply means that if a country is doing so, its leaders need to go slowly and be aware that moving too fast, or not making the hard decisions that need to be made in an economy, will lead to serious difficulties.

Uganda

President Yoweri Museveni of Uganda.

Uganda has an area of 93,070 square miles and a fast-growing population of over 39 million. A variety of languages are spoken, including Bantu, Swahili, and English. Its religions are Christian, Muslim, and a variety of tribal sects. Uganda lies on the equator and has an average elevation of 4,000 feet above sea level. Its central fertile

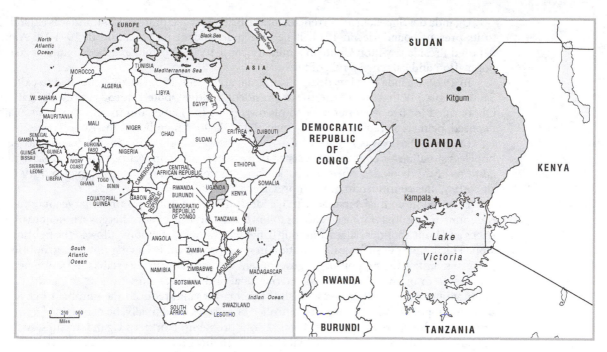

Map of Africa (left); Map of Uganda (right).

Uganda: **Selected Statistics**

Population: 39.5 million
  Urban: 17%
  Rural: 83%
Population growth rate: 3.2%
  Age distribution
    Under 15: 48%
    15–64: 50%
    Over 64: 2%
Fertility rate: 5.71 per woman
Birth rate per year per 1,000 population: 43
Death rate per year per 1,000 population: 10
Infant mortality: 56 per 1,000

Life expectancy at birth
  Male: 54
  Female: 57
Religions
  Protestant: 45%
  Roman Catholic: 39%
  Muslim: 14%
  Other: 2%
School life expectancy: 10 years
Literacy rate among those aged 15 and older: 78%
GDP: $88.6 billion (purchasing power parity)
GDP per capita: $2,400 (purchasing power parity)
Population below poverty line: 19.7%
Cell phone subscriptions: 60 per 100 inhabitants
Internet users: 22%

plateau is bounded to the east and west by the mountains of the Great Rift Valley. Annual rainfall is about 40 inches, and temperatures generally remain between 60°F and 85°F.

Uganda's biggest problem is a lack of political coherence; it comprises a dozen major tribes, of which the Bantu-speaking groups form the majority. The Ugandan tribes in the south are now the most numerous and have given their tribal name to the whole country. Most people depend on agriculture for a living, although some of the northern tribes are also wandering herders. Illiteracy is extremely high. Most agriculture consists of subsistence and livestock farming, although Uganda remains one of the world's largest producers of coffee, which accounts for almost all of its export earnings.

Uganda developed, in its current form, as a British protectorate in 1894, and was extended to its present boundaries in 1914. It became independent in 1962, and in 1971 Idi Amin deposed President Milton Obote in a military coup. In 1972, Amin expelled Uganda's Asian population and launched a rule of terror.

In 1979, Uganda was invaded by Tanzania, and Amin fled. (In 2000, he died in exile in Saudi Arabia.) With Amin's exile, the ex-president, Milton Obote, returned to rule the nation. Obote ruled for five years but favored his own tribe, the Langi, and in mid-1985 was again deposed, being replaced by a military man, Tito Okello, a member of the Acholi tribe.

In 1986, Okello was replaced by Yoweri Museveni, who turned what seemed to be a hopeless situation—a country that existed more in name than in reality, a country that earlier editions of this book described as a basket case— into a more politically stable country that since 1987 has continued to grow impressively.

How did he do this? First, he kept his idealism; he did not appropriate large amounts of the country's wealth for himself and his followers. Second, he opened his government to other tribes and built a political alliance among tribes that, although tenuous, allowed the fighting to stop. Third, he reduced major corruption in government while leaving minor corruption in place to maintain the support of the government workers. Fourth, he established a sufficiently stable system of laws that allowed international and domestic investment to occur. Fifth, although he was a socialist, he established free markets and reduced the number of government monopolies and government-controlled businesses. And finally, he maintained a strong army under his control. Uganda still has serious problems. Northern Ugandan cities, such as Kitgum, are still recovering from a civil war in which more than 200,000 people died and many others moved to refugee camps.

It should be noted that the commendable economic performance in Uganda has not led to political reform. The ruling party, the NRM, dominates and makes it difficult or impossible for other parties to compete. If a competing party starts to do well, it generally experiences a government investigation that discovers that it has violated a rule or law, and the leader is

What is the Role for the Guiding Elite in a "Democracy"?

The case studies presented in this chapter raise important questions about government and democracy. In the West there is a strong ideological belief that democracy is the best system of government. This view is held without a full recognition of how dependent a functioning democracy is on a culture and on an established rule of law that limits the actions of elected leaders and those that did not get elected.

When the opposition's goal is seen as undermining the existing system, that opposition will be put down by the leaders, under the belief that they are saving the system. In the United States that is implicit, since both main parties were, until recently, seen as sharing similar core values. In China, Venezuela, and Uganda, the ruling parties see their role as protecting core values that they believe their opponents do not hold. Thus, they justify their repression of other parties as a necessary foundation for their democracy.

In recent years the United States' complacency over its own democracy is being tested with the election of Donald Trump. His election shocked many of the elite, a number of whom believed that he did not share their core values. Consistent with this belief there was a push to try to figure out ways to remove him from office through impeachment, and some of the elite were looking for actions that could be interpreted as impeachable offenses. But for many in the United States, especially those in rural Middle America and Southern states, Trump came closer to capturing aspects of their core values of individual freedom and responsibility than did the mainstream candidates from either main party. That's why he won the election. They saw the push to impeach a legitimately elected leader as itself close to a violation of the core principles of democracy.

What lesson do we learn from the three case studies? Democracy can be fragile and has many dimensions. Countries and scholars should be hesitant to claim that their system is best or to condemn other systems which are different than theirs. Keep the core values as inclusive as possible. When individuals in society begin seeing their differences as differences involving core values, democracy will be less likely to work.

threatened with jail. President Museveni argues that while multiparty democracies suit Western societies, which divide horizontally by class, they only deepen divisions within African societies, which are vertically split along ethnic or regional lines. He says that, given the ethnic problems Uganda faces, Western-style democracy is not appropriate for Uganda or most other African nations. He argues that Western countries should consider the results of his rule and not worry about whether it has a Western-style democracy. Uganda's arrangement of severely restricted, though not totally banned, alternative political parties is known as the "**Movement system.**"

An example of the control that Museveni's party exerts can be seen in the election of 2006, which Museveni won handily. An important reason why is that his main opponent was arrested and charged with treason and rape just months prior to the election. In 2011 and 2016 Museveni continued the harassment of opponents, having them arrested for treason and other crimes, before the election. Both times Museveni was reelected with over 60 percent of the vote, although both outside observers and internal opponents objected to the election as being rigged in Museveni's favor. Museveni is in his mid-70s and would not have been eligible to run for reelection. But he changed the Constitution to allow him to run, just as he had earlier changed the Constitution to allow him to be in office for more than two terms.

Museveni's Movement system is a challenge to Western scholars who support democracy as it is practiced in Western countries. The problem is that in developing countries with many competing ethnic groups, Western-style democracy often leads to enormous corruption and civil war. Museveni argues that, given that reality, developing African countries need an idealistic broad group committed to state stability and preventing corruption to oversee the playing out of political democracy. He sees his Movement as providing that for Uganda, and after he leaves office, he has called for the Movement to remain—not as a political party but as an organization overseeing state stability and preventing corruption. The problem is whether any group will be able to provide checks on the Movement if they lose their idealism. More and more, Western observers who were previously supportive see the Movement turning into an autocracy that stifles democracy.

Conclusion

In considering the choices a developing country must make, you will see the game of society played in its entirety. The individuals who succeed in making the right choices launch their countries into prosperity and political stability. Those who make the wrong choices leave their countries in poverty.

The preceding descriptions have been necessarily brief. You can find more information on the web and in the library, and you'll need a lot more information before you can make reasonable choices. Even if you don't take that step-for-social-science into the library, keep your eyes and ears open for stories about these and other countries in the newspapers; in news magazines such as *Time* or the *Economist;* and on television and the Internet—because these countries will be in the news. The issues of social science surround you and will continue to surround you all your life.

 Study and **Review**

Key Points

- Six problems facing all developing countries are the political consensus problem, the corruption problem, the economic problem, the debt problem, the population problem, and the brain drain problem.
- Each of these problems is interrelated with the others and is deeply ingrained in the culture of the society.
- Reasonable suggestions for a potential leader of a developing country include keeping an open

mind, recognizing the difficulties, and maintaining idealism.
- Policy options for developing countries include political options, economic options, foreign policy options, population options, and brain drain options.
- To truly understand the problems of developing countries, we must do case studies of specific countries.

Some Important Terms

brain drain (426)
BRIC countries (418)
Cultural Revolution (431)
debt restructuring (425)
developing countries (418)

foreign aid (424)
international debt (425)
Least-Developed Country (418)
"Movement system" (437)
NGO (424)

per capita output (425)
political consensus (421)
soft power (432)
World Bank (423)

Questions for Review and Discussion

General Questions

1. What is the chief characteristic that identifies a country as developing?
2. Name three groups of developing countries, and state briefly what distinguishes one group from another.
3. If a developing country cannot find a way to hold itself together, what is likely to happen to it?
4. Why might democracy not be the best choice of political system for a developing country?
5. Are there any good things to be said for autocratic government? If so, what are some of them?
6. What are some of the abuses in which a corrupt government indulges?
7. A poor country might solve its problems by becoming richer. How can a poor country save and invest?
8. Aid to developing countries from the governments of developed countries has been decreasing. Give some of the reasons.
9. Some developing countries have borrowed so much money from foreign banks that they are having great difficulty paying it back. What is likely to happen in such countries?
10. What problems does rapid population growth present to a developing country? Are there any advantages to rapid population growth in developing countries?
11. How can a developing country acquire the human skills, training, and valuable ideas it needs in order to compete in modern industrial society?
12. Are there guaranteed solutions to the problems of developing countries? If so, describe some of the solutions.
13. What were your proposals for the development of the country of Hopelandia?

Internet Questions

1. Go to https://www.youtube.com/watch?v=XTyXmtwXl_Q and watch the video. What is the Riversands Incubation Hub?
2. Watch the video at https://www.youtube.com/watch?v=y5kSEPuwGCQ. What are the main reasons for supporting IFAD? Can you think of any costs?
3. Go to https://www.youtube.com/watch?v=jxPA3xkSpJY and watch the video. Based on this video, should Latin America be concerned about the effects of climate change?
4. Look at the UN page on identifying Least Developed Countries at https://www.un.org/development/desa/dpad/least-developed-country-category.html. What are the criteria for determining if a country is an LDC? Which criterion do you think is most important?
5. Go to the International Monetary Fund page, http://www.imf.org/external/np/exr/glossary/index.asp. What is the HIPC Initiative?

For Further Study

Books to Explore

Cohen, Jessica, and William Easterly, *What Works in Development? Thinking Big and Thinking Small*, Washington, DC: The Brookings Institution, 2009.

Collier, Paul, *The Bottom Billion: Why the Poorest Countries Are Failing and What Can Be Done about It*, New York: Oxford University Press, 2007.

Easterly, William, *The White Man's Burden: Why the West's Efforts to Aid the Rest Have Done So Much Ill and So Little Good*, New York: Penguin, 2007.

Easterly, William, *The Tyranny of Experts: Economists, Dictators, and the Forgotten Rights of the Poor*, New York: Basic Books, 2015.

Epstein, Helen C., *Another Fine Mess: America, Uganda, and the War on Terror*, New York: Columbia Global Reports, 2017.

Epstein, Gerald, *Capital Flight and Capital Controls in Developing Countries*, Cheltenham: Edward Elgar, 2005.

Gallegos, Raul, *Crude Nation: How Oil Riches Ruined Venezuela*, Lincoln, NE: Potomac Books, 2016.

Guest, Robert, *The Shackled Continent: Power, Corruption, and African Lives*, Washington, DC: Smithsonian Books, 2004.

Hung, Ho-fung, *The China Boom: Why China Will Not Rule the World*, New York: Columbia University Press, 2015.

Isegawa, Moses, *Snakepit (Uganda)*, New York: Knopf, 2004.

Meredith, Martin, *The Fate of Africa: A History of the Continent Since Independence*, New York: Public Affairs, 2011.

Sachs, Jeffrey, *The End of Poverty: Economic Possibilities for Our Time*, New York: Penguin, 2005.

Tripp, Aili Mari, *Museveni's Uganda: Paradoxes of Power in a Hybrid Regime*, Boulder, CO: First Forum Press, 2010.

Wasserstrom, Jeffrey, *China in the 21st Century: What Everyone Needs to Know*, New York: Oxford University Press, 2010.

Internet Sites to Explore

"http://www.china-embassy.org/eng" The Chinese Embassy.

"http://www.eepsea.net" Economy and Environment Program for Southeast Asia.

"http://www.imf.org" International Monetary Fund.

"https://ustr.gov/trade-agreements/free-trade-agreements/north-american-free-trade-agreement-nafta" NAFTA.

"http://www.statehouse.go.ug/" Uganda.

"http://www.usaid.gov" U.S. Agency for International Development.

"https://www.hrw.org/americas/venezuela" Human Rights Watch: Venezuela.

"http://www.worldbank.org" The World Bank.

International Institutions and the Search for Peace

After reading this chapter, you should be able to:

- Explain the statement, "War is merely a continuation of politics by other means."
- Define the policy of pre-emption and explain its implications for international harmony
- Describe the usefulness and limitations of international law
- List the three most important organs of the United Nations
- Summarize the United States' position on the United Nations
- Summarize the current outlook for peace
- Give a history of the Arab-Israeli conflict

Nothing is more important than the war on war.

—Pope Leo XIII

In 2017, North Korea tested an intercontinental ballistic missile (ICBM) capable of reaching anywhere in the Unites States. North Korean leader Kim Jong-un warned the United States that he had a launch button on his desk, and he wasn't afraid to use it. U.S. President Donald Trump responded to him on Twitter, calling Kim Jong-un Rocket Man. He tweeted: "Will someone from his depleted and food starved regime please inform him that I too have a Nuclear Button, but it is a much bigger & more powerful one than his, and my Button works!"

President Trump's bravado and approach to international diplomacy worried many observers, but the approach of his predecessors also provoked concern. Either they were being too accommodating to other countries, or they were being too belligerent. There is clearly no one right way and it may be that all ways are wrong, and it is only after the fact that we can make a reasonable judgement about success. Currently, the United States is "ending" wars in Afghanistan and Iraq after more almost two decades of fighting. But even as those wars were declared ended for the United States, there was still fighting going on, and the U.S. was involved in that fighting. Specifically, U.S. troops were on the ground in both countries, which are plagued by internal divisions and civil wars. And it wasn't only there. To varying degrees the United States was also involved in internal wars in Libya, Yemen, and Syria, and other Middle Eastern countries were deeply troubled. Much of the U.S. involvement in these wars could be tied to the War on Terror.

The War on Terror began as a U.S. response to September 11, 2001, when **Al-Qaeda**, a fundamentalist Islamist terrorist group, hijacked airplanes and crashed them into New York's World Trade Center and the Pentagon in Washington, DC. In response, the United States declared a general war on terrorism and adopted a **policy of pre-emption**—a policy under which the United States would attack terrorists wherever they were found, even before they had committed acts of terrorism. This policy of pre-emption, which became known as the

Bush Doctrine because it was implemented by then President George W. Bush, led the United States into the Iraq and Afghanistan wars. Unfortunately, those wars did not reduce terrorism, but rather spread it.

Two aspects of the policy of pre-emption were highly controversial—the first was that the United States declared that it had the right to go into any sovereign country and fight terrorists, and if the country harbored terrorists, that country would be considered a terrorist country and thus subject to U.S. attack. Second, those attacks could be based on suspicions and clandestinely gathered information, which would be hard for any other country to verify.

Both the Iraq and Afghanistan wars were much more expensive and costly to conduct than originally predicted. The Iraq War cost thousands of U.S. lives and more than $1 trillion; after a quick defeat of the Saddam Hussein government, it led to civil strife in Iraq that is still ongoing today. A similar outcome occurred with Afghanistan.

Iraq and Afghanistan were just two of the areas in which the United States was involved. The United States' difficulties there led Iran and North Korea to take strong stands against U.S. demands about what they should do. North Korea developed nuclear weapons and missiles that could reach the United States. Iran worked on developing a nuclear program, but agreed to suspend that work in exchange for a removal of UN economic sanctions against it. President Barack Obama accepted the deal but President Trump questioned it, and in 2018 he withdrew the United States from the deal. In addition, Russia is conducting what many call a grey zone war in Ukraine, whereby it conducts actions, such as sending unmarked troops to fight, but claims not to be involved with their actions, which just avoids forcing a reaction by the United States. Russia entered directly into the conflict in Syria as it supported President Bashar al-Assad, and the United States supported the rebels, even while both Russia and the United States were fighting the Islamic State in Iraq and Syria (ISIS), a group classified as terrorists. China is exerting its power in the Far East. It is developing its navy and making claims of control for much of the South China Sea, going so far as to add fill to atolls, thereby turning them into islands on which it can build air bases, which strengthen its claim to the South China Sea.

Such actions reflect a changing world order. The United States' economic and political hegemony (almost total dominance), which developed with the breakup of the former Soviet Union in the 1980s, has ended, and China, the European Union, and Russia have filled the void. Even relatively small nations, such as Venezuela and Bolivia, have felt themselves able to thumb their noses at the United States—calling it a paper tiger whose time has passed. Such conclusions are premature: The United States remains the dominant power in the world, but the world is highly complex and that power is limited.

President Bush's successor, Barack Obama, recognized that, and in response to what was called the **Arab Spring**—a series of popular revolts against autocratic Arab leaders who did not allow free elections—the United States took a much less prominent role; some called it "leading from behind." It supported the rebellions but withheld direct involvement until other nations had committed themselves to an effort and agreed to take lead roles. Thus, for example, in Libya, the United States did not get involved until the Arab League, a group of surrounding Arab countries, had committed themselves to the overthrow of the old regime. Even then, the United States provided only backup support for NATO, allowing other NATO countries to take a lead role in the bombing support provided for the rebellion. The United States took a similarly limited role in Syria.

The results have also been problematic. Both Syria and Libya have experienced civil war and are far less stable than they were before. Hundreds of thousands of refugees have left those countries, attempting to immigrate to other safer countries. These civil wars allowed militant terrorist groups, such as the Islamic State (IS, formerly ISIS), to take over large sections of both of those countries, forcing the United States into the fight. The fight against IS eliminated its control over territory, but did not eliminate IS, which remains a dangerous terrorist group that attacks targets around the world. It seems that neither leading from the front, nor leading from behind, provides a good answer to dealing with the political strife in other countries.

President Trump's foreign policy is different. He calls it his America First policy, and it has involved his making strong statements about the need for the United States to get better outcomes in agreements. But his actions have been somewhat less provocative—more like Bush's than Obama's, but still measured compared to the bravado of his belligerent tweets.

In this chapter we consider the broad issues of war and peace in the specific context of the international institutions that have developed to help maintain international relations. We also examine how these institutions are related to U.S. foreign policy, and explore why it is so hard to avoid war, and why, despite that, we continually try to do so.

*T*he Problem of War

War is hell. Besides the lives lost and the trillions of dollars spent, war brings about enormous social and cultural changes. World War I paved the way for the success of communism in the former USSR, it helped to bring on the Great Depression of the 1930s, and it unleashed forces that produced fascism in Italy and National Socialism (Nazism) in Germany. Similarly, World War II changed the nature of the world, bringing an end to the colonial empire system. Likewise, the recent U.S. wars have led to quite different results than anticipated by most in the U.S. government when they began them, and the full effects of those wars will not be known for many years.

The Causes of War

Few things are certain about war, but it seems that inevitably it is the other side that started it, and that the stated cause of the war will mask other underlying causes. Analyzing the causes of war is not a task about which a person can afford to be dogmatic. We can point to many forces at work and can reason as to how the forces work, but we cannot with exactitude draft any formula that will fully explain, evaluate, and relate the many pressures, conditions, emotions, ambitions, and practices behind international discord. Karl von Clausewitz, an influential German general and military strategist of the nineteenth century, argued that "war is merely a continuation of politics by other means." When peaceful methods do not accomplish their objectives, countries consider force.

Destruction in Jobar, Damascus

© Alamy

Generally speaking, identifying forces that tend to bring about war is easier than explaining or evaluating them. Factors that may contribute to bringing on war include the desire of a nation for power, economic rivalries, religious and political divisions (such as those in Yemen and Sudan), social unrest, the ambitions of political and military leaders, fanatical devotion to revolutionary ideologies (as in some Middle Eastern countries), intense ethnic rivalry among various groups, the desire for security or territory (as in Israel), the need to protect a country's national honor, or simply mistaken ideas about another country's intentions.

Because states are the work of human beings, inquiry into the causes of war goes back to the nature of human beings. Although psychologists and biologists admit that war may seem to reflect the impulses and emotions of humans—anger, fear, suspicion, and frustration—the general opinion is that people are not so made that they require war for the satisfaction of their basic drives. Their war making is believed to depend more on acquired attitudes, beliefs, and points of view than on their inherent nature.

The nation-state, as typified by public opinion and by its leaders, may be sensitive, quick to take offense, and hasty to retaliate. In the 2003 Iraq War, once the United States had decided that Saddam Hussein was harboring "weapons of mass destruction," negotiations proved fruitless, even though in the end it was clear that Iraq had no such weapons.

Within states or within the community of states as a whole, certain conditions often add to the chances of war at any given time. Poverty in a nation may produce a restlessness that breeds civil strife, and this in turn may result in international war or lead to dictatorships that foster warlike conditions. Dissension or economic depression within a state may cause governments to welcome war in order to establish national unity or to create a diversion from internal problems incapable of solution. When a spirit of militarism has been developed within a nation, as it had in Germany in the 1930s, touching off a war is relatively simple. That same spirit of militarism exists, although to a lesser extent, in the Middle East today, which is one of the reasons that area has been the site of numerous wars and is also why it is likely to be the site of more trouble in the future.

Among conditions in the international community conducive to war is a sharp ideological split, like the one that, up until the early 1990s, existed between the former Soviet Union and its allies on the one hand and the United States and its allies on the other. In the early 2000s, the religious differences among certain groups are turning into ideological splits that are highly conducive to war.

The existence of a power vacuum of sizable proportions is another hazardous condition in the world community, and it is frequently found when an empire has just been demolished or an alliance has broken down. Thus, the breakup of the Soviet Union, while reducing the ideological friction between the former Soviet Union and the United States, produced numerous tinderboxes in Eastern Europe and in the former Soviet Union itself. It also changed international political dynamics, and there was no effective counterbalance to the United States, allowing the United States to enter into small wars without any expectation of serious reprisals from other countries. This did not reduce tensions. Instead, in many observers' eyes, the United States' unbridled use of power has contributed both to terrorism and to the support that terrorism gets in a number of countries. Thus, terrorism may be seen as a type of reprisal.

Finally, the sudden rise of a nation state that challenges another often leads to conflict. This was pointed out by the Greek Historian Thucydides, and has acquired the name the **Thucydides Trap**—when fear of growth of another country's power leads to actions that lead to war. China's recent rise has all the makings of the Thucydides Trap.

Approaches to the Problem of War

Throughout history, most people have probably desired peace, though in some tribal societies war—in combination with customs such as war dances, headhunting, and scalp collection—became an integral part of the group culture. War helped to give life meaning by providing danger, excitement, and opportunities for winning prestige. Nevertheless, the quest for peace goes back at least to the biblical prophet Isaiah's long look ahead to the time when "nation shall not lift up sword against nation, neither shall they learn war anymore."

Ever since nation-states began to develop in the late Middle Ages, various poets, philosophers, and politicians have presented plans for maintaining peace. These peacemakers include Dante, King Henry IV of France, William Penn, and Immanuel Kant. But none of the plans were practical, nor did they reach the masses or receive serious consideration from governments.

Diplomacy.   Disputes are, or at least seem to be, inevitable among people, bullies and ninety-pound weaklings alike. The alternative to a slugfest is reasonable discussion, which on the international level is called diplomacy. The problems of states are first of all handled by diplomats, usually with success. Occasionally, however, diplomacy fails. Because a serious dispute that gets out of hand can result in war, states genuinely anxious to stay at peace will keep their diplomats at work as long as any hope of a solution exists. Throughout the history of the nation-state, diplomacy has done much to avoid war.

The contributions of diplomacy to peace include the efforts of third states as well as the parties to disputes. A disinterested state may try to get disputants together for further negotiations when they reach a deadlock and when unfortunate developments appear imminent; or, injecting itself a little further into a controversy, a third state may attempt **mediation**—a procedure that calls on the mediating government to make suggestions for solutions, thus concerning itself with the merits of the issues involved. For example, European countries tried to mediate a dispute between the United States and Iran about Iran's nuclear power program. Similarly, the United States has been trying to mediate the ongoing dispute between Israel and the Palestinian Authority.

The U.S. role of mediator between the Palestinians and the Israelis was made more difficult in 2017 when President Trump announced that the United States would move its embassy to Jerusalem, which Israel had made its capital. The Palestinians objected since that move seemed to prejudge issues about Jerusalem that were supposed to be part of a final peace agreement between Israel and the Palestinians. In response, they said that they would no longer see the United States as an "honest broker," which is a term used to describe a neutral mediator in a dispute.

*T*rump Diplomacy

In Chapter 1 I introduced you to book smarts, which complemented street smarts. There are many other types of "smarts." Smarts are really just an understanding and knowledge of the unspoken language of how things are expected to be done. Another of these smarts is what might be called "diplomacy smarts." Diplomats speak a different language than do you and I. It is a language that is understood by other diplomats, but which those of us on the outside often have a difficult time interpreting. For example, diplomats are sickeningly cordial; they always say nice things, but the say them in such a way that other diplomats know they they are really saying something else. For example, the statement "We had a cordial conversation" probably means "we accomplished diddly squat." The advantage of diplomatic smarts is that it keeps the conversation going, and put a pleasant façade on what are often angry confrontations. Like Captain Louis Renault, they are "shocked" by knowledge that they know full well isn't shocking. The language is based on the belief that if we're talking, it's better than if we're fighting, and that being cordial keeps us talking.

The disadvantage of diplomacy smarts is that many of the issues separating the two disputing parties never get raised. One of the reasons President Trump is treated so cordially (interpret "not liked in the least"—and that's being diplomatic) by many elite diplomats is that he refuses to follow the "diplomacy smarts" rules. He tweets out statements that make diplomats cringe, and which undermine all the cordiality that diplomats have worked so hard to maintain. He takes strong positions, then the next week switches his tone and takes another position, as if he were a different person.

While Trump's approach to diplomacy has problems, it also has benefits—it allows the underlying hostilities between the participants to be more openly considered and possibly allows for new ways of dealing with the deep underlying differences to be found. Consider the North Korean negotiations, in which neither Trump nor Kim Jong-un played by standard diplomatic rules. Instead they exchanged hostile tweets. But then they met face to face and agreed to move toward peace at a much quicker pace than standard diplomacy would have ever allowed. Whether their alternative approach works or not remains to be seen. But, in my view, their approach is not one which demonstrates their lack of understanding of diplomacy smarts, as many commenters have suggested it is. Rather it is a frustration with the hypocrisy of diplomacy smarts and an attempt to develop an alternative way of dealing with difficult issues. Trump is attempting to redefine "diplomacy smarts."

In recent years, a number of countries such as Timor Leste, Kenya, Nepal, Somalia, Sudan, and Nigeria—both independently and through the United Nations—have relied on outside mediation activities. When mediation breaks down, the mediators must choose whether to become actively involved by providing peacekeeping forces or military force to achieve what they consider to be a fair resolution to the problems, or, less frequently and very reluctantly, to give up, admitting that some situations are, at least for a time, immune to outside influence.

International Government.   As we have seen, governments, for all their problems, generally maintain order within their boundaries by providing alternative mechanisms for settling disputes. Thus, it is only natural that some of the proposals for preventing war between nation-states have involved an international government, or at least some option other than war, for settling disputes on an international level. These include the international courts and the **United Nations (UN)**, an organization of independent states that debates, and sometimes does something about, international problems. Together, these institutions comprise the rudimentary beginnings of world government, although when nations do not like the decisions, they generally disregard them. Thus, when the UN failed to officially sanction war against Iraq, the United States attacked anyway, with some U.S. government officials declaring the UN irrelevant. However, later, when the United States wanted Iran to end its nuclear program, it relied on the authority of the UN as the reason why Iran had to comply. More recently, in late 2017, the United States announced that it was reducing its dues payments to the UN because the UN had denounced the United States' formal recognition of Jerusalem as the capital of Israel.

International Law and International Courts.   For centuries, the ideal of a world ordered by a unified system of law has persisted. The ancient Greek city-states applied among themselves an elemental body of rules relating to matters such as diplomacy, treaties, and war. In Rome there was a *jus gentium*, or forum, to regulate the relations of the diverse peoples within the empire. As soon as the system of nation-states got under way centuries ago, it began constructing for itself a body of law. Hugo Grotius, a Dutchman, usually is referred to as the founder of modern **international law**—the system of rules on rights and duties of states in their mutual relations—because of his systematic organization and discussion of the law of his day in his famous book entitled *The Law of War and Peace* (1625). Often, however, emphasis was put on what nations ought to do rather than on their customary behavior.

By the nineteenth century, the actual practices of states in their relations to one another began to be stressed more and more in discussions of international law, and less attention was paid to what they ought to do from the point of view of abstract justice. Today, established procedures in the form of custom, treaties, conventions, and formal agreements are the chief basis of international law. Its subject matter is extensive, embracing items such as the recognition of new states and governments, diplomatic privileges and immunities, the acquisition of territory, nationality, extradition, the treatment of aliens, commerce, the jurisdiction of states, the responsibility of states, the beginning of war, the conduct of war, and the effect of war on treaties.

The Usefulness and the Limitations of International Law.   The usefulness of international law in the maintenance of order and peace among nations has always been limited. No international system of criminal law and prosecution has been established to date, although the UN has established laws related to war and international conduct of countries. To enforce these laws it has created an International Court of Justice (commonly known as the World Court) and an International Criminal Court. These international laws concern war crimes and crimes against humanity, defined as crimes that "are particularly odious offenses in that they constitute a serious attack on human dignity or grave humiliation or a degradation of one or more human beings." Debates often arise about what a war crime is or whether a crime reaches the level of a crime against humanity, especially when those accused are still in power. But deposed leaders, or leaders who have lost a war, often find themselves subject to such charges.

A country's submission to an international court's justice is voluntary, and there are no effective means available to the community of states for the enforcement of the law. A violator may be threatened by the injured party, it may be the object of retaliatory measures, and in the last analysis it may be challenged in war. But these are not orderly procedures comparable to the methods possessed by a state for enforcing laws internally. For example, in the mid-1980s, when the United States was found to be in violation of international law with its policy in Central America, and especially in Nicaragua, it simply ignored the ruling.

Despite these deficiencies of the community of states, the usefulness of international law should not be underestimated. Nations may be able to violate the law and get away with it, but they much prefer not to do so, for they do not like to be regarded as lawbreakers. A bad reputation can be harmful to a state, even a powerful one such as the United States. The fact that nations constantly appeal to the standard of the law in their communications and negotiations with each other, both in claiming rights and in meeting their obligations, is evidence that they at least like to appear law-abiding.

In recent history, many states discovered the high costs of having a bad reputation (due to a consistent violation of international law). For example, South Africa finally ended more than four decades of apartheid in response to significant pressure that included economic sanctions and condemnations. More recently, Iran and North Korea have undertaken actions that have led to international condemnation and UN sanctions.

*T*he United Nations

The United Nations is the closest institution we have to a world government. The UN was formed in reaction to a surge of enthusiasm after World War II for a world organization able to keep the peace. On August 24, 1941, Prime Minister Winston Churchill of Great Britain and U.S. President Franklin D. Roosevelt announced in the famous Atlantic Charter the need for a "permanent system of general security." On January 1, 1942, soon after the United States entered the war, a UN Declaration was signed confirming the objectives of the Atlantic Charter. This declaration gave the UN, which was established on October 24, 1945, its name. The primary purpose of the UN, according to Article 1 of the charter, is maintaining "international peace and security."

The UN is not the first attempt at a worldwide organization designed to keep the peace. The first comprehensive approach to the problem of war by a group of states was written into the Covenant of the League of Nations in 1919 following World War I. This organization failed, however, to receive the international support necessary to make it a viable world organization. Although the United States was cooperative, it never became a member, and in 1939, after numerous ineffective attempts to use the League as an arbitration tool, it folded.

The most important organs of the UN are the Security Council, the General Assembly, and the Secretariat. The **Security Council**—the legislative body that has "primary respons-ibility for the maintenance of international peace and security"—is the most powerful organ of the UN. The council deals with international disputes and decides when aggression is taking place or when there is a threat to the peace. It is composed of fifteen nations, of which five—the People's Republic of China, France, Russia (which took over the seat of the former Soviet Union), the United Kingdom, and the United States—are permanent members. The other ten members are nonpermanent and are elected by the General Assembly for terms of two years, with the elections staggered so that five new countries come into office each year.

The Security Council must have the affirmative vote of nine of its members. When an issue is procedural in nature, any nine suffice, but in all other matters, the nine must include all

The Security Council of the United Nations adopting a resolution.

© Alamy

five permanent members of the council. On major questions, each of the five permanent members has a **veto**—a vote that forbids or blocks the making of a decision. This veto has been used relatively often, reducing the Security Council's ability to make decisions on controversial issues. For example, in 2009, the United States wanted a resolution imposing strong sanctions on North Korea for its testing of nuclear weapons, so it turned to the UN Security Council. However, it could not get the support of the other four permanent members, any one of which had veto power, so it had to modify its resolution and settle for weaker sanctions.

Similarly, in 2012, when most countries favored a proposal to make the Palestinian territory a member of the UN, the United States threatened to veto it, which would prevent it, since such a change required approval by the Security Council. However, it could not stop the change in the status of the Palestinian territory from a nonvoting observer "entity" to that of a nonvoting observer state, since that required only General Assembly support. This change allowed Palestinians to join UN organizations, and to pursue cases against Israel at the International Criminal Court.

The **General Assembly** is a UN legislative body that includes representatives of all the member states. It meets annually and concerns itself "with any questions or matters within the scope of the present charter or relating to the powers and functions of any organs provided for in the present charter." It has no legislative power, but it discusses a wide variety of international problems. When it arrives at a decision, it is in the form of a recommendation, either to states or to other organs.

The **Secretariat** is the UN executive arm. It is headed by the secretary-general, who is elected by the General Assembly and traditionally holds the post for a period of five years. In 2018 the secretary-general was Antonio Guterres. The Secretariat carries out a variety of organizational, research, publication, and communication functions, and the secretary-general plays an important role in diplomacy among states.

Is the UN Worth It?

When the UN began, there was great hope for using it as a vehicle for resolving disputes among nations without resort to violence, and for discussion that could prevent war in the future. Initially, the UN was dominated by the United States and its allies, with the former Soviet Union the odd country out. Because it had different views, the Soviet Union used its veto to stop a wide variety of activities. As the UN expanded from its initial 55 members to its approximately 193 members today, the general tenor of the organization changed. The new states tended to disagree with the United States, and in the 1970s and 1980s the UN was often at odds with U.S. policy. This led the United States to be far less supportive. For example, the United States also chose not to sign the Law of the Sea treaty developed by the UN, and it withdrew from the United Nations Educational, Scientific, and Cultural Organization (UNESCO) in 1984, claiming extraneous politicization and "an endemic hostility toward the institutions of free society, particularly those that protect the free press, free markets, and, above all, individual human rights." An assistant secretary of state said, "When UNESCO returns to its original principles, the United States would be in a position to return to UNESCO."

This change was reflected in U.S. voting in the Security Council. Whereas in the early years of the UN, the United States never used its veto, in the 1970s and 1980s the United States used its veto power relatively often to prevent action by the UN. In the late 1980s, the nature of the UN changed from what it was in the 1970s and early to mid-1980s. Changes in the former Soviet Union and China made agreement in the Security Council more likely, and the UN more often reflected U.S. desires. This agreement within the UN with regard to U.S. desires gave more legitimacy to U.S. actions in maintaining the peace and achieving its international goals.

During the presidency of George W. Bush, the UN was not supportive of many U.S. positions, and the U.S. reaction was to withdraw—if not in fact, at least in principle—and look to other means of handling international disputes. That's precisely what it did in 2003. When it was clear that the UN would not sanction war against Iraq to eliminate weapons of mass destruction, but instead wanted to give UN weapons inspectors more time to determine whether Iraq had such weapons, the United States simply went to war on its own together with what it called the Coalition of the Willing.

With the election of Barack Obama in 2008, the U.S. attitude toward the UN became much more supportive and cooperative, and the United States' relationship with the UN improved. That changed with the election of Donald Trump who once again put the United States in conflict with many UN positions. For example, in 2017, when the UN General Assembly voted to condemn the United States for its recognition of Jerusalem as the capital of Israel, the United States announced that it would reduce funding for the UN. This is important because the U.S. contribution makes up a bit over one-fifth of the UN's budget (see Figure 22.1). Because of its large contribution to funding, the UN has been forced to take notice of the U.S. position, and has often modified its positions in order to be more in accordance with U.S. desires. The UN, like most other institutions, is subject to the golden law of economics—"He who's got the gold makes the rules." The UN funding sources have been changing over the last decade. Specifically, the United States' and Japan's funding are decreasing and China's funding is increasing. Thus, in the future the UN will likely not be as responsive to U.S positions as it has been in the past, and a bit more responsive to China's positions. This is another example of China's growing role in the world economy and in global affairs.

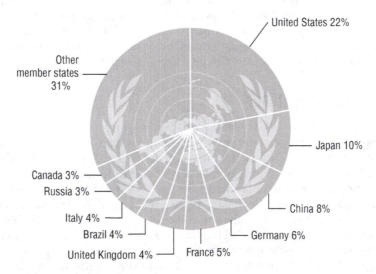

Figure 22.1

Approximate assessments for paying for the United Nations, 2016–2018.

The UN's Role in Keeping the Peace

Supporters of the UN point out that for all its problems, the UN is still the only world force for peace that we have, and therefore argue that it is important. To see its importance let's consider how it has contributed to keeping the peace and how it can continue to do so.

In the event of a "threat to the peace, breach of the peace, or act of aggression," the Security Council may invoke **sanctions**—diplomatic, economic, or military punitive actions undertaken through a collective security system—against the state that is to blame. The charter lists three types of coercive measures:

1. severance of diplomatic relations
2. the complete or partial interruption of economic relations with the dissident state
3. the use of armed forces

The amount of pressure that diplomatic sanctions produce would ordinarily be limited. The more powerful economic sanctions are seldom tried. They were imposed on Iraq in the 1990s and on Syria in 2011. These actions were partially successful. A couple of more recent examples have been more successful. For example, sanctions were instrumental in bringing Iran to the bargaining table, with the United States and the UN agreeing to eliminate their sanctions in return for Iran limiting its nuclear program. Even when President Trump withdrew the United States from the agreement, Iran held back on restarting its nuclear program, as Europe tried to offset some of the U.S. sanctions that would be reinstituted. Trump's hope is that he can gain an even better deal, in which Iran not only gives up its nuclear program, but it also reduces it support of groups that the United States sees as supporting terrorism.

Another example of recent sanctions are the strong economic sanctions imposed on North Korea in response to its development of its nuclear weapons program. Initially, those sanctions had little effect; the North Korean leader, Kim Jong-un, called them an "act of war" and he expanded the program. That provoked a response from President Trump, and led to the harsh rhetoric on both sides that I began the chapter with. But then the rhetoric stopped; the two leaders had a meeting, and, as President Trump put it, they fell in love. They agreed to move toward peace, eliminating nuclear weapons from North Korea in exchange for a lifting of the sanctions. Whether that will actually come to pass remains to be seen.

Military sanctions are supposed to be the final recourse of the UN in its peacemaking efforts. To make the system function more smoothly, the charter imposes on each member of the organization the duty of contributing to the UN military force, with the Security Council responsible for defining each member's contribution to the joint effort, should an occasion for military sanctions arise.

Impressive as the charter provisions regarding military sanctions may appear at first glance, in fact they have been of limited value. When the North Koreans attacked South Korea on June 25, 1950, the Security Council had no military force on which it could draw because no agreements

The demilitarized zone between South and North Korea.

had been reached about what members were expected to provide. The failure to make those agreements had resulted from the inability of the Military Staff Committee to specify the general principles that such agreements should embody; no nation had yet undertaken a definite obligation with respect to any possible joint military action.

When the report came that South Korea had been invaded, a meeting of the Security Council was immediately called to deal with the problem. The council urgently asked for a cessation of hostilities and a withdrawal of the invading troops. Because two days later the ceasefire order had not been respected, the Security Council set to work to apply military sanctions against North Korea. This action would undoubtedly have been vetoed by the former Soviet Union had its delegates been present, but months earlier they had withdrawn from the UN meetings in anger because Taiwan, rather than China, had been given the Chinese seat in the organization. Because the Soviet delegate was not present at the ensuing Security Council meeting, the council was able to call for a ceasefire and authorize a UN-led military action—the Korean War, which lasted from 1950 to 1953.

Since then, the UN has had some successes in keeping the peace—the Suez Canal Crisis, helping to end the Iran-Iraq War, and helping to end the internal conflict in Angola; it has also had failures. The largest of these failures involved its diplomatic attempt to keep the peace in the Middle East. When Iraq invaded Kuwait, the UN imposed economic sanctions against Iraq and authorized military force to achieve Iraq's withdrawal from Kuwait. These authorizations occurred in the Security Council and were supported by the former USSR and accepted by China (both of which had veto power).

The UN hoped the economic sanctions and the threat of war would bring about a diplomatic solution. No diplomatic solution was found, and in 1991 the UN authorized the use of force to achieve the directives. However, instead of establishing a UN military force, the UN simply authorized the United States to lead a coalition in a war against Iraq. The U.S.-led forces quickly won the war, and the UN played a key role in establishing the framework under which Iraq surrendered. It also played an important role in assisting refugees from the war and in undertaking weapons inspections.

The UN did not maintain those weapons inspections, and in the early 2000s, Iraq expelled the UN inspectors, leading to intense diplomatic negotiations. In fall 2002, the United States pushed the UN to give Saddam Hussein an ultimatum, and in spring 2003, Hussein let the weapons inspectors back in to Iraq. Despite this concession, the United States was not satisfied with the progress made in finding weapons of mass destruction. The United States pushed the UN to declare Iraq in material breach of the earlier peace accord agreements and to allow the use of military force to ensure compliance.

When it became clear that the Security Council was not going to authorize force at this time, the United States, together with Great Britain, declared that a UN mandate was unnecessary and attacked Saddam Hussein to "eliminate weapons of mass destruction" and thereby help protect the world from terrorism. In response to the attack, there were significant anti-war activities, especially in Europe, where a large majority of the population opposed the U.S./United Kingdom unilateral action.

Once in control, the United States found little in the way of weapons of mass destruction—the given reason for the war. Despite this, because the initial attack went well, and because Saddam Hussein was deposed, even many who opposed the war felt the outcome was a good thing, because Hussein had been a brutal dictator. Immediately after Hussein's overthrow, a large majority of the U.S. population supported it—the "it dussint matter why we dunnit as long as we wunnit" approach to war.

After starting the war without UN approval, the United States took major control of the establishment of a new government in Iraq, freezing the UN out of much of the process. Essentially, it told the UN, "We will do what we want; if you condone it, we will let you play a role; if you don't, we will do what we want anyway."

That attitude did not sit well with the rest of the world, and the United States' actions generated significant anti-U.S. feelings outside the United States. But there was also an

UN peacekeepers on duty.

© AP images

acceptance of the "realpolitik"—the United States had unsurpassed military power—and thus there was little that other countries could do if the United States decided to use that power. In many people's eyes, the UN had lost any effective role in providing for peace and security in the world. The United States had usurped it. Despite its military strength, the United States found that winning the peace was much more difficult than winning the war. As the difficulties of maintaining the peace became enormous, the United States went back to the UN, asking for its help.

The United States again turned to the UN when it wanted to limit Iran's nuclear program to ensure that Iran did not develop nuclear weapons. It won UN support for sanctions against Iran if it did not end its nuclear program, but to win that support it had to reduce its demands, limiting those demands to suspending its nuclear agreement, and not limiting other activities, such as supporting groups that the United States considered terrorist, or developing long-range missiles. Another incident that demonstrates the way the United States interacts with the UN occurred in 2006 when Israel bombed Lebanon in response to Hezbollah's (a political group within Lebanon) capture of two of its soldiers. Most countries of the world wanted a resolution requiring Israel to stop the bombing and to introduce a ceasefire. The United States did not go along; instead the United States delayed, giving Israel additional time to achieve its military objectives. Eventually, the United States agreed to a limited UN peacekeeping force and an Israeli withdrawal.

As you can see, the U.S. relationship with the UN has been a pragmatic one: When working with the UN will serve U.S. interests, the United States works with it; when it does not serve U.S. interests, it doesn't. Even before President Trump's America First policy the United States has retained the right to act unilaterally when it perceives that its vital interests are being challenged.

The failure of many UN peacekeeping attempts has led to a UN report calling for a permanent UN-controlled army so that the UN will have "the tools" to address any conflict situation. Because countries are reluctant to give up autonomy to the UN, there may be some increase in and modernization of the UN peacekeeping department, but the troops will likely remain "on loan" from individual nations. The problem is one of control. The UN does not have the high-level military structure to successfully direct the operations even if it gets the troops. Therefore, control generally falls to one country. And, if a peacekeeping state becomes unhappy with the action, it can simply recall its troops, as India did with its troops in Sierra Leone in 2000.

In considering the UN, a key point to remember is that the UN is not a super state. It cannot force individuals or states to accept its decisions, and often it simply lacks the ability to impose its will on the member states. All it can do is impose sanctions, which are methods of exerting pressure on recalcitrant states. In imposing sanctions, two basic handicaps limit its effectiveness: (1) its member states retain their sovereignty, and (2) much of the power of the world is concentrated in a few powerful states, and unless these states concur and choose to use the UN as a vehicle to achieve their ends, the UN will not be effective.

Other UN Approaches

Some of the other approaches the UN has tried include the following:

- Registration of treaties in order to avoid obstructive secret treaties
- Further development of international law
- Promotion of education through the programs of UNESCO
- Encouragement of regional arrangements devoted to the preservation of peace
- International control of nuclear energy
- Regulation of national armaments, including missiles and nuclear weapons.

The practice of having treaties registered and published by the Secretariat has become firmly established, and although it does not guarantee that secret agreements will be eliminated, it does reduce the chances of their existence. An International Law Commission has tried to promote the progressive development of international law, and it has made headway slowly. The programs of UNESCO have aimed at the furtherance of fundamental education, technical and vocational education, the exchange of books between nations, the exchange of students, and many other objectives, all designed to produce a better international outlook on the part of people everywhere. However, these methods for advancing the cause of peace are necessarily slow and their results somewhat uncertain.

Efforts to establish international control of nuclear energy and national armaments began in 1963 under the direction of President John F. Kennedy, and they were formalized in 1968 with the Treaty on the Non-Proliferation of Nuclear Weapons (NPT), which provided for nonnuclear nations to forgo nuclear bomb development in exchange for aid in building peaceful nuclear power programs. Nations with the bomb were ordered to reduce armaments. Despite UN efforts, about fifty nations failed to sign the agreement. The UN's International Atomic Energy Agency (IAEA) has supervisory power over this treaty, but its authority and capabilities are limited. Thus, in 2003, when North Korea decided to develop a nuclear bomb, it simply expelled the UN observers who had been there expressly to ensure this did not happen. Other countries also tried to retain that option.

Given its limited sanctions and tools, the UN has not been especially successful in stopping even small wars, and it certainly has not been capable of coercing the largest and most powerful members of the international community. Even when dealing with small conflicts among member nations, the UN currently has no facility to force anyone to follow its policy. Thus, in the Iran-Iraq War in the mid-1980s, the UN was unable to enforce a ceasefire for years simply because the countries refused to obey the order. Only in 1988, when both countries chose to have a ceasefire, could the UN "enforce" its policy. Loyal supporters of the UN still hope that in time it will develop into an organization capable of maintaining international law, order, and justice. As the world grows smaller and smaller and as the range and deadliness of weapons increase, the need for such an organization becomes ever greater.

*T*he Outlook for Peace

The beginning of the new millennium was marked by the end of the Cold War and the beginning of a period of U.S. domination in the world militarily and politically. This changed the nature of the outlook for peace. The fears associated with the Cold War and the "communist threat," that filled the United States in the 1950s and 1960s are gone. Today, the communist threat, as interpreted then, seems a long way behind us, and it is hard to believe that in the 1950s and early 1960s, U.S. schools conducted air raid drills in which students practiced what to do in case of a Russian attack, and U.S. families built and stocked air raid shelters. For the United States, at least, such imminent threats are minimal, but other threats have replaced them.

The rise of U.S. dominance has provoked an anti-U.S. backlash and the development of terrorist cells throughout the world whose goal is to inflict harm on the United States and make it pay for its "bullying ways." This is particularly true among some Arab and Islamic groups who feel that the United States has been biased in its support of Israel in the Israeli-Palestinian conflict. The power of these groups was seen in the 9/11 attacks on the Pentagon and the World Trade Center and in the terrorist bombing of the United States and U.S.-ally institutions around the world. To fight such threats, the United States has established a war on terrorism, an ongoing war in which the United States claims the right to attack terrorists with pre-emptive strikes. Unfortunately, each of these strikes convinces others of the United States' bullying ways and leads more to join the terrorist cause, or at least to implicitly or explicitly support the terrorist cause. What the right mix of strength and understanding is for the United States to follow is still much in debate.

Those countries that have been accused of supporting or harboring terrorists can be pushed in two ways—they can succumb and stop their support of terrorism, or they can follow policies that may prevent attack, such as surreptitiously developing nuclear weapons, as North Korea, and likely Iran, have done. Their reasoning was that such a capability, and a willingness to use it, would prevent a U.S. attack and give them prestige on the world stage.

Ironically, the decline of fear of a global nuclear disaster has increased the likelihood of regional conflicts and the possibility that those regional conflicts could be nuclear. Why? Because a decreased fear that any regional conflict will pit two superpowers against each other in irreconcilable positions frees nations from automatically expecting a small war to lead to a large war. But simply because the expectation of a large war is reduced, it is not necessarily the case that the actual probability of a large war is reduced, and regional conflicts might, in fact, lead to such irreconcilable positions and the possibility of World War III. Just as fights between siblings can erupt at any time, so too can disagreements among supposedly friendly nations.

For example, after the fall of the Soviet Union in 1991, the United States and Russia seemed to come to an agreement that both were committed to peaceful coexistence. It has, however, been an uneasy alliance. A dispute between the two about how to deal with Ukraine led to military clashes as Russian portions of Ukraine attempted to gain more autonomy from Ukraine. The fighting was substantial for a while, but ultimately a shaky ceasefire was reached. However, relations between Russia and the United States deteriorated; the United States and the European Union claimed that Russia was aiding the pro-Russian fighters and imposed economic sanctions against Russia. In response, Russia imposed economic sanctions against the United States and the European Union. Both remained in place even after the ceasefire.

Similar clashes occurred in Syria in 2015 and 2016, where both the United States and Russia claimed to be fighting terrorists, and both conducted bombing raids against the terrorists. But they interpreted terrorists differently. Russia saw all those fighting President Assad as terrorists since they saw him as the legitimate leader of Syria. The United States saw only one of those groups, IS, as terrorists. The United States saw others fighting Assad as "freedom fighters" who were legitimately trying to take over power from Assad, who the United States did not recognize as the legitimate leader of Syria. Starting in 2016, Russia increased its military presence in Syria and the United States decreased its presence, leading Syrian forces, which Russia supported, to improve their positions and take control of more of the country. By late 2018 President Assad had gained control over much of Syria.

In 2017, Kim Jong-un increased his testing of nuclear weapons and the rockets by which they could be delivered. President Trump took a hard line on this development, leading to the Rocket Man exchange with which we began the chapter. Kim Jong-un's response to Trump had Kim calling Trump a "mentally deranged U.S. dotard." (Dotard means a senile person.) In many people's eyes this war of words placed the world closer to nuclear war than did the Cuban Missile crisis in the 1960s. But then, as discussed above, the threat disappeared, at least temporarily, as the two leaders entered into a reciprocal admiration agreement. Observers

World Trade Center attacks, September 11, 2001.

© Alamy

hoped that the new friendship would lead to peace, but with such volatile leaders many worried that the pendulum would shift the other way.

While, as of the time of writing this, U.S. relations with China are reasonably friendly, the two countries have a number of disputes that could erupt at any time. One dispute involves trade; President Trump, claiming that China had not followed the trade agreements in place, imposed tariffs on some Chinese goods; China retaliated, and the United States responded by threatening even more tariffs. China did likewise. Another area of concern involves geopolitics as China is extending its influence throughout the world, both militarily and economically. Economically, in 2016, it established the Asian Infrastructure Development Bank that gives it a larger role in Asian economic development. Militarily, it claimed territory on the East China Sea; that would preclude U.S. military ships from large parts of that sea. China is also developing cyber war capabilities and hacking U.S. computers (just as the United States likely hacks China's computers); and it is developing weapons that can challenge the U.S. control of space. So while both are currently committed to peaceful cooperation, that commitment is a surface commitment that could break down quickly.

In considering the various arguments on both sides, it is important to recognize that "right" is almost inevitably a gray area, and each side will often do what is politically and economically in its own interest. This means that we can expect that any government with the power to do so will attempt to impose its will on the world. It is a maxim of politics that power corrupts and absolute power corrupts absolutely. The only way peace will have a chance is if those possessing power do not interpret to their advantage what is "right" in the large number of gray areas. Unfortunately, there have not been many examples of such objective interpretation of what is "right" in history. Instead, history has contained many more examples of the view that "might makes right."

Trouble Spots of the World

The war on terrorism has less of a specific geographic component than did previous wars. Terrorists could be anywhere—they could be living right next door. Similarly, the damage from terrorism is not limited to some far-off country. It could be right here in the United

States, as was made clear with the World Trade Center attack. Terrorism is likely to be exacerbated by geographically specific fights, and unfortunately, around the world there are a number of festering problems, and in this section, we shall review some of them. Let's start with Africa.

African Stability.   During the post-World War II period, many African countries won their independence from European colonial nations, but that independence has been marked by bloody internal strife, coups d'état, and disputes over borders with neighboring countries. Few of the countries have the underlying social infrastructure necessary for a democratic government, so the governments have generally been autocracies, and the fights have been over which and what type of autocracy will rule.

Many African nations have strong ethnic divisions. Because of the historically imposed boundaries that combine competing ethnic groups, there will likely be continuing internal wars and fights throughout the 2000s. Examples include Somalia, where fighting between competing groups has led to famine and civil war; Rwanda, where fighting between the Tutsis and Hutus has torn the country's social fabric apart; the Sudan and South Sudan, which separated in 2011, only to end up in armed conflict. Yet another example is Zimbabwe, where, until 2018, the government of Robert Mugabe clung to power through the use of intimidation and violence towards opposition leaders. In 2018 a new government came in; whether the new government will be a change for the better remains to be seen. Nigeria has been stable, but a terrorist group, Boko Haram, remains a powerful disruptive force.

Latin American Stability.   Let's next turn to Latin America. Latin America is no longer as troubled a region as it was when it was a location for a proxy war between the competing superpowers. But it is still troubled, with gangs extorting protection money from businesses and terrorizing citizens who challenge their power, and controlling larges areas in a number of central and South American countries. It was that trouble that led to caravans of migrants leaving their countries and trying to emigrate into the United States.

An example of the problems caused by that competition between superpowers was the bloody civil wars in Nicaragua and El Salvador in the early 1980s as both the United States and the former Soviet Union jockeyed for position. Those problems have ended, but significant problems remain.

Some of these problems are simply leftover antagonisms from the earlier conflicts. Others result from the large disparities in income within countries, the weak democratic traditions in many of them, and the powerful drug cartels. Venezuela's democracy had been essentially dismantled by Presidents Chavez and Maduro. This led to political strife and a breakdown of people's faith in government being responsive to the will of the people. It also led to economic sanctions being imposed on Venezuela by the United States. Combined this led to a severe economic depression in Venezuela and a breakdown of order. In many countries drug cartels and gangs often operate at will; they are the law, not the government. Even Mexico, one of the most stable Latin American countries, finds itself fighting to get control over the drug cartels. Thousands of innocent civilians have been caught in the crossfire, killed in fights either between various cartels or between the government and the cartels.

Stability in the Former Soviet Republics and Eastern Europe.   In recent years Russia and Ukraine have been in dispute over how Eastern Ukraine, which is culturally connected to Russia, should be governed, with Russia supporting armed groups who are fighting the Ukrainian government. In 2014, Russia annexed Crimea, which had been part of Ukraine, ostensibly to protect Russian speakers there. The United States and the European Union objected, and provided some financial support for Ukraine; they also imposed economic sanctions on Russia, which responded with economic sanctions against Western companies. As of 2019, the tension continued.

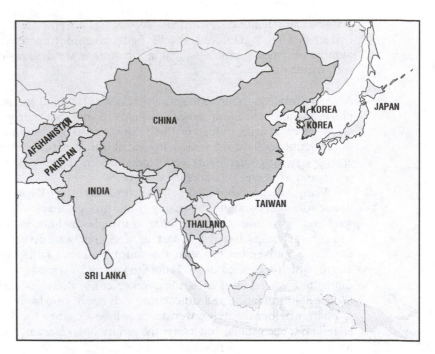

Some potential Asian trouble spots: India–Pakistan border; North–South Korea border; Chinese–Indian border and Tibetan region of China; Afghanistan.

Stability in the Far East and Indochina.   In 2018, North Korea was still of concern because it has developed a nuclear bomb and missiles that can send them throughout the world. The United States stated that North Korea should not have nuclear weapons, and in 2017 there was a war of tweets between President Trump and the North Korean leader, Kim Jong-un. As I discussed earlier, in 2018 that changed to a lovefest between the two leaders, but it was a lovefest on highly shaky grounds.

Even if the North Korean problem is resolved, the Far East will likely experience significant potential for instability, with the growth of China into a world economic and military power that can challenge the United States, creating the Thucydides Trap. As mentioned above, China is claiming control over 90 percent of the South China Sea, an area that extends far beyond its coastline, and which includes areas that other Far East countries claim as their own. To strengthen its claims to the sea, it has taken over atolls (rings of coral reef or a series of islets creating shallow lagoons in the ocean), and is building islands out of them and then placing military bases on them. The United States has objected but has not done anything to stop them. China-U.S. relations remain a trouble spot.

Tension in the Middle East.   The Middle East has been a source of tension and instability in the world for the last forty years, and it remains a serious trouble spot. There are actually two related problems there: governing problems within the Arab states and tensions between Arab states and Israel.

Governing Problems in the Middle East.   Like most former colonial areas in which a country has been created by colonies, rather than emerging on its own, the Middle East has had a difficult time creating a state that represents the will of the people. Instead, most Middle Eastern countries have been ruled by autocrats who have come from one tribe in the region and who have maintained control, not through democratic means, but rather through oppression and fear. These autocrats also often have become corrupt. For many businesses in

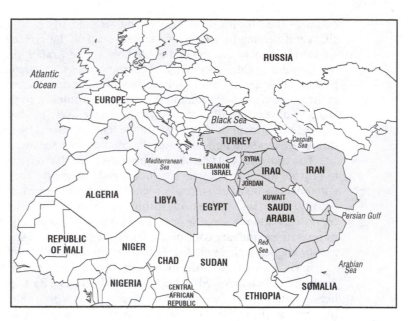

The Middle East and surrounding countries.

these countries, in order to get a permit to do anything, you have to pay bribes and do what the government wants. It is the cost of doing business.

This situation has led to difficult choices for the United States and its allies. Often, the authoritarian regimes have been willing to support U.S. policies contrary to the will of their population, which has led to their getting U.S. support and aid, even though they did not allow free elections and were repressive. The leaders have been seen as strong friends of the United States, causing them to be disliked by the population, which strongly opposes U.S. policy in support of Israel. Hosni Mubarak in Egypt is an example. He ruled Egypt for more than thirty years with strong U.S. government support. The United States turned a blind eye to the lack of free elections and his legal sanctions preventing the Muslim Brotherhood from running for office, even though that party had significant support in the population.

The contradictions came to a head in what has become known as the Arab Spring—the 2011 uprisings of the population in Tunisia, Libya, Egypt, Yemen, and Syria, with smaller uprisings in other Middle Eastern countries. What set it off was a single incident. A Tunisian street vendor set himself on fire on December 17, 2010, as a protest against the harassment and humiliation that he felt had been inflicted on him by a municipal official and her aides. They had confiscated his vegetable cart for conducting business without a license, which required him to pay bribes to the government officials. That protest struck a chord with people all over the Middle East who could not find jobs and were sick of paying bribes. Demonstrations against the Tunisian government grew and then spread across the Middle East, causing the Tunisian leader to resign, the Egyptian leader to be overthrown and arrested, and civil wars in Libya and Syria to erupt.

The United States supported the freedom the people were demanding, but it also had supported many of the previous leaders, so it found itself in a difficult position—whether to support the leaders or the protesters. Unfortunately, the new governments that formed after the protests were in many cases unable to govern, and they lost the support of the people. Consider, for example, Egypt. Initially, after the Arab Spring uprising, the Muslim Brotherhood candidate, whom the United States opposed, won the election. However, he quickly lost the support of the people, and there was essentially a coup d'état and the head of the armed forces, Abdel Fattah el-Sisi became president. His rule became increasingly authoritarian; he outlawed the Muslim Brotherhood, and arrested any candidate who seemed as if he had a chance of beating him in an election. Essentially he created an authoritarian government almost identical to the one that existed before the Arab Spring.

One intractable problem is that unemployment in the regions among the youth is often 40 percent or higher, and the new governments have no better ways of providing jobs for people at the wages they want than did the older governments. In fact, the fighting and uncertainty associated with the fall of the old regimes have likely made the problems worse. When one combines that economic reality with the tension caused by tribal and religious rivalries, one can understand the difficult times the countries are having.

The countries will fall into two groups—those that have sufficient oil income they can use to provide their citizens with significant material goods, such as Kuwait and Saudi Arabia— and others without such income, such as Egypt and Yemen. Those with sufficient income can use it to maintain relative calm within the country. Those without it either have to resort to repressive authoritarian rule or they fall into crisis. For example, Egypt dealt with the problem by reverting to military control after an attempt at democracy. Yemen fell into a civil war with groups aligned with Saudi Arabia fighting groups aligned with Iran.

Even countries that had income to placate their citizens faced problems. Saudi Arabia, Turkey, and Iran jockeyed for leadership of the Middle East, leading to contentious proxy wars between the various factions. Saudi Arabia's war with Yemen was intended to limit Iranian influence in the region, and Iran's support of Syria was designed to increase its influence.

Middle Eastern politics are further complicated by internal tensions among different sects of Islam. For example, Iran is ruled by Shiites, while Saudi Arabia, as well as other Middle Eastern countries, is ruled by Sunnis, even though much of its population is Shiite. This means that Saudi Arabia is concerned about Iran gaining too much influence in the region, because it might empower its Shiite minority to revolt.

Clearly, politics in the Middle East is complicated, and we have not even discussed the many different Sunni and Shiite sects, which often have quite different agendas. Many of these agendas are never directly stated, and often are even contrary to stated positions, which means that the statements any official makes often have double or triple meanings and need to be interpreted with care. Middle East "diplomatic smarts" is a highly nuanced version of diplomatic smarts. It is more like playing Go than playing Chess.

Palestinian-Israeli Tensions.   The problems just outlined would be more than enough for any region, but they are exacerbated by tensions with Israel. Practically since the beginning of history, the Middle East has been a virtual hotbed of warring peoples. The countries of the area, such as Libya, Syria, Iraq, Israel, and Iran, have periodically fallen under the influence of rulers from many different nations. During World War I, the area was occupied by French and British troops, and between 1922 and 1939 the Jewish population in Palestine (now Israel) rose from 84,000 to 445,000. The land they bought and occupied had been previously owned by absentee landlords, and the displaced Arabs who had previously rented the land remained hostile to the new settlers. The land became disputed territory.

As the Jewish population increased, so did **Zionist**—views of an individual who supports the establishment and expansion of a Jewish homeland—activities. During World War II, Zionist forces fought on the side of the Allies, but continually reminded the Allied forces that their own central motive was to seek independence for a Jewish nation. The area in which the nation was proposed was a British protectorate, and in 1942 Britain passed the Biltmore Program, which called for the first steps to be taken to secure Palestine for the Jews. It provided for unrestricted Jewish immigration into Palestine and eventual establishment of a Jewish commonwealth.

Palestinian Arabs, meanwhile, did not put up a united resistance to the Zionists. Therefore, at the end of World War II, the Palestinian Arabs had only the League of Arab States (Egypt, Syria, Lebanon, Transjordan, Iraq, Saudi Arabia, and Yemen) to turn to. They voiced opposition to the Biltmore Program. Britain, undecided about how the situation should be handled, called for the establishment of a binational state in Palestine, and refused to admit some 100,000 European Jewish refugees to the area. Another outbreak of violence caused the UN to intervene. On September 1, 1947, the UN commission of inquiry called for the division of the territory into two states—one Arab and one Jewish.

The Arabs, who constituted a majority in both the "states" the UN had created, refused the order and thus the Palestinian War began. The well-organized Zionist forces overcame the Arabs, and by May 1948 they had obtained control not only of the Jewish share of Palestine but the Arab share as well. On May 14, 1948, the state of Israel was proclaimed. Since that time there has been continual strife between Israel and its surrounding Arab neighbors. The first outbreak of violence was the Suez War in 1956, when Israel staged a surprise attack on Egypt in the Sinai area. In 1967, the tensions broke into war again, and in what is called the Six-Day War, Israel made large territorial gains, taking land from Egypt and Jordan. Israel continued to occupy the territory it won in the war, citing the need for national security. In 1973, Arab forces attacked Israel in an attempt to regain their land, and sporadic fighting continued until mid-1974 when both sides agreed to a ceasefire.

In 1967, the UN Security Council passed what has come to be known as **Resolution 242**, which called for the return of land and property taken by Israel during the wars. In 1974 the UN General Assembly recognized the Palestine Liberation Organization (PLO), giving it permanent observer status at the UN. Israel rejected this, citing security reasons and arguing that it could not give land back to a group committed to the annihilation of Israel. In response, Israel began to establish Jewish settlements in the occupied land.

Some hope of accord existed in 1979, as Egypt and Israel agreed to a peace treaty calling for Israel's withdrawal from the Sinai Peninsula, but the more difficult Palestinian question was skirted. That question eventually led to continued fighting and war as Israel invaded Lebanon in 1982 in an attempt to eliminate the PLO. As a result of this fighting, much of Beirut, the capital of Lebanon, fell into ruins as Israel, the PLO, and Syria struggled for political power in the area. In Lebanon, the many internal groups are differentiated by intense religious, political, and economic rivalries, and they fight bitterly with each other, while, at the same time, outside interests, such as those of Syria and Israel, attempt to enforce their own versions of order on the country. In the early 1990s, a Syrian-backed faction took control, and it looked as though the long ordeal in Lebanon was finally coming to an end. Conflict still existed, however, in south Lebanon, where Lebanese troops attempted to regain land occupied by fighting PLO guerrillas and

Palestinian demonstrators throw stones at Israeli soldiers during a clash in the West Bank of the Palestinian territory.

The Most Elusive Gift of All

If you asked most sane and temperate men and women throughout the world what they wanted most for the holidays,

their first choice wouldn't come in a magnificent box with a fancy ribbon.

They couldn't find it on a colorful page of a fat Christmas catalog.

They wouldn't see it glistening out at them from a window of a smart boutique.

Because it's the most precious and elusive gift of all...:

PEACE ON EARTH

United Technologies advertisement.

Israelis. The Golan Heights, which was once part of Syria but was annexed by Israel in 1981 and settled by Israeli citizens, remained in dispute.

In August 1993, the Israeli Prime Minister, Yitzhak Rabin, and the chairman of the PLO, Yasser Arafat, signed a historic peace accord to bring to a conclusion almost five decades of incessant turmoil and conflict. Israel agreed to turn over specific regions of the West Bank and Gaza Strip to the Palestinian Arabs, who would administer them as autonomous divisions. The negotiations leading toward final settlement continued with enormous fights and complaints on both sides. Those fights and complaints continued through the 1990s and early 2000s. In 2003, in retaliation for suicide bombings, Israel sent in its army and occupied much of the West Bank and Gaza, destroying and laying siege to PLO headquarters and houses of suspected terrorists and their relatives. The United States and other Western countries urged both sides to follow a Roadmap to Peace, which required both Palestinians and Israelis to move simultaneously toward peace, with the Palestinian police force stopping the militant Palestinians from attacking Israelis and the Israeli forces withdrawing from Palestine and stopping settlements. Few believed that the Roadmap would work, but all believed that it was best to try.

In 2006, Israel conducted a unilateral withdrawal from part of the Palestinian territory, annexed other parts of the Palestinian territory that Israel had occupied in previous wars, and began building a wall separating Palestinians from the annexed territories.

Arafat's successor party, Fatah, signed a peace treaty with Israel, and then lost an election to Hamas, which did not accept the existence of Israel and was far more militant. Hamas vowed never to accept Israel's right to exist, leading Israel to break off peace negotiations and to begin a policy of assassinating Hamas leaders. That led to further violence, and in 2006, Hezbollah, a militant group in Lebanon, entered the fight. Israel attacked Lebanon as well as the Palestinian territory, arguing that the Lebanese government had not contained Hezbollah. Israeli bombing raids killed thousands of Lebanese civilians, and Hezbollah indiscriminately launched thousands of missiles at Israel. Moderates were caught in the middle, as both sides became more and more radicalized.

In 2009, President Obama reached out to the Arab and Palestinian communities and stated that he opposed expansions of Israeli settlements in occupied Palestinian territory. This had always been U.S. stated policy, but earlier the United States had looked the other way and not imposed any penalties on Israel for its repeated violations. That policy changed when Donald Trump won the presidential election in 2016. With Trump's election U.S. policy became much more accepting of settlements, and of Israel. The United States threatened to stop providing financial aid for Palestinians, and recognized Jerusalem as Israel's capital, even though the Palestinians also claimed it as their capital. The Palestinians strenuously objected but there was little they could do.

Conclusion

In summary, international politics is anything but settled and clear. Often there is no formal resolution to a conflict, but despite this, the conflict will fade away with time, as both sides realize that they are better off letting the conflict fade away rather than face it directly. But the threat of a conflict escalating into a military fight is always there. Social scientists have no answers from these conflicts. But what social scientists hope is that by considering them in a reflective way the various sides can see the advantages of getting along, and of reasonable compromise. As Pope Leo XIII put it in the opening epigraph to this chapter, "nothing is more important than the war on war."

 Study and **Review**

Key Points

- If countries do not get what they want, and they have the power to do so, they often go to war to get it.
- International law is a good idea, but it lacks any way of enforcing its decisions.
- Three principal organs of the UN are the General Assembly, the Security Council, and the Secretariat.
- The United States did not pay its dues for UNESCO for the same reason that Billy takes his ball away if he doesn't like the way the game is going.

- The new world order is to be determined collectively by the major powers, primarily the United States. The U.S. policy of pre-emption made it the ultimate arbiter of right and wrong in the world.
- With the rise of China, U.S. hegemony is being challenged.
- The Arab-Israeli conflict has many dimensions and affects the area like a cancer that has metastasized.

Some Important Terms

Al-Qaeda (429)
Arab Spring (430)
General Assembly (434)
international law (433)
mediation (432)

policy of pre-emption (429)
Resolution 242 (445)
sanctions (436)
Secretariat (435)
Security Council (434)

Thucydides Trap (443)
United Nations (UN) (432)
veto (434)
Zionist (445)

Questions for Review and Discussion

General Questions

1. How do you explain the prevalence of wars throughout human history?
2. Is the threat of war over with the end of the Cold War? Explain your position.
3. Is President Trump's America First policy a reasonable basis for diplomacy? Why or why not?
4. Explain the statement that war is "merely a continuation of politics by other means."
5. Explain how diplomacy is used to prevent war.
6. What are some of the reasons that international government cannot prevent all wars?
7. What are the three most important organs through which the UN acts?
8. What is the difference between the UN General Assembly and the UN Security Council?

9. How does the veto power of the Security Council hinder the search for peace? Are there any ways the veto power helps the search for peace?
10. Discuss some of the accomplishments of the UN.
11. What are some of the worst trouble spots in the world today? Can you think of ways to deal with any of these problems?
12. Give a brief history of the Arab-Israeli conflict.
13. What is meant by the new world order? Was there more or less stability in the world under this order?
14. What is the most significant problem the world faces?
15. How would we know if the war on terrorism is justified?
16. If Mexico established a policy of pre-emption, how would the United States likely respond?

17. If the amount of money now spent on weapons systems could be used for something else, what do you think the money should be spent on?

Internet Questions

1. Go to https://peacekeeping.un.org/en/where-we-operate. What are the current UN peacekeeping operations?
2. What is the mission statement of the International Committee of the Red Cross? Consult its website, https://www.icrc.org.
3. According to Graça Machel, the UN expert on the impact of war on children (see https://www.unicef.org/graca/), why are children particularly vulnerable to land mines?
4. Go to the UN website http://www.un.org/en/about-un/index.html. Who is the current Secretary-General, and when did he take office?
5. Using the International Peace Bureau site, http://www.ipb.org/ , what is the Sean MacBride Peace Prize?

*F*or Further Study

Books to Explore

Allison, Graham, *Destined for War: Can America and China Escape Thucydides's Trap*. New York: Houghton Mifflin Harcourt, 2017

Annan, Kofi, *Interventions: A Life in War and Peace*, New York: Penguin Press, 2012.

Basic Facts About the United Nations, New York: United Nations Publications [Updated regularly].

Carter, Jimmy, *Palestine: Peace not Apartheid*, New York: Simon and Schuster, 2006.

Chua, Amy, *Political Tribes: Group Instinct and the Fate of Nations*, New York: Penguin Press, 2018.

Ferguson, Niall, *The War of the World: Twentieth-Century Conflict and the Descent of the West*, New York: Penguin, 2006.

Haass, Richard, *The World in Disarray: American Foreign Policy and the Crisis of the Old Order*, New York: Penguin Random House, 2017.

Hemon, Aleksandar, and Peter van Agtmael, *Behind the Glass Wall: Inside the United Nations*, New York: MCD, 2017.

Kennedy, Paul, *The Parliament of Man: The Past, Present, and Future of the United Nations*, New York: Random House, 2006.

Kissinger, Henry, *World Order*, London: Penguin Press, 2014.

Meisler, Stanley, *United Nations: A History*, New York: Grove Press, 2011.

Schake, Kori, *Safe Passage: The Transition from British to American Hegemony*, Cambridge, MA: Harvard University Press, 2017.

Internet Sites to Explore

"http://www.cwps.org" Center for War/Peace Studies.

"https://www.icj-cij.org" The International Court of Justice.

"http://www.oecd.org" Organization for Economic Co-operation and Development.

"http://www.un.org/en/index.html" The United Nations.

"https://en.unesco.org" United Nations Educational, Scientific and Cultural Organization.

"http://www.wfwp.org" Women's Federation for World Peace International.

"http://www.who.int/en" The World Health Organization.

Index

Note: Page numbers in **bold** type refer to **tables**
Page numbers in *italic* type refer to *figures*
Page numbers followed by 'n' refer to notes
Page numbers followed by 'p' refer to photographs